THE SALE OF GOODS

The Sale of Goods

M.G. BRIDGE

Hind Professor of Commercial Law
University of Nottingham
Director of Research, Norton Rose

OXFORD UNIVERSITY PRESS

OXFORD
UNIVERSITY PRESS

Great Clarendon Street, Oxford OX2 6DP

Oxford University Press is a department of the University of Oxford.
It furthers the University's objective of excellence in research, scholarship,
and education by publishing worldwide in

Oxford New York

Athens Auckland Bangkok Bogotá Buenos Aires Calcutta
Cape Town Chennai Dar es Salaam Delhi Florence Hong Kong Istanbul
Karachi Kuala Lumpur Madrid Melbourne Mexico City Mumbai
Nairobi Paris São Paulo Shanghai Singapore Taipei Tokyo Toronto Warsaw

with associated companies in Berlin Ibadan

British Library Cataloguing in Publication Data
Data available

Library of Congress Cataloging in Publication Data
Data available

ISBN 0-19-825871-2
ISBN 0-19-876535-5 (Pbk)

Printed in Great Britain
on acid-free paper by
Biddles Ltd., Guildford and King's Lynn

Foreword

to the paperback edition

On the occasion of this launch of *The Sale of Goods* in a paperback edition, the publishers have been kind enough to allow me some space to take account of the more significant developments in the law since the casebound version was prepared.

The House of Lords in *Stocznia Gdanska SA* v *Latvian Shipping Co* ([1998] 1 All ER 883, applying *Hyundai Heavy Industries Co Ltd* v *Papadopoulos* [1980] 1 WLR 1129) has reaffirmed the proposition that shipbuilding contracts are not to be regarded as simple contracts of sale. The construction and design elements, treated as part of a seller's consideration distinct from the proprietary transfer of the completed ship, make such contracts hybrid in nature. When, therefore, instalments of the purchase price had already fallen due and payable at the time the sellers exercised an express right of rescission (so-described) under the contract, that right to payment was not removed by the rescission. Furthermore, given the nature of the contract, there had not occurred a total failure of consideration when the contract was rescinded. Consequently, if the outstanding instalments had been paid, they could not have been recovered by the defaulting buyers.

The classification of the contract was also an important issue in *St Albans City and District Council* v *International Computers Ltd* ([1996] 4 All ER 481), which appeared too late for detailed treatment in the casebound edition of this book. It concerned software provided under an agreement for the supply of a computer system. The trial judge was of the view that software was 'probably' goods under section 61(1) of the Sale of Goods Act ([1995] FSR 686, 699) since '[p]rograms are . . . of necessity contained in some physical medium'. In the Court of Appeal, Sir Iain Glidewell took the matter further when saying that the disk carrying a program was goods under the Act, although the program *per se* was not. He went on to say that the quality of the program stored on the disk was a matter for section 14 of the Sale of Goods Act, and hence strict liability, in the same way as strict liability would follow in the case of defective instructions in a car maintenance manual. From this position, he went on to consider the case of a program directly transferred by the licensor to the user's system without the user receiving any tangible thing. This case would fall outside the Sale of Goods Act, as well as outside the Supply of Goods and Services Act 1982, and so liability should have to exist at common law. In the learned judge's view, the implied term that the parties 'must have intended' in such a case would be one of strict liability that the program be reasonably fit for its purpose. With respect, this goes beyond the business efficacy approach to implied terms. The contract would be perfectly effective with a minimal implied term based upon the licensor taking reasonable care.

The above *obiter* statements are controversial. It is correct enough to say that no proper distinction is to be drawn between instructions stored on a computer disk and instructions stored in a book. In the case of complex goods supplied with a manual, it is uncontroversial too that the goods assessed for compliance with section 14 include the manual without which they cannot be used (*Wormell* v *RHM Agriculture (East) Ltd* [1986] 1 WLR 336; *Amstrad plc* v *Seagate Technology Inc*, unreported 9 May 1997). The same cannot quite be said of a computer program. It is not a case of the disk being unusable without a program: the disk is merely the integument of the program. Again, where a system is supplied, it is not properly a case of hardware being unusable without software: the hardware is only the means by which the software can be used and enjoyed. In the computer world, tangible things are supplied for the purpose of using dominant intangible things. In the world of cars and video recorders, intangible instructions are supplied for the better use of tangible things. This points to the supply of software being classified as the provision of services attracting fault-based and not strict liability. Unless this is so, the prospects presented by Sir Iain Glidewell for authors of non-fiction books are daunting. If his words were extended from instructions to information (and how can the two be separated?) then authors should take out liability insurance and preface their work with well-drawn exclusion clauses. Furthermore, professionals such as solicitors and architects should feel some trepidation. If the supply of just a program (without a disk) telling the user how to do something attracts strict liability, why should this not also be so for a solicitor's letter of advice? The relieving answer that the latter is providing a service and that section 13 of the Supply of Goods and Services Act lays down a standard of due care for contracts for services invites the response that the supply of a program should also be treated as the supply of a service, even if it comes with a disk.

Another issue of classification presented itself in *Forthright Finance Ltd* v *Carlyle Finance Ltd* ([1997] 4 All ER 90). Forthright supplied on finance terms over three years (see below) a Ford Cosworth car to Senator, which in turn sold the car to Carlyle in furtherance of a conditional sale agreement between Carlyle and Griffiths. Forthright sued Carlyle in conversion, the sale by Senator to Carlyle being implicitly treated as unlawful. The question was whether the agreement between Forthright and Senator was one of conditional sale or hire purchase. If it was one of hire purchase, Carlyle had no defence to the conversion action. It was common ground that Griffiths acquired good title to the car as a private purchaser under Part III of the Hire Purchase Act 1964, but that Act gave no protection to Carlyle, a trade or finance purchaser. If, however, the contract between Forthright and Senator was a conditional sale, Senator, as one in possession of goods that it had agreed to buy, could pass good title to Carlyle under section 25 of the Sale of Goods Act. Section 25 does not apply to consumer conditional sales, but the court treated the Forthright-Senator contract as a non-consumer contract because it fell outside the financial limits of the Consumer Credit Act 1974.

The Court of Appeal held that the Forthright-Senator contract was a conditional sale agreement, though styled a hire purchase contract. The interesting feature of the agreement, placing it between orthodox drafts of hire purchase and conditional sale contracts, was that it required Senator to pay all of the instalments making up the price of the car. Senator thereupon would be deemed to have exercised a hire purchaser's option so as to acquire title to the car 'unless the hirer has told the owner before that time that such is not the case'. Since Senator had to pay all of the instalments, the agreement was held to be in both substance and form a conditional sale agreement. Forthright's attempt to protect itself from subsequent trade or finance purchasers was dismissed as 'specious'. One may add that it was evidently most unlikely that Senator would exercise its quit option having paid the price in full or even in advance of performing its obligation to pay in full. An agreement to buy can therefore exist even if the buyer has an option to put the goods back on the seller. In principle, this should be so whether the buyer with such an option is or is not paid for the goods upon resale to the original seller.

Part III of the Hire Purchase Act 1964 was also present in *Keeble* v *Combined Lease Finance plc* (Court of Appeal, 6 March 1996). The sole issue was whether, in the case of a car bailed to two partners each jointly and severally liable to the finance company, a good title could be passed under the Act by only one of them to a *bona fide* private purchaser. The court held that 'the debtor' in section 27(1) meant 'the persons, or either of them, to whom the vehicle is bailed'. Consequently, the finance company's technical argument failed and the private purchaser acquired good title under the Act.

In *Atari Corp (UK) Ltd* v. *Electronic Boutique Stores Ltd* ([1998] 1 All ER 1010), a number of interesting issues arose concerning sale or return agreements. First of all, the question whether the buyer's conduct amounted to an acceptance of the goods was treated as an aspect of construction of the particular arrangement. The sellers had applied for

Foreword to the paperback edition

summary judgment under RSC Order 14 and the Court of Appeal disposed of the dispute by exercising its powers under Order 14A instead of merely giving the buyers leave to defend. The central point of the case is that sale or return buyers are bailees who have an option to decide whether to buy the goods in their possession. Although nothing was made of the buyers' duty to pay on 30 November, prior to the expiry of the option period on 31 January, one could imagine a case where there is a defeasible sale, possibly with a limited entitlement to reject the goods. In the present case, however, the arrangement between the parties, though treated as a contract, was held to be not one of sale. Phillips LJ was of the view (at 1018) that the seller cannot withdraw his offer to sell, a proposition which he appears to believe flows from the language of section 18, rule 4. It is hard to see why this should be so. Phillips LJ's observation prompts the question whether the buyer has provided consideration for the option or whether the Act has dispensed with fundamental contractual doctrine. It would be difficult to construct the former whilst leaving the buyer with a true option; one should also be slow to recognise radical changes to contract law produced by incidental effect in a statute.

Atari involved the acquisition of computer games which were dispersed to a number of the buyers' stores. The buyers gave notice that they would be returning large numbers of a particular game at a time when the numbers of returnable stock were unknown, they had not been assembled at a central point and they were also not immediately available to the sellers. Construing this particular agreement, the court concluded that the notice was valid. It gave a clear generic description of the goods; the stock to be returned did not have to be immediately ready for collection and could subsequently be ascertained. It was not necessary to decide whether the stock had to be ready by 31 January, but possibly the case that it had to be (Waller LJ at 1015). If the buyers, despite their non-acceptance of the stock, later sold it or some of it, their earlier notice would remain valid though they would commit the tort of conversion in respect of the sold stock. It is interesting to note a tendency in *Atari* to treat the buyers' non-acceptance under section 18, rule 4, in a way similar to a buyer's rejection of non-conforming goods under section 35. This may not be a desirable tendency: the length of a reasonable period under the two sections should not be supposed to be the same. It is better to speak of a buyer's non-acceptance rather than rejection of the goods. There is also a statement in the case that a failure to hand over the stock immediately would be a conversion if the notice stated that it was immediately ready for collection (Waller LJ at 1016). This statement, if correct, extends the tort of conversion, without statutory justification in the Torts (Interference with Goods) Act 1977, into a simple failure or refusal to deliver, territory previously occupied by the tort of detinue. The final point is that the sale or return agreement was construed as severable in quantities to be determined by the buyers acting unilaterally when selling on the stock. Similarly, the sale of some stock would not be an act adopting the transaction in respect of stock not yet sold on.

An important case on waiver and acceptance of goods is *Glencore Grain Rotterdam BV* v *Lebanese Organisation for International Commerce* ([1997] 4 All ER 514). It deals with the controversial principle in *Panchaud Frères SA* v *Ets. General Grain Co* ([1970] 1 Lloyd's Rep 53), that a c.i.f. buyer of goods may, by his conduct in accepting documents that reveal a breach of the seller's physical responsibilities in respect of the goods, be thereafter debarred from rejecting the goods themselves. The issue is one that will be dealt with in greater detail in the book on international sale of goods that I am currently preparing for Oxford University Press. For the moment, it is enough to observe that the Court of Appeal, in a case dealing with the refusal of f.o.b. sellers to load a ship without founding that refusal on the buyers' unlawful demand for freight prepaid bills of lading, has kept the principle alive. It 'may represent a species of estoppel' (at 527). The court noted a lack of support for Winn LJ's emergent doctrine of fair conduct (in *Panchaud Frères*) but, concerned at the unfairness that might arise if a party were allowed to revert to his contractual rights, supported *Panchaud Frères* as a decision on estoppel by conduct. The court was also prepared to recognise *Panchaud Frères* as authority for a common law rule of acceptance of the goods (cf. section 35 of the Sale of Goods Act) occurring when the documents themselves were accepted, which is questionable in view of the shortage of time allowed to c.i.f. buyers to inspect documents.

Recent cases have demonstrated the difficulty of determining on the facts whether sufficient time has passed for the buyer to accept goods according to section 35 of the Sale of Goods Act (*Peakman* v *Express Circuits Ltd* (Court of Appeal, 3 February 1998); *Owner Drivers Radio Taxi Service Ltd* v *CTL Group Ltd* (2 May 1995). Reported cases give little assistance to courts on this matter.

The *Peakman* case also gives support, in actions for damages for breach of warranty under section 53 of the Sale of Goods Act, to making an award based on the cost of rectifying defects in the goods. A more difficult question concerning damages under this section presented itself in *Bence Graphics International Ltd* v *Fasson UK Ltd* ([1997] 4 All ER 979) where the Court of Appeal, by a majority, departed from well-established law (*Slater* v *Hoyle & Smith* [1920] 2 KB 11) that sub-sale contracts should be disregarded when assessing the buyer's damages for breach of warranty of quality under section 53 of the Sale of Goods Act. The presumptive rule is that damages should be assessed by reference to the value of the sub-warranty goods at the time of delivery; this rule corresponds to the reference to the market at the due date of delivery in cases of non-delivery and non-acceptance. The sellers in *Bence* delivered to the buyers a large quantity of cast vinyl film used by the buyers in manufacturing decals for the container industry. In breach of express and implied terms in the contract, the film failed to survive in a legible state. In awarding the buyers damages amounting to the price paid, the trial judge treated the film as worthless. He noted that, though the buyers had not been sued by sub-buyers of the decals, they remained exposed to such claims and might have suffered a loss of business reputation.

The decision was reversed by the Court of Appeal and the buyers' damages limited to the prorated contract price for the small quantity of vinyl remaining in their hands. According to Otton LJ, the *Slater* case, which involved cloth that the buyers bleached and sold on, was to be distinguished from the present case in that here the goods sold on by the buyer (decals) were different from those bought by the buyer (vinyl film). This factual distinction plainly does not stand up and the other majority judge, Auld LJ, was quite right to say so. In Otton LJ's view, the sellers had rebutted the presumptive reference to the diminished value of the goods in section 53(3). Damages were to be assessed by reference to the resale of the decals, which was sufficiently contemplated by the parties under the remoteness of damage rule. The sellers possessed quite detailed knowledge of the buyers' resale needs. Otton LJ does not put it in quite so many words but, since the buyers incurred no liability for the decals resold, they should recover no damages for the film that was used in these sales. Auld LJ's judgment goes deeper into the principles of damages recovery but his conclusion is the same as Otton LJ's. He adds that the contemplation of sub-sale losses displaces the value approach in section 53(3). Certainly, a plaintiff should not recover both for that would amount to double-counting. The dissenting judge, Thorpe LJ, was content to fall back on the finding of the trial judge that the sellers had failed to carry the burden of showing the parties' intention to displace the presumptive rule in section 53(3). (Liquidated damages clauses apart, does the application of section 53(3) turn on the intention of the parties?)

In a case like this, there are two opposing approaches to consider. The first, exemplified by *Slater* and those cases adhering to the market rule, is that the systematic integrity of the rule counts more than the need for accurate compensation in individual cases. The section 53(3) rule is easier to administer than one that demands a close scrutiny of subsequent contracts. Furthermore, it may be seen as easing the forensic burden of a plaintiff who cannot be sure if and when he might be faced with a claim by sub-buyers and who is unable to prove with the necessary exactitude a loss of business reputation. A loss of value claim for damages provides for such a plaintiff a rough and ready equivalent to unaccrued and unprovable losses and also expedites litigation. In support of this approach, it is noteworthy that there is no precisely stated rule of factual causation in the Sale of Goods Act. The opposite approach, which was favoured by the majority in *Bence*, is that damages in a case like the present should follow the normal approach to damages assessment and focus on the remoteness rule and the actual loss caused to the present plaintiff. It leaves unanswered the question whether, in the interest of consistency, the same approach should be adopted in the future for cases of non-delivery and non-acceptance. Finally, it would be interesting to speculate about a clause that excluded liability for contemplable business losses incurred by the plaintiff buyer. Would the court say that the value measure was excluded by the contemplation and that the plaintiff should recover nothing in the face of an effective exclusion clause? Or would it say that, taking all the circumstances into account, the presumptive rule in section 53(3) had not been displaced after all? The latter seems more likely.

Finally, there have been recent developments in Europe to consider. The most significant of these is that the green paper on *Guarantees for Consumer Goods and After-Sales Services* (COM(93)509) has now reached the stage of a proposed Commission directive (COM(1998)217) pursuant to Article 189b of the amended Treaty of Rome (for an earlier draft, see Department of Trade and Industry, 'Proposals for a European Parliament and Council Directive on the Sale of Consumer Goods and Associated Guarantees: Second Consultation Document' (21 July 1997); R Bradgate, 'Consumer Guarantees: the EC's Draft Directive' [1997] 1 *Web JCLI*). This directive, agreed by European Consumer Ministers (see Department of Trade and Industry Press Release P/98/304) would affect current law on consumer sale of goods agreements in the following respects.

The coverage of the directive is spelt out in Article 1. 'Consumer goods' are any 'moveable' goods supplied by sellers (in the plural) to consumers (in the plural); a 'seller' is someone who sells, or supplies on exchange terms, in the course of his trade, business or profession; and a 'consumer' is a natural person 'acting' (on the stage?) for reasons not related to his trade, business or profession. The drafting is shoddy, and not to be excused on the ground that it lays down only the general principles, and the directive is obscure on the relationship of a particular seller to a particular consumer. Although there is no stated link between the seller and the consumer, the tenor of the directive is that the consumer acquires new goods and the obvious example of its application is indeed where the consumer is the immediate buyer. But there seems nothing to prevent the application of the directive in favour of a third party consumer to whom the buyer (who may not pass the test of a consumer) requires the seller to deliver the goods directly. The goods have to conform to the contract in that they must comply with the description given them by the seller and possess the qualities of any proffered sample or model, be fit for the purposes for which goods of the same type are commonly supplied as well as fit for any particular purpose made known to the seller at the contract date, and have quality and performance standards that the consumer is entitled to expect, 'partly' ('particularly'?) in view of the public statements made by the seller or producer when advertising or labelling the goods (Article 2). This obligation of quality, fitness and description should be applied by English courts in the same way that sections 13-15 of the Sale of Goods Act are applied except that the directive extends the seller's legal guarantee to take account of expectations engendered by producers' statements. The obligation has its antecedents in the common law, though it appears to have been imported into the directive *via* the Vienna Convention on the International Sale of Goods 1980 (see Article 35). It is unlikely that civil law countries in Europe would apply description in the technical sense understood in England. This raises the interesting question whether an English court enforcing the directive should treat express warranties and representations emanating from the seller as part of description for the purpose of the directive. It is submitted that, in the interest of harmonisation of law within the EU, it should.

Under the directive, the seller will be responsible for non-conformity in the goods existing at the time of delivery and becoming 'manifest' within two years (Article 3.1), unless the consumer agrees to conclude the contract though aware of the lack of conformity (Article 2.3). Once the consumer notifies the seller of non-conformity, the two-year period is suspended until the seller's obligations are fulfilled (Article 7). Any non-conformity becoming manifest within six months of delivery is rebuttably presumed to have existed in the goods at the time of delivery (Article 3.3). The Department of Trade and Industry is of the view that Article 3.1 does not impose a durability requirement. In the sense that it is the *non-conformity* that must appear within two years of delivery, the DTI is right: goods may be conforming and not last two years (e.g., Beaujolais Nouveau). Yet Article 3.1 cannot be said to impose a limitation period since it requires that the non-conformity appear within two years and not that the consumer take action within two years. What Article 3.1 seems to do is to protect the seller from liability for latent defects that become manifest after the two year period. It is a provision that guillotines the consumer's rights under Article 2; it does not impose an additional durability requirement on the seller. It is not inconceivable that, under the Sale of Goods Act, a consumer would be able to trace a fault in the goods appearing after two years to the condition of the goods on delivery and hold the seller responsible for it. This possibility would remain after the implementation of the directive (Article 7).

It is in the remedies provision that the departure of the draft directive from English law is most marked. First of all, a consumer paying instalments as agreed with the seller may suspend payment until the lack of conformity is put right (Article 4). Furthermore, upon notification to the seller of the non-conformity of the goods, the seller is bound 'without unreasonable delay' to offer to replace the goods free of charge or to repair them (Article 3.4). (It is not clear what is the sanction for the seller's failure to comply with this duty, though any (implied) period in which the consumer must choose his remedy is likely to be extended.) The consumer may then choose freely either 'claim' (*sic*) offered except where only one of them is 'economically appropriate' regarding 'the seller's interests' and 'reasonable' to the consumer.

Where neither remedy is 'possible' (presumably a remedy both economically inappropriate and unreasonable would not be 'possible'), or if an attempted repair does not make good a lack of conformity, the purchaser may demand either a price reduction or 'rescission' of the contract (Article 3.4). Rescission, the prospect of which should encourage sellers to repair if they get the chance, ought to correspond to contractual termination as understood in England. The obligations of the seller regarding replacement goods are the same as for the original goods and the guarantee period recommences upon replacement (Article 3.5). The price reduction action is inspired, not by the consumer's right to abate a part of the price under section 53(1) of the Sale of Goods Act, but rather by the Roman *actio quanti minoris*, which appears in the Vienna Convention as Article 50. The difference between Article 50 and section 53(1) is that under the former the consumer could throw back on the seller a part of any market fall occurring after the contract date. Subject to this, Article 3.4, in an open-ended fashion, seems to give the consumer the powerful remedy of rejection of the goods and termination of the contract for a much longer period than that available under the Sale of Goods Act. (An earlier draft would have confined the remedies of rescission and replacement to one year from an unstated date.) The directive says nothing about the consumer who has had the valuable use of the goods for a lengthy period before rescinding the contract and claiming the return of the price in full.

Article 3 also contains a provision releasing the seller from liability for 'public statements' made by the producer if the seller did not know and could not have known of the statement, or corrected the statement or shows that the consumer could not have been influenced to buy the goods by the statement (Article 3.2). A seller held liable for a non-conformity due to an act of commission or omission of the producer or of any intermediate seller or intermediary is permitted to claim over against that person 'under the conditions laid down by national law' (Article 3.7). If this statement means only what it appears to mean, it says nothing worth saying. It does not provide that liability under the directive can be transmitted to any of those parties. It appears to mean, for example, that a seller sued successfully by a consumer under legislation incorporating the directive may sue its own seller for a breach of one of the implied terms in sections 13–14 of the Sale of Goods Act, seeking to recover consequential damages pursuant to section 54, to the extent allowed by current English law.

The draft directive also contains a number of provisions on express, or commercial, guarantees. They must be in a written document and contain stated information (Article 6.2); informal warranties given by sellers would seem to fall outside this provision. They must also place the consumer in a better provision than that provided by national rules governing the sale of consumer goods (Article 6.1). This latter provision appears to be sensible and useful only if one makes the assumption that the guarantee is designed to supersede those same national rules and, under the relevant law, would be contractually effective in so doing.

Finally, rights under the directive may not be waived or excluded by means of contractual terms or agreements concluded with the seller before notification of lack of non-conformity (Article 9.1).

26 May 1998

Preface

The origins of this work lie in a book that I wrote when on the Faculty of Law of McGill University, Montreal. It was entitled *Sale of Goods* (1988) and addressed the subject from a Canadian perspective. Thanks to Oxford University Press, I have been able to 'patriate' this book but have, in the process, produced much more than an update of that 1988 book. Large parts of the book have been extensively rewritten; relatively few sentences have emerged from the process unscathed. There have of course been a substantial number of changes in sales law in the last decade, which is somewhat surprising given the relative paucity of case law in a mature subject. The most important developments have been statutory ones, notably the Sale and Supply of Goods Act 1994 and the Sale of Goods (Amendment) Act 1995. The former recasts the old merchantable quality implied term as the implied term of satisfactory quality. Apart from tinkering with the definition of the term, the Act in rechristening that term points to the fundamental shifts in the pattern of sale transactions that have occurred in the last hundred years or so. The latter statute, introducing a major proprietary reform, creates interests by way of tenancy in common in bulk goods, a matter of no small interest to the bulk commodities trade but not confined to that trade.

The focus of this work is the English law of sale. A series of statutory reforms of the last thirty years have given it an identity separate from its counterparts in other Commonwealth jurisdictions. It is with some regret that I note the passing of a *ius commune* of sale in common law countries. The old American Uniform Sales Act was modelled by Williston on our Sale of Goods Act 1893. It disappeared with the arrival of Article 2 of the Uniform Commercial Code in the 1950s. But there was no practice of citing American cases in this country, so the rupture was more apparent than real. Commonwealth statutes were largely identical to the 1893 Act, apart from some differences in drafting techniques. English statutory definitions referred to above, together with major changes in the receiving countries, such as Australia's Trade Practices Act, will create difficulties of transferring authorities between jurisdictions, even as the courts of this country show a refreshing willingness to look overseas for inspiration. This disintegration of sales law is, nevertheless, inevitable if it is to keep pace with the society in which it is embedded: the law of sale is not a museum piece. This is very much a book on the English law of sale. It should be consulted with care by those interested in the Scots treatment of the subject since, in important respects, Scots law departs from English law. Commonwealth authority is cited where it is either practically relevant or of sufficient interest to throw light on English law.

This is a book concerned with the general, domestic law of sale. It aims, not merely to lay out the English law of sale, but also to prescribe and criticize. The best service an author can provide for the professional and scholarly communities is to furnish them with a thoroughgoing examination of principle that will equip them to understand, and not merely to know, the subject. Otherwise the book would soon become about as useful as an out-of-date railway timetable. It is therefore important to appraise the subject of sale with an evolutionary eye. Many apparent oddities in the law were accurate enough expressions of the case law codified for the first time in 1893. Understanding their origin is more than half of the way towards dealing with them. Although our Sale of Goods Act dates from 1979, it is just the 1893 Act as modified by a series of statutes, designed mainly to equip the law to deal with consumer transactions, together with a few very minor changes of style introduced for no apparent reason. The 1979 Act falls well short of a modern recasting of sales law. It is questionable how long the Act can survive in its present form as a general sales statute. The work of the Law Commission in the field adds up to a fairly compelling case for the separation of the consumer and commercial laws of sale.

One of the difficulties facing a writer, dealing with sale, is knowing where to draw the line between the special law of sale and the general law of contract. As a matter of principle, this question became for me subordinate to the maximum permitted length of the manuscript. Sale is probably the most important of the special contracts; it cannot be mastered without a solid understanding of general contract law. Some account must therefore be taken of the general law, but it would be pointless to reproduce in great detail areas that had best be consulted in the general contract (and tort) textbooks. Export sales are not treated as such but case law is examined to the extent that it applies the rules concerning delivery, payment and proprietary matters. In addition, this book deals with consumer material only in so far as it bears upon the private law relationship of seller and buyer. It cannot therefore be regarded as a consumer law text. Transactions similar to sale are referred to quite copiously but the overwhelming concern of the book is with sale itself. Finally, although it is easy to think of sales law as a branch of applied contract law, that is true only in part. A very substantial portion of sales law is personal property law and I hope I have done justice to it.

I owe much to the support and encouragement of Richard Hart and his colleagues at Oxford University Press. Furthermore, when the process of retyping and editing was threatening to overwhelm me, I became indebted to the Nottingham University Law Department administrator, Linda Wright, who arranged for outside assistance at short notice. I also wish to record my gratitude for the efforts of Sandra Frisby who gave me invaluable assistance as a summer research student. Finally, my thanks and apologies go to my family, who do not share my peculiar fascination with sales law but who, like any conscientious buyer, paid the price.

University of Nottingham
26 July 1996

Table of Contents

Table of Cases

Table of Statutes

Statutory Instruments

County Court Rules

Supreme Court Rules

United States of America

Table of International Instruments

1

Introduction and Conclusion of the Contract

Background to Modern Sale of Goods Legislation

Sale of goods is a specialized branch of the general law of contract. Its case law has been of fundamental importance in assisting the development of the general law. In two principal respects, however, the special law of sale of goods stands apart from general contract law. First, unlike most nominate contracts, sale involves a conveyance of the seller's property interest in the goods in favour of the buyer, which, together with the abundance of reported sales decisions, lends a degree of autonomy to this branch of the law. Secondly, and quite strikingly in view of the paucity of statutes in general contract law, sale has its own statutory code, the Sale of Goods Act 1979, which is for the most part a reworking of its 1893 predecessor.

Far from separating sales law from the general law of contract, a reference to it is directed by the Act where none other of its provisions apply.[1] Yet the process of reabsorption of sale by the general law, prompted by the gaps that appear in a code over time and by the mass of decisions that encrust particular provisions of the Act, is disguised by the way that syllabuses and textbook writers have delineated sale as a category apart.

Most of the law of sale, a branch of commercial law, is the product of nineteenth century developments.[2] Prior to this, Lord Mansfield had fostered the integration of the law merchant into the common law by making the latter responsive to the customs and usages of the former,[3] just as Lord Holt, a half century earlier, had laid the foundation of the common law treatment of negotiable instruments.[4] Nevertheless, the major features of the modern law of sale, such as the passing of property and risk, the implied terms of description, fitness for purpose, and merchantable quality, and the remedies for breach of contract were laid down in a series of nineteenth century judgments ranging from the time of Lord Ellenborough to Lord Blackburn. The enactment in 1893 of the Sale of Goods Act[5] was the coping-stone of this development.

[1] S. 62(2).   [2] K. Llewellyn, (1939) 52 *Harv. LR* 725, 740–6.
[3] W. S. Holdsworth, *A History of English Law* (1903 ff., Methuen and Sweet & Maxwell, London, 17 vols.), xii (1938), 524–42.
[4] *Ibid.*, vi (1924), 519–22.   [5] 56 & 57 Vict., cap. 71.

A consequence of this course of progression is that the present Sale of Goods Act 1979, a re-enactment of the 1893 Act with intervening amendments and minor statutory changes, faithfully reflects the type of sale agreement that preoccupied the courts in that century. This case law was mainly concerned with small commodities agreements and the sale of goods for industrial use and consumption. It can be traced into the provisions of the 1893 Act. Large-scale commodities agreements on forward delivery terms involving the transfer of documents find no mention in the 1893 Act or even in its 1979 successor. Further, the difficulties experienced in reforming the statutory provisions on the implied terms, discharge for breach, and acceptance, dealt with by the Sale and Supply of Goods Act 1994, are rooted in the fact that the law was not codified on the basis of decisions arising out of the dealings in consumer durables and complex manufactured goods that are prominent in modern case law.[6]

The Sale of Goods Act 1979 cannot be described as an attempt to revise the law of sale to meet late twentieth century conditions. The law therein was not overhauled and subjected to the rigorous scrutiny needed for such a task. Rather, a number of important, though, in the greater scheme of things, incidental, reforms of the 1960s and 1970s were consolidated alongside a few minor changes of drafting style. Those reforms affected the definition of the implied terms of title, description, merchantable quality, and fitness for purpose; the ability of the seller to exclude these obligations; the relationship between the buyer's right to examine the goods and to reject them if they are defective; and the exceptions to the rule of *nemo dat quod non habet*. Further changes of similar importance, advocated by the Law Commission,[7] were implemented by the Sale and Supply of Goods Act 1994 without changing the original structure inherited from the 1893 Act. In addition, a Sale of Goods (Amendment) Act 1994 was passed to abolish the rule of market overt in the transfer of title to goods. The Department of Trade and Industry, in the same year again, issued a consultative document dealing with the quality of consumer goods, but this has not so far produced legislative change.[8] In 1995, another Sale of Goods (Amendment) Act was passed, this time to permit prepaying buyers to acquire an undivided interest in bulk goods.

Any discussion of the merits of a radical revision of sales law should start from the position that the Sale of Goods Act is largely presumptive and rarely mandatory. Those with a mind to exclude or vary its provisions are, for the most part, unimpeded in their efforts, though the combined force of statutory inertia and contractual brevity should not be

---

[6] K. Sutton, (1969) 7 *Alta LR* 130, 173; Lord Diplock, (1981) 15 *UBC LR* 371, 373–4.
[7] *Sale and Supply of Goods* (Law Com. No 160, 1987).
[8] For prospective developments in the area of consumer guarantees, see Ch. 8 below.

underestimated. What cannot be said is that an archaic statute, essentially Victorian, is stifling commerce. Even if there were any truth in this, commerce is resilient enough to absorb such an irritant in the way that an oyster envelopes a grain of sand. In any case, an aging statute increasingly defers to case law responsive to changes in commercial practice.[9]

Account should be taken of the work that has taken place on the unification of international sales law,[10] which began in the 1930s under the auspices of the Institute for the Unification of Private Law. These efforts resumed after the Second World War in the 1950s and produced two conventions that were adopted at a diplomatic conference sponsored by the Dutch Government. The conventions dealt with the formation of international sale of goods contracts and with the law governing the sales themselves. Neither convention exercised strong international appeal, and a fresh reform initiative was taken by the United Nations Commission on International Trade Law, which culminated in a 1978 draft Convention on International Sale of Goods that was unanimously approved at a diplomatic conference held in Vienna in 1980. The Convention has now been ratifed by more than forty countries, accounting for the greater part of world trade, and the isolation of the United Kingdom, which has so far failed to ratify, is becoming increasingly obvious. Drawing from a wide array of civil and common law experience, and responsive to the commercial needs of different types of economies, the Convention rests upon the inherited wisdom and authority of no particular legal system. UNCITRAL provides a documentary service about the national case law interpreting the Convention[11] but there is no authoritative supranational source to provide *amicus curiae* opinions. Those national courts producing the first crop of persuasive decisions will set the tone for the Convention's future interpretation. English courts will therefore have no part to play in the interpretation of the Convention, apart perhaps from the occasional case where they may be called upon to apply, as the proper law of a contract, a law that incorporates the Convention.

Code and Common Law

A legitimate criticism of the common law is that its finely-calibrated character, responsive to infinite shades of practical reality, is purchased at the cost of a complexity that places its comprehension beyond the

[9] G. Gilmore, (1948) 57 *Yale LJ* 1341.
[10] For an historical account of these developments, see J. Honnold, *Uniform Law for International Sales* (2nd edn., Kluwer, Devente, 1991).
[11] CLOUT: Case Law on Uncitral Texts. There is also an information service organized by Pace University of New York available on the Internet: see http://www.cisg.law.pace.edu.

reach of all but a select number of academics, judges, and practitioners.[12] The complexity of modern case law complements the complexity
of modern statutes. It is salutary to compare in the 1979 Act the pristine
sections of the 1893 Act with the late twentieth century additions: the former are open-textured and simple, while the latter are contorted by the
draftsman's attempts to provide for every eventuality.

The 1893 Act was consequent upon the simplification of procedure
and the abolition of the forms of action,[13] together with the substitution
of a mass of judge-made legal rules for the unrecorded factual judgments
of juries.[14] It is a compendium of clear rules that has come under stress
in modern conditions as the pendulum between law and fact has swung
increasingly in favour of the latter, a tendency due in no small part to the
infusion of the common law with a benevolent judicial discretion at the
expense of legal inflexibility.[15] The Sale of Goods Act 1893 recorded a
process that over the nineteenth century had substituted a network of
legal rules for a laconic and unsystematic mass of jury decisions.[16] The
line between fact and law has been redrawn in modern times in favour of
the former, although this has come too late for the civil jury, now almost
completely disappeared.

Confidence in statutory codes as universal solvents is inversely proportional to the number of years that have passed since their enactment; the
same holds true for civilian codes. The Sale of Goods Act may not be a
code in the sense understood by a civilian jurist, since it is confined to a
special contract (sale) and permits penetration by the general uncodified
law to fill its lacunae, but it can rightly be called a codification for the conscious attempt to summarize rather than reform the antecedent case
law.[17] Unlike a statute such as the Consumer Credit Act 1974, which manufactures its own concepts and largely consigns the antecedent case law
to oblivion, the Sale of Goods Act is very much a creature of the common
law that it summarized. A thorough understanding of the Act cannot be
attained without a journey to the case law that prompted the statutory
provisions, however much this might be deplored by those who argue
that statutes supply a fresh start and wholly supersede earlier case law.

[12] See the criticisms of Lord Diplock about the cost and needless complexity of modern
legal argument fuelled by the multiple citation of authority in, e.g., *Lambert* v. *Lewis* [1982]
AC 225.
[13] Holdsworth, n.3 above, ix (3rd edn., 1944), 247–335.
[14] The virtues of a clear rule are promoted in M. Chalmers, (1903) 19 *LQR* 10;
Holdsworth, n. 3 above, xi (1938), 315–18.
[15] P. S. Atiyah, (1980) 65 *Iowa LR* 1249.
[16] The right to terminate for breach was firmly established as a matter of law by cases
such as *Bentsen* v. *Taylor, Sons & Co. (No. 2)* [1893] 2 QB 274. Perhaps the best-known example is the laying down of rules governing remoteness of damage in contract. See *Hadley* v.
Baxendale (1854) 9 Ex. 341; Simpson, (1979) 46 *U Chi LR* 533.
[17] Chalmers, n. 14 above.

Be that as it may, the classic approach to a codifying statute, uttered in the full and optimistic flush of the statute's youth, is given by Lord Herschell in respect of the Bills of Exchange Act 1882,[18] like the Sale of Goods Act 1893 a product of Sir Mackenzie Chalmers's draftsmanship. He said that the starting point should be the natural meaning of the statutory text itself, 'uninfluenced by any considerations derived from the previous state of the law', and that recourse should be had to the antecedent case law only in exceptional cases, for example, if the text was unclear or if it adopted a term of art that could be clarified by a discussion of the cases. Besides the economy of effort that comes with not 'roaming over a vast sea of authorities', the court also avoids the risk of misreading provisions of a reforming or clarifying nature, not literally based upon earlier cases.[19]

But in our legal tradition, the accretion of case law impedes direct access to the text and the text itself becomes absorbed eventually by the common law. The words of Lord Herschell might have seemed to lack currency in the case of sale were it not for the introduction of a statutory definition of merchantable quality in 1973, renamed with some modification as satisfactory quality in 1994. This has prompted two divergent judicial approaches to its interpretation: the one seeking an answer to its meaning in the text itself, and the other looking to the case law on which it was modelled.[20] Further, an argument in favour of turning from time to time to the pre-1893 case law is that the provisions of the Act are sometimes based upon common law reasoning that is now outmoded. Chalmers faithfully recorded the law as he saw it, though it should be understood that certain changes were made to the 1893 Act in its progression through Parliament. Condensing sales law as it did, the Sale of Goods Act encouraged later observers to see as flaws in the Act rules that were a perfect reflection of the contemporary law that had been codified.[21] A similar judgement is that Chalmers, the author of the highly

[18] *Bank of England* v. *Vagliano Bros.* [1891] AC 107. For a defence of the merits of the Sale of Goods Act in promoting legal simplicity, see A. Diamond, (1968) 31 *MLR* 361, 368–70.

[19] But for references to the Sale of Goods Act 1893 codifying rather than the reforming law, see e.g. *Bristol Tramways & Carriage Co. Ltd* v. *Fiat Motors Ltd* [1910] 2 KB 831, 836; *Harris* v. *Tong* (1930) 65 OLR 133, 137 (Can.); *Healing Sales Pty. Ltd* v. *Inglis Electrix Pty. Ltd* (1968) 121 CLR 584, 612 (Windeyer J).

[20] For a statement of the need to examine pre-codification authorities, see *M/S Aswan Engineering Establishment Co.* v. *Lupdine Ltd* [1987] 1 WLR 1. For the opposite view, see *Rogers* v. *Parish Motors (Scarborough) Ltd* [1987] 2 All ER 232 (Mustill LJ) and *Marimpex Mineralöl Handels GmbH* v. *Louis Dreyfus et Cie GmbH* [1995] 1 Lloyd's Rep. 167, 179. Assuming the latter approach to an unhelpful statutory definition, how should a court dealing with 'satisfactory quality' approach cases decided under the 'old' s. 14(6) definition of merchantable quality? See further the examination of the pre-1973 authorities in *Cehave NV* v. *Bremer Handelsgesellschaft mbH* [1976] QB 44.

[21] The Ontario Law Reform Commission, *Report on Sale of Goods* (1979), i, 23–4, refers to a number of rules as 'original defects'. But, to take one example, the 'artificial restrictions

successful Bills of Exchange Act 1882, nodded when he laid out the inferior Sale of Goods Act 1893.[22] With imaginative and informed interpretation, the Act can be brought back into line with contemporary contract law. Sales law and contract law alike are dynamic and must respond to changing patterns of commercial activity. On occasion, the resolution of a modern problem may need the antecedents of the statutory text to be scrutinised with no small care. To understand the pedigree of sales law is not to practise legal antiquarianism.

Sale of Goods Act and Common Law

The Sale of Goods Act is less than a code, for section 62(2) directs a reference to the general law when the Act itself is silent:[23]

The rules of the common law, including the law merchant, except in so far as they are inconsistent with the provisions of this Act, and in particular the rules relating to the law of principal and agent and the effect of fraud, misrepresentation, duress or coercion, mistake or other invalidating cause, apply to contracts for the sale of goods.

This section shows that the Act was never designed to be comprehensive and inward-looking; rather, it expresses a framework of mainly presumptive rules complementing the general law.[24] A number of sections state that the intention of the parties is paramount,[25] thereby emphasizing they are free to strike their own bargain.[26] Sales law and general contract law are both affected by forces abridging contractual freedom, and

on the remedies of a buyer in a sale of specific goods' were in fact a faithful reflection of a lingering *caveat emptor* ethic.

[22] Gower, Foreword to P. S. Atiyah, *The Sale of Goods* (Pitman, London, 1963) ('perhaps, his least happy effort'). A similar judgment is that of K. Llewellyn, who referred to the Act as drafted 'not by Blackburn nor by Bramwell, nor yet by Hamilton or Kennedy, but by merely an able lawyer who knew his Bills and Notes': (1937) 37 *Col LR* 341, 409.

[23] M. Chalmers, *The Sale of Goods Act, 1893, Including the Factors Acts, 1889 & 1890* (4th edn., Butterworths, London, 1899), 6: '[T]he contract of sale . . . [i]n part . . . is governed by principles peculiar to itself, and in part by principles common to all [consenual and bilateral] contracts. . . . The Act, except incidentally, deals only with the first-mentioned principles. The principles of law which govern the contract of sale, in common with all other consensual contracts, are outside its scope. But they are saved by sect.[62(2)]'.

[24] Introduction to the 1st edn. of Chalmers, *ibid.*, and reproduced in all subsequent editions of the work: 'Sale is a consensual contract, and the Act does not seek to prevent the parties from making any bargain they please. Its object is to lay down clear rules for the case where the parties have either formed no intention, or failed to express it.'

[25] Particularly apparent in Part IV (Performance of the Contract).

[26] Expressed most strongly by Jessel MR in *Printers & Numerical Registering Co.* v. *Sampson* (1875) LR 19 Eq. 462, 465: '[I]f there is one thing which more than another public policy requires it is that men of full age and competent understanding shall have the utmost liberty of contracting, and that their contracts when entered into freely and voluntarily shall be held sacred and shall be enforced by Courts of justice.'

by the need to strike a reasonable balance between freedom and intervention.

Section 62(2) has proved its value in the past when enabling courts to avoid inflexibility in the Sale of Goods Act. Thus section 7 was not applied in one case where the goods had never existed and therefore could not be said to have perished for the purpose of initial impossibility;[27] and the Act's classification of implied contractual terms as conditions and warranties was held in another case not to impede the application of intermediate stipulation analysis to express terms of the contract.[28] Applied in this corrective fashion, section 62(2) works to prevent the divergence of sales law from an evolving general law.

Equity

In another respect, however, section 62(2) has fostered just such a divergence. It makes no reference to the rules of equity. Does 'the rules of common law' mean common law and equity as opposed to statute, or common law in the narrower sense that excludes equity? The question has proved to be particularly troubling in the areas of equitable proprietary interests and, in certain Commonwealth jurisdictions, the equitable rule of innocent misrepresentation.[29]

The issue concerning innocent misrepresentation is whether the lenient equitable test for an actionable misrepresentation, that a statement merely induce the making of a contract,[30] or the common law rule, that it induce in the mind of the listener a fundamental mistake,[31] applies to sale of goods agreements. In England, the matter has long been settled in favour of the equitable view.[32] But the New Zealand Court of Appeal in *Riddiford* v. *Warren*[33] took the opposite view for these reasons. First, innocent misrepresentation had never formed part of sales law before sale was codified, as opposed to reformed, by statute. The reference in section 62(2) to 'misrepresentation' was therefore to the common law rule. Moreover, a lenient misrepresentation rule could subvert the statutory scheme of contractual terms and remedies for breach.[34] We shall see later in this text that English courts have moved by other means

---

[27] *McRae* v. *Commonwealth Disposals Commission* (1951) 84 CLR 377.
[28] *Cehave NV* v. *Bremer Handelsgesellschaft mbH*, n. 20 above.
[29] *Riddiford* v. *Warren* (1901) 20 NZLR 572; *Watt* v. *Westhoven* [1933] VLR 458.
[30] *Redgrave* v. *Hurd* (1881) 20 Ch D 1; *Torrance* v. *Bolton* (1872) LR 8 Ch. App. 118.
[31] *Kennedy* v. *Panama, New Zealand and Australian Royal Mail Co. Ltd* (1867) LR 2 QB 580.
[32] See e.g. the recent example of *Naughton* v. *O'Callaghan* [1990] 3 All ER 191, where the issue does not rate a mention.   [33] N. 29 above.
[34] *Watt* v. *Westhoven*, n. 29 above, 463: 'Much of the language, and the arrangement in which the Act has codified the common law, would have to be revised to accommodate a doctrine whereby every warranty could become a condition, and every inducing statement not warranted would be a condition also.'

to prevent such subversion from occurring.[35] Secondly, the issue was not to be resolved in accordance with the rule that, in cases of conflict between law and equity, the rules of equity shall prevail. There was no conflict to resolve since innocent misrepresentation had never been extended to 'mercantile contracts for the sale of goods' in the years before the fusion of law and equity.

However faithful *Riddiford* v. *Warren* may have been to the pre-code law of sale, it is motivated by the regrettable view that the Sale of Goods Act froze the living law. Chalmers may well have believed that sales law had reached the acme of its development before the Act, but a sensible view of the draftsman's intention would see section 62(2) as incorporating the general law as it exists from time to time so as to retain the affinity between sale and the general law.

An approach similar to the one in *Riddiford* v. *Warren* has exercised a more general and lasting appeal in respect of the transfer of equitable proprietary rights between seller and buyer. In contrast with its laconic treatment of common law misrepresentation, the Act deals at length with the passing of the legal, or general, property in goods.[36] A buyer who has obtained this general property may, if the seller becomes insolvent before delivery, assert this property right against the seller's creditors, secured and unsecured. A buyer unable to show that such a conveyance has taken place, but to whom equitable proprietary rights have been transferred, would receive upon the seller's insolvency equivalent protection.[37] Despite nineteenth century authority favouring the buyer, the dominant view in this century is that there is no room in sales law for the passing of implied equitable proprietary rights.[38] The question why some equitable rules have been incorporated in sales law while others, in the interest of commercial stability and convenience, have not, has not received a judicial airing.

In numerous other respects, equity plays an uncontroversial part in contemporary sales law. Any argument that promissory estoppel,[39] injunctive relief,[40] and rectification,[41] to name just three examples, are

[35] *Leaf* v. *International Galleries* [1950] 2 KB 86; M. G. Bridge (1986) 20 *UBC LR* 53; Ch. 5 below.   [36] Ch. 3 below.

[37] *McEntire* v. *Crossley Bros.* [1895] AC 457, 461; *Madell* v. *Thomas* [1891] 1 QB 230, 238.

[38] *Re Wait* [1927] 1 Ch. 606; *Leigh and Sillavan Ltd* v. *Aliakmon Shipping Co. Ltd* [1986] AC 785.

[39] The rule has been applied in numerous commodities cases as a last ditch attempt to curb the application of the strict law on termination for breach: e.g., *Société Italo-Belge pour le Commerce et l'Industrie* v. *Palm and Vegetable Oils (Malaysia) Sdn. Bhd.* [1981] 2 Lloyd's Rep. 695; *Peter Cremer* v. *Granaria BV* [1981] 2 Lloyd's Rep. 583; *Bremer Handelsgesellschaft mbh* v. *Finagrain, Cie Commerciale Agricole et Financière SA* [1981] 2 Lloyd's Rep. 259; *Bremer Handelsgesellschaft mbh* v. *C. Mackprang Jnr.* [1979] 2 Lloyd's Rep. 221.

[40] e.g. *Sky Petroleum Ltd* v. *VIP Petroleum Ltd* [1974] 1 WLR 576.

[41] *United States of America* v. *Motor Trucks Ltd* [1924] AC 203; *F. E. Rose (London) Ltd* v. *W. H. Pim Jnr. & Co. Ltd* [1953] 2 QB 450.

excluded by the Act would receive short shrift. Other equitable institutions, such as relief against forfeiture,[42] remain of doubtful scope in sale
of goods cases, not because of anything in the Act but because their own
doctrinal limitations may restrict their operation. The problem of
equity's relationship with the common law centres today, not so much
upon the scope of the Act, but rather upon the extent to which equitable
rules and institutions are free to develop by expansion or even by retraction after the administrative fusion of the two systems.[43] This in turn presents the questions whether such a refurbished equity is greatly different
from a common law renewed by an infusion of discretion and sensitivity
to particular fact, and whether the two systems are converging to produce a unification of substantive law.

Law Merchant

Section 62(2) explicitly incorporates the rules of the law merchant. The
law merchant was the source of the unpaid seller's right of stoppage *in
transitu*[44] and it continues still to invigorate the common law.[45] It is not,
however, some body of immutable, supranational law proceeding from
the will of a higher sovereign, or even an all-encompassing *opinio juris*,
but rather the sum of trade usages and customs practised from time to
time and upon which commercial parties are presumed to conduct their
dealings.[46] They are binding either as implied terms of the contract or
because they colour its interpretation; they may therefore be ousted by a
contrary agreement.[47] In modern times, the proliferation of standard-
form agreements has diminished the scope for implied terms based
upon trade usage,[48] so that in a very real sense now the law merchant is
the totality of standard forms.

Section 62(2) would exclude the law merchant where it is inconsistent
with the Act. To understand how far this reservation hampers the law

---

[42] *Stockloser* v. *Johnson* [1954] 1 QB 476; *Barton Thompson & Co. Ltd* v. *Stapling
Machines Co.* [1966] Ch. 499; *Sport Internationaal Bussum BV* v. *Inter-Footwear Ltd* [1984]
1 WLR 776.

[43] *United Scientific Holdings Ltd* v. *Burnley Borough Council* [1978] AC 904; *Federal
Commerce & Navigation Co. Ltd* v. *Molena Alpha Inc.* [1978] QB 927, 974; Goodhart and
Jones, (1980) 43 *MLR* 489.

[44] *Gibson* v. *Carruthers* (1841) 8 M & W 321; Ch. 10 below.

[45] Lord Devlin, *Samples of Lawmaking* (OUP, London, 1962), 'The Relation between
Commercial Law and Commercial Practice' (Lecture 2); L. Trakman, *The Law Merchant:
The Evolution of Commercial Law* (Fred B. Rothman & Co., Littleton, Colo., 1983).

[46] *Goodwin* v. *Robarts* (1875) LR 10 Ex. 337; *Edelstein* v. *Schuler & Co.* [1902] 2 KB 144. For
the requirement that custom must be reasonable, see *Produce Brokers Co.* v. *Olympia Oil
and Cake Co.* [1916] 2 KB 296, 298.

[47] *Palgrave, Brown & Son Ltd* v. *SS Turid (Owners)* [1922] 1 AC 397; *Brown* v. *Byrne* (1854)
2 E & B 703 (reluctance to find inconsistency between established custom and bill of lading).

[48] Lord Devlin, n. 45 above.

merchant, it is necessary to quantify the mandatory content of the Sale of Goods Act. It cannot be that the law merchant is excluded every time the Act lays down presumptive rules of agreement, for this would concede it a very small role to the law merchant[49] and would create an inconsistency between trade usages and other sources of express and implied terms. Since the binding force of trade usage itself depends upon presumptive agreement, the inroads it makes into the Act are surely as great as those made by inconsistent express and implied terms. The rules regarding the passing of property and risk in c.i.f. contracts,[50] inconsistent with the presumptive rules of the Act, may be regarded as binding on the parties by virtue of either implied agreement or of trade usage.

But there are provisions in the Act that may not be excluded by the parties. Parties may not provide for the general property in unascertained goods to pass to the buyer before the goods become ascertained;[51] any inconsistent trade usage should be excluded under section 62(2). The Act also deals with the proprietary relationship between original owner and subsequent transferee in a group of sections dealing with the rule of *nemo dat quod non habet* and its exceptions.[52] The law merchant has been relied upon in the past to extent the scope of the negotiability principle to novel types of securities.[53] Were it to manufacture new exceptions to the *nemo dat* rule, this would be in contravention of the comprehensive scheme of title resolution laid down in the Act and so could not be recognized.

CONCLUSION OF THE CONTRACT

This section of the Chapter is devoted to certain aspects of the contractual formation process that merit attention in a specialist sale of goods text. No attempt will be made to dispose of matters that had best be left to the general contract texts. Mention will be made here of formalities; of special statutory provision for abuses and potential abuses in the process of concluding a sale of goods contract; and of offer and acceptance, contractual capacity and certainty, to the extent that they are dealt with specifically in the Sale of Goods Act.

---

[49] Since rules of presumptive agreement are particularly apparent in the area of delivery, where trade usage is most likely to intrude, the point speaks for itself.

[50] *Comptoir d'Achat et du Boerenbond Belge S/A* v. *Luis de Ridder Lda* [1949] AC 293; Ch. 4 below.

[51] See s. 16; Ch. 3 below.   [52] Ss. 21–26.

[53] *Goodwin* v. *Robarts*, n. 46 above (scrip); *Edelstein* v. *Schuler & Co.*, *ibid.* (bearer bonds).

Formalities

Between 1677 and 1954, sale of goods agreements for goods exceeding £10 in value could be enforced only if they were evidenced by a note or memorandum of the agreement signed by the party against whom enforcement was sought. Two statutory exceptions to this writing requirement existed: where the buyer had actually received and accepted the goods; and where the buyer had made some advance payment.[54] These exceptions created for sale of goods contracts an extended equivalent of the equitable doctrine of part performance applicable to contracts involving the sale of land, the existence of which was recognized by statute[55] before the writing requirement was tightened for land in such a way as to leave no room for the continuing existence of part performance.[56] The writing requirement for sale of goods gave rise to a body of very complex law[57] which was severely criticized by Stephen and Pollock in one of the most polemical law review articles ever written.[58] In 1954, the need for writing was abolished by the Law Reform (Enforcement of Contracts) Act.[59] The current position, as expressed in section 4 of the Sale of Goods Act 1979, is that no formal requirements of any kind are exacted for sale of goods agreements under the Act, which may be concluded in any way that evidences the appropriate contractual intention. Section 4, however, is without prejudice to other statutes imposing formal requirements that extend to certain sale of goods agreements.[60] Among these are the Bills of Sale Acts 1878–91.

Briefly, these statutes promote two quite different policies: they protect needy debtors against certain types of grasping behaviour by creditors, and they supposedly protect outside creditors from the deceptive appearances created when a debtor appears to be in unencumbered possession of chattels, but in reality has signed away his rights to a particular creditor. The Bills of Sale Acts impose a most demanding formal and written procedure once the parties to a bill of sale have decided to reduce their agreement to writing.[61] In modern times, there are very few registered bills of sale and the statutory repeal of the legislation would

---

[54] This provision originated as s. 17 of the Statute of Frauds 1677, 29 Car. II, cap. 3, and was re-enacted with changes as s. 4 of the Sale of Goods Act 1893.

[55] S. 40(2) of the Law of Property Act 1925.

[56] Law of Property (Miscellaneous Provisions) Act 1989.

[57] The writing requirement is still in existence in a number of Commonwealth jurisdictions. See M. G. Bridge, *Sale of Goods* (Butterworths, Toronto, 1988), 75–95.

[58] (1885) 1 *LQR* 1.

[59] S. 1.

[60] See, e.g., sale of goods contracts that are consumer credit agreements: Consumer Credit Act 1974, ss. 60 ff.

[61] *Newlove* v. *Shrewsbury* (1888) 21 QBD 41; *Charlesworth* v. *Mills* [1892] AC 231. The Acts do not themselves demand that the agreement take a written form.

probably leave little mark on the law.[62] A wide variety of document is caught by the statutory definition of a bill of sale:[63] it is by no means confined to agreements that borrow the form of a sale of goods contract. The subject is best left to specialist texts.[64]

Unsolicited Goods

The Unsolicited Goods and Services Act 1971[65] was passed to deal with one particular abusive practice in the formation of contracts,[66] namely, the practice of inertia selling, by which goods were sent without prior request to recipients with the accompanying information that they were to be considered sold at the stated price unless the recipients declared in time their intention not to buy the goods. There is no doubt that many recipients, whether through inertia or a less-than-perfect understanding of the principles of contract formation, paid the demanded price and kept the goods. The key provision of the Unsolicited Goods and Services Act is section 1(1) which provides that, as between the sender and the unwilling recipient, the latter may 'use, deal with or dispose of [the goods] as though they were an unconditional gift to him' and the sender's rights in the goods shall be extinguished. Before the recipient can act under section 1(1), a number of points have to be satisfied. First, the goods have to be sent with a view to the recipient acquiring them. This would protect the sender if the goods were mistakenly sent to the wrong person or to the wrong address. The recipient would need to think long and hard about treating the goods as a gift if there is a possibility, based on evidence not available to the recipient, that a mistake of this

---

[62] Nevertheless, non-corporate mortgages and charges, created by individuals and partnerships, are registered under the Acts, while their corporate equivalents are registered under ss. 395 ff. of the Companies Act 1985.

[63] S. 4 of the Bills of Sale Act 1878.

[64] See especially *Halsbury's Laws of England* (4th edn., Title: 'Bills of Sale' by R. M. Goode, Butterworths, London, 1992).

[65] Amended by the Unsolicited Goods and Services (Amendment) Act 1975.

[66] Other practices may be dealt with under powers conferred on the Director-General of Fair Trading by Part II of the Fair Trading Act 1973. Pyramid sales are the subject of particular treatment under the 1973 Act: ss. 118–22 and the Pyramid Selling Schemes Regulations 1989, SI 1989/2195 (as amended). Likewise the duty on the Director-General to encourage the preparation of codes of practice by particular trade associations: s. 124(3) of the 1973 Act. Doorstep selling is a practice that obviously can give rise to abuses taking the form of denial of choice and harassment in the formation of contracts: see the European Council of Ministers' Directive 85/577/EEC, [1985] OJ L372/31, implemented by the Consumer Protection (Cancellation of Contracts Concluded away from Business Premises) Regulations 1987, SI 1987/2117. Distance or direct selling is not so obviously liable to give rise to abuses: see the European draft directives at [1992] OJ C156/14 and [1993] OJ C308/18, and the Commission Recommendation at [1992] OJ L156/21. For details on the above, see G. G. Howells and S. Weatherill, *Consumer Protection Law* (Dartmouth, Aldershot, 1995), chs. 8, 16.

kind has occurred. Secondly, the sender is protected if the recipient had no reasonable cause to believe that the goods were sent for the purpose of acquisition by a trade or business. Circumstances could arise where it is no easy matter for the recipient to read the mind of the sender.[67] Thirdly, the recipient must not have requested the goods or have agreed to return them. Finally, the sender must not have taken the opportunity to repossess the goods within six months of the recipient obtaining possession of them, or within thirty days of a prescribed notice given by the recipient for the sender to collect the goods, whichever comes first.

Auctions

Although Part II of the Sale of Goods Act is entitled 'Formation of the Contract', the one provision dealing with the formation of contracts, section 57 on auction sales, is located elsewhere in the Act. Section 57(2), in providing that the contract is concluded when the auctioneer announces this by the fall of the hammer or in some other customary way, codifies one of the earliest common law rules on contract formation.[68] The bidder consequently makes the offer which, in accordance with ordinary contract principle, the auctioneer is free to accept or refuse.[69] The contract concluded in this way relates to the particular lot announced to be the subject of the bidding, unless this presumptive rule is displaced in the circumstances.[70] There is an exception to the binding nature of a contract concluded by the auctioneer's announcement. It arises where bidders have been notified that the auction is subject to a reserve or upset price.[71] If a sale is announced by the auctioneer below this price, it has been held[72] that an auctioneer refusing to complete the contract in these circumstances may not be sued by the successful bidder for breach of his warranty of authority.[73] The auctioneer also clearly lacks the actual authority to bind the principal. Furthermore, having notified the reserve price, the auctioneer cannot bind the principal on the ground of apparent authority.

Besides an auction being notified as subject to a reserve or upset price, it may also be notified as subject to a right to bid by or on behalf of the seller.[74] Where a right to bid is thus reserved, the seller, or any single person in his stead, is entitled to bid at the auction.[75] If no such notification is made, it is unlawful for the seller to bid or to employ someone else to

---

[67] Where is the burden of proof? Presumably on the recipient.

[68] See *Payne* v. *Cave* (1789) 3 TR 148. On auction sales generally, see F. Meisel and B. W. Harvey, *Law and Practice of Auctions* (2nd edn., OUP, London, 1995).

[69] *British Car Auctions* v. *Wright* [1972] 3 All ER 462.   [70] S. 57(1).

[71] S. 57(3).   [72] In *McManus* v. *Fortescue* [1907] 2 KB 1.

[73] Under the rule in *Collen* v. *Wright* (1857) 8 E & B 647.

[74] S. 57(3). The right to bid must be 'reserved expressly'.   [75] S. 57(6).

bid.[76] An auctioneer, moreover, who knowingly takes such a bid also acts unlawfully.[77] The Act goes on to provide that a sale concluded after an unlawful bid may be treated as fraudulent by the buyer.[78]

A number of questions about reserve prices and rights to bid are left unanswered by the Act. First, it is not clear what is the position where a reserve price has not been notified but the auctioneer withdraws the goods. The Act provides no assistance at all in such cases and does not even say that withdrawal of the goods is wrongful. Secondly, the Act is unclear on the consequences of an unlawful bid being made, or of the goods being knocked down to the seller or his agent. No sanction or civil right in favour of one or more disappointed bidders or potential bidders is stated in the Act but there is an argument that the auctioneer should be liable in the circumstances on a collateral contract for breach of an undertaking to sell to the highest legitimate bidder.[79] The difficulty is that section 57(2), in accordance with normal contract principle, gives the auctioneer freedom to accept or refuse a bid. Furthermore, the auctioneer has not positively undertaken to sell to the highest legitimate bidder. Thirdly, the successful bidder may treat the 'sale' as fraudulent when an unlawful bid has been made, but what is the position if the property has not yet passed so that the contract of sale has not yet matured into a sale?[80] Common sense would require 'sale' to be read broadly to include also contracts of sale so that the seller could not recover from damages from a non-accepting buyer.[81] Fourthly, although the buyer may presumably rescind the contract for fraud, after an unlawful bid, in accordance with the limits imposed for rescission in such cases, the question of damages is not so easy where, for example, the buyer has lost the right to rescind. Presumably, damages would lie in the tort of deceit against the seller, but it is not clear whether only the seller would be liable or whether the auctioneer would also be liable, with joint and several liability between the two. Section 57(5) deems the sale to be fraudulent and not the behaviour of those acting unlawfully in making or permitting bids when the auction is conducted. The auctioneer is not a party to the contract of sale.[82]

---

[76] S. 57(4).   [77] *Ibid.*   [78] S. 57(5).

[79] *Warlow* v. *Harrison* (1859) 1 E & B 309. This argument could also be used where the goods are simply withdrawn.

[80] See s. 2(4). A likely construction where payment has not yet been made.

[81] It would be ridiculous to require the buyer to pay before taking proceedings.

[82] For other legislation on abusive auction practices, see the Mock Auctions Act 1961 (criminal penalties) and the Auctions (Bidding Agreements) Act 1969 (bidding rings).

Capacity

Part II of the Sale of Goods Act contains limited provision on contractual capacity. It has nothing to say about corporate capacity.[83] Section 3 deals only with the purchase of 'necessaries', leaving all other matters arising in connection with capacity to buy and sell and matters of property to the general law.[84] Section 3 deals with minors and persons who are not competent to contract as a result of mental incapacity or drunkenness. A minor is someone who has not yet attained the age of 18.[85] According to section 3(2), the incapacitated person must pay a reasonable price for necessaries that are sold and delivered. This raises three major points. First, 'necessaries' are defined in general terms by section 3(3) as 'goods suitable both to the condition in life of the minor' or other incapacitated person and to his actual requirements at the time of the sale and delivery. The definition has been particularly hard to apply in the case of minors. The question whether goods are necessaries is a mixed question of law and fact, so that there must be some evidence on which a finding to that effect can be made.[86] It is the seller who carries the burden of proving that the goods are necessaries[87] and, given the nature of the test, it will often be a difficult burden to discharge. The seller will have to show that the goods are necessaries, having regard not only to the condition in life of the minor, but also to the minor's existing provision of goods of that kind.[88]

Secondly, section 3(2) applies only to necessaries 'sold and delivered'. Where the goods have not yet been delivered, or have been delivered but the property has not yet passed to the buyer, the common law applies and does not give a clear answer to the question whether either or both of the seller and buyer are bound.[89] Since the minor lacks capacity to contract,[90] there is no reason to give the protection of a binding contract

---

[83] See *Palmer's Company Law* (ed. by G. K. Morse and others, Sweet & Maxwell, London, looseleaf), i, Pts 2–3.

[84] See the standard contract texts.

[85] The Family Law Reform Act 1969 reduced the age from 21 and so, to a large extent, eliminated the problem of minors' contracts.

[86] *Ryder* v. *Wombwell* (1868) LR 4 Ex. 32.   [87] *Ibid.*; *Nash* v. *Inman* [1908] 2 KB 1.

[88] *Nash* v. *Inman*, n. 87 above. For the difficulties of a seller who lacks knowledge, see *Johnstone* v. *Marks* (1887) 19 QBD 509. For details of nineteenth century case law showing the consumer needs of sons of the nobility, see G. H. Treitel, *The Law of Contract* (9th edn., Sweet & Maxwell, London, 1995), 495–6.

[89] See *Nash* v. *Inman*, n. 87 above; *Roberts* v. *Gray* [1913] 1 KB 520 (services).

[90] The position of mentally incapable buyers is different. If the seller is unaware of the mental disorder, he need not rely upon s. 3 but may enforce the contract at common law: *Baxter* v. *Portsmouth* (1826) 5 B & C 170. Otherwise the contract may be avoided by the mentally incapable party: *Imperial Loan Co.* v. *Stone* [1892] 1 QB 599. A drunkard is liable on a contract at common law unless his condition is so extreme as to be known to the other party: *Gore* v. *Gibson* (1843) 13 M & W 623.

to a seller who can help himself by refusing to deliver, or by taking proceedings for the recovery of goods, in which he has reserved the general
property, against a minor unlawfully retaining possession. Nor is there
any reason to give the minor a right to compel further performance of the
contract by demanding that the seller deliver the goods or convey the
property in them. Thirdly, the contractual price is displaced by the reference to a reasonable price. That is consistent with the price recoverable
on a restitutionary basis under the old count of goods sold and delivered.[91] It is not necessarily predicated upon a binding contract. Section
3(2) does not include the count of goods bargained and sold, applicable
where the property had passed but delivery had not yet been made. A
seller dealing with a minor in these circumstances is protected by the
unpaid seller's right of retention in section 39 and the right of resale in
section 48. Such a seller does not need the protection of a personal action
as well. Section 3 can therefore be rationalized as minimal legislative
intervention designed to avert an unjustified enrichment of the minor. It
would take a modern rationalization of the law to interpret it as a partial
codification of the law dealing with the enforcement of contracts against
minors.

Unstated Price

Section 8(1) of the Sale of Goods Act, after making the obvious point that
the parties are at liberty to settle the price in the contract, goes on to say
that it 'may be left to be fixed in a manner agreed by the contract, or may
be determined by the course of dealing between the parties'. Section 8(2)
then states that the buyer must pay a reasonable price[92] where 'the price
is not determined as mentioned in sub-section (1)'. There is an ambiguity at the heart of this provision which captures the difficulty of knowing
how far the law is prepared to go in enforcing uncertain contracts for the
sale of goods. The question is whether the word 'determined' is to be
read as 'actually determined' or as 'to be determined'. If it is the former,
then section 8(2) is literally capable of application to cases where the parties have prescribed a method of determining the price,[93] but for one reason or another the agreed machinery has broken down. If section 8(2)
bears the latter meaning, however, it will apply only where the contract
fails to create machinery for establishing the price. It will thus certainly
apply where the contract says nothing at all about the price; arguably, it
will also apply where the price is indirectly described in terms of a cur-

---

[91] Discussed in the context of contractual certainty, text accompanying nn. 95–100
below.
[92] Defined in the usual way in s. 8(3) as dependent upon the particular circumstances.
[93] With the exception of the particular method dealt with by s. 9.

rent or future standard that is treated as though it were self-executing, such as a 'fair price' or a 'reasonable price'. As the law has developed, it seems likely that the former approach is correct, at least to the extent that the contractual relations of the parties are well enough defined for there to be a binding contract at common law to which section 8(2) can apply.[94]

Section 8(2) was codified on the basis of a number of nineteenth century authorities where nothing was said about the price.[95] In most of these decisions, the seller's consideration had actually been executed, by delivery of the goods to the buyer or to an agent of the buyer, such as a carrier. Where this had occurred, it was not necessary to assess the buyer's liability in terms of any special or express contract between them. Indeed, it could be assumed that there was no special contract to embarrass resolution of the matter, which was handled off the contract in the *indebitatus* count of goods sold and delivered. The buyer was rendered liable in a price action, and an amount was adjudged owing that was the reasonable, fair, or market value of the goods at the time of their delivery.[96] So far, this line of development would not extend to cases where the seller wished to pursue a damages action for non-acceptance under an executory contract. This decisive step was taken in *Hoadly* v. *M'Laine*[97] where a carriage was manufactured to the buyer's specifications[98] and the buyer held liable, on the basis of the reasonable value of the carriage, in a damages action.[99] Doubts have nevertheless been expressed in Australia in recent times about whether section 8(2) should apply to executory contracts.[100]

Section 8 deals with only one source of uncertainty in a sale of goods contract, the amount of the price. It does not deal with elements such as the amounts of delivery and payment that have to be made under an instalment contract, or the time and place of delivery,[101] which are left to

---

[94] A problem of an obvious chicken-and-egg character raised in *May & Butcher Ltd* v. *The King* (1929) [1934] 2 KB 17n.

[95] See in particular *Valpy* v. *Gibson* (1847) 4 CB 837; *Acebal* v. *Levy* (1834) 10 Bing. 376.

[96] See text preceding n. 94 above. [97] (1834) 10 Bing. 482.

[98] And was thus not a standard market item where the seller might have been expected to find another buyer.

[99] Carrying the law beyond the more restrictive statements in *Acebal* v. *Levy*, n. 95 above, 382, by Tindal CJ, who also gave the judgment in *Hoadly* v. *M'Laine*, n. 97 above.

[100] *Hall* v. *Busst* (1960) 104 CLR 206, 233–4 (Menzies J). Menzies J was prepared to distinguish *Hoadly* as a work and materials contract, so that the buyer would be liable in a restitutionary *quantum meruit* action for a reasonable price on completion of the work. Windeyer J, dissenting on a different point in *Hall* v. *Busst*, supported *Hoadly* and the reading it directed of s. 8(2). To this effect, see also *Wenning* v. *Robinson* (1964) 64 SR(NSW) 157; *Montana Mustard Seed Co.* v. *Gates* (1963) 42 WWR 303.

[101] See, e.g., *Hillas & Co. Ltd* v. *Arcos Ltd* (1932) 147 LT 503; *Custom Motors Ltd* v. *Dwinell* (1975) 61 DLR (3d) 342.

the common law.[102] The prevailing approach is for the courts to strive for the enforcement of agreements, on the ground that a transaction intended to be binding should as far as possible be upheld: *verba sunt intelligenda ut res magis valeat quam pereat.*[103] In this connection, the old distinction between executory and executed contracts survives to the extent that a greater judicial willingness to enforce an incomplete agreement is likely to be presented in executed consideration cases,[104] if only because the prejudice suffered by the plaintiff if the defendant is released from his undertaking will probably be greater in such a case.[105] A court is likely to enforce a contract even if sense cannot be made of one of its terms, if that term is plainly unimportant or meaningless,[106] but will not thus intervene if the term is important and sense cannot be made of it,[107] or if a particular method of valuation chosen by the parties has broken down and was not necessarily designed to produce the fair or reasonable price that would be reached by the trier of fact.[108] One particular stumbling block to enforcement in the past has been the assertion that the courts will not intervene where the price is to be settled by the parties themselves at a future date, on the ground that an agreement to agree is not a contract known to law,[109] just as there cannot be a contract to negotiate.[110] But a contract where the quantity of goods has been left to future agreement has been upheld.[111] The prohibition on enforcing an agreement to agree is a shibboleth that should not command unswerving support in a modern and flexible law of contract. This is particularly so

---

[102] See the general contract texts.

[103] *Hillas & Co. Ltd* v. *Arcos Ltd*, n. 101 above.

[104] *British Bank for Foreign Trade* v. *Novinex Ltd* [1949] 1 KB 623.

[105] *Foley* v. *Classique Coaches Ltd* [1934] 2 KB 1; *Mack & Edwards (Sales) Ltd* v. *McPhail Bros.* (1968) 11 SJ 211.

[106] e.g. *Nicolene Ltd* v. *Simmonds* [1953] 1 QB 543 ('the usual conditions of acceptance apply').

[107] e.g. *Scammell* v. *Ouston* [1941] AC 251 ('balance of purchase price can be had on hire purchase terms').

[108] See, e.g., *Re Nudgee Bakery Pty. Ltd's Agreement* [1971] Qd. R 24, where a five-year contract for flour requirements prescribed payment at the maximum level permitted by a regulatory contract without providing for the case where the statute was repealed. Also *Kidston* v. *Sterling and Pitcairn Ltd* (1920) 61 SCR 193 (Can: parties could not agree on what they meant by 'market price' in seven-year supply contract, except that it did not mean the market price).

[109] *May & Butcher Ltd* v. *The King*, n. 94 above. See also *Courtney and Fairbairn Ltd* v. *Tolaini Bros. (Hotels) Ltd* [1975] 1 WLR 297. *May & Butcher* was distinguished in a case involving a lease with an option to purchase the reversion at a price to be agreed, not by the parties themselves, but by valuers appointed by each of the parties: *Sudbrook Trading Estate Ltd* v. *Eggleton* [1983] 1 AC 444.

[110] *Ibid.* On the difficulties involving the enforcement of 'lockout agreements', preventing the parties from dealing with third parties during the negotiation process, see *Walford* v. *Miles* [1992] 1 All ER 453; *Pitt* v. *PHH Asset Management Ltd* [1994] 1 WLR 327.

[111] *F. & G. Sykes (Wessex) Ltd* v. *Fine Fare Ltd* [1967] 1 Lloyd's Rep. 53 (buyer's requirements over five years of 30–80,000 broiler chickens with the precise figure to 'be agreed').

where the parties intend to be contractually bound and the consequences of holding otherwise would be unduly prejudicial to one of them,[112] or where they are dealing at arm's length in goods that are traded on a market, so that they may be presumed likely to arrive in any event at a price directed by market forces. The *May & Butcher* objection that section 8(2) is brought into play only when an agreement passes the test of a binding contract at common law[113] may be countered in the following way. Section 62(2) introduces common law contract rules into sale of goods contracts only to the extent that these are not inconsistent with the provisions of the Act. Since the prohibition on enforcing agreements to agree appears to contradict the literal wording of section 8(1) and (2), it would seem that such agreements should be enforced in accordance with the terms of the section, whatever might be the position under the general law of contract.[114]

Section 9 of the Sale of Goods Act deals with contracts where the price is to be settled by a third-party valuer. Subsection (1) deals with two cases. First, where the valuation machinery breaks down because the designated valuer cannot or will not do the job, the agreement is avoided.[115] Secondly, where the machinery thus breaks down but a part or all of the goods are delivered to and appropriated by the buyer,[116] the buyer is bound to pay a reasonable price on the basis of an *indebitatus* count for goods sold and delivered.[117] Section 9(2) then goes on to create a special statutory action in damages where either the buyer or the seller is at fault in causing the valuation machinery to break down: it could, for example, deal with a case where one of the parties refuses to carry out an undertaking to name one of two agreed joint valuers.[118] There is no justification for the special treatment in section 9 of this one aspect of contractual formation. It would be better to allow such issues to be resolved by the general law of contract, or by a sufficiently general statutory text that embraced other examples of obstructive behaviour in the bargaining process. This would allow the law to develop unimpeded by a nineteenth century approach to formation in one corner of the law. There seems every reason nowadays to apply a fair or reasonable price where

[112] Especially the case in output and requirements contracts where one party's needs or capacity are monopolized by the other.

[113] A similar problem presents itself with the Vienna Convention on Contracts for the International Sale of Goods 1980: compare Arts. 14 and 55.

[114] There is a problem with interpreting the Act in this way: the Act does not as such define 'contract', which arguably should be interpreted according to the general law.

[115] S. 9(1) codifies *Cooper* v. *Shuttleworth* (1856) 25 LJ Ex. 114.

[116] The property, it seems, would thereupon pass.

[117] This codifies *Clark* v. *Westrope* (1856) 18 CB 765.

[118] S. 9(2) would reverse the actual result in *Vickers* v. *Vickers* (1867) LR 4 Eq. 529, 535–6 (Page-Wood V-C: 'this particular case . . . tries the principle to the utmost').

two parties each appoint a valuer but the machinery breaks down because of one of those valuers;[119] yet section 9(1) states that the agreement is avoided.

[119] Cf. *Sudbrook Trading Estate Ltd* v. *Eggleton*, n. 109 above.

2

Definition and Subject Matter of the Sale of Goods Contract

Section 2(1) defines a sale of goods contract for the purpose of the Act as one 'whereby the seller transfers or agrees to transfer the property in the goods for a money consideration called the price'. Sale is to be distinguished from other contracts in that it involves the transfer of ownership (that is, the property) in goods (as opposed to other items) for money (as opposed to some other type of consideration). Ownership is a notion that should be treated with some care in personal property law. For present purposes,[1] it may be seen as the best available possessory right to a thing. If any of these three elements of ownership, goods, or money is absent, the contract will not be one of sale of goods for the purpose of the Act, no matter how similar in spirit it may be to such a contract. The fate of such cognate transactions will be dealt with later in this chapter.

DEFINITION OF 'GOODS'

These are defined by section 61(1) as including 'all personal chattels other than things in action and money' and in particular 'emblements, industrial growing crops, and things attached to or forming part of the land which are agreed to be severed before sale or under the contract of sale'. Personal chattels consist of what remains of property after land and chattels real (leasehold interests in land) are abstracted.[2] Once things in action[3] and money[4] are also removed, the personal chattels that may be the subject of a sale of goods agreement consist of those tangible, movable items that we call things in possession.

The definition of goods therefore embraces all personal chattels (with

---

[1] Discussed in the text accompanying nn. 155–60 below.

[2] For the common law distinction between personalty and realty, see J. Williams, *Principles of the Law of Personal Property etc.* (14th edn., by T. Cyprian Williams, Sweet & Maxwell, London), 1–6.

[3] So called because rights in them cannot physically be vindicated by taking possession and so depend upon legal proceedings. See *Torkington* v. *Magee* [1902] 2 KB 427, 430. Lord Blackburn said the expression extended to 'all personal chattels that are not in possession': *Colonial Bank* v. *Whinney* (1886) 11 App. Cas. 426, 439–40.

[4] Hard to classify as a thing in possession or a thing in action: see M. G. Bridge, *Personal Property Law* (Blackstone, London, 2nd edn. 1996), 6.

the above exceptions). Large and unusual items such as ships[5] and air-craft,[6] certainly personal chattels, are therefore dealt with by the Act,[7] from whose provisions special statute may depart in their case.[8] The particular mention of various types of crop and agricultural produce in the above definition needs to be explained in the light of the legislative history governing the observance of forms in sales of land and of goods.

Before 1954, contracts for the sale of goods above a certain value had to be evidenced in writing. This requirement, introduced in section 17 of the Statute of Frauds 1677 for the sale of 'goods, wares and merchandandizes' (not defined in the statute),[9] was continued by section 5 of the Sale of Goods Act 1893 for 'goods', defined in terms almost identical to those used in the 1979 Act. Section 4 of the Statute of Frauds also required writing for the sale of 'lands, tenements and hereditaments or any interest in or concerning them' (again not defined). It was superseded by a similar requirement in section 40 of the Law of Property Act 1925, which defined land in lengthy terms, specifically referring to buildings and minerals.[10] When section 40 was repealed by the Law of Property (Miscellaneous Provisions) Act 1989, which introduced a more stringent writing rule, land itself was not defined in the new Act.

Crops and Natural Produce

For writing purposes, it is important to distinguish goods and land,[11] since contracts concerning the latter are invalid if not in writing. Unfortunately, a reading of the case law and the definition of 'goods' in the Sale of Goods Act suggests that crops and other agricultural produce are capable of being both goods and land. In principle, things attached to land form part of the land: thus, while a conveyance of land does not include chattels upon the land, attached things, even if not expressly listed, will pass to the transferee.[12] It is commonly contemplated that crops and natural produce will be severed, at seasonal intervals in the case of crops, and treated as goods. Where severance is contemplated pursuant to contract, the question is whether the contract must comply

---

[5] *Behnke* v. *Bede Shipping Co. Ltd* [1927] 1 KB 649; *McDougall* v. *Aeromarine of Emsworth Ltd* [1958] 3 All ER 431.

[6] See *United Dominions Trust (Commercial) Ltd* v. *Eagle Aircraft Services Ltd* [1968] 1 All ER 104.

[7] Ships are, however, excluded by the Vienna Convention on the International Sale of Goods 1980, Art. 2(e).

[8] Note the provisions governing the register of ships and their ownership: Merchant Shipping Act 1995, ss. 8–16.

[9] The words 'wares and merchandizes' seem to add nothing to 'goods'.

[10] S. 205(1)(ix).   [11] M. G. Bridge (1986) 64 *Can. Bar Rev.* 58.

[12] *Saunders* v. *Pilcher* [1949] 2 All ER 1097; *Dyck* v. *Dyck* [1926] 3 WWR 762; *Shewchuk* v. *Seafred (No. 2)* [1927] 2 WWR 207.

with section 2 of the 1989 Act or might be made by informal means, as is permitted by the Sale of Goods Act. It cannot safely be assumed that, just because such items are 'goods' for the purpose of the latter Act, a contract for their sale need not satisfy any writing requirement for land. Had the sanction for non-compliance with the writing requirement for land remained unenforceability, it might have been arguable that the plaintiff should have been allowed to characterize and enforce the contract as one for the sale of goods: the Sale of Goods Act in section 60 states that rights and liabilities declared by the Act may be enforced by action. But the Law of Property (Miscellaneous Provisions) Act 1989 now provides that a contract for the disposition of an interest in land 'can only be made in writing'.[13] To allow such a contract to be enforced as a sale of goods contract is too sharp an inroad into a recently enacted statute to be a likely outcome of litigation.

Nineteenth-century Case Law

The nineteenth-century cases characterizing crops and produce as either goods or land are difficult to follow and summarize. Abinger CB once said that no general rule laid down in one case was not contradicted in another.[14] Numerous criteria were brought into play in Statute of Frauds cases: whether it was the buyer or the seller who was to sever growing things from the soil;[15] the putting of those things into a deliverable state and the intention of the parties to pass the property in them before or after severance;[16] the practical necessity of the buyer having an interest in the land in order to enter upon it and effect a severance;[17] the introduction of human labour into the growing process;[18] the intention of the parties to have mature growths severed immediately after the contract so that after the contract the soil serves only as a natural warehouse;[19] and the collateral issues of whether for the purpose of execution of judgments the growing things would have been treated as goods, and whether for the purpose of descent on death they would have gone to the next-of-kin (goods) or the heir-at-law (land).[20] Implicit in some of these older authorities is a confusion between contract and conveyance, namely, that because the property in future crops cannot pass before

---

[13] S. 2.   [14] *Rodwell* v. *Phillips* (1842) 9 M & W 501, 505.

[15] *Evans* v. *Roberts* (1826) 5 B & C 829.   [16] *Smith* v. *Surman* (1829) 9 B & C 561.

[17] *Crosby* v. *Wadsworth* (1805) 6 East 602 as discussed in *Evans* v. *Roberts*, n. 15 above; *Jones* v. *Flint* (1839) 10 A & E 753.

[18] *Evans* v. *Roberts*, n. 15 above; *Scorell* v. *Boxall* (1827) 1 Y & J 396.

[19] *Parker* v. *Staniland* (1809) 11 East 362; Sjt. Williams's notes to *Duppo* v. *Mayo* (1670) 1 Wms. Saund. 275, 276 (6th edn., 1845 by E. V. Williams). These reports were edited on various occasions, and it is the last edition, subsequently incorporated in the ER, that is referred to here.

[20] *Rodwell* v. *Phillips*, n. 14 above; *Scorell* v. *Boxall*, n. 18 above; *Evans* v. *Roberts*, n. 15 above; *Jones* v. *Flint*, n. 17 above.

they come into existence, so a contract for their sale cannot concern goods. Further, the application of multiple criteria in some cases compounds the difficulty of stating the law, and the sparseness of reasoning in others encourages a search for an overarching rule that fits the results if not the reasoning in the cases.

Lord Blackburn was responsible for the central position given to the passing of property in sales law. In a magisterial classification of the cases, he said that, if the property in growing things were to pass after severance, the contract was one of sale of goods; but if it were to pass before severance, it was not a sale of goods contract at all and might or might not concern land under section 4 of the Statute of Frauds.[21] Although early editions of *Benjamin* supported this thesis,[22] there was only partial backing for it in the cases, which are more fully explained as follows.

In the case of *fructus naturales*, the spontaneous growth of the soil such as timber or grass, the contract disposed of an interest in land if the buyer was to sever,[23] and of an interest in goods if the seller was to sever.[24] But the cases consistent with this distinction rely upon other reasons: if the seller severed, the contract could be seen as reserving in him a controlling intention to pass the property only after the growing things acquired the identity of goods upon severance;[25] if the buyer severed, he could be seen as needing at least a limited proprietary interest in the land in order to carry out that purpose.[26]

Fructus industriales, namely fruits and crops grown by the labour of the agricultural year, were treated as goods no matter who was responsible for their severance,[27] even if they were not in a mature state at the contract date.[28] The probable reason was that a buyer did not need any-

[21] *Blackburn on Sale* (2nd edn., 1885 by W. C. Graham, Stevens, London), 4–15.

[22] e.g. J. P. Benjamin, *A Treatise on the Law of Sale of Personal Property* (2nd edn., Sweet & Maxwell, London, 1873), 91–93.

[23] *Smith* v. *Surman*, n. 16 above; *Evans* v. *Roberts*, n. 15 above; *Emmerson* v. *Heelis* (1809) 2 Taunt. 38 (extended to *fructus industriales*).

[24] *Crosby* v. *Wadsworth*, n. 17 above; *Scorell* v. *Boxall*, n. 18 above; *Carrington* v. *Roots* (1837) 2 M & W 248.

[25] *Smith* v. *Surman*, n. 16 above.

[26] *Crosby* v. *Wadsworth*, n. 17 above; *Jones* v. *Flint*, ibid.

[27] *Evans* v. *Roberts*, n. 15 above; *Parker* v. *Staniland*, n. 19 above; *Warwick* v. *Bruce* (1813) 2 M & S 205; *Jones* v. *Flint*, n. 17 above; *Sainsbury* v. *Matthews* (1838) 4 M & W 334; Sjt. Williams's notes to *Duppo* v. *Mayo*, n. 19 above. But see the inconsistent results in *Rodwell* v. *Phillips*, n. 14 above, and *Emmerson* v. *Heelis*, n. 23 above; also the result in *Waddington* v. *Briscoe* (1801) 2 B & P 452, where the speculative nature of a contract for the supply of crops encouraged a disapproving court to deny the exemption from stamp duty accorded by the Stamp Act, 55 Geo. 3, cap. 184, to contracts for the sale of goods, wares and merchandise.

[28] *Evans* v. *Roberts*, n. 15 above; *Jones* v. *Flint*, n. 17 above; *Sainsbury* v. *Matthews*, n. 26 above. This was also the view of Scrutton LJ in *English Hop Growers Ltd* v. *Dering* [1928] 1 KB 174, 178–9.

thing so enduring as an interest in land to achieve a purpose whose success depended upon dispatch.[29] Where the crops were mature at the date of the contract and had to be severed immediately, there was the further reason that the soil had no more to give and served merely as a natural warehouse for the crops.[30] Any divergence between *fructus naturales* and *fructus industriales* was narrowed by the controversial decision in *Marshall* v. *Green*,[31] which extended the warehouse principle to *fructus naturales*.

Statutory Definition

Interpreted literally, the statutory definition of 'goods' set out above significantly extended the definition to be drawn from the cases. This definition clearly gives support to the Blackburn proprietary thesis and, though not explicitly, is by virtue of its width consistent with the natural warehouse principle in *Marshall* v. *Green*.[32] In practical terms, any extension of the definition would lie in the area of *fructus naturales* where the buyer severs. It is hard to say what the draftsman meant when inserting the expression 'industrial growing crops' but it seems designed to serve as the Scots equivalent of *fructus industriales*,[33] just as 'emblements' has come loosely to mean the same thing.[34]

English decisions based on the statutory definition give some support for the view that it should be given its literal meaning. It seems to have been assumed in *Kursell* v. *Timber Operators and Contractors Ltd*[35] that the grant to a buyer of a licence to sever timber in a Latvian forest over a fifteen-year period was a transaction caught by the Sale of Goods Act. A contract permitting the buyer to enter land and sever timber was regarded in *James Jones & Sons Ltd* v. *Earl of Tankerville*[36] as a sale of goods contract and thus amenable to specific performance under the Sale of Goods Act. In contrast, the Privy Council, construing a New Zealand tax statute in *Kauri Timber Co Ltd* v. *Commissioner of Taxes*,[37] held that a buyer's right to cut and haul timber was an interest in land: the natural warehouse principle in *Marshall* v. *Green*[38] could not be applied since the contract required a lengthy occupation of the land by the buyer until the timber reached maturity. Further, an Australian court

---

[29] *Jones* v. *Flint*, n. 17 above.   [30] *Parker* v. *Staniland*, n. 19 above.
[31] (1875) 1 CPD 35.   [32] *Ibid.*
[33] But the expression is not a term of art in Scots law: *Benjamin's Sale of Goods* (5th edn., 1997 by A. G. Guest and others), §1–092.
[34] Chalmers used emblements and *fructus industriales* interchangeably: M. Chalmers, *The Sale of Goods Act, 1893, Including the Factors Acts, 1889 & 1890* (4th edn., Butterworths, London, 1899), 117. But see the technical meaning of emblements in *Benjamin's Sale of Goods*, n. 33 above, §1–092.
[35] [1927] 1 KB 298.   [36] [1909] 2 Ch. 440.
[37] [1913] AC 771, not cited in *Kursell*, n. 35 above.   [38] N. 31 above.

has held that a contract conferring the right to enter land to harvest nuts from trees conferred a profit à prendre, and was not a contract of sale of goods since the buyer was under no obligation to sever.[39] The Court of Appeal in *Saunders* v. *Pilcher*[40] held that a conveyance of land to a buyer included also the natural produce growing on the land, but it was not denied that the scope of 'goods' had been extended by the Act. There seems no reason to doubt that crops and natural produce might be the subject of both a sale of land and sale of goods agreement.

It is submitted that the definition of 'goods' should be given a straight-forward reading and the Act be applied even to cases where the buyer, pursuant to an obligation to do so, effects severance of natural produce, with the possible exception of contracts where the buyer is given an interest in land pending a lengthy maturing of the produce. Difficulties may arise where the definitions of goods and land overlap: we have seen that this may happen with regard to the writing requirement. There may also be a title dispute between a purchaser of land and a purchaser of goods. This is unlikely to be a problem apart from cases where the seller of crops or produce that have attained maturity then sells the land before the crops or produce have been severed. A similar difficulty could arise with fixtures. Where property has a dual existence as land and goods, the rule of *nemo dat quod non habet* together with its exceptions could resolve title disputes.[41] Statutory rules for the registration of interests in land may have to be followed by the buyer of crops or produce if his interest is to be asserted successfully against a later buyer of the land.

Fixtures

Chattels attached to land have long been treated as land for various legal purposes.[42] They vest in the owner of the land once they are so attached to the land as to comply with the legal test of a fixture and accompany the land when it is conveyed.[43] Whether a chattel becomes a fixture depends upon a dual test consisting of a factual element and an intentional element: the degree of attachment of the chattel to the land and the object and purpose of the attachment.[44] In addition, even if a chattel becomes a fixture in this way, as between a landlord and a tenant it may be a

[39] *Warren* v. *Nut Farms of Australia Pty. Ltd* [1981] WAR 134.
[40] [1949] 2 All ER 1097.
[41] A radically different approach would treat the acquirer of an interest in land as paramount in all cases: see Ontario Law Reform Commission, *Report on Sale of Goods* (1979), i, 70.
[42] H. Bennett, 'Attachment of Chattels to Land' in N. Palmer and E. McKendrick (eds.), *Interests in Goods* (Lloyd's of London Press, London, 1993).
[43] *Lavery* v. *Pursell* (1889) 39 Ch. D 508; *Lee* v. *Risdon* (1816) 7 Taunt. 188.
[44] *Hellawell* v. *Eastwood* (1851) 6 Ex. 295.

tenant's fixture or a landlord's fixture.[45] Those fixtures in the former category attached by the tenant under the lease may be removed by the tenant, pursuant to a common law right, at the end of the lease, whereupon they are reinvested with the character of chattels. Consistently with this entitlement, an agreement by a tenant to transfer this right of severance is not treated as disposing of an interest in land; nor is it treated as a sale of goods agreement.[46]

There is surprisingly little authority for the case where the owner of land agrees to sell fixtures to a buyer whilst retaining ownership of the land itself. Before the enactment of the Sale of Goods Act, it might have been useful to ask whether fixtures were akin to growing crops and who was to sever them, and whether it was significant that the parties might or might not have intended the property in them to pass before severance. In *Lavery* v. *Pursell*,[47] Chitty J held that a contract permitting a buyer to sever building materials from land concerned land for the purpose of section 4 of the Statute of Frauds. In one Canadian case, where it was the seller who was to sever a saw-mill together with its machinery at the end of the logging season, the court surprisingly concluded that the contract concerned land.[48] Regardless of whether it is the seller or the buyer who is to sever, the definition of 'goods' in the Sale of Goods Act is broad enough to embrace all sales of a fixture to be severed from land under the contract.

Minerals and Energy

Similar principles apply where the buyer extracts minerals under a contract of sale. The closest analogy is with *fructus naturales*, where it is the buyer who severs. Despite the breadth of the statutory definition, however, there seems to be great reluctance to treat contracts for buyer severance other than as sale of land agreements,[49] the justification apparently being that the words in the definition of goods 'attached to or forming part of the land' ought to be read *eiusdem generis* with emblements and industrial growing crops. The natural warehouse principle of *Marshall* v. *Green*[50] will not serve to extend the definition of goods for items like minerals that have never derived sustenance from the land.

---

[45] *Halsbury's Laws of England* (4th edn., Butterworths, London, 1994), xxviii(1) (Title: 'Landlord and Tenant'), paras. 143 ff.

[46] *Lee* v. *Gaskell* (1876) 1 QBD 700; *Devine* v. *Callery* (1917) 40 OLR 505 (Can.).

[47] N. 43 above.

[48] *McPherson* v. *US Fidelity and Guaranty Co.* (1914) 33 OLR 524.

[49] See British Columbia Law Reform Commission, *Report on the Statute of Frauds* (1977), 11. Royalty agreements are treated, however, as involving neither a sale of goods nor a sale of land: *Emerald Resources Ltd* v. *Sterling Oil Properties Management Ltd* (1969) 3 DLR (3d) 630, affd. (1971) 15 DLR (3d) 356.

[50] N. 31 above.

Thus in *Morgan* v. *Russell & Sons*,[51] the sale of a heap of slag and cinders resting on the land was held to dispose of an interest in land. In rejecting the statutory extension of the definition of 'goods', this approach is restrictive and out of line with other types of thing attached to or part of land.

Forms of energy, such as electricity or gas, are less easily seen as tangible physical movables. Assuming that all problems of severance from the soil have been resolved, a transaction involving forms of energy ought to be treated as a sale of goods contract for the purpose of the Act provided that the relationship between seller and buyer is one of private contract.[52] The sale of bottled gas is clearly governed by the Act;[53] also, it seems, the sale of gas in a less neatly packaged way.[54] One Canadian case accepts that steam for heating purposes was tangible personalty under a tax statute, but its supply took place under a contract for services since the residue of steam was returned to the supplier in the form of a vapour.[55] The supply of other things such as electricity and water should be seen as a sale of goods transaction even if the thing is supplied in a formless, unpackaged way.[56]

Body Parts

In this developing area of law, the focus has not been mainly on whether a contract for the sale of parts of the human body is a contract of sale of goods for the purpose of the Sale of Goods Act. There are vital preliminary questions to be resolved, namely, whether parts of the human body are capable of ownership and whether contracts for their disposition are illegal under statute.[57] For centuries, human hair has been bought and

[51] [1909] 1 KB 357. See also *Mills* v. *Stokman* (1967) 116 CLR 61; *McNeil* v. *Corbett* (1907) 39 SCR 608 (Can.); *Saskatoon Sand & Gravel* v. *Steve* (1973) 40 DLR (3d) 248 (gravel to be extracted by the buyer).

[52] For a discussion of statutory entitlement ousting private sale, see *Pfizer Corpn* v. *Minister of Health* [1965] AC 512.

[53] *Marleau* v. *People's Gas Supply Co. Ltd* [1940] 4 DLR 433; *Bradshaw* v. *Boothe's Marine Ltd* [1973] 2 OR 646.

[54] See *Erie County Natural Gas and Fuel Co. Ltd* v. *Carroll* [1911] AC 105; *Tilbury Town Gas Co. Ltd* v. *Maple City Oil and Gas Co. Ltd* (1915) 35 OLR 186 (Can.).

[55] *Re Social Services Tax Act* (1970) 74 WWR 246.

[56] The supply of power (whether in the form of 'gas, electricity or any other motive power') was treated as occurring under a sale, and therefore attracting fitness for purpose liability, in *Bentley Bros.* v. *Metcalfe & Co.* [1906] 2 KB 548, though the court was uncertain about the precise definition of the subject matter. The question whether a supply of electricity was a sale of goods was left open in *County of Durham Electrical Power Distribution Co.* v. *IRC* [1909] 2 KB 604. The supply of any form of power, heating, refrigeration or ventilation is treated as a sale of goods rather than services for VAT purposes: Finance Act 1972, s. 5(4). Electricity is excluded from the Vienna Convention on the International Sale of Goods 1980, Art. 2(f).

[57] See generally G. Dworkin and I. Kennedy (1993) 1 *Medical LR* 291.

sold without controversy; and it is a commonplace that human skeletons are owned by medical students and bought and sold accordingly. Unless a contract for the sale of such items is illegal, there is every reason to treat it as a contract for the sale of goods. The liability of the seller, however, has caused acute difficulties. North American case law has dealt with the responsibilities of a supplier of blood,[58] a matter of acute importance if the blood carries hepatitis or is HIV-infected. One recent Canadian case has succeeded at the expense of doctrinal coherence in avoiding the conclusion that a doctor supplying HIV-infected semen for artificial insemination owes the recipient the strict warranty obligations of a seller of goods.[59] Another concluded that a hospital patient, not billed for the cost of blood supplied, did not provide a money consideration; consequently, the Sale of Goods Act did not apply.[60] Furthermore, the fact that blood fell outside normal commercial channels of distribution made the case an inappropriate one for fashioning common law warranties akin to the strict implied terms in the Sale of Goods Act.[61] As regards illegality, transplant surgery has shown that body organs have a transfer value, whether they come from corpses or from living transferors. The Human Organ Transplant Act 1989[62] makes it an offence to make or receive payment for organs[63] removed from dead or living persons.

Things in Action and Money

The statutory definition of 'goods' excludes things in action and money, which is consistent with the pre-Act case law. This exclusion would affect documentary intangibles. In consequence, shares in a company (unless for special reasons the share certificates themselves have become collectors' items and are bought and sold accordingly) are not goods under the Act. In *Colonial Bank* v. *Whinney*,[64] shares were found to be things in action under bankruptcy legislation. Lord Blackburn thought they were personal chattels but not goods; they were outside section 17 of the Statute of Frauds since the property in them did not pass by delivery. In

---

[58] e.g. *Perlmutter* v. *Beth David Hospital* (1954) 123 NE 2d 792 (service not sale); *Reilly* v. *King County Central Blood Bank Inc.* (1972) 492 P 2d 246 (sale); R. Magnusson, 'Proprietary Rights in Human Tissue' in N. Palmer and E. McKendrick (eds.), n. 42 above, 254–6. For Australian authority on the question whether blood can be 'goods', see *E* v. *Australian Red Cross Society* (1991) 105 ALR 53; *PQ* v. *Australian Red Cross Society* [1992] 1 VR 19.

[59] *ter Neuzen* v. *Korm* (1993) 103 DLR (4th) 473.

[60] *Pittman Estate* v. *Bain* (1994) 112 DLR (4th) 257.

[61] *Quaere* the position under the Supply of Goods and Services Act 1982, s. 1? Would it depend upon whether the patient was receiving NHS or private treatment?

[62] In s. 1.

[63] An organ is defined as 'any part of a human body consisting of a structural arrangement of tissues which, if wholly removed, cannot be replicated by the body': s. 7(2).

[64] (1886) 11 App. Cas. 426.

accordance with the express language of the Act, however, an undivided interest in goods may be the subject matter of a sale of goods contract.[65]

Money itself may not be goods, for otherwise the exchange of money for a money consideration called the price could be regarded as a sale of goods contract instead of a loan or a moneylending agreement, clearly a more natural representation of the transaction. Where, nevertheless, currency and bank notes have attributes enhancing their face value,[66] rarity for example, these additional attributes will be sufficient to give them the character of goods for the purpose of the Act. Again, if money is treated as a commodity instead of a medium of exchange, authority exists for treating the money as goods, at least for the purpose of a special statute.[67]

Shares in Goods[68]

According to section 2(2): 'There may be a contract of sale between one part owner and another.' The parties may be joint tenants or tenants in common and their interests may arise in varying degrees. More difficult is the case, not covered by section 2(2), where a co-owner wishes to sell an undivided share in goods to an outside buyer, since it was held, before the Sale of Goods (Amendment) Act 1995, that an undivided share is not goods but a chose in action.[69] There are also licensing cases holding that members of unincorporated associations do not buy the drinks supplied to them but obtain on terms a distribution of the property owned by the association.[70] For contracts concluded before the implementation of the Sale of Goods Act (Amendment) 1995,[71] the position is as follows. The effect of section 2(2) is to modify the definition of goods to admit shares disposed of between co-owners. The provisions of the Sale of Goods Act thus apply to such contracts, with the presumable exception of section

---

[65] Discussed in the text accompanying nn. 68–76 below.

[66] *Moss* v. *Hancock* [1899] 2 QB 111 (restitution of stolen property). See also statements about the difference between goods and currency in *Banque Belge pour l'Etranger* v. *Hambrouck* [1921] 1 KB 321, 326, 329 (recovery of stolen money not yet passed into currency).

[67] *R* v. *Vanek* [1969] 2 OR 724 (Can.) (bags of silver coin under export licence statute). Naturally, the mischief of individual statutes will have an enlarging or diminishing effect on the scope of 'goods'.

[68] See Law Commission, *Sale of Goods Forming Part of a Bulk* (Law Comm., London, 1993, Law Com. No. 215); L. S. Sealy and R. J. A. Hooley, *Text and Materials in Commercial Law* (Butterworths, London, 1994), 215–16.

[69] *Re Sugar Properties (Derisley Wood) Ltd* [1988] BCLC 146.

[70] *Graff* v. *Evans* (1882) 8 QBD 373; *Trebanog Working Men's Club & Institute Ltd* v. *Macdonald* [1940] 1 KB 576. The light thrown on the civil aspect of sale of goods by tax, licensing, and criminal cases is often unilluminating.

[71] Taking effect on 19 Sept. 1995.

16,[72] since otherwise the contract under section 2(2) could never be executed. Where a co-owner's share in goods is the subject of a contract with an outside buyer, section 2(2) does not apply. Nevertheless, by common law analogy,[73] the relevant provisions of the Sale of Goods Act could be applied to a contract concerning the sale of an undivided share.[74] Where the Sale of Goods (Amendment) Act 1995 applies, the position now is that an undivided share in goods is within the definition of goods in the Sale of Goods Act. This is accomplished by the addition to that definition of the words 'and an undivided share in goods'.[75] Furthermore, where the subject matter of a contract is a share in an identified bulk, this is defined as specific goods,[76] with the result that section 16 again will have no application.

Computer Software

Computer hardware is obviously goods and it has been said that a contract for the sale of both hardware and software (but not software alone) is a contract of sale of goods.[77] The real question is whether the supplier of software owes the due care obligation of the supplier of services or the strict obligations of the seller of goods.[78] A book would certainly be regarded as goods but information or advice therein would be subjected to a due care standard. So it should be with software, the seller being strictly liable only for the physical materials on which the programme is written.[79]

A 'MONEY CONSIDERATION CALLED THE PRICE'

A contract of sale of goods under the 1979 Act is one where the buyer pays a money consideration called the price. Certain difficulties arise where

---

[72] Which requires as a matter of law that the contract goods be first ascertained before the property in them can pass to the buyer.

[73] S. 62(2).

[74] Again, s. 16 should be excluded. See Law Com. No. 215, n. 68 above, paras. 2.5–6, Ch. 3 below.

[75] S. 2(c) of the 1995 Act amending s. 61(1) of the Sale of Goods Act. See further Ch. 3 below.

[76] S. 2(d) of the 1995 Act amending s. 61(1) of the Sale of Goods Act.

[77] *Toby Constructions Products Pty. Ltd* v. *Computer Bar (Sales) Pty. Ltd* [1983] 2 NSWLR 48.

[78] Discussed Ch. 7 below.

[79] In *St Albans City and District Council* v. *International Computors Ltd* [1995] FSR 686, an Unfair Contract Terms Act 1977 case, the trial judge treated software containing a database as goods. In the Court of Appeal ([1996] 4 All ER 481), Sir Ian Glidewell was of the view that the supply of a computer programme attracted strict and not fault-based liability though the programme was not 'goods'. See also G. Gretton [1996] *JBL* 524.

goods are exchanged or traded in for other goods: these will be examined below when the sale of goods contract is compared to similar transactions. The present purpose is to distinguish money from similar forms of payment.

The most obvious forms of money are coins and bank notes, in other words legal tender. In this country, coinage is issued exclusively by the Royal Mint in accordance with Treasury permission.[80] Banknotes are issued exclusively by the Bank of England,[81] the denominations and overall amounts being the subject of Treasury approval.[82] It should be no objection to the buyer's consideration consisting of money that it be in a foreign currency. The essence of money for present purposes is that it is a freely-circulating medium of exchange.[83]

A clear and liquidated financial advantage accruing to the 'seller' will not, however, amount to money as such: money is not the same as money's worth. Thus an agreement to transfer leasehold land in return for the transferee agreeing to assume substantial rent payments has been held not to be a sale.[84] Similarly, the transferor of shares paid with shares in the transferee company (who alternatively might have taken a stated money price for the transferred shares) does not sell them to the transferee.[85] But it is no objection to the characterization of an agreement as one of sale that the buyer pays with a cheque or banker's draft, for here the instrument serves as conditional payment[86] until the bank, acting as agent for the buyer, puts the seller in funds with the amount of the cheque or draft. The instrument itself may not be money but it is the means by which the seller obtains money.

An instrument may be given in payment for goods supplied where it serves as absolute and not conditional payment. It has been held in one old case[87] that the contract is not one of sale but one of barter (or exchange) of the instrument against the goods. The buyer of seven pipes of Guernsey red wine paid the seller with a bill of exchange drawn by one stranger on another and due on a later date, without recourse against the

---

[80] Coinage Act 1971.   [81] Bank Charter Act 1844.

[82] Currency and Bank Notes Act 1954; Currency Act 1983.

[83] See *Moss* v. *Hancock*, n. 66 above; also Case 7/78 *R.* v. *Thompson* [1978] ECR 2247 (ECJ) (Krugerrands and UK coin not goods under EEC Treaty).

[84] *Robshaw Bros. Ltd* v. *Mayer* [1957] Ch. 125. It is questionable that it is a binding contract at all as opposed to a gift with a burden attached to it: see *Thomas* v. *Thomas* (1842) 2 QB 851. A promise of land for the extinguishment of an antecedent debt was held not to be a sale in *Simpson* v. *Connolly* [1953] 1 WLR 911.

[85] *Re Westminster Property Group Plc* [1984] 1 WLR 1117, approved [1985] 2 All ER 426 (CA).

[86] *Currie* v. *Misa* (1875) LR 10 Ex. 153, 163, rev'd. other grounds (1876) 1 App. Cas. 554; *Re Romer & Haslam* [1893] 2 QB 286, 296, 300, 303; *Royal Securities Corpn. Ltd* v. *Montreal Trust Co.* (1966) 57 DLR (2d) 666.

[87] *Read* v. *Hutchinson* (1813) 3 Camp. 352. See also *McGlynn* v. *Hastie* (1918) 44 OLR 190 (Can.: barter of hogs for cheque drawn by third party on bank).

buyer if the bill were dishonoured. When the bill became due, it was dishonoured by the drawee, whereupon the seller brought action against the buyer in debt on one of the old money counts, namely, for goods sold and delivered. The seller's action failed because the goods had been bartered and not sold; the buyer had never undertaken to pay a money sum.

Accepting that the buyer in the above case was not liable to pay when the drawee defaulted, it does not necessarily follow that the contract may not be treated as one of sale. An alternative argument is that the payment of the money consideration is entrusted under the contract to a third party but that the seller takes the risk of third party default and so may not have recourse to the buyer in that event.[88] This approach may be useful in dealing with the relationships arising out of the use of trading checks, which are vouchers issued by a lender to a borrower and used by the latter, who trades them in for goods at certain nominated retail outlets, pursuant to arrangments between those outlets and the lender.[89] The borrower uses the checks exactly as though they are cash, yet they lack the universality of money. In *Davis* v. *Customs and Excise Commissioners*,[90] the court concluded that a contract of sale had been entered into between the borrower and the retailer, so that value added tax could be levied. Moreover, the court also resisted the argument that there had been a sale of goods by the retailer to the lender, but delivered at the latter's request to the borrower.

Credit Cards

The above case is of assistance in analysing the relationships arising out of the acquisition of goods by means of a bank credit card.[91] The cardholding buyer presents the card in payment to a seller who has pre-existing arrangements with the issuer of the card to accept the use of the card in payment. The seller makes a graphite impression of the card on a sales voucher signed by the cardholder, or captures information from the card by 'swiping' it before issuing duplicate till receipts. The seller then presents the voucher or till receipt to the issuer who pays the face amount less an agreed discount. From the cardholder's point of view, it is like a deferred cash transaction, with payment of the sale price eventually being made to the issuer. The payment mechanism differs from payment by means of a cheque drawn by a buyer on his bank in that,

---

[88] A variation of this is that both parties are discharged if the cheque is dishonoured: see s. 2(3) (a contract of sale may be absolute or conditional).

[89] See the Crowther Committee Report on *Consumer Credit* (HMSO, London, 1971, Cmnd 4596), i, ch. 2.4.1 ff.

[90] [1975] 1 WLR 204.   [91] M. G. Bridge (1977) 28 *NILQ* 382.

whereas the cardholder always draws on a line of credit provided by the issuer, a buyer paying by cheque receives credit only if the account on which the cheque is drawn is in debit or is a special loan account. The bank credit card differs in terms of degree from trading checks in that many fewer sellers will accept trading checks than credit cards.

Unlike the case of trading checks, where the seller receives payment from the lender without discount, the seller is paid less than the face amount of the voucher by the card issuer. While the grant of a discount from seller to issuer comes close to being a notorious fact, the amount of it is not, and there is usually no disclosure of either by the issuer to the cardholder. The contract between seller and cardholder should remain nonetheless a contract of sale of goods, with the filling in of the sales voucher constituting the agreed method of paying the price.[92]

Certain problems, however, remain. First, there is the question of contractual certainty, which is a problem in that most cardholders never know the final price received by the seller.[93] This is unlikely to matter in practice, since certainty is usually a problem in executory contracts and one of the advantages of bank credit cards is that they accelerate the execution of contracts. A second problem concerns the liability of the cardholder to the seller if the issuer fails to honour the sales voucher. This is a small risk, but it has been settled that, as a matter of construction, the cardholder and seller agree on a paymaster, the issuer, with no recourse against the cardholder if the issuer defaults.[94] In this respect, bank credit card payment differs from payment by means of a cheque or under a banker's letter of credit.[95] This would not prevent the contract between seller and cardholder from being one of sale of goods.[96] Thirdly, if the view is taken that the issuer is the agent of the cardholder in effecting payment to the seller, it might be argued that the undisclosed discount by seller to issuer is a secret profit which the agent issuer should disgorge to its principal, the cardholder.[97] Any such difficulty, if it arises, could be resolved if issuers took it in themselves to make full and frank disclosure of their discounts to their cardholders.[98] If it should be argued that the

---

[92] A contract of sale of goods is defined in s. 2(1) as one in which the seller agrees to transfer the property in goods to the buyer for a money consideration: it does not say that the price must come from the buyer. The buyer's duty to pay (s. 27) may be modified or excluded (s. 55) so that the seller looks to a third party instead for payment. For the joint and several liability of that third party for misrepresentations and breaches of contract by the seller, see Consumer Credit Act 1974, ss. 56 and 75 and Bridge, n. 91 above.

[93] Ch. 1 above.   [94] *Re Charge Card Services Ltd* [1989] Ch. 497.

[95] *W. J. Alan & Co.* v. *El Nasr Export and Import Co.* [1972] 2 QB 189.

[96] N. 92 above.

[97] On agency and secret profits, see *Bowstead on Agency* (16th edn., 1996 by F. M. B. Reynolds, Sweet & Maxwell, London), §§6–038, 6–044, 6–075 and Art. 48; *Phipps* v. *Boardman* [1967] 2 AC 46; *Keogh* v. *Dalgety* (1916) 22 CLR 402; *Aas* v. *Bentham* [1891] 2 Ch. 144.

[98] *Hippisley* v. *Knee Bros.* [1905] 1 KB 1.

strict rules on secret profits ought to apply only to those agents who negotiate the formation and terms of contracts, which issuers do not, it must be said that the law supports no such distinction. In addition, credit card issuers come within the spirit of the rules governing secret profits. They hold out to sellers that acceptance of their credit cards will increase business volume and their discount has a manifest tendency to drive up selling prices at the expense of cardholders, who may be denied the cash discounts sometimes given to other buyers.

Trading Stamps

Finally, similar problems are posed by trading stamps accumulated on certain purchases and then later surrendered for goods. The supply of goods for stamps was examined in a Canadian case, where the court appears to have concluded that the surrender of intrinsically worthless trading stamps for goods was a barter contract and not a sale of goods.[99] The trading stamps could not therefore be seen as a money consideration. A similar approach underlies legislation passed on the assumption that it was necessary to ensure that the supply of goods in return for trading stamps attracts the same obligations concerning description, fitness, and quality of the goods as are laid down by the Sale of Goods Act.[100] If the issuer is paid for the stamps before or when they are issued by retailers to their customers, then this payment is divorced from any subsequent transaction involving the surrender of accumulated stamps by those customers in return for goods. It cannot therefore be said that the supplier of the goods receives stamps in order to recover the price of goods supplied from some other paymaster. The stamps themselves lack the currency of money, so, though perhaps money's worth, are not money.

BASIC STATUTORY DISTINCTIONS

The implementation of the Sale of Goods Act is based on sets of key definitions. These definitions are of major importance in the application of the passing of property rules. The sale of goods is a hybrid of contract and conveyance in which the contractual and proprietary aspects of the transaction are virtually inseparable, in contrast with the sale of land where the contract and the conveyance are formally and chronologically

---

[99] *R.* v. *Langley* (1899) 31 OR 295.
[100] Trading Stamps Act 1964, s. 4, as amended by s. 16(1) of the Supply of Goods (Implied Terms) Act 1973. Trading stamp transactions are excepted contracts under the Supply of Goods and Services Act 1982, s. 1(2)(c).

distinct.[101] Under the Sale of Goods Act, the passing of property from seller to buyer is the fulcrum on which depend issues as diverse as the incidence of risk, the impact of frustration, the seller's entitlement to recover as a debt the unpaid price, and the rights of buyer and seller in the event of the other's bankruptcy. As this last item shows, the passing of property does not merely provide the key to the resolution of contract problems between the parties *inter se*; it also affects strangers to the contract and may be significant for certain statutory, non-sale purposes where it is important to identify the owner of the goods. The definitions in the Sale of Goods Act do not bear upon the passing of property as an end in itself, but rather as a medium through which contractual rights and liabilities are resolved.

Contract and Conveyance

The Act defines 'contract of sale' as comprised of 'an agreement to sell' and 'a sale'.[102] The former is merely the description of the contract at the executory stage; the latter, in its pure form, refers to the actual conveyance of the goods, though sometimes it designates the cumulation of contract and conveyance arrived at when the contract is executed. Consistent with this latter usage is section 2(6): 'An agreement to sell becomes a sale when the time elapses or the conditions are fulfilled subject to which the property in the goods is to be transferred.' Section 2(4) recognizes that, under some contracts of sale, the property in the goods passes automatically by virtue of the conclusion of the contract itself: 'Where under a contract of sale the property in the goods is transferred from the seller to the buyer the contract is called a sale.' Here, the contract and conveyance are thoroughly fused and inseparable. According to section 2(5) on the other hand: 'Where under a contract of sale the transfer of the property in the goods is to take place at a future time or subject to some condition later to be fulfilled the contract is called an agreement to sell.' In this case, the contract and conveyance may be chronologically distinct, but the absence of forms in the passing of property in goods renders it just an incident in the performance of the contract.

The Act also provides in section 61(1) that ' "sale" includes a bargain and sale as well as a sale and delivery'. This is an unexplained reference to the old common (or *indebitatus*) counts of goods bargained and sold and goods sold and delivered.[103] These counts were simplified actions identifying in abbreviated form the circumstances in which the seller

---

[101] M. G. Bridge (1986) 20 *UBC LR* 53.   [102] S. 2(1), (4)–(5).
[103] E. Bullen and S. Leake, *Precedents of Pleadings in Personal Actions in the Superior Courts of the Common Law* (3rd edn., Sweet & Maxwell, London, 1868), 35–40.

could maintain a debt action for the price. Briefly, if the seller were unable to fit his case into either of these counts, he could not sue in debt but was generally limited to a damages action against the buyer for non-acceptance. The factor uniting the two counts was the passing of property in the goods: the count of goods bargained and sold applied where the property had passed, usually on the conclusion of the contract, but delivery had not occurred; the count of goods sold and delivered lay when the property passed at a later time and delivery had been made. It was always possible for the seller to maintain a right to sue in debt if he stipulated in the contract that the buyer was to pay for the goods at a date prior to the passing of property: the buyer's duty to pay thus became a condition precedent to the seller's duty to convey the goods to the buyer.[104] To succeed in his debt action, however, the seller would have to continue holding himself ready and willing to convey the goods to the buyer on the eventual payment of the price, and would be disqualified if he conveyed the goods to a third party in the meantime.[105] These rules establishing the scope of the seller's debt action are preserved, albeit in different language, in section 49 of the Act.

Broadly speaking, sale is the event on which a seller's breach of contract action passes from damages to debt, though in the latter instance the seller has always been free to elect to sue for damages instead.[106] Sale is also significant in determining whether a buyer denied delivery of the goods may pursue an action in the tort of conversion; such a buyer may thereby succeed in establishing the right to immediate possession[107] needed for bringing an action of this kind. A right to immediate possession does not necessarily follow the passing of property to the buyer, for example, where the buyer has not yet paid and payment is a contractual condition of delivery.[108] Conversely, a buyer may already be in

---

[104] See Sjt. Williams's notes to *Pordage* v. *Cole* (1669) 1 Wms. Saund. 319, Rule 1; *Dunlop* v. *Grote* (1845) 2 C & K 153.

[105] *Laird* v. *Pim* (1841) 7 M & W 478; *Lamond* v. *Davall* (1847) 9 QB 1030.   [106] S. 50.

[107] *Marquess of Bute* v. *Barclays Bank Ltd* [1955] 1 QB 202; *Rodgers* v. *Kennay* (1846) 9 QB 594, 596; *Jarvis* v. *Williams* [1955] 1 WLR 71; *International Factors Ltd* v. *Rodriguez* [1979] QB 351. Although the right to immediate possession may suffice for conversion, the better view is that possession at the time of the wrong is needed for trespass: F. Pollock and R. Wright, *An Essay on Possession in the Common Law* (OUP, London, 1888), 28; *Penfold's Wines Pty. Ltd* v. *Elliott* (1946) 74 CLR 204. See also E. H. Warren (1936) 49 *Harv. LR* 1084.

[108] *Lord* v. *Price* (1874) LR 9 Ex. 54. In *Chinery* v. *Viall* (1860) 5 H & N 288, where sheep had been bought on credit and left in the possession of the seller *qua* agent, the buyer had title to sue without payment or tender of payment. In actions against the seller where the property has passed but the unpaid seller has a lien for the price, the unlawful action of the seller will terminate the lien and endow the buyer with the right to immediate possession so as to be able to sue the seller in conversion: *Gurr* v. *Cuthbert* (1843) 12 LJ Ex. 309. A mere contractual expectancy of receiving goods is not equivalent to the right to immediate possession of them: *Jarvis* v. *Williams*, n. 107 above. It may be, however, that the property need not have passed for a buyer in conversion to have the right to immediate possession: *International Factors Ltd* v. *Rodriguez*, n. 107 above.

possession of goods though the property has not yet passed under the contract of sale. His possession of the goods will support an action in trespass or conversion against a third-party tortfeasor, or against a seller who is guilty of a wrongful interference with the goods.[109] A buyer with the right to immediate possession may, where the seller has wrongfully not delivered, elect to sue for damages for non-delivery instead of in conversion. Commonly, there will be little difference between these two actions since specific delivery (in a tort action), just like specific performance (in a contract action), is rarely awarded to the buyer.[110] The greater frequency of the seller's debt action for the price, when contrasted with the buyer's correlative action for the recovery of the goods themselves, has been the subject of disparaging comment.

Conditional Contracts

The Act also provides in section 2(3) that a 'contract of sale may be absolute or conditional'. Such a condition often holds up the execution of the contract, that is, the passing of the property.[111] Perhaps the commonest example is a conditional sale contract whereby the buyer obtains possession of the goods and agrees to pay the price by deferred instalments, the property passing upon payment of the final instalment. A contractual condition may also qualify the performance of provisions other than those relating to the passing of property. The word 'condition' is quite possibly the most ambiguous in the contract lexicon.[112] The conclusion of a binding contract may be held up pending the occurrence of an external condition.[113] Or one or more obligations of a binding contract may be suspended until an internal condition has been fulfilled. In the latter case, the internal condition may be non-promissory, in that neither party has undertaken that it will or will not occur.[114] Or it may be promissory, so that the party bound is answerable in damages while the other is entitled to discharge himself from the contract.[115]

---

[109] *The Winkfield* [1902] P 42; *Wilson* v. *Lombank Ltd* [1963] 1 WLR 1294; *Healing (Sales) Pty. Ltd* v. *Inglis Electrix Pty. Ltd* (1968) 121 CLR 584 (also a breach of the quiet possession warranty in s. 12(2)(b): *Chinery* v. *Viall*, n. 108 above.

[110] *Cohen* v. *Roche* [1927] 1 KB 169 (specific delivery); *Behnke* v. *Bede Shipping Co. Ltd* [1927] 1 KB 649 (specific performance). See Ch. 10 below.

[111] Ch. 3 below.   [112] See S. Stoljar (1953) 69 *LQR* 485.

[113] As in the 'subject to contract' cases: *Winn* v. *Bull* (1877) 7 Ch. D 29; *Von Hatzfeldt-Wildenberg* v. *Alexander* [1912] 1 Ch. 284, 288–89; *Astra Trust* v. *Adams & Williams* [1969] 1 Lloyd's Rep. 89.

[114] It was common in the 19th century for goods to be sold on a 'to arrive' basis so the seller was not bound in the event of the goods failing to reach their destination: *Calcutta and Burmah Steam Navigation Co.* v. *De Mattos* (1863) 32 LJQB 322, affd. (1864) 33 LJQB 214. But the courts leant against interpreting contracts to exculpate the non-delivering seller: *Fragano* v. *Long* (1825) 4 B & C 219.

[115] *Trans Trust SPRL* v. *Danubian Trading Co. Ltd* [1952] 2 QB 297. This is the sense in which the word is used in the sections dealing with the termination of the contract for

Existing and Future Goods

Section 5(1) of the Act states: 'The goods which form the subject of a contract of sale may be either existing goods, owned or possessed by the seller, or goods to be manufactured or acquired by him after the making of the contract of sale, in this Act called future goods.'

This distinction between existing and future goods comprises the universe of goods: all goods are either one or the other and may not be both. The purpose of this distinction appears to be two-fold: first of all, it resolves any doubt that future goods may lawfully be the subject of a contract of sale.[116] The common law has not always been sympathetic to futures and forward delivery trading[117] and, as stated above, there has also been a discernible tendency to confuse an impossible conveyance of future goods with a feasible agreement to convey future goods once they become existing goods. This point is bolstered by section 5(2), which provides that the seller's acquisition of future goods may depend upon a contingency.[118] Whether the seller will be liable in the event that he does not acquire the goods is a different matter: that depends upon the construction of the contract.[119] Secondly, the Act in section 5(3) makes it clear that there can be no passing of property in future goods.[120] This provision recognizes the physical impossibility of the seller's transferring the property in goods that do not exist, or that exist but are not owned by him.[121]

---

breach and with the seller's duties in respect of title, description, fitness, and quality of the goods.

[116] *Ajello* v. *Worsley* [1898] 1 Ch. 274.

[117] As an example of a number of early sale of goods cases, see *Lorymer* v. *Smith* (1822) 1 B & C 1, 2. The Statute of Frauds (Amendment) Act (Lord Tenterden's Act) 1828, 9 Geo. IV, cap. 14, s. 7, reproduced in substance as s. 5(2) of the Sale of Goods Act, recognized the existence of such contracts as binding sale of goods agreements. For the exploded belief that such contracts were wagers on commodity prices, see *Bryan* v. *Lewis* (1826) Ry. & Moo. 386. See also K. Llewellyn (1937) 37 *Col. LR* 341, 351 n. 21 (reference to 16th-century market regulations and the forbidden practice of forestalling).

[118] It seems to be a particular application of s. 2(3), though s. 5(2) does not deny the possibility of a seller warranting that future goods will become existing goods.

[119] *Watts* v. *Friend* (1858) 10 B & C 446; *Hale* v. *Rawson* (1858) 4 CB(NS) 85. For the *buyer* claiming a contractual right not to take future goods, see *Messervey* v. *Central Canada Canning Co.* [1923] 3 WWR 365; *Wingold* v. *William Looser & Co. Ltd* [1951] 1 DLR 429.

[120] *Lunn* v. *Thornton* (1845) 1 CB 379; *Belding* v. *Read* (1865) 3 H & C 955, 961 ('there cannot be a prophetic conveyance').

[121] But note that s. 5(1) appears to include, in the definition of existing goods, goods that the seller possesses but does not own. It may be that the seller of such goods may, prior to acquiring ownership from the third party owner, divest himself of the whole of his entitlement in the goods on the proprietary transfer (see Ch. 3 below). As soon as the seller acquires proprietary rights from the owner, the buyer's title would then be automatically fed. The seller's contractual responsibility in respect of that transfer, however, would fall under s. 12.

Another effect of section 5(3) is that a contract is not invalidated just because the subject matter does not exist as defined by the Act.[122] Even if the seller purports to transfer the property in future goods before they become existing goods, he will be treated as having undertaken to transfer the property once they become existing goods by manufacture or acquisition as the case may be.[123]

A purported present conveyance of future goods will not automatically be converted by the Act or by common law into an effective conveyance at the moment future goods become existing goods. At common law, it has always been impossible to direct the passing of property in goods at some future date without performing a fresh act of conveyance.[124] Nevertheless, a category of goods with a potential existence, such as the unborn young of particular animals or the crop of a particular field owned by the seller, has long been recognized at common law as an exception to this rule, so that a fresh conveyance is not needed when the goods come into existence.[125] This common law exception is the general rule in equity which, looking on that as done which ought to be done, transmits automatically the equitable property in goods, in response to a purported present conveyance, once the goods have come into existence.[126] The equitable rule, however, does not assist volunteers, namely those who have given no consideration for the purported present conveyance.[127] As will be discussed in a later chapter,[128] it was never clear to what extent these equitable rules applied to ordinary contracts of sale that were not designed as part of a scheme to provide security for a loan. Furthermore, as the present authorities hold, it seems that the Sale of Goods Act concedes no part or very little part to equitable rules concerning the passing of property.[129]

Specific and Unascertained Goods

Specific goods are those 'identifed and agreed on at the time a contract of sale is made'.[130] The Act also makes references to unascertained

---

[122] See also s. 5(2) and n. 117 above.   [123] In accordance with s. 27.

[124] *Lunn* v. *Thornton*, n. 120 above; *Langton* v. *Higgins* (1859) 4 H & N 402. The same effect would be achieved if the buyer took possession under a licence to seize: *Congreve* v. *Evetts* (1854) 10 Ex. 298; *Hope* v. *Hayley* (1856) 5 E & B 830.

[125] *Grantham* v. *Hawley* (1603) Hob. 132; *Grass* v. *Austin* (1882) 7 OAR 511 (Can.).

[126] *Holroyd* v. *Marshall* (1862) 10 HLC 191; *Tailby* v. *Official Receiver* (1888) 13 App. Cas. 523; *Collyer* v. *Isaacs* (1881) 19 Ch. D 342.

[127] *Re Ellenborough* [1903] 1 Ch. 697.   [128] Ch. 3 below.

[129] *Ibid.*; *Re Wait* [1927] 1 Ch. 606.

[130] S. 61(1). This now includes an identified undivided share in goods: s. 2(d) of the Sale of Goods (Amendment) Act 1995, amending the definition of specific goods in s. 61(1) of the Sale of Goods Act.

goods,[131] which are nowhere defined. By inference, however, unascertained goods are all those goods that, at the date of the contract, are not specific goods. Just as the distinction between existing and future goods exhausts all goods at the contract date, so too does the distinction between specific and unascertained goods. But the two sets of distinctions do not quite rotate on the same axis. Existing goods may be either specific or unascertained, while future goods are nearly always unascertained and specific goods are almost always existing goods. An identified second-hand reaper owned and possessed by a third party at the contract date, and thus future goods, was regarded as specific goods in *Varley* v. *Whipp*.[132] A contract to sell a fungible item possessed in bulk by a seller in his store room will involve goods that are both existing and unascertained.

Quasi-specific Goods

Two refineménts have to be introduced to the distinction between specific and unascertained goods. First, the parties may contract for the sale of unascertained goods but limit the seller's power of selection to a specific bulk. A seller may be required to supply widgets from the stock currently in his store room just as, in an example used by Chalmers,[133] a seller may undertake to supply a number of bottles of a particular vintage of wine from the larger stock currently lying in his cellar. These quasi-specific goods remain in principle unascertained goods since it cannot be said of any particular widget or bottle in the larger stock whether it has been identified and agreed upon at the contract date. The seller's power of selection may be constrained in varying degrees between the cases of unlimited selection and quasi-specific goods. A seller, for example, may have to supply amber durum wheat shipped from a Pacific Coast port in July. Although these are not quasi-specific goods, the seller's choice is limited: he may not tender to the buyer amber durum wheat of the same quality as the contract demands shipped from a Great Lakes port in a different month.

Quasi-specific goods cannot be treated as specific goods where the Act lays down particular rules for specific goods, as it does for example in sections 6–7 for initial and subsequent impossibility of performance arising out of the perishing of goods.[134] Indeed, the Act itself makes it plain that the passing of property rules for specific goods cannot be applied to

---

[131] Ss. 16 and 18, Rule 5. They are also referred to in their later ascertained state in ss. 17(1) and 52.

[132] [1900] 1 QB 513. See also *Bannerman* v. *Barlow* (1908) 7 WLR 859 (Can.); *J. I. Case Threshing Machine Co.* v. *Fee* (1909) 10 WLR 70.

[133] *The Sale of Goods Act, 1893* (4th edn., Butterworths, London, 1899), 19–20 ('five dozen of the '74 champagne wine in my cellar'). See *Howell* v. *Coupland* (1876) 1 QBD 258.

[134] *H. R. and S. Sainsbury Ltd* v. *Street* [1972] 1 WLR 834.

quasi-specific goods.[135] Yet this hybrid category of quasi-specific goods has certain of the characteristics of specific goods and, even if a provision of the Act does not apply to it, careful thought should be given to the application of that provision by analogy or as the statutory expression of a broader and relevant common law principle.

Ascertained Goods

The second refinement concerns ascertained goods which appear to defy the binary classification of goods as specific or unascertained. Ascertained goods, along with specific goods, are eligible for specific performance.[136] Ascertained goods do not exist in that state at the contract date: they are goods initially unascertained that have subsequently been identified to the contract.[137] At that date, the impediment to the passing of property in unascertained goods, laid down by the Act and motivated by the same consideration of impossibility that prevents the property passing in future goods, is lifted.

Summary

The distinction between specific and unascertained goods formerly had a dramatic impact on the incidence of contractual rights and duties. It is much less important nowadays.[138] In principle, as the Act maintains, the property in specific goods passes at the contract date and in unascertained goods at a later date.[139] Judicial interpretation of the relevant provisions has blunted this distinction in the area of the passing of property, partly at least to avoid the application of the now-repealed rule that specific goods could never be rejected by the buyer if the property in them had already passed.[140] The distinction retains its force in the contractual areas of discharge for initial and subsequent impossibility.[141] For much of the nineteenth century, the distinction was important for the incidence of the seller's obligations concerning the quality and fitness of goods. The rule of *caveat emptor* was more effective in diluting the obligations of the seller of specific goods than those of the seller of unascertained goods.[142] This discrepancy showed a tendency to diminish during the course of the nineteenth century though it persisted to a lesser degree in a disguised form in the Act.[143]

---

[135] S. 16. See also *Re Wait*, n. 129 above.   [136] S. 52.

[137] *Re Wait*, n. 129 above, 630 (Atkin LJ).

[138] The distinction did not feature in the draft bill attached to the Ontario Law Reform Commission, *Report on Sale of Goods* (1979). A periphrastic reference to specific goods emerges in the Canadian Uniform Sale of Goods Act, s. 92(2). See Alberta Institute of Law Research and Reform, *The Uniform Sale of Goods Act 1982* (Report No. 38), 203–4.

[139] S. 18, Rule 1, Rule 5.   [140] Misrepresentation Act 1967, s. 4(1).

[141] Ss. 6–7.   [142] Ch. 7 below.

[143] In the former presumptive denial of rejection rights in the case of specific goods.

General and Special Property

A sale of goods contract requires the seller to transfer the 'property' in goods to the buyer:[144] 'property' is defined as 'the general property in goods and not merely a special property'.[145] No definition is given for 'special property'.

Personal property law is vague on the definition of its basic concepts. The Sale of Goods Act does not speak of ownership, and for a good reason. At common law, proprietary rights are protected from tortious interference by means of personal actions requiring the plaintiff to be in possession or have the right to immediate possession at the time of the wrong.[146] Before the enactment of the Torts (Interference with Goods) Act 1977, the position was as follows. A plaintiff succeeded in a conversion action because his possessory right was superior to the defendant's.[147] The judgment operated finally as between the parties to the action without having an *in rem* effect on strangers. Only in exceptional cases was the defendant permitted to resist the plaintiff's possession-based claim by pointing to the superior possessory right (the *ius tertii*) of a third party.[148] Such relativity of right as between plaintiff and defendant hardly accorded with anything so absolute as ownership.[149] It was quite consistent with this lack of absoluteness that delivery up of the disputed thing was not available as a remedy until quite recent times;[150] even today, it is infrequently awarded.[151]

The 1977 Act abolished the *ius tertii* defence and promoted the joinder of multiple actions involving the same disputed goods.[152] It also made

---

[144] S. 2(1).   [145] S. 61(1).

[146] *The Winkfield* [1902] P 42; *Marquess of Bute* v. *Barclays Bank Ltd* [1955] 1 QB 202. According to F. Pollock and R. Wright, *An Essay on Possession in the Common Law* (OUP, London, 1888), 5, 'so feeble and precarious was property without possession, or rather without possessory remedies . . . that Possession largely usurped not only the substance but the name of Property'. For the recovery in damages of the full value of the chattel by the bailee, see *The Winkfield*, above, and *The Joanna Vatis* [1922] P 92. Owners out of possession were given a new remedy in the form of an action on the case for damage done to their reversionary interest in *Mears* v. *London and South Western Railway Co. Ltd* (1862) 11 CB(NS) 850.

[147] *Buckley* v. *Gross* (1863) 3 B & S 566; *Bird* v. *Town of Fort Frances* [1949] OR 292 (Can.).

[148] Where the defendant had not interfered with the plaintiff's possession and was not the plaintiff's bailee: *Leake* v. *Loveday* (1842) 4 M & G 972; *Biddle* v. *Bond* (1865) 6 B & S 225. A defendant unable to plead the *ius tertii* might yet defend the action on the authority of the true owner: *Biddle* v. *Bond*, above; *Rogers Sons & Co.* v. *Lambert & Co.* [1891] 1 QB 318. He could also plead eviction by title paramount: *Ross* v. *Edwards* (1895) 73 LT 100.

[149] The language of ownership is probably attributable to the influence of 19th century factors legislation. See generally G. Battersby and A. D. Preston (1972) 35 *MLR* 268.

[150] Common Law Procedure Act 1854, s. 78.

[151] Ch. 10 below; *General and Finance Facilities Ltd* v. *Cook's Cars (Romford) Ltd* [1963] 2 All ER 314. For a case where the court exercised its discretion in favour of the claimant, see *Howard E. Perry & Co. Ltd* v. *British Railways Board* [1980] 1 WLR 1375 ('Steel is gold').

[152] Ss. 8–9.

provision for the avoidance of the overcompensation that came with the award of full damages to plaintiffs with only a limited possessory interest; the defendant was concomitantly protected from multiple liabilities exceeding the value of the goods.[153] The 1977 changes may betoken the start of a movement towards absolute ownership going beyond the text of the Act itself; they do not affect the earlier[154] provisions of the Sale of Goods Act.

The general property in goods can therefore be understood as encapsulating the best possessory right there can be in the contract goods, a possessory right that is good against the whole world. If even such a possessory right seems fugitive, it should be remembered that goods, in contrast with land, which is permanent and ineradicable, have always been regarded at common law as transient and so hardly deserving of the complex proprietary structure (the doctrine of estates) that is capable of dividing land in a multiple fashion among various owners and over time.[155]

Quite simply, the general property in goods is the most exalted interest that the law deems personal property fit to have: nothing more enduring is necessary for a species of property that does not last forever. But even this modestly stated interest may not be the interest that the buyer and seller have agreed that the former shall have. It is common for a limited interest to be the subject of a sale agreement,[156] even an interest that is precarious to a degree unknown by the parties.[157] Notwithstanding such shortcomings in the seller's proprietary interest, the contract should still be regarded as one governed by the Sale of Goods Act. To reach this result, the above definition of general property needs to be modified. For the contract to be one of sale, it is necessary for the seller to transfer or agree to transfer the whole of his interest in the goods, and not reserve a part of that interest unconditionally or direct the buyer to hold the goods on bailment terms, for a bailee's interest is but a special property in the goods.[158] The difference between general and special property will nevertheless in certain cases appear to be quantitative,[159] but that is hardly

[153] Ss. 5(3), 7.
[154] In the sense that they were brought forward from the 1893 Act.
[155] J Williams, *Principles of the Law of Personal Property* (14th edn., 1894 by T. Cyprian Williams, Sweet & Maxwell, London), 44.
[156] S. 2(2) deals with sales beween part owners.
[157] S. 12(3) permits limited title sales.
[158] *The Odessa* [1916] AC 145 (terminology criticized); *Nyberg* v. *Handelaar* [1892] 2 QB 202; *Donald* v. *Suckling* (1866) LR 1 QB 585; O. W. Homes, *The Common Law* (Little Brown, Boston, Mass., 1881), 242. For the proprietary interest of a commercial pledgee of documents of title, see *Burdick* v. *Sewell* (1884) 13 QBD 157, 174 (Bowen LJ dissenting), revd. *sub nom Sewell* v. *Burdick* (1884) 10 App. Cas. 74, 92–3 (Lord Blackburn); *Harper* v. *Godsell* (1870) LR 5 QB 422, 426 (Blackburn J) (delivery warrants); *The Orteric* [1920] AC 724.
[159] e.g. the lease of goods for a period equal to their useful life. From an early date, a finder has been considered to hold the chattel under the terms of a deemed bailment, yet

unusual given the extent to which the notion of relativity of right has pervaded this area of law. In the last resort, what matters is the scope of the interest that the seller warrants will be transferred and not the interest the seller succeeds in transferring.[160]

THE CONTRACT OF SALE AND RELATED TRANSACTIONS INVOLVING GOODS

Though the issue is rather less important than it used to be, it may still be important for various reasons to distinguish sale of goods contracts from related contracts involving the transfer of goods. It should not be forgotten, however, that much of the Sale of Goods Act consists of *prima facie* rules, departed from in numerous types of sale contracts, and of duties that may be excluded subject to external statutory controls. Furthermore, section 62(2) exists to prevent the divergence of sales law from the general law of contract.

The scope of the Act may present itself in different contexts. No longer do sale of goods contracts have to be evidenced in writing when related contracts need not be.[161] Furthermore, as regards the quality and fitness of goods supplied under transfer contracts akin to sale, such as work and materials contracts, the courts displayed a willingness at common law to mimic the statutory terms of fitness and quality even before these were enacted in the Supply of Goods and Services Act 1982. Nevertheless, the rules in the Act on the passing of property and on the seller's action for the price find no statutory counterpart in legislation dealing with related contracts. These rules may be applied by analogy outside the Act, an expedient adopted for the implied terms of quality and fitness before these were expressly enacted in separate legislation. What precisely is meant by application by analogy is a different matter. A statute might serve as a policy inspiration for innovation in the common law.[162] It might even be argued that cases outside the Sale of Goods Act fall within

where the true owner is not to be found it is in practical terms indefeasible. See W. Laidlaw (1931) 16 *Cornell LQ* 286, 287. The same idea was implicit in the 14th century extension of the writ of detinue to finders: Williams, n. 2 above, 16. See also *Newman* v. *Bourne and Hollingsworth* (1915) 31 TLR 209.

[160] 'The purpose of the contract [of sale] is that the seller divests himself of all proprietary rights in the thing sold in favour of the buyer': M. Chalmers, *The Sale of Goods Act, 1893* (4th edn., Butterworths, London, 1899), 3.

[161] The writing requirement was repealed by the Law Reform (Enforcement of Contracts) Act 1954, s. 1.

[162] *The Queen in Right of Canada* v. *Saskatchewan Wheat Pool* (1983) 143 DLR (3d) 9; *Bhadauria* v. *Board of Governors of Seneca College* (1979) 105 DLR (3d) 707, revd. (1981) 124 DLR (3d) 193.

the equity of the statute.[163] These approaches hardly fit a codifying statute like the Sale of Goods Act which, in its 1893 form, drew upon case law that also sustained contracts akin to sale of goods. The Act in this respect may be regarded as evidence of the common law that applied to related contracts, or the common law that would have developed had it not been cut off by the process of enactment and confined to sale of goods, the most important of a group of like transactions. The enactment of a codifying statute should not be relied upon to prevent the cross-pollination between sale and related contracts that would certainly have occurred if sales law had remained uncodified.

Work and Materials Contracts

Work and materials[164] contracts fall within a spectrum running from services to sale of goods. A contract to supply services, such as transport or dry-cleaning, is not a sale of goods contract. Nor is it a work and materials contract.[165] There are, however, few contracts for services where only labour is supplied: even a dry-cleaner supplies wire coat hangers. Work and materials differ from services in that goods supplied are integral, not collateral, to the supplier's performance. At the other end of the spectrum, a sale of goods contract may include services, for example, the sale of a kitchen appliance with a labour and parts warranty, or the sale of a fixture which the seller agrees to dismantle prior to delivery.[166] Labour is inherent in the manufacture and distribution of goods, so the distinction between sale of goods and work and materials is one of degree.

It is therefore necessary to explore the conjunction of labour and goods before drawing a line between sale of goods and work and materials. Labour and goods may be blended in an integrated way in the manufacturing process, as where a painter produces a portrait in oils[167] and a dentist a set of dentures.[168] Or the labour may be collateral to goods

---

[163] J. Landis, 'Statutes and the Sources of Law' in *Harvard Legal Essays* (Harvard University Press, Boston, Mass., 1934). See also J. Landis (1965) 2 *Harv J of Leg.* 7.

[164] An expression preferred herein to labour and materials.

[165] But the two are sometimes confused: *Grouse Mountain Resorts Ltd* v. *Bank of Montreal* (1960) 25 DLR (2d) 371.

[166] *Underwood* v. *Burgh Castle Brick Co.* [1922] 1 KB 343.

[167] *Robinson* v. *Graves* [1935] 1 KB 579 (work and materials); *Isaacs* v. *Hardy* (1884) Cab. & El. 287 (sale of goods). In such cases, the law tends towards work and materials: *Dodd and Dodd* v. *Wilson* [1949] 2 All ER 691 (inoculation of cattle). But see *Philip Head & Sons Ltd* v. *Showfronts Ltd* [1970] 1 Lloyd's Rep. 140 (installation of carpet).

[168] *Lee* v. *Griffin* (1861) 1 B & S 272 (sale); *Samuels* v. *Davis* [1943] 1 KB 526 (sale). See also *Marcel (Furriers) Ltd* v. *Tapper* [1953] 1 All ER 15 (sale of fur jacket made to order); *Deta Nominees Pty. Ltd* v. *Viscount Plastic Products Pty. Ltd* [1979] VR 167 (sale of custom-built manufacturing dies); *Lockett* v. *A. and M. Charles Ltd* [1938] 4 All ER 170; *Gee* v. *White Spot Ltd* (1986) 7 BCLR (2d) 235 (Can.) (sale of restaurant meal).

that are made serviceable, as where a plumber installs a furnace[169] or a garage fits replacement parts in a car.[170] Sometimes labour is both integral and collateral, as where boilers are built and then installed.[171] In so far as labour and goods are capable of being separated, it might be argued that the Sale of Goods Act should be applied to that part of the transaction concerning goods, the remainder being governed by a separate regime.[172] The abolition of the writing requirement and the enactment of the Supply of Goods and Services Act 1982 have created the opportunity to move away from definitive questions and ask more specific questions.[173] Where labour and goods are inseparably blended, the Act could be applied to the ingredients used, if not to the overall product. Support for this type of partial application of the Sale of Goods Act, however, is not to be found in the case law.

If a transaction concerning the product of labour and goods must be classified definitively as a sale of goods or supply of work and materials, the choice seems to lie among three possible tests. First, the transaction may be seen in substance or essence as one or the other; secondly, a comparative value test may be applied to determine whether the goods or the labour have the greater financial value; or thirdly, the transaction may be seen as a sale of goods contract if the property in some goods is conveyed and these goods are not wholly incidental to the transaction. Drawing the line between sale of goods and work and materials has in the past been distorted in favour of the latter by the judicial desire in some cases to avoid the old writing requirement for sale of goods.

In *Lee* v. *Griffin*,[174] the plaintiff dentist contracted to prepare two sets of false teeth. When his patient died before payment, her executor, citing

---

[169] *British American Paint Co.* v. *Fogh* (1915) 24 DLR 61 (*semble* sale, but out of line with other authorities).

[170] *Stewart* v. *Reavall's Garage* [1952] 2 QB 545 (work and materials); *G. H. Myers & Co.* v. *Brent Cross Service Co.* [1934] 1 KB 46 (work and materials); *Sterling Engine Works* v. *Red Deer Lumber Co.* (1920) 51 DLR 509 (work and materials).

[171] *Anglo-Egyptian Navigation Co.* v. *Rennie* (1875) LR 10 CP 271 (work and materials). See also *Clark* v. *Bulmer* (1843) 11 M & W 243 (installation of engine: work and materials); *Fairbanks Soap Co.* v. *Sheppard* [1953] 1 SCR 314 (Can.) (building of machinery: work and materials); *Wolfenden* v. *Wilson* (1873) 33 UCQB 442 (Can.:manufacture and installation of tombstone: sale *sed quaere?*).

[172] It has been recognized that a transaction may be mixed: *Hyundai Heavy Industries Co. Ltd* v. *Papadopoulos* [1980] 1 WLR 1129 (contract for sale of ship to be built contained features making it akin to work and materials and services contracts). See also *Pritchett & Gold* v. *Currie* [1916] 2 Ch. 515 (sale of storage battery later to be installed); *Matheson* v. *Meredith* (1955) 1 DLR (2d) 332. Cf. *H. Parsons (Livestock) Ltd* v. *Uttley, Ingham & Co. Ltd* [1978] QB 791. But shipbuilding contracts are usually treated as sale of goods contracts: *Reid* v. *Macbeth & Gray* [1904] AC 223; *McDougall* v. *Aeromarine of Emsworth Ltd* [1958] 3 All ER 431.

[173] Such as: how strict is the liability of a garage when installing new parts? Or when checking existing parts?

[174] N. 168 above. See the thorough review in *Deta Nominees, ibid.*

the absence of writing, declined to pay. The contract was held to be one of sale of goods and thus unenforceable. Blackburn J purportedly applied a substance test, but considered it satisfied if the property in goods was transferred by one party to the other. The breadth of his approach is evident in the example he gives of the sculptor who, despite all his art and labour,[175] is a seller of the statue he makes. The comparative value test was firmly rejected by the court,[176] which also excluded from the category of sale supplies of collateral goods, such as the paper used by an attorney for an opinion and the book produced by the printer.[177] It is hard to see why these are excluded by the letter of the test applied by Blackburn J, who was plainly yielding to the imperative of an impressionistic judgment guided by some sense of substance.

The leading modern statement of the law, *Robinson* v. *Graves*,[178] concerned a contract to paint a portrait of the defendant's future wife, which was held to be one of work and materials. The reasoning is unpersuasive and the court is unsure whether it is applying or departing from *Lee* v. *Griffin*,[179] a case hard to distinguish on its facts. Some emphasis was placed on the degree of co-operation required of the sitter as tending towards work and materials, but the same could be said of a patient whose mouth is modelled for dentures. The core of the decision in *Robinson*, however, was that a contract was in substance one for work and materials where the value of the skill well exceeded that of the accompanying materials.[180] This pragmatic blend of language accepted and rejected in *Lee* v. *Griffin* is unproductive of precision and encourages the search for differences of degree between for example a photographer who produces quick passport photographs[181] and one who prints portraits, or between a society painter and a street artist. In defence of *Robinson*, however, the court seemed unwilling to allow an unconscientious contract-breaker to put up the defence of non-compliance with the sale of goods writing requirement.

A particular difficulty along the line between work and materials and sale of goods occurs in those cases where materials are supplied by a customer to be made up into a new product. The supply of the new product by the manufacturer is unlikely to be treated as a sale of goods if no goods

---

[175] Exceeding in value the materials.

[176] 'I do not think that the test to apply to these cases is whether the value of the work exceeds that of the materials': n. 168 above, 278.

[177] *Ibid.*, 277–8. But see *Canada Bank Note Engraving and Printing Co.* v. *Toronto Railway Co.* (1895) 21 OAR 462 (printing of a special debenture form a sale of goods), purportedly applying *Lee* v. *Griffin*, n. 168 above.

[178] N. 167 above. Criticized trenchantly in *Deta Nominees*, n. 168 above.

[179] N. 168 above.

[180] N. 167 above, 585–6 and 589–90.

[181] Cf. *R.* v. *Howarth* [1920] 2 WWR 1043 (sale of enlarged photograph).

of the manufacturer are used in the process.[182] The position is more complicated if the manufacturer's own goods are added to the customer's. There is support for the view that such a contract is one of sale,[183] but this conclusion would be unattainable if the customer never intended to convey the property in his materials to the manufacturer and the preponderance of the materials came from the customer rather than the manufacturer. In this case, the manufacturer's materials would under the rule of accession vest in the customer once they were irrevocably attached to the customer's materials[184] and there would be nothing to convey to the customer.

To a large extent, the repeal of the writing requirement has robbed this issue of any practical significance. Even before the enactment of the Supply of Goods and Services Act 1982, the House of Lords in *Young & Marten Ltd* v. *McManus Childs Ltd*[185] was prepared to extend by analogy implied terms of fitness and quality in the Sale of Goods Act to related transactions since it would be invidious for the strength of warranty rights to be determined by the side of the line on which a transaction fell.[186] In the Canadian case of *Borek* v. *Hooper*,[187] a painting was commissioned to fill a particular space in the purchaser's home. The painting cracked and the court, ruling in favour of the purchaser, applied a common law warranty of fitness for purpose, not to the painting as such, but to the materials used. It is unlikely that the Supply of Goods and Services Act 1982 Act would permit such a distinction between the ingredients and the final product, but it would probably be immaterial in most cases. Modern legislation also enacts a standard of due care for the supply of services[188] so that, whilst the line between sale of goods and work and materials may not be important for warranty reasons, the line between services and goods will be.[189]

---

[182] One possibility is a contract for services, but the property in new goods vests under the *specificatio* rule in the manufacturer, so a work and materials contract (at least) ought to be required if the property is later to be transferred to the supplier of the materials.

[183] *Dixon* v. *London Small Arms Co. Ltd* (1876) 1 App. Cas. 632, *per* Lord Penzance.

[184] *Scott Maritimes Pulp Ltd* v. *B. F. Goodrich Canada Ltd* (1977) 72 DLR (3d) 680. The issue was not resolved in *Simplex Machine Co. Ltd* v. *McLellan, McFeely & Co. Ltd* [1928] 3 WWR 255.

[185] [1969] 1 AC 454. See also *Helicopter Sales (Australia) Pty. Ltd* v. *Rotor-Work Pty. Ltd* (1974) 132 CLR 1; *Hart* v. *Bell Telephone Co. of Canada Ltd* (1976) 26 OR (2d) 218; *G. H. Myers & Co.* v. *Brent Cross Service Co*, n. 170 above.

[186] Lord Upjohn in *Young & Marten*, n. 185 above, 473 ('most unsatisfactory, illogical, and indeed a severe blow to any idea of a coherent system of common law').

[187] (1994) 18 OR (2d) 470.

[188] Supply of Goods and Services Act 1982, s. 13.

[189] Ch. 7 below.

Barter and Trade-in Agreements

Where goods are supplied in return for goods, the transaction is one of barter (or exchange).[190] The absence of a money consideration means it is not a sale of goods and so the rules governing actions for the price will not apply.[191] Extending these rules by analogy will not assist a claimant if a liquidated money value cannot be assigned to the undelivered goods.

It is sometimes possible to construe a barter as back-to-back sales with a mutual set-off of the prices owed, but this may only be done if a cash-value can be assigned to the subject matter of the transaction.[192] In some running account agreements, the periodic striking of a settlement figure should give the supplier in credit a debt action.[193] Some transactions may be analysed as requiring the recipient of goods to pay cash subject to an option to supply goods instead.[194] This inference will be a likely one if a cash price is first agreed before the buyer is given the option.[195]

Trade-in agreements, as well as the similar promotional agreements under which money and vouchers are supplied for goods, merit a separate mention. Lord Reid was of the view that the party giving the mixed consideration in a promotional transaction was not a buyer of goods,[196] but the Act does not require an exclusively money consideration. If the seller's consideration (goods) may be adulterated with some labour, why may not the buyer's (money) with some goods?

Suppose the seller of a new car wishes to sue for the price a defaulting buyer who agreed to pay with cash and a trade-in. This should be permissible if a price was agreed and the buyer given the option of paying a stated amount in the form of the trade-in.[197] A buyer who defaults is not exercising his option to pay part of the price in kind.

---

[190] *Pearce* v. *Brain* [1929] 2 KB 310. The Sale of Goods Bill originally contained a provision applying its provisions *mutatis mutandis* to contracts of exchange, but this was deleted in the House of Commons Select Committee: Chalmers, *The Sale of Goods Act, 1893* (4th edn., Butterworths, London, 1899), 5.

[191] *Harrison* v. *Luke* (1845) 14 M & W 139; *W. J. Albutt & Co.* v. *Riddell* [1930] 4 DLR 111; *R* v. *Langley* (1899) 31 OR 295 (Can.).

[192] e.g. *Aldridge* v. *Johnson* (1857) 7 E & B 855; *Messenger* v. *Greene* [1937] 2 DLR 26 (goods exchanged at 'regular prices'); *Saxty* v. *Wilkin* (1843) 11 M & W 622; *Hands* v. *Burton* (1808) 9 East 349. But see *Davey* v. *Paine* [1954] NZLR 1122 (explicable on apparent authority grounds).

[193] e.g. *Ingram* v. *Shirley* (1816) 1 Stark 185.

[194] *South Australian Insurance Co. Ltd* v. *Randell* (1869) LR 3 PC 101 and similar cases discussed below.

[195] *Gordon* v. *Hipwell* [1951] 2 DLR 733.

[196] *Chappell & Co. Ltd* v. *Nestlé Co. Ltd* [1960] AC 87, 109. Cf. *Buckley* v. *Lever Bros.* [1953] OR 704. See also *Mason & Risch* v. *Christner* (1920) 48 OLR 8 (Can.).

[197] See *G. J. Dawson (Clapham) Ltd* v. *Dutfield* [1936] 2 All ER 232. See also *Forsyth* v. *Jervis* (1816) 1 Stark 437. A trade-in was however treated as an exchange in *Davey* v. *Paine* [1954] NZLR 1122.

A further complex problem in trade-in transactions is whether both parties deal in the dual capacities of buyer and seller. Is the dealer entitled to the benefit of whatever implied terms might be available if he were the buyer of the trade-in vehicle? The liability of trade sellers being greater than private sellers, this question is more significant if the trade-in supplier is also in the motor trade. It should not unduly strain matters to regard both parties as sellers under back-to-back transactions with a set-off and outstanding cash balance.[198]

Bailment Agreements

Bailment is a transaction in which possession of goods is transferred from bailor to bailee, whether for a fixed, determinable, or indeterminate term, on the understanding that the goods will be returned at the end of the term, or transferred to or held on behalf of someone else at the bailor's direction.[199] In those cases where the bailee pays hire for the enjoyment of the goods, it is his acquisition of only a special property that distinguishes the bailment from a sale.[200] The distinction between sale and bailment fades away in practical terms where depreciating goods are hired to a bailee for the rest of their useful life, or under that form of bailment called hire purchase where a purchase option is given to the bailee. Bailment is usually a consensual relationship[201] which in most cases flows from a contract between bailor and bailee, though in some cases it is gratuitous.[202] Sometimes the bailor will pay the bailee for his services in relation to the goods; sometimes the bailee will pay the bailor for his enjoyment of them. It is the latter of these cases that approximates more to a sale of goods agreement, from which it is to be distinguished by the transfer under the bailment of only a special property in the goods in return for a sum called hire, representing, not the value of the goods themselves, but the value of their use.

---

[198] This was done in *Smith* v. *Billard* (1922) 55 NSR 502 (Can.) even though there had been no valuation of the trade-in. Cf. *Mason & Risch*, n. 196 above.

[199] N. E. Palmer, *Bailment* (2nd edn., Sweet & Maxwell, London, 1992); W. Jones, *An Essay on the Law of Bailment* (1781); G Paton, *Bailment in the Common Law* (Stevens, London, 1952); *Motor Mart Ltd* v. *Webb* [1958] NZLR 773.

[200] But see *Motor Mart*, n. 199 above, where the court treated a conditional sale agreement as a bailment: *sed quaere?* See also the reservation of title cases discussed Ch. 3 below.

[201] With the exception of involuntary bailment, and quasi-bailments such as that based upon a finding.

[202] Despite attempts to fit it into a contract mould, it is submitted that this is the better rationalization, on the facts presented, of *Bainbridge* v. *Firmstone* (1838) 8 A & E 743. See C. Davidge (1925) 41 *LQR* 433 and Sir F. Pollock's sharp observation, *ibid.*, 440.

Hire Purchase

Hire purchase[203] is functionally similar to conditional sale, a transaction plainly covered by the Sale of Goods Act. It developed in the furtherance of statutory avoidance. As a credit-granting transaction, permitting the hirer to enjoy goods before paying for them in full, hire purchase was distinguishable from a security bill of sale and free from bills of sale legislation prescribing stiff formalities and registration procedures.[204] Furthermore, it was not lending, and so the bailor finance companies were free from the Moneylenders Acts.

Unlike hire purchase, a security bill of sale involves the sale of goods to a lender defeasible upon the repayment of the loan.[205] Although the law condones artificial transactions, it does not permit parties to enter into wholly fictitious 'sham' transactions.[206] In contrast, hire purchase is an agreement to hire goods, the hire being payable in instalments, with an option to purchase exercisable for usually a nominal amount after all the instalments of hire have been paid.[207] However much commercial sense it might make to acquire the general property in the goods for a nominal sum,[208] the hirer is not someone who has bought or agreed to buy goods;[209] consequently, the bailor's title is secure against good faith purchasers from the bailee.[210]

---

[203] R. Goode, *Hire Purchase Law and Practice* (2nd edn., Butterworths, London, 1970); A. G. Guest, *The Law of Hire Purchase* (Sweet & Maxwell, London, 1966).

[204] *McEntire* v. *Crossley Bros.* [1895] AC 457.

[205] The transaction in *Beckett* v. *Tower Assets Co.* [1891] 1 QB 1 was held not to be a chattel mortgage, where the lender first bought the goods at a friendly distress sale before returning the goods to the borrower on hire purchase terms. See also *Manchester, Sheffield and Lincolnshire Railway Co.* v. *North Central Wagon Co.* (1888) 13 App. Cas. 554, 567–8; *W. J. Albutt & Co. Ltd* v. *Riddell*, n. 191 above; *Re Estate of Smith & Hogan Ltd* [1932] SCR 661 (Can.).

[206] *Ibid.*; *Re Watson* (1890) 25 QBD 27; *Polsky* v. *S. and A. Services* [1951] 1 All ER 185; *Stoneleigh Finance Ltd* v. *Phillips* [1965] 2 QB 537; *Snook* v. *West Riding Investments Ltd* [1967] 1 QB 786.

[207] *Helby* v. *Matthews* [1895] AC 471.

[208] *Warman* v. *Southern Counties Car Finance Corpn.* [1949] 2 KB 576, 582. The hirer will be liable to maintain the hire for a minimum period and will have to face a minimum payments clause if desiring to withdraw from the agreement before that date. This minimum sum is a primary alternative to the hire that was agreed to be paid over the instalment period. See *Associated Distributors Ltd* v. *Hall* [1938] KB 83; *Bridge* v. *Campbell Discount Co. Ltd* [1962] AC 600. It is not a liquidated damages clause, and thus not open to scrutiny as a penalty. The rule against penalties applies only to secondary obligations liability: *Protector Endowment Loan & Annuity Co.* v. *Grice* (1880) 5 QBD 592; *Wallingford* v. *Directors, &c, of the Mutual Society* (1880) 5 App. Cas. 685; *Re Emerald Christmas Tree Co.* (1979) 105 DLR (3d) 75. Confined to the improper commutation of primary into secondary liability, its function is not to police the fairness of contracts.

[209] *Helby* v. *Matthews*, n. 207; above *Lee* v. *Butler* [1893] 2 QB 318. Cf. *R. E. MEL Industries Ltd* (1981) 121 DLR (3d) 103.

[210] *Helby* v. *Matthews*, n. 207 above. See Ch. 9 below.

Pledge

Pledge is a form of bailment[211] in which possession of goods or documents of title to goods is granted to a pledgee as security for a loan.[212] This loan is not comparable to the price paid by a buyer since, unlike the payments made by a hirer, it is not related to the use and enjoyment of the pledge itself by the pledgee. The pledgee has only a special property;[213] consequently, the analogy with sale is slender. At common law, the pledgee may sell the pledge if the pledgor defaults on repayment of the loan, though any surplus realised will have to be turned over to the pledgor.[214]

Sale or Return and Sale on Approval

A more compelling analogy with sale of goods is afforded by those bailments called sale or return and sale on approval in which the bailee obtains possession with an option to buy the goods at a stated price, no hire being paid in the meantime. In a sale or return, a potential buyer acquires the goods with an eye to their resale, a common arrangement in certain businesses such as bookselling. Sale on approval refers to the acquisition of goods for the personal enjoyment of the potential buyer, a transaction familiar to stamp-collecting juveniles. Legislation hostile to the sending of unsolicited goods[215] has reduced certain types of sales on approval.

Though they may ripen into a sale, in neither type of bailment has the bailee 'bought or agreed to buy' the goods.[216] The Sale of Goods Act deals with sale or return and sale on approval in section 18, Rule 4, which lays down certain rules for the formation of a contract of sale pursuant to the option given by the bailor.[217] Upon conclusion of the contract, the seller's property passes immediately to the buyer, which is consistent with the presumptive rule that the property in specific goods passes to

---

[211] *Coggs* v. *Bernard* (1703) 2 Ld. Raym. 909.

[212] *Chitty on Contracts*, (27th edn., Sweet & Maxwell, London, 1994 by A. G. Guest and others); Palmer, n. 199 above; E. I. Sykes and S. Walker, *The Law of Securities* (5th edn., Law Book Co., Sydney, 1993).

[213] *Carter* v. *Wake* (1877) 4 Ch. D 605; *Sewell* v. *Burdick* (1884) 10 App. Cas. 74.

[214] *Ex p. Hubbard* (1886) 17 QBD 690, 698; *Halliday* v. *Holgate* (1868) LR 3 Ex. 299; *Burdick* v. *Sewell* (1884) 13 QBD 159, 174 (Bowen LJ). Pledge is described as a security half way between a lien and a mortgage by Willes J in *Halliday* v. *Holgate*, above, 302. For the position governing that type of pledging known as pawnbroking, see the Consumer Credit Act 1974, ss. 114–121.

[215] The Unsolicited Goods and Services Act 1971, as amended by the Unsolicited Goods and Services (Amendment) Act 1975.

[216] In this respect, the position is like hire purchase, discussed above. Cf. *Marten* v. *Whale* [1917] 2 KB 480, where the party in possession was not so under 'a mere option to buy'.

[217] Ch. 3 below.

the buyer at the contract date. These bailments should be distinguished from those defeasible sales where the buyer is entitled to return the goods and annul the sale within certain limits including time. Such transactions are regular sales unless and until the buyer's divesting option is exercised.[218] The option to return the goods may involve placing the interim risk of loss on the buyer,[219] but the presumptive rule seems to put the risk on the seller in the absence of special language in the agreement.[220]

Defeasible sales of this type may be barely distinguishable from sales where the buyer is given wider rights of rejection than those arising under the Act.[221] Suppose a buyer rejects goods under a provision in the contract allowing him to do so if he is not satisfied with the goods. As a matter of construction, it may be difficult to determine whether the buyer determines the contract because of a discharging breach by the seller or pursuant to a non-promissory condition, his own lack of satisfaction. Only in the former case will the buyer be entitled to damages. The further the buyer goes beyond the entitlement given by the Act, it is submitted, the more should a court tend to construe as non-promissory the event giving rise to the right of rejection.

Loans for Consumption

The relation between sale and bailment emerges in an interesting way in a number of cases, mainly from the Commonwealth, involving grain stored in an interim fashion in grain elevators prior to one of three events: its eventual return to the depositor; the return of an equivalent quantity and standard of grain;[222] and the sale of the grain to the elevator company.[223] The depositor's objective will normally be the sale of the grain, though he may simply want it stored or treated prior to its use for seeding and animal feed purposes. If the producer sells the grain, this may occur some time after its initial deposit in the elevator.

Where under the agreement the grain is deposited in a special bin, isolated from other depositors' grain, the contract gives rise to a bailment,[224] even though a later sale may be contemplated. The general

---

[218] *The Vesta* [1921] 1 AC 774; *Ward* v. *Cormier* (1910) 39 NBR 567 (Can.).

[219] The custom of the trade imposed it on the buyer in *Bevington* v. *Dale* (1902) 7 Com. Cas. 112.

[220] *Elphick* v. *Barnes* (1880) 5 CPD 321, following *Head* v. *Tattersall* (1872) LR 7 Ex. 7.

[221] *Patterson* v. *Lane* (1921) 60 DLR 252.

[222] The grain is inspected and graded for this purpose.

[223] The depositor may have a sale option; cf. sale or return where the option is exercised by the buyer. Or the elevator company may exercise a purchase option on the producer's failure to remove the grain or its equivalent amount by a certain date.

[224] *Isaac* v. *Andrew* (1877) 28 UCCP 40 (Can.); *Cargo* v. *Joyner* (1899) 4 Terr. LR 64 (Can.); *Lawlor* v. *Nicol* (1898) 12 Man. LR 244 (Can.).

property in the grain remains in the bailor. Until recently,[225] it could have been said with some confidence that grain commingled as part of a common stock vests in the elevator company, whose obligation to return an equivalent amount under what is a contract of barter is in the nature of a debt obligation and not a proprietary matter. Unlike Roman law, where the real contract of *mutuum* constituted a loan of fungibles for consumption, the common law of bailment required a return of the very goods bailed, in their original or altered form.[226] Consequently, a loan of cattle, to be returned, either as the original cattle or their comparable substitutes, with a number of their young, was held not to be a bailment.[227]

In *Mercer* v. *Craven Grain Storage Co*,[228] however, the House of Lords, without considering prior authority, concluded in the most summary of terms that a bailment survived an agreed mixing where the bailee had authority to extract goods from the common stock and substitute other goods for them.[229] In that case, the bailors sometimes removed their grain from storage to execute sale transactions and sometimes ordered the bailee to deliver directly to the buyers. The case concerned an action in conversion[230] by the bailors against the bailee, which had exceeded its authority to sell by disposing of grain for less than the minimum stipulated price and was in no financial position to pay the proceeds to the bailor. Bailment arrangements of the above sort would involve the treatment of the various bailors as tenants in common of the commingled goods, liable to share rateably the losses arising from any shrinkage in the bulk.

The tenancy in common idea, successfully pressed by the bailors in *Mercer*, had earlier been invoked sparingly by the common law,[231] and was seemingly inconsistent with the bailee having the freedom to deal beneficially with the common stock.[232] It was to be found where the owner of goods was not privy to their mixing by a bailee, which might

---

[225] See now the House of Lords decision in *Mercer* v. *Craven Grain Storage Ltd* [1994] CLC 328; L. Smith (1995) 111 *LQR* 10.

[226] *Chapman Bros.* v. *Verco Bros. and Co. Ltd* (1933) 49 CLR 306; *South Australian Insurance Co. Ltd* v. *Randell* (1869) LR 3 PC 101.

[227] *Crawford* v. *Kingston* [1952] OR 714. Cf. *Harding* v. *Commissioner of Inland Revenue* [1977] 1 NZLR 337.

[228] N. 225 above. See also *Busse* v. *Edmonton Grain & Hay Co. Ltd* [1932] 1 WWR 296.

[229] The bailment agreement contained a clause reserving title in the bailors.

[230] The principal point was whether the bailee had an arguable defence to the bailors' claim that they had sold the grain without authority. Apart from this, the bailors, to succeed in conversion, would need to show a right to immediate possession stemming from their retained ownership.

[231] *Laurie and Morewood* v. *Dudin and Sons* [1926] 1 KB 223. Cf. *Inglis* v. *Stock* (1885) 10 App. Cas. 263, 267.

[232] *Chapman Bros.* v. *Verco Bros. and Co. Ltd*, n. 226 above.

occur accidentally[233] or through the actions of a wrongdoer, often a bailee.[234] In addition to *Mercer*, tenancy in common has been incorporated in a recent statute.[235] Furthermore, where the depositor knows no more than that his goods might be mixed with those of an identical kind belonging to others, it seems that the transaction gives rise to a tenancy in common between this depositor and others on the ground that the depositor has not done enough to surrender his property interest in full.[236] In *Re Stapylton Fletcher Ltd*,[237] certain buyers of vintage wine authorized the seller to hold their wine in the seller's different capacity as warehouseman. The goods having been ascertained,[238] the buyers' property in the wine survived the removal of the wines from the seller's trading stacks and its storage commingled with the wines of others in warehouse stacks. Although there was nothing in the warehouse stacks to indicate ownership of particular bottles or cases, the seller's meticulous stock record was valuable evidence of an intention that the buyers were not to be divested of property rights by the fact of commingling in this way.

It is not clear to what extent the inference of tenancy in common at common law is dependent upon intention, whether it is express[239] or implied.[240] Consequently, it is difficult to know how far the *Mercer* decision may be taken outside its immediate facts, given the inadequate treatment that the subject received in the House of Lords. Assuming the relevance of intention, and that a bailment leading to a tenancy in common will not be inferred from the simple mixing of goods with the consent of the depositor, complex problems could arise from multiple deposits of different types. If there are depositors with different intentions, then the warehouse would presumably stand in for those who fail to show the requisite intention to retain an interest by way of tenancy in common.

The practical problems arising out of commingled bailment cases concern the risk of loss, by fire for example, and the insolvency of the bailee. Where the general property is transferred to the warehouse or elevator company, as would happen in the case of an exchange or sale of the goods, the risk of loss will pass to transferee but the risk of insolvency will

---

[233] *Spence* v. *Union Marine Insurance Co.* (1868) LR 3 CP 427.

[234] *Indian Oil Corpn* v. *Greenstone Shipping SA* [1988] QB 345, departing from earlier dicta of Lord Moulton in *F. S. Sandeman & Sons* v. *Tyzack and Branfoot Steamship Co. Ltd* [1913] AC 680, penalising the wrongdoer by vesting the whole of the commingled goods in the person whose goods were wrongfully mixed. See P. Matthews [1981] *CLP* 159.

[235] The Sale of Goods (Amendment) Act 1995, discussed Ch. 3 below. The language of tenancy in common is not expressly used in the Act.

[236] See *Re Stapylton Fletcher Ltd* [1994] 1 WLR 1181. [237] *Ibid.*

[238] Under s. 16: discussed Ch. 3 below.

[239] As in *Mercer* (the reservation of title clause), n. 225 above.

[240] As in *Re Stapylton Fletcher Ltd*, n. 236 above.

be assumed by the transferor. The position is reversed if there is a bailment. It is probably easier to insure against fire than someone else's insolvency, and the spate of insolvencies in recent times means that developments like the *Mercer* case are a source of encouragement to those depositing goods for storage and similar purposes.

Gift

Unlike the civil law, the common law does not treat a gift as a species of contract. Rather, it is a gratuitous conveyance of the general property complete upon delivery,[241] coupled with an intention on the donor's part to vest the general property in the donee. A promise to give, unless made by way of deed,[242] is unenforceable at common law for lack of consideration. Furthermore, equity will not perfect an imperfect gift and so will not intervene by, for example, inferring a fictitious trust in favour of the donee.[243]

Promotional Schemes

The distinction between gift and sale emerges under certain promotional schemes where the buyer obtains a 'gift' with the contract goods. *Esso Petroleum Co. Ltd* v. *Customs and Excise Commissioners*[244] involved the supply of coins celebrating a sporting event with the purchase of a minimum quantity of petrol. The question was whether the coins had been produced for 'general sale', in which case their supply would attract purchase tax. The various analytical possibilities were that the coins were the subject of a gift, or were supplied under an innominate collateral contract separate from the sale of the petrol, or were sold to the customer together with the petrol for the same money consideration. On the first possibility, tax could not be levied in the absence of any contractual obligation relating to the coins. Nor could it be levied on the second possibility, since the customer's consideration, entry into the main contract of sale, was not itself a money consideration, which meant that the coins had not been sold. Only on the third possibility would tax be payable. By a majority,[245] the House of Lords held that tax was not payable, the majority of four being equally divided between the first two

---

[241] *Irons* v. *Smallpiece* (1819) 2 B & Ald. 551; *Re Ridgway* (1885) 15 QBD 447; *Cochrane* v. *Moore* (1890) 25 QBD 57; *Re Cole* [1964] Ch. 175.
[242] Which demonstrates the vestigial hold of the old writ of covenant.
[243] *Richards* v. *Delbridge* (1874) LR 18 Eq. 11; *Jones* v. *Lock* (1865) 1 Ch. App 25.
[244] [1976] 1 WLR 1.
[245] Lord Fraser dissented. *Chappell & Co. Ltd* v. *Nestlé Co. Ltd* [1960] AC 87 does not help to solve the problem since in that case the mixed consideration came from the buyer and not the seller.

possibilities.[246] It is submitted that the court should clearly have pre-ferred the second. The first hypothesis would not meet the legitimate complaints of qualifying customers denied the coins after buying the petrol, and oil companies are not benevolent institutions. The third pos-sibility was rightly rejected: the garages were seeking to expand their petrol sales, not to diversify their trading activities.

Agency Agreements

It may be uncertain whether goods are delivered to a recipient in his capacity as buyer or as agent on behalf of the remitting principal. The issue is one of construction of the underlying agreement and therefore one of law.[247] The issue may arise in various contexts. A buyer may wish to rescind a contract for a fraudulent misrepresentation committed by someone further up the distribution chain, possible if that person was the undisclosed principal of the apparent seller but not otherwise.[248] Or a problem of title transfer may arise in which it is important to know in what capacity a person is in possession of goods.[249]

In construing the agreement, a court, though guided by the label cho-sen by the parties, will not be bound by their characterization of the rela-tionship. Parties' conduct is more important than what they say.[250] Where a contract described the plaintiffs as 'sole selling agents' of the defendants' bricks, the price to be paid by them not being fixed but set-tled at 90 per cent of the retail price paid by builder customers, the con-clusion was that the agent was really a buyer.[251] It has also been stated that someone may be an agent even if he is allowed to retain any surplus over a minimum sale figure.[252]

Agents establish privity of contract between their customers and their principals; this is a consequence and not a diagnostic test of agency.[253]

[246] Lords Wilberforce and Simon took the view that there was a collateral contract (sec-ond hypothesis) while Viscount Dilhorne and Lord Russell came down in favour of gift (first hypothesis).

[247] *W. T. Lamb & Sons* v. *Goring Brick Co.* [1932] 1 KB 710. See also *Snelgrove* v. *Ellingham Colliery* (1881) 45 JP 408.

[248] *Garnac Grain Co. Inc.* v. *H. M. F. Faure & Fairclough Ltd* [1966] 1 QB 650, affd. [1968] AC 1130n. The buyer was held to be purchasing so as to resell the goods to the original seller.

[249] *Weiner* v. *Harris* [1910] 1 KB 285.

[250] *W. T. Lamb & Sons* v. *Goring Brick Co*, n. 247 above; *International Harvester Co. of Australia Pty. Ltd* v. *Carrigan's Hazeldene Pastoral Co.* (1958) 100 CLR 644; *Ex p. White* (1871) LR 6 Ch. App 397, 399, affd. *sub nom John Towle & Co.* v. *White* (1873) 29 LT 78, 79.

[251] *W. T. Lamb & Sons* v. *Goring Brick Co*, n. 247 above. See also *W. Y. McCarter, Burr Co. Ltd* v. *Harris* (1922) 70 DLR 420.

[252] *Ex p. Bright* (1879) 10 Ch. D 566: but other factors favoured agency in the illustration given by Jessel MR.

[253] For the possibility that the property in goods passes through a commission agent without privity of contract being established between principal and third party, see *Ireland* v. *Livingstone* (1874) LR 5 HL 395.

Similarly unhelpful in diagnosis is the case of the agent asked to procure goods at a price not exceeding a stated figure, who owes his principal a duty of diligence to acquire the goods as cheaply as possible, accounting for any savings made.[254] Any duty to account will be consequent on the relationship being sale or agency. Perhaps the most helpful indication of agency is the degree of control exercised by one party over the activities of another,[255] though in certain cases, as where a manufacturer wishes to preserve the integrity of its distribution network, sellers may have considerable control over buyers.[256] If a person receiving goods is paid a percentage of the mark-up instead of being exposed to the market with its advantages and disadvantages, this points towards agency.[257] Likewise if he need not pay for them until paid in turn by his customer.[258] A close integration of two businesses, common with exclusive distributorships and output and requirements contracts, will not necessarily influence judicial interpretation in favour of agency.[259] The choice between agency and sale is unlikely to affect the degree of protection afforded the more dependent of two integrated businesses against a too-hasty rupture of the relationship, perhaps the most difficult problem arising out of such transactions.

Security Agreements

Certain security agreements borrow the form of a contract of sale. Though similar in economic purpose to a conditional sale, which certainly comes under the Sale of Goods Act, a security bill of sale is accorded special treatment precisely because it is a sale only in formal terms. It consists of an outright sale by a mortgagor who remains at all material times in possession of the goods, the conveyance to the mortgagee buyer being defeasible on the occurrence of a condition, namely, the repayment in full of the loan made by mortgagee to mortgagor.[260] Since the use and enjoyment of the goods by the mortgagee is not contemplated by the parties, it would be inappropriate to apply the provisions of the Act regarding, for example, delivery, quality, fitness, and damages.[261] Hence section 62(4) of the Act provides: 'The provisions of this Act about contracts of sale do not apply to a contract in the form of a

---

[254] *Ireland* v. *Livingstone*, n. 252 above.   [255] *Weiner* v. *Harris*, n. 249 above.

[256] *Dunlop Pneumatic Tyre Co. Ltd* v. *Selfridge & Co. Ltd* [1915] AC 847.

[257] *Weiner* v. *Harris*, n. 249 above.   [258] *Ibid.*

[259] *Decro-Wall International SA* v. *Practitioners in Marketing Ltd* [1971] 2 All ER 216. Similarly, franchise agreements.

[260] *Keith* v. *Burrows* (1876) 1 CPD 722, 731.

[261] The mortgagee may previously have sold the goods to the mortgagor before taking back a security bill of sale. The initial sale would thus be a genuine sale and governed by the Act in the usual way.

contract of sale which is intended to operate by way of mortgage, charge, pledge, or other security.'

The question is whether section 62(4) excludes the operation of the whole of the Act or only those provisions that operate between buyer and seller *inter se*. Excluded from the latter group would be those sections concerning title transfer arising out of a contract of sale but concerning disputes between parties who are not buyer and seller. If a conditional buyer is in principle a buyer in possession under section 25 of the Act,[262] and thus able to overreach the seller's title when disposing of the goods to a good-faith transferee, it is difficult to see why the grantor of a security bill of sale should not be a seller left in possession of the goods by the buyer under section 24 with similar disposing powers.[263] Both conditional sales and security bills may be used to acquire goods on financed terms and both pose the risk of deception of third parties by the party given or left in possession by the owner of the goods. Section 62(4) can be sensibly confined to the terms of the contract of sale so as to give disposing power to the grantor of the bill. Further, had the draftsman sought to exclude the whole Act, it would have been easy enough to say just that by omitting the words 'about contracts of sale'.

[262] Subject to the position in consumer contracts, discussed Ch. 9 below.
[263] But there is no provision in consumer legislation excepting security bills of sale from s. 24 of the Sale of Goods Act.

3

The Passing of Property

Sale of goods is a hybrid transaction in which, in keeping with its informal and fast-moving nature, matters of contract and conveyance are hard to separate. The passing of property in goods is a fulcrum on which depend issues as diverse as the seller's entitlement to sue for the price,[1] the incidence of risk of loss or casualty to the goods,[2] and the position of buyer and seller on the other's bankruptcy. It may also affect the remedies of the parties, including specific performance and, until the law was changed in 1967,[3] the buyer's right of rejection. The whereabouts of the property may affect third parties as it touches upon liability in conversion,[4] insurable interest, liability to tax, criminal responsibility,[5] and the amenability of the goods to execution and insolvency creditors.[6] Lord Blackburn was largely responsible for the central position occupied by the passing of property in sales law;[7] in our own century, Llewellyn has trenchantly criticized the 'lump' concept of title (or property), namely the use of property to resolve divergent issues by mechanical means without heeding their different functional considerations.[8] There are signs of the 'narrow issue thinking' he favoured in cases on risk, but, to take other examples, it does not seem much in evidence in actions for the price and the rights of pre-paying buyers when the seller becomes insolvent.

THE RULE STRUCTURE

It was long after the passing of property was first permitted by manual delivery and then by a deed of transfer that it could be accomplished

---

[1] S. 49(1).   [2] S. 20.   [3] Misrepresentation Act, s. 4(1); Ch. 3, below.

[4] The plaintiff must show possession or the right to immediate possession at the time of the tort. The incidence of property will also come into play in the adjustment of complex liabilities: Torts (Interference with Goods) Act 1977, ss. 7–9.

[5] e.g. *Edwards* v. *Ddin* [1976] 1 WLR 942.

[6] *Re Wait* [1927] 1 Ch. 606; *Carlos Federspiel & Co. SA* v. *Charles Twigg & Co. Ltd* [1957] 1 Lloyd's Rep. 240.

[7] As the full title of his treatise, usually known as *Blackburn on Sale*, shows: *A Treatise on the Effect of the Contract of Sale on the Legal Rights of Property and Possession in Goods, Wares and Merchandise.*

[8] 'Through Title to Contract and a Bit Beyond' (1938) 15 *NYU LR* 159.

purely in accordance with the intention of the contracting parties,[9] which today is the dominant rule. In principle, the passing of property has been emancipated from physical delivery, but in practice the two events largely coincide.

The paramountcy of intention is established in section 17 but the parties' intention is checked in the case of unascertained and future goods, where the property may only pass once the goods become respectively ascertained and existing.[10] A purported present sale will not automatically become a sale once the goods become existing goods;[11] the parties must also agree their unconditional appropriation to the contract. The same result should hold true for a purported sale of unascertained goods though section 16 does not explicitly say so. These rules have been supplemented by the Sale of Goods (Amendment) Act 1995. It is now possible for an undivided share to pass to the buyer by way of tenancy in common where the buyer has paid and the goods are to come from a bulk that has been identified to the contract at or subsequent to the contract date.[12] The Act is unclear on the process by which the buyer's interest in the bulk is transformed into the general property in ascertained and unconditionally appropriated goods. This is discussed below.

Except where the seller gives up possession but retains the property in the goods as security for the payment of the price, it is relatively uncommon for buyer and seller to express their intention concerning the passing of property. The Act encourages an inquiry into 'the terms of the contract, the conduct of the parties and the circumstances of the case'[13] but sets out in section 18 presumptive rules of intention if such inquiry is fruitless. By these rules,[14] the property in specific goods passes at the contract date, unless the goods have to be put in a deliverable state, or the seller has to weigh, measure, or test them to determine the price. In sale or return and similar transactions, the property passes as soon as the contract is concluded because the goods are necessarily specific at that time. Unascertained and future goods are dealt with together in the one rule, which requires their 'unconditional appropriation' to the contract by one party with the 'assent' of the other; a particular application of the rule is then given for the case where a carrier is employed to deliver the goods.

[9] *Cochrane* v. *Moore* (1890) 25 QBD 57.

[10] S. 16 (unascertained goods); s. 5(3) (sale of future goods treated as agreement to sell).

[11] *Lunn* v. *Thornton* (1845) 1 CB 379. There is an exception for goods with a potential existence: *Grantham* v. *Hawley* (1615) Hob. 132, discussed Ch. 2 above.

[12] S. 1(3) of the 1995 Act, adding a new s. 20A to the Sale of Goods Act with effect from 19 Sept. 1995.

[13] S. 17(2). 'It is impossible to imagine a clause more vague than this, but I think it correctly represents the state of the authorities when the Act was passed': *Varley* v. *Whipp* [1900] 1 QB 513, 517 (Channell J).

[14] Discussed in the text accompanying n. 18 ff. below.

Rather untidily tacked on to this scheme of rules is section 19, dealing with cases where the seller 'reserve[s] the right of disposal' of goods,[15] whether specific or later 'appropriated' to the contract, that are delivered to the buyer or to a carrier or other bailee. Before the Act, it was not clear whether such action by the seller reserved in him the property in the goods or asserted the continuance of a lien over them, at least in those cases where the seller retained control of shipping documents.[16] This lack of clarity is evident in the failure of section 19 to state bluntly that the seller retains the property and to integrate section 19 into the scheme of the preceding sections.

As for contracts involving the transfer of goods that are not contracts of sale, such as barter contracts and work and materials contracts, there is a distinct shortage of authority on the passing of property from transferor to transferee. It is likely that the rules of the Sale of Goods Act would be applied,[17] a court being perhaps not too astute to say that this is done as a matter of analogy.

SPECIFIC GOODS

Section 18, Rules 1–3

Section 18, Rule 1

Section 18, Rule 1, provides: 'Where there is an unconditional contract for the sale of specific goods in a deliverable state the property in the goods passes to the buyer when the contract is made, and it is immaterial whether the time of payment or the time of delivery, or both, be postponed.'[18] The closing words appear to limit severely the chance of finding a contrary implied intention.[19] Yet, in modern times, the courts have been prepared to find a way round this presumptive rule,[20] which is founded on the fiction that a delivery of the goods to the buyer is deemed to have occurred upon the conclusion of the contract.[21] There is some

---

[15] *James* v. *The Commonwealth* (1939) 62 CLR 339.

[16] Ontario Law Reform Commission, *Report on Sale of Goods* (1979), ii, 342–4.

[17] *Koppel* v. *Koppel* [1966] 1 WLR 802 (barter). Cf. *Flynn* v. *Mackin & Mahon* [1974] IR 101.

[18] *Tarling* v. *Baxter* (1827) 6 B & C 360; *Simmons* v. *Swift* (1826) 5 B & C 857; *Martindale* v. *Smith* (1814) 1 QB 389; *Gilmour* v. *Supple* (1858) 11 Moo. PC 551. The place where the property passes is where the goods happen to be at the contract date: *Badische Anilin und Soda Fabrik* v. *Hickson* [1906] AC 419.

[19] On the search for intention, see *Re Anchor Line (Henderson Bros.) Ltd* [1937] Ch. 1.

[20] They were encouraged to do so by the old s. 11(1)(c) of the 1893 Act which, before its amendment by s. 4(1) of the Misrepresentation Act 1967, in concert with s. 18, Rule 1, deprived the buyer of specific goods of the right of rejection for breach of condition where the property passed at the contract date.

[21] *Dixon* v. *Yates* (1833) 5 B & Ad. 313, 340: 'The very appropriation of the chattel is equivalent to delivery by the vendor, and the assent of the vendee to take the specific chattel, and to pay the price, is equivalent to his accepting possession' (Parke B).

small justification for the rule if the parties are *inter praesentes* and all that is left to do is for the buyer to carry away the goods.[22] The presumptive rule is that delivery occurs at the seller's place of business,[23] where the specific goods will usually be found, and the seller may exercise a lien to prevent the buyer from taking away the goods before payment if credit is not allowed under the contract.[24] Here, a fusion of the contract and the conveyance may well accord with the expectations of the parties. But the goods may be elsewhere and delivery may be delayed, and these variations cause the fiction to break down.

Until quite recent times, section 18, Rule 1, was applied almost as an ineluctable rule of law, consistently with the declared immateriality of postponing delivery or payment. It has also been applied though the seller had further duties to perform, such as cutting standing hay[25] and delivering the goods to a carrier.[26] The property has been held to pass with the fall of the auctioneer's hammer, despite the unknown reputation of the successful bidder.[27] It has also passed despite the goods being in the hands of a bailee who has not yet attorned to the buyer.[28]

The existence of an inconsistent intention ousting section 18, Rule 1, was considered at length in *Re Anchor Line (Henderson Brothers) Ltd*[29] where the buyers of an electric crane on instalment terms were to have 'the entire charge and responsibility for the crane'. They were to pay a 'deferred purchase price'; references were made to the 'completion of the purchase'; and the instalments covered 'interest' and 'depreciation'. On the liquidation of the buyers, the court held the property remained with the sellers. More recently, an inconsistent intention has been said to be quite easily found;[30] there may be little formal authority to support this,[31] but it is consistent with a modern concern with insolvency and with the abundance of property-retention devices in instalment and deferred payment contracts. The presumptive rule in section 18, Rule 1, is not as strong today as it used to be.

Perhaps the most important reason for easing the strictness of Rule 1 was its earlier role[32] in preventing the buyer of specific goods from reject-

---

[22] *Tarling* v. *Baxter*, n. 18 above ('where there is an immediate sale and nothing remains to be done by the vendor as between him and the vendee' (Bayley J)).

[23] S. 29(2).   [24] S. 39(1)(a); Ch. 10 below.

[25] *Tarling* v. *Baxter*, n. 18 above.   [26] *Craig* v. *Beardmore* (1904) 7 OLR 674 (Can.).

[27] *Dennant* v. *Skinner* [1948] 2 KB 164. Cf. *Dobson* v. *General Accident Fire and Life Assce. Corpn. plc* [1990] 1 QB 274, where the court avoided passing of property issues in holding that a loss could be claimed under a theft clause in an insurance policy where goods were delivered in return for a stolen, and therefore valueless, building society cheque.

[28] *Richardson* v. *Gray* (1869) 29 UCQB 360 (Can.).   [29] N. 19 above.

[30] *R. V. Ward Ltd* v. *Bignall* [1967] 1 QB 534, 545 (Diplock LJ).

[31] See also *Minister for Supply and Development* v. *Servicemen's Co-operative Joinery Manufacturers Ltd* (1952) 82 CLR 621, 635, 640.

[32] N. 20 above.

ing them if the seller committed a discharging breach of contact. If the property passed at the contract date, the buyer was denied rejection rights altogether. Initially it was a question of a buyer, having paid, whose abstract enjoyment of the general property meant he could never assert the total failure of consideration that was necessary to ground an action to recover the money.[33] This was because the contract had first to be rescinded *ab initio* before such an action could be maintained.[34] Oddly, the denial of rejection was then extended to cases where the buyer had not yet paid when he sought to reject, since no sensible distinction could be drawn between non-paying and prepaying buyers.[35] The apparent result was the complete denial of rejection and termination rights where the property in specific goods had passed to the buyer.[36] It was never clear why the same result should not also apply where the property passed in ascertained goods.[37] This position was preserved in statutory amber, the Sale of Goods Act, at a time when developments in the general law of contract were destroying the logical underpinnings of the position.[38]

Judicial assaults on the combined effect of section 18, Rule 1, and the old section 11(1)(c) focused on language in the latter provision permitting its ouster by a contrary intention; they also raked over the meaning in Rule 1 of 'unconditional' and 'deliverable state' in decisions that are still relevant in the application of the rule. This approach began with *Varley* v. *Whipp*[39] where the contract was for a second-hand self-binding reaper, new the previous season when it had cut fifty to sixty acres, and currently at Upton where it had not been seen by the buyer. When the

[33] See, e.g., *Hunt* v. *Silk* (1804) 5 East 449; *Street* v. *Blay* (1831) 2 B & Ad 456.

[34] *Weston* v. *Downes* (1778) 1 Dougl 23; *Towers* v. *Barrett* (1786) 1 TR 133. The common law process of rescission was not flexible enough to allow for a minor monetary adjustment. Cf. the American position: S. Williston (1901) 14 *Harv. LR* 317, 421, and American Law Institute, *Restatement of the Law of Contracts* (1939), §349, as reformulated in broader discretionary language in *Restatement of the Law Second [:] Contracts* (1982), §384(2)(b).

[35] *Street* v. *Blay*, n. 33 above.

[36] Subject to a contrary term in the contract: see *Head* v. *Tattersall* (1872) LR 7 Ex. 7; *Rowland* v. *Divall* [1923] 2 KB 500 (Atkin LJ).

[37] But see *Perkins* v. *Bell* [1893] 1 QB 193, 198 (right of rejection lost with passing of property). One view was that the appropriation of non-conforming ascertained goods did not pass the property, since the buyer had not assented to the appropriation of such goods: *Ollett* v. *Jordan* [1918] 2 KB 41. Note that, for unascertained goods, the presumptive rule (Rule 5) turns on the appropriation of goods that conform to the contract description. The idea behind this was to preserve the buyer's right of examination (Ch. 5 below) notwithstanding the prior delivery of the goods to the carrier as the buyer's agent. This view can be seen also in Atkin LJ's opinion that the property in c.i.f. goods does not pass upon the documentary transfer if the buyer has not had the opportunity to examine: *Hardy* v. *Hillerns & Fowler* [1923] 2 KB 490, 499. See also M. G. Bridge (1986) 20 *UBC LR* 53, 100, n. 23.

[38] e.g. the modern orthodoxy of prospective contractual termination: *Heyman* v. *Darwins Ltd* [1942] AC 356; *Photo Production Ltd* v. *Securicor Transport Ltd* [1980] AC 827; *Johnson* v. *Agnew* [1980] AC 367.

[39] [1900] 1 QB 513.

machine arrived by rail at its destination, the buyer found it to be old and much-used. According to Channell J, who did not explain why, the property had not passed since the contract was not 'unconditional'.[40] One possible interpretation of this ambiguous word is that the contract contains no promissory conditions,[41] which is a rather implausible creature. Less implausible is a contract that contains no promissory conditions that have been breached by the seller, which may have been what Channell J had in mind. One suggestion is that the commission of a discharging breach by the seller prevents the property passing,[42] but there is nothing explicit in the Act to the effect that the passing of property is dependent upon compliance by the seller with the promissory conditions that the goods are fit for their purpose or are of satisfactory quality. The idea that 'unconditional' refers to the absence of a breach of promissory condition by the seller may be narrowed further to breaches of the description condition in section 13. In the case of specific goods, the description condition requires the seller to tender goods that conform to their contractual identity,[43] a test consonant with that employed in cases of common law mistake. Hardly an exacting obligation, this would be breached where the goods supplied were different in kind from those called for by the contract. In most specific goods contracts, where the goods are seen by buyer and seller, there is normally little prospect of the description obligation being breached, but the goods in *Varley* v. *Whipp* had never been seen by the buyer and their variance from the contract language was so marked that it could truly be said that the goods supplied were not the contract goods.

Nevertheless, the word 'unconditional' has to be construed as it appears in section 18, Rule 1, and not just as it might be understood in the judgment of Channell J. Its likely meaning is that it connotes an event that the parties have expressly or impliedly intended to mark the passing of property. Such an event is one that may or must happen after the contract date. In section 18, Rules 2–3, the property in specific goods presumptively passes when various acts of weighing, testing and putting the goods into a deliverable state have been carried out. These, it is submitted, are events of the kind referred to in more general terms in section 18, Rule 1, under the umbrella word 'unconditional'. Other events could be found in the express or implied agreement of the parties, which a modern court might be readier to find in the teeth of the strong language of Rule 1. It might be agreed, for example, that the property will pass only

---

[40] [1900] 1 QB 517.

[41] See *Taylor* v. *Combined Buyers Ltd* [1924] NZLR 627; *Armaghdown Motors Ltd* v. *Gray* [1963] NZLR 518.

[42] N. 37 above.   [43] Ch. 7 below.

after the buyer has had a chance to inspect or test the goods[44] or upon the clearance of a cheque used by the buyer in payment.[45]

Section 18, Rule 2

Section 18, Rule 1, also requires the goods to be in a 'deliverable state', defined as 'such a state that the buyer would under the contract be bound to take delivery of them'. This requirement may be seen as a specific instance of a conditional contract. It should be read with section 18, Rule 2, which provides that if specific goods have to be put in a deliverable state, the property presumptively passes when this is done and the buyer has notice thereof. In the cause of giving rights of rejection to the buyer of specific goods, it has been argued in the past[46] that goods are not in a deliverable state if the buyer is entitled to reject them because of the seller's discharging breach, for in such a case the buyer is not bound to take delivery. This approach is uncomfortably circular and is not good law. With the statutory changes in 1967 enhancing the rejection rights of buyers of specific goods, it is no longer needed for their protection.

The words 'deliverable state' can now sensibly be confined to the performance by the seller of duties, such as packing, repair, dismantling, and servicing between the contract date and delivery. This state of affairs is dealt with by section 18, Rule 2.[47] A good example is *Underwood Ltd* v. *Burgh Castle Cement and Brick Syndicate*.[48] The seller of a horizontal condensing engine was to put it free on rail in London. The machine weighed thirty tons and was bolted to and embedded in concrete, and so had to be detached and dismantled before delivery to the carrier. Until this was done, it was in no state to be delivered.[49] Goods are not prevented from being in a deliverable state just because the seller has yet to deliver them to a carrier: they do not have to be in a *delivered* state for the property to pass. Nor will the passing of property be delayed under Rule 2 if certain acts have to be performed by a third party, for example by a warehouseman as agent for the buyer.[50]

---

[44] Cf. *Head* v. *Tattersall*, n. 36 above.

[45] See *Godts* v. *Rose* (1855) 17 CB 229; *Shepherd* v. *Harrison* (1871) LR 5 HL 116; *Kidd* v. *Harden* [1924] 3 WWR 293.

[46] P. S. Atiyah (1956) 19 *MLR* 315.

[47] If such activities are to be performed by the buyer, as in *Kursell* v. *Timber Operators and Contractors Ltd* [1927] 1 KB 298, the case will come under the general language of s. 18, Rule 1.   [48] [1922] 1 KB 343.

[49] *Ibid.*, 345 (Bankes LJ): 'A "deliverable state" does not depend upon the mere completeness of the subject matter in all its parts. It depends on the actual state of the goods at the date of the contract and the state in which they are to be delivered by the terms of the contract.' See also *Wilde* v. *Fedirko* [1920] 1 WWR 866; *McDill* v. *Hilson* [1920] 2 WWR 877 (seller agreed to polish furniture already paid for by buyer). It would be interesting to see if a court would so readily apply s. 18, Rule 2, where the risk of damage to the goods is not the issue but rather the insolvency of the seller.

[50] *Rugg* v. *Minett* (1809) 11 East 210.

Once goods have been put into a deliverable state, the buyer must be given notice of this before the property will pass under Rule 2.[51] This notice is actual and not constructive, so in one case the property did not pass when the seller completed repairs to a car but failed to inform the buyer.[52] Like any other presumptive rule, however, Rule 2 may be excluded by contrary agreement. This occurred in *Young* v. *Matthews*[53] where 1.3 million bricks were sold in return for the surrender by the buyer of a bill of exchange drawn on the seller. The seller's foreman pointed to three clamps of finished, burning, and unbaked bricks from which delivery was to be made and responded yes to the question: 'Do I clearly understand that you are prepared, and will hold and deliver this said quantity of bricks?' The seller became bankrupt before delivery, but the court held that the property in the bricks had already passed to the buyer despite their not being in a deliverable state, a result in accord with the unusual circumstances of the case.[54]

Section 18, Rule 3

Section 18, Rule 3, provides that where, under a contract for the sale of specific goods in a deliverable state, the seller has to 'weigh, measure, test or do some other act or thing for the purpose of ascertaining the price', the property will not pass until this act has been done and the buyer given notice.[55] This rule, said to be 'somewhat hastily adopted from the civil law',[56] was firmly established at common law before the codification of sale. In *Rugg* v. *Minett*,[57] where the buyer bought at auction two lots of turpentine, whose contents could only be determined once another twenty-five lots had been topped up from the two lots, the property did not pass until this was done. Likewise, the property in a stack of bark sold at so much a ton did not pass where it had to be weighed 'and the concurrence of the seller in the act of weighing was necessary'.[58] Even where the contract is an entire one, it has been held that the property may pass in some of the goods though not the residue when the seller's acts are incomplete.[59]

---

[51] Notice was introduced into the original Sale of Goods Bill on a Scottish suggestion that it would be unfair to put the risk on a buyer who did not know that the property had passed.

[52] *Jerome* v. *Clements Car Sales Ltd* [1958] OR 738.   [53] (1866) LR 2 CP 127.

[54] The court was generous: the goods had not been ascertained from bulk (see K. Llewellyn (1938) 15 *NYU LR* 159, 172, n. 20). Estoppel would not assist the buyer in view of the seller's insolvency.

[55] Like the rest of the rule, notice can be dispensed with by contrary intention: *Begert* v. *Parry* (1922) 70 DLR 233.

[56] *Blackburn on Sale* (2nd edn., Stevens, London, 1885 by J. C. Graham), 175.

[57] N. 50 above.

[58] *Simmons* v. *Swift* (1826) 5 B & C 857. See also *Logan* v. *Le Mesurier* (1847) 6 Moo. PC 116; *Gilmour* v. *Supple* (1858) 11 Moo. PC 551; *Acraman* v. *Morrice* (1849) 8 CB 449.

[59] *Rugg* v. *Minett*, n. 50 above.

If the measurements have been taken leaving only mechanical arithmetical tasks to be performed, the property will pass.[60] Furthermore, the acts in Rule 3 are concerned with ascertaining the price and so the rule does not apply where a lump sum for the goods, unaffected by the acts to be performed, has already been agreed.[61] Rule 3 does not apply if the acts in question, even if connected with ascertaining the price, are those of the buyer or of a sub-buyer.[62]

Sale or Return and Sale on Approval

According to section 18, Rule 4, where goods are sent on approval or on sale or return or similar terms, the property will pass when the buyer 'signifies his approval or acceptance to the seller or does any other act adopting the transaction'. Alternatively, it will pass if the buyer retains the goods, without notifying the seller of his rejection of them, beyond either a reasonable time or the time stipulated by the seller for the return of the goods.

Although expressed in terms of passing of property, these are elliptical rules of contract formation stating that the property passes as soon as the contract of sale is concluded, a point not always appreciated. Until that moment arrives, there is no contract of sale as defined by the Sale of Goods Act, since the 'buyer'[63] has not yet bought or agreed to buy the goods. Prior to the contract of sale, the goods, it is submitted, are held on contractual bailment terms,[64] the buyer having an option to purchase them. To be distinguished from contractual bailments of this sort are contracts of sale in which the buyer is given a wide right of rejection of the goods within a stated period. A binding contract of sale has been concluded in such a case but the buyer's entitlement may delay the passing of property (and perhaps also the risk) until the buyer runs out of time to exercise his right of rejection.[65]

The issues arising under Rule 4 are not usually (though they may be) those at stake when the passing of property is considered, such as the incidence of risk and the insolvency of either party and the seller's right

[60] *Tansley* v. *Turner* (1835) 2 Bing. NC 151.
[61] *Lockhart* v. *Pannell* (1873) 22 UCCP 597 (Can.).
[62] *Turley* v. *Bates* (1863) 2 H & C 200; *Nanka-Bruce* v. *Commonwealth Trust* [1926] AC 77.
[63] Note: the language of seller and buyer will be used in this discussion of Rule 4 even where the arrangement under which the goods are delivered has not yet become a contract of sale.
[64] See the more tentative view in *Benjamin's Sale of Goods* (5th edn., 1997 by A. G. Guest and others), §5–043, but how else can the buyer's position be described?
[65] *Elphick* v. *Barnes* (1880) 5 CPD 321 is a case of this kind. *Quaere* the binding character of the contract where the buyer's right of rejection appears to be unfettered as it was in *Elphick?* In French law, such potestative (or self-enabling) clauses in contracts are null and void: C. Civ. Arts. 1170, 1174.

to sue for the price. The most common issue is a title dispute between the seller and a transferee by way of sale or pledge from the buyer, where the buyer disposes of the goods without paying the seller. It is in the seller's interest to argue that the buyer did not accept his offer in accordance with Rule 4; consequently, the property did not pass to the buyer who is therefore unable to transmit title to the transferee. The transferee will be concerned to argue that a contract of sale was concluded between seller and buyer; the property passed and accordingly a general or special property was transferred by buyer to transferee under the later disposition.

The Buyer's Acceptance

The acceptance of the buyer that concludes the contract of sale and thus triggers the conveyance under Rule 4 may take three forms: first, a declared acceptance like any other contractual acceptance; secondly, conduct that is consistent with an intention to accept the offer; and thirdly, retention of the goods beyond the time stipulated by the seller or beyond a reasonable time. This last mode of acceptance is difficult to reconcile with the rule that a contract may not be concluded by the offeree's silence.[66] The preoccupation of Rule 4 with title transfer issues, and its failure to refer explicitly to contract formation, encourages a rather literal reading of the rule at the expense of orthodox contract principle. The provisions of the Act may of course override the rules of common law contract. Nevertheless, since section 18, Rule 4, fails to state that the seller can stipulate for acceptance by silence, and since there is no contract of sale before the buyer's acceptance, Rule 4 should as far as possible be read in harmony with contract formation rules,[67] especially since the buyer is exercising an option.[68] The buyer's acceptance by effluxion of time should only arise if his retention of the goods can plausibly be interpreted as conduct evincing an intention to accept, bolstered perhaps by previous arrangements between the parties or by what was said by the seller when possession of the goods was given to the buyer. Taking possession of goods is a consensual act that can supply the necessary conduct, whereas receipt of a contractual offer is a passive affair. Even if the rules of contract formation were designed to give way to special statutory provision in this case, Rule 4 does not permit a seller to practise inertia selling on the buyer by sending goods without prior

---

[66] *Felthouse* v. *Bindley* (1862) 11 CB(NS) 869, affd. (1863) 7 LT 835.

[67] Cf. *May and Butcher Ltd* v. *The King* [1934] 2 KB 17n (HL), for the view that the reasonable price rule in s. 8(1) cannot be invoked until an agreement passes the threshold test of a binding contract at common law. The rules of the common law continue to apply to contracts of sale of goods if they are not inconsistent with the provisions of the Act: s. 62(2).

[68] Cf. *Holwell Securities Ltd* v. *Hughes* [1974] 1 WLR 155.

request and unilaterally defining the time of acceptance.[69] Its wording turns upon 'delivery' to the buyer, which requires a *voluntary* transfer of possession.

The first mode of acceptance in Rule 4, signifying the buyer's approval or acceptance, needs no comment, but the second mode, performing an act adopting the transaction, has proved troublesome. In *Kirkham* v. *Attenborough*,[70] where the language of the Act was criticized, the 'transaction' in Rule 4 was interpreted as the agreement of sale proposed by the seller when bailing the goods to the buyer. When the latter, who had received the goods on sale or return terms, pledged them with the defendant pawnbroker, he was held thereupon to have adopted the transaction. At the very moment of the pledge, the property in the goods passed from the seller to the buyer, and the special property in turn to the defendant transferee.[71] Consequently, the special property conveyed in turn by the buyer to the pawnbroker was strong enough to resist the demands of the seller. In *Kirkham*, the court did not interpret the buyer's behaviour in terms of an objective intention to accept the seller's offer; rather, the court was impressed by the fact that his action was inconsistent with his 'free power'[72] to return the goods. Besides drifting somewhat from the orthodoxy of contract formation, this approach does not sit well with authority that an unauthorized sub-pledge is not as such an act of conversion.[73] Similarly, apart from any fraudulent intentions of the bailee, the pledge of goods may always be redeemed and the goods returned within the stated time or a reasonable time. The *Kirkham* approach might also be better suited to a sale or return where the buyer sub-sells, since a sub-sale is the very transaction contemplated by the sale or return. It seems less suited to a pledge or to any disposition of the goods under a sale on approval, which contemplates that the buyer will use and consume the goods.

Further light is cast on the adopting act in *Genn* v. *Winkel*,[74] a case involving two further sub-bailments of the goods on sale or return terms, which lends support for the following two propositions. First, the adoption by a sub-bailee of a proposed sale will feed adoptions back up the bailment chain, so that the buyer may become bound even if not aware of the sub-bailee's adopting act. If the sub-bailment itself were seen as equivalent to a pledge in inhibiting the buyer's 'free power' to return the goods, then consistency with *Kirkham* v. *Attenborough* would require a

---

[69] On the sending of unsolicited goods, see Ch. 1 above.

[70] [1897] 1 QB 201, followed in *London Jewellers Ltd* v. *Attenborough* [1934] 2 KB 206.

[71] *Whitehorn Bros.* v. *Davison* [1911] 1 KB 463.

[72] N. 70 above, 203 (Esher MR). See also *ibid.*, 204 (Lopes LJ), and the bailee's 'free control [over the goods] so as to be in a position to return them'.

[73] *Donald* v. *Suckling* (1866) LR 1 QB 585.   [74] (1912) 107 LT 434.

sale to be concluded earlier at the moment of sub-bailment, unless the initial seller authorized the sub-bailment. More consistent with *Kirkham* is the second proposition from *Genn* v. *Winkel*, that once the offer of a sub-bailment takes place on terms permitting the sub-bailee to retain the goods beyond the time for acceptance given to the buyer, then the buyer thereby adopts the seller's offer.[75] So, if A bails goods on sale or return terms to B for fourteen days and B sub-bails the goods to C for a period stated to be longer or capable of being longer, B will at the point of sub-bailment be deemed to have adopted A's offer.

A further difficulty of adoption concerns the buyer who makes personal use of the goods. Where the transaction is a sale on approval, some degree of use is contemplated by the nature of the arrangement but not, it is submitted, such use as appreciably diminishes the value of the goods, at least in the absence of clear permission to the contrary. If the transaction is one of sale or return, the transaction may on its construction permit the buyer to allow potential sub-buyers some degree of use of the goods for trial purposes. But a sale or return arrangement may become a sale if the buyer makes an unauthorized personal use of the goods.[76] Any assertion of title going beyond the authority to act conferred by the seller ought to be sufficient to adopt the transaction.[77]

The lapse of a reasonable time, arising under the third mode of acceptance in Rule 4, was considered in *Poole* v. *Smith's Cars (Balham) Ltd*,[78] where the court, in holding that the time had elapsed under a sale or return between two car dealers, considered a number of factors, including the declining second-hand car market at that time of the year, the rapid depreciation of the car, the seller's repeated requests for the return of the car, and the evidently temporary ('holiday arrangement') character of the bailment. The question is one of fact and degree. The reasonable time in Rule 4 may elapse after the buyer has become bankrupt. The risk of this is not assumed by the seller, so the failure of the buyer or his trustee in bankruptcy to return the goods will not mean that the property in the goods passes to the buyer and thence to the trustee.[79]

A buyer who is negligent in looking after the goods during the option period should not thereby be seen as adopting the transaction,[80] but will be liable in tort as a negligent bailee and in that capacity will bear the

---

[75] (1912) 107 LT 434 (Buckley LJ).

[76] Consider the conduct of the buyer's salesmen in *Poole* v. *Smith's Car Sales (Balham) Ltd* [1962] 2 All ER 482 using the car for their own purposes.

[77] Like conversion but without the restricting effect of s. 11(3) of the Torts (Interference with Goods) Act 1977 (denial of title alone is not a conversion). See *Astley Industrial Trust* v. *Miller* [1968] 2 All ER 36—registering the car.

[78] N. 76 above.					[79] *Re Ferrier* [1944] Ch. 295.

[80] e.g. by retaining destroyed goods or goods that have had to be repaired beyond a reasonable time.

burden of disproving personal negligence.[81] A mechanical application of section 18, Rule 4, should not be used to justify substituting an absolute contractual obligation for a duty of care in negligence, by deeming a contract of sale to be concluded by the passage of time where the buyer is unable to return destroyed goods. The result should be the same if the accident to the goods happens down a bailment chain.[82] A more difficult case is dishonesty down the bailment chain. In *Ray* v. *Barker*,[83] the buyer was held to have adopted the transaction as a consequence of a fraudulent pledge further down the chain. Since the bailee trusts to the integrity and credit of the sub-bailee, however, it is surely appropriate to say that he undertakes *qua* the seller to accept the risk of default of the sub-bailee, and of subsequent sub-bailees too.

Exclusion of Rule 4

Since it is based upon presumed intention, *Rule 4* can be displaced by contrary agreement. The lesson of *Kirkham* v. *Attenborough* was learnt by the seller of jewellery in *Weiner* v. *Gill*[84] where the agreement on which goods were bailed on sale or return, stated: '[G]oods had on approbation or on sale or return remain the property of Samuel Weiner until such goods are settled for or charged.' This displayed a contrary intention, allowing the seller to assert his title against the defendant pledgee. But *Weiner* v. *Gill* was not the last word on the battle between seller and innocent transferee. As will later be shown, words like 'sale or return' are not conclusive of the nature of a transaction if the court believes that on its true construction the agreement is one of agency, where the principal who owns the disputed goods is liable to be challenged by the innocent transferee on different grounds.[85] Rule 4 has been excluded elsewhere because the plain intention of the parties was that the property should only pass on a cash payment.[86] If the buyer declares an intention not to accept the offer, his subsequent conduct in relation to the goods has been held not to be an acceptance,[87] though it could be a conversion of them.

---

[81] *Houghland* v. *R. R. Low (Luxury Coaches) Ltd* [1962] 1 QB 694.

[82] *Genn* v. *Winkel*, n. 74 above, 109 (Vaughan Williams LJ).

[83] (1879) 4 Ex. D 279.   [84] [1906] 2 KB 574.

[85] *Weiner* v. *Harris* [1910] 1 KB 285, discussed Ch. 9 below. For the difference between sale or return and agency, see *Re Nevill* (1870) LR 6 Ch. App. 397. See also *W. T. Lamb & Sons* v. *Goring Brick Co. Ltd* [1932] 1 KB 710, *The Kronprinzessin Cecilie* (1917) 33 TLR 292 and the cases on reservation of title, discussed in the text accompanying nn. 301 ff. below.

[86] *Percy Edwards Ltd* v. *Vaughan* (1910) 26 TLR 545. See also *Whitehorn Bros.* v. *Davison*, n. 71 above, 483–4.

[87] *Swenson* v. *Lavigne* [1925] 3 DLR 681. See also *Ellis* v. *Mortimer* (1805) 1 B & P NR 257.

UNASCERTAINED AND FUTURE GOODS

Ascertainment and Existence

Although the intention of the parties is paramount in the passing of property, this is subject to the goods having become existing and ascertained.[88] Since the Sale of Goods (Amendment) Act 1995, a buyer will in some cases acquire as tenant in common an undivided share in a bulk before ascertainment of the particular goods that the seller intends to deliver under the contract.[89] The incidents of this tenancy in common, which is anyway confined to special cases, are somewhat different from the general property in the goods that the buyer acquires once the rules in sections 16–19 of the Act have been satisfied. Consequently, although the 1995 tenancy-in-common rules have in a practical sense modified the law on ascertainment and the significance of ascertainment, the established position in the Sale of Goods Act will first be considered before attention is turned to the 1995 changes.

Some assistance is given by the Act in determining when future goods come into existence, namely, upon their manufacture or acquisition by the seller.[90] Crops and produce in an immature state should also be future goods; hence the property in grapes still on the vine will not pass.[91] In a contract for the sale of a ship to be built, it is common for parties to stipulate that the property in the inchoate structure will pass as it is added to from time to time,[92] and nothing in sections 5 and 16 is inconsistent with such an intention. Courts have been reluctant to give effect to clauses providing that the property will pass in materials fashioned for a ship, even before they become part of the ship by accession,[93] possibly because the contract is for the sale of a ship and not of building materials, which before attachment constitute future goods.[94]

---

[88] Ss. 5(3) and 16.

[89] Discussed in the text accompanying nn. 180 ff. below. The Act does not in fact explicitly use the language of tenancy in common.

[90] S. 5(1).   [91] *Orr* v. *Danforth Wine Co.* [1936] OWN 306 (Can.).

[92] *Clarke* v. *Spence* (1836) 4 A & E 448; *Seath* v. *Moore* (1886) 11 App. Cas. 350; *Reid* v. *MacBeth & Gray* [1904] AC 223; *Sir James Laing & Sons Ltd* v. *Barclay, Curle & Co. Ltd* [1908] AC 35; *Re Blyth Shipbuilding & Dry Docks Co. Ltd* [1926] Ch. 494. In the absence of such a clause, there appears to be 'a strong *prima facie* presumption' against the passing of property in incomplete work: *Seath* v. *Moore*, above, 370 (Lord Blackburn); *Sir James Laing & Sons*, above. See also *Re Royal Bank of Canada and Saskatchewan Telecommunications* (1985) 20 DLR (4th) 415.

[93] *Seath* v. *Moore*, n. 92 above, and *Re Blyth Shipbuilding, ibid.* (where this seems to be treated as a rule of law).

[94] But it may be possible to provide for the property to pass in unattached parts by clear drafting: *North Western Shipping & Towage Co.* v. *Commonwealth Bank of Australia Ltd* (1993) 118 ALR 453, 481 (Fed. CA).

Ascertainment

Not defined by the Act, ascertainment[95] occurs once goods have subsequently been identified to the contract.[96] Goods bought in by a seller with the intention of fulfilling a sale obligation, which thereby become existing goods, may not yet be ascertained. That will happen when they are identified to the particular contract at hand by a process of earmarking such as labelling or packaging.[97] If the seller merely promises or represents that he holds the agreed goods for the buyer, this is not enough to ascertain the goods from the seller's existing or after-acquired stock. This was the position in *Re Goldcorp Exchange Ltd*[98] where a seller misled investors into believing that, when they paid for precious metals, the seller would store the appropriate quantity on their behalf in a vault free of charge. The seller's statements did not as such identify to the contract existing metals in the seller's possession answering to the contract description or future metals coming in, in which latter case there was the added difficulty of not knowing how such metals could be identified amongst a range of competing contracts of sale.

Goods will be treated as unascertained even if they are a fungible portion of a specific or ascertained bulk, at least until separation occurs.[99] Another way of putting it is that the relevant quantity is not appropriated to the contract before separation.[100] The property, for example, will therefore not pass in a quantity of newsprint if the seller retains an unascertained portion.[101] A graphic illustration of this approach is *Re Wait*,[102] where Wait agreed to sell to the buyer on c.i.f. Avonmouth terms 500 tons of Western White Wheat from a parcel of 1,000 tons shipped by one of Wait's own suppliers on the *m.v. 'Challenger'*.[103] Although the buyer paid the contract sum, no property in the goods passed for reasons expressed by Atkin LJ as follows: '[N]o 500 tons of wheat have ever been

---

[95] See the discussion in Law Commission, *Sale of Goods Forming Part of a Bulk* (1993 Law Com. No. 215) Part II.

[96] *Re Wait* [1927] 1 Ch. 606; *Thames Sack & Bag Co. Ltd* v. *Knowles & Co. Ltd* (1918) 88 LJKB 585; *Re Western Canada Pulpwood & Lumber Co.* [1929] 3 WWR 544.

[97] For a loose approach to ascertainment in cases where goods of the type and quantity agreed to be sold are then warehoused rather than delivered to the buyer, see *Re Stapylton Fletcher Ltd* [1994] 1 WLR 1181, discussed below.

[98] [1995] 1 AC 74. See also *Re London Wine Co. (Shippers) Ltd* (1979) [1986] PCC 121.

[99] *Gillett* v. *Hill* (1834) 2 Cr. & M 530; *Swanwick* v. *Sothern* (1839) 9 A & E 895; *Campbell* v. *Mersey Docks and Harbour Board* (1863) 14 CB(NS) 412; *Boswell* v. *Kilborn* (1858) 15 Moo. PC 309; *Jenkyns* v. *Usborne* (1844) 7 Man. & Gr. 678.

[100] *Healy* v. *Howlett & Sons* [1917] 1 KB 337.

[101] *Ross* v. *Eby* (1877) 28 UCCP 316 (Can.).   [102] N. 96 above.

[103] Note the disagreement between Atkin LJ, who thought that any parcel of 500 tons on the *Challenger* could have been tendered, regardless of the identity of the shipper, and Sargant LJ, who thought the opposite. The latter was surely correct given the clause in the contract naming the particular shipper and releasing Wait in the event of his named shipper failing to perform.

earmarked, identified or appropriated as the wheat to be delivered . . . under the contract. The buyers have never received any bill of lading, warrant, delivery order or any document of title representing the goods.'[104] *Re Wait* would therefore support the passing of property to a buyer of the 1,000-ton bulk receiving the bill of lading against payment but not to two cash-paying buyers of 500 tons each.[105]

The buyer of goods contained in a specific or ascertained bulk was sometimes fortunate even before the Sale of Goods (Amendment) Act 1995. In one case, ascertainment of the buyer's share occurred by exhaustion when it was isolated after other orders from the same bulk had been executed by delivery.[106] In another case, the buyers would have failed, but for the happy accident of buying from a different seller the remainder of the goods left in the specific bulk with their own unascertained portion.[107] It would have been legal pedantry of the worst kind to deny the buyers on the ground that neither contractual portion had been ascertained when the two taken together had been. Furthermore, section 16 does not apply where the contract is for the sale of an undivided share in specific goods belonging to the seller, rather than a severable quantity of goods in that bulk.[108] Formerly, this was because the contract was not a sale of goods contract. The new definition of 'goods'[109] includes an undivided share in goods. This means that sales of undivided shares are now governed by the Sale of Goods Act. But they are specific goods[110] and thus still unaffected by section 16 of the Sale of Goods Act. The property in an undivided share can therefore pass without payment being made by the buyer.[111] The buyer may also be able to benefit from a personal estoppel against a third party,[112] such as a warehouseman who

---

[104] N. 96 above, 629.

[105] For the difficulties posed by s. 16 to the modern practice of bulk shipments of commodities, see B. Davenport [1986] *LMCLQ* 4, discussing the Dutch case of *The Gosforth*, 20 Feb. 1985, Rotterdam Comm. Ct., unreported.

[106] *Wait & James* v. *Midland Bank* (1926) 31 Com. Cas. 172.

[107] *Karlshamns Oljefabriker* v. *Eastport Navigation Co. Ltd (The Elafi)* [1982] 1 All ER 208. This result, and the one in *Wait & James*, is incorporated in s. 1(2) of the 1995 Act, amending the rules on unconditional appropriation by adding a new s. 18, Rule 5(3),(4), to the Sale of Goods Act 1979.

[108] Law Com. No. 215, paras. 2.5–6.

[109] In s. 61(1) of the Sale of Goods Act as amended by s. 2(c) of the Sale of Goods (Amendment) Act 1995.

[110] Pursuant to s. 2(d) of the 1995 Act amending s. 61(1) of the Sale of Goods Act.

[111] For the distinction between subject-matter and shares thereof, in the constitution of a trust and the application of the certainty rule, compare *Re London Wine Co. (Shippers) Ltd*, n. 98 above, with *Hunter* v. *Moss* [1994] 1 WLR 452, criticized by D. Hayton (1994) 110 LQR 335. See also *Holland* v. *Newbury* [1997] 2 BCLC 369.

[112] Because the estoppel gives rise to a personal right (see *Re London Wine Co. (Shippers) Ltd*, n. 98 above) the insolvency of a seller renders worthless any estoppel against him: *Re Goldcorp Exchange Ltd*, n. 98 above.

attorns to the buyer[113] when the buyer's quantity has not yet been ascertained.

Overcoming section 16

The seller in *Re Wait* did not provide the buyer with a delivery document of any kind, which was arguably a breach of his c.i.f. obligations. Suppose however that a seller performs all his personal obligations[114] under a contract where the goods are held in an undivided bulk by a carrier or warehouseman.[115] In one case concerning the risk of adulteration of white spirit, the Court of Appeal departed from the 'lump' concept of title in holding that, notwithstanding the property remaining in the seller, the risk had passed to the buyer from the time when the buyer could have called for delivery of his portion of the bulk.[116] Could the same approach be adopted in cases of seller insolvency? Blackburn J once said that he was 'very much inclined to struggle very hard' to prevent the 'monstrous hardship' of a windfall benefit to the seller's creditors in such circumstances.[117] Before the Sale of Goods (Amendment) Act 1995, attempts to assist buyers by overcoming the section 16 impediment to the passing of property were made with the assistance of equitable ideas[118] and the common law notion of tenancy in common.[119] These attempts proved unsuccessful.

Equitable Property Rights

Although *Re Wait* is an apparently decisive authority against the buyer acquiring equitable rights to the contract goods by operation of law,[120] it is worth tracing the antecedent law before the case is considered at length. Before the codification of sale, the Privy Council had held that a

---

[113] See *Laurie and Morewood* v. *Dudin and Sons* [1926] 1 KB 223; *Woodley* v. *Coventry* (1863) 2 H & C 64; *Knights* v. *Wiffen* (1870) LR 5 QB 660; *Henderson* v. *Williams* [1895] 1 QB 521.

[114] The seller may of course be in breach for non-delivery if a third party, such as a warehouseman, fails to do something, e.g., attorn to the buyer.

[115] See the sympathetic approach to the buyer of the Canadian court in *Coffey* v. *Quebec Bank* (1869) 20 UCCP 110, 113, affd. (1869) 20 UCCP 555. Cf. *Re Rose* [1952] Ch. 499 (gift of shares and equitable interest in donee prior to registration of transfer by company).

[116] *Sterns Ltd* v. *Vickers Ltd* [1923] 1 KB 78.

[117] *Martineau* v. *Kitching* (1872) LR 7 QB 436, 454.

[118] Rejected in *Re Wait* [1927] 1 Ch. 606, discussed below. See Law Reform Commission of Western Australia, *Discussion Paper on Equitable Rules in Contracts for the Sale of Goods* (Project no. 89, 1995), ch. 4 (especially paras. 4.35 ff).

[119] The buyer's argument to this effect was implicitly rejected, presumably because of its inconsistency with s. 16, by the Court of Appeal in *Laurie and Morewood* v. *Dudin and Sons*, n. 113 above. Cf. *Inglis* v. *James Richardson & Sons* (1913) 29 OLR 229 (Can.).

[120] It was not challenged head on in *Re Goldcorp Exchange Ltd* [1995] 1 AC 74. See also *Re Stapylton Fletcher Ltd* [1994] 1 WLR 1181.

seller purportedly negotiating a non-negotiable bill of lading in favour of a bank had nevertheless succeeded in conveying an equitable title.[121] Although not a case of unascertained goods, this decision was significant in applying equitable proprietary principles where the seller had intended but failed to transfer a legal proprietary right. It might yet be significant where a seller transfers a bill of lading to an undivided part of a bulk with the intention of passing the general property in the quantity covered by the bill of lading to the buyer.[122] There were other pre-codification decisions from which a buyer of unascertained goods could draw considerable comfort. In *Hoare* v. *Dresser*,[123] a broker, acting as the *del credere* agent of a seller of three cargoes of timber, accepted a number of the seller's drafts, in return receiving copies of the charterparties of two of the vessels carrying the goods and the promise of bills of lading when the loading was completed. The House of Lords held that he acquired an equitable interest in the goods upon loading even though he never received the bills of lading. Furthermore, in the leading case of *Holroyd* v. *Marshall*,[124] a textile manufacturer, as security for a debt, assigned by way of mortgage[125] all present and future machinery in the mill until the debt was paid. The House of Lords held that the creditor had automatically acquired an equitable interest in the future machinery upon its acquisition by the debtor, since a court of equity would order the performance of the contract to assign the machinery. At law, a deed assigning future property was, to the extent of that property, void in law[126] and a fresh conveyance of each item of machinery would be required as and when it came into existence.

Equity gave effect to a purported present assignment of future property by treating it as a promise to assign the goods.[127] Treating that as done which ought to be done, equity viewed the contract to assign as a perfected assignment as soon as it was able to 'fasten upon' the goods, that is, upon their coming into existence.[128] Even if this event occurred during the assignor's insolvency, the equitable assignment would take effect.[129] An issue never adequately resolved was whether the promise to convey had to be linked to the completed assignment by compliance

---

[121] *C. P. Henderson & Co.* v. *Comptoir d'Escompte de Paris* (1873) LR 5 PC 253.

[122] The transfer of a bill of lading carries with it the property rights intended by the transferor: *Sewell* v. *Burdick* (1884) 10 App. Cas. 74. On the failure of the law prior to 1995 to satisfy commercial expectations, see Law Com. No. 215, paras. 3.3–4.

[123] (1859) 7 HLC 290.   [124] (1862) 10 HLC 191.

[125] A defeasible sale: *Keith* v. *Burrows* (1876) 1 CPD 722.

[126] *Lunn* v. *Thornton* (1845) 1 CB 379; explained as an application of the maxim *nemo dat quod non habet* by Willes J (*arguendo*) in *Chidell* v. *Galsworthy* (1859) 6 CB(NS) 471, 473.

[127] See P. Matthews [1981] *LMCLQ* 40.

[128] *Tailby* v. *Official Receiver* (1888) 13 App. Cas. 523.

[129] *Collyer* v. *Isaacs* (1881) 19 Ch. D 342. But it would not apply to property coming into the hands of a bankrupt upon his discharge from bankruptcy: *ibid.*

with the doctrine of specific performance. In *Holroyd* v. *Marshall*,[130] Lord Westbury said that the assignee was entitled to relief provided the contract was such 'as a court of equity would direct to be specifically performed'.[131] On the face of it, this limitation would give little scope for equitable assignment in commercial sales contracts where goods almost always lack the unique quality needed if the discretionary remedy of specific performance is to be successfully invoked.[132] Furthermore, the law is also reluctant to grant specific performance outside cases of specific or ascertained goods.[133]

Lord Westbury, nevertheless, gave as an example of a valid equitable assignment a contract for the sale of 'five hundred chests of the particular kind of tea which is now in my warehouse in Gloucester',[134] which, not without some ambiguity, is a contract for the supply of an unascertained part of a specific bulk. This example using commonplace goods tells against taking too literally the reference to specific performance, and alone should be enough to refute the argument that equitable rights may only be assigned where the remedy of specific performance is available. Yet Lord Westbury's example was phrased in another report quite differently as one for the sale, not of an unascertained part of a specific bulk, but of specific goods.[135] Even if the claimant is able to surmount the specific performance barrier, however high it is erected, more recent authority denies that the availability of specific performance necessarily means that the buyer has an equitable interest in the subject matter of the contract.[136] In the later case of *Tailby* v. *Official Receiver*, Lord Westbury's specific performance limitation was interpreted as confined to the particular example he used to show that equitable rights are more than shadowy things.[137] Another attempt to neutralize Lord Westbury's words came in a case where Cotton LJ stated that the specific performance limitation applied only where the contract was wholly executory and not where the assignee had already performed his part of the bargain, for in such a case damages would not be an adequate remedy.[138]

---

[130] N. 124 above. [131] N. 124 above, 211.

[132] The limitation would surely exclude the (run of the) mill machinery in *Holroyd* v. *Marshall*, n. 124 above.

[133] See s. 52 of the Sale of Goods Act, discussed in the text accompanying n. 103 above.

[134] N. 124 above, 209.

[135] The Law Journal report records 'a contract to sell *the* five hundred chests of a particular kind of tea which are now in my warehouse in Gloucester' (emphasis added): (1862) 33 LJ Ch 193, 196. Predictably, the resultant ambiguity was relied upon in *Re Wait*, n. 118 above, to attack the notion of equitable property rights in sales law.

[136] *Re London Wine Co. Ltd* (1979) [1986] PCC 121; *Re Stapylton Fletcher Ltd* [1994] 1 WLR 1181.

[137] N. 128 above, 545–8 (Lord Macnaghten).

[138] *Re Clarke* (1887) 36 Ch. D 348, 352. See also Buckley LJ in *Swiss Bank Corpn* v. *Lloyds Bank Ltd* [1982] AC 584, 595 (Buckley LJ). For conflicting statements on whether the defendant's insolvency should incline a court to grant specific performance, see *Anders Utkilens*

Prior to the passing of the Sale of Goods Act in 1893, the prospects for a prepaying buyer therefore appeared encouraging.

Re Wait

The effect of the Act on equitable proprietary rights in sales law was considered in *Re Wait*.[139] The prompt date for payment by the buyer was thirty-three days after Wait had sight of the bill of lading (which covered the whole parcel of 1,000 tons) from his own seller. Although this seemed a normal c.i.f. contract, where the buyer might have demanded a documentary tender that included a bill of lading,[140] the buyer paid the seller after being invoiced for the agreed sum without receiving a bill of lading or indeed any other delivery document. Wait hypothecated the bill of lading to his bank as security for his overdraft and paid the price received from the buyer into his general account. The bank, acting unilaterally, transferred this credit item a few days later into a separate loan account that had been debited with the sum advanced to Wait upon the hypothecation. Before delivery of the 500 tons could be made to the buyer, Wait was made bankrupt and the official receiver's representative obtained the bill of lading by discharging the debt from the loan account, thus leaving the buyer's payment as a credit. At no material time did the 500 tons due to the buyer ever become separated from bulk.

The trial judge declined to award specific performance of the contract but held that the buyer's payment was trust money earmarked for a special purpose and so should be repaid to the buyer.[141] The Divisional Court in Bankruptcy, however, ordered specific performance but the Court of Appeal by a majority overturned the award on the ground that the goods had never become 'specific or ascertained' for the purpose of section 52 and specific performance.[142] It further held that the buyer had no equitable property in the 1,000 ton bulk.[143] No argument relating to a

---

Rederei A/S v. *O/Y Louise Stevedoring Co. A/B* [1985] 2 All ER 669, 674 (it should not) and *Eximenco Handels AG* v. *Partredereit Oro Chief* [1983] 2 Lloyd's Rep. 509, 521 (it should).

[139] [1927] 1 Ch. 606, strongly criticized by Sir F. Pollock (1927) 43 *LQR* 293. For delivery terms see the text accompanying n. 103 above.

[140] *Quaere* a bill of lading that dealt with an unascertained portion of a larger bulk?

[141] For such a trust to arise, the buyer's money must be sufficiently dedicated to the purpose of acquiring the goods that it not may be mingled with the seller's other moneys and it must be returned if the dedicated purpose cannot be performed: see M. G. Bridge (1992) 12 *OJLS* 333 and the case law therein discussed, including *Barclays Bank Ltd* v. *Quistclose Investments Ltd* [1970] AC 567 and *Re Kayford Ltd* [1975] 1 All ER 604. In *Re Goldcorp Exchange Ltd* [1995] 1 AC 74, the buyer's argument that his money was received by the seller in the capacity of fiduciary failed because the buyer's purpose in making payment was to fulfil his sale obligations and there was no restriction imposed on the use by the seller of the money.

[142] N. 139 above, 616–21 and 630–4.

[143] Before the trial judge, the buyer had also claimed a charge over the bulk to secure repayment of the purchase money.

trust of the purchase money was made by the buyer by the time the action reached this stage.

Of the majority judges, Lord Hanworth MR pointed to the specific performance limitation in Lord Westbury's judgment in *Holroyd* v. *Marshall*[144] and held also, in effect, that an equitable appropriation would have to pass the test of ascertainment in section 16.[145] Atkin LJ too referred to Lord Westbury and held also there could be no equitable assignment of the buyer's 500 tons enforceable by equitable lien or charge over the 1,000 ton bulk arising from 'the mere sale[146] or agreement to sell'.[147] The Act was a complete codification of property rights arising out of the contract of sale:

It would have been futile in a code intended for commercial men to have created an elaborate structure of rules dealing with rights at law, if at the same time it was intended to leave, subsisting with the legal rights, equitable rights inconsistent with, more extensive, and coming into existence earlier than the rights so carefully set out in the various sections of the Code.[148]

Furthermore, to grant the relief sought by the buyer would 'also appear to embarrass to a most serious degree the ordinary operations of buying and selling goods, and the banking operations which attend them'.[149] Despite Atkin LJ's concerns, however, it is surely not too important to worry about the bank advancing money to the seller against a pledge of the shipping documents.[150] If the bank has notice of the equitable interest granted to the buyer, it is forewarned and can take its own precautions; and if it is not aware of this interest, its own special legal property will prevail against or override[151] the buyer's equitable interest.

Atkin LJ did concede that a 'seller or a purchaser may, of course, create any equity he pleases by way of charge, equitable assignment or any other dealing with or disposition of the goods, the subject matter of sale; and he may of course create such equity as one of the terms expressed in the contract of sale'.[152] No such special provision had in his view been

---

[144] (1862) 10 HLC 191.   [145] N. 139 above, 622.

[146] *Quaere* s. 2(4)?   [147] N. 139 above, 636.   [148] *Ibid.*, 635–6.

[149] N. 139 above, 629–30. Note also his criticism of the difficulty in determining when an equitable property passed to the buyer: *ibid.*, 635.

[150] His concern was that the efficacy of a seller's pledge of the shipping documents with a bank would be undermined if the bank's knowledge of the existence of a contract of sale were to be treated as knowledge of equitable interests arising thereunder: *ibid.*, 639–40. Why should it?

[151] Depending upon whether the pledge precedes the equitable assignment or vice versa.

[152] N. 139 above, 636. This concession is not referred to by Lord Brandon in *Leigh and Sillavan Ltd* v. *Aliakmon Shipping Ltd* [1986] AC 785, 812–13, when he adopts Atkin LJ's views on the need to exclude equitable proprietary principles from the scope of the Sale of Goods Act. The concession, however, is mentioned explicitly by Lord Mustill in *Re Goldcorp Exchange Ltd*, n. 141 above, where he too adopts Atkin LJ's views.

made in the present case.[153] Nor did he feel drawn to intervene in favour of the buyer on grounds so inherently vague as dishonesty (or, supposedly, equitable fraud). The general hostility of Atkin LJ's remarks towards the equitable infiltration of commercial law, however, has succeeded in concealing his concession that the parties could create equitable rights under a contract of sale if they put their minds to it in the proper way. But to the extent that equitable rights would create real impediments to the operation of the seller's activities, as they would if they encumbered a portion of the seller's trading stock,[154] a court would require a great deal of persuading that equitable rights were genuinely intended by the parties.[155]

Sargant LJ, dissenting in *Re Wait*,[156] plainly believed that Wait had appropriated the particular cargo of 1,000 tons from which to fulfil his sale obligations to the buyer. He considered that an equitable interest would have passed to the buyer from the time of appropriation if the buyer had agreed to buy the whole of the 1,000 ton bulk, and the same conclusion should follow on the present facts since in both cases it would be fraud or dishonesty for the seller to divert the wheat from the contract with the buyer.[157] Equitable assignment, in his view, was not tied to the doctrine of specific performance and, though the 500 tons had never been ascertained, they were nevertheless ascertainable at the time when it was sought to enforce the contract.[158] Finally, the Sale of Goods Act had not put paid to equitable interests arising out of sale of goods contracts and the equitable assignment could be implemented by specific performance since the goods in question could be regarded as 'specific goods' under section 52.

For practical purposes, *Re Wait* put an end to the idea of an implied equitable assignment in sales law,[159] despite a majority view that the result would have been different if the seller had undertaken to deliver the buyer's 500 tons out of the 1,000 tons for which he held a bill of lading.[160] Recent confirmation of the effect of *Re Wait* comes from the Privy Council decision in *Re Goldcorp Exchange Ltd*,[161] which also stands for a

---

[153] N. 139 above, 635.
[154] The seller could not deal freely with stock the subject of a trust.
[155] *Re Goldcorp Exchange Ltd*, n. 141 above, 91, 96–7.
[156] N. 139 above, especially 644–7, 655–6.
[157] On this point, see also *Clark* v. *Scottish Imperial Insurance Co.* (1879) 4 SCR 192 (Can.) (Ritchie J).
[158] See also Bowen LJ in *Re Clarke*, n. 138 above, 355.
[159] But see *Electrical Enterprises Pty. Ltd* v. *Rodgers* (1989) 15 NSWLR 473, where the court gave the seller of goods an equitable (non-possessory) lien over them, declining to follow the *Re Wait* view that the Sale of Goods Act fully codified property rights.
[160] Hanworth MR and Sargant LJ. Atkin LJ insisted, against a plain reading of the contract, that the seller could have tendered from any shipment on board the *Challenger*.
[161] N. 141 above; McKendrick (1994) 110 *LQR* 514.

refusal to infer a fiduciary relationship from ordinary contractual dealings or to impose constructive trust, equitable lien, and restitutionary proprietary rights simply because the seller has failed to abide by his promises and representations regarding the holding of earmarked goods for the buyer. From the buyer's point of view, this case was weaker on its facts than *Re Wait* since there was no question of an identified bulk to be charged with equitable rights.

Tenancy in Common

It is noteworthy that the Law Commission, when it considered the problem of insolvency and bulk goods, recommended a reform favouring the pre-paying buyer based, not upon equitable ideas, but upon the common law doctrine of tenancy in common. Such a buyer, unless the parties otherwise agreed, would obtain an undivided share in an identified bulk, until his share was separated in the normal course.[162] The Commission's proposal was that tenants in common of the bulk would share rateably any shrinkage of the bulk, but that any of them removing or receiving his contract quantity from the bulk should be protected from liability to other tenants suffering a shortfall.[163] The recommendations of the Law Commission were enacted as the Sale of Goods (Amendment) Act 1995 (discussed below).

The position before the 1995 changes, where there was a specific or ascertained bulk and various unsatisfied buyers therefrom, was that those buyers could not be treated without more ado as tenants in common of the undivided bulk.[164] It was not enough that the seller's creditors would obtain a windfall benefit from the accident of non-ascertainment from the bulk, or that the buyers had a common interest, or at least no adversity of interest, in the face of the seller's insolvency. Nevertheless, in *Re Stapylton Fletcher Ltd*,[165] decided after the Law Commission report, it was held that, just as a tenancy in common can be imposed by law in the case of a wrongful mixing of goods,[166] so there was nothing to prevent the parties impliedly or expressly agreeing for the seller to hold the buyer's goods mixed in common with those of other buyers.[167] In that case, sellers of wine, exercising rigorous stock controls,

---

[162] The Commission's proposals, in line with the views of consultants, were confined to sales out of a particular bulk: Law Com. No. 215, n. 95 above, paras. 3.10 and 4.1. For discussion of the report and the working paper, see A. Hudson [1989] *LMCLQ* 420; R. Bradgate and F. White [1994] *LMCLQ* 315.

[163] *Ibid.*, paras. 4.19–21.

[164] *Laurie and Morewood* v. *Dudin and Sons* [1926] 1 KB 223; *Karlshamns Oljefabriker* v. *Eastport Navigation Corpn (The Elafi)* [1982] 1 All ER 208, 214. See Law Com. No. 215, n. 95 above, paras. 2.4 and 2.7.

[165] [1994] 1 WLR 1181; N. Campbell [1996] *JBL* 199.

[166] See *Indian Oil Corpn.* v. *Greenstone Shipping SA* [1988] QB 345.

[167] *Quaere* a tenancy in common between the seller and one or more buyers?

conscientiously segregated cases of wine, the subject of various contract of sales, by removing the wine from their ordinary trading stacks and transferring it to their warehouse stacks.[168] Even though it could not be said that individual buyers' wines had been earmarked before being submerged in a common pool, the court held first that the wines of those buyers had thereby been ascertained under section 16. The test of ascertainment was to be understood differently where sellers made a constructive delivery to themselves as warehousemen as opposed to an actual delivery to the buyer.[169] A less controversial feature of the case was the next step taken by the court, namely, the inference from the parties' conduct of a tenancy in common of the wine in the warehouse stacks. This conclusion was reached even though the cases of wine in those stacks were not allocated to particular warehousing contracts and there was nothing to show to which warehousing contract cases of a particular type and vintage of wine belonged. The meticulous records of the warehouse, however, revealed the names of those who were entitled in gross to share those cases. In the event of loss or breakages in the common warehouse pool, each buyer would bear the burden rateably with the other tenants in common according to their respective shares. The tenancy in common result in this case is equally applicable to goods delivered by the seller and mingled with identical or compatible goods of the buyer, in circumstances where the seller does not intend to pass the property in the goods to the buyer.[170] On its own terms, the case is unlikely to be of assistance to a buyer in a case like *Re Wait*.

Buyers and Insolvent Sellers

Before we turn to the Sale of Goods (Amendment) Act 1995, it is useful to consider a further aspect of the case for intervention on behalf of the buyer. If section 16 may not be applied[171] in a way favourable to the buyer, then any intervention on his behalf, by means of equitable rules or by statutory means, should not be a matter of mere legal technique under broad rubrics such as 'fraud' and 'dishonesty'. It should as a matter of principle be asked why the buyer should rank ahead of the insolvent seller's other creditors.[172] The Law Commission did assert that 'insolvency law has to accept the rules of property law as it finds them'[173] and implied that removing anomalies from existing law does not inter-

---

[168] *Re London Wine Co. Ltd* (1979) [1986] PCC 121 was distinguished by the existence of a defined bulk coupled with this process of segregation: n. 165 above, 1194.

[169] N. 165 above, 1199.

[170] See P. Watts (1990) 106 *LQR* 552, discussing *Coleman* v. *Harvey* [1989] 1 NZLR 723; A. Hudson [1991] *LMCLQ* 23.

[171] As it was in *Re Stapylton Fletcher Ltd*, n. 165 above.

[172] See *Re Goldcorp Exchange Ltd* [1995] 1 AC 74, 99.

[173] Law Com. No. 215, n. 95 above, para. 3.19.

fere with the rules of distribution on insolvency.[174] But it is difficult to see a proposed major reform, prompted by a report dealing with the problems raised by a long-established body of law, as responding to a mere anomaly. There is much to be said in this area of law for confronting the issue of insolvency head on. The best starting point for preferring the prepaying buyer is Atkin LJ's statement in *Re Wait*:

> If a seller of goods delivers them to a buyer before payment, trusting to receive payment in due course, and the buyer becomes bankrupt, the seller is restricted to a proof, and can assert no beneficial interest in the goods. There seems no particular reason why a different principle should prevail where a buyer hands the price to the seller before delivery of the goods trusting to receive delivery in due course. In both cases credit is given to the debtor, and the buyer and the seller take the well known risk of the insolvency of their customer.[175]

A seller who delivers the goods before payment is well able to see the risk and guard against it by reserving the general property. The prepaying buyer is not so well positioned and may be unaware that his goods form an undifferentiated part of a bulk.[176] A matter of critical importance raised in this passage is whether 'credit' is granted by the prepaying buyer to the seller or, more accurately, whether the buyer advances money to the seller with the intention of financing the latter's business, accepting the risk of relegation to the status of an unsecured creditor if he does not actively bargain for a security. In *Re Wait*, the buyer did not advance the price to permit Wait to obtain the goods from his shipper. The contract was an ordinary c.i.f. transaction contemplating the transfer of the general property, through the medium of the bill of lading, against payment. It is arguable that the adventitious circumstance of the contract quantity being submerged in a larger bulk baffled the expectations of the parties that the buyer would become the owner of the contract goods upon payment. Credit is not the practice in commodity transactions and a case can be made for intervention in favour of the buyer where otherwise the seller's creditors would obtain a windfall benefit. Those who take an insolvency risk commonly charge a premium commensurate with the risk, which is not the case with prepaying buyers of part of a bulk cargo.

It is easily overlooked that one example of a prepaying buyer who does not extend credit to the seller, and indeed receives it from the seller, is the buyer on instalment terms where the seller retains the general property until payment in full has been made. Canadian cases on conditional sales, seemingly attracted by the analogy of a security bill of sale where the grantor has an equity of redemption in the goods, support the view

---

[174] *Ibid.*   [175] [1927] 1 Ch. 606, 640.
[176] Or that there is not even a bulk: *Re Goldcorp Exchange Ltd*, n. 172 above.

that an equitable or other limited interest, measured by the instalments paid from time to time, passes to the buyer.[177] These cases are consistent in approach with English hire purchase cases allowing the finance company, in a conversion action against a third party tortfeasor, to recover only damages limited to the unpaid balance on the hire purchase agreement.[178] The normal conversion award, based upon the value of the goods, would be more consistent with the *legal* structure of the hire purchase agreement, under which the finance company retains the full beneficial and legal ownership until the hirer can and does exercise the option to purchase.[179]

Sale of Goods (Amendment) Act 1995

Be that as it may, the Sale of Goods (Amendment) Act 1995[180] implemented the above tenancy in common proposals of the Law Commission. According to section 20A of the Sale of Goods Act 1979,[181] where 'the goods or some of them form part of a bulk', the buyer acquires an 'undivided share in the bulk' and becomes an owner in common of the bulk[182] unless the parties agree otherwise. Two conditions have to be satisfied before this proprietary interest arises. First, the bulk in question[183] must be identified in the contract or by subsequent agreement between the parties. A difficult case, common in international commodity sales, is the seller who issues a notice of appropriation (or declaration of shipment) indicating that the buyer's goods will come from a named ship. Of itself, this does not refer to a particular portion of that ship's cargo, defined by one or more bills of lading, sufficiently for an undivided share to pass to the buyer.[184] This difficulty will in practice be resolved by

---

[177] *C. C. Motor Sales Ltd* v. *Chan* [1926] SCR 485, 491; *Workmen's Compensation Board* v. *US Steel Corpn.* (1956) 5 DLR (2d) 184; *Commercial Credit Corpn.* v. *Niagara Finance Corpn.* [1940] SCR 420; *Rogerson Lumber Co. Ltd v. Four Seasons Chalet Ltd* (1980) 29 OR (2d) 193. See also the old system of lien notes: A. Hogg (1924) 2 *Can. Bar Rev.* 491.

[178] *Belvoir Finance Co. Ltd* v. *Stapleton* [1971] 1 QB 210; *Wickham Holdings Ltd* v. *Brooke House Motors Ltd* [1967] 1 All ER 117.

[179] Other examples showing that the law does not stop at the formal structure of hire purchase include *Whiteley* v. *Hilt* [1918] 2 KB 808 (assignability of option rights); *Transag Haulage Ltd* v. *Leyland DAF Finance plc* [1994] BCC 356 (relief against forfeiture); Consumer Credit Act 1974, ss. 90, 132 (limits on the right of repossession).

[180] J. Ulph [1996] *LMCLQ* 93; R. Goode, *Commercial Law* (2nd edn., 1995), 228–31, 246–7.

[181] As added by s. 1(3) of the 1995 Act.

[182] Evidently with other buyers in the same position and/or the seller, to the extent that the seller retains an interest in the bulk.

[183] Defined as 'a mass or collection of goods of the same kind which . . . is contained in a defined space or area . . . and is such that any goods in the bulk are interchangeable with any other goods therein of the same number or quantity': s. 2(a) of the 1995 Act, adding a new definition to s. 61(1) of the Sale of Goods Act.

[184] See the views of Atkin LJ, expressed in *Re Wait*, n. 175 above, that the sellers could have performed the contract out of any cargo on the *Challenger*, and not just that portion of the cargo for which they held a bill of lading: discussed at n. 103 above.

compliance with the second condition demanded by section 20A before the buyer will acquire an undivided share, which is that the buyer must have made payment for that share. In international commodity sales where goods are shipped in bulk, payment will be made against the transfer to the buyer of a delivery order.[185] The undertaking of the ship to surrender the relevant cargo, which makes the delivery order effective, will have been given upon the surrender by the seller to the ship of one or more bills of lading. The receipt by the buyer of the delivery order will therefore be predicated upon the identification of the bulk by that bill of lading.

Certain difficulties arising from the implementation of the above provisions of the 1995 Act are dealt with in the same legislation. First, the size of the buyer's share is a rateable one corresponding to the ratio between the bulk and the the quantity of the goods for which payment has been made by the buyer.[186] Any 'delivery'[187] out of the bulk to a buyer who has made only a part payment will be 'ascribed' to that payment.[188] This means that the buyer's undivided share in the remaining bulk will be diminished to the extent that he acquires the property in delivered goods. The buyer's property interest, whether it takes the form of an undivided share or the property in goods or both, will not by virtue of this legislation exceed the payment made. Secondly, any shrinkage in the bulk, which could occur for various reasons including natural wastage, theft, or default of the seller, will be borne rateably by the various tenant buyers according to the size of their respective shares in the bulk.[189] Thirdly, deliveries[190] out of the bulk to individual buyers may override the undivided shares of co-owners to whom delivery has not been made. Section 20B(1)(a) of the Sale of Goods Act[191] provides that co-owners are deemed to consent to such deliveries out of the bulk to fellow co-owners entitled to receive such delivery. A buyer receiving delivery in full in this way is not required to indemnify fellow co-owners who later bear a disproportionately large share of any shrinkage that has occurred in the

[185] For the meaning of which see Ch. 6 below.
[186] S. 2(3) of the 1995 Act, adding s. 20A(3) to the Sale of Goods Act. The buyer's share may therefore increase incrementally as payment is progressively made. The size of the buyer's share corresponds directly to the size of the part payment (a unit pricing approach): s. 1(3) of the 1995 Act adding s. 20A(6) to the Sale of Goods Act.
[187] This can take the form of a passing of property in the relevant goods falling short of a physical delivery: s. 2(b) of the 1995 Act amending the definition of delivery in s. 61(1) of the Sale of Goods Act.
[188] S. 1(3) of the 1995 Act adding s. 20A(5) to the Sale of Goods Act.
[189] S. 1(3) of the 1995 Act adding s. 20A(4) of the Sale of Goods Act. This provision does not address the position of a co-owning seller, whether or not responsible for the shrinkage. Common law principles would reach the same result as s. 20A(4) in the case of an innocent seller: *Spence* v. *Union Marine Insurance Co.* (1868) LR 3 CP 427; M. G. Bridge, *Personal Property Law* (Blackstone, London, 1993), 83–4.
[190] In the extended sense referred to above.   [191] Added by s. 1(3) of the 1995 Act.

bulk.[192] Similarly, this consent of co-owners of the bulk extends under section 20B(1)(b) to 'any dealing with or removal, delivery or disposal of the goods' by one of their number. This could refer to a contract between a buyer and a sub-buyer and should not merely condone the act of the buyer but also protect from suit the sub-buyer.[193] It could also include a seller's decision to let a buyer have delivery of goods in the bulk even before that buyer makes payment. Further, there is general language in section 20B(2) protecting those who act within the area of the above consents. A warehouseman, for example, effecting delivery would be protected from liability in conversion. Finally, the contractual rights of a buyer benefiting from the various proprietary rights conferred by sections 20A–B remain unaffected by the legislation.[194]

Four significant points arising out of the 1995 Act should also be mentioned. First, although it does not say so explicitly, the Act creates an interim position in the passing of property from seller to buyer: the buyer's undivided share as tenant in common of the bulk will be superseded by the general property in the contract goods after the buyer's goods have been separated from the identified bulk. Secondly, there is the relevance of the unconditional appropriation rules in section 18, Rule 5. It is submitted that the buyer's undivided share should not be erased after ascertainment just because Rule 5 has not yet been satisfied.[195] It would be a curious property right of the buyer's if it could be unilaterally divested by the seller in separating the buyer's goods from bulk. This would be inconsistent with the notion of ownership in common, especially if the seller had retained an interest in the bulk so as to be one of those owners in common. The seller's act of ascertainment could, if necessary, be seen as the act of an agent acting on behalf of the buyer, the owner of the separated share. Section 18, Rule 5, a rule of presumptive intention, could also be seen as excluded by a contrary intention.

Thirdly, there is the relationship between the new sections 18, Rule 5(3),(4), and 20A. Although a buyer will not acquire an undivided interest under the latter provision until payment is made, once the bulk is exhausted by other buyers' claims, leaving only the non-paying buyer with a claim to receive goods from that bulk, the property in the remaining goods will pass to that buyer pursuant to section 18, Rule 5(3),(4). The

---

[192] S. 20B(3)(a). But co-owning buyers are free to agree otherwise amongst themselves: s. 20B(3)(b). In what circumstances, unless they all contract with the seller on the same standard form making such provision, might such a bargain be struck?

[193] It would have been preferable to define the sub-buyer's title. Further, it would seem that this sub-buyer is protected even if the same bulk is not at any time appropriated to the sub-sale.

[194] e.g. any action against the seller for non-delivery of agreed goods would remain.

[195] Discussed below.

unpaid seller will have, however, the protection of a lien over the goods until payment is made.[196] It is perhaps curious that section 20A does not give a non-paying buyer an undivided share leaving the seller to be protected by that same lien. Fourthly, as noted earlier, an undivided interest is now defined as goods under the Sale of Goods Act 1979. This does not mean that a sub-buyer (who may not yet have paid) of unascertained goods in a bulk automatically becomes the buyer of an undivided share just because the buyer acquires an undivided share in the bulk upon payment. The distinction between the sale of an undivided share and the sale of unascertained goods in a specific or identified bulk remains. The 1995 Act builds upon and preserves that distinction even as it brings both transactions within the amended Sale of Goods Act 1979.

The 1995 Act may usefully be set alongside a 1993 reform to the British Columbia Sale of Goods Act.[197] This reform grants to a consumer buyer,[198] to the extent of any prepayment made, a 'lien' against such goods in the seller's possession and destined for sale, the property in which has not passed to a different buyer, as correspond with the contract description or (where relevant) any sample of the goods. There is no need for any bulk to be appropriated to the contract, a clear point of departure from our 1995 Act. Furthermore, it is not clear whether this 'lien' is of an equitable or common law nature; it seems to be *sui generis*. First, a 'trustee-in-bankruptcy'[199] with no knowledge of the lien is not liable for dealings with the goods. Secondly, the lien is discharged when goods are 'appropriated'[200] to a 'sale'.[201] Thirdly, the buyer's lien ranks ahead of 'other security interests'[202] under the province's modern personal property security legislation, which has abandoned any distinction between common law and equitable interests. Fourthly, the buyer's lien, as against other buyers' similar liens, is treated as in the nature of a tenancy in common in that the shortage of any available goods to satisfy all liens entails the rateable abatement of the buyers' several claims. Fifthly, the equitable principles of marshalling govern in the case of competing buyers' liens, meaning that a buyer's lien will be released in favour of

[196] Sale of Goods Act, s. 39(1)(a).
[197] The Consumer Protection Statutes Amendment Act SBC, c. 1993, s. 27, adding ss. 73–80 to The Sale of Goods Act RSBC 1979, c. 370. See the comment by the Chairman of the British Columbia Law Reform Commission (A. Close) at (1995) 25 *Can Bus LJ* 127 and the criticism of the draft proposal by M. G. Bridge at (1989) 5 *Banking and Finance LR* 171.
[198] One who buys 'primarily for personal, family or household purposes'. The reform is designed to deal with mail order and similar transactions.
[199] This includes sheriffs, liquidators, and even receivers.
[200] Whatever that means.
[201] Contract of sale or sale properly so called? *Semble*, the buyer under this 'sale' need not have paid. *Quaere*, sales by trustees, liquidators, and (some) receivers acting as agents of the insolvent seller, and by sheriffs and (other) receivers who do not act in that capacity?
[202] Which includes mortgages, charges, and title reservations.

other buyers' liens to the extent that that buyer has other security (broadly defined) to reinforce his claim to goods or the return of his purchase price. A final point to note about this legislation is that the buyer does not merely have a lien over the seller's goods but also a lien over 'any account in a savings institution in which the seller usually deposits the proceeds of sale'. There is thus no need to comply with the requirements of a *Quistclose* trust;[203] the interesting question of how such a lien is to be reconciled with a competing claim by that savings institution falls outside the scope of this text. It should be noted that the two liens, over goods and accounts, both apply in securing either the performance of the contract by the delivery of goods or the reimbursement of any money prepaid.[204]

Unconditional Appropriation

Once the embargo placed by section 16 on the passing of property is lifted, by the goods becoming ascertained,[205] the way is open for the property to pass according to the intention of the parties. Failing an actual intention, the presumptive intention in section 18, Rule 5(1), is as follows:

Where there is a contract for the sale of unascertained or future goods by description, and goods of that description and in a deliverable state are unconditionally appropriated to the contract, either by the seller with the assent of the buyer or by the buyer with the assent of the seller, the property in the goods then passes to the buyer; and the assent may be express or implied, and may be given either before or after the appropriation is made.

It is possible, where ascertainment from an agreed bulk is delayed, for an agreed unconditional appropriation to be held in suspense until the act of ascertainment occurs.[206] A review of the case law fails to reveal a differential application of the rule depending upon the issue at stake, whether it is a matter of risk or the seller's bankruptcy or the seller's entitlement to sue for the price. Indeed, attempts by litigants to manipulate the rule according to context once attracted disparaging comment in the Privy Council.[207] Yet it cannot be said that the approach to unconditional appropriation has been wholly consistent in the cases: as will be seen,

---

[203] Referred to at n. 141 above.

[204] The seller decides whether to perform or repay. This appears to give him in all cases where the liens exist an option to terminate contracts of sale, subject to the buyer's right to claim damages for breach of contract if the prepaid money is returned.

[205] Likewise the embargo on future goods in s. 5(3) lifted when they become existing goods.

[206] See *The Elafi* [1982] 1 All ER 208. This has been confirmed by legislation: s. 1(2) of the Sale of Goods (Amendment) Act 1995, adding a new s. 18, Rule 5(3),(4), to the 1979 Act.

[207] *Gilmour* v. *Supple* (1858) 11 Moo. PC 551.

much depends upon the seller's delivery obligations. The passing of property, as shown by Rule 5(1), is a consensual act. Indeed, it is shaped almost as a contract, with one of the parties offering particular goods to another who then accepts them.[208]

Appropriation is an ambiguous word and the case law is unhelpful in elucidating it. Baron Parke once ascribed to it three meanings in a well-known but obscure passage.[209] To isolate the meaning of the word, it helps for analytical purposes to define three stages in the passing of property in unascertained goods: first, an appropriation by one party; secondly, a further act by that same party that renders the appropriation unconditional; and thirdly, the assent of the non-appropriating party (whether to the appropriation or the making of it unconditional is not clear but unlikely to be significant). Subject to one exception,[210] appropriation *simpliciter* appears to mean only the ascertainment of the goods.[211] A seller would thus appropriate from existing stock by setting aside goods intended for the fulfilment of a particular sale contract. Appropriation from future stock would be accomplished, for example, upon the later receipt of stock specially bought in for a particular resale commitment, or upon the completion by a manufacturing seller of a production run set up for a particular buyer, or upon a setting aside of goods out of a general consignment bought in or manufactured.

In certain international sales conducted on c.i.f terms, appropriation works as follows. Goods are said to be appropriated to the contract when the seller passes on to the buyer details of their shipment, including the identity of the ship, in a notice of appropriation (or declaration of shipment). It is common for goods to be thus appropriated when they are an unascertained part of a larger bulk thereby rendered specific, such as 10,000 tonnes of soya bean meal from the 50,000 tonnes on board the named ship. This process of appropriation, unlike the examples of appropriation given above, locks the seller in to delivering goods from that ship, but they can be any 10,000 tonnes thereon.[212] The property in the goods, even if ascertained from the bulk,[213] will not usually pass by

---

[208] This contractual feature is not as well developed here as it has been for sale of land where the contract of sale may merge in the later conveyance.

[209] *Wait* v. *Baker* (1848) 2 Ex. 1, 8–9: 'The word appropriation may be understood in different senses. It may mean a selection on the part of the vendor, where he has the right to choose the article which he has to supply in performance of his contract. . . . Or the word may mean, that both parties have agreed that a certain article shall be delivered in pursuance of the contract, and yet the property may not pass in either case. . . . "Appropriation" may also be used in another sense . . . viz. where both parties agree upon the specific article in which the property is to pass, and nothing remains to be done in order to pass it.'

[210] See the use of the word in c.i.f. sales discussed in the next para. below.

[211] This would correspond to the first of Baron Parke's meanings, n. 209 above.

[212] Subject to the right, if it exists, to substitute another appropriation.

[213] As where the seller appropriates the entire contents of a particular hold.

virtue of this appropriation,[214] but the seller has lost his contractual freedom to appropriate to the contract goods from any other source.

The next step is to determine what it is about an appropriation that makes it unconditional. There are two broad alternative approaches. First, if an appropriation takes place when particular goods are applied to the contract, it is unconditional if the seller's decision is, or later becomes, demonstrably a firm one. Secondly, an appropriation becomes unconditional when a seller puts it out of his physical power to reverse the effect of the appropriation. The former approach is based upon the idea of election.[215] The appropriation of a cargo by a c.i.f. seller, who thereby loses his contractual freedom to supply goods from an alternative source,[216] would be unconditional if Rule 5 turned on election. The effect of the unconditional appropriation, however, might be inhibited by the non-ascertainment of the buyer's quantity or by a reservation by the seller under section 19 of his right of disposal. Similarly, election may explain the Canadian case where the manufacturer of certain cars was bound to deliver them to a carrier and, before doing so, prepared drafts for the buyer with accompanying invoices and certificates identifying the cars by serial number. The buyers accepted the drafts and, though the cars were never delivered, the court held that they had been unconditionally appropriated to the contract.[217] Consistent too with the election approach is *Pignataro* v. *Gilroy*[218] where the property in a quantity of rice, to be delivered at the seller's premises, passed when the buyer failed to collect the goods after being notified by the seller that they were ready. The real difficulty in the case concerned the buyer's assent to the seller's unconditional appropriation: it seems to have been assumed that the seller's work of appropriation was complete when the goods were set aside for the buyer. The buyer had earlier inspected the rice from which the contract quantity was to come and had taken a sample. Elsewhere, an appropriation[219] effective to pass the property has been found when the seller filled containers supplied by the buyer, even though the goods

---

[214] Because the seller will reserve the right of disposal under s. 19 until payment is made: discussed in the text accompanying nn. 262 ff. below.

[215] *Heyward's Case* (1595) 2 Co. Rep. 35a. For the modern definition of election, see *Peyman* v. *Lanjani* [1985] Ch. 457, discussed Ch. 6 below.

[216] But see *Borrowman, Phillips & Co.* v. *Free & Hollis* (1878) 4 QBD 500 for the view that the appropriation of a cargo that does not comply with the contract is binding on the seller only if the buyer accepts it. *Sed quaere?*

[217] *Hayes Bros. Buick-Opel-Jeep Inc.* v. *Canada Permanent Trust Co.* (1976) 15 NBR (2d) 166.

[218] [1919] 1 KB 459. The goods were deliverable on *ex* warehouse terms, for the meaning of which see *Fisher Reeves and Co. Ltd* v. *Armour and Co. Ltd* [1920] 3 KB 614.

[219] The word 'unconditional' is not used, which is typical of the pre-Act authorities. This makes *Wait* v. *Baker*, n. 209 above, difficult to apply today. The word is also absent in s. 19(1).

were not delivered to the carrier.[220] In both cases, however, the goods were to be supplied from a specific bulk[221] and the result is consistent with the c.i.f. example given above. These cases involve one or both of the following: a contractual commitment to deliver from a specific bulk and a statement to the buyer that the appropriation has been made.

Outside the above cases, the election approach is open to the criticism that little separates a mere appropriation from one that is unconditional, and that it begs the question whether a setting aside by the seller is tentative or final. The result in other cases accords with the view that an appropriation becomes unconditional when the seller is physically unable to change his mind.[222] This may explain the view of Atkin J in *Stein, Forbes & Co* v. *County Tailoring Co.*[223] that the appropriation of a seller who does not mean the buyer to have the goods before payment is only a conditional one.[224] Further, in *Carlos Federspiel & Co. SA* v. *Charles Twigg & Co. Ltd*,[225] the seller, who had been paid by the buyer, was bound to ship a quantity of bicycles and tricycles at a UK port, and so had packed the goods into crates labelled with the buyer's name and address. The seller was awaiting a ship bound for a Central American port when a receiver was sent in by one of the seller's creditors. Consequently, delivery never took place. Pearson J held that the property had not passed[226] and stated that unconditional appropriation[227] occurs with the last act of the seller's performance under the contract, which is tantamount to delivery or constructive delivery. The constructive delivery that occurs where a third party bailee attorns to the buyer, which puts a change of mind beyond the reach of the seller, marks the moment when the property passes.[228] Constructive delivery may also be found where the seller holds the goods as bailee for the buyer. This accommodates the above cases of the buyer's containers, where a constructive (more accurately a

[220] *Aldridge* v. *Johnson* (1857) 7 E & B 855; *Langton* v. *Higgins* (1859) 4 H & N 402.

[221] The whole bulk in the case of *Langton*, n. 220 above.

[222] See *Edwards* v. *Ddin* [1976] 1 WLR 942 (property passed when petrol fed into the tank of the defendant's car). Cf. *R.* v. *Thomas* [1928] 2 WWR 608 (passing of property conditional upon payment being made); *Addy* v. *Blake* (1887) 19 QBD 478; *Noblett* v. *Hopkinson* [1905] 2 KB 214. As for the possibility that a tenancy in common arises in a commingled mass, see P. Watts (1990) 106 *LQR* 552.

[223] (1916) 88 LJKB 448.

[224] See also *Godts* v. *Rose* (1855) 17 CB 229. But that seller could be protected by a lien and does not need the general property as such.

[225] [1957] 1 Lloyd's Rep. 240. *Quaere* the seller who ships goods under the terms of a sea waybill entitling him, as against the carrier, to change the identity of the named consignee when the goods are in transit.

[226] Cf. the Canadian case of *NEC Corpn.* v. *Steintron Electronics Ltd* (1985) 50 CBR (NS) 91, where, on similar facts, the court held that the property had passed since the seller in practice always shipped out goods already addressed to the named buyer.

[227] Pearson J speaks of appropriation but means unconditional appropriation.

[228] *Laurie and Morewood* v. *Dudin and Sons* [1926] 1 KB 223; *Wardar's Import and Export Co. Ltd* v. *W. Norwood & Sons Ltd* [1968] 2 QB 663.

fictitious) delivery was found in the act of filling them.[229] They were explained in *Re Stapylton Fletcher Ltd*[230] as cases where the seller constituted himself a bailee of the contract goods. In that case, the court held that certain goods had been unconditionally appropriated to a sale contract when they were removed from the seller's trading stock and then shortly afterwards mixed with similar goods destined for other buyers and held by the seller on warehouse terms.

Unconditional Appropriation and the 1995 Act

Although the Sale of Goods (Amendment) Act 1995 is not couched in the language of unconditional appropriation, it must be asked what effect its provisions might have on the existing law in this area. As stated above, a buyer, to the extent of any payment made, acquires an undivided interest by way of tenancy in common in 'a bulk which has been identified either in the contract or by subsequent agreement between the parties'.[231] The Act defines 'bulk' as a 'mass or collection of goods of the same kind', whose components are interchangeable and which is 'confined in a defined space or area'.[232] Suppose that in *Carlos Federspiel & Co. SA* v. *Charles Twigg & Co. Ltd*[233] there had been two pre-paying Costa Rican buyers and they had both been informed by the sellers that their goods, bicycles of the same type, had been set aside and were awaiting shipment in the sellers' loading bay. It is arguable that this would amount to the agreed identification of a bulk so as to confer a proprietary interest on each buyer. This conclusion would be easier to reach if the crates were not addressed and were so positioned that the two parcels of goods were not separated. If only one buyer were informed of the readiness of the goods for dispatch, only that buyer, on the face of it, could claim that there is an identified bulk.

Suppose now that the sellers failed to inform either buyer that his goods are in the loading bay. This prompts the question what is meant by identification 'either in the contract or by subsequent agreement'. Section 18, Rule 5(1), permits unconditional appropriation with an added assent to amount to a transfer of the property in the goods; as we shall see, that assent is frequently implied in advance of the appropriation. This is an implied agreement of sorts, but it might be difficult to see a similar passive response by the buyer to a seller's message as the basis for a 'subsequent agreement' under section 20A. It could not easily be seen either as an identification 'in the contract'. Finally, if there is only

---

[229] *Langton* v. *Higgins*, n. 220 above (Bramwell B); *Aldridge* v. *Johnson, ibid.* (Crompton J).
[230] [1994] 1 WLR 1181.
[231] S. 20A of the Sale of Goods Act as added by s. 1(3) of the 1995 Act.
[232] S. 61 of the Sale of Goods Act as added by s. 2(a) of the 1995 Act.
[233] N. 225 above.

one quantity of goods laid out in the loading bay for only one buyer, who is informed that the goods are ready for shipment, it is not easy to see that the goods constitute a 'bulk', but it seems perverse to deny such buyer a proprietary interest if, in the case outlined above, two buyers together had each an undivided interest. It would also be odd to deny an interest to the two buyers on the ground that their goods had been separated and identified to each of them so as not to form a commingled mass. The incoherence between the 1995 changes and the existing law on unconditional appropriation seems destined to cause future trouble. A relaxation of section 16 and its requirement of ascertainment, following upon the enactment of section 20A, does not sit easily with a continuing strict approach to section 18, Rule 5.

Scope of Rule 5(1)

Rule 5(1) requires the goods to be in 'a deliverable state', which here has the same meaning as in Rule 1.[234] Rule 5(1) was not satisfied where carpets, brought to the buyer's premises, had not yet been fitted by the seller.[235] But the goods must answer to the contractual description if the property is to pass under Rule 5.[236] The scope of description used to be larger for unascertained than for specific goods. In recent years, there has been a discernible tendency to diminish the scope of description so that, far from embracing all the stated attributes of unascertained goods, it is confined for specific and unascertained goods alike to the identity of the goods.[237] Consequently, the property will not often nowadays be prevented from passing under Rule 5(1) by a failure to meet the contractual description. Where the buyer's assent to an unconditional appropriation by the seller is implied, which is quite common, it might also be said that the buyer does not authorize the seller to appropriate to the contract goods not conforming to the basic standard of the contractual description. The property will not pass if the seller tenders goods other than the agreed contract quantity.[238] Courts are also markedly reluctant to recognize that the property in goods the subject of an entire contract passes incrementally as they are delivered into the hands of a carrier.[239]

---

[234] Discussed in the text accompanying nn. 47–50 above.

[235] *Philip Head & Sons Ltd* v. *Showfronts Ltd* [1970] 1 Lloyd's Rep. 140. See also *Hendy Lennox Ltd* v. *Grahame Puttick Ltd* [1984] 1 WLR 485; *Anderson* v. *Morice* (1876) 1 App. Cas. 713 (Lord Blackburn: incomplete loading of ship, *sed quaere*? since the section speaks of deliverable and not delivered state.

[236] *Vigers* v. *Sanderson* [1901] 1 KB 608; *Hammer and Barrow* v. *Coca-Cola* [1962] NZLR 723, 731.

[237] Discussed Ch. 10 below.

[238] *Cunliffe* v. *Harrison* (1851) 6 Ex. 903; *Levy* v. *Green* (1859) 1 E & E 969.

[239] *Bryans* v. *Nix* (1839) 4 M & W 775; *Anderson* v. *Morice*, n. 235 above. See however *Colonial Insurance Co. of New Zealand* v. *Adelaide Marine Insurance Co.* (1886) 12 App. Cas. 128 where the court was plainly concerned to give the buyer an insurable interest in cargo

Assent

Rule 5(1) requires the assent of one party to the other's unconditional appropriation.[240] It may take the form of an authority given by the buyer to the seller to appropriate, as where the contract calls for payment against shipping documents[241] Or it may be given by a third party, such as the carrier,[242] acting thus as agent for the buyer. A seller delivering to a carrier other than the one nominated by the buyer will therefore not have the buyer's assent to the unconditional appropriation.[243] The assent is often implied: in *Pignataro* v. *Gilroy*,[244] the court was prepared to find the buyer's assent in his failure to respond for a month to the seller's notification that the goods were ready for collection. Yet the assent is real enough:[245] even an unlawful repudiation of the contract by the buyer will effectively withdraw his assent to an unconditional appropriation by the seller.[246] Denied the buyer's co-operation in the passing of property, the seller is unable to sue for the price as a debt[247] and must be content with a damages action for non-acceptance of the goods. The absence of an earlier assent by the buyer has prevented the property from passing even though the goods have been marked in some way with the buyer's name.[248] Where the assent given is express and takes place after the seller has appropriated the goods, that act of appropriation is more likely to be treated as unconditional than a similar appropriation preceded by an implied assent.[249]

Assent needs to be considered in connection with the buyer's right of examination of the goods,[250] which has had an impact on both the passing of property and the buyer's right to reject non-conforming goods. In the last century, it was common to assert that the buyer lost his right to reject by failing to examine the goods at or before delivery. If such an

loaded from time to time. The courts have not denied the incremental passing of property as goods are removed from storage: *Rohde* v. *Thwaites* (1827) 6 B & C 388; *Aldridge* v. *Johnson*, n. 220 above.

[240] See *Godts* v. *Rose*, n. 224 above; *Campbell* v. *Mersey Docks and Harbour Board* (1863) 14 CB(NS) 412, 415–16.

[241] *Ginner* v. *King* (1890) 7 TLR 140.

[242] *Blackburn on Sale* (2nd edn., Stevens, London, 1885 by J. C. Graham), 139–40.

[243] *Copp* v. *Rhindress* (1921) 67 DLR 782; *Pullan* v. *Speizman* (1921) 67 DLR 365.

[244] [1919] 1 KB 459.

[245] See *Jenner* v. *Smith* (1869) LR 4 CP 270; *Atkinson* v. *Bell* (1828) 8 B & C 277.

[246] *Sells Ltd* v. *Thomson Stationery Ltd* (1914) 6 WWR 731; *Butterick Publishing Co.* v. *White & Walker* (1914) 6 WWR 1394; *Mason & Risch Ltd* v. *Christner* (1918) 44 OLR 146, affd. (1920) 48 OLR 8 (Can.) (revocation of seller's agency to make unconditional appropriation).

[247] *White & Carter (Councils) Ltd* v. *McGregor* [1962] AC 413.

[248] *Xenos* v. *Wickham* (1867) LR 2 HL 296, 316; *Mucklow* v. *Mangles* (1808) 1 Taunt 318. Or designed for the buyer's special use: *Atkinson* v. *Bell*, n. 245 above.

[249] See *Xenos* v. *Wickham*, n. 248 above; *Donaghy's Rope and Twine Co.* v. *Wright Stephenson & Co.* (1906) 25 NZLR 641.

[250] S. 34. Discussed Ch. 5 below.

examination did take place, it could be regarded as providing the buyer's assent to the seller's unconditional appropriation of the goods.[251] The relaxation of the buyer's right of examination, so as to permit it and a concomitant rejection of the goods to take place upon their arrival, may explain why, until it became clear that the passing of the property was no bar to a later rejection of the goods,[252] some courts held that the property did not pass before examination.[253] Examination may therefore have encouraged courts generally to conclude that the property passed later rather than sooner in the case of unascertained goods.

The different delivery obligations of the seller have a bearing upon the moment property passes. We have seen that where the buyer is to take delivery of the goods from the seller's premises, a number of cases hold that the property passes even before such delivery takes place. Where the seller undertakes personally to deliver the goods to the buyer's establishment or residence, there appears to be no general rule, the property in some cases passing before delivery[254] and in others upon delivery to the buyer at destination.[255] The passing of property upon delivery is a likely construction where the sale is not on credit terms and the buyer is to pay upon receipt of the goods.

Rule 5(2) and Carriers

Where an independent carrier is employed by the parties, the position is dealt with by Rule 5(2) in these terms:

Where, in pursuance of the contract, the seller delivers the goods to the buyer or to a carrier or other bailee or custodier (whether named by the buyer or not) for the purpose of transmission to the buyer, and does not reserve the right of disposal, he is to be taken to have unconditionally appropriated the goods to the contract.

Though its relationship to Rule 5(1) is not expressly stated, Rule 5(2) appears to be a particular application of the former rule. With its reference to the right of disposal,[256] Rule 5(2) could fairly be read as meaning that the property passes no later than delivery to the carrier, leaving Rule 5(1) satisfied if, for example, the buyer has expressly assented to an

---

[251] *Naugle Pole & Tie Co.* v. *Wilson* [1929] 3 WWR 730. Examination could also be assent to a later ascertainment from a specific bulk: *Rohde* v. *Thwaites*, n. 239 above. Cf. *Wardar's Import and Export Co. Ltd* v. *W Norwood & Sons Ltd* [1968] 2 QB 663.

[252] *Colonial Insurance Co. of New Zealand* v. *Adelaide Marine Insurance Co*, n. 239 above; *McDougall* v. *Aeromarine of Emsworth Ltd* [1958] 1 WLR 1126.

[253] e.g. *Perkins* v. *Bell* [1893] 1 QB 193.

[254] *Pletts* v. *Beattie* [1896] 1 QB 519; *Furby* v. *Hoey* [1947] 1 All ER 206.

[255] *Noblett* v. *Hopkinson* [1905] 2 KB 214 (*semble*); *Caradoc Nurseries Ltd* v. *Marsh* (1959) 19 DLR (2d) 491; *Coupland* v. *Elmore* [1928] 1 WWR 380; *R.* v. *Chappus* (1920) 48 OLR 189 (Can.).

[256] See s. 19 (shipping documents transferred after delivery to carrier).

appropriation before the goods are placed in the carrier's hands. Nevertheless, the effect of enacting Rule 5(2) in specific terms is to make it hard to argue that the property passes before delivery.[257] It may pass of course after delivery if the seller still has duties to perform.[258] In Canadian decisions where the seller's delivery duty is expressed as f.o.b. the place of destination, the courts have decisively rejected the argument that the expression f.o.b. is designed only to indicate that the seller is to pay for the cost of carriage.[259] Instead, they have held that the term indicates an intention to defer the passing of property.[260] Rule 5(2) applies only to carriers and not to warehouses. Consequently, where a warehouse attorns to the buyer, the property should pass at that time and before the buyer collects the goods.[261]

RESERVING THE RIGHT OF DISPOSAL

The purpose of section 19 is to counter the presumptive passing of property rules in section 18, which it does by stating that contracting for the sale of specific goods, or appropriating[262] goods to a contract for unascertained goods, will not pass the property if the seller reserves the right of disposal. The draftsman might simply have left the matter to be determined by an application of the intention rule in section 17, which overrides the presumptive rules in section 18, but the additional text in section 19 has the merit of avoiding doubts about implied intention. The reservation of the right of disposal most often concerns unascertained goods and delays the passing of property after a delivery or constructive delivery. But it can also affect specific goods where, given that presumptively the property passes at the date of the contract, it may happen before delivery.[263] Where the contract is for unascertained goods, the

---

[257] *Carlos Federspiel & Co. SA* v. *Charles Twigg & Co. Ltd* [1957] 1 Lloyd's Rep. 240; *Atkinson* v. *Plimpton* (1903) 6 OLR 566 (Can.); *William Blackley Ltd* v. *Elite Costumes Ltd* (1905) 9 OLR 382. The Post Office is a carrier for this purpose: *Badische Anilin und Soda Fabrik* v. *Basle Chemical Works* [1898] AC 200. The rule is of course subject to a contrary intention: *Mooney* v. *Lipka* [1926] 4 DLR 647; *National Coal Board* v. *Gamble* [1959] 1 QB 11. The court declined to find a contrary intention where it was the seller's practice to insure goods dispatched to its customers in *H. B. McGuiness Ltd* v. *Dunford* (1958) 13 DLR (2d) 622.

[258] *National Coal Board* v. *Gamble*, n. 257 above (weighing the goods).

[259] *Winnipeg Fish Co.* v. *Whitman Fish Co.* (1909) 41 SCTR 453; *Steel Co. of Canada Ltd* v. *The Queen* [1955] SCR 161; *Beaver Specialty Ltd* v. *Donald H Bain Ltd* (1973) 39 DLR (3d) 574. If the delivery term were f.o.b. the place of shipment, the buyer would have to arrange and pay for freight.

[260] See also *Re Grainex Canada Ltd* (1987) 34 DLR (4th) 646.

[261] *Laurie and Morewood* v. *Dudin and Sons* [1926] 1 KB 223; *Wardar's Import and Export Co. Ltd* v. *W. Norwood & Sons Ltd* [1968] 2 QB 663.

[262] *Sc.* unconditional appropriation.

[263] *Re Shipton, Anderson & Co. and Harrison & Co.* [1915] 3 KB 676. Reserving the right of disposal of specific goods may not happen after the contract date if the property has

seller may reserve the right of disposal unilaterally by taking the requisite action. If a seller reserves the right of disposal when he was bound, under the contract, to appropriate the goods unconditionally on delivering them to the carrier, the seller's action will be no less effective as a reservation for that reason.[264]

Reserving the right of disposal is commonly done in documentary international sales of unascertained goods taking place on f.o.b., c.i.f. or similar terms, the very case contemplated by the section.[265] Despite delivery to the carrier, who is presumptively the agent of the buyer,[266] the property will normally pass when shipping documents are subsequently tendered to the buyer in return for payment. A more prolonged form of security for payment is the conditional sale, whereby the property passes upon payment of the last instalment due under the contract. Unlike the functionally similar hire purchase and equipment leasing transactions, this transaction is governed by the Sale of Goods Act. In recent years, trade suppliers of goods have developed an appreciation of their rights under the Sale of Goods Act. The practice has grown of sellers expressly retaining the property in goods after delivery. In order to bridge the gap between the short commercial life of the contract goods and the eventual date of payment, sellers have also sought by a variety of drafting devices to acquire rights in goods made by the buyer with the aid of the contract goods, or in the proceeds of a sub-sale of these or the original contract goods.[267]

Where the seller reserves the right of disposal after delivering the goods to the carrier, the normal reason is that the seller is seeking security for the payment of the price,[268] though there are other reasons. For example, a seller may wish to pledge the bill of lading issued by the carrier as security for a loan bridging the period between delivery and payment by the buyer,[269] or may wish for tactical reasons to delay as long as

already passed. The seller does not have the unilateral right to divest the buyer of the general property.

[264] *Gabarron* v. *Kreeft* (1875) LR 10 Ex. 274. See also *The San Nicholas* [1976] 1 Lloyd's Rep. 8, where the contract provided for the property to pass upon shipment but the sellers took out a bill of lading providing for delivery to their own order. Lord Denning thought there was at least a *prima facie* case that the property in the goods passed upon the transfer of the bill of lading. But surely there would have to be evidence of the sellers' intention to reserve the right of disposal, just as it is a matter of intention whether and to what extent property rights are transferred with the bill of lading: *Sewell* v. *Burdick* (1884) 10 App. Cas. 74.

[265] S. 19(2),(3).

[266] This is true of f.o.b. contracts (*Wait* v. *Baker* (1848) 2 Ex. 1) but clearly a fiction in the case of c.i.f. buyers (Ch. 6 below).

[267] Discussed in the text accompanying nn. 314 ff. below.

[268] *Wait* v. *Baker*, n. 266 above.

[269] *The Albazero* [1977] AC 774; *Ross T. Smyth & Co. Ltd* v. *T. D. Bailey, Son & Co.* [1940] 3 All ER 60.

possible the appropriation of the goods to contracts with different consignees.[270]

In international sales, reserving the right of disposal occurs most often in the presumptive case set out in section 19(2), namely where an order bill of lading[271] naming the seller (or an agent, such as a bank) as consignee is issued by the carrier and retained by the seller.[272] A seller taking a bill of lading in this form is free to indorse it at a later date in favour of the buyer who will need it to take delivery of the goods from the carrier at the port of discharge. It is a question of fact whether a particular seller's behaviour accords with this presumed intention.[273] In *The Albazero*, Brandon J at first instance[274] saw ample evidence to rebut any presumption that the sellers had reserved the right of disposal in order to secure payment by the buyers. The sellers, a major oil company, did not intend to pledge the bill of lading or tender it for cash payment from the buyer; the oil had been sold on credit; and sellers and buyers were associated companies. Nevertheless, because the stated destination in the bill of lading was 'Gibraltar for orders', whereas the contractual destination was Antwerp, Brandon J concluded, in view of the sellers' manifest desire to keep for as long as possible their strategic freedom to divert the cargo to another customer at a different port of discharge, that the presumed intention in section 19(2) to reserve the right of disposal had not been rebutted.

Nature of the Seller's Reservation

Section 19 does not say precisely what is the proprietary effect of reserving the right of disposal, and the lack of explicit connection between this section and the previous sections dealing with the passing of property is

---

[270] *The Albazero*, n. 269 above (Brandon J).

[271] Though the statutory presumption does not apply, a seller on the facts is likely to reserve the right of disposal when retaining other delivery documents such as delivery warrants and orders which, though not documents of title at common law, are in fact effective means of securing delivery from carriers and other bailees. Also if the seller consigns goods to himself under a non-negotiable waybill, reserving the right to give the carrier fresh delivery instructions.

[272] Before the enactment of the statutory presumption, the Court of Exchequer Chamber in *Browne* v. *Hare* (1859) 4 H & N 822 had declined to overturn a jury finding that the taking out of a bill of lading 'unto shippers' order or their assigns' did not show an intention to reserve the general property. The approach of the court was coloured by its view that a seller who reserved the right of disposal could not be said to have shipped the goods *free* on board as required by the contract, a view that would not be entertained today: see *Mitsui & Co. Ltd* v. *Flota Mercante Grancolombiana SA (The Ciudad de Pasto)* [1988] 2 Lloyd's Rep. 208, 213.

[273] *Browne* v. *Hare*, n. 272 above. The reservation must not occur too late or the seller will be taken to have unconditionally appropriated the goods: *Ogle* v. *Atkinson* (1814) 5 Taunt. 759.

[274] N. 269 above, 799.

curious. If securing payment of the price were the only reason for this arrangement, it could plausibly be argued that the unpaid seller needs no more than a lien[275] over the shipping documents after unconditionally appropriating the goods on delivery to the carrier. The bill of lading is the only effective way in which the goods can be constructively handled in transit[276] and the carrier is both entitled and bound to deliver the goods only to the lawful holder of the bill of lading.[277] Even if the property has passed to the buyer, an unpaid seller would be able to rescind the contract and resell the goods in the circumstances provided for by section 48[278] and would be able to negotiate the bill of lading made out in his name to a second buyer. The problem with this reasoning is that, if a lien were all that the seller obtained, one would expect to see section 19 refer explicitly to lien and the section itself located in that part of the Act dealing with the real rights of the unpaid seller. Further, in the case of a seller who pledges shipping documents, a lien interest in the underlying goods would not be enough because a lien is not transferable[279] and the pledgee would obtain no interest in the goods for the advance to the seller.[280] Hence, it makes sense for such a seller to retain the general property when reserving the right of disposal. Moreover, a seller who has not appropriated the goods to a particular contract of sale when the bill of lading is issued cannot but be treated as having reserved the general property.[281] Although the requirements of sections 16 to 18 for the passing of propery have not been met, it should be noted that such a seller will often be factually or legally committed to tendering the shipping documents under a particular contract. For example, a seller with an unappropriated shipment in hand and an f.o.b. contract to perform may not be able to find another shipment for that contract within the time allowed by the contract for delivery, or may not be able to find another cargo on the same ship, which was nominated by the buyer and has now left port. In some circumstances, the act of shipping goods that accord with a particular contract may be seen as an election by the seller to appropriate the shipment to that contract.[282] It should be otherwise if the seller has more than one contract to perform under which this

---

[275] S. 41.

[276] But by notices of appopriation, the goods may be made the subject of repeated c.i.f. contracts in string trading conditions.

[277] Ch. 6 below. [278] Ch. 10 below.

[279] *Donald* v. *Suckling* (1866) LR 1 QB 585; *Franklin* v. *Neate* (1844) 13 M & W 481 (but see the discussion of mercantile agency and the factor's lien: Ch. 9 below). A lienee cannot sell the lien, nor may it be taken in execution by a sheriff: *Legg* v. *Evans* (1840) 6 M & W 36. Although a lienee has no power of sale at common law (*Thames Iron Works Co.* v. *Patent Derrick Co.* (1860) 1 J & H 93), a seller in these cicumstances would resort to the power of sale in s. 48.

[280] *Van Casteel* v. *Booker* (1848) 2 Ex. 691. [281] *The Albazero*, n. 269 above.

[282] *Wait* v. *Baker*, n. 266 above, 9 (500 qtrs of barley).

shipment could have been made. In a c.i.f. string, a seller relaying a notice of appropriation becomes contractually committed to supply documents concerning goods on the named ship.

The cases recognizing that the seller has reserved the right of disposal usually treat the seller as having retained the general property in full,[283] the implication being that the buyer has no proprietary interest. As will later be seen, the buyer in such cases commonly bears the risk from an earlier date and therefore has an insurable interest in the goods, which may be referred to ambiguously as though it were a property interest.[284] In a minority of cases the buyer is recognized as having at least some interest in the goods by way of a derogation from any general property of the seller.[285] One case refers to the seller as having (only) a 'hold' over the goods, going beyond the 'right to retain possession' and involving a power of resale on default by the buyer.[286]

If it were felt that in some cases the seller needs no more than a lien over the shipping documents then, instead of trying to diminish the proprietary effects of reserving the right of disposal, an alternative approach would be to deny that the seller has reserved the right of disposal at all. The rebuttable presumption in section 19(2) has been stated to be a weak one where payment is the only goal sought.[287] It has been rebutted where the seller's purpose in taking out an order bill of lading in his own name was because he feared the buyer would reject the goods and so wished to make certain he had an insurable interest in them.[288] But the presumption was not rebutted in one case where the seller procured from the master of the buyer's own ship a bill of lading deliverable to order.[289]

Non-statutory Examples of Reservation

Outside the express language of section 19(2), the right of disposal was held to have been reserved where the seller, refused to comply with the

---

[283] *James* v. *The Commonwealth* (1939) 62 CLR 339, 378; *Wait* v. *Baker*, n. 266 above; *Mirabita* v. *Imperial Ottoman Bank* (1878) 3 Ex. D 164 (Cotton LJ); *The Miramichi* [1915] P 71; *The Prinz Adalbert* [1917] AC 586. In *Ross T. Smyth*, n. 269 above, 68, Lord Wright thought it essential.

[284] This seems the best explanation of the judgment of Bramwell LJ in *Mirabita*, n. 283 above.

[285] In *Van Casteel* v. *Booker*, n. 280 above, where the goods had been loaded on the buyer's own ship, the court was content to say only that the reserving seller had preserved his right of stoppage *in transitu*.

[286] *Ogg* v. *Shuter* (1875) 1 CPD 47, 50–1 (Lord Cairns LC).

[287] *The Parchim* [1918] AC 157, 170–1, referred to as decided on 'very special facts' in *The Kronprinsessan Margareta* [1921] 1 AC 486, 516 (Lord Sumner).

[288] *Joyce* v. *Swann* (1864) 17 CBNS 84. See also *The Albazero*, n. 269 above.

[289] *Van Casteel* v. *Booker*, n. 280 above: seller's right of stoppage therefore preserved when otherwise it would have been lost since a delivery to the buyer's ship is a delivery to the buyer. See also *Turner* v. *Liverpool Docks Trustees* (1851) 6 Ex. 453.

contract by shipping goods on the buyer's account, but instead procured the issuance of the bill of lading naming a fictitious person as consignee.[290] A reservation has also been recognized where goods are stated in the bill of lading to be simply deliverable to order.[291] Where the bill of lading is made out to buyer or order, the act of the seller in retaining possession of the bill of lading in this form is likely to be treated as a reservation,[292] but not if the evidence shows the seller intended the buyer to have the general property.[293] As a matter of principle, there is something to be said for the view that the seller thereby retains only a lien over the shipping documents since, while the contract remains on foot, the goods cannot be appropriated to any other contract of sale. Nevertheless, while still the holder of the bill of lading, the seller may indorse the bill so as to require the carrier to deliver to a different named consignee.[294] There seems no reason, therefore, to distinguish different cases of reservation of the right of disposal according to the named consignee.

Bill of Lading and Bill of Exchange

Even if the bill of lading is delivered to the buyer, it does not follow that the seller thereby surrenders the right of disposal. Section 19(3) states that, where the seller transmits the bill of lading to the buyer together with a draft bill of exchange for the price, the buyer must return the bill of lading if he does not accept the draft.[295] The provision makes no distinction between bills of lading naming the buyer or those naming the seller as consignee. It further provides that the property in the goods does not pass to the buyer who wrongfully retains the bill of lading, which codifies those cases that more precisely held that the seller's intention to pass the property to the buyer is conditional upon the buyer's acceptance of the draft.[296] The proprietary consequences of a bill

---

[290] *Gabarron* v. *Kreeft* (1875) LR 10 Ex. 274.

[291] *James* v. *The Commonwealth*, n. 283 above, 380; *Shepherd* v. *Harrison* (1871) LR 5 HL 116, 128, 131; *Van Casteel* v. *Booker*, n. 280 above.

[292] *Hansson* v. *Hamel and Horley Ltd* [1922] 2 AC 36, 43 (Lord Sumner); *The Kronprinsessan Margareta*, n. 287 above. Note that in *Arnhold Karberg & Co.* v. *Blythe Green Jourdain & Co.* [1915] 2 KB 379, 387, Scrutton J states that in such a case the buyer acquires the general property on tendering the price whereas, in other cases where the right of disposal is reserved, the property passes upon payment.

[293] *Ladenburg & Co.* v. *Goodwin, Ferreira & Co.* [1912] 3 KB 275: also stating that the transfer of the general property did not affect the right of stoppage in transit for non-payment.

[294] *Mitchell* v. *Ede* (1840) 11 Ad. & E 888, 903; *Elder Dempster Lines Ltd* v. *Zaki Ishag* [1983] 2 Lloyd's Rep. 548, 555.

[295] The buyer has no lien over the bill of lading for any freight paid: *Rew* v. *Payne Douthwaite* (1885) 53 LT 932.

[296] *Shepherd* v. *Harrison*, n. 291 above; *Brandt* v. *Bowlby* (1831) 2 B & Ad. 932; *Jenkyns* v. *Brown* (1849) 14 QB 496; *Wilmshurst* v. *Bowker* (1841) LJCP 161. Cf. *Key* v. *Colesworth* (1852) 7 Ex. 594.

of lading being indorsed and delivered depend upon the intention of the indorser.[297] The seller may intend not to pass the property to the buyer[298] though there is a strong presumption that this was intended where the seller indorses and delivers a bill of lading to the buyer.[299] Even if no property interest passes to the buyer on the indorsement and delivery of a bill of lading, the buyer will be a buyer in possession of a document of title and thus empowered to transfer good title to a *bona fide* purchaser.[300]

Reservation of Title Clauses

In domestic sales, it is common for unpaid sellers to reserve the right of disposal after delivery to the buyer by means of a *Romalpa* clause, which takes its name from the leading modern case that focused attention on the seller's right of reservation.[301] The practice developed because unpaid sellers, permitting the property to pass in the conventional way under section 18, find themselves at a disadvantage upon the insolvency of the buyer. The first call on the buyer's assets will come from secured and preference creditors, and the seller will join other unsecured creditors in receiving on average a very small insolvency dividend hardly worth the expense of lodging a proof with the buyer's liquidator or trustee in bankruptcy.[302] The great advantage to a seller of reserving the general property in the goods is that, until the property passes, no ownership rights vest in the buyer and therefore the goods cannot fall within a security granted by the buyer, before or after the contract of sale is concluded, to one or more creditors, or vest in the liquidator or trustee. A further advantage is that a property reservation clause need not be registered in the way that a security by way of charge or mortgage has to be if a secured creditor is to be able to assert his rights against third parties and the liquidator or trustee of the grantor of the security.[303]

---

[297] *Sewell* v. *Burdick* (1884) 10 App. Cas. 74; *Sanders Bros.* v. *Maclean & Co.* (1883) 11 QBD 327; *Burgos* v. *Nascimento* (1908) 11 LT 71; *The Orteric* [1920] AC 274.

[298] *Leigh and Sillavan Ltd* v. *Aliakmon Shipping Ltd* [1986] AC 785.

[299] *Dracachi* v. *Anglo-Egyptian Navigation Co.* (1868) LR 3 CP 190; rebutted in *Aliakmon Shipping*, n. 298 above.

[300] Under s. 25(1) of the Sale of Goods Act or s. 9 of the Factors Act 1889. See *Cahn* v. *Pockett's Bristol Channel Steam Packet Co. Ltd* [1899] 1 QB 643.

[301] *Aluminium Industrie Vaassen BV* v. *Romalpa Aluminium Ltd* [1976] 1 WLR 676. See generally G. McCormack, *Reservation of Title* (2nd edn., Sweet & Maxwell, London, 1995); S. Wheeler, *Reservation of Title Clauses* (OUP, London, 1991); *Palmer's Company Law* (ed. G. K. Morse and others, Sweet & Maxwell, London, looseleaf), ii, ch. 13; L. S. Sealy and R. J. A. Hooley, *Text and Materials in Commercial Law* (Butterworths, London, 1994), 407–25; N. Palmer (1993) 6 *J of Cont. Law* 175.

[302] The treatment given to unsecured creditors is criticized as a 'raw deal' by Templeman LJ in *Borden (UK) Ltd* v. *Scottish Timber Products Ltd* [1981] Ch. 25, 42.

[303] Companies Act 1985, ss. 395 ff.

An inherent limitation on the seller's rights is that goods supplied tend to depreciate, or else they have an ephemeral existence before being resold or consumed or transformed in identity by the buyer. To counter this limitation, sellers have drafted clauses purporting: (a) to reserve by an 'all moneys' clause the general property in goods supplied until the whole of the buyer's indebtedness to the seller, and not just the price owed for the goods supplied, has been paid off; (b) to reserve rights in goods newly manufactured by the buyer that incorporate the goods supplied by the seller; (c) to claim the proceeds of sale of goods resold by the buyer.[304] In summary, sellers have been successful with adequately drafted clauses (including all moneys clauses) to the extent of the original goods supplied, but have failed in their attempts to reserve property rights in money proceeds and newly manufactured goods. They have been unable to persuade courts that these extended rights are truly reserved rights as opposed to rights granted by the buyer, with the consequence that courts have characterized sellers' efforts as charges. Since unpaid sellers invariably fail to register these extended rights as charges, they are worthless in the event of the buyer's insolvency or receivership. This is understood if not always stated in the cases: a seller unsuccessful in reserving the general property is plainly seen to have lost despite the empty compensation of having a charge over the assets of the buyer. A further complicating feature of *Romalpa* litigation, rendering it difficult to make universal statements, is that the scope of the seller's rights may be affected by concessions made in the course of litigation and by the particular language used in the clause.

Where the contract goods remain in the buyer's possession in an unaltered state, the courts have given effect to a simple reservation clause, even if the buyer is given liberty to transform or consume the goods before payment is made.[305] This accords with sections 17 to 19 of the Sale of Goods Act, which make it plain that the property cannot pass to the buyer without the co-operation of the seller.[306] Provided the seller's intention is clear, it does not matter if other parts of a clause expressing this intention operate as a charge on the buyer's assets.[307] No particular words need be used by the seller, for example, describing the buyer as an agent, bailee[308] or fiduciary. If, however, the seller purports to reserve

---

[304] For a more elaborate classification of these clauses, see G. McCormack, *Reservation of Title* n. 301 above, 2.

[305] *Romalpa*, n. 301 above; *Clough Mill Ltd* v. *Martin* [1985] 1 WLR 111.

[306] Note that s. 19(1) refers to the seller reserving the right of disposal 'by the terms of the contract *or appropriation* (emphasis added)'. Even if the seller has contracted to pass the property to the buyer at an earlier date, yet his action in reserving the right of disposal may be effective to inhibit the passing of property.

[307] *Clough Mill Ltd* v. *Martin*, n. 305 above.

[308] An inappropriate way to describe a buyer in possession: *E. Pfeiffer Weinkellerei-Weinenkauf GmbH* v. *Arbuthnot Factors Ltd* [1988] 1 WLR 150; *Borden (UK) Ltd* v. *Scottish*

'equitable or beneficial ownership', this has been held to be a charge.[309] The reason is that the clause amounts to an outright transfer of the general property to the buyer, coupled with a grant back to the seller of the beneficial ownership in the goods. The premise given for this two-stage analysis, that the bare legal title cannot directly be conveyed to the buyer, is not as a matter of principle to be reconciled with the decision of the House of Lords in *Abbey National Building Soc.* v. *Cann*,[310] that the equitable interest of a mortgagee building society in a dwelling was carved out of the ownership of the dwelling before the proprietary residue[311] vested directly in the buyer granting the mortgage. There was no *scintilla temporis* in which full legal and beneficial ownership vested in the buyer before the grant to the building society. Nevertheless, the pitfall presented by *Re Bond Worth Ltd*[312] is easily avoided if the clause by one means or another makes it plain that the seller is reserving the general property in the goods.[313]

Altered Goods

For the reservation clause to remain effective, the goods have to retain their identity, which will be lost if they are irrevocably attached to a larger chattel or if they are so altered by the manufacturing process that they cannot be said to be the goods supplied by the seller. In the case of irrevocable attachment (or *accessio*), the rule is that ownership of the lesser thing vests in the owner of the greater thing. In *Hendy Lennox (Industrial Engines) Ltd* v. *Grahame Puttick Ltd*,[314] the incorporation of diesel engines identified by serial numbers in generator sets did not amount to *accessio* because the process could be reversed by several hours' work without damaging the separated parts. Where goods are altered in the manufacturing process and lose their identity, it is a case of *specificatio*, and the operator, whose labour brings about the alteration, becomes the owner.[315] It is a question of degree whether the goods have been sufficiently altered to lose their identity. Thus the identity of the goods supplied is lost where fibre was worked into yarn and subsequently into

---

Timber Products Ltd, n. 301 above(Bridge LJ). *Aliter Clough Mill Ltd* v. *Martin*, n. 305 above, 116 (Robert Goff LJ).

[309]   *Re Bond Worth Ltd* [1980] Ch. 228.

[310]   [1991] 1 AC 56, overruling *Church of England Building Soc.* v. *Piskor* [1954] Ch. 533. See R. Gregory (1990) 106 *LQR* 551. But *Re Bond Worth Ltd*, n. 309 above, was said to survive *Abbey National Building Soc.* v. *Cann* in *Stroud Architectural Systems Ltd* v. *John Laing Construction Ltd* [1994] BCC 18.

[311]   The bare legal title plus the equity of redemption.   [312]   N. 309 above.

[313]   It should avoid any reference to equitable or beneficial ownership.

[314]   [1984] 2 All ER 152.

[315]   *Chaigley Farms Ltd* v. *Crawford, Kaye & Grayshire Ltd* [1996] BCC 957.

carpet,[316] leather is cut and stitched into handbags,[317] and resin incorporated in chipboard.[318] In the last case, the court declined to trace the resin into the chipboard so as to give the seller a shared interest in the final product; it was impossible to work out the contributions of seller and buyer to that product. Some generosity to the unpaid seller is to be found in one case deciding that logs retained their identity despite being cut into planks[319] and in another that goods surrender their original identity when they lose all significant value as raw materials, the implication being that some degree of transformation by the buyer's efforts is not fatal to that original identity.[320] Where goods are supplied and blended by the buyer with identical goods, then, subject to a tenancy in common argument, it will be difficult for the seller to assert that a title retention clause remains effective.[321]

All-moneys Clauses

An all-moneys clause, by which the seller reserves the general property until all the buyer's indebtedness to the seller is paid off, will be effective. The rules in the Sale of Goods Act making the passing of property a matter of contractual intention are not confined to payment of the contract price. This was confirmed by the House of Lords in *Armour* v. *Thyssen Edelstahlwerke AG*.[322] Where a seller supplies the buyer on a recurring basis, it means that past indebtedness can always be brought forward and attached to any goods of the seller in the buyer's possession, even if part or the whole of the price for these goods has been paid. The effectiveness of this approach to reservation demands that the clause be inserted in all contracts for the supply of goods to the buyer since the seller cannot know in what order the buyer will consume those supplies. It was the view of the House of Lords in *Armour* that a seller availing himself of his reservation rights and repossessing the goods was under no obligation to account to the buyer for any surplus realised on resale exceeding the buyer's indebtedness.[323] This is certainly the case where the seller terminates the contract of sale for the buyer's discharging breach[324] but it has been said that a seller will have to account for any

---

[316] *Re Bond Worth Ltd*, n. 309 above.   [317] *Re Peachdart Ltd* [1984] Ch. 131.
[318] *Borden (UK) Ltd* v. *Scottish Timber Products Ltd*, n. 302 above.
[319] *Pongakawa Sawmill Ltd* v. *New Zealand Forest Products Ltd* [1992] 3 NZLR 304.
[320] *Modelboard Ltd* v. *Outer Box Ltd* [1992] BCC 945.
[321] But see *Forsythe International (UK) Ltd* v. *Silver Shipping Co. Ltd* [1994] 1 WLR 1334, 1338, where it was common ground between the parties that the title retention clause of a supplier of bunker fuels was still good against a charterer purchasing the fuels, even though (*semble*) the fuels were mixed with bunker fuels already on board ship.
[322] [1991] AC 339.   [323] Cf. the position of a mortgagee.
[324] *Clough Mill Ltd* v. *Martin*, n. 305 above. But a buyer unable to recover surplus value might have a restitutionary right to the recovery of excessive sums paid: Robert Goff LJ, *ibid.*

surplus in the (unlikely) event of the contract remaining on foot at all times.[325] A seller is most likely to realize a surplus where durable items have been supplied on various occasions under the terms of all-moneys clauses, or where part of the price of appreciating goods has been paid.[326] Any attempt to make the seller account for a surplus comes close to treating him as a mortgagee realising his security and to treating the reservation itself as a registrable charge.

The above view of the seller's entitlement to retain resale moneys, applicable to all-moneys and simple reservation clauses, is entirely orthodox: the effect of the clause is that the seller reserves the full legal property until the attached condition has been met by the buyer. The buyer does not have a property interest in the goods, though there may be in rare circumstances relief from forfeiture of his possessory interest given to a buyer prepared to pay the sum due.[327] To succeed, the buyer[328] must show that the principal purpose of the reservation clause was to secure payment of the price by the buyer pursuant to the contract. This requirement should not pose a great problem in practice, but the buyer will usually be in severe difficulties in further showing a substantial windfall to the seller over and above the sum due under the contract.[329]

Extended Title Reservation

It was stated above that a seller, relying upon a simple reservation clause, may not follow the goods once they lose their identity in the manufacturing process. But what is the effect of a clause that purports to reserve in the seller the general property in those newly manufactured goods? Robert Goff LJ in *Clough Mill Ltd* v. *Martin*[330] gave considerable comfort to the draftsmen of such extended clauses. That case involved various consignments of yarn that had not lost their identity, but the reservation clause stated that the ownership of the yarn 'shall be and remain with' the seller even if the yarn were 'incorporated in or used as material for other goods'. Robert Goff LJ had difficulty seeing why such a clause, vesting the property in new goods in the seller from the moment of their creation, amounted to the conferment by the buyer of a right on the seller by way of charge, even though, but for the clause, the rules of property law would have vested ownership of the new goods in the buyer. With

---

[325] *Ibid*. Robert Goff LJ attributes the seller's duty to account to an implied term in the contract. But it is not easy to see why the implication of such a term should be necessary to give business efficacy to the contract or why it should apply only if the contract has not been terminated. See also N. Palmer (1993) 6 *J of Cont. Law* 175, 182–3.

[326] *Clough Mill Ltd* v. *Martin* [1985] 1 WLR 111 (Robert Goff LJ).   [327] Ch. 10 below.

[328] More likely receiver or liquidator bringing proceedings in the buyer's name.

[329] *Transag Haulage Ltd* v. *Leyland DAF Finance plc* [1994] BCC 356.

[330] N. 326 above.

respect, this reasoning is hard to support. It is the essence of a successful reservation clause that its effects require no proprietary input from the buyer: the seller declines to participate in the process of an assented to unconditional appropriation that would pass the property to the buyer under section 18, Rule 5. The clause referred to by Robert Goff LJ requires the buyer to surrender property rights to the new goods conferred by the rules of *accessio* and *specificatio*.[331] Furthermore, a different view of the matter was taken by Buckley LJ in *Borden (UK) Ltd* v. *Scottish Timber Products Ltd*[332] who thought it 'impossible' for the seller to reserve the property in a new item that 'originates' with the buyer. In this area of law, results speak louder than words. Robert Goff LJ himself went on to say that the above clause was in fact a charge. It gave no credit for any value added by the buyer in the form of labour and materials, and the learned judge could not believe the parties intended the seller would have the windfall benefit that would accrue under a reservation clause in a contract terminated for the buyer's discharging breach.[333] The prospect of two suppliers of raw materials, each relying upon a clause like that in *Clough Mill*, also pointed to its treatment as a charge despite the 'violence' this did to the language used.[334]

The remaining area of difficulty concerns the money proceeds of sub-sales of the goods[335] by the buyer. In *Aluminium Industrie Vaassen BV* v. *Romalpa Aluminium Ltd*,[336] a quantity of aluminium foil was supplied under a contract containing a clause providing that 'ownership ... will only be transferred to purchaser when he has met all that is owing' to the seller. The clause also stated that the buyer was 'fiduciary owner' of new goods made with the foil and had to 'hand over ... claims' against sub-buyers to the seller. The seller was held entitled to trace into the money proceeds from sales of the foil even though nothing was explicitly said in the contract about these proceeds. The court found between the buyer and the seller a fiduciary relationship, as required to trace in equity.[337] Roskill LJ, in particular, saw nothing inconsistent in a buyer disposing of the foil to a sub-buyer as principal whilst acting as the seller's agent or bailee.

Romalpa is a flawed decision. The seller conceded that the buyer held the foil as a bailee,[338] and it seems to have been assumed that bailees and

---

[331] As well as in cases of commingling.   [332] [1981] Ch. 25, 46.

[333] See also *Re Peachdart Ltd*, n. 317 above (where the parties, supplier of leather and manufacturer of handbags, 'must have intended' a charge); *Specialist Plant Services Ltd* v. *Braithwaite* [1987] BCLC 1; *Ian Chisholm Textiles Ltd* v. *Griffiths* [1994] BCC 96.

[334] *Clough Mill Ltd* v. *Martin*, n. 326 above (Robert Goff LJ).

[335] The same considerations would apply to the money proceeds of new goods in the unlikely event of the seller successfully demonstrating that the clause was not a charge.

[336] [1976] 1 WLR 676.

[337] See *Re Diplock* [1948] Ch. 465; *Chase Manhattan Bank NA* v. *Israel-British Bank Ltd* [1981] Ch. 105.

[338] *Re Bond Worth Ltd* [1980] Ch. 228 ('of crucial importance').

agents receive proceeds as fiduciaries in all cases. It was later stated that they only presumptively received proceeds as fiduciaries[339] and, more recently, even the existence of a presumption has been doubted.[340] Later cases, dealing with express proceeds clauses, have set down constraints to be satisfied if these clauses are not to be treated as registrable charges. These constraints, in practical terms impossible to satisfy,[341] drive home the message that it is not for the parties to deem their relationship to be a fiduciary one or one of agency if in objective commercial terms they are conducting an arm's length sale.[342]

The constraints are as follows. First, the seller must require the proceeds to be kept segregated from other assets of the buyer.[343] Secondly, to the extent the seller's interest in the proceeds is defeasible upon payment of the contract price, that interest will be regarded as a charge.[344] Thirdly, any requirement that the buyer shall account only for such proceeds as equal the price due under the sale contract will be regarded as inconsistent with the beneficial interest in the proceeds vesting first in the seller.[345] Fourthly, language in the sale contract requiring the seller to transfer or pass on claims against sub-buyers is not consistent with the seller's claim that those rights were vested in him from the date of their creation.[346] Fifthly, a fixed period of credit that does not match the cycle in which the buyer receives the proceeds of a resale will tend towards the conclusion that a proceeds clause amounts to a charge.[347] The obstacles facing the seller seeking a non-registrable interest in money proceeds seem insuperable.

---

[339] *Hendy Lennox (Industrial Engines) Ltd* v. *Grahame Puttick Ltd* [1984] 2 All ER 152, referring to *Boardman* v. *Phipps* [1967] AC 46, 127 (Lord Upjohn) and *Re Coomber* [1911] 1 Ch. 723. See also L. Sealy [1962] CLJ 69.

[340] *Re Andrabell Ltd* [1984] 3 All ER 407. See also *E. Pfeiffer Weinkellerei-Weinenkauf GmbH* v. *Arbuthnot Factors Ltd* [1988] 1 WLR 150. On the difficulty of establishing a fiduciary relationship in an ordinary sale contract see *Re Goldcorp Exchange Ltd* [1995] 1 AC 74; *Compaq Computer Ltd* v. *Abercorn Group Ltd* [1991] BCC 484.

[341] '[I]t is almost inevitable . . . that where the contract seeks to confer upon the seller a right to look for satisfaction of the price to property which is worth more than that amount (or to a sum of money which exceeds the price which is owed), the courts will construe the transaction as one involving a charge': L. S. Sealy and R. J. A. Hooley, *Text and Materials in Commercial Law* (Butterworths, London, 1994), 414.

[342] Cf. the more lenient attitude of the courts in other areas of the law relating to charges: *Welsh Development Agency* v. *Export Finance Co. Ltd* [1992] BCLC 48, with which contrast *Curtain Dream plc* v. *Churchill Merchanting Ltd* [1990] BCC 341.

[343] *Hendy Lennox (Industrial Engines) Ltd* v. *Grahame Puttick Ltd*, n. 339 above; *Re Andrabell Ltd*, n. 340 above.

[344] *Tatung (UK) Ltd* v. *Galex Telesure Ltd* (1989) 5 BCC 325; *Compaq Computer Ltd* v. *Abercorn Group Ltd*, n. 340 above.

[345] *Re Andrabell Ltd*, n. 340 above; *Pfeiffer Weinkellerei-Weinenkauf GmbH* v. *Arbuthnot Factors Ltd*, ibid.

[346] *E. Pfeiffer Weinkellerei-Weinenkauf GmbH* v. *Arbuthnot Factors Ltd*, n. 340 above.

[347] *Re Andrabell Ltd*, n. 340 above.

4

Risk, Mistake, and Frustration

Risk and frustration may conveniently be treated in proximity since the operation of frustration is bounded by the transfer of risk. Risk is associated with the price: it determines when the buyer must pay for goods accidentally damaged, lost or destroyed. Where a contract is frustrated, it is automatically discharged.[1] The primary effect of this is to excuse the party, usually the seller, whose performance is affected by the frustrating event from liability for breach of contract. The buyer would, even without the dissolving effect of frustration on the contract, usually have the defence of the seller's non-performance of a condition precedent.[2] Although the passage of risk to the buyer ousts the operation of frustration, frustration may still be in issue when risk remains with the seller. Since mistake[3] also deals with the same subject matter of material mishap to the goods, there is a tendency to apply it with the same degree of rigour as frustration as a contractual dispensing agent. It is therefore convenient to treat mistake and frustration in sequence. It is just possible for there also to be a degree of intersection between mistake and risk, though it is unlikely that any contract on its construction will transfer to the buyer the risk of loss occurring before the contract is even concluded.

---

[1] *Hirji Mulji* v. *Cheong Yue Steamship Co. Ltd* [1926] AC 497; *Bank Line Ltd* v. *Arthur Capel & Co.* [1919] AC 435; *Tamplin Steamship Co. Ltd* v. *Anglo-Mexican Petroleum Co.* [1916] 2 AC 397. The treatment of frustration in this text is necessarily limited. For further detail, consult the standard contract texts.

[2] e.g. the hirer of the music hall in *Taylor* v. *Caldwell* (1863) 3 B & S 826 need not have benefited from an implied condition, that the concert hall continue to exist, excusing both parties when the hall burnt down. It would be enough that the owner, unable to tender the hall to the hirer, could not comply with the condition precedent to the hirer's duty to pay. The burning down of the hall could be raised as a defence by the owner if sued by the hirer for failing to make the hall available as agreed. A similar approach to this is adopted by Art. 79 of the Vienna Convention on the International Sale of Goods 1980, which in stated conditions 'exempts' from liability the non-performing party leaving the other party's position to be determined by the performance and avoidance rules elsewhere stated in the Convention.

[3] Largely confined in this text to initial impossibility. For further detail, consult the standard contract texts.

RISK

Risk is dealt with in four sections of the Sale of Goods Act[4] which, though concerned with the location of risk between buyer and seller, is not at all explicit about its contractual consequences. Risk is a proprietary notion that has to be translated into the language of contractual rights and duties:[5]

The truth is that risk is a derivative, and essentially negative, concept—an elliptical way of saying that either or both of the primary obligations of one party shall be enforceable, and that those of the other party shall be deemed to have been discharged, even though the normally prerequisite conditions have not been satisfied. That is to say, the legal consequences attaching to 'the risk' fall to be defined purely in terms of the parties' other duties and the corresponding rights and remedies: the seller's right to claim the price, and the buyer's right to resist payment or demand its return; and the right to claim damages (*e.g.*, for non-delivery or non-acceptance) or to resist such a claim.

Meaning of Risk

Suppose goods are destroyed or damaged by an accidental fire while in the possession of a bailee, such as a warehouseman. If the risk of loss remains with the seller, the seller cannot call on the buyer to pay the price or sue for damages for the buyer's refusal to accept a tender of ashes or damaged goods.[6] The buyer is entitled to refuse a tender of defective goods and, if delivery has already occurred before the casualty to the goods, he will hold the goods at the disposal of the seller.[7] If the property has passed to the buyer while the risk remains with the seller, a possible though infrequent occurrence, the property, having passed only conditionally, will revest in the seller.[8] Further, if the buyer has already paid the price, he may recover this as money had and received on a failure of consideration. Despite its baneful effect in the past on the buyer's right to reject specific goods for breach of condition,[9] the passing of property has not prejudiced the buyer's claim where the risk has

---

[4] Ss. 7, 20, 32(3), and 33. It also appears inferentially in s. 32(2) where the buyer may displace the allocation of risk if the seller makes an unreasonable contract with the carrier on behalf of the buyer.

[5] L. Sealy [1972B] *Camb. LJ* 225, 226–7. On risk, see also Lawson (1949) 65 *LQR* 352; D. Fitzgerald (1996) 9 *J of Cont. Law* 206.

[6] Whether the seller would be liable for damages for non-delivery depends upon the operation of frustration.

[7] Subject to contrary agreement, the buyer need not return the goods to the seller: s. 36.

[8] *Head* v. *Tattersall* (1872) LR 7 Ex. 7; *May* v. *Conn* (1911) 23 OLR 102 (Can.); Sealy, n. 5, above 239.

[9] Ch. 3 above.

remained with the seller.[10] If the buyer elects to retain damaged but serviceable goods, or a lesser quantity than that agreed, there is authority supporting his recovery of a portion of the price paid.[11] And if in such a case he has not yet paid, the buyer would presumably pay the agreed price subject to an abatement for the affected goods.

If the risk of loss is on the buyer, the seller may sue for the price even though not fulfilling the normal preconditions for maintaining a price action. He will be unable to make a tender of sound goods, which is presumptively demanded before the buyer can be called upon to pay,[12] and if the risk is on the buyer but the property remains with the seller, he may be unable to appropriate the goods to the contract with the assent of the buyer, so as to comply with the usual requirement of a price action that the property have passed.[13] Besides the seller being deemed to have fulfilled all conditions precedent to an action for the price, the effect of risk being on the buyer is that he may not sue for damages for non-delivery.[14]

In some instances, the buyer's duty to pay may be conditioned either as to time or amount by an event that can no longer occur as a result of the accident to the goods. If the buyer was bound to pay so many days after delivery, which cannot now occur,[15] it seems reasonable to date this obligation from the time when delivery should otherwise have probably occurred.[16] Sometimes, the exact quantity of the goods on arrival or delivery serves to quantify the price. In *Martineau* v. *Kitching*,[17] the risk of loss of sugar loaves destroyed in a fire was on the buyer. Each loaf weighed between thirty-eight and forty-two pounds and the practice was for the buyer to pay on the prompt date either a sum equivalent to the actual weight, if delivery had already been made, or an approximate sum to be subsequently adjusted. The fire destroyed any chance of calculating the actual weight of the loaves but the buyer was bound to pay a sum 'ascertain[ed] . . . as nearly as you can'.[18] A similar case involved the arrival weight of a cargo of ice,[19] where the buyer's liability was to pay 'fair estimation of its value'[20] at the time the ship went down.

---

[10] *Head* v. *Tattersall*, n. 8, above 14.

[11] In the breach case of *Ebrahim Dawood Ltd* v. *Heath Ltd* [1961] 2 Lloyd's Rep. 512, where the buyer, electing to keep some of the goods tendered under the now-repealed s. 30(3), was allowed to recover that portion of the price corresponding to the rejected goods. See also *Devaux* v. *Connolly* (1849) 8 CB 640; *Behrend* v. *Produce Brokers Ltd* [1920] 3 KB 530; *Westdeutsche Landesbank* v. *Islington LBC* [1994] 1 WLR 938; Sealy, n. 5. above.

[12] S. 28 in concert with the various conditions dealing with description, fitness, and quality.

[13] S. 49(1).

[14] The seller will not 'wrongfully' have refused or neglected to deliver under s. 51(1).

[15] Cf. *Alexander* v. *Gardner* (1835) 1 Bing. NC 671.

[16] Sealy, n. 5 above, prefers payment to be made in 'a reasonable time'.

[17] (1872) LR 7 QB 436.   [18] *Ibid.*, 456.

[19] *Castle* v. *Playford* (1872) LR 7 Ex. 98.   [20] *Ibid.* 99.

Allocation of Risk

The main provision on the allocation of risk is section 20(1):

Unless otherwise agreed, the goods remain at the seller's risk until the property in them is transferred to the buyer, but when the property in them is transferred to the buyer the goods are at the buyer's risk whether delivery has been made or not.

Presumptively, therefore, risk and property march hand in hand[21] though it is the mark of more enlightened judicial authority that the two should be separated where this accords with the common intention of the parties, an intention that should readily be inferred when a yoking together of property (especially the presumptive rule in section 18, Rule 1) and risk would produce an inconvenient or unjust result.[22] It is not clear what is the effect on risk of the creation of an undivided share of a specific or identified bulk by the Sale of Goods (Amendment) Act 1995. It is significant, however, that section 20 was not amended so as presumptively to pass the risk once such an interest arose in favour of a paying buyer. In most of the cases where such an interest arises, the particular common law rules on the allocation of risk in f.o.b. and c.i.f. contracts[23] will govern. Apart from these cases, it was surely right not to harness risk to an undivided interest, which will arise precisely because the buyer has not yet obtained delivery of the goods. Indeed, the failure to amend section 20 may be seen as offering some support for the view that the transfer of risk according to property rather than possession should not readily be recognized.

   The refusal of the common law to permit the property to pass in an ascertainable but unascertained part of a specific bulk has already been noted.[24] Were the law to insist dogmatically on risk accompanying property, a seller might bear the risk of loss of goods lying in a warehouse for months after abandoning all pretensions to deal with them. In *Sterns Ltd v. Vickers Ltd*,[25] the sellers sold 120,000 gallons of white spirit out of a 200,000 gallon bulk kept in their name in a warehouse. The sellers procured from the warehouse a delivery warrant addressed to the order of the buyer. The buyer indorsed the warrant to a sub-buyer who appeared at the warehouse several months later with it, only to discover a deterioration in the quality of the spirit affecting its specific gravity. This seems to have been due to the wrongful behaviour of the warehouse company

---

   [21] It is common in the cases for the property first to be located prior to ascertaining risk. Occasionally, risk will be located first by a court searching for the whereabouts of property.
   [22] *Martineau* v. *Kitching*, n. 17 above; *Sterns Ltd* v. *Vickers Ltd* [1923] 1 KB 78; K. Llewellyn (1938) 15 *NYU LR* 159.
   [23] Discussed in the text accompanying nn. 59 ff. below.
   [24] Ch. 3 above.   [25] N. 22 above.

in topping up the tank with spirit of a different specific gravity. It was understood, in both the sale and sub-sale, that storage costs and insurance charges should be borne by buyer and sub-buyer respectively. In an action by the sellers, the court held that the risk of deterioration had passed to the buyer. The property in the goods, not yet in the buyer,[26] would doubtless have passed on payment and transfer of the warrant but for the non-separation of the 120,000 gallons. Further, the sellers, in procuring from the warehouse a warrant addressed to the buyer, which bound the warehouse to the buyer,[27] had performed their delivery obligation and there was nothing more for them to do under the contract.[28] The buyer could have collected the spirit at any time thereafter.

A contrasting case is *Healy* v. *Howlett & Sons*,[29] where the seller of fish caught off the west coast of Ireland consigned to his own order 190 boxes of mackerel, which included an unascertained portion of twenty boxes that he had agreed to sell to the London buyer. Because of a delay in the rail journey to Dublin, the fish missed the scheduled Holyhead boat and had deteriorated to the point of unacceptable quality when the seller's agent at Holyhead, about half way into the transit, separated the buyer's boxes. An invoice sent too late, after the conclusion of the contract, put the 'sole risk' on the buyer, but this document was rightly disregarded. It seemed that the seller consigned the fish to his own order as far as Holyhead only to conceal from competitors the identity of his buyers. But for the delayed separation of the buyer's boxes, the property would probably have passed to the buyer when the fish began its journey in Ireland and before it missed the boat.[30] An arguable case can therefore

[26] It is noteworthy that on similar facts Blackburn J in *Martineau* v. *Kitching*, n. 17 above, 454, would strive to prevent the passing of property from producing an artificial solution in both risk and insolvency cases. In his view, it would be a 'monstrous hardship' for the buyer in a case like *Martineau* to have to lodge an insolvency proof: 'I should be very much inclined to struggle very hard to find any legal reason for saying that, though the risk remained in the sellers, yet the property had passed to the buyers as soon as they made payment.'

[27] The warehouse had thus attorned to the buyer, but not to the sub-buyer. See Ch. 6 below. A delivery warrant is not a document of title at common law: *ibid*. Consequently, indorsees have no rights against the issuer of the warrant in the absence of attornment. A warrant is, however, a document of title in the extended statutory sense for the purpose of exceptions to the *nemo dat* rule of title transfer: Ch. 9 below.

[28] N. 22 above, 85 (Scrutton LJ). Although the buyer, in transferring the delivery order to the sub-buyer, might also be said to have done all that was required under the contract, the failure of the buyer thus to confer on the sub-buyer direct rights against the warehouse does not make the transfer of risk to the sub-buyer a foregone conclusion. Yet it would not be sensible to leave the goods at the buyer's risk for months after the sub-buyer has received an indorsed delivery order, unless the point is made that in such circumstances the buyer should procure from the warehouse a fresh delivery order in the name of the sub-buyer and thus an attornment to the sub-buyer.

[29] [1917] 1 KB 337.

[30] The report does not record the shipping terms or the incidence of the duty to pay freight to the carrier(s), though the quoted price probably included the cost of carriage.

be made that the buyer should have borne the risk of deterioration but the court, seemingly drawn by the supposed indivisibility of property and risk, ruled otherwise.

Risk and Quality Obligations

A difficult practical problem concerns perishable goods that deteriorate in transit. Normally, when goods are delivered to the carrier, the risk will pass at that time.[31] When perishable goods arrive at their destination unfit for consumption, it may be difficult to know whether this is due to the seller's breach of contract in not shipping goods that are of satisfactory quality and fit for the buyer's purpose or to an event that occurred in transit while the goods were at the buyer's risk. It depends on the evidence going to the state of the goods upon shipment. The goods must then have been capable of standing the rigours of a normal voyage and of satisfying fitness and quality standards for a reasonable period thereafter so as to allow for disposal.[32] Thus in *Mash & Murrell Ltd* v. *Joseph I. Emmanuel Ltd*,[33] the seller of Cyprus spring potatoes shipped c. & f. Liverpool was held liable at trial for the fact that upon arrival they were found to be unfit for consumption. The evidential difficulties in such a finding should not be underestimated. The decision was reversed on appeal because the voyage had not been normal: the damage to the potatoes had occurred as a result of their lying unventilated in a port of call for five days. The risk therefore fell upon the buyer.[34]

Where the transit is unusually long, the buyer will on similar grounds bear the risk of loss attributable to the length of the voyage, unless the buyer's stated purpose embraces a voyage of this length[35] or the seller expressly warrants that the goods will stand a 'long haul'.[36] Where the

---

[31] Either because of the combined presumptive effects of ss. 18, Rule 5, and 20, or because the parties to a documentary sale have expressly or impliedly provided for the risk to pass then and the property at a later date when the shipping documents are transferred against payment.

[32] *Healy* v. *Howlett & Sons*, n. 29 above (Ridley J).

[33] [1961] 1 WLR 862, revd. on the facts [1962] 1 WLR 16. See also *Beer* v. *Walker* (1877) 46 LJQB 677; *Ollett* v. *Jordan* [1918] 2 KB 41, 47 (Atkin LJ); *Hardwick Game Farm* v. *Suffolk Agricultural and Poultry Producers' Association Ltd* [1964] 2 Lloyd's Rep. 227, 270; *Oleificio Zucchi SpA* v. *Northern Sales Ltd* [1965] 2 Lloyd's Rep. 496, 517; *Georgetown Seafoods Ltd* v. *Usen Fisheries Ltd* (1977) 78 DLR (3d) 542. Cf. *Cordova Land Co. Ltd* v. *Victor Bros. Inc.* [1966] 1 WLR 793, where the court drew a distinction between perishable goods like potatoes, where description and quality standards might have to be met by the goods on arrival, and goods like the present animal hides, where this was not the case.

[34] See also *Davidson* v. *Bigelow & Hood Ltd* [1923] 1 DLR 1175.

[35] For the purpose of s. 14(3): discussed Ch. 7 below.

[36] e.g. *Tregunno* v. *Aldershot Distributing Co-operative Co. Ltd* [1943] OR 795 (Can.). A similar result follows if the buyer is responsible for the mode of carriage and the damage to the goods stems from the chosen mode: *Kelly, Douglas & Co. Ltd* v. *Pollock* (1958) 14 DLR (2d) 526.

court is faced with a conflict between findings that the goods were sound when shipped and that nothing unusual occurred in transit, it is likely as a matter of evidence that any extraordinary deterioration in the goods will be put down to a hidden flaw in them, and thus made the responsibility of the seller.[37] In international sales forms, however, it is common for the contract to stipulate that a certificate of inspection will be conclusive evidence as to their quality upon shipment, the object being to direct an aggrieved buyer away from the seller and in the direction of the carrier or the insurance company. In such sales, furthermore, evidence about the condition of the goods upon shipment may be found in the bill of lading, which may state that the goods were or appeared to be in good condition, or which may be claused to indicate they were defective.

Risk and Carriage

Even if the risk is on the buyer while the goods are in transit, the seller may still be liable if loss or deterioration is due to an unreasonable contract of carriage made by the seller with the carrier. According to section 32(2):

Unless otherwise authorised by the buyer, the seller must make such contract with the carrier on behalf of the buyer as may be reasonable having regard to the nature of the goods and the other circumstances of the case; and if the seller omits to do so, and the goods are lost or damaged in course of transit, the buyer may decline to treat the delivery to the carrier as a delivery to himself or may hold the seller responsible in damages.

Where the seller could, for the same freight charge, have put the goods on rail at the carrier's risk, subject only to the reasonable burden of the carrier inspecting the packing, it was unreasonable to ship at the buyer's risk.[38] In one Canadian case, a seller who, in breach of the contract of sale, failed to stipulate with the railway carrier that cabbages should be carried in heated wagons was held liable when they suffered frost damage after being left unheated in a railway siding.[39] Since the carrier was never under an obligation to keep the railway wagons heated, the buyer's only recourse was against the defaulting seller. A seller who does make a proper contract does not, of course, guarantee that the carrier will comply and does not answer for the carrier's breach of the contract of carriage.[40]

Section 32(2) should apply regardless of whether the seller contracts

---

[37] *Barnes* v. *Waugh* (1906) 41 NSR 38 (Can.).
[38] *T. Young & Sons* v. *Hobson and Partner* (1949) 65 TLR 365.
[39] *B. C. Fruit Market Ltd* v. *National Fruit Co.* (1921) 59 DLR 87.
[40] *Van Zonnefeld & Co.* v. *Gilchrist* (1915) 8 OWN 4 (Can.).

with the carrier as principal or as agent for the buyer.[41] The provision gives the buyer a choice of remedies. If the buyer chooses to regard the seller as having failed to deliver, this should mean that the buyer may decline to pay the price or, having paid it, recover the price as on a failure of consideration. The buyer should also have an action for damages for non-delivery. The buyer's right to treat the seller's action as a discharging breach of the contract of sale would appear not to depend upon the degree of damage suffered by the goods in transit. But the buyer's rights under section 32(2), it is submitted, should depend on there being a causal link between the seller's default and the buyer's prejudice, which will be absent in those cases where the buyer could have corrected that default before the damage was done.[42] Where the buyer elects to sue for damages, there is no reason to suppose that the measure of damages is anything other than that under section 53.[43]

Similar to section 32(2) is section 32(3), which establishes the presumptive rule that, where goods are 'sent' by sea by seller to buyer, in circumstances where insurance is usually carried, a failure by the seller to give such 'notice' as to enable the buyer to insure the goods in transit means that the goods will be at the seller's risk.[44] This provision comes from Scots law[45] and does not sit comfortably with English practice in the area of international documentary sales on c.i.f. and f.o.b. terms. In such contracts, the risk is on the buyer from shipment,[46] which is the case dealt with by section 32(3). That provision is ousted by contrary implication in the case of c.i.f. contracts, since insurance is the responsibility of the seller.[47] It should apply to c. & f. contracts, at least in those cases where the seller is not contractually bound to take out insurance for the buyer's account. It is however awkward in c.& f. cases to speak of goods being 'sent' to the buyer instead of the seller tendering a shipping document issued under a contract of carriage. A similar awkwardness is present with f.o.b. contracts, where delivery to the carrier on shipment is

[41] The former will be the case with c.i.f. contracts and the latter would apply in the case of certain f.o.b. contracts.

[42] *Mayhew* v. *Scott Fruit Co.* (1921) 21 DLR 54 9 (goods dispatched to wrong address and buyer doing nothing about it).

[43] Discussed Ch. 10 below.

[44] Although the provision as such is clearly confined to sea transit, it may well be that a common law analogue would be fashioned under s. 62(2) for other forms of transport such as multimodal transportation.

[45] *Wimble, Sons & Co.* v. *Rosenberg & Sons* [1913] 3 KB 743 (Hamilton LJ).

[46] In c.i.f contracts, the cargo may be appropriated to the contract after shipment, whereupon the risk passes retrospectively to the buyer. Discussed in the text accompanying nn. 67 ff. below.

[47] *Law and Bonar Ltd* v. *British American Tobacco Co. Ltd* [1916] 2 KB 605. But it might apply in the unlikely case of a buyer wanting a usual type of insurance cover going beyond the insurance required under a c.i.f. contract: *ibid.*, 608–9.

tantamount to delivery to the buyer since the carrier is presumptively the buyer's agent.[48]

The difficulty in applying section 32(3) to f.o.b. contracts came to a head in the leading case of *Wimble Sons & Co* v. *Rosenberg & Sons*.[49] It concerned a contract for the sale of 200 bags of rice f.o.b. Antwerp, under which the sellers, informed after the contract date that Odessa was the destination, were responsible for shipping as required by the buyers and were left to select the ship.[50] Information about the ship was first sent to the buyers four days after the ship foundered upon leaving harbour. The buyers had not yet effected insurance since it was their practice to do so only after notification of the name of the ship on which the goods were loaded. They refused to pay, citing the sellers' non-compliance with section 32(3). By a majority decision, the Court of Appeal found for the sellers. Of the two judges who thought that section 32(3) applied to f.o.b. contracts,[51] Vaughan Williams LJ thought that section 32(3) required an actual notice and was not dispensed with because the buyer might already have sufficient knowledge to insure.[52] Buckley LJ, on the other hand, thought the requirements of the provision could be and had been met in the shape of the knowledge already possessed by the buyers. Hamilton LJ agreed with Buckley LJ on this point[53] though his preference was for holding that section 32(3) had no application to f.o.b. contracts. So there were clear (though differently constituted) majorities that the provision applied, that no formal notice was required, and that the buyers had sufficient knowledge. They knew the port of discharge and did not need to know the name of the ship since they could have effected insurance on an Odessa voyage by a ship or ships to be declared.

Sometimes the seller 'agrees to deliver . . . at his own risk' the goods to some place other than where they are when sold.[54] In such a case, section 33 states a presumptive rule that this assumption of risk does not include 'any risk of deterioration in goods necessarily incident to the course of transit'. This provision should apply where the seller's agreement to

---

[48] S. 32(1).   [49] N. 45 above.

[50] Presumptively the f.o.b. buyer selects the ship: see *Pyrene Co. Ltd* v. *Scindia Navigation Co. Ltd* [1954] 2 QB 402.

[51] Vaughan Williams and Buckley LJJ. The former stated that 'the word "send" covers every obligation of the seller in reference to effecting or securing the arrival of the goods . . . at their destination'. The latter thought 'send' was equivalent to transmit or dispatch. Dissenting on this point, Hamilton LJ thought that the sellers could not send the goods to the buyers by sea when they had already delivered the goods to the buyers' agent, the carrier, upon shipment.

[52] On the facts, his lordship thought the buyer did not already know enough.

[53] See also *Northern Steel and Hardware Co. Ltd* v. *John Batt and Co. (London) Ltd* (1917) 33 TLR 516.

[54] *Quaere* does 'sold' refer to contract or conveyance? It makes more sense to say the former though the latter accords with the technical language of the Act.

assume the risk is express or implied, or where in accordance with the presumptive rule in section 20(1) the risk remains with the seller. Section 33, with its limited allocation of necessary risk to the seller, should not be read so as to detract from the broader allocation of risk to the seller under the special provisions of section 32(2) and (3). In particular, section 33 should not be allowed to undermine the normal rule that, where the risk is on the buyer, the seller must still ship goods that will not in a normal transit deteriorate to the point of unsuitability.[55] It would be odd if the seller's quality obligations were to be diluted just because the risk of loss had been assumed by the seller under section 33.

Section 33 is based on a case where a quantity of iron dispatched by canal rusted in transit.[56] It was held that this was a necessary incident of canal transport and so had to be borne by the buyer. In modern conditions, a different result should follow where the goods can be packed or treated to obviate such a risk by a method usual in the trade, or where they must be so dealt with if on arrival they are to pass the tests of fitness and quality laid down by the implied terms in section 14 of the Act.[57] Peaches cannot be expected to be as fresh on arrival as on shipment, but they can be expected to be fit for human consumption on distribution to consumers through the normal retail channels.[58] The word 'necessarily' is likely to be quite strictly interpreted nowadays and it is hard to imagine a modern instance of the application of the section.

Risk and Export Sales

As stated earlier, risk presumptively passes to the buyer on shipment, when the services of an independent carrier are used, because that is when the property in the goods presumptively passes. This will not be the case with those contracts where the seller undertakes to deliver the goods to the buyer in the country of destination, whether from the ship itself (*ex* ship) or at some inland point such as a warehouse (arrival). In such cases, the risk will be on the seller during transit.[59] With other shipping terms, such as c.i.f. and f.o.b., the seller will commonly reserve the right of disposal until payment is made on the documentary exchange.[60]

[55] *Winnipeg Fish Co.* v. *Whitman Fish Co.* (1909) 41 SCR 453; *Georgetown Seafoods Ltd* v. *Usen Fisheries Ltd* (1977) 78 DLR (3d) 542.

[56] *Bull* v. *Robison* (1854) 10 Ex. 342. See also *Lewis* v. *Barré* (1901) 14 Man. LR 32 (Can.).

[57] In *Bull* v. *Robison*, n. 56 above, the goods were admittedly unmerchantable on arrival, but a modern water shipment of equivalent length would surely require shipment below deck by the seller or in a container, methods denied to a 19th-century canal shipment by barge.

[58] *Mash & Murrell Ltd* v. *Joseph I. Emmanuel Ltd* [1961] 1 WLR 862; *Beer* v. *Walker* (1877) 46 LJQB 677.

[59] *Yangtse Insurance Asscn.* v. *Lukmanjee* [1918] AC 585, 589 (Lord Sumner).

[60] So as to reserve the general property: Ch. 3 above.

It is neverthless settled that the risk impliedly passes as from shipment in c.i.f.[61] and on shipment in f.o.b.[62] contracts. The difference in formulation stems from shipment taking place pursuant to a pre-existing f.o.b. contract of sale, whereas shipment commonly occurs before the goods are appropriated to a c.i.f. contract and sometimes even before the c.i.f. contract is concluded. It can therefore be transferred retrospectively in c.i.f. contracts. One possible meaning of shipment is that it occurs at the time and point when the goods cross the ship's rail,[63] but a preferable view is that it happens when the seller's duty regarding the physical delivery of the goods to the carrier has been accomplished.[64] If the contract of sale permits the seller to tender to the buyer a 'received for shipment' bill of lading,[65] the risk might therefore pass before the goods are placed on board. It is more likely that the contract will require an 'on board' bill of lading, in which case the seller's responsibility will cease only when the loading has been completed. Perhaps the most principled approach to the matter is to regard the risk as being transferred at the moment when the carrier becomes responsible for the goods and thus protected by insurance cover and able to benefit from limitations of liability under international conventions.[66]

In c.i.f contracts, the consequences of the risk being on the buyer as from shipment are even today not thoroughly resolved. In *Couturier* v. *Hastie*,[67] the seller was not permitted to recover the price on a tender of shipping documents relating to a cargo of specific goods that had perished before the conclusion of the contract. This decision therefore supports the view that in a c.i.f. contract the retrospective transfer of the risk of loss to the buyer will stop at the contract date. But the decision does not rule out a similar backdating of the risk of damage, as opposed to loss, and it does not prevent the parties from making whatever contractual provision for the allocation of risk they wish as long as they sufficiently demonstrate their intentions. The c.i.f. buyer will have a valuable insurance policy as well as the prospect, as assignee of the seller's rights, of an action against the carrier. Yet the allocation of the risk of pre-contract loss is an unlikely construction of a contract for unascertained goods where the seller is aware of the loss before

[61] *Comptoir d'Achat et du Boerenbond Belge S/S* v. *Luis de Ridder Lda (The Julia)* [1949] AC 293; *Biddell Bros.* v. *E. Clemens Horst Co.* [1911] 1 KB 934. As for the meaning of 'shipment', see *Anderson* v. *Morice* (1875) LR 10 CP 609, affd. (1876) 1 App. Cas. 713.

[62] *Stock* v. *Inglis* (1884) 12 QBD 564; *The Parchim* [1918] AC 157, 168.

[63] Criticized in the f.o.b. case of *Pyrene Co. Ltd* v. *Scindia Navigation Co. Ltd*, n. 50 above.

[64] See *Benajmin's Sale of Goods* (5th edn., 1997 by A. G. Guest and others), §20–075.

[65] It might do for some c.i.f. contracts, though not for contracts where the seller must place the goods free *on board*. Discussed further, Ch. 6 below.

[66] N. 64 above, §20–075. See the Hague-Visby Rules as set out in the Carriage of Goods by Sea Act 1971.

[67] (1853) 9 Ex. 102, affd. (1856) 5 HLC 673.

concluding the contract or before even appropriating the goods. The courts are reluctant to treat c.i.f. contracts as purely a sale of documents.[68] If such a seller had a range of c.i.f. buyers from whom to select the recipient of the shipping documents, there is the further complication of deciding the principles on which such a selection might be made. And if the seller actually knew of the loss before entering into the particular contract of sale, any construction that the buyer must be satisfied with only the documents would to all intents and purposes be untenable.

Suppose the seller appropriates to the contract a cargo that perishes after the contract date but before the appropriation. At first sight, the c.i.f. risk rule requires the buyer to bear the loss,[69] but it has been powerfully argued that the risk should remain with the seller, seemingly regardless of whether the seller knew of the loss before the notice of appropriation.[70] Certainly, if the seller did know of the loss at that time, the difficulty mentioned above of discovering on what basis a seller with a number of purchasers should single one of them out makes itself felt again. Authorities dealing with c.i.f. contracts containing prohibition clauses, where the seller's capacity to perform across a wide contractual front is impaired by a governmental embargo on shipment, appear to favour any reasonable action by the seller in apportioning whatever performance capability he retains amongst his various buyers.[71] This

---

[68] See *Arnhold Karberg & Co.* v. *Blyth, Green, Jourdain & Co.* [1916] 1 KB 495, where Scrutton J at first instance states that 'a c.i.f. sale is not a sale of goods, but a sale of documents relating to goods' ([1915] 2 KB 379, 388). In the Court of Appeal, Bankes and Warrington LJJ state, however, that a c.i.f. contract is a sale of goods to be performed by the delivery of documents (above, 510, 514). McCardie J in *Manbre Saccharine Co. Ltd* v. *Corn Products Co. Ltd* [1919] 1 KB 198, 203, referred to the difference of opinion in *Arnhold Karberg* as 'one of phrase only', saying for his part that delivery in a c.i.f. contract was effected by a delivery of goods and not documents (*ibid.*, 202). In *James Finlay & Co. Ltd* v. *N. V. Kwik Hoo Tong Handel Maatschappij* [1929] 1 KB 400, 407–8, Scrutton LJ thought it unnecessary to say whether a c.i.f. contract was a sale of goods or of documents, but he still thought there was a lot to be said for the documents view. See also *Ross T. Smyth & Co. Ltd* v. *T. D. Bailey, Sons & Co.* [1940] 3 All ER 60, 68, where Lord Wright stated that a c.i.f. contract was a sale of goods contract, and *Hindley & Co. Ltd* v. *East Indian Produce Co. Ltd* [1973] 2 Lloyd's Rep. 515, where a c. & f. contract was stated to be a sale of goods contract to be performed by the delivery of documents. On balance, this is the preferred view, with the addition that the documents in question should evidence that the seller has entered into proper contracts of carriage and insurance. The transfer of the documents should also be effective in assigning to the buyer rights under the above contracts.

[69] See *Produce Brokers Co. Ltd* v. *Olympia Oil Co. Ltd* [1917] 1 KB 320, 329–30 (Scrutton LJ), disapproving *Re Olympia Oil and Cake Co. and Producers Co.* [1915] 1 KB 253 (Div. Ct.), but revd. on other grounds [1916] 1 AC 314; J. Feltham [1975] *JBL* 273. The judgment of Scrutton LJ, above, has been explained as turning on the construction of the particular contract: *Benjamin's Sale of Goods* n. 64 above, §19–074.

[70] *Benjamin's Sale of Goods*, n. 64 above, §19–073.

[71] See *Westfälische Centrale Genosschenscfaft GmbH* v. *Seabright Chemicals Ltd* (unreported), cited in *Bremer Handelsgesellschaft mbH* v. *Continental Grain Co.* [1983] 1 Lloyd's Rep. 269; M. G. Bridge, 'The 1973 Mississippi Floods: "Force Majeure" and Export

approach, which may usefully be adapted to unappropriated damaged cargoes and to partly damaged bulk cargoes destined for numerous buyers, could also be adopted for lost cargoes. To say that a seller may not appropriate a lost cargo strikes at the principle of retrospective risk allocation, though some room would still be left for that principle if retrospectivity were permitted to apply to damaged as opposed to lost cargoes. It would in many cases be impracticable to conduct a minute evidentiary inquiry in order to discover whether damage to cargo occurred before or after appropriation.

There is case law support for retrospective risk allocation in the case of lost cargoes. In *C. Groom Ltd* v. *Barber*,[72] the sellers appropriated a cargo of Hessian cloth on board the *City of Winchester* to their contract with the buyer the day before the ship, which had been sunk two weeks previously, was posted as a loss at Lloyd's. Atkin J held that the seller was entitled to be paid against a tender of the usual shipping documents even if the goods had not been 'appropriated' at that time. He stated that on the facts there had apparently been no appropriation, but, since he was refuting the seller's argument that the buyer had to be in a position to pass the property in the goods upon the documentary tender, it is clear that he was talking of appropriation in the proprietary sense, and not in the sense of attaching a descriptive source to the contract goods. In *Manbre Saccharine Co. Ltd* v. *Corn Products Co. Ltd*,[73] the sellers, with knowledge of the loss of the ship, appropriated a quantity of corn starch on the *Algonquin* to their contract with the buyers. The buyer's defence pointed to the significance of the seller's knowledge. Curiously, however, McCardie J did not focus on this point in his judgment and was content to hold that the sellers were entitled to be paid against documents representing a cargo lost before tender.[74]

Cargoes are commonly sold on c.i.f. terms in string. Where the practice of the trade is content with an insurance policy covering certain risks, there seems little reason for halting the loss before the string is fully formed. Otherwise, a seller, who may have carefully matched his purchase and sale commitments, thus avoiding a speculative long or short position in the market, would be left with an insurance policy covering loss and a possible breach of contract action for non-delivery against him by a buyer to whose contract he cannot now appropriate a cargo. Nevertheless, the Divisional Court in *Re Olympia Oil and Cake Co. Ltd*[75]

Prohibition' in E. McKendrick (ed.), *Force Majeure and Frustration of Contract* (2nd edn., Lloyd's of London Press, London, 1995).

[72] [1915] 1 KB 316.   [73] N. 68 above.

[74] The seller had taken out war risk insurance but the insured value, though markedly higher than the contract price, was lower than the market price at the date of the appropriation.

[75] N. 69 above.

held that the seller could not appropriate a lost cargo.[76] When the same case went before the Court of Appeal at a later stage of its confused judicial and arbitral existence, under the name of *Produce Brokers Co. Ltd* v. *Olympia Oil and Cake Co. Ltd*,[77] Scrutton LJ stated in trenchant terms that the earlier decision was wrong.[78] Furthermore, the Court of Appeal upheld an arbitral finding that there was a custom in the oil seed trade by which a buyer had to accept an appropriation originating with the head seller even if the intermediate seller knew of the loss before appropriating the cargo to the contract with the buyer.

The difficulties in this area arise, not because buyers dislike having to claim under an insurance policy (for it is usually the case in commodities sales to insure in excess of the contract value), but because the lost cargoes question arose during the First World War. At that time, war risk was not covered in many c.i.f. contracts[79] and the insurance rights of a buyer of a cargo lost through enemy action were therefore worth nothing. The problem could still arise with any risk falling outside the customary insurance obligations of the c.i.f. seller or where a rising market produces a loss in excess of the insurance value.

Risk and Breach of Contract

Where the seller commits a discharging breach of contract, the relation of this to risk poses a problem. Suppose damage to or destruction of the goods is due to the very breach committed by the seller. A car, for example, is destroyed in an accident caused by a defect in its steering. The modern view is that the passing of the property to the buyer is no bar to its revesting in the seller when the goods are lawfully rejected by the buyer.[80] The same could be said of risk. The seller cannot seriously argue against the buyer's right of rejection (or notional rejection of lost goods) in the above case on the ground that the buyer bore the risk, because this would nullify the buyer's rights of rejection and contractual termination.

Where, however, the goods are damaged or destroyed for reasons unconnected with the seller's discharging breach, the position is more

---

[76] Two members of the court (Shearman and Avory JJ) thought the fact of the cargo being lost before appropriation was enough, while the third, Rowlatt J, based his decision in favour of the buyer on the ground that the seller knew of the loss at the time of the appropriation.

[77] N. 69 above.   [78] *Ibid.* 330.

[79] Sometimes war risk was expressly stated to be for the buyer's account: *C. Groom Ltd* v. *Barber*, n. 72 above.

[80] *R. V. Ward Ltd* v. *Bignall* [1967] 1 QB 534. On the property passing only conditionally in such a case, see *Colonial Insurance Co. of New Zealand* v. *Adelaide Marine Insurance Co.* (1886) 12 App. Cas. 128; *Hardy & Co.* v. *Hillerns and Fowler* [1923] 2 KB 490, 499 (Atkin LJ); *Kwei Tek Chao* v. *British Traders & Shippers Ltd* [1954] 2 QB 459, 487–8; *McDougall* v. *Aeromarine of Emsworth Ltd* [1958] 3 All ER 431, 437.

complex. If the buyer would have rejected the goods on discovering the breach, there is an argument that it would be unreasonable to oblige him to bear the interim risk. There is also a supporting property argument, that goods failing to accord with the contract description will not pass to the buyer under the presumptive rule in section 18, Rule 5. In *Head* v. *Tattersall*,[81] the seller of a horse warranted that it had hunted with the Bicester hounds and undertook to take it back if by a certain date the buyer should discover this was not so. The buyer found out in time that the horse was an imposter, but not before it had died. The court decided that the buyer was entitled to recover the price. It is not clear whether the seller had as such committed a breach of contract or whether the buyer's discovery was a non-promissory condition precedent to his right to reclaim the money, but the difference between the two should not affect the location of the interim risk.

The reversal of risk in a less exotic case than *Head* v. *Tattersall* appears more questionable, especially since, nowadays, the buyer's right of rejection may endure for a significant period beyond the point and time of delivery.[82] Furthermore, to leave the risk with the buyer avoids a very difficult speculation, informed by self-serving argument from the buyer, about whether the buyer would or would not have gone on to reject the goods. Finally, there is the insurance argument that a buyer should insure goods in his possession and the seller may reasonably not have insurance coverage. This argument weighed heavily with a New Zealand court which ruled that the risk of accidental fire rested on the buyer who, at the relevant time, had not decisively rejected the goods for their failure to conform to sample.[83] The court conceded that upon rejection a defeasible property in the buyer could revest in the seller, so its decision is not based upon a mechanical attachment of property and risk. In addition, the court did not deprive the buyer of the right to reject because of the buyer's delay in exercising it, so the decision cannot be explained away on that ground.[84] On balance, unless the contract expressly or impliedly permits the buyer to reverse the risk, which is a possible interpretation of *Head* v. *Tattersall*, it is submitted that the risk of interim loss arising from events not connected with the non-conforming character of the goods should remain with the buyer. In many cases, this point of principle will

---

[81] (1872) LR 7 Ex. 7.   [82] Ch. 5 above.

[83] *Canterbury Seed Co. Ltd* v. *J. G. Ward Farmers' Association Ltd* (1895) 13 NZLR 96. See also A. Hudson 'Conformity of Goods on Passing of Risk' in D. Feldman and F. Meisel (eds.), *Corporate and Commercial Law* (Lloyd's of London Press, London, 1996).

[84] The fire occurred four days after the buyers' letter failed unequivocally to state a rejection of the goods. In the court's opinion, n. 83 above, 110: 'Until the vendors were informed of the election so to divest [the property, consequent upon rejection] they would not be expected to insure the goods or be justified in dealing with them.'

not need to be settled: the event that damages or destroys the goods will prevent the buyer from proving the existence of a discharging breach.

Risk and Delayed Delivery

Section 20(1), which states the presumptive date of transfer of the risk to the buyer, is subject to the contrary intention of the parties. It is also ousted under section 20(2) 'where delivery has been delayed through the fault of either buyer or seller'. In that event, 'the goods are at the risk of the party at fault as regards any loss which might not have occurred but for such fault'. This provision contemplates two types of case: first, where the property (and hence the risk) has passed to the buyer, as presumptively it does with specific goods at the date of the contract,[85] but the buyer has been prevented by a defaulting seller from taking delivery; and secondly, where the property in the goods (and hence the risk) remain with the seller, who is unable to pass the property by unconditional appropriation to the buyer because of the latter's delay. There is little case law. Both examples of the provision would seem to be most necessary in a legal system that links together risk and property indissolubly, which is not the case under the Sale of Goods Act. The first example is also of reduced significance because of the modern judicial reluctance to hold that the property in specific goods passes before delivery.[86] It has, nevertheless, been applied where a c.i.f. seller interferes with the discharge by the carrier of goods to the buyer.[87] Even though a c.i.f. contract does not as such require the seller to 'deliver' the goods to the buyer,[88] the bill of lading contract, under which the buyer acquires rights against the carrier, does indeed require the carrier to deliver the goods to the buyer,[89] and the seller who persuades the carrier not to do so is guilty of delaying delivery to the buyer.

The second example of section 20(2) was applied in *Demby Hamilton & Co. Ltd* v. *Barden*[90] which concerned the delivery by instalments of apple juice sold by sample and a buyer who was at fault in not issuing delivery instructions. The great difficulty of complying with the sample except by furnishing each instalment from the same bulk led the court to the conclusion that the buyer could not delay the seller in the expectation that stocks on hand would be sold to other buyers and the buyer's demands met from stocks newly manufactured by the seller. There had,

---

[85] S. 18, Rule 1, in conjunction with s. 20(1).   [86] Ch. 3 above.

[87] *Gatoil International Inc.* v. *Tradax Petroleum Ltd* [1985] 1 Lloyd's Rep. 350.

[88] See *Congimex Cia Geral SARL* v. *Tradax Export SA* [1983] 1 Lloyd's Rep. 250.

[89] Ch. 6 below.

[90] [1949] 1 All ER 435. See also the extension in *Gillespie* v. *Hamm* (1899) 4 Terr. LR 78 (Can.: delay in payment by conditional buyer in possession).

in effect, been an appropriation of a particular bulk to the contract, though, because of non-ascertainment, the property had not, and could not have, passed in the undelivered instalments. Consequently, when the balance of the contract quantity became putrid, the buyer bore the loss. Given the language of section 20(2), it is difficult to defend a Canadian case which left on the seller the risk of loss where, had the buyer taken timely delivery, the agreed horses would have been in a place where they could not have contracted the disease that killed them.[91]

Section 20(2) is therefore most likely to be applied to specific goods or to unascertained goods in a larger bulk, the bulk having been specific at the date of the contract or ascertained by subsequent appropriation. The provision recognizes, by transferring only that portion of the risk attributable to delay, that the risk may be divided between seller and buyer.[92] If the risk is displaced under section 20(2), it does not merely release from his obligations the party freed from the risk. This party may also sue for the price or damages for non-acceptance (if he is the seller), or sue to recover the price or damages for non-delivery (if he is the buyer).[93] In the latter case, the seller is unlikely to be assisted by the frustration defence since the loss or damage will be the product of his own culpable delay.

Section 20(3) preserves the responsibility of the buyer or seller as bailee notwithstanding the allocation of risk elsewhere in the section. The bailee of goods must take reasonable care of them and bears the burden of demonstrating that such care has been taken.[94] This provision will certainly apply where possession is transferred or retained for purposes collateral to the contract of sale.[95] More loosely, section 20(3), or an equivalent common law principle,[96] will apply wherever there is a separation of possession and risk under a contract of sale. The result in section 20(3) can sometimes be reached by other means. For example, the risk of loss to goods in the seller's possession may, because of the buyer's delay, have been transferred under section 20(2). In this case, the answer to the problem of the careless seller/owner can be found in the words of section 20(2) itself: the loss or damage to the goods cannot be attributed to the buyer who delays taking delivery. Further, suppose that, under section 20(1), the risk has passed to the buyer but not yet the property.

---

[91] *Collins* v. *Wilson* [1922] 3 WWR 1086.
[92] For another example of divided risk, see *Rugg* v. *Minett* (1809) 11 East 210.
[93] *Allied Mills Ltd* v. *Gwydir Valley Oilseeds Pty. Ltd* [1978] 2 NSWLR 26.
[94] *Houghland* v. *R. R. Low (Luxury Coaches) Ltd* [1962] 1 QB 695.
[95] *Wiehe* v. *Dennis Bros.* (1913) 29 TLR 250: the sellers retained a Shetland pony called 'Tiny' so it could continue to collect for 'Our Dumb Friends League' at the Olympia Horse Show.
[96] Some difficulty arises in seeing the seller retaining the general property in the goods as a bailee for the buyer.

The seller's quality and fitness obligations should prevail over the transfer of risk and prevent him from charging the buyer with the consequences of his own carelessness; he may also be liable in damages for non-delivery or defective delivery.

Risk and Third-party Tortfeasors

A buyer to whom the risk of loss or damage is transferred will suffer the effect of tortious damage committed by third parties for whom the seller is not responsible. It is well settled that the buyer who bears the risk, but has neither property nor possession, has an insurable interest in the goods.[97] But such a buyer has very real difficulties in suing the third party in tort. The tort of trespass requires the plaintiff to have been in possession of the goods at the time the third party interferes with them, while a plaintiff suing in conversion must have had either possession or the right to immediate possession at the time of the wrongful act.[98] For negligence, the plaintiff must have either the property or possession.[99] Unlike conversion, where damages are calculated according to the value of the goods at the date of conversion,[100] damages in negligence will measure the actual injury suffered by the plaintiff. These should however come to the full value of the goods, notwithstanding the plaintiff having only the possession but not the property, if the plaintiff bears the risk as between himself and the other party to a contract of sale.[101]

The question of risk and standing to sue in tort poses the greatest problems in the area of ocean transport where the carrier is guilty of losing, damaging, or misdelivering the goods. To accommodate c.i.f. and related contracts, provision was made by the Bills of Lading Act 1855 for the statutory assignment to the buyer of the benefits and burdens of the contract of carriage taken out by the seller.[102] Because this assignment took place in narrowly defined circumstances, and the law on the subject was not reformed until the Carriage of Goods Act 1992, it meant that a buyer who could not sue the carrier for breach of contract was driven instead to seek an action in tort. In *Margarine Union GmbH* v. *Cambay Prince Steamship Co. Ltd*,[103] the buyer of goods to whom the risk had passed was denied an action in negligence when the carrier transported copra in an unfumigated vessel. At the time of the carrier's wrongdoing, the buyer

---

[97] *Inglis* v. *Stock* (1885) 10 App. Cas. 263; *The Parchim* [1918] AC 157.
[98] Ch. 8 below.   [99] *Leigh and Sillavan Ltd* v. *Aliakmon Shipping Ltd* [1986] AC 785.
[100] *General & Finance Facilities Ltd* v. *Cook's Cars (Romford) Ltd* [1963] 1 WLR 644.
[101] *Quaere* the effect of the defendant's ability to plead the *ius tertii* in consequence of s. 8 of the Torts (Interference with Goods) Act 1977?
[102] S. 1.
[103] [1969] 1 QB 219. Assumed to be correct in *Karlshamns Oljefabriker* v. *Eastport Navigation Co. Ltd (The Elafi)* [1982] 1 All ER 208.

had no proprietary interest in the copra. The law of tort, apart from exceptional cases, will not permit the recovery of damages for economic loss, such as that suffered by a buyer in having to pay the seller the price of lost or damaged goods. Nevertheless, the risk-bearing c.i.f. buyer was permitted to recover in *Schiffhart & Kohlen GmbH* v. *Chelsea Maritime Ltd*[104] on the ground that a c.i.f. buyer was within the reasonable contemplation of the negligent carrier and there were no reasons of a policy nature to preclude recovery.

As part of a general clampdown on recovery in the tort of negligence for economic loss, the House of Lords in *Leigh and Sillavan Ltd* v. *Aliakmon Shipping Ltd*[105] refused an action to the risk-bearing buyer and signalled in the most emphatic terms a return to *Margarine Union*. In the Court of Appeal,[106] where the buyer was similarly denied, it had been emphasized by the majority that allowing the buyer to sue the carrier in tort would permit him to evade the limitations on liability imposed by the Hague Rules for contract actions against carriers,[107] and would disturb the economic balance between the relations of buyer and seller and of carrier and cargo-owner.[108] In the House of Lords, the buyer was sacrificed in the general interest of certainty of tort liability. The court was attracted by the prospect of a bright line separating liability and immunity in tort, and it saw such a line in the rule denying economic loss recovery to a plaintiff in consequence of property damage caused by the defendant to a third party.

The buyer in this case was unable to sue in contract under the Bills of Lading Act 1855, because the bill of lading had been indorsed in favour of and delivered to the buyer, not to transfer the general property, but to permit the buyer as agent for the seller to collect and warehouse the goods at the port of discharge. The buyer and seller had initially contracted on c. & f. terms before varying their contract to provide for delivery *ex* warehouse on arrival of the goods. Consistently with the contract being initially a c.& f. contract, the risk of damage in transit remained upon the buyer notwithstanding the variation. In the court's view, the buyer at the moment of variation ought to have secured an assignment of the seller's contract rights against the carrier or else an undertaking by the seller to sue the carrier on behalf of the buyer in the event of damage to the cargo. There was not truly any gap in the law that had to be filled by an extension of tort liability since the buyer could have obtained

---

[104] [1982] QB 481, followed in *The Nea Tyhi* [1982] 1 Lloyd's Rep. 608.
[105] N. 99 above.   [106] [1985] 2 WLR 289.
[107] The same limitations are imposed by the Hague-Visby Rules (Art. IV *bis*(1)) in the case of tort actions against carriers. Although the report in *Aliakmon Shipping* does not say so, the country of shipment (South Korea) was not a party to the Brussels Convention adopting the Visby amendments.
[108] N. 106 above, 301, 313–14.

protection from contract law. Furthermore, the House of Lords refused to accede even to a duty of care made subject to the carrier's contractual defences against the seller contained in the bill of lading.

As much as one sympathizes with the court's yearning for simple law, the result gives the carrier a windfall immunity. It also imposes an unrealistically high standard of legal circumspection on international traders in unusual circumstances demanding rapid action. If the immunity of negligent stevedores is predicated upon the integral nature of contracts involved in the distribution and carriage of goods overseas,[109] it is difficult to see why this integrality should not also be recognized in the interest of buyers in circumstances like those arising in *Leigh and Sillavan Ltd* v. *Aliakmon Shipping Ltd*.[110] The opening up, by the Carriage of Goods by Sea Act 1992, of contractual actions against the carrier to a wide range of buyers[111] is designed to prevent problems of this kind from arising in the future. Nevertheless, if there are gaps in the coverage of the Act,[112] experience in this area of commercial activity shows they will be discovered in litigation sooner rather than later.

Risk and Delivery

The Sale of Goods Act, in linking the passing of risk to the passing of property, has been criticized for ignoring insurance realities, in particular that the person in possession of goods is nearly always the one better placed to insure them.[113] There is much force in this since delivery, which is the voluntary transfer of possession, is usually a visible event.[114] But the rule in section 20(1) is only a presumptive one and the modern law on the passing of property ties it in with delivery, so any statutory reform associating risk with possession rather than property would yield modest results in practice. One area where it would be prudent to delay the passing of risk notwithstanding delivery is where the goods are delivered to the post office or to a courier for transmission to a non-commercial buyer.[115] The commercial seller would know how and when to insure against loss or damage in transit; the non-commercial buyer would not. It may be that this position is recognized informally in commercial prac-

---

[109] [1975] AC 154.   [110] N. 99 above.

[111] The most striking feature of s. 2(1) of the Act is that the right to sue the carrier is unhitched from the passing of property. It may be exercised by the holder of a bill of lading, by the person to whom delivery is to be made under a non-negotiable sea waybill, and by the holder of a ship's delivery order.

[112] See S. Baughen [1994] *JBL* 62.

[113] P. S. Atiyah, *The Sale of Goods* (9th edn., Pitman, London, 1995 by J. N. Adams), 305.

[114] An obvious exception is constructive delivery, e.g., where a warehouseman attorns to a new bailor.

[115] Ontario Law Reform Commission, *Report on Sale of Goods* (1979), i, 267.

tice by such sellers not charging their buyers with the risk of loss or damage in transit.[116]

FRUSTRATION

The Sale of Goods Act treats explicitly only a small portion of the law on frustration of contracts. The relevant provision is section 7: 'Where there is an agreement to sell specific goods and subsequently the goods, without any fault on the part of seller or buyer, perish before the risk passes to the buyer, the agreement is avoided.'[117] There are no reported cases bearing directly upon the section. It applies only to agreements to sell specific goods. When section 18, Rule 1, was applied less flexibly than it is now, the presumptive contract for specific goods was a sale and not an agreement to sell. Moreover, section 7 treats only one supervening event, namely, the perishing of the goods. This includes both the physical destruction of the goods and any drastic change that alters their commercial identity.[118] Section 7 does not deal with unascertained goods, nor, probably, with unascertained goods from a specific bulk. Even if the seller is able to tender goods differing in no material respect from the agreed specific goods, he may not do so: specific goods are unique and irreplaceable, even if their exact counterparts can be found elsewhere.

Frustration and Risk

As section 7 is formulated, its relationship to risk is unclear. Risk is directed mainly to the question whether the buyer has to pay the price, whereas frustration usually answers the question whether the seller, unable to make a conforming tender of goods, is released from paying damages to the buyer. If the risk remains with the seller by virtue of section 20(1), it should not be assumed that the parties intended that the seller should answer to the buyer for the accident to the goods. Risk has two meanings that ought not to be confused: first, the statutory meaning in the Sale of Goods Act that determines whether the buyer should still pay despite the accident to the goods; and secondly, the meaning it has

---

[116] R. Cranston, *Consumers and the Law* (2nd edn., Weidenfeld & Nicholson, London, 1984), 169 (referring to customer good will). It is common for buyers to pay an additional sum representing, not just postage and packing, but also insurance.

[117] See the criticisms of the Ontario Law Reform Commission, n. 115 above, ii, 366–8.

[118] For the meaning of which, see the insurance case of *Asfar & Co. Ltd v. Blundell* [1896] 1 QB 123, where the dates at the bottom of the river could no longer be described as dates and could only be used for distilling industrial alcohol. See also *Turnbull v. Rendell* (1908) 27 NZLR 1067 (where the seller should have been held to warrant that 'table potatoes' were still capable of answering that description).

when the contract upon its construction visits the harsh consequences of an event more or less upon the designated risk-bearer. The Sale of Goods Act is only concerned with the *transfer* of risk and the effect this has upon the buyer's obligations. It does not deal with the broader reaches of contractual risk-allocation. If the contract explicitly places the risk of loss upon the seller, this goes beyond the limited effect of section 20(1), which is that the risk has not passed to the buyer. The contractual clause may well signify the parties' intention that the seller shall be liable in damages for an inability to tender conforming goods; the statutory provision merely entails that the buyer need not pay the price.

A related question concerns the buyer to whom the risk of loss has passed. Section 7 is explicitly excluded in this case. The clear implication is that the contract would not be frustrated. If the contract were frustrated, the transfer of risk would be confined to damage or loss falling outside the notion of perishing in section 7. This is, if not an impossible construction of sections 7 and 20(1), at least an unlikely one. Where the buyer has both risk and possession, the above implication is even stronger and where, in addition to these two, the buyer also has the general property, the implication that the contract remains on foot is irresistible.

If the supervening event is one with which section 7 is not concerned, such as a governmental embargo on trading or a requisition of goods,[119] risk in the Sale of Goods Act sense is unlikely to provide a solution to the problem. Whether the buyer or seller remains liable under the contract will be determined by ordinary principles of contractual construction and frustration. In *Kursell* v. *Timber Operators and Contractors Ltd*,[120] the contract was for the sale of all the trees of stated dimensions in a Latvian forest. The forest was nationalized and the court concluded that the property (and therefore also the risk) in the trees had not passed to the buyer since the trees were not in a deliverable state under section 18, Rule 1. In consequence, the contract was held to be frustrated. Even if the property, and seemingly also the risk, had passed, Scrutton LJ was of the view that the doctrine of frustration would still operate given that so much remained to be done under the contract. The contract had a full fifteen years to run, during which the buyer was to have had the use of the seller's sawmill and plant when felling the trees. If this view is correct, it would surely govern only in exceptional circumstances like those in *Kursell*.

[119] Governmental requisition was treated as perishing 'in a sense' in *Re Shipton, Anderson & Co. and Harrison & Co.* [1915] 3 KB 676, where the problem was solved by the court construing the particular contract. Governmental acts are invariably made the subject of express *force majeure* and prohibition of export clauses in international commodities contracts.
[120] [1927] 1 KB 298.

Frustration and Fault

Section 7 does not apply where specific goods perish owing to the fault of buyer or seller. As seen above, the fault of either party in delaying delivery will subject that party to the risk arising from the delay.[121] Where this results in the transfer of the risk of loss to the buyer, both his fault and the passing of risk will prevent the implementation of section 7. Where the seller is responsible for the delay, his fault blocks the application of the section. In neither case should the party at fault be able to take comfort from general contractual principles, for there is no relief given for self-induced frustration. Delay, as contemplated by section 20(2), should be considered as fault in section 7 whenever delivery is not taken or made at the contractually agreed time, whether this is a fixed date or a reasonable period.

If the seller is negligent in losing or damaging the goods in his possession, he should be liable in damages for non-delivery. Any argument that liability ought to be in the tort of negligence founders if the buyer did not have the property in the goods at the time.[122] If the fault is that of the buyer in possession, the buyer should have to pay the price if the risk or the property has passed. If neither has passed, then the buyer's liability will have to be in damages for negligence given the absence of a contractual alternative. If the goods are lost, it is likely that the price and the contractual and tortious measures of damages will all yield the same or approximately the same sum.[123]

Frustration and Quality Obligations

Another difficulty concerns the relationship between the seller's fitness and quality obligations (in section 14)[124] and section 7. In *Horn* v. *Minister of Food*,[125] a farmer agreed to sell a specific clamp of potatoes, thirty-three tons in weight, on terms providing for delivery instructions over a five- to seven-month period starting from the contract date. The contract recognized that the potatoes would suffer some deterioration but imposed a duty on the seller to cover them so as to minimize that deterioration. When a seam of rot was discovered in the potatoes some five months after the contract date, the buyers refused to give delivery instructions. The seller's action against the buyers[126] succeeded since,

---

[121] S. 20(2).   [122] See discussion in the text accompanying nn. 97 ff. above.
[123] An indemnity and an expectation valuation of the article will produce different results only in the case of non-market items: L. L. Fuller and A. Perdue (1936) 46 *Yale LJ* 52.
[124] Ch. 7 below.   [125] [1948] 2 All ER 1036.
[126] It seems to have been for the price, though it is not easy to see how the seller qualified for the right to sue for the price under s. 49.

though the goods were not of merchantable quality, the parties had by their agreement substituted for this obligation a duty on the seller to take reasonable care of the potatoes, which had been duly performed.

The court might equally have said that the risk of post-contract deterioration had been transferred contractually to the buyers, although the property was to pass only upon delivery. It had to rule out section 7 to reach the result it did, on the dubious ground that, though all thirty-three tons of potatoes rotted before delivery, the potatoes were still potatoes and so could not be said to have perished.[127] A better view, it is submitted, was that the outright destruction of the potatoes was at the risk of the buyers owing to their delay in giving delivery instructions, section 20(2) thus overriding section 7 because of the buyers' fault. Alternatively, the court might have said simply that the parties had displayed a contrary intention ousting section 7.[128]

Apart from special facts like those in *Horn*, deterioration in perishable goods between contract and delivery is likely to be at the risk of the seller, who will consequently be liable for supplying unfit or unsatisfactory goods. Where there is accidental loss or destruction of specific goods for reasons not connected with natural decaying processes, the seller should normally be able to invoke the frustration principle in section 7, or an equivalent common law provision.[129]

Frustration and Foresight

Nothing in section 7 precludes its application simply because the risk of perishing was foreseen by the parties at the contract date. Just because a risk is foreseen does not mean that the parties have implicitly agreed that the seller shall bear responsibility for it.[130] A failure to make explicit provision for an event may signify hope that it will not occur or an inability to reach agreement about it. But it may also in some cases amount to an implicit allocation of risk ousting the application of the doctrine of frustration. For example, a seller who undertakes to sell a herd of cattle, despite a nearby outbreak of foot-and-mouth disease, to a distant buyer unaware of the disease, should, if the cattle become infected or are slaughtered, be prevented from relying upon section 7 and compelled to pay damages for non-delivery. Section 7 could, with a little difficulty, be treated as impliedly excluded. In such a case, a court is very unlikely to conclude both that the property in the herd passed at the contract date to the buyer under section 18, Rule 1, and that the risk passed simultaneously under section 20.

---

[127] Cf. n.118 above.   [128] Assuming it may be excluded: see discussion on s. 6 below.
[129] If the goods have not perished.
[130] *Ocean Tramp Tankers Corpn.* v. *V. O. Sovfracht* [1964] 2 QB 226.

Partial and Temporary Frustration

The orthodox position, enacted by section 7, is that frustration operates automatically to discharge both parties prospectively from the contract. The effect of frustration is therefore felt by the contract as a whole rather than by the particular obligation affected by the outside event. This is unfortunate in that it denies flexibility to a court where the impossibility of performance is only temporary or partial in effect. If the seller cannot deliver the whole of the agreed specific goods because a portion has perished, may not the buyer demand delivery or the seller demand acceptance of the remainder? If a contract calls for the delivery of the goods on a certain date and a governmental embargo of temporary duration prevents delivery on that date, may not either party, even in the absence of contractual provision, demand performance when the embargo is lifted on the ground that the contract has only been suspended?[131] Would this depend upon whether the time of delivery was of the essence of the contract? The principle that frustration automatically discharges contracts receives its strongest expression from a line of cases on supervening illegality, where public policy prevented either party from demanding partial or delayed performance of the contract.[132]

The drawbacks to the orthodox position can be seen in two decisions dealing with the partial perishing of future goods to be derived from a specific location, a case that falls outside section 7. In *Howell* v. *Coupland*,[133] a farmer agreed to sell '200 tons of regent potatoes grown on land belonging to [the farmer] in Whaplode'. When the contract was made, twenty-five of the Whaplode acres had been sown with potatoes and the remaining forty-three acres were later sown. A disease subsequently attacked the crop, through no fault of the farmer. The eighty tons of potatoes that were produced were delivered to the buyer who nevertheless brought an action for non-delivery of the remaining 120 tons. The Court of Appeal found an implied condition precedent to the farmer's duty to deliver that the potatoes should not have been destroyed for reasons beyond the control of the farmer: 'It was not an absolute contract of delivery under all circumstances, but a contract to deliver so many potatoes, of a particular kind, grown on a specific place, if deliverable from that place.'[134]

---

[131] On suspension generally, see J. Carter 'Suspending Contract Performance for Breach' in J. Beatson and D. Friedmann (eds.), *Good Faith and Fault in Contract Law* (OUP, London, 1995).

[132] *Hirji Mulji* v. *Cheong Yue Steamship Co. Ltd* [1926] AC 497; *Bank Line Ltd* v. *Arthur Capel & Co.* [1919] AC 435; *Tamplin Steamship Co. Ltd* v. *Anglo-Mexican Petroleum Co.* [1916] 2 AC 397. On partial and temporary frustration, see G. H. Treitel, *Frustration and Force Majeure* (Sweet & Maxwell, London, 1994), ch. 5.

[133] (1874) LR 9 QB 462, affd. (1876) 1 QBD 258.   [134] *Ibid.* 261.

A notable feature of the decision is the room it leaves for the construction of the contact. If the potatoes had been damaged rather than destroyed by the disease, again through no fault of the farmer, they would not have been in a deliverable state, so the farmer would not be liable for non-delivery or able to insist that the buyer take them in their damaged state. No issue arose as to the buyer's or seller's right to insist on delivery of the eighty tons grown, for delivery had already occurred. In the court below,[135] Blackburn J said there was an implied term of the contract that each party should be free if the crop perished. If the contract were entire and indivisible, this would mean that neither party could have compelled delivery of the eighty tons. If the contract, however, could be interpreted to require delivery of a part crop, then the farmer would only have been *pro tanto* released by the supervening event. The buyer would not have been entitled to demand 120 tons of potatoes from another source. The clear description given in the contract to the potatoes would have precluded that.

The seller's duty to deliver the lesser quantity was clarified nearly 100 years later in *H. R. & S. Sainsbury Ltd* v. *Street*,[136] which concerned a contract for the whole of the 1970 harvest of feed barley, estimated by the parties at 'about 275 tons', to be grown on the defendant's farm. In a bad harvest, only 140 tons were grown and the farmer wished to be released from the contract to find another buyer for his barley at the higher prevailing market rate. The buyer, disclaiming any right to sue for short delivery, recovered damages for non-delivery of the barley actually grown. According to the court, section 7 did not apply for it dealt only with goods existing at the contract date. Rather, the relevant provision was section 5(2), which states that '[t]here may be a contract for the sale of goods the acquisition of which by the seller depends on a contingency'. With respect, this provision was almost certainly drawn to prevent contracts to sell future goods from being treated as unlawful wagers on commodity prices, and to allow parties to buy and sell goods on an arrival basis.[137] A better approach would be to admit the common law under section 62(2) and construe the contract to reach the result.

The court's decision, that the buyer could call for delivery of the reduced crop, is not clear whether this is a matter of option or obligation on the buyer's part,[138] although the market price made it an option that any buyer would want to exercise. The court constructed an implied condition from 'the presumed intention of reasonable men' that the buyer was entitled to delivery. Presumably, if there had been a glut leading to a fall in the market, the same presumed intention should have permitted

---

[135] N. 133 above. [136] [1972] 1 WLR 834.
[137] See *Hale* v. *Rawson* (1858) 4 CB(NS) 85.
[138] Cf. UCC, Art. 2–613(b) (buyer's option).

the seller to call on the buyer to accept at the contract price a harvest in excess of 275 tons.[139] The decision is to be welcomed for admitting the flexibility that comes with construction of the contract and for not holding that the contract was automatically frustrated. The common law of frustration surrenders more easily to the contrary intention of the parties than does the unyielding language of section 7.

A similar constructive approach could be applied to delayed performance. Since the common law does not rewrite contracts, it will not impose a suspension on contracting parties where no warrant exists for this in the contract.[140] In commercial sales contracts, the time of delivery is normally of the essence of the contract.[141] The buyer may, however, waive timely performance by the seller,[142] in which case the seller may not insist the contract is discharged for his own breach.[143] Where the delay is due to causes for which the seller is not responsible, it may be that contractual performance by the seller is impossible even though the contract is not frustrated according to the stringent common law test. There may be, for example, a condition of a particular contract that the goods be put on rail on a stated date and, owing to industrial action, the cancellation of rail services on that date. In such a case, even though time is of the essence, the buyer ought to be able, though not bound, to waive timely performance, while the seller has a defence to an action for damages for late delivery.[144] Eventually, either a temporary restraint upon performance will be lifted or the delay will mature into a frustrating delay.[145] On the construction of some contracts, it might be possible to say that time is not of the essence, or that the performance period is elastic, where the delay is due to events for which the seller is not contractually responsible.[146] In such a case, the seller would also be entitled to insist that the contract remain on foot.

Partial frustration can emerge in another guise too. Suppose specific goods are to be delivered in more than one instalment, payment to occur

[139] If the estimate were the seller's, there would probably be an implied term that it be a reasonable one.

[140] *Sanschagrin* v. *Echo Flour Mills Co.* [1922] 3 WWR 694. Contractual suspension is a common feature of *force majeure* clauses in international commodity sales forms: see M. G. Bridge, 'The 1973 Mississippi Floods: "Force Majeure" and Export Prohibition' in E. McKendrick (ed.), *Force Majeure and Frustration of Contract* (2nd edn., Lloyd's of London Press, London, 1995).

[141] Ch. 6 below.   [142] *Charles Rickards Ltd* v. *Oppenhaim* [1950] 1 KB 616.

[143] Discharge is at the injured buyer's election: *Photo Production Ltd* v. *Securicor Transport Ltd* [1980] AC 827.

[144] See G. H. Treitel, *The Law of Contract* (9th edn., Sweet & Maxwell, London, 1995), 785–7, for a discussion of cases of temporary unavailability of the subject matter of the contract.

[145] *Jackson* v. *Union Marine Insurance Co. Ltd* (1875) LR 10 CP 125.

[146] e.g. *Brenner* v. *Consumers Metal Co.* (1917) 41 OLR 534 (Can.: delivery 'as soon as possible').

after all deliveries have been made. After some instalments have been delivered, the remainder perish in a frustrating incident before the risk passes to the buyer. In the perhaps unlikely event of the contract being construed as entire and indivisible, delivery in full is a condition precedent to the buyer's duty to pay the price, which leaves no room for apportioning the price under the contract. If still in possession of the goods, the buyer has the option under section 30(1) of the Sale of Goods Act of rejecting them or retaining and paying for them at the contract rate.[147] This provision, which enacts a form of implied contract on *quantum valebant* terms, avoids the need to consider whether retaining the goods is a matter of option or obligation for the buyer, a point not clarified by the law on partial frustration.[148] If the goods have been disposed of or consumed by the buyer before the frustrating incident, section 30(1) would not apply, since it contemplates the buyer accepting the goods notwithstanding the short delivery. Nor would there be any scope for section 1(3) of the Law Reform (Frustrated Contracts) Act 1943 which, upon a frustration of the contract, requires the recipient of a 'valuable benefit' to pay a 'just sum', since the Act has no application to contracts for specific goods frustrated by the perishing of the goods.[149] The provisions of the Act could however apply to other frustrating events, such as governmental requisition,[150] in which event payment at the contract rate is probably the most likely outcome. As for the case where a portion of the specific goods perish, whether or not the contract as a whole is sufficiently disturbed for it to be frustrated, a court seeking a just result is likely to make a restitutionary award based upon the contract rate.

The same case of specific goods where a part of the goods perish also causes difficulties if the buyer has paid a portion or the whole of the agreed price in excess of any benefit received before the event destroying the remainder of the goods. On the face of it, the buyer is not able to demonstrate the total failure of consideration needed to support an action for money had and received. It has nevertheless been argued that the effect of the risk being on the seller means that the seller cannot retain a sum in excess of the benefit conferred upon the buyer.[151] It is doubtful that so much can be read into the fact that the risk has not yet passed to the buyer,[152] but predictable that a modern court will strive to avoid an unjustified enrichment of the seller and fashion a result akin to

[147] There is no good reason to confine this provision to cases of breach of contract.

[148] See above discussion of *Sainsbury* v. *Street*, n. 136 above.

[149] S. 2(5)(c). Or to specific goods contracts where the risk has passed to the buyer or indeed to any contracts to which s. 7 of the Sale of Goods Act applies.

[150] Provided the risk has not passed to the buyer: *ibid.*

[151] P. S. Atiyah, *The Sale of Goods* (9th edn., Pitman, London, 1995 by J. N. Adams), 314. *Aliter* Treitel, n. 144 above, 830–1 (pointing to the difficulties of apportioning the price).

[152] See the discussion on risk above.

what could have been achieved under the 1943 Act had it been applicable.[153]

The final problem arising out of partial frustration concerns the seller of goods from a specific bulk or location who, owing to a supervening event such as governmental requisition or prohibition of export, has not or cannot procure sufficient goods of the contract description to satisfy all of his contractual commitments. May he fulfil those contracts that he can, pleading that the remainder are frustrated? Or is he obliged to perform the contracts in order of seniority? Or may or must he apportion such goods as he has or can procure amongst all of his outstanding contracts? There is high authority consistent with the view that, if a seller chooses to fulfil some of his contracts in full to the exclusion of the rest, he cannot plead frustration of the contracts he does not perform, since the frustration is self-induced.[154] This places the seller in an invidious position. A series of cases dealing with governmental prohibition of shipment, all based upon contract forms that contain express prohibition clauses, would appear to protect the seller against the self-induced frustration argument and sanction any reasonable behaviour on the seller's part in response to his various legal, as opposed to moral, commitments.[155] This might, depending on the circumstances, involve a *pro rata* allocation amongst all of the seller's contracts.[156] These prohibition clauses did not then and do not now deal in detail with the partly-capable seller. The result they support could sensibly extend to all cases, whether or not the contract contains an express clause, where the seller has properly incurred a range of contractual commitments before the supervening event.[157]

[153] A number of authorities sanction the recovery of a part of the prepaid price where the consideration has partly failed, as where the seller fails to deliver all of the agreed goods or where the buyer rejects some of the goods for misdescription. See *Devaux* v. *Connolly* (1849) 8 CB 640; *Biggerstaff* v. *Rowatt's Wharf Ltd* [1896] 2 Ch. 93, 100, 105; *Behrend & Co. Ltd* v. *Produce Brokers Co. Ltd* [1920] 3 KB 530, 535; *Ebrahim Dawood Ltd* v. *Heath Ltd* [1961] 2 Lloyd's Rep. 512; *Westdeutsche Landesbank* v. *Islington LBC* [1994] 1 WLR 938. The number of such claims is likely to rise in consequence of the increased rights of partial rejection introduced by the Sale and Supply of Goods Act 1994: Ch. 5 below.

[154] *Maritime National Fish Ltd* v. *Ocean Trawlers Ltd* [1935] AC 524; *J. Lauritzen AS* v. *Wijsmuller BV (The Super Servant Two)* [1990] 1 Lloyd's Rep. 1.

[155] *Bremer Handelsgesellschaft mbH* v. *Continental Grain Co.* [1983] 1 Lloyd's Rep. 269, 282; *Intertradex SA* v. *Lesieur-Tourteaux SARL* [1977] 2 Lloyd's Rep. 146, 155, [1978] 2 Lloyd's Rep. 509, 513; *Bremer Handelsgesellschaft mbH* v. *Vanden-Avenne Izegem PVBA* [1978] 2 Lloyd's Rep. 109, 115, 128, 131; *Bremer Handelsgesellschaft mbH* v. *C. Mackprang Jnr.* [1979] 1 Lloyd's Rep. 221, 224; *Westfälische Centrale Genossenschaft GmbH* v. *Seabright Chemicals Ltd* (unreported), cited in *Bremer Handelsgesellschaft mbH* v. *Continental Grain Co.*, above; *Pancommerce SA* v. *Veecheema BV* [1982] 1 Lloyd's Rep. 645, revd. on other grounds [1983] 2 Lloyd's Rep. 304.

[156] Bridge, 'The 1973 Mississippi Floods: "Force Majeure" and Export Prohibition' in E. McKendrick (ed.), *Force Majeure and Frustration of Contract* (2nd edn., Lloyd's of London Press, London, 1995).

[157] Cf. *The Super Servant Two*, n. 154 above.

Frustration and Unascertained Goods

Section 7 does not deal with unascertained goods from a specific bulk or with generic goods whose source of supply is delimited by the contract.[158] The orthodox view is that the seller of unascertained goods can always go to market to buy in fresh supplies if the anticipated source dries up.[159] Likewise, a buyer will be unable to plead frustration if the markets he had in mind for distributing the goods become closed to him.[160] Just as a seller is not prevented from buying in merely because of a steep rise in commodity prices,[161] so a buyer can always find another market if he incurs the necessary expense or reduces his prices sufficiently. The law of frustration gives relief from impossibility, not economic hardship. If a more generous measure of relief is sought by the parties, then an express clause to that effect should be inserted in the contract.[162]

If, however, the contractually stipulated source of supply cannot provide the goods, as where the contract flour was to come from a mill that burned, the contract will be frustrated.[163] If the contractually agreed method of shipment or delivery becomes impossible, the contract will also be frustrated.[164] Neither party may unilaterally alter contractual shipment or delivery terms, even if the alteration imposes a lesser burden on the other party.[165] Where a method of shipment or delivery is contemplated by the parties rather than required by the contract, the

---

[158] e.g. soya bean meal of US origin shipped from a Gulf of Mexico port within a stated period.

[159] *Blackburn Bobbin Co.* v. *T. W. Allen & Sons* [1918] 2 KB 467; *Exportelisa SA* v. *Giuseppe Figli Soc. Coll.* [1978] 1 Lloyd's Rep. 433. See also *Ross T. Smyth & Co. Ltd (Liverpool)* v. *W. N. Lindsay Ltd (Leith)* [1953] 1 WLR 1289.

[160] *Congimex Cia Geral de Comercia SARL* v. *Tradax Export SA* [1983] 1 Lloyd's Rep. 250 (buyer of goods c.i.f. Lisbon unable to land them could still tranship them or have them oncarried to another country); *Wingold* v. *William Looser & Co. Ltd* [1951] 1 DLR 429; *Atlantic Paper Stock Ltd* v. *St Anne-Nackawic Pulp & Paper Co.* [1976] 1 SCR 580 (Can.).

[161] See *Davis Contractors Ltd* v. *Fareham Urban District Council* [1956] AC 696; *Samuel* v. *Black Lake Asbestos and Chrome Co. Ltd* (1920) 48 OLR 561 (Can.: unprofitability due to increased cost of mineral abstraction).

[162] See essays by A. Berg, M. Furmston, and E. McKendrick in E. McKendrick (ed.), n. 156 above.

[163] *Sanschagrin* v. *Echo Flour Mills Co.* [1922] 3 WWR 694. See also *Howell* v. *Coupland* (1876) 1 QBD 258; *Re Badische Co. Ltd* [1921] 2 Ch. 331; *E. Hulton and Co. Ltd* v. *Chadwick and Taylor Ltd* (1918) 34 TLR 230.

[164] See *Nickoll & Knight* v. *Ashton, Edridge & Co.* [1901] 2 KB 126; *Vancouver Milling & Grain Co. Ltd* v. *C. C. Ranch Co. Ltd* [1924] 2 DLR 569; *Brenner* v. *Consumers Metal Co*, n. 146 above.

[165] *Maine Shipping Co.* v. *Sutcliffe* (1918) 87 LJKB 382. *A fortiori* the party whose performance has become impossible cannot be required to provide an alternative and more onerous performance: *Nile Co. for the Export of Crops* v. *H. & J. M. Bennett (Commodities) Ltd* [1986] 1 Lloyd's Rep. 555 (buyer stopped by governmental act from paying cash against documents not bound to open an irrevocable letter of credit instead).

contract will be frustrated only if its foundation has been altered in a way that satisfies the stringent common law test. One party's factual expectation regarding performance does not constitute the legal basis for peformance. For this reason, a c.i.f. Hamburg contract for the sale of a quantity of Sudanese groundnuts shipped from a Red Sea port was held not to be frustrated when the consequence of the closure of the Suez Canal was that the groundnuts had to endure a journey two or three times as long *via* the Cape of Good Hope.[166] The failure of a source of supply contemplated by only one of the parties will not frustrate the contract;[167] where the source is contemplated by both parties, the event will have to satisfy the common law test for frustration.[168]

Consequences of Frustration

At common law, discharge for frustration operates prospectively so that any loss lies where it falls. Contractual performance due or already rendered remains undisturbed; future liabilities are discharged. Before the landmark decision in *Fibrosa Spolka Akcyjna* v. *Fairbairn Lawson Combe Barbour Ltd*,[169] the law worked against the interest of a pre-paying buyer who received no actual benefit before the contract was frustrated. If the buyer sought to recover his money on the ground of a total failure of consideration, he was met with the successful objection that, upon the conclusion of the contract, he did receive something of value, namely, the seller's promise to supply the goods which remained binding until the frustrating event.[170] The House of Lords in *Fibrosa* overcame this objection in holding that consideration in the formation of contracts was not to be confused with consideration in the quasi-contractual action for the recovery of money. The latter signified benefit actually received rather than benefit promised. This reasoning would still be needed for those sale of contracts falling outside the 1943 Act if the buyer is to recover money paid.[171]

The Law Reform (Frustrated Contracts) Act 1943 modified the common law rule that frustration discharges a contract prospectively. The starting point is that moneys paid may be recovered and moneys payable

---

[166] *Tsakiroglou & Co. Ltd* v. *Noblee Thorl GmbH* [1962] AC 93. Cf. *Holland American Metal Corpn.* v. *Goldblatt* [1953] OR 112 (Can.).

[167] *Blackburn Bobbin Co.* v. *T. W. Allen & Sons*, n. 159 above ('Finnish birch timber' could have come from existing stocks in England when imports from Finland became impossible).

[168] Cf. *Re Badische Co. Ltd* (supervening illegality), n. 163 above; *E. Hulton and Co. Ltd* v. *Chadwick and Taylor Ltd, ibid.*

[169] [1943] AC 32, overruling *Chandler* v. *Webster* [1904] 1 KB 593.

[170] *Chandler* v. *Webster*, n. 169 above.

[171] See also discussion above on partial failure of consideration.

before the frustrating event need no longer be paid.[172] Important exceptions are then grafted on to this rule. First, a party who has incurred
expenses in performing the contract may, within the discretion of the
court, retain or recover from the sum paid or payable an amount that
does not exceed such sum.[173] Secondly, if one of the parties has conferred upon the other a valuable benefit, he is entitled, again subject to
the discretion of the court, to recover from the other a sum equivalent to
the value of this benefit.[174] Applied to a simple sale of goods contract, the
rule that moneys paid or payable may be recovered or retained amounts
to a concession to the interests of buyers, while the exceptions for benefits and expenses redress the countervailing interests of sellers.

MISTAKE

The subject matter of mistake is dealt with in only two places in the Sale
of Goods Act: first, in section 6; and secondly, in section 23, which deals
with the transfer of title to goods under a voidable contract.[175] The
greater part of the law of mistake is remitted to the general law of contract; it is incorporated in sales contracts by virtue of section 62(2) and
will not be treated in this text.[176]

According to section 6: 'Where there is a contract for the sale of specific
goods, and the goods without the knowledge of the seller have perished
at the time when the contract is made, the contract is void.' Section 6 is
supposedly based upon *Couturier* v. *Hastie*,[177] a case that repays careful
examination.

The contract was for the sale of a specific cargo of corn on board the
Kezia Page. Unknown to the parties, the cargo had already overheated
and had been sold in Tunis by the ship's master; it had thus ceased to
exist for commercial purposes. The seller nevertheless demanded payment, tendering the shipping documents, which included an insurance
policy, under this early version of a c.i.f. contract. The buyer refused to
accept the documents and pay the price, citing the non-existence of the
cargo at the contract date. Consequently, the seller sued for the price of
the cargo the *del credere* agent who had negotiated the sale, the liability
of this agent turning upon whether the buyer was entitled to refuse payment. The trial judge ruled that it was a condition of the contract that a
cargo was in existence and capable of delivery, so the seller could not

---

[172] S. 1(2).   [173] *Ibid.*
[174] S. 1(3). See Robert Goff J in *BP Exploration Co. (Libya) Ltd* v. *Hunt (No. 2)* [1979] 1 WLR
783, affd. [1981] 1 WLR 232 and [1983] 2 AC 352.
[175] Discussed Ch. 9 below.   [176] See the standard contract texts.
[177] (1853) 9 Ex. 102, affd. (1856) 5 HLC 673.

recover. Reversing this decision, the Court of Exchequer held that the seller could validly tender documents relating to goods lost before the conclusion of the contract. This decision was reversed by the Court of Exchequer Chamber, which held that the buyer had not taken the risk of casualty to the goods before the contract, and that it was the basis of the contract that the cargo was in existence at the date the contract was concluded. The seller had therefore not made a valid tender. This ruling was upheld in the House of Lords where it was stressed that the decision turned upon the construction of the particular contract, which was conditioned on the goods being in existence at the contract date.

Nowhere in any of the judgments is there a reference to mistake or voidness. The case is entirely consistent with the use of constructive conditions precedent.[178] The decision was that the seller, having failed to satisfy the condition of making a good tender, could not complain about the buyer's refusal to pay the price. It does not rule out the possibility or the presumption that sellers warrant the existence of specific goods at the contract date. The plaintiff seller's liability was never put to the test since there was no counterclaim for damages for non-delivery. Yet Chalmers interpreted *Couturier* as holding that contracts for the sale of goods that have perished at the contract date are void for mistake,[179] and this view has subsequently been followed in the case law.[180] Section 6 enacts what appears to be an inflexible rule of law making no allowance for a contrary intention that the seller should be contractually liable if by words or conduct he expressly or impliedly warrants or represents the existence of the goods.

These difficulties came to the surface in the highly persuasive decision of the Australian High Court in *McRae* v. *Commonwealth Disposals Commission*[181] where a government agency, inviting salvage bids, negligently asserted the existence of a specific wreck on a non-existent reef in the Pacific Ocean. Section 6 was held inapplicable on the ground that goods that never existed cannot have perished. Carefully reviewing *Couturier*, the High Court found that the common law position was based upon constructive conditions precedent and not upon the idea that certain contracts are void for mistake. Hence it declined to invoke any principle identical to the one in section 6 *via* the common law gateway of section 62(2).

---

[178] According to Sir F. Pollock (Introduction to the Revised Reports, i, vi): '*Couturier v. Hastie* . . . shows how a large proportion of the cases which swell the rubric of relief against mistake in the text-books (with or without protest from the text-writer) are really cases of construction.'

[179] *The Sale of Goods Act, 1893* (4th edn.,Butterworths, London, 1899), 19.

[180] *Barrow, Lane & Ballard Ltd* v. *Phillip Phillips & Co.* [1929] 1 KB 574.

[181] (1951) 84 CLR 377.

In *McRae*, the buyer was suing the seller for damages representing his out-of-pocket expenses in equipping a salvage expedition. The issue could not be resolved simply by holding that the seller had failed to make a good tender. Starting from the constructive principle that sellers normally warrant the existence of specific goods, the court found such a warranty had been impliedly given by the seller. It was plainly influenced by the high degree of negligence displayed by the seller, an attitude consistent with the modern tendency to introduce fault into the test of promissory intention for express warranty.[182] Similar evidence of the influence of tort law is to be found in the court's denial to the buyer of expectation damages founded on the notional value of the wreck, which was impossible to evaluate, and in its award instead of a reliance measure based upon the buyer's wasted expenses.

Tort law provides one way round section 6 and its apparent disallowance of contractual liability. A seller negligent in asserting the existence of goods could be held liable for negligent misstatement and subjected to a tortious measure of damages.[183] Where the seller is not negligent but plainly undertakes that the goods are in existence, it is not so easy. It may be possible to construe a collateral contract based on the seller's implied undertaking that the goods exist. Since entry into even an illegal contract has been held to be sufficient consideration for a collateral promise,[184] the same should hold true for entry into a void contract. Yet it is difficult to see this as other than an illusory consideration. Another possibility is to say that section 6, in common with the other contractual provisions[185] of the Sale of Goods Act, may always be excluded by a contrary agreement, express or implied. Such contrary agreement imposing liability on the seller may be found in the warranty itself. Alternatively, it may be that the parties agree that the buyer shall assume the risk of pre-contract loss. Section 55 permits the parties to exclude 'any right, duty or liability' arising by implication of law under a contract of sale. Though the rule in section 6 seems to be, if anything, the very negation of rights, duties, and liabilities, a court would probably invoke section 55 if it felt it had to avoid the effect of section 6, even though the latter provision, unlike so many others in the Act, does not expressly permit a contrary intention or use the language of presumption.

Section 6 deals only with perishing.[186] It has nothing to say about embargoes or other forms of governmental intervention. Nor does it as

---

[182] Ch. 8 below.

[183] *Hedley Byrne & Co. Ltd* v. *Heller & Partners Ltd* [1964] AC 465. In an appropriate case, these should include the loss of an alternative expectation: *V. K. Mason Construction Ltd* v. *Bank of Nova Scotia Ltd* (1985) 16 DLR (4th) 598.

[184] *Strongman (1945) Ltd* v. *Sincock* [1955] 2 QB 525.

[185] As opposed to those dealing with the *nemo dat* rule and title transfer: Ch. 9 below.

[186] Discussed at n. 118 above.

such apply to the perishing of goods other than specific goods. Where unascertained goods are agreed to be sold under a broad description, it is unlikely that the unavailability of such goods to the seller would vitiate the contract. The position could be different if descriptive words closely delimit the source of the contract goods, and should most certainly be different if the seller's obligation is to supply an undivided part of a specific bulk. In all these cases falling outside section 6, the court, it is submitted, should have recourse to the common law approach espoused in *McRae*.[187]

The rule in section 6 does apply to specific goods that have perished in part. In *Barrow, Lane & Ballard Ltd* v. *Phillip Phillips Ltd*,[188] where the contract concerned a batch of 700 bags of Chinese ground nuts lying at a wharf, 109 bags had, without the parties' knowledge, already been stolen by unknown persons. The contract was entire and indivisible, so the diminished quantity could not be used towards a proportionate abatement of the price. The court held that the contract was void and, to be consistent with principle, would have had to reach the same result if even a much smaller quantity had been stolen, at least where the seller could not make a tender within the ungenerous margins allowed by the maxim *de minimis non curat lex*. The seller consequently had to bear the risk of additional theft occurring after the contract date. Before the shortfall became known, the buyer had removed 150 bags from the wharf and paid a proportion of the contract price into court. Although a *quantum valebant* undertaking could not be inferred from the buyer's consumption of these bags in ignorance of the theft or thefts, a modern court would impose on a recalcitrant buyer a restitutionary duty to pay in such circumstances. In some cases, the contract might expressly or impliedly allow the seller such a wide tolerance in matters of quantity that the buyer would be liable at the contract rate for goods delivered.[189]

---

[187] N. 181 above. And in the second part of Lord Atkin's speech in *Bell* v. *Lever Bros.* [1932] AC 161.

[188] N. 180 above.

[189] *Goldsborough, Mort & Co. Ltd* v. *Carter* (1914) 19 CLR 429 (after bad weather, seller could muster only 890 sheep instead of 'about' 4,000).

5

Termination of the Contract for Breach

This Chapter deals with the right of an injured party to terminate the contract as a result of the other party's breach. This right, dependent upon the status of the term infringed or upon the consequences of the breach, may in some cases be affected by a cure of defective performance by the breaching party. Particular complications arise under documentary sales. In the case of a buyer, the right to terminate is lost when the goods have been accepted; there are similar rules governing the loss of the right to rescind for innocent misrepresentation. Termination is sometimes called discharge for breach[1] and, more rarely nowadays, rescission for breach, which has to be distinguished from rescission *ab initio* for actionable misrepresentation.

Termination operates prospectively: the injured party is released from further performance and the breaching party's unperformed primary obligations are commuted into secondary obligations to pay damages.[2] An important feature of termination, when the existence of the right has prompted litigation, is that it frees the injured party from a market risk imposed by the contract. For example, when the market price for goods declines after the contract, a buyer will often be keen to take advantage of termination rights consequent upon late delivery or the delivery of non-conforming goods. This will permit the acquisition of cheaper substitute goods from a different source. It is not obvious that a buyer terminating a contract because the goods are not reasonably fit for purpose should thereby be able to acquire substitute goods that are fit, and at a lower price that takes account of market decline after the date of the first contract.[3] The buyer retaining goods has to absorb the fall in their market value.[4] The long-standing position of English law is that the motive behind the exercise of termination rights, particularly the desire to use technical rights to escape from a losing contract, does not qualify or

[1] Cancellation is not uncommon in the US; avoidance is used in the Vienna Convention on International Sale of Goods 1980.

[2] *Photo Production Ltd* v. *Securicor Transport Ltd* [1980] AC 827.

[3] Contrast this with damages, where the object is to put the plaintiff in the position he would have occupied if the contract had been performed: *Wertheim* v. *Chicoutimi Pulp Co.* [1911] AC 301; *Proctor & Gamble Philippine Mfg. Corpn.* v. *Kurt A. Becher GmbH & Co.* [1988] 2 Lloyd's Rep. 21. Ch. 10 below.

[4] But cf. the odd case of *Naughton* v. *O'Callaghan* [1990] 3 All ER 191, discussed Ch. 10 below.

exclude those rights. This must now be reconsidered in the light of the Sale and Supply of Goods Act 1994, which in certain instances prevents an unreasonable termination where the breach of an implied condition in the Sale of Goods Act produces slight consequences.

DISCHARGE: CONDITIONS, WARRANTIES, AND INTERMEDIATE STIPULATIONS[5]

A line has to be drawn to separate cases where termination rights do and do not lie for a breach of contract.[6] Numerous factors might be considered in marking out this line. Advocates of individual responsibility might stress the importance of contractual undertakings and use the goad of extensive termination rights to encourage the performance of contractual promises, as penalty clauses might if they were lawful. Termination might also be favoured by those arguing that it is futile to imprison parties in a continuing embittered relationship, and that freeing them to seek their opportunities elsewhere might avoid economic waste. This approach would be consistent with a bias against termination for short-term relationships where future co-operation is not in prospect, on the ground, for example, that the buyer may be better placed than the seller to avoid economic waste in using defective goods. Supporters of the consumer interest, however, would see in extensive terminations rights an effective lever for redressing the imbalance between a business seller and a consumer buyer.[7] Other countervailing considerations pit the conviction, that the needs of certainty and forward-planning favour strict and predictable law, against the belief that the merits of the parties can only fairly be considered in view of the consequences of the breach. This latter approach could take account of considerations of hardship, and would, for example, permit a distinction between the tardy manufacturer of machinery designed for the buyer's unique specifications and the tardy supplier of commodities, for which a market can always be found. An argument against strict termination rights is that they permit the assertion of technical claims by a party when the market has swung against him, thus undermining the broad allocation of market risk agreed upon at the outset of the contract.

[5] M. G. Bridge (1983) 28 *McGill LJ* 867; J. Carter, *Breach of Contract* (2nd edn., 1991); New South Wales Law Reform Commission, *Working Paper on the Sale of Goods (Warranties, Remedies, Frustration and Other Matters)* 1975; R. Bradgate, 'Rejection and Termination in Contracts for the Sale of Goods', in J. Birds, R. Bradgate, and J. Villiers, *Termination of Contracts* (Wiley Chancery, London, 1995).

[6] Ontario Law Reform Commission, *Report on Sale of Goods* (1979), i, 145–50; Alberta Institute of Law Research and Reform, *The Uniform Sale of Goods Act* (Report no. 38, 1982), 140–57. [7] Law Commission, *Sale and Supply of Goods* (Law Com. No. 160, 1987).

Breach of Contract Principles Before the Codification of Sale

Prior to the rise of *assumpsit* in the sixteenth century, what we would now call contractual actions were enforced by the writs of debt and covenant.[8] Neither debt nor covenant focused on the mutuality of promises in a consensual transaction. Debt transcended the modern range of contract in dealing with the liability to pay a liquidated sum of one who had obtained a *quid pro quo*;[9] covenant dealt with the unilateral obligation to perform a promise made under seal. The emergence of *assumpsit* brought with it the idea that mutual and executory promises are binding because each is consideration for the other.[10] Only later did this interdependence also assist in defining the right of termination for breach.[11] To this extent, the dependency of contractual promises upon each other determined the order in which they were to be performed. Hence the failure by one party to perform a promise might have the consequence that the promise of the other party did not spring. A different principle, failure of consideration, reigned where a contract had been imperfectly executed by one party and the other sought termination. The challenge facing the legal system was to accommodate these two principles of dependent promises and failure of consideration within a unitary doctrine of termination for breach.

Kingston v. *Preston*[12] contains the classical exposition of the dependency principle. It swept aside the formalist approach of earlier authority and ruled that the order of performance turned upon 'the evident sense and meaning of the parties'.[13] In that case, despite the absence of a formal connection between a vendor's promise to transfer his business and the purchaser's promise to give security for future payments, the court ruled that the purchaser had to perform first, for otherwise the vendor would be robbed of a major inducement to contract. Lord Mansfield

---

[8] See A. W. B. Simpson, *A History of the Common Law of Contract [:] The Rise of Assumpsit* (OUP, London, 1975); S. F. C. Milsom, *Historical Foundations of the Common Law* (2nd edn., Butterworths, London, 1981); C. H. Fifoot, *History and Sources of the Common Law [:] Tort and Contract* (Stevens, London, 1949); T. Plucknett, *A Concise History of the Common Law* (5th edn., Butterworths, London, 1956); J. H. Baker, *An Introduction to English Legal History* (3rd edn., Butterworths, London, 1990); S. Stoljar, *A History of Contract at Common Law* (Australian National University Press, Canberra, 1975). For the view that the importance of the penal bond in the development of contract law has been understated, see A. W. B. Simpson (1966) 81 *LQR* 392.

[9] See *United Australia Ltd* v. *Barclays Bank Ltd* [1941] AC 1, 26 (Lord Atkin).

[10] See *Norwood* v. *Norwood and Read* (1558) 1 Plowd. 180, 182 ('every contract executory is an *assumpsit* in itself'); *Slade's Case* (1602) Co. Rep. 92(b).

[11] This was not immediately obvious. See *Nichols* v. *Raynbred* (1615) Hob. 88, where Nichols could sue Raynbred on his promise to pay without averring that he was ready and willing to deliver the agreed cow. Raynbred's remedy for breach was a cross action.

[12] (1773), unreported but recounted in *Jones* v. *Barkley* (1781) 2 Dougl. 684, 689–91.

[13] *Ibid.* 691.

divided contractual promises into three categories:[14] first, independent promises, where a party's failure to perform sounds only in damages and does not release the other from performing his promise; secondly, dependent promises, where a party's promise is dependent upon prior performance of his promise by the other; and thirdly, concurrent dependent promises, where each party's performance is dependent upon prior performance by the other. The evident circularity in the last category was broken by allowing the plaintiff to aver readiness and willingness to perform as a condition precedent to suing the defendant for his failure to perform.[15]

If the above dependency rules were uncompromisingly applied, a party unable to complete performance, and thus unable to aver performance of all conditions precedent to the other's duty to perform, would leave the other in possession of the fruits of incomplete performance. To avoid such enrichment, the other was required to perform and bring a cross action for damages for defective performance.[16] This is shown by the great case of *Boone* v. *Eyre*,[17] where the vendor of a plantation and the slaves upon it received from the purchaser the agreed sum of £500 but was denied the agreed annuity of £160. The purchaser pleaded that the vendor was not lawfully possessed of the slaves. In the court's view, the vendor's breach went only to a part of the consideration bargained for by the purchaser and could be compensated in damages. Judgment for the purchaser would have allowed him to retain the plantation at an undervalue.[18]

The result in *Boone* v. *Eyre* was explained in *Duke of St Albans* v. *Shore*[19] in terms of the inequality of damages, namely, that to deprive the vendor of his annuity would inflict upon him a loss out of all proportion to the loss suffered by the purchaser when the contract was breached.[20] In *Duke of St Albans* itself, the purchaser was entitled to refuse to complete the purchase of a farm upon discovery that the vendor had cut down a large number of trees. The vendor could not recover in his debt action

---

[14] *Ibid.* 690–1. See C. Morison, *Rescission of Contracts* (Stevens, London, 1916), 61–9, who points out that Lord Mansfield was speaking of *covenants*, that is, promises under seal. If his words were meant to be so confined, the later cases seem not to have restricted them in this way.

[15] See *Jones* v. *Barkley*, n. 12 above; Sale of Goods Act, s. 28.

[16] See Sjt. Williams's famous notes to *Pordage* v. *Cole* (1669) 1 Wms. Saund. 319, 320.

[17] (1777) 1 H Bl. 273. See also *Campbell* v. *Jones* (1796) 6 TR 570.

[18] Sjt. Williams attached importance to the fact that the contract had been performed in part: n. 16 above. The seller could not have recovered the value of the plantation on the common count of *quantum valebat* since this would have been inconsistent with the terms of an open (that is, unrescinded) contract: see *Cutter* v. *Powell* (1795) 6 TR 320.

[19] (1789) 1 H Bl. 270.

[20] *Ibid.* 279. For a modern decision actuated by this principle and applying it through the medium of damages assessment, see *Jacob & Youngs Inc.* v. *Kent* (1921) 129 NE 889 (NY).

'unless [he] has done all that it was incumbent on him to do'.[21] Assuming the breach to be no more serious than the breach of the vendor in *Boone,* there was a vital distinction between the two cases. The purchaser had obtained no benefits under the contract in *Duke of St Albans* when declining to proceed further with performance. The related ideas of inequality of damages and the receipt of a valuable benefit pointed to a critical distinction between executory and partly-executed contracts.[22]

The stage was now set for bringing together valuable benefit, inequality of damages, dependency of promises, and failure of consideration within a unitary system of termination rules, which occurred during the nineteenth century. Contractual termination was treated as a question of law and therefore outside the province of the jury, a development contemporaneously affecting also the remoteness of damages rules.[23] The intention of the parties, as manifested in the contract itself, was the paramount principle governing termination.[24] This intention might be that each and every breach should permit termination.[25] In the absence of such an express intention, a jury considering the hypothetical range of consequences flowing from the breach of a particular term would state the effect of any breach on 'the substance and foundation of the adventure'.[26] The judge would then decide whether the range of consequences was so serious that any breach of the term should permit termination.[27] Because of the close identification of the term and its consequences, the practice developed of labelling as conditions[28] those terms whose every breach gave rise to termination rights, instead of as warranties coupled with a condition precedent.[29] Terms that did not give rise to termination rights were known simply as warranties, a confusing usage since all inducing statements made with contractual intention were also known

---

[21]　(1789) 1 H Bl. 278.

[22]　See *Ellen* v. *Topp* (1851) 6 Ex. 424 (but not trivial benefit: *ibid.* 442); *Graves* v. *Legg* (1854) 9 Ex. 710, affd. (1857) 2 H & N 210; *Hoare* v. *Rennie* (1859) 5 H & N 19; *Simpson* v. *Crippen* (1872) LR 8 QB 14; *Honck* v. *Muller* (1881) 7 QBD 92.

[23]　*Hadley* v. *Baxendale* (1854) 9 Ex. 341; J. Danzig (1975) 4 *J Leg. Stud.* 249.

[24]　Bridge, n. 5, above 881–4, discussing *Bettini* v. *Gye* (1876) 1 QBD 183; *Poussard* v. *Spiers* (1876) 1 QBD 410; *Bentsen* v. *Taylor, Sons & Co. (No. 2)* [1893] 2 QB 274.

[25]　*Bettini* v. *Gye,* n. 24 above, 187: 'Parties may think some matter, apparently of very little importance, essential; and if they sufficiently express an intention to make the literal fulfilment of such a thing a condition precedent it will be' (Blackburn J).

[26]　*Bentsen* v. *Taylor, Sons & Co. (No. 2),* n. 24 above.

[27]　A question of construction, and therefore one of law.

[28]　A stern critic of this technique was S. Williston. The use of 'condition' in this way seems to date from *Glaholm* v. *Hays* (1841) 2 Man. & Gr. 257. See also J. L. Montrose [1964] *CLJ* 60, 75–82; F. M. B. Reynolds (1963) 79 *LQR* 534, 534–40. This practice remains the clearest way of conveying the parties' meaning (but see *Wickman Machine Tool Sales Ltd* v. *L Schuler AG* [1974] AC 235). On the need for clear language, see *Bowes* v. *Chalyer* (1923) 32 CLR 159, 182.

[29]　See Diplock LJ in *Hongkong Fir Shipping Co. Ltd* v. *Kawasaki Kisen Kaisha* [1962] 2 QB 26, 71.

as warranties.[30] Some of these latter terms might be important enough to pass the above test of a promissory condition.

This new terminology supplanted the language of mutual and dependent promises and encouraged certainty by cataloguing the status of specific terms of commercial contracts such as sale and charterparties. But it also promoted rigidity by disregarding the effects produced by specific breaches of contract,[31] thus eclipsing or concealing the failure of consideration principle. The Sale of Goods Act is imbued with the language of conditions and warranties to a degree that impedes the search for a flexible solution to problems. Not entirely suppressed, however, the failure of consideration principle has been transformed into various rules controlling in some measure the extensive termination rights granted by the Act.

Statutory Termination Rules Before the Sale and Supply of Goods Act 1994

Chalmers claimed the Sale of Goods Act 1893 'endeavoured to reproduce as exactly as possible the existing law'.[32] The terminology of conditions and warranties, expounded in key cases leading up to the 1893 Act, is therefore writ large in the Act and in its successor, unchanged in this respect, the Act of 1979. A significant, though partial, reform is contained in the Sale and Supply of Goods Act 1994. Apart from this last development, a superficial reading of the Sale of Goods Act might encourage the view that termination rights can by a process of construction be predicted in all cases at the outset of the contract.

The starting point is section 11(3):

Whether a stipulation in a contract of sale is a condition, the breach of which may give rise to a right to treat the contract as repudiated, or a warranty, the breach of which may give rise to a claim for damages but not to a right to reject the goods and treat the contract as repudiated, depends in each case on the construction of the contract; and a stipulation may be a condition, though called a warranty in the contract.

Section 11(3) does not explicitly state that all stipulations in contracts of sale are either conditions or warranties, but that is the implication. It denies, moreover, that a breach of warranty could ever give rise to termination. Furthermore, until the 1994 Act, the Sale of Goods Act did not in the list of events preventing the buyer from rejecting the goods and

---

[30] Ch. 8 below.

[31] *Hongkong Fir Shipping Co. Ltd* v. *Kawasaki Kisen Kaisha*, n. 29 above.

[32] Introduction to the 1st edn. of M. Chalmers, *The Sale of Goods Act, 1893* (Butterworths, London, 1894) and reprinted in subsequent editions.

terminating the contract[33] list minor or trivial injury. The comprehensive pretensions of section 11(3) are bolstered by the binary technique of the draftsman in section 61(1) in defining only 'warranty', leaving 'condition' to be understood as any stipulation that is not a warranty. Since a warranty is 'collateral to the main purpose of [the] contract', a condition must therefore be not collateral, that is, integral to the main purpose. The conclusion that slight breaches of condition never disallow termination, while serious breaches of warranty never permit it, seems ineluctable in interpreting the 1979 Act before the 1994 changes.

The above binary view is reinforced by the way that the Sale of Goods Act classifies the various implied terms. Thus the seller's duties regarding his right to sell, description, satisfactory quality,[34] fitness for purpose and correspondence with sample are stated to be conditions.[35] On the other hand, the seller's duties regarding the buyer's quiet possession and the freedom of the goods from encumbrances are classed as warranties.[36]

This binary approach treats termination entitlement as a matter of *a priori* construction of the contract. In the language of the old law, it is as if termination depended exclusively upon the dependent promises rules. What therefore became of failure of consideration and cognate ideas, such as the receipt of benefit, inequality of damages and partial execution? There are a number of responses to this.

First, failure of consideration is preserved in effect by section 31(2) of the Act, which deals with severable instalment contracts, where discharge from the outstanding portion of a partly executed contract turns 'on the terms of the contract and the circumstances of the breach'. This involves a consideration of the factual circumstances of the breach. Secondly, failure of consideration is free to invade duties of the buyer and the seller, notably those concerning the time, manner, and content of delivery and payment and acceptance duties, which are not designated by the Act as conditions or warranties. Duties of delivery and acceptance in section 27 escape classification as conditions or warranties. In addition, according to section 10:

(1) Unless a different intention appears from the terms of the contract, stipulations as to time of payment are not of the essence of a contract of sale.

(2) Whether any other stipulation as to time is or is not of the essence of the contract depends upon the terms of the contract.

This permits courts to be flexible and look to the consequences of breach. Moreover, even (for example) if timely payment by the buyer were construed as not of the essence of the contract, a failure to pay

---

[33] Ss. 11(2), 35.
[34] As merchantable quality has become with effect from the 1994 Act.
[35] Ss. 12(1) and 13–15.   [36] S. 12(2).

would over time become non-payment rather than late payment[37] and the seller would be able to terminate. The seller cannot be expected to abide by the contract until the crack of doom because timely payment is not of the essence of the contract. Thirdly, the Act does not expressly provide that the doctrine of conditions and warranties applies also to express terms of the contract.[38]

Fourthly, the Sale of Goods Act contains a number of provisions attesting to the importance of execution and benefit in defining termination entitlement. The implied terms of quiet possession and freedom from encumbrances,[39] which connote interference after the event with the beneficial enjoyment of goods, are designated as warranties that never give rise to termination rights. The receipt of a benefit was also implicit in the now-repealed provision that, if the property in specific goods passed at the date of the contract, the buyer could not reject the goods for breach of condition.[40] The quasi-contractual origins of this provision show it to have been fed by the inability of a buyer, who had obtained even the abstract property in goods, to rescind the contract *ab initio*, at that time a necessary precondition to an action for the recovery of money on a failure of consideration.[41]

Fifthly, the acceptance rules in section 35 clearly recognize the distinction between executory and executed contracts for the purpose of termination. Though there is no explicit link to section 35, section 11(2), which states that a buyer may waive a breach of condition by the seller and elect instead to treat it as a breach of warranty, is the inspiration behind the later provision. Section 11(4) echoes section 11(2) in stating that acceptance means that a breach of condition by the seller can only be treated as a breach of warranty. The circumstances in section 35 in which the buyer accepts the goods are threefold: when the buyer intimates an acceptance to the seller, when after delivery he performs an act inconsistent with the ownership of the seller, and when he retains the

---

[37] Williston stressed that it was 'desirable to distinguish between a breach of promise to do a thing and a breach of promise as to the time when it shall be done': S. Williston and G. Thompson, *A Treatise on the Law of Contracts* (rev. edn., Baker Voorhis, New York, 1936), iii, §845.

[38] But s. 11(3) could be so interpreted. Discussed further below.   [39] S. 12(2).

[40] S. 11(1)(c) of the Sale of Goods Act 1893 in combination with s. 18, Rule 1.

[41] *Cutter* v. *Powell* (1795) 6 TR 320; *Weston* v. *Downes* (1778) 1 Dougl. 23; *Towers* v. *Barrett* (1786) 1 TR 133; *Hunt* v. *Silk* (1804) 5 East 449; *Street* v. *Blay* (1831) 5 B & Ad. 456. For a fuller explanation see M. G. Bridge (1986) 20 *UBC LR* 53. On the notions of execution and benefit undermining strict terms, see *Behn* v. *Burness* (1863) 3 B & S 751, 755–6. *Graves* v. *Legg* (1854) 9 Ex. 710 asserts that the difference for termination purposes between executory and executed contracts did not affect the initial characterization of a term as a condition precedent, with which cf. *Ellen* v. *Topp* (1851) 6 Ex. 424 (construction of contract 'varied by matter *ex post facto*'). This last proposition was criticized in *Wallis, Son & Wells* v. *Pratt & Haynes* [1911] AC 394, 400, tacitly disapproving of Farwell LJ in the court below at [1910] 2 KB 1003, 1018.

goods beyond a reasonable time even though not intimating acceptance. All three cases are consistent with an election to retain the goods and sue for damages, but the third, probably the most common in practice, is also consistent with execution and benefit analysis.

It may be argued that the reason the Act treats so many of the implied terms as conditions is that initially a very short time was contemplated between delivery and acceptance, during which the buyer would be unlikely to derive a practical benefit from the contract. Canadian cases in particular have stretched the meaning of a reasonable time in extending the buyer's right of rejection.[42] It is noticeable that, in so doing, the courts have often stressed that the breach of an implied condition binding the seller in the circumstances amounts to a fundamental breach or otherwise produces grave effects. Such a buyer is unlikely to derive a net benefit from the contract.[43] The result is not dissimilar to the two-tier approach to rejection in the US Uniform Commercial Code, consisting of successive rights of rejection and revocation of acceptance,[44] the latter lying in stated cases where the value of the goods to the buyer is substantially impaired.

Section 35 does not mount a head-on assault on the doctrine of conditions and warranties but undermines it covertly. A term that for remedial purposes must be treated as a warranty is still essentially a condition.[45] The corollary to the proposition, once a condition always a condition, is the proposition, once a warranty always a warranty. The Sale of Goods Act contains no overt concession to the failure of consideration principle by allowing termination for factually serious breaches of warranty. This is not too surprising, since the Act is so strict in classifying the important implied terms as conditions, thus obviating a need to invoke failure of consideration.

Slight Breach and the Sale and Supply of Goods Act 1994

A new section 15A, inserted in the Sale of Goods Act by section 4 of the Sale and Supply of Goods Act 1994,[46] limits the right to terminate for breach of the implied description, quality, and fitness conditions in sections 13 to 15 in the following terms:

---

[42] Discussed at n. 151 and the text accompanying n. 197 below.
[43] See also *Rowland* v. *Divall* [1923] 2 KB 500, discussed Ch. 9 below.
[44] UCC, Arts. 2–602, 608.
[45] See *Wallis, Son & Wells* v. *Pratt & Haynes* [1910] 2 KB 1003, *per* Fletcher Moulton LJ (dissenting), whose judgment was adopted as a model statement of the law by the House of Lords, n. 41 above.
[46] In force as of 3 Jan. 1995. See M. G. Bridge [1995] *JBL* 398.

(1) Where in the case of a contract of sale—

    (a) the buyer would, apart from this subsection, have the right to reject goods by reason of the breach on the part of the seller of a term implied by section 13, 14 or 15 . . ., but

    (b) the breach is so slight that it would be unreasonable for him to reject them,

then if the buyer does not deal as a consumer, the breach is not to be treated as a breach of condition but may be treated as a breach of warranty.[47]

Subsection (3) goes on to place on the seller the burden of persuasion of showing that the terms of sub-section (1) have been met, which in practice will not be easy to discharge. There is also a provision curtailing the buyer's rights under section 30 where the seller delivers too many or too few goods and the shortfall or excess is so slight that it would be unreasonable for the buyer to reject the goods.[48]

Section 15A, confined to non-consumer sales, was recommended by the Law Commission in its report on *Sale and Supply of Goods*.[49] The reasons there given for a reform of the Sale of Goods Act with perceived minor practical consequences are as follows. In taking advantage of rejection and termination rights for slight breaches of condition, the buyer was sometimes able to put on the seller a disproportionate loss, a version of the inequality of damages argument.[50] The buyer in so doing might reverse the effect of a market risk that under the contract had gone against him,[51] one of the consequences of a lawful termination. The introduction of a control like that in section 15A would therefore, in this one specific case, prevent action being taken by the buyer in bad faith,[52] although the Law Commission took care to say that the buyer's motive in terminating a contract was not a matter for review.[53] These two positions are not easily reconciled. So as probably not to upset the commodities markets, the new provision is considered not to overrule those authorities that state that the time of delivery in commercial contracts is normally of the essence of the contract,[54] although an advantageous

---

[47] Similar provisions have been introduced into the Supply of Goods (Implied Terms) Act 1973 for hire purchase agreements (s. 11A) and into the Supply of Goods and Services Act 1982 for other contracts of proprietary transfer (s. 5A) and for hire contracts (s. 10A).

[48] S. 30(2A).　　　[49] Law Com. No. 160, 1987.　　　[50] *Ibid.*, para. 4.1.

[51] Para. 4.5.　　　[52] Para. 4.18.　　　[53] Para. 4.19.

[54] Para. 4.24. But note that timely delivery is historically explained in terms of description: *Bowes* v. *Shand* (1877) 2 App. Cas. 455; *Kwei Tek Chao* v. *British Traders and Shippers Ltd* [1954] 2 QB 459, 480–1. So, too, in more recent times has been the condition that an f.o.b. seller deliver goods at the nominated port of shipment: *Petrograde Inc.* v. *Stinnes Handels GmbH* [1995] 1 Lloyd's Rep. 142. Do these cases apply s. 13 or concern express conditions inspired by the content of s. 13? Could a stipulation be both an express condition and part of the s. 13 description condition, and if so, could a buyer freely elect in favour of the former to avoid the application of s. 15A? In the litigious world of commodities trading,

termination to recapture a lost market movement is likely to be particularly in evidence in such cases. It is noticeable too from the text of section 15A that it does nothing to undermine the strictness of section 12(1) and the seller's right to sell.[55] If a small amount is left outstanding under a financed conditional sale, and the finance house demands that sum from a sub-buyer, the latter will be able to invoke the full rigour of section 12(1) against the intermediate seller.

An argument supporting section 15A is that it would avoid the compulsion to give a slanted application of the implied conditions of fitness and quality in the Act.[56] The new provision certainly accords with the practice in international commodities contracts of making a price allowance for damaged goods. In many such cases, the buyer is the party better able to make economic use of sub-standard goods. An additional benefit could be the avoidance of tortured interpretations of the meaning of description in section 13 of the Act.[57] It is possible too that the threat of the section may persuade a buyer to permit a seller to cure a defect or other non-conformity in the goods supplied, which would go some little way to redress the Law Commission's recommendation that the seller not be given a statutory right to cure. The provision in section 15A applies only where the consequences of the breach are so slight that it would be unreasonable for the buyer to reject the goods. It should not prevent rejection where the breach cannot be described as slight but the buyer is unreasonable in, for example, turning down an offer of cure. The slight breach limitation on termination is a long way from the test of a discharging breach laid down in *Hongkong Fir Shipping Co. Ltd* v. *Kawasaki Kisen Kaisha*,[58] which few claimants would be able to satisfy in practice, and falls considerably short of the test for a material breach required by Scots law.[59] The Law Commission is surely right to conclude that it will therefore be of infrequent application[60] but perhaps has not estimated sufficiently the disruptive possibilities in a structural reform like this one.

The parties are permitted expressly or impliedly to oust section 15A.[61] Nothing in the text of the new provision states that this will be subject to the controls laid down for exclusion clauses in the Unfair Contract Terms Act 1977.[62] It would not be easy anyway to see how the 1977 Act could apply to an implied exclusion. As for an express exclusion, the 1977 Act was not amended to take account of the Sale and Supply of Goods Act

these questions will one day be asked. The systemic certainties of these terms being treated as conditions may therefore be undermined by s. 15A.

[55] Ch. 9, below.

[56] The Law Commission mentions *Millars of Falkirk* v. *Turpie* 1976 SLT 66 but might also have referred to the unconvincing conclusion on merchantable quality of the Court of Appeal in *Cehave NV* v. *Bremer Handelsgesellschaft mbH* [1976] QB 44.

[57] Ch. 7, below.				[58] [1962] 2 QB 26.				[59] S. 11(5).

[60] N. 49 above, para. 4.21.				[61] S. 15A(2).				[62] Ch. 8 below.

but, in section 3, does contain a provision that on the face of it might embrace a buyer's written standard terms excluding section 15A. But there is an insuperable difficulty. Section 15A constrains the buyer's rights under section 11 of the Sale of Goods Act, and a clause excluding section 15A would be one that lifts an impediment to the exercise of the buyer's statutory rights. Section 3(2) of the 1977 Act is designed to prevent a party from excluding or restricting liability when in breach of contract or claiming to render no performance or a performance substantially different from that which was reasonably expected. This is a long way from dealing with a clause ousting section 15A and the limits it places on the exercise of the buyer's statutory rights under section 11 of the Sale of Goods Act. Any argument that the clause restricts the buyer's liability to pay the purchase price for the goods appears strained.

Lastly, just as the decision not to pursue the seller's right to cure a defective tender in consumer cases gave leverage to the consumer buyer in dealings with the seller, so too would the retention of the present strict law serve the same purpose. Hence section 15A is confined to non-consumer cases, namely, those cases that do not pass the test of a consumer transaction in the 1977 Act.[63] It may seem hard on retailers to leave them exposed to strict termination rights exercised by consumer buyers, yet be disabled by section 15A from terminating the contract *qua* their own suppliers. But this is a particular example of the general problem they face when their conditions of sale differ from those on which they acquired the goods.[64] It should also be remembered that the loss felt by their consumer buyers may not be the same as the loss they seek to pass on to their suppliers. Moreover, they may already have lost the right to reject the goods under section 35. Finally, if they have been exposed to the termination of their own sales contracts, it may be that their own attempts to terminate would not fall foul of section 15A.

Termination Developments in Modern Contract Law

Any conviction that the doctrine of conditions and warranties, as codified in the Sale of Goods Act, was of general application to all contracts and their terms, was jolted by *Hongkong Fir Shipping Co. Ltd* v. *Kawasaki Kisen Kaisha*.[65] A quality obligation in a time charter, namely the owner's duty to provide a seaworthy ship, was neither a condition, whose every breach would permit the charterer to terminate, nor a warranty, whose breach could only ever give rise to a damages claim. Rather, it belonged to a large group of intermediate terms permitting termination only if the injured party were deprived of substantially the whole of the contracted-

[63] N. 49 above, para. 4.8. For the definition of consumer transactions, see Ch. 8 below.
[64] N. 49 above, para. 4.26.   [65] N. 58 above.

for benefit. Alternative language of long standing would refer to a failure of consideration, a frustrating breach, and a breach going to the root of the contract.[66] At the heart of the case lies the idea that it is not so much the status of the term breached that governs the existence of termination rights, but rather the impact of the events flowing from the breach on the injured party's bargain.[67] Indeed, the judgment of Diplock LJ for a time put in doubt the parties' freedom to define all future outcomes of a breach as going to the root of the contract by designating it as a condition.[68] According to Diplock LJ, certain complex undertakings, like the owner's duty to provide a seaworthy ship, cannot be classified simply as conditions or warranties since the range of outcomes produced by a breach can run from the trivial to the serious, from a rusty nail on the deck to broken down engines.[69]

The Mihalis Angelos,[70] a case concerning an 'expected ready to load' clause in a voyage charter, displays a reaction against the emphasis placed in *Hongkong Fir* on defining termination rights by reference to events. The shipowner was in breach by failing honestly and reasonably to believe that the ship would be ready to load in Hanoi by the stated date. In concluding that the clause was a condition, the court laid particular emphasis on long-standing commercial authority and usage,[71] a clear concession to the importance of commercial certainty.[72]

The above cases do not draw a clear line between conditions and intermediate stipulations for clauses other than the ones under review. Nor do they relate the autonomy of the parties in grading contractual terms to the role of the court in quantifying the severity of a breach. Neither case, moreover, has anything to say about the reconciliation of their divergent approaches within the statutory framework of sale of goods

---

[66] There is little to choose between the various formulations, but the preferred approach in this text is for root (or radical breach) language (see *Davidson* v. *Gwynne* (1810) 12 East 381).

[67] N. 58 above, 68–9. Cf. *Peter Lind and Co.* v. *Constable Hart and Co.* [1979] 2 Lloyd's Rep. 248, 253.

[68] Nothing in Diplock LJ's judgment supports the view that the parties may *a priori* define any breach of a contractual term as having this effect. Cf. Blackburn J in *Bettini* v. *Gye* (1876) 1 QBD 183, 187, and see the criticism of Diplock LJ's judgment by Megaw LJ in *Bunge Corpn.* v. *Tradax Export SA* [1981] 2 All ER 513, 536–7.

[69] N. 58 above, 69–71.

[70] *Maredelanto Cia Naviera SA* v. *Bergbau Handels GmbH* [1971] 1 QB 164. See D. Greig (1973) 89 *LQR* 93.

[71] T. Scrutton, *Scrutton on Charterparties and Bills of Lading* (10th edn., Sweet & Maxwell, London, 1921) (an edition for which Scrutton retained responsibility); *Finnish Govt.* v. *H. Ford & Co. Ltd* (1921) 6 Ll LR 188; *Samuel Sanday & Co.* v. *Keighley Maxsted & Co.* (1922) 27 Com. Cas. 296.

[72] N. 70 above, 199 and 207, where Edmund Davies and Megaw LJJ approved the language of Williams J in *Behn* v. *Burness* (1863) 3 B & S 751, 759, asserting that the time of a ship's arrival was of prime importance to a charterer 'considering winds, markets and dependent contracts'.

agreements.[73] In *Cehave NV* v. *Bremer Handelsgesellschaft mbH*,[74] the *Hongkong Fir* approach was imported into sales law. The contract called for the shipment 'in good condition' of a quantity of citrus pulp pellets for compounding into cattle feed.[75] A substantial portion of the shipment had suffered from overheating. The buyers, having paid against shipping documents, rejected the goods and sought the return of the price. In a falling market at the port of discharge, they repurchased the goods, through an agent at a judicial sale, for a price significantly below their value as damaged goods.[76] Beside throwing the market risk back on the sellers, the buyers therefore benefited from the distress sale. Later, by carefully eking out the goods, they used them all in compounding feed. By their own actions, they showed that damages would have been a perfectly adequate remedy for the breach.

In finding for the sellers, the court in *Cehave* had to confront the obstacle of the statutory doctrine of conditions and warranties. A rather startling aspect of the case was that, despite the serious damage to the goods, the sellers were held not to be in breach of the merchantable quality condition.[77] This difficulty out of the way, the court unanimously concluded that the express shipment term was not a contractual condition.[78] Consequently, the buyers were entitled to terminate only if the breach went to the root of the contract, which plainly it did not. For the binary system of conditions and warranties laid down in the Sale of Goods Act, the court in accommodating express terms substituted a different binary system.[79] This system would still admit the possibility of contractual conditions, established as such by statute, party choice, and commercial usage, though no court would liberally add to the known stock of conditions.[80] In addition, there would be the residuum of contractual terms, namely warranties, the normal remedy for whose breach would be damages but which would afford 'back-up'[81] termination rights if the breach went to the root of the contract. Besides its discordance with the

---

[73] But treating *Hongkong Fir* as concerning the sale of goods, the 'seller's' obligation to tender a conforming ship might well have been a condition but the 'buyer's' right of rejection might have been lost by acceptance under s. 35.

[74] *The Hansa Nord* [1976] QB 44. See also *Total International Ltd* v. *Addax BV* [1996] 2 Lloyd's Rep. 333.

[75] Cl. 7 of the form 200 of the now-defunct Cattle Food Trade Association.

[76] The contract price was £100,000, the market price at delivery for sound goods was £86,000, and a reasonable price allowance for the damage would have been £20,000. In 'an astonishing sequence of events', n. 74 above, 55–6 (Denning MR), the buyers' agents paid £33,720 for the goods at the judicial sale and turned them over at that price to the buyers.

[77] Ch. 7 below. See M. G. Bridge (1983) 28 *McGill LJ* 867, 898–9.

[78] No case law existed to show that it was.

[79] N. 74 above, 73 (Roskill LJ) and 84 (Ormerod LJ). Lord Denning, *ibid.* 61, however, saw contractual terms as falling into three categories, conditions, warranties, and intermediate stipulations.

[80] N. 74 above, 70–1 (Roskill LJ).   [81] A phrase of Ormerod LJ: n. 74 above, 83.

language of the Act, in particular section 11(3), which implies that the doctrine of conditions and warranties extends to *all* contractual stipulations, and not just implied terms, this view does not accommodate statutory implied warranties, which in no circumstances permit termination for breach.[82] But this is a minor difficulty. The approach in *Cehave* may not be one of unimpeachable fidelity to the language of the Act, but the court's decision represents a determined effort to avoid a rift between sales law and a constantly changing general contract law.[83]

Cehave was not the last swing of the pendulum. A later House of Lords decision, *Bunge Corpn.* v. *Tradax Export SA*,[84] pointed the way to strict termination rights in the case of time of performance of primary obligations in international commodities contracts, a line that for the most part was confirmed in subsequent decisions.[85] The contract was for the f.o.b. bulk shipment of soya bean meal from an American Gulf of Mexico port, under which the buyers were to give the sellers fifteen days' notice of expected readiness to load. When the buyers were four days late in giving the notice, the sellers terminated the contract and sued for damages on a falling market.[86] The buyer's breach did not go to the root of the contract so the seller had to establish that the buyer's duty was a condition. At all levels it was held to be a condition, largely because of the need to promote certainty in the forward-planning and contractual management aspects of the international commodities trade and to simplify dispute settlement. Difficult issues of damages entitlement, protracted trials and complex time of the essence clauses could all be avoided by treating time obligations as conditions.[87] Lord Wilberforce went as far as to deny any role to intermediate stipulations in dealing with time obligations in commercial contracts since 'there is only one kind of breach possible, namely to be late'.[88] Yet the prejudice of a party receiving late

---

[82] Ss. 11(3), 61(1). See Bridge, n. 77 above, 898–9.

[83] N. 74 above, 60, 72–3, 82–3. See also the description case of *Harlingdon and Leinster Enterprises Ltd* v. *Christopher Hull Fine Art. Ltd* [1991] 1 QB 564.

[84] [1981] 2 All ER 513, affirming the decision of the Court of Appeal, which had reversed Parker J.

[85] *Toepfer* v. *Lenersan-Poortman NV* [1980] 1 Lloyd's Rep. 143; *Cie Commerciale Sucres et Denrées* v. *Czarnikow Ltd (The Naxos)* [1990] 3 All ER 641; *Gill & Duffus* v *Soc. pour l'Exportation des Sucres* [1985] 1 Lloyd's Rep. 621. *Aliter, Phibro Energy* v. *Nissho* [1991] 1 Lloyd's Rep. 38. A less strict approach is taken to incidental obligations: *Bremer Handelsgesellschaft mbH* v. *Vanden Avenne-Izegem SA* [1978] 2 Lloyd's Rep. 109; *State Trading Corp.* v. *Golodetz* [1988] 2 Lloyd's Rep. 182.

[86] It is not clear why the sellers defied conventional wisdom.

[87] See Lord Lowry, n. 84 above, 545–6. This speed and consistency of result is of course a by-product of making termination rights a pure matter of construction and therefore of law. See the deference paid to the views of arbitrators and trade boards at the same time as the sovereignty of the courts is asserted: *ibid.* 532 (Megaw LJ) and 553 (Lord Roskill). See also Lord Radcliffe's discussion of the respective roles of arbitrator and judge in the frustration case of *Davis Contractors Ltd* v. *Fareham UDC* [1956] AC 696, 730.

[88] *Ibid.* 541. See also Megaw LJ, 534.

performance frequently mounts from day to day, so as eventually to deprive him of substantially the benefit for which he bargained. A further reason for the outcome was that the seller's subsequent duty of timely shipment was a condition, so the buyer's anterior duty to give notice had to be one too.[89]

Bunge Corpn. v. *Tradax SA* makes it possible to predict termination rights with some degree of precision. First, the decision accepted in principle intermediate stipulations whilst denying their application to time provisions in commercial contracts. The autonomy of the parties in grading a contractual term as a condition if they so wished—a freedom put in some doubt by *Hongkong Fir*—was also underwritten.[90] In consequence, the approach to termination rights is a two-fold one: first, the construction of the contract to see if the term breached was a condition; and secondly, failing this, the appraisal of the effects of the breach to see if it went to the root of the contract.[91] As a summary of the antecedent law, *Bunge* suggests a basic distinction between quality and time obligations.[92] The former are particularly apt for an intermediate stipulations approach, though the implied conditions of quality, fitness, and description are put beyond the reach of this by the Sale of Goods Act. If they give rise to a slight breach, the new section 15A can prevent unreasonable termination, but this is quite a long way from the intermediate stipulations approach.

In the case of commodities contracts at least, time obligations would usually be conditions even if not expressed to be such. In the case of consumer contracts, where less importance is attached to time than in the commodities markets, it might be preferable to permit termination only when the consequences of breach assume serious proportions,[93] though even here it is questionable whether the confining *Hongkong Fir* test should be applied to consumer buyers in its full rigour. For different reasons, time provisions in contracts for the sale of non-market items, such as complex machinery, commonly designed or tailored to the buyer's particular specifications, should not as a matter of course be construed

[89] *Ibid.*, in the House of Lords, 542, 543, and 553 (Lords Wilberforce, Scarman, and Roskill); in the Court of Appeal, 532 and 540 (Megaw and Browne LJJ). This does not logically follow: Ch. 6 below.

[90] N. 84 above, 536–7 (Megaw LJ) and 552 (Lord Roskill). See also the judgments in the *Hongkong Fir* case of Sellers and Upjohn LJJ: [1962] 2 QB 26, 60 and 63. The right of parties to designate a term as a condition was upheld in *Lombard North Central Plc* v. *Butterworth* [1987] QB 527.

[91] See also Denning MR in *Cehave*, n. 74 above.

[92] N. 84 above, 534 (Megaw LJ) and 541 (Lord Wilberforce).

[93] *Allen* v. *Danforth Motors Ltd* (1957) 12 DLR (2d) 572. Cf. *Charles Rickards Ltd* v. *Oppenhaim* [1950] 1 KB 616, where the buyer, who had throughout made it clear that he needed the car for a continental trip, waited patiently for the agreed distant delivery date.

impliedly as conditions.[94] The prejudice suffered on termination by the defaulting seller might be out of all proportion to the injury suffered on breach by the buyer. Furthermore, the opportunities for delay in such contracts are manifold and not always easily countered; sellers may, for example, rely upon the arrival of parts from their suppliers. The contracts themselves commonly involve a protracted process of negotiation, giving the buyer an opportunity to insert an express condition, and contain liquidated damages clauses for delay, thereby suggesting that termination should not arise for every breach.

THE BUYER'S RIGHTS OF EXAMINATION AND REJECTION

General

A buyer exercising a right to terminate the contract may thereby reject a non-conforming tender of goods by the seller and refuse to accept tenders that would, but for the termination, have fallen due at a future date. Although termination entails rejection, it does not necessarily follow as a matter of logic that a buyer entitled to reject goods is thereby entitled to or does terminate the contract.[95] When the principle of cure is examined below, the significance of this gap between rejection and termination will become apparent.

The Sale of Goods Act is not explicit in its treatment of termination and rejection and their effect upon the rights and duties of the parties. There is no definition at all of termination or of any of its synonyms such as discharge, rescission for breach, or cancellation. Sometimes, the Act refers to the entitlement of a party to treat the contract as repudiated for the other's breach,[96] but it does not say what in practical terms that means. The precise meaning of rejection is not stated in the Act, though the Act does recite the circumstances in which the right is lost by the buyer's acceptance of the goods[97] and refers to one instance of rejection, the refusal to accept a tender of non-conforming goods, when providing that the buyer is under no obligation to return the goods to the seller.[98]

The link between termination and rejection is left obscure. Certainly, where the seller is in breach of a statutory implied warranty, the buyer may neither reject the goods nor treat the contract as repudiated.[99] The Act says merely that a breach of condition 'may give rise' to a right to treat

---

[94] *Fairbanks Soap Co.* v. *Sheppard* [1953] 1 SCR 314.
[95] But see *Kwei Tek Chao* v. *British Traders and Shippers Ltd* [1954] 2 QB 459, 480, where Devlin J treats rejection as tantamount to termination.
[96] Ss. 11(3),(4), 31(2), and 61(1) ('warranty').   [97] S. 35.   [98] S. 36.
[99] Ss. 11(3) and 61(1).

the contract as repudiated.[100] It also fails to say precisely when a breach of condition occurs, whether on the tender of non-conforming goods, or on the expiry of the delivery period where time is of the essence, or in the event of a frustrating delay where time is not of the essence.[101] In grading certain implied terms as conditions, the Act does not relate them explicitly to rejection. It also expressly recites rejection rights where the seller is long or short on delivery, but again fails to state the consequences of this as a matter of termination.[102]

Despite the imprecision of the Act, it may be stated with some confidence that, apart from the possible right of a seller to cure a defective tender, a breach of condition, or the commission of any other discharging breach allows the buyer to terminate the contract. Furthermore, subject again to the possibility of cure, a buyer is allowed to reject goods tendered by the seller as and when the seller commits a breach of condition.[103]

Examination

The buyer's right of examination is to be found in section 34 which as reformed[104] now reads:

Unless otherwise agreed, when the seller tenders delivery of goods to the buyer, he is bound on request to afford the buyer a reasonable opportunity of examining the goods for the purpose of ascertaining whether they are in conformity with the contract and, in the case of a contract for sale by sample, of comparing the bulk with the sample.

This section is the old section 34(2) with the addition to its main provision of a specific example of its application to sales by sample.[105] The former sub-section (1) has, for the sake of clarity, been reworked into the body of section 35, which deals with the loss of a buyer's right of rejection consequent upon acceptance of the goods. This move is the latest step in an attempt to devise a protocol clearly showing that the examination rule takes precedence over the acceptance rules.[106] It evidences the conflict that has emerged over the years between the two sections as the commercial and legal practice of examination has changed.

This change can be seen in the place of examination. The nineteenth century cases reveal that the buyer's assent to an unconditional

---

[100] S. 11(3).   [101] See the discussion of cure below.   [102] S. 30.
[103] This discussion assumes that the contract is entire. For severable instalment contracts, see the text accompanying nn. 214 ff. below.
[104] Sale and Supply of Goods Act 1994, s. 2(2).
[105] Drawn from the former text of s. 15.
[106] See the earlier difficulties posed by *Hardy & Co. (London)* v. *Hillerns & Fowler* [1923] 2 KB 490.

appropriation of the goods by the seller and his examination of the goods were one and the same act. It was not as such the passing of property in unascertained goods that prevented the buyer from rejecting them but rather the buyer's approval of goods after examination or his waiver[107] of this right to examine. The equivalent rule for specific goods, most of which would have been examined or available for examination before the contract, prevented rejection after the passing of property and was based upon the idea of a notional delivery to the buyer at the contract date.[108] For local deliveries in particular, the place of examination was the seller's premises, which is the presumptive place of delivery[109] and therefore the place where the buyer presumptively makes payment.[110] A buyer satisfied with his examination of goods unconditionally appropriated by the seller would thereupon intimate to the seller that he was accepting them[111] and make payment. In such a case, the buyer's right of rejection would therefore be evanescent and commonly lost altogether if the buyer waived the right to examine or conducted a brief examination at the point of delivery.[112]

The link between the seller's premises and examination was necessarily broken where buyer and seller were separated by a distance and the services of a carrier were employed to transport the goods to the buyer. What seems to have been a rule that the place of examination was the seller's premises was relaxed as it became established that the buyer could examine on the arrival of the goods.[113] The carrier might have been able to provide a deemed assent to the seller's unconditional appropriation but not to examine and accept the goods on the buyer's behalf. In some cases, the link between assent and examination was not easily sundered: they held that a buyer examining the goods away from the seller's premises had not given prior assent to the seller's unconditional appropriation of non-conforming goods to the contract.[114] The passing of property would not nowadays pose an obstacle to the buyer's examination and rejection of the goods. A right of examination was necessarily postponed in the case of goods sold whilst in transit.[115] Similarly, goods

---

[107] See the waiver principle in s. 11(2).

[108] *Dixon* v. *Yates* (1833) 5 B & Ad. 313. Ch. 3 above.   [109] S. 29(2).

[110] S. 28 and Ch. 6 below.   [111] The first case of acceptance in s. 35.

[112] *John Hallam Ltd* v. *Bainton* (1919) 45 OLR 483 (Can.).

[113] *Bragg* v. *Villanova* (1923) 40 TLR 154; *Thames Canning Co.* v. *Eckhardt* (1915) 34 OLR 72 (Can.); *Tower Equipment Rental Ltd* v. *Joint Venture Equipment Sales* (1975) 9 OR (2d) 453 (Can.).

[114] *Ollett* v. *Jordan* [1918] 2 KB 41. In *Hardy & Co.* v. *Hillerns & Fowler* [1923] 2 KB 490, 499 Atkin LJ states that the property in c.i.f. goods does not pass upon the documentary transfer until the buyer has had an opportunity to examine the goods. See also *Perkins* v. *Bell* [1893] 1 QB 190, 198: rejection right surrendered on passing of property upon delivery.

[115] Thus the right of inspection in c.i.f. contracts is deferred: *Polenghi Bros.* v. *Dried Milk Co. Ltd* (1904) 92 LT 64; *E. Clemens Horst Co.* v. *Biddell Bros.* [1912] AC 18.

such as frozen fish could not adequately be inspected until the process of thawing at destination permitted it.[116] The point is not usually taken nowadays that the place of delivery is the place of examination.[117] In other cases, where buyer and seller contemplated that the goods would be examined by a distant sub-buyer, it might be their intention to postpone examination by or on behalf of the buyer to that place and time.[118] The shift of the place of examination excited fears in some cases that certain buyers might unscrupulously exploit the distance of the seller in extracting concessions.[119]

Section 34 does not define what amounts to an examination of the goods. At one extreme, it could be a brief and superficial inspection of the outward aspect of the goods; at the other, it could be a prolonged and beneficial use of the goods in service. The range embraces goods as diverse as natural commodities and manufactured items but the section 34 case law does not overtly reveal any difference in the understanding of examination for the purpose of dealing with these two types of goods. What is clear is that the law has not surrendered to the possibility that examination could extend to the latter of the above extremes. One objection to such a concession is that it would bring the buyer's right of examination into even more conflict with the acceptance bars to rejection in section 35.[120] The right of examination has, nevertheless, been extended to the hidden characteristics of goods, even when this has entailed some degree of destructive testing.[121] Postponing examination and extending its scope, however, is responsible for the battle for precedence in modern times between sections 34 and 35, resolved firmly in favour of the former.

Section 34 provides that the seller is bound on request to afford the buyer a reasonable opportunity to examine the goods but it makes no mention of the sanction for non-compliance. Certainly, a refusal to permit the buyer to examine may be seen as destroying the lawfulness of the

[116] *Winnipeg Fish Co.* v. *Whitman Fish Co.* (1909) 41 SCR 453.

[117] e.g. *Bernstein* v. *Pamson Motors (Golders Greeen) Ltd* [1987] 2 All ER 220. See however *Long* v. *Lloyd* [1958] 2 All ER 402, 406 where the court, dealing with the sale of a second-hand lorry, stated that apart from special circumstances the buyer should examine upon delivery. This now appears anachronistic.

[118] *Molling & Co.* v. *Dean & Son Ltd* (1901) 18 TLR 217; *A. J. Frank & Sons Ltd* v. *Northern Peat Co.* [1963] 2 OR 415 (Can.). Where goods cannot practicably be examined at the point of delivery, the right of examination will be deferred: *Heilbutt* v. *Hickson* (1872) LR 7 CP 438; *Grimoldby* v. *Wells* (1875) LR 10 CP 391.

[119] *Szymanowski and Co.* v. *Beck and Co.* [1923] 1 KB 457, 467 ('rejection ... as a lever to extort a reduction in the price'); *Re Faulckners Ltd* (1917) 38 DLR 84.

[120] Notably the retention of the goods beyond a reasonable time and the performance of an act inconsistent with the ownership of the seller. *Bernstein*, n. 117 above: a reasonable time is not the time needed to discover a hidden defect in the goods.

[121] *Heilbutt* v. *Hickson*, n. 118 above; *Toulmin* v. *Hedley* (1845) 2 Car. & K 157; *Winnipeg Fish Co*, n. 116 above; *Reevie* v. *White Co. Ltd* [1929] 4 DLR 296.

seller's tender so that the seller may not complain if the buyer refuses to accept and pay for the goods.[122] It has been said that a refusal to allow examination is a discharging breach.[123] This may be justified on the ground that the seller's conduct amounts to a repudiation or prevents due delivery in circumstances where time is of the essence of the contract.

Apart from consumer transactions, a buyer may waive, or under the terms of the contract surrender, the right of examination. The latter is commonly done in international commodity sales where disinterested inspection agencies issue certificates that are final and binding on the parties.[124] This system meets the concerns of a seller about having to dispose of rejected goods in a distant place. To a degree, that seller, if already paid by the buyer against shipping documents, has the tactical upper hand since it is up to the buyer to reject the goods and take steps to recover the price.[125] Under section 35(2),[126] the buyer is not bound by an acceptance of the goods, taking the form of an intimation of acceptance or the performance of an act inconsistent with the ownership of the seller, where the buyer has not had a chance to examine the goods. Although the buyer's examination rights for the purpose of section 35 may be waived or surrendered,[127] this is not allowed if the buyer is a consumer.[128] In non-consumer sales, a waiver, not amounting to a variation of the contract, of the right to examine should not be caught by the Unfair Contract Terms Act. The only relevant provision, section 3, applicable to a buyer doing business on the seller's written standard terms, governs the use of contract terms. A post-contract waiver of rights in a delivery note, for example, is not a contract term. Section 3 could extend to a surrender of the right to examine in the contract itself, but the difficult and technical argument would have to be made that the seller is excluding a liability to return the purchase price as a consequence of the rejection of the goods.[129]

---

[122] *Isherwood* v. *Whitmore* (1843) 11 M & W 347.

[123] *Lorymer* v. *Smith* (1822) 1 B & C 1.

[124] See, e.g., *Alfred C. Toepfer* v. *Continental Grain Co.* [1974] 1 Lloyd's Rep. 11; *Berger & Co. Inc.* v. *Gill & Duffus SA* [1984] AC 382. Questions may arise whether such a provision is confined to defects of quality: *N. V. Bunge* v. *Cie Noga d'Importation et d'Exportation SA* [1980] 2 Lloyd's Rep. 601 (admixture of soya oil and groundnut oil).

[125] The buyer has no lien for the recovery of the price: see *J. L. Lyons & Co.* v. *May and Baker Ltd* [1923] 1 KB 685; *Kwei Tek Chao* v. *British Traders & Shippers Ltd* [1954] 2 QB 459.

[126] Sale and Supply of Goods Act, s. 2(1).

[127] As implied by s. 35(3) for non-consumer cases.

[128] The definition of a consumer sale is taken from the Unfair Contract Terms Act 1977, Ch. 8 below.

[129] What if the buyer has not yet paid?

Acceptance

Section 11(4) provides that the buyer of goods under a non-severable contract[130] loses the right of rejection, and thus may not treat the contract as repudiated, after acceptance of the goods or a part of them.[131] This provision is made expressly subject to the new section 35A which permits such a buyer, if there is no express or implied contrary intention,[132] to reject non-conforming goods while accepting all those goods that are unaffected by the seller's breach.[133] The breach has to be serious enough that the buyer could have rejected the goods in their entirety, since section 35A does not manufacture a right of rejection where none existed before. If, for example, the seller were to sell a job lot, described as goods of varying quality and condition, the buyer would not be entitled to isolate in that lot those goods that fall below the average standard and reject them, when the goods as a whole comply with the conditions of description, fitness, and quality in sections 13 to 14. A more difficult question concerns the buyer who, under the new section 15A, would be unreasonable in rejecting goods for a slight breach of one or more of these implied terms.[134] Could the buyer reject a portion of the goods and retain all the rest? It might appear reasonable for the buyer to do this but section 35A requires that the buyer first have a right to reject the goods and section 15A deprives the buyer of the right of rejection.[135] The answer would therefore seem to be no.

Partial Rejection

The right of partial rejection, created whenever there has been a breach of condition, express or implied, or other breach going to the root of the contract, is an enlargement of the previous right of partial rejection given

[130] On entire and severable contracts see Ch. 6 below.

[131] This provision does not apply to consumer conditional sale contracts, which for this purpose are treated as hire purchase contracts: Supply of Goods (Implied Terms) Act 1973, s. 14 (see below). A buyer is a consumer who deals as a consumer for the purpose of Part I of the Unfair Contract Terms Act 1977: *ibid*.

[132] S. 35A(4). The difficulties stated above in applying the provisions of the Unfair Contract Terms Act to implied exclusions of s. 15 apply here too. S. 35A contains no equivalent to s. 35(3), which in consumer cases preserves the buyer's right to examine notwithstanding waiver or contrary agreement.

[133] S. 35A(1)(b). This does not take away the right of a buyer in receipt of an excess tender to accept only that quantity required by the contract: s. 30(2).

[134] The question also arises where the buyer is prevented from rejecting goods for slight deficiencies or surpluses: s. 30(2A).

[135] S. 15A: 'Where . . . the buyer would, apart from this subsection, have the right to reject goods . . .'.

[136] *W. Barker Jnr. & Co. Ltd* v. *E. T. Agius Ltd* (1927) 33 Com. Cas. 120; Law Com. No. 120, paras. 6.6 ff.

to the buyer for a breach of the seller's description obligation.[136] Section 30(4), stating this latter right, has now been repealed[137] because of its absorption by the more extensive provision in section 35A. Partial acceptance will often make good commercial sense and can be seen at work already in the cases where the parties have voluntarily agreed upon it.[138] It can often be the solution that minimizes the losses caused by the tender of non-conforming goods. The buyer exercising the new right of partial rejection must retain all conforming goods but may also, if he wishes, retain some of the non-conforming goods.[139] In the exercise of these rights, the buyer may not break up a commercial unit of goods; an acceptance of any of the goods in a unit is a deemed acceptance of all the goods in that unit.[140] Although the new provision does not say so, the buyer should pay for the goods retained at the contract rate, which is the rule laid down for short delivery by section 30(1). Similarly, if the buyer has already paid, so much of the contract price as corresponds to the rejected goods should be recoverable as on a failure of consideration.[141]

Meaning of Acceptance

Section 35 lays down three ways in which the buyer, by accepting the goods, loses the right of rejection. It should not be forgotten that an injured party may elect to treat a breach of condition as a breach of warranty. Nevertheless, the requirements of an election are so stringent[142] that it is difficult to conceive of such a case that does not fall within the heads of acceptance, especially the first, in section 35. These three acceptance heads are, first, an intimation to the seller that the buyer is accepting the goods; secondly, the performance after delivery of an act inconsistent with the seller's ownership; and thirdly, the retention of the goods after the lapse of a reasonable time.

Before these different modes of acceptance are considered, it is useful to consider two matters: the diverse meanings of acceptance in sales law and the common law underpinning of the statutory notion of acceptance

---

[137] Sale and Supply of Goods Act, s. 3(3).

[138] *Manifatture Tessile Laniera Wooltex* v. *J. B. Ashley Ltd* [1979] 2 Lloyd's Rep. 28; *Molling* v. *Dean* (1901) 18 TLR 217 (seller stamped the names of different sub-buyers on a consignment of 40,000 books). It is also common in the international commodity sale forms. A significant number of Canadian cases have in the past permitted partial acceptance despite the Act or (for pre-Act cases) the entire contracts rule. See M. G. Bridge, *Sale of Goods* (Butterworths, Toronto, 1988), 297–8.

[139] S. 35A(1)(b). Law Com. No. 160, para. 6.11.

[140] S. 35(7). Law Com. No. 160, paras. 6.12–13. Examples given are individual volumes in a set of encyclopædias and one of a pair of shoes.

[141] Partial recovery claims are not uncontroversial but are sanctioned by a number of authorities: see *Devaux* v. *Connolly* (1849) 8 CB 640; *Biggerstaff* v. *Rowatt's Wharf Ltd* [1896] 2 Ch. 93, 100, 105; *Behrend & Co. Ltd* v. *Produce Brokers Co. Ltd* [1920] 3 KB 530, 535; *Ebrahim Dawood Ltd* v. *Heath Ltd* [1961] 2 Lloyd's Rep. 512.

[142] *Peyman* v. *Lanjani* [1985] Ch. 457.

in section 35. In modern sales law, acceptance has at least three meanings. First, as one of the exceptions to the written evidence requirement, which is still to be found in some jurisdictions with an Act based upon the imperial Sale of Goods Act 1893, it is behaviour, sometimes prior to the receipt of goods,[143] that acknowledges the existence of a contract of sale.[144] This meaning of acceptance should be distinguished from the second meaning, the acceptance that forecloses rejection rights under sections 11(4) and 35.[145] The third meaning emerges from section 27, which speaks of the buyer's duty to accept and pay for the goods, the correlative of the seller's duty of delivery, which is needed to allow the seller to effect delivery. This form of acceptance occurs upon the transfer of possession, actual or constructive, to the buyer. The buyer must receive the seller's tender, which may occur in various ways, for example, through the agency of a carrier under section 32(1).

These three meanings reveal the explosion of the idea of acceptance as it has been pressed to perform different functions. The old written evidence acceptance might well precede the section 27 acceptance which will almost always precede the section 35 acceptance. It is the section 27 meaning that is the essential meaning of acceptance; the others represent departures from the norm. Acceptance as an exception to the written evidence requirement was accelerated to provide alternative unwritten evidence, while acceptance under section 35 was set back in order to accommodate to some degree the buyer prejudiced by hidden faults in complex manufactured goods.

The setting back of acceptance in section 35 has not been accomplished uniformly throughout the cases and has occurred to a greater degree in Canada than in England. So much uncertainty has been generated that a buyer can rarely be confidently advised whether rejection is still an available remedy. Though it will not dissipate the uncertainty, an exploration of the common law underpinning of section 35 would at least rationalize it. Section 11(2) provides that a buyer may elect to treat a breach of condition as a breach of warranty. When this provision is harnessed to acceptance in sections 11(4) and 35, acceptance may be seen as a statutory variant of election,[146] the idea being that the buyer's section 35 conduct evinces an objective intention to pursue only a damages remedy. In a similar vein, it has been said that a buyer may be estopped from rejecting the goods,[147] though modern acceptance cases do not ask whether the seller has relied to his detriment or altered his position as a result of the buyer's behaviour. Election and estoppel are not to be

---

[143] *Morton* v. *Tibbett* (1850) 15 QB 428; *Cusack* v. *Robinson* (1861) 1 B & S 299.
[144] S. 5(3) of the 1893 Act.   [145] *Abbot & Co.* v. *Wolsey* [1895] 2 QB 97.
[146] See *The Kanchenjunga* [1990] 1 Lloyd's Rep. 391.
[147] *Heilbut* v. *Hickson* (1872) LR 7 CP 438, 451.

confounded, since the former turns on a manifest choice of remedies by the buyer and the latter on reliance by the seller.[148] Whichever principle is brought in to support the notion of acceptance in section 35, it can justify an extension of the acceptance period when the seller requests an opportunity to correct faults in the goods or takes his time when responding to the buyer's complaints. Can such a seller fairly assert an irrevocable choice of remedies by the buyer or claim to have been put off balance by the buyer's behaviour? The new section 35(6)(a) states that the buyer will not be deemed to have accepted the goods merely because 'he asks for, or agrees to, their repair by or under an arrangement with the seller'. This may suspend the lapse of a reasonable time in section 35 but it leaves unanswered the question whether prolonged and intensive use as the buyer awaits action by the seller might still be an acceptance.

An alternative route to the relaxation of section 35 is to be found in section 11(4) which points to an implied or express term permitting rejection of the goods after acceptance.[149] Another possibility, not evident on the face of section 35, is that a buyer who has derived no benefit from the goods should be entitled to reject them.[150] This may be used to rationalize the Canadian cases, mentioned above, invoking the doctrine of fundamental breach to allow a belated rejection of the goods.[151] This particular approach has yet to commend itself to English courts. A related idea, expressed in negative terms, that the buyer may not reject if the goods cannot be restored to the state they were in at the contract date, was rejected by the Law Commission for inclusion in section 35.[152] It would have strengthened further the post-contract bargaining position of retailers, and there was no evidence of difficulties in practice making a case for such a reform. This last point is explicable at least in part by the brevity of the acceptance period.

Intimation of Acceptance

The first head of acceptance in section 35 is the buyer's intimation of acceptance to the seller. It was stated above that the origin of this head of

[148] Discussed Ch. 6 below.

[149] *Rowland* v. *Divall* [1923] 2 KB 500, 507; *O'Flaherty* v. *McKinlay* [1953] 2 DLR 514; *Bannerman* v. *White* (1861) 10 CB(NS) 844; *Head* v. *Tattersall* (1872) LR 7 Ex. 7.

[150] See *Behn* v. *Burness*, n. 72 above; *Poulton* v. *Lattimore* (1829) 9 B & C 259 (useless seed).

[151] *Lightburn* v. *Belmont Sales Ltd* (1969) 69 WWR 734; *Beldessi* v. *Island Equipment Ltd* (1973) 41 DLR (3d) 147; *Gibbard Hereford Farms Ltd* v. *Massey-Ferguson* (1974) 10 NSR (2d) 272; *Grafco Enterprises Ltd* v. *Schofield* [1983] 4 WWR 135. Some Canadian cases have demanded grave consequences attendant upon a breach the longer the buyer has possession of the goods before rejection: *Lightburn* v. *Belmont Sales Ltd, ibid.*; *Barber* v. *Inland Truck Sales Ltd* (1970) 11 DLR (3d) 469; *Gibbons* v. *Trapp Motors Ltd* (1970) 9 DLR (3d) 742; *Cushman Motor Works of Canada Ltd* v. *Laing* (1919) 49 DLR 1.

[152] Law Com. No. 160, para. 5.40. But note that this is one of the grounds for losing the right to rescind for misrepresentation.

acceptance lay in the practice of buyers, examining goods at the seller's premises, acceding to the seller's delivery of them under the contract, which would account for the rather vague word 'intimation'. This head of acceptance is rarely applied nowadays[153] but the Law Commission was concerned lest it be invoked by sellers procuring the buyer's signature to a delivery note containing an acceptance statement.[154] As seen above, the problem was resolved in the 1994 Act by providing that an intimation of acceptance would not be deemed an acceptance under section 35 before the buyer had had a reasonable opportunity to examine the goods.[155] Furthermore, consumer buyers could not waive their rights under this provision.[156]

It is not easy to see how a buyer, when not in the presence of the seller, can intimate his acceptance of the goods without expressly informing the seller that they will be retained despite their deficiencies. Letters of complaint will not readily be construed as intimating acceptance, even if they are insufficiently clear to be a rejection.[157] On the other hand, a demand that the seller do something or the goods will be rejected may leave it too late for the buyer eventually to reject.[158] Rejection, not defined by the Act,[159] requires a clear intention on the buyer's part to throw the goods back on the seller,[160] and a statement to that effect will carry no weight if the buyer's actions are not consistent with the statement.[161] The new section 35(6)(a), applicable to all three heads of acceptance, puts it beyond any doubt that a buyer asking for or agreeing to a repair by the seller does not thereby intimate an acceptance of the goods.

Acts Inconsistent with the Seller's Ownership

The second head of acceptance in section 35 is the performance by the buyer of an act inconsistent with the seller's ownership, perhaps the most difficult head of acceptance to understand.[162] Once it was settled

---

[153] *Staiman Steel Ltd* v. *Franki Canada Ltd* (1985) 53 OR (2d) 93. The Ontario court was unable to discover another case decided under this head.

[154] Law Com. No. 160, para. 5.20. [155] S. 35(2).

[156] S. 35(3). An exclusion of non-consumer buyers' rights would be subject to the Unfair Contract Terms Act 1977: see Law Com. No. 160, para. 5.24.

[157] *Varley* v. *Whipp* [1900] 1 QB 513.

[158] *Lee* v. *York Coach and Marine* [1977] RTR 35.

[159] The parties themselves may prescribe the permitted method of rejection: *Cockshutt* v. *Mills* (1905) 7 Terr. LR 392 (Can.).

[160] *Couston, Thomson & Co.* v. *Chapman* (1868) LR 2 HL 250 (Sc.): 'clear and distinct notification of the breaking off of the contract'. See also *Grimoldby* v. *Wells* (1875) LR 10 CP 391.

[161] *Graanhandel T. Link BV* v. *European Grain & Shipping Ltd* [1989] 2 Lloyd's Rep. 531 (persisting with a sale of rejected goods for the account of the sellers despite the sellers' refusal to give buyers authority to sell on their behalf). See also *Morton* v. *Chapman* (1843) 11 M & W 534; *Vargas Pena Apezteguia* v. *Peter Cremer GmbH* [1987] 1 Lloyd's Rep. 394. Cf. *Tradax Export SA* v. *European Grain & Shipping Ltd* [1983] 2 Lloyd's Rep. 100.

[162] See Law Com. No. 160, para. 5.33.

that the buyer's right of rejection was no longer encompassed by examination at the point of delivery, this head was bound to cause problems of interpretation and degree. For example, although the buyer of goods for personal consumption may reject them even after some degree of beneficial use, the degree of wear and tear might reach a point where the buyer's inability to return the goods in substantially the same condition as when they were delivered amounts to the performance of an inconsistent act.[163] A handling of the goods short of this point may be seen as authorized by the seller and therefore as consistent with the seller's ownership.[164] Rejection has been allowed where a portion of the goods have been destroyed by a method of testing that was the only way to reveal hidden flaws.[165] Sometimes, however, the goods may be so worthless that the distinction between resisting payment or demanding the return of the price, on the one hand, and claiming damages for breach of warranty of quality, on the other, is barely worth drawing.[166]

Subject to the conduct of a prior examination, the transfer by the buyer of proprietary rights to a third party has been treated as an inconsistent act. This was so in one case where the buyer granted a security bill of sale over plumbing supplies.[167] If, however, the goods supplied fall within a pre-existing security over future property granted by the buyer, this should not be regarded as an inconsistent act. That security attaches automatically to the goods and not as a result of any further voluntary act on the part of the buyer.[168] The revesting in the seller of the property in the goods should normally override equitable interests in those goods acquired in the meantime by a third party. If the recovery of the goods by the seller from the buyer is not prejudiced, the courts tend to resist the finding of an inconsistent act.[169] The resale of the goods by the buyer is

---

[163] Law Commission, *Sale and Supply of Goods*, Consultative Document No. 58 (1983), 45.

[164] But see *Armaghdown Motors Ltd* v. *Gray Motors Ltd* [1963] NZLR 5 (registration of vehicle in buyer's name an inconsistent act: surely wrong).

[165] *Heilbut* v. *Hickson*, n. 147 above (Brett J; cf. other judgments); *Winnipeg Fish Co.* v. *Whitman Fish Co.* (1909) 41 SCR 453 (testing by consumption). Excessive destructive testing might amount to an inconsistent act: *Harnor* v. *Groves* (1855) 15 CB 667; *Heilbut* v. *Hickson*, above. Likewise the incorporation of goods in other goods or in a building: *Charles Henshaw & Sons Ltd* v. *Antlerport* [1995] CLC 1312 (Ct. of Session).

[166] N. 150 above and accompanying text. There is high authority in Canada that a seller, faced with a damages claim, has the burden of proving the residual value of the goods which will be considered worthless in the absence of such proof: *Massey Harris Co.* v. *Skelding* [1934] SCR 431; *Ford Motor Co.* v. *Haley* [1967] SCR 437; *Evanchuk Transport Ltd* v. *Canadian Trailmobile Ltd* (1971) 21 DLR (3d) 246. *Sed quaere?*

[167] *Meta's Ltd* v. *Diamond* [1930] 3 DLR 886.

[168] *Tailby* v. *Official Receiver* (1888) 13 App. Cas. 523.

[169] *Fisher, Reeves & Co. Ltd* v. *Armour & Co. Ltd* [1920] 3 KB 614, 624, Scrutton LJ (making tentative plans to resell the goods); *J. & S. Robertson (Australia) Pty. Ltd* v. *Martin* (1955) 94 CLR 30 (claiming from the insurer).

precisely the kind of inconsistent act contemplated by section 35,[170] but a number of difficulties, the subject of statutory intervention on two occasions, have arisen where goods have been delivered to a sub-buyer before the buyer has examined them.

At the centre of the debate lies the Court of Appeal decision in *E. Hardy & Co. (London) Ltd* v. *Hillerns & Fowler*,[171] which involved the sale of Argentinian wheat on c.i.f. London terms. On outturn in England, the buyers broke bulk and consigned parcels to a number of sub-buyers before suspicions that the goods were non-conforming were confirmed by their sub-buyers. They then sought to reject the goods and the question was whether the act of reselling and forwarding the goods was inconsistent with the seller's ownership. There was a finding of fact that, at the time they performed these acts, the buyers had not had sufficient time to examine the goods. The buyers would obviously not have wished to incur the added expense of warehousing the goods before conducting an examination of them. As the Act then stood, there was nothing in sections 34 and 35 to establish which of them took precedence. The court concluded that sections 34 and 35 were independent of each other and the buyers had lost the right to reject under section 35.

In *Hardy*, the seller took no part in the delivery to the sub-buyers. In an earlier case,[172] books were packed by the seller for an ocean voyage and marked with the American sub-buyer's name. The sub-buyer rejected the books and the buyer shipped them back to England before rejecting them. The rejection was held to be effective. The United States was the agreed place of examination and the buyer recovered the two-way carriage costs to the sub-buyer since they were within the reasonable contemplation of buyer and seller.[173] Nevertheless, the restrictive rule in *Hardy* was extended in *E. & S. Ruben Ltd* v. *Faire Bros. & Co. Ltd*[174] where, as interpreted by the court, the delivery of rubber sheeting was made at the seller's premises before the seller, as agent for the buyer, shipped the goods to the sub-buyer. It was held that the buyer could not reject the goods when these were rejected by the sub-buyer since the act of dispatching them to the latter's premises was inconsistent with the seller's ownership. On similar facts, *Ruben* was distinguished in the New Zealand case of *Hammer and Barrow* v. *Coca Cola Export Corpn.*[175] where a quantity of yo-yos were delivered by the seller to a Christchurch carrier destined, as the seller knew, for an Auckland sub-buyer. Because

---

[170] *Parker* v. *Palmer* (1821) 4 B & Ald. 387 (buyer put defective goods up for auction and bought them in himself); *Morton* v. *Chapman*, n. 161 above.

[171] N. 106 above. See also *Parker* v. *Palmer*, n. 170 above.

[172] *Molling* v. *Dean* (1901) 18 TLR 217.

[173] This case was criticized in *Hardy*, n. 106 above.

[174] [1949] 1 KB 254; L. C. B. Gower (1949) 12 *MLR* 368.   [175] [1962] NZLR 723.

Auckland was held to be the place of examination, the carriage of the goods was not an inconsistent act and the buyer could still reject the goods. Similarly, in the Canadian case of *A. J. Frank & Sons Ltd* v. *Northern Peat Co.*,[176] the Ontario seller consigned a quantity of rail to the Ontario buyer's order in a Quebec town. When the Quebec sub-buyer rejected the goods, the buyer recovered possession of them and rejected them, lawfully in the view of the court since the Quebec town was the place of examination.[177]

When section 35 of the Sale of Goods Act was amended in 1967,[178] sub-section (1) was declared subject to section 34. This was designed to reverse the result in *Hardy*,[179] though it still remained open to sellers to claim that a buyer not availing himself of an opportunity to examine the goods had waived his right to do so, thus accepting the goods. In the post-1994 sub-section (2), the buyer is 'not deemed to have accepted' the goods by the performance of an inconsistent act under sub-section (1)[180] until he has had a reasonable opportunity to examine them for conformity. The point is also made explicitly in the new sub-section (6)(b) that the delivery of the goods to another under a sub-sale or other disposition is not a deemed acceptance. Presumably, since the Act, as it always has done, says 'not deemed to have accepted', instead of 'deemed not to have accepted', there may be cases where the seller can draw on additional behaviour of the buyer to show the performance of an inconsistent act. The new provisions go on to state that a consumer buyer may not waive his rights under sub-section (2), thereby implicitly recognizing that a non-consumer buyer may. The unanswered question is why a buyer, who voluntarily chooses to dispatch goods without delay to a sub-buyer, can be said not to have had an opportunity to examine them, at least in those cases where the seller is unaware of the resale plans.

The relaxation of the inconsistent act rule in section 35 prompts the question where should rejection take place. Section 36 states that the buyer refusing to accept the goods after delivery need only intimate to the seller that he is refusing them and need not return them to the seller. This pitches the behaviour of the buyer at a standard lower than is commonly met in commercial life. The section does not refer to, and may not

---

[176] [1963] 2 OR 415.

[177] See also *Winnipeg Fish*, n. 165 above: frozen fish could only be inspected when it had thawed out at the sub-buyer's premises

[178] By the Misrepresentation Act, s. 4(2).

[179] Despite the criticism that the *Hardy* case has attracted over the years, the result—that defective goods should not be thrown back on a c.i.f. seller but should be the subject of a price allowance—is expressly required by the principal commodities trading forms, e.g., GAFTA 100, cl. 5.

[180] S. 35(1) refers to an act after delivery to the buyer. This must also include delivery by the seller directly to the sub-buyer, or the inconsistent act rule would have no application at all in such cases.

have been designed to deal with, a delivery under a sub-sale. A seller having to recover the goods from an inaccessible place or an unco-operative sub-buyer could suffer considerable hardship. It might have been better if the changes to section 35 had dispensed with the inconsistent act doctrine[181] so as to allow rejection where the buyer was able to place the goods at the disposal of the seller. Any expenses incurred by the buyer in making arrangements to recover the goods could, within the bounds of the remoteness rule, be compensated in damages.

The final difficulty raised by the inconsistent act doctrine, untouched by the 1994 reforms, is how can a buyer to whom the property in the goods has passed perform an act inconsistent with the seller's ownership. This has been the subject of inquiry in the case of documentary sales on c.i.f. terms. It is settled law that the c.i.f. buyer normally acquires the property in the goods when paying against the exchange of shipping documents. A view once entertained, however, was that the property did not pass on the documentary exchange but later, when the buyer had an opportunity to examine the goods.[182] The better, but uncomfortably circular, view is that the inconsistent act refers to the reversionary entitlement of the seller that would have sprung at the moment of rejection but for the inconsistent act.[183] An outmoded view has it that a discharging breach of contract prevents the property from passing in the first place.[184]

A last point presented by the *Hardy* case concerns sub-sales performed by an exchange of shipping documents. Dealings with the documents, as they are passed down a c.i.f. sales string, will not be treated as inconsistent acts that take away any right to reject the goods themselves once they are landed.[185]

Lapse of Time

The third acceptance head in section 35 is the lapse of a reasonable time. This is the most difficult of the heads to apply in practice since it is very much fact-based,[186] though the paucity of reported disputes[187] helped to

[181] As was initially proposed at the consultative stage for consumer sales by the Law Commission: n. 163 above (paras. 4.85–88) but later rejected in the Report (Law Com. No. 160, para. 5.37).

[182] In the *Hardy* case: [1923] 2 KB 490, 499 (Atkin LJ). Not the position that the paying buyer would want to put forward if the seller became insolvent in the meantime.

[183] *Ibid.* 496 (Bankes LJ).

[184] Expressed in *Ollett* v. *Jordan* [1918] 2 KB 41. See now the *Hardy* case, n. 182 above, 499 (alternative view of Atkin LJ); *McDougall* v. *Aeromarine of Emsworth Ltd* [1958] 1 WLR 1126; *Kwei Tek Chao* v. *British Traders & Shippers Ltd* [1954] 2 QB 459, 487–8; *Colonial Insurance Co. of New Zealand* v. *Adelaide Marine Insurance Co.* (1886) 12 App. Cas. 128, 140.

[185] *Kwei Tek Chao*, n. 184 above: the *Hardy* case, n. 182 above, 499 (Atkin LJ).

[186] Law Com. No. 160, para. 2.48: '[N]o limit on the number of factors which the court is entitled to take into account.'

[187] In England. There have been quite a lot in Canada.

persuade the Law Commission not to recommend statutory change, and in particular not to introduce fixed periods for different classes of goods.[188] It has been said that a buyer's interest in rejecting goods, instead of suing for damages for diminished value, is stronger where goods are bought for consumption rather than resale.[189] A reselling buyer will often be able to find a market even for defective goods, though care may be needed in settling the terms of such a resale if the buyer's reputation is not to be injured.

The lack of English case law requires some explanation. A buyer, particularly one who is a consumer, requires a degree of nerve to exercise rejection rights. First of all, the uncertainty of the rejection period makes it difficult to give advice on the subject. Further, if the buyer has paid for the goods, they will have to be put out of commission if the rejection is to pass the test of unequivocality. Although rejected goods need not be returned to the seller,[190] the buyer of a defective car, for example, is likely to wait a long time for the seller to come and collect it and may not have the resources to provide for alternative transport in the meantime. All the while, the car will be depreciating and suffering from neglect. Returning the car and keys to the seller may prove to be tactically more effective. If payment is outstanding, the buyer faces a problem common to all contracting parties exercising uncertain termination rights. If the buyer has inadvertently accepted the goods, a repudiation of the contract will turn out to be unlawful and the buyer will be open to an action by the seller.

Various factors may be considered in determining the lapse of a reasonable time but the time needed to discover a latent defect is not one of them,[191] although the speedy discovery of a defect may abridge the time given to the buyer.[192] Furthermore, as stated above, it is not likely that the notion of examination can be stretched to cover beneficial use in service and take advantage of the subordination of the acceptance rules to the buyer's right of examination. But the complexity of the goods may bear upon the length of the period: the buyer of a bicycle would have to reject sooner than the buyer of a nuclear submarine.[193] The nature of the

[188] Law Com. No. 160, para. 5.19. Creating a fixed period or periods would be open to the same criticisms as creating fixed durability periods under s. 14.

[189] J. Honnold (1949) 97 *U Penn LR* 457, 469. Also, as the trading forms for agricultural commodities recognize, where such goods are used in a buyer's manufacturing process.

[190] S. 36. It is not clear what duty, if any, is owed by the buyer to the seller in respect to the custody and care of rejected goods. Should the buyer incur reasonable expenses in looking after the goods, these should be recoverable as consequential damages under s. 54.

[191] e.g. *Bernstein* v. *Pamson Motors (Golders Green) Ltd* [1987] 2 All ER 220. See also *Laurelgates Ltd* v. *Lombard North Central Ltd* (1983) 133 NLJ 720.

[192] *Couston, Thomson & Co.* v. *Chapman* (1872) LR 2 HL 250.

[193] *Bernstein*, n. 191 above. This is difficult to reconcile with the court's view that the period is not computed by the time taken to discover a defect. For the view that the complexity of the intended function of goods defines the time for rejection, see *Charles Henshaw & Sons Ltd* v. *Antlerport* [1995] CLC 1312 (Ct. of Session).

fault may be material, especially if the buyer monitors it for a short while before determining that it is serious enough to warrant decisive action.[194] It has also been said that the period should not be extended in favour of the buyer, since it is commercially desirable for the seller to close his ledger.[195] Nevertheless, a seller facing a damages claim for breach of contract is in no position to close his ledger on the transaction. The intensity of use of the goods by the buyer is likely to be relevant: here, the lapse of time shades into the performance of an inconsistent act. Where the rejection of the goods would amount to a grave business decision against a seller disputing liability, and might imperil future relations with the seller, a buyer may be entitled to take some time to consider his position carefully.[196] Canadian cases have permitted the rejection of goods many months after delivery on the ground that their continued use in service by the buyer is causing significant business losses,[197] but English courts are unlikely to be so generous to a buyer who can mitigate business losses by acquiring substitute goods from another source.

The computation of a reasonable time is an elastic affair but the period is unlikely to extend beyond a few weeks and may be shorter. In *Bernstein* v. *Pamson Motors (Golders Green) Ltd*,[198] the plaintiff's new car broke down 'on its first proper trip' on a motorway less than four weeks after he had acquired it. In that time, it had been driven for only 140 miles. The fault was a minor one and easily, though expensively, put right, but the defendant sellers were in breach of the merchantable quality condition.[199] Nevertheless, the plaintiff informed the defendants the day after the breakdown that he was rejecting the car and refused to collect it from the defendants' garage, where it was later repaired under the manufacturer's guarantee and made 'effectively as good as new'. The buyer had waited too long.[200] It is questionable, however, that the court would have been so strict if the buyer had correctly believed that the fault in the car threatened future problems. The gravity of the fault may well affect the length of the acceptance period.

[194] See *Baynham* v. *North West Securities Ltd*, 7 Dec. 1982, discussed in *Bernstein*, n. 117 above, 227.

[195] *Bernstein*, n. 191 above.

[196] *Manifatture Tessile Laniera Wooltex* v. *J. B. Ashley Ltd* [1979] 2 Lloyd's Rep. 28; *Fisher, Reeves and Co. Ltd* v. *Armour and Co. Ltd* [1920] 3 KB 614 at 624 (Scrutton LJ).

[197] *Public Utilities Commission of Waterloo* v. *Burroughs Business Machines* (1974) 6 OR (2d) 257; *Burroughs Business Machines Ltd* v. *Feed-Rite Mills (1962) Ltd* (1973) 42 DLR (3d) 303, affd. [1976] 1 SCR *v.* (computer systems).

[198] N. 191 above.

[199] A piece of sealant had entered the lubrication system and interrupted the flow of oil to the camshaft.

[200] See *Long* v. *Lloyd* [1958] 2 All ER 402, a misrepresentation case where the right to rescind was lost after less than a week, the court following the acceptance rules in s. 35. A modern court would not take such a strict view.

An appeal in the *Bernstein* case was compromised. In *Rogers* v. *Parish (Scarborough) Ltd*,[201] the buyer of a car, itself the replacement for an unsatisfactory model returned after a few weeks, was rejected by the buyer six months after the delivery of the original vehicle and after it had been driven without satisfaction for 5,500 miles. During that time, there had occurred a series of inspections and attempted repairs. The defendants attempted on appeal to argue that the buyer was too late to reject but, since the matter had not been taken in the pleadings and in the court below, and hence critical findings of fact about the course of dealings had not been made, the Court of Appeal refused to allow the matter to be raised. It is a matter of speculation, therefore, how much the various interventions by the seller might have extended the acceptance period. As seen above, section 35(6) now provides that the buyer in these circumstances does not thereby accept the goods,[202] but the provision is not explicit about the suspension of time while repairs are being attempted. It seems reasonable to suppose, however, that time stands still while the seller's efforts are continuing.[203] The Law Commission initially recommended a provision stating that the acceptance period was to be extended in these circumstances but prudently drew back from a complex provision.[204] This is yet another matter that can be factored into the standard of a reasonable time in section 35.

Other Contracts and Affirmation

The above rules in section 35 apply to sale of goods agreements with the exception of consumer conditional sale contracts. Section 14 of the Supply of Goods (Implied Terms) Act 1973 requires the latter agreements to be treated in the same way for present purposes as hire purchase contracts. The right to reject goods under a hire purchase contract, in common with other contracts for the transfer of a proprietary interest in goods[205] and with hire contracts,[206] turns upon the common law doctrine of affirmation.[207] A contract is affirmed by an injured party who elects to keep it on foot.[208] If election is to be understood in the way advanced by the Court of Appeal in *Peyman* v. *Lanjani*,[209] as existing only if the elector is aware, not only of the fact of a serious breach but also of the choice of remedies available,[210] then few hire purchase agreements

---

[201] [1987] 2 All ER 232.   [202] Cf. *Long* v. *Lloyd*, n. 200 above.
[203] But cf. *Lee* v. *York Coach and Marine* [1977] RTR 35.
[204] Law Com. No. 160, para. 5.42.
[205] Supply of Goods and Services Act 1982. See Ch. 7 below.
[206] See *Guarantee Trust of Jersey Ltd* v. *Gardner* (1973) 117 SJ 564.
[207] See Law Com. No. 160, paras. 2.50 ff.
[208] For affirmation generally, see G. H. Treitel, *The Law of Contract* (9th edn., Sweet & Maxwell, London, 1995), 354–6.
[209] [1985] Ch. 457.   [210] See Ch. 6 below.

would ever be affirmed. As much as this laxity may accord with the imperative of consumer protection, it has little to commend it for non-consumer contracts involving the supply of goods. There is some evidence of leniency in respect of a hire purchase bailee's right to reject goods. In *Yeoman Credit Ltd* v. *Apps*,[211] the bailee paid hire for three months despite the presence of serious defects in a car and retained possession for a further two months before the finance company repossessed the car with the bailee's consent. Holroyd Pearce LJ, attracted by the analogy of a simple hire contract, was of the view that the 'continuing repudiation' by the finance company meant that the right to reject remained alive throughout the period. This continuous breach reasoning was, however, rejected by the Court of Appeal in *UCB Leasing Ltd* v. *Holtom*[212] A different approach, also favourable to the hire purchase bailee, is evident in *Farnworth Finance Facilities Ltd* v. *Attryde*,[213] where the bailee of a motor cycle was held not to have affirmed the contract by electing to retain it. He had used the cycle for five or six weeks after its return from the manufacturer, where it had been sent for repairs. The effect of election is that a bailee who has not discovered defects in goods may still reject them despite a lapse of time that would be fatal to a buyer under section 35 of the Sale of Goods Act.

INSTALMENT CONTRACTS

The Sale of Goods Act lays down special rules for the termination of instalment contracts, their point of departure being the distinction between entire and severable contracts, which is of less significance in sales law than in certain other branches of contract law. The typical problem to which this distinction speaks concerns an act whose performance in full is a condition precedent to payment by the other contracting party. For this reason, a builder who is to be paid only when the building has been completed cannot demand payment under the contract until this has been done.[214] If, for example, the builder cannot finish because of lack of funds, there is a risk of the site owner being enriched at the expense of the builder.

Various attempts have been made over the years to dull the sharp edge of this rule by creating exceptions. The retention of the land, with its incomplete building, by the owner gives no comfort to the builder: the

---

[211] [1962] 2 QB 508.   [212] [1987] RTR 362.
[213] [1970] 2 All ER 774. See also *Laurelgates* v. *Lombard North Central Finance* (1983) 133 NLJ 720 (10 months and a number of repairs); *Jackson* v. *Chrysler Acceptances Ltd* [1978] RTR 474, 480–1.
[214] *Sumpter* v. *Hedges* [1898] 1 QB 673.

owner enjoying his land will not be seen as impliedly undertaking to pay for the incomplete work.[215] But it has been established that substantially completing the building permits the builder to claim the price under the contract, subject to the owner's counterclaim for damages for the cost of completing the work to standard.[216] No appreciable need has been felt for such a substantial performance rule in sales law. Goods are movable; buildings are not. A buyer retaining a defective or short tender of goods accepts them and therefore will have to pay for them. Nevertheless, there will be some cases where the rigour of entire contracts analysis could produce hardship, an example being the seller manufacturing machinery to the buyer's specifications and installing it in the buyer's premises over time.[217] The prejudice of a seller who finds goods of this nature thrown back on his hands could be substantial, and the acceptance rules in the Act would do nothing to lessen it.[218] In appropriate cases, the doctrine of substantial performance could be invoked to require the buyer in fact to retain the machinery and claim damages from the seller.[219] Restitutionary analysis might also be appropriate where the buyer has consumed or dispersed a portion of the contract goods before discovering his right to avoid the contract under section 6 because the goods in their entirety did not exist at the contract date.[220]

Builders may take steps under the contract to protect themselves from the consequences of incomplete performance. The contract may, and commonly does, provide that instalments of the price are payable once the building arrives at designated stages of completion. This renders the contract severable: the designated stages are made conditions precedent to the payment of the stated instalments of the price. A similar application of the principle of severability is at work in section 31 of the Sale of Goods Act which departs from the doctrine of conditions and warranties in laying down a separate rule for terminating instalment contracts.[221] Even before the enactment of the new section 35A and the rule of partial

---

[215] *Sumpter* v. *Hedges* [1898] 1 QB 673.

[216] *H. Dakin & Co. Ltd* v. *Lee* [1918] 1 KB 566; *Hoenig* v. *Isaacs* [1952] 2 All ER 176.

[217] *Appleby* v. *Myers* (1867) LR 2 CP 651; *Fairbanks Soap Co.* v. *Sheppard* [1953] 1 SCR 314 (Can.).

[218] Cf. *Carter* v. *Scargill* (1875) LR 10 QB 564 (benefit and incomplete performance in the sale of a business).

[219] But see *Appleby* v. *Myers*, n. 217 above (no enduring benefit); *Fairbanks Soap, ibid.* (abandonment).

[220] See *Barrow, Lane & Ballard Ltd* v. *Phillip Phillips & Co.* [1929] 1 KB 574 (buyer voluntarily paid for goods consumed before apprised of short tender).

[221] The distinction laid down by the Act between instalment and non-instalment transactions does not repeal the common law distinction between entire and severable contracts. There may be severable contracts that are not instalment transactions (e.g. *Longbottom* v. *Bass, Walker & Co.* [1922] WN 245) and entire contracts under which the goods are deliverable in instalments (e.g. *Boyd* v. *Sullivan* (1888) 15 OR 492 (Can.)). See Ontario Law Reform Commission, *Report on Sale of Goods* (1979), ii, 541–54.

acceptance, the buyer's acceptance of one or more instalments did not prejudice his right to reject the remainder if he could later establish a right to terminate the contract.[222]

Termination of Instalment Contracts

Section 31 does not expressly deal with the rejection of individual instalments, a matter for common law principles and section 35A(2), but it does deal with the termination of the contract as it affects the outstanding balance of performance. According to section 31(2), where the seller makes 'defective deliveries in respect of one or more instalments', it depends upon the terms of the contract and the circumstances of the case whether the breach is a repudiation of the whole contract or a severable breach giving rise to 'a claim for compensation but not to a right to treat the whole contract as repudiated'. The section applies the same rule where the buyer does not take delivery or pay for the goods.

The language of section 31(2) raises a number of points. First, it applies only to goods 'delivered by stated instalments, which are to be separately paid for'. Although the Act does not translate instalment contracts into the language of entire and severable contracts, these are certainly severable contracts. In addition, certain contracts for instalment deliveries excluded by section 31(2), for example, because the size of each instalment is not 'stated' or because the intervals and amounts of payment do not match the instalments,[223] would be severable contracts, except where payment comes in one lump sum.[224] Severable contracts falling outside section 31(2) would be governed by equivalent common law principles brought in through section 62(2).[225]

The second point rising from section 31(2) is that it applies to breaches of both seller and buyer, though in practice it is more often the delivery obligations of buyer and seller, rather than the payment obligation of the buyer,[226] to which the subsection is applied. This versatility explains why the provision speaks of 'compensation' rather than damages: a seller unable to treat the buyer's breach as a repudiation wll have a lesser remedy that may include an action for the price of instalments

[222] Sale of Goods Act, ss. 11(4), 31(2).

[223] See *Jackson* v. *Rotax Motor & Cycle Co.* [1910] 2 KB 937; *Regent OHG Aisenstadt und Barig* v. *Francesco of Jermyn Street* [1981] 3 All ER 327 (where the court, erroneously it is submitted, applied s. 31(2)).

[224] N. 221 above. The new rule of partial rejection in s. 35A would avoid any hardship caused by the buyer under an entire contract accepting a portion of the goods before defects in the remainder come to light.

[225] So the result in *Regent OHG Aisenstadt*, n. 223 above, should remain the same.

[226] But see, e.g., *Mersey Steel and Iron Co.* v. *Naylor Benzon & Co.* (1884) 9 App. Cas. 434; *Bloomer* v. *Bernstein* (1874) LR 9 CP 588; *Decro-Wall International SA* v. *Practitioners in Marketing Ltd* [1971] 1 WLR 361.

delivered.[227] Thirdly, the injured party's termination rights are dressed up in the language of repudiation, which is the present disavowal of,[228] or declared or manifest inability to carry out,[229] future obligations in a manner sufficiently serious to permit the injured party to anticipate future non-performance by terminating the contract.[230] Trivial breaches will not by mere repetition or the threat of repetition thereby become repudiatory.[231] A genuine disagreement about the interpretation of a contract will not be a repudiation just because it is ill-founded.[232] But a repudiation was found where the buyer demanded credit before accepting future deliveries, when the contract required payment on delivery,[233] and in another case where the buyer demanded a price allowance for past deliveries before accepting future deliveries.[234]

Correct as it is to say that an ill-founded interpretation is not as such repudiatory, and that a refusal to perform must be clear and absolute,[235] the impact of a declared misinterpretation on the future performance of the contract must be considered. For example, if the buyer makes it clear that he will not accept a tender from the seller in a way that conforms to the seller's (correct) interpretation of the contract, the seller will be entitled to terminate: the buyer may not impose unilaterally even a minor variation of contract on the seller and the seller is entitled to assume the refusal of his tender when the time comes.[236] Again, if it is the seller who is insistent that he will tender in a way departing from the contract standard, it will depend upon whether at the delivery date the buyer could have rejected the seller's tender. A breach of contract is not the more potent for being anticipatory.[237]

---

[227] See *Workman, Clark & Co. Ltd* v. *Lloyd Brazileño* [1908] 1 KB 968, 978–9. (The seller's entitlement to the first instalment of the price having fallen due, the seller was entitled to recover this without reference to the resale of the goods to a third party.)

[228] See the buyer's language in *Taylor* v. *Oakes, Roncoroni and Co.* (1922) 127 LT 267.

[229] *Foran* v. *Wright* (1989) 64 ALJR 1, 9, 17; *British and Beningtons Ltd* v. *North Western Cachar Tea Co. Ltd* [1923] AC 48; *Rawson* v. *Hobbs* (1961) 107 CLR 466; *Universal Cargo Carriers Ltd* v. *Citati* [1957] 2 QB 401; *Anchor Line Ltd* v. *Keith Rowell Ltd* [1980] 2 Lloyd's Rep. 351.

[230] See, e.g., *Withers* v. *Reynolds* (1831) 2 B & Ad. 882; *Geddes Bros.* v. *American Red Cross* [1921] 1 WWR 185.

[231] *Freeth* v. *Burr* (1874) LR 9 CP 208; *Decro-Wall*, n. 226 above.

[232] *Woodar Investment Development Ltd* v. *Wimpey Construction UK Ltd* [1980] 1 WLR 277; *Sweet & Maxwell Ltd* v. *Universal News Service Ltd* [1964] 2 QB 699.

[233] *Withers* v. *Reynolds*, n. 230 above.

[234] *McCowan* v. *McKay* (1901) 13 Man. LR 590 (Can.).

[235] See *Chilean Nitrate Sales Corpn.* v. *Marine Transport Co. Ltd (The Hermosa)* [1982] 1 Lloyd's Rep. 570, 572–3.

[236] See *Warinco AG* v. *Samor SpA* [1979] 1 Lloyd's Rep. 450. For the buyer who refuses to pay for past deliveries over which the seller has surrendered his lien, see *Yeast* v. *Knight & Watson* [1919] 2 WWR 467 (not a repudiation). The buyer was seeking to suspend payment until the second delivery was made and was rightly suspicious of the seller's intention to deliver.

[237] See *Afovos Shipping Co. SA* v. *R. Pagnan & Fgli.* [1983] 1 WLR 195, 203, where Lord

Section 31(2), by employing the concept of repudiation, predicts the future of the contract in the light of the breaching party's past and present performance. It therefore says nothing about the rejection of delivery instalments already accepted, which according to severable contracts analysis must be retained by the buyer. Where there is a general refusal or renunciation, the injured party is entitled to assume the worst.[238] If, however, the repudiation has to be inferred from the present defective performance of a party not expressing a wish to renounce the contract in full, a difficult inquiry is launched which must take account, *inter alia*, of the chances of the breach being repeated in future.[239] Consequently, in *Maple Flock Co. Ltd* v. *Universal Furniture Products (Wembley) Ltd*,[240] where the breach affected only one instalment out of about sixty-five and occurred a quarter of the way through the delivery schedule, and was moreover a freak occurrence unlikely to be repeated, the court held that the buyer could not treat the seller's breach in delivering contaminated rag flock as a repudiation of the remainder of the contract.

Although section 31(2) employs the forward-looking concept of repudiation, the injured party's termination rights are not in practice estimated without account being taken of the impact of past and present breaches.[241] So in one case calling for the delivery of 1,100 pieces of timber where the seller tendered a non-conforming first instalment of 750 pieces, the court, though basing its judgment on the inference of future breaches from the tender of this defective instalment, could not but have

Diplock's requirement that the breach in future deprive the innocent party of substantially the whole benefit of the contract should be read as including also any threatened breach of a condition. See on this point *Foran* v. *Wright*, n. 229 above, 5 (Mason CJ), 14 (Brennan J). See also *Federal Commerce & Navigation Co. Ltd* v. *Molena Alpha Inc* [1979] AC 757, 779 (Lord Wilberforce).

[238] *Freeth* v. *Burr*, n. 231 above; *Mersey Steel and Iron Co.* v. *Naylor Benzon & Co*, n. 226 above.

[239] *Dickinson* v. *Fanshaw* (1892) 8 TLR 271; *Maple Flock Co. Ltd* v. *Universal Furniture Products (Wembley) Ltd* [1934] 1 KB 148.

[240] N. 239 above.

[241] *Berliner Gramophone Co.* v. *Phinney and Co. Ltd* (1921) 57 DLR 596, 601–2 ('often "the last straw" which causes trouble'). Cf. *Nitrate Corpn. of Chile Ltd* v. *Pansuiza Cia de Navigacion SA* [1980] 1 Lloyd's Rep. 638, 653, affd. *sub nom Chilean Nitrate Sales Corpn.* v. *Marine Transport Co. Ltd*, n. 235 above. Acceptance of defective instalments in the past is no waiver of the buyer's rejection rights concerning the same defect in future instalments: *Bremer Handelsgesellschaft mbH* v. *Deutsche Conti Handelsgesellschaft mbH* [1981] 2 Lloyd's Rep. 112. Even if such instalments may no longer be rejected, it is submitted they may still be weighed at a later date in assessing the impact of the seller's breach under s. 31(2). The more advanced in performance a contract is that has been satisfactorily performed in the past, the harder it will be to terminate the balance of the contract under s. 31(2): see *Cornwall* v. *Henson* [1900] 2 Ch. 298.

[242] *Millars' Karri & Jarrah Co.* v. *Weddel, Turner & Co.* (1908) 11 LT 128. See also *Maple Flock Co. Ltd* v. *Universal Furniture Products (Wembley) Ltd*, n. 239 above, 158 (serious single breach may be enough).

been influenced by the preponderant volume of that instalment.[242] Moreover, the leading modern case, *Maple Flock Co. Ltd* v. *Universal Furniture Products (Wembley) Ltd*, though looking at the chances of repeated breaches, also took into account the quantitative ratio of the present breach to the contract as a whole. In some cases, the court may have to consider the combined effect of a breach and an external event, for which the party in breach is not responsible and therefore not liable in damages, in determining whether the overall event is serious enough to permit termination.[243]

Another difficulty emerging from section 31(2) concerns the timing of the breach and raises the question whether an early failure to perform, particularly in respect of the first instalment, is more serious than a later failure. In *Hoare* v. *Rennie*,[244] a contract called for 667 tons of Swedish iron to be delivered June to September in four approximately equal instalments. The seller tendered twenty-one tons in June whereupon the buyer repudiated the contract. The Court of Exchequer held the buyer's repudiation to be justified since the contract had begun 'at the outset ... with a breach'. Since the buyer had received no benefit, there was no difficulty in putting the parties back in *statu quo ante*.[245] This decision was trenchantly criticized in *Simpson* v. *Crippen*,[246] where 6–8,000 tons of coal were to be delivered over a year in approximately equal monthly instalments. The buyer having sent for delivery of only 158 tons in the first month, the seller repudiated the contract at the start of the second month. The court held that the buyer's breach in taking less than the agreed quantity went only to a part of the consideration bargained for and the seller's repudiation was therefore unlawful.

The court in *Honck* v. *Muller*[247] had difficulty in reconciling these two cases. In that case, the buyer failed to take delivery of the first instalment of 2,000 tons of pig iron deliverable in three monthly instalments. Bramwell LJ stated the vital significance of a default on the first instalment and a repudiation by the injured party before any deliveries were made since a 'contract ... part performed ... cannot be undone'.[248] Now the facts of *Honck* v. *Muller*, where the breach went to a third of the contractual quantity, could justify its divergence from *Simpson* v. *Crippen*, where the breach affected less than one-twelfth of the agreed amount, if both were to be subject to a simple repudiatory breach test. Moreover, on the facts of *Honck* v. *Muller*, a buyer who defaults on the first instalment

---

[243] *Nitrate Corpn. of Chile Ltd* v. *Pansuiza Cia De Navigacion SA*, n. 241 above, 649.
[244] (1859) 5 H & N 19.   [245] Prospective termination is a modern notion.
[246] (1872) LR 8 QB 14.   [247] (1881) 7 QBD 92.
[248] *Ibid.* 98–9. See also Baggallay LJ, 101–2. In *Coddington* v. *Paleologo* (1867) LR 2 Ex. 193, the first instalment was for an unstated amount, but the decision went off on a point of interpretation.

may default also on the second and third; a buyer who accepts delivery of the first instalment but defaults on the second may default again only in respect of the third instalment. This factual difference apart, no reason in law justifies distinguishing between the first and subsequent instalments.

Rejecting Particular Instalments

As noted above, section 31(2) does not state whether, for example, a buyer may reject a defective instalment of goods in circumstances where he may not terminate the contract as a whole. It has been said that a 'contract for the sale of goods by instalments is a single contract, not a complex of as many contracts as there are instalments under it'.[249] Although this may seem to deny severable rejection rights, there is considerable case law support for the buyer's right to reject non-conforming instalments, even if the buyer has lost the right to terminate the contract or has not yet acquired it.[250] Since section 31(2) does not on its terms apply to the rejection of individual instalments, it would seem that rejection would depend upon the application of the normal principles relating to conditions, warranties, and intermediate stipulations. A breach of the satisfactory quality term in section 14(2) in respect of an instalment should therefore permit the rejection of the instalment, subject to a claim by the seller that the buyer should not be allowed to reject if the consequnces of the breach are slight and rejection would be unreasonable.[251] The existence of severable rejection rights is implicit in section 35A(2) which permits the buyer to accept only a part of a non-conforming instalment and reject the rest. In certain cases, where the contractual timetable has been disturbed and deliveries have not been made at the agreed times, courts have been prepared to conclude that the contract

---

[249] *Maple Flock*, n. 239 above, 154. This is so even if the contract contains a clause providing that each delivery is a separate contract: *Panoutsos* v. *Raymond Hadley Corpn. of New York* [1917] 2 KB 473; *Ross T. Smyth & Co. Ltd* v. *T. D. Bailey Son & Co.* [1940] 3 All ER 60; *J. Rosenthal & Sons* v. *Esmail* [1965] 1 WLR 1117; *Robert A. Munro and Co. Ltd* v. *Meyer* [1930] 2 KB 312, 332; *Re Grainex Canada Ltd* (1987) 34 DLR (4th) 646.

[250] See *Sierichs* v. *Hughes* (1918) 42 OLR 608 (Can.); *Molling & Co.* v. *Dean & Son Ltd* (1901) 18 TLR 217; *Jackson* v. *Rotax Motor & Cycle Co.* [1910] 2 KB 937; *Regent OHG Aisenstadt und Barig* v. *Francesco of Jermyn Street* [1981] 3 All ER 327. *Quaere* may a buyer treat the timely delivery of an instalment as of the essence in respect of that instalment when the balance of the contract may not be terminated because the effects of the breach are not sufficiently severe?   [251] S. 15A.

[252] On abandonment generally, see Ch. 6, below. Where a party requests a delivery not to be made, an application of waiver or variation principles might support the mutual intention that delivery be postponed, with the consequence that it does not lapse: *Tyers* v. *Rosedale and Ferryhill Co. Ltd* (1875) LR 10 Ex. 195. Some of the above difficulties stem from an approach to anticipatory repudiation treating it as an offer to rescind on terms: see *Geddes Bros.* v. *American Red Cross* [1921] 1 WWR 185; P. M. Nienabr [1962] CLJ 213; F. Dawson [1981] *CLJ* 83.

has lapsed *pro tanto* by a process of mutual abandonment.[252] The seller may not make a subsequent late tender and is not thereby released from liability in damages.[253] As we shall see when we look at cure, a distinction may be drawn between rejection and termination, which supports severable rejection rights while the contract remains on foot.

In an earlier chapter,[254] it was noted that English courts accord a place in sales law to innocent misrepresentation, although it is not dealt with in the Sale of Goods Act, and section 62(2), when incorporating the rules of common law, makes no mention of the rules of equity. Although some Commonwealth cases[255] have denied the availability of rescission once the contract has been executed, section 1(b) of the Misrepresentation Act 1967 put it beyond doubt that execution[256] was no bar to rescission. Section 1(b) therefore confirmed the antecedent case law, which permitted rescission notwithstanding execution.[257]

Rescission and Rejection

The same section[258] similarly provides that the fact of a misrepresentation becoming a term of the contract is no bar to rescission for innocent misrepresentation. Unlike the abolition of the execution bar to rescission, this provision has left difficulties in its wake. Rescission *ab initio* and termination are different remedies: one is retrospective and the other prospective, but they both involve the return of the goods to the buyer. A buyer able to return the goods and resist payment of or recover the price, and who has no interest in pressing a damages claim,[259] will be indifferent to whether this process is accomplished by a retrospective dismantling or a prospective truncation of the contract.[260] Nevertheless,

---

[253] F. Dawson [1981] *CLJ* 83. See also *De Oleaga* v. *West Cumberland Iron & Steel Co. Ltd* (1879) 4 QBD 472.

[254] Ch. 1 above.   [255] See M. G. Bridge (1986) 20 *UBC LR* 53.

[256] Not the passing of property but the fact that 'the contract has been performed'. Canadian cases also equate execution with delivery of the goods: Bridge, n. 255 above.

[257] *T. & H. Harrison* v. *Knowles and Foster* [1918] 1 KB 608; *Leaf* v. *International Galleries* [1950] 2 KB 86; *Long* v. *Lloyd* [1958] 2 All ER 402; *Goldsmith* v. *Roger* [1962] 2 Lloyd's Rep. 249. *Aliter Armstrong* v. *Jackson* [1917] 2 KB 822. Note how, in the above cases concerning specific goods, rescission for misrepresentation gave an opportunity for buyers to return them when the rules on breach, prior to the enactment of s. 4 of the Misrepresentation Act, deprived such buyers altogether of the right of rejection if the property had passed at the contract date (which remains the presumptive rule).

[258] S. 1(a).   [259] e.g. because the market is falling.

[260] For cautionary remarks about the ambiguity of rescission, see *Mersey Steel and Iron Co.* v. *Naylor Benzon & Co.* (1882) 9 QBD 648, 671.

the rules on rescission for misrepresentation are not identical to acceptance as defined in section 35. The right to rescind is lost when one of the rescission bars intrudes, namely, the acquisition of third-party rights in the subject matter of the contract, or the affirmation of the contract by the party to whom the misrepresentation is made, or the lapse of a reasonable time, or the alteration of the subject matter making impossible a true *restitutio in integrum*. Consequently, the question that needs to be addressed is whether an attempt should be made to subordinate the rescission rules to the rules on rejection and termination. This will require an understanding of the role accorded to equitable remedies when invoked to supplement the common law as well as an analysis of section 1(a) of the Misrepresentation Act.

Equity developed to redress the rigours of the common law.[261] Rescission for innocent misrepresention emerged in its present general form,[262] unconfined to those contracts falling within the province of equity in the years preceding the fusion of the courts of equity and common law, at a time when common law fraud was undergoing a rigorous definition,[263] and the inference of warranties from pre-contractual representations was substantially restricted to prevent the award of damages for a mere representation.[264] Fraud may still be defined in restrictive terms, but rights based upon express warranty have so far expanded in modern times that it is difficult to see any rigours left at common law for equity to redress. In addition, since 1967, damages have been available for negligent misrepresentation. It could also be argued that the continuance of broad rescission rights is at odds with the *Hongkong Fir*[265] exhortation to look for serious consequences flowing from a breach rather than at the executory classification of a term as a condition or warranty. Subject to section 2(2) of the Misrepresentation Act, a contract may be rescinded for a misrepresentation that only in part induces entry into a contract. Furthermore, equity should not be staked to its pre-fusion boundaries but should as required expand or retract.[266] All of this makes a case that rescission for innocent misrepresentation should not be permitted once the misrepresentation becomes a term of the contract, but that is the very opposite of what is provided by section

---

[261] Supporting the loss of rescission rights, see P. S. Atiyah (1959) 22 *MLR* 76. The Law Reform Committe has drawn attention to the sometimes drastic nature of rescission when compared to the veniality of some representations: Tenth Report of the English Law Reform Committee on *Innocent Misrepresentation* (Cmnd. 1782, HMSO, London, 1962), para. 11. See Misrepresentation Act 1967, s. 2(2), for the discretion to award damages instead of rescission. See also J. Unger (1963) 26 *MLR* 292, 293.

[262] *Redgrave* v. *Hurd* (1882) 20 Ch. D 1.

[263] *Derry* v. *Peek* (1889) 14 App. Cas. 337.

[264] *Heilbut, Symons & Co.* v. *Buckleton* [1913] AC 30; Ch. 8 below.

[265] [1962] 2 QB 26.

[266] See *United Scientific Holdings Ltd* v. *Burnley Borough Council* [1978] AC 904.

1(a). Consequently, if the case made above, that the role of innocent misrepresentation in sales law should be controlled, is sufficiently compelling, such control will have to be exercised in either of two ways. First, the discretion given to courts in section 2(2) of the Misrepresentation Act, to award damages in lieu of rescission, might be widely exercised. Secondly, the rules governing the loss of the right to rescind might be aligned with the acceptance rules in section 35.

The first of these approaches ought to be uncontroversial once the case is successfully made that rescission is unduly generous to the claimant compared to the relief afforded by breach-of-contract principles. The criticism that rescission for misrepresentation can too easily undo a contract that could not be terminated for breach is not satisfactorily answered by asserting that the common law 'is dealing with discharge by acceptance of repudiation, equity with a vice inherent in the formation of a contract'.[267] Section 2(2) empowers a court to declare a contract subsisting (or revive one that has been rescinded by a self-executing act of rescission) if this is equitable considering the nature of, and the harm caused by, the misrepresentation and the loss caused by rescinding the contract. The second approach imports the difficulty of knowing how far it can be pressed: should it be confined to cases where the buyer has a right to reject goods for breach of condition, or should it also play a part where the misrepresentation is incorporated in the contract as a mere warranty whose breach does not give rise to a right to terminate the contract?

It is possible that the lapse of time needed for rescission to be denied is longer than the reasonable period stipulated for an acceptance in section 35. The buyer in *Bernstein*[268] could not readily be accused of the type of delay that in equity is treated as laches, namely delay that amounts to acquiescence or induces detrimental reliance by the seller.[269] Furthermore, the commission of an act inconsistent with the ownership of the seller is not as such a bar to rescission.[270] It must therefore be asked whether the right to rescind for misrepresentation survives the loss of the right to reject under section 35.

---

[267] R. P. Meagher, W. M. C. Gummow, and J. R. F. Lehane, *Equity[:]Doctrines and Remedies* (3rd edn., Law Book Co., Sydney, 1992), para. 1314.

[268] [1987] 2 All ER 220.

[269] *Erlanger* v. *New Sombrero Phosphate Co.* (1878) 3 App. Cas. 1218, 1279 ('due diligence' in the light of 'notice or knowledge'). See further Meagher, Gummow, and Lehane, n. 267 above, ch. 36.

[270] It is technically possible that the right to rescind might be lost before the buyer accepts the goods: *restitutio in integrum* is not one of the heads of acceptance in s. 35. No court is likely to cut down the s. 35 period for this reason.

Aligning Rescission and Rejection Rights

In *Leaf* v. *International Galleries*,[271] the plaintiff bought a picture entitled 'Salisbury Cathedral' from the sellers, who represented it as the work of Constable. Five years later, the plaintiff, intending to sell the picture, discovered it was not a Constable. He returned it and asked for the price to be reimbursed. At trial, the plaintiff's modest demand seems to have been treated as an action for the recovery of the price consequent upon rescinding the contract for innocent misrepresentation, the plaintiff having resisted the judge's invitation to claim damages for breach of warranty. Rescission, denied at trial because the contract had been executed, was refused for different reasons in the Court of Appeal. According to Denning LJ, the right to rescind for misrepresentation should be refused when the right to reject for breach of condition had been lost; the statement in question was a condition and the right to reject had lapsed.[272] Jenkins LJ appeared to reverse the trial judge's finding that rescission was not barred by laches,[273] while Evershed MR, observing that undoing transactions late in the day would undermine finality in business matters, agreed with Denning LJ that rescission should not lie when acceptance precludes rejection.[274]

Leaf gives less than a full explanation why rescission should be subordinated to the termination rules of the Sale of Goods Act, though it contains statements that misrepresentation is 'less potent' than a breach of condition[275] and that the availability of a common law damages remedy lessens the need to resort to equitable remedies.[276] Nothing was said to the effect that the Act established a comprehensive remedial structure that could only be upset by the irruption of innocent misrepresentation.

The decision in *Leaf* is squarely based upon the primacy of common law breach of contract over innocent misrepresentation. Yet it is at risk of being overturned as a result of section 1(a) of the Misrepresentation Act whose effect is that the incorporation of a misrepresentation as a term of the contract does not take away the right to rescind if rescission would have been available but for such incorporation. Although this provision was enacted to deal with the case of a misrepresentation that becomes a warranty, it is equally capable of embracing the circumstances of *Leaf*. This would be most undesirable.

Prior to section 1(a), there was significant support for the view that the incorporation of a misrepresentation as a mere warranty took away the

---

[271] [1950] 2 KB 86; L. C. B. Gower (1950) 13 *MLR* 362.
[272] *Ibid.* 90. This same approach was adopted in *Long* v. *Lloyd* [1958] 2 All ER 402.
[273] *Ibid.* 92.   [274] *Ibid.* 94–5.   [275] *Ibid.* 90–1.   [276] *Ibid.* 95.

right to rescind.[277] In favour of subsuming the misrepresentation in the term is the idea that breach of contract generates the superior right[278] and that it dispenses with the need to resort to equity for rescission. Section 1(a) would not, however, prevent a court from exercising its discretion to declare the contract subsisting under section 2(2). A more difficult question is whether the approach adopted in *Leaf* to cap rescission rights could be employed to similar effect in the case of a warranty whose breach does not give rise to a right to terminate the contract and therefore does not bring into play the acceptance heads in section 35. If rejection rights are non-existent, it would be decidedly odd if a buyer were able to rescind in the case of a subsequent warranty when he would not have been able to do so if the misrepresentation had become a condition of the contract. One solution to this would be to cap rescission if, had the misrepresentation become a condition, the right to reject would have been lost under section 35. But this in its turn would highlight the oddity of rescission being available in the case of a misrepresentation, not significant enough to become a term of the contract at all, when it would have been denied had the misrepresentation become a term. These difficulties point to the superior solution that it would be better to extirpate rescission for innocent misrepresentation altogether from sales law.[279] This would come close to the conclusion in the New Zealand case of *Riddiford* v. *Warren*[280] that innocent misrepresentation has no place in sales law, but on the above view there would remain the right to damages for negligent misrepresentation under section 2(1) of the Misrepresentation Act. In a climate hostile to changes in sales law that might somehow deprive consumers of a present advantage,[281] it is unlikely that this solution would ever receive the legislative backing it needs to succeed.

REJECTION AND DOCUMENTARY SALES

A c.i.f. contract is a documentary sale in that the seller's normal duty to deliver goods is substituted by a duty to ship or cause them to be shipped

[277] Supporting the loss of rescission rights are *Pennsylvania Shipping Co.* v. *Cie Nationale de Navigation* [1936] 2 All ER 1167; *Zien* v. *Field* (1963) 43 WWR 577. Asserting the opposite view are *Cie Nationale des Chemins de Fer Paris–Orléans* v. *Leeston Shipping Co.* (1919) 2 Ll. LR 235; *Academy of Health and Fitness Pty. Ltd* v. *Power* [1973] VR 254.

[278] In one case, incorporation as a warranty was not fatal to rescission because the recovery of damages would have been of little practical value to the plaintiff: *Academy of Health and Fitness Pty. Ltd* v. *Power*, n. 277 above.

[279] See the alternative solution of Gower, n. 270 above, where he would deem all misrepresentations to be contractual conditions so as to prevent rescission where rejection was no longer available.

[280] (1901) 20 NZLR 572.   [281] A strong theme in Law Com. No. 160.

and a duty to tender certain documents evidencing that carriage and insurance contracts have been entered into on appropriate terms.[282] In transit, the goods are represented by a transport document, classically a bill of lading,[283] which is their documentary expression until the transit comes to an end. The orthodox view is that the buyer has separate rights of rejection and termination arising out of documentary breaches and breaches concerning the quality and timely shipment of the goods,[284] but the true position is a little more complex than this. The rejection of documents will entail the rejection of the goods, since the c.i.f. seller may not unilaterally alter the contract and tender the goods physically on shore.[285] Likewise, the rejection of the goods will require the buyer to place any documents already received at the disposal of the seller.

Documentary and Physical Breach

A seller may commit separate documentary and physical breaches arising out of the same facts. In *James Finlay & Co. Ltd* v. *N. V. Kwik Hoo Tong Handel Maatschappij*,[286] where goods were shipped out of time under a bill of lading falsely dated, the seller was guilty both of late shipment and of breaching an implied contractual duty that the bill of lading be correctly dated. Devlin J in *Kwei Tek Chao* v. *British Traders and Shippers Ltd*,[287] another case of late shipment and false dating of the bill of lading, stated that the right to reject non-conforming documents is distinct from the right to reject non-conforming goods. The former arises on tender and the latter only when the goods are landed and found after examination not to conform to the contract.[288] The acceptance of a falsely dated bill of lading will therefore not prevent the buyer from rejecting the goods for late shipment.[289]

---

[282] The seller's documentary duties are considered in Ch. 6 below.

[283] *Sanders* v. *Maclean & Co.* (1883) 11 QBD 327, 341.

[284] *Kwei Tek Chao* v. *British Traders and Shippers Ltd* [1954] 2 QB 459.

[285] *Orient Co. Ltd* v. *Brekke & Howlid* [1913] 1 KB 532.

[286] [1929] 1 KB 400. See also *Hindley & Co. Ltd* v. *East India Produce Co. Ltd* [1973] 2 Lloyd's Rep. 515. Cf. *Johnson* v. *Taylor Bros. & Co. Ltd* [1920] AC 144, where the court declined to allow a writ to be served out of the jurisdiction when the failure to tender documents in England stemmed from a failure to ship them in Sweden.

[287] N. 284 above.

[288] It is more correct to say that the right to reject the goods arises after the buyer has acquired the documents. According to Lord Diplock in *Berger & Co. Inc.* v. *Gill & Duffus SA* [1984] AC 382, the c.i.f. buyer's right to reject the goods arises after they are unconditionally appropriated to the contract. This would occur once the seller's reservation of the right of disposal is released on the buyer paying against the documents.

[289] Subject to the buyer's waiver of late shipment (*Panchaud Frères* v. *Ets. General Grain Co.* [1970] 1 Lloyd's Rep. 53), which is not to be inferred lightly (*Procter and Gamble Phillipines* v *Peter Cremer* [1988] 3 All ER 843). Where the bill of lading is falsely dated but shipment is timely, the buyer does not have a separate right of rejection of the goods (*Procter & Gamble Philippine Mfg. Corpn.* v. *Kurt A. Becher GmbH & Co.* [1988] 2 Lloyd's Rep. 21).

If the goods are landed and it transpires that the seller has committed breaches of the fitness, quality or description conditions,[290] the buyer will not be prevented from rejecting the goods by dint of an earlier acceptance of the documents. Furthermore, the buyer's right to reject the goods will not be barred under section 35 by dealings with the documents inconsistent with the seller's ownership, such as pledging the documents or even delivering them to a sub-buyer in a sales string.[291] The application of section 35 here would be most inconvenient and would bar the exercise of rights of rejection of the goods in sales strings. In *Kwei Tek Chao*, Devlin J stated that the buyer acquired on the documentary exchange a conditional property in the goods that would be resolved by condition subsequent on a later, lawful rejection of the goods.[292] A pledge or resale of the documents amounts only to a dealing in this conditional property and does not touch the seller's conditional reversion; only an interference with the latter would deprive the buyer of a later entitlement to reject the goods.[293] The appeal to commercial convenience is more persuasive than the appeal to legal logic.

In a c.i.f. contract, the buyer's duty to pay against documents before examining the goods[294] in a real sense allocates to the buyer the commercial risk of having to pursue the seller to recover the price once the goods are proved to be defective. The free flow of shipping documents in c.i.f. transactions requires that the buyer not be permitted to go behind documents regular on their face so as to exercise prematurely a right of rejection of the goods. Attempts by buyers to do precisely this have produced difficulties as demonstrated in the following cases.

In *Braithwaite* v. *Foreign Hardwood Co.*,[295] the contract was for the sale of about 100 tons of Honduras rosewood to be delivered in instalments and paid for against bills of lading. The dispute centred on a shipment of sixty-three tons, whose documents the buyers rejected for reasons that later proved groundless. Later, the buyers discovered that a portion of the shipment fell short of the cargo standard,[296] by which time the seller had accepted the buyers' repudiation and resold the cargo to a third party. In the seller's action for damages for non-acceptance, the question was whether the buyers' refusal of the documents could be justified by their later discovery. The trial judge made an allowance against the seller's damages for the qualitative shortcomings of the shipment, which was accepted (rather grudgingly) by the majority of the Court of

---

[290] In the standard trading forms, fitness and quality discrepancies are usually the subject of a price allowance.

[291] *Kwei Tek Chao* v. *British Traders and Shippers Ltd*, n. 284 above.

[292] *Berger & Co. Inc.* v. *Gill & Duffus SA*, n. 288 above, 395 ('trite law').

[293] N. 284 above, 485–8.

[294] *E. Clemens Horst Co.* v. *Biddell Bros.* [1912] AC 18. Discussed Ch. 6 below.

[295] [1905] 2 KB 543.   [296] Probably to a minor extent.

Appeal.[297] By repudiating the contract, the buyers were regarded as having waived the seller's future obligation that the goods conform.[298]

A number of questions are prompted by *Braithwaite*.[299] First, does the decision undermine the orthodox proposition that an injured party has the right to terminate a contract even if he is unaware of his legal entitlement to do so, or even cites a different (and ill-founded) reason for doing so?[300] Secondly, supposing that the buyers would have been entitled to reject the shipment on arrival (which was perhaps unlikely), did this mean that they were entitled to reject a prior tender of shipping documents regular on their face? Thirdly, if the buyers had no such right to reject conforming documents, what effect did their repudiation, and the seller's later acceptance of it, have on the seller's future duty concerning the quality of the goods? Fourthly, if the seller's duty in respect of the goods were waived by the buyers' earlier repudiation, how far did this waiver go and, in particular, was it relevant in assessing the seller's damages for the buyer's non-acceptance of the documents?[301] Finally, what bearing does the case and its ensuing treatment have on the proposition that the integrity of documentary transactions should be safeguarded for reasons of commercial convenience?

Braithwaite clearly troubled the trial judge and Court of Appeal in *Taylor* v. *Oakes, Roncoroni & Co.*[302] A number of instalments of rabbit skins had been taken by the buyers before they repudiated the contract in the light of the sub-buyer's refusal to take further skins, prompted by adverse market conditions. The seller claimed damages for non-acceptance, whereupon the buyers discovered a breach of description in respect of skins already delivered. Nevertheless, the seller's breach was held to be severable and so the buyers were not entitled to terminate the balance of the contract. Two points of interest emerge from the case.

---

[297] N. 295 above, 552 ('damages [assessed] from the point of view of common sense rather than strict law').

[298] *Ripley* v. *M'Lure* (1849) 4 Ex. 34. See also *Cort* v. *Ambergate, Nottingham, and Boston etc. Railway Co.* (1851) 17 QB 127 (contract-breaker unable to enter plea traversing other party's averment of readiness and willingness to perform).

[299] In support of the decision, see *Continental Contractors Ltd* v. *Medway Oil and Storage Co. Ltd* (1925) 23 Ll. LR 124, revd. other grounds (1926) 25 Ll. LR 298. Doubt was cast on it by Lord Sumner in *British and Beningtons Ltd* v. *North Western Cachar Tea Co. Ltd* [1923] AC 48, 70. It clearly bothered the court in *Taylor* v. *Oakes, Roncoroni & Co.* (1922) 127 LT 267 and was left open by Lord Pearson in *J. Rosenthal & Sons Ltd* v. *Esmail* [1965] 1 WLR 1117. See also *Fercometal SRL* v. *Mediterranean Shipping Co. SA* [1989] 1 AC 788; *Foran* v. *Wright* (1989) 64 ALJR 1.

[300] Among the many authorities, see *Boston Deep Sea Fishing & Ice Co.* v. *Ansell* (1889) 39 Ch. D 339; *British and Beningtons Ltd* v. *North Western Cachar Tea Co. Ltd*, n. 299 above; *Arcos Ltd* v. *E. A. Ronaasen & Son* [1933] AC 470.

[301] A premature rejection of the shipment does not as such prejudice a seller who cannot in time appropriate a substitute shipment to the contract.

[302] N. 299. above This seems to have been a c.i.f. contract or a close equivalent.

First of all, the buyers unsuccessfully argued that account should be taken of the seller's likely ability to comply with the contract in future. The buyer's repudiatory breach, once accepted by the sellers, rendered irrelevant, even (it seems) for the purpose of calculating the sellers' damages, any consideration of the sellers' readiness and willingness to perform in future.

Secondly, the various judges in *Taylor* were concerned to distinguish *Braithwaite* so as to maintain the right to terminate a contract in those cases where the injured party failed to state a reason for so doing. Two judges in *Taylor*[303] asserted that in *Braithwaite* no actual tender of the shipping documents had taken place.[304] Instead, the seller had merely declared his intention to tender those shipping documents and had accepted the buyers' repudiation before doing so. The reason for this distinction was the belief that the buyers in *Braithwaite* could lawfully have rejected even conforming documents, provided they betokened a non-conforming cargo that could be rejected, even if the buyers were unaware of the non-conformity in the cargo when rejecting the documents. Although the reasoning is incomplete, one may surmise that the two judges in *Taylor* saw the act of tendering the documents as appropriating the cargo they represented, triggering a discharging breach regarding the goods themselves. Since no such tender occurred, no discharging breach ever took place. But the true explanation of *Braithwaite* may be more simple. It seems to have concerned a c.i.f. contract, though the report fails to say so. If that is correct, the seller could not be in breach with respect to the cargo before the buyer actually accepted the shipping documents.

Another point stemming from *Braithwaite* concerns one possible interpretation of this obscure case, that the seller had not accepted the buyers' repudiation. It is orthodox law that a party, faced with a repudiation by the other, may elect either to accept the repudiation and bring the contract to an end, or to affirm the contract. In the latter case, the affirming party keeps the contract alive for all purposes, including the raising of subsequent defences by the party who had previously repudiated the contract.[305] Furthermore, the affirming party remains liable to fulfil the contract for his own part, and thus runs the risk that the contract will be terminated against him for his own future non-

---

[303] N. 299, above 269 (Greer J at trial), 271 (Bankes LJ). Scrutton and Atkin LJJ (at 271, 272) left the point open.

[304] Relying upon equivocal language of Collins MR at [1905] 2 KB 543, 549 (the seller was 'ready to hand over' the bill of lading). See also *Esmail* v. *J. Rosenthal & Sons Ltd* [1964] 2 Lloyd's Rep. 447, 466 (Salmon LJ); *Fercometal SARL* v. *Mediterranean Shipping Co. SA,* n. 299 above, 804–5.

[305] *Avery* v. *Bowden* (1855) 5 E & B 714.

performance.[306] There is no third choice available to the party faced with a repudiation, namely, 'to affirm the contract and yet be absolved from tendering further performance unless and until [the repudiating party] gives notice that he is once again able and willing to perform'.[307]

On the *Taylor* proposition that the seller's future ability to perform becomes irrelevant once he accepts the buyer's repudiation, it has been persuasively argued that an unlawful repudiation by one party, while freeing the other from having to show a readiness and willingness to perform at the future date when his performance would fall due, does not however dispense the latter 'from having to show at the time of the repudiation he was disposed and able to complete the contract had it not been renounced' by the other party.[308] By this reasoning, a seller who would have gone on to commit a discharging breach of contract should not be able to reap a windfall from the buyer's premature repudiation and sue the buyer for breach. It has been cogently asserted that a party who lacks the capacity to perform, at a time when the other wilfully repudiates the contract, himself commits an anticipatory repudiation.[309]

Damages and Prospective Physical Breach

There is an alternative approach to the incapable seller, particularly useful perhaps if there is uncertainty concerning the degree of proof of his future incapacity. It is submitted that account might be taken when assessing damages of how the seller would probably have performed at the future date.[310] This approach would dispense the seller from having to show a prior disposition and willingness to perform as a condition for bringing suit against the buyer, but would take account of his performance potential in settling damages, since the buyer should be held liable only for such losses as he actually causes.[311] This approach could extend also to inevitable future non-performance. In *The Mihalis Angelos*,[312] where the charterers prematurely terminated a charter that

---

[306] *Fercometal SARL* v. *Mediterranean Shipping Co. SA*, n. 299 above (charterer invoked cancellation clause because ship not ready to load); *Segap Garages Ltd* v. *Gap Oil (Great Britain) Ltd, The Times*, 24 Oct. 1988.

[307] *Fercometal SARL*, n. 299 above, 805. Cf. *Foran* v. *Wright*, n. 299 above, 5 (Mason CJ), 16 (Brennan J).

[308] F. Dawson (1980) 96 *LQR* 239, relying upon the language of Lord Campbell CJ in *Cort* v. *Ambergate, Nottingham, and Boston etc Rly. Co.*, n. 298 above, 144.

[309] *Foran* v. *Wright*, n. 299 above, 9 (Mason CJ), 17 (Brennan J), relying upon *British and Beningtons Ltd* v. *North Western Cachar Tea Co. Ltd*, n. 299 above; *Rawson* v. *Hobbs* (1961) 107 CLR 466; *Universal Cargo Carriers Corpn.* v. *Citati* [1957] 2 QB 401.

[310] See the inconclusive discussion in *Bunge Corpn.* v. *Vegetable Vitamin Foods (Private) Ltd* [1985] 1 Lloyd's Rep. 613.

[311] *Quinn* v. *Burch Bros. (Builders) Ltd* [1966] 2 QB 370; *Cia Financiera Soliada SA* v. *Hamoor Tanker Corpn. Inc. (The Borag)* [1981] 1 WLR 274.

[312] *Maredelanto Cia Naviera SA* v. *Bergbau-Handel GmbH* [1971] 1 QB 164.

they would certainly have been entitled and would have wished to terminate at a later date, nominal damages only were awarded the shipowners.

The above line of reasoning and the documentary integrity of c.i.f. transactions came together in *Berger & Co. Inc.* v. *Gill & Duffus SA*.[313] The contract was for 500 tonnes of Argentinian bolita beans c.i.f. Le Havre and provided that an inspector's certificate of quality on discharge was to be final. The sellers' documentary tender did not include this certificate, so the buyers declined to pay, and eventually the sellers accepted the buyers' repudiation as terminating the contract. The House of Lords held that the quality certificate procured on discharge was not one of the documents that the seller had to tender in order to demand payment of the buyer. Consequently, the buyers' conduct was wrongful[314] and the sellers were entitled to damages for non-acceptance. This result is quite consistent with the long-standing rule that a c.i.f. buyer does not have the right to examine the goods on discharge before making payment.[315] It transpired that the certificate evidenced that the goods came up to the contractual standard, but their Lordships considered what the position would have been if the goods were non-conforming. In their view, consistently with the result in *Braithwaite*,[316] account should be taken of the possibility that the buyers would have gone on to recover damages representing any deficiency in the goods coming to light once they were landed. The court's willingness to discount the sellers' damages, even though the sellers' physical duties in respect of the goods had not yet fallen due and now, as a result of the termination of the contract never would, is consistent with general contract principle. The purpose of a damages award is to put the plaintiff in the position he would have occupied if the defendant had performed the contract. Assuming, then, that the buyers had paid the sellers in *Berger*, the sellers would thereupon be in breach if the goods were non-conforming and open to a damages action by the buyers. If, for example, the buyers had then been able to reject the goods, and in the estimation of the court would have done so, the sellers' damages for the buyers' earlier breach should be discounted in the light of that possibility. This could, in certain cases, produce a nominal damages award, which for all practical purposes would lift from the c.i.f. buyer the commercial risk of having to pay before seeing the goods.

---

[313] [1984] AC 382.

[314] The House firmly disapproved of contrary judgments in the Australian High Court in *Henry Dean & Sons (Sydney) Ltd* v. *O'Day Pty. Ltd* (1927) 39 CLR 330 (Knox CJ and Higgins J).

[315] *E. Clemens Horst Co.* v. *Biddell Bros.* [1912] AC 18.

[316] Curiously ignored in the arguments and the judgment.

CURE AND TERMINATION

Earlier in this Chapter, the lack of explicit statutory connection between the buyer's right to reject and right to terminate was discussed. Suppose the seller tenders goods that the buyer is entitled to reject. Does this mean that the buyer may *ipso facto* terminate the contract? Or may the seller make amends by resubmitting a conforming tender? Does the answer depend upon whether the delivery date or period has expired, or upon whether the time of delivery is of the essence of the contract? If cure[317] is permitted, must it take the form of substituting different goods, or may the seller tender the original goods in a repaired or modified condition? What is the significance here of specific goods, and should one look at language of description and at the process of appropriating goods to the contract? If cure is to be allowed, should it lie wherever the breach is serious enough on the facts to justify termination, or should it be confined to cases where the buyer is abusively seeking to terminate for breach of condition? Should the buyer be given the right to demand cure so that, if it is not provided, a non-discharging breach by the seller can be converted into a discharging breach? As regards consumer goods supplied with a manufacturer's warranty, there is an argument that the buyer's expectations may reasonably be defined in terms of the entire package purchased by the consumer, which includes the manufacturer's warranty and the after-sales service.[318] Seen in this way, cure could be regarded as an integral part of the seller's performance.

In 1983, the Law Commission noted that 'there is great uncertainty... as to the existence or extent of the seller's right to repair or replace defective goods'.[319] The Commission put forward for consultation a number or remedial regimes incorporating the notion of cure in consumer sales.[320] In its 1987 Report, however, the Commission rejected the statutory introduction in consumer sales of a seller's right to cure, because it gave leverage to sellers against buyers and posed complex practical problems of implementation.[321] For non-consumer sales, the Commission's provisional recommendation for consultation purposes was that cure should not be introduced: the circumstances of such sales were complex and cure would in many cases be impracticable.[322] Its rejection of cure in consumer cases fortified the Commission in its provisional recommendations.[323] It should be noted, however, that the new rules on termination for slight breach in sections 15A and 30(2A) deal with one

---

[317] R. J. Adhar [1990] *LMCLQ* 364; Apps [1994] *LMCLQ* 525; R. M. Goode, *Commercial Law* (2nd edn., Penguin, London, 1995), 363–6.
[318] But see Ch. 7 below.   [319] Consultative Document No. 58, para. 2.38.
[320] *Ibid.*, paras. 4.36 ff.   [321] Law Com. No. 160, paras. 4.13 ff.
[322] N. 319 above, paras. 4.52 ff.   [323] Law Com. No. 160, paras. 4.16 ff.

problem that the introduction of cure was designed to counter, namely, abusive termination for trivial breaches. Furthermore, the stance of the Law Commission does not affect the present existence of a doctrine of cure in so far as it may be garnered from various corners of sales law. The Commission did not conduct a survey of the area.

Tender and Cure

Before the authorities are discussed, a general assessment of the existing position is in order. Suppose the seller tenders goods, originally unascertained, that are not of satisfactory quality. The buyer may refuse them on tender. This will prevent the passing of property in them if the presumptive rule in section 18, Rule 5, operates. Or the buyer may take delivery and reject them within the section 35 acceptance period. If the buyer refuses the seller's tender, and there is further time to perform, denying the seller the right to make a tender of substitute goods would be tantamount to saying that defective tenders are *per se* repudiatory breaches, regardless of whether in the particular circumstances the buyer justifiably loses faith in the seller's ability to produce a conforming tender. The Sale of Goods Act does not say *when* the seller commits a breach of condition concerning the quality or fitness of goods. It is unlikely that the seller's duty will spring before the time of sale or, which in practice will be the same thing, delivery. This would appear to allow the seller time to make a second tender if goods answering the contract description[324] are available. This second tender will have to be of substitute goods: repaired goods would probably fall foul of any description in the contract requiring them to be new.[325] The second tender[326] would have to be made within the delivery period where time is of the essence.[327] Where time is not of the essence, there seems no reason to prevent a late cure if it occurs before the delay assumes frustrating proportions.[328]

If the buyer has taken delivery, the question of cure becomes more difficult. The seller will be in breach and the existence of any cure entitlement has two formidable obstacles to surmount. First, if the seller is to be prevented from exercising a right to terminate the contract for breach of condition under section 11(3), it may be necessary to find an implied term, stemming from business efficacy,[329] to that effect. This seems very

[324] Discussed Ch. 7 below.

[325] See *Annand & Thompson Pty. Ltd* v. *Trade Practices Commission* (1979) 40 FLR 165.

[326] If this too is defective, the seller may in the circumstances have committed a repudiatory breach.

[327] A general entitlement for the seller to cure would in effect convert all breaches into time breaches. The buyer would terminate because the seller had failed to deliver conforming goods on time.

[328] See Lord Devlin [1966] *CLJ* 192, 203.   [329] *The Moorcock* (1889) 14 PD 64.

unlikely. A slightly more promising approach is to observe that a breach of condition *may* under section 11(3) give rise to a right to reject goods and treat the contract as repudiated. The difficulty here is that section 11(3) appears to link the buyer's rejection of the goods seamlessly to treating the contract as repudiated, thus leaving no room for the implication of some step, control, or constraint between those two actions of the buyer. Secondly, the act of appropriating goods to a contract with the consent of the buyer may fix a description on them so that the seller may not unilaterally recall and substitute them.

In the case of specific goods, their uniqueness will prevent a seller from substituting them. The carrying out of any repairs will pose the same descriptive difficulties as were observed above for unascertained goods. For both specific and unascertained goods, the obligations of the seller discussed concerned the fitness and quality of the goods. But there may be other seller's duties, whose breach permits the buyer to terminate, that afford greater scope to cure. For example, the strict duties concerning the contract quantity in section 30 are not expressed as contractual conditions. In consequence, section 11(3) does not come into play. Various duties relating to the delivery of the goods in export sales may, as we shall see, allow some scope for cure.

The case most commonly cited in favour of cure is *Borrowman Phillips & Co.* v. *Free & Hollis*.[330] The c.i.f. sellers of a quantity of corn declared their intention to tender a cargo aboard the *Charles Platt* but the buyers declared they would not accept it because the sellers did not have the shipping documents to hand. Subsequently, the sellers offered a cargo aboard the *Maria D* for which they had a correctly dated bill of lading. The buyers also refused this offer on the ground that the sellers could not substitute the first cargo, and were sued successfully by the sellers for damages for non-acceptance. Reversing the trial judge on this point, the Court of Appeal ruled that the sellers had not irrevocably appropriated the cargo of the *Charles Platt*. The judgments are not as clear as they might be, but it seems that the sellers had merely offered to tender a cargo, and the offer never became binding because it was not accepted by the buyers. It is not clear from the judgments as a whole whether this was because the sellers' initial offer was tentative or whether it could only have become binding if it had been accepted by the buyer. The latter seems likely, so the case is similar to that, discussed above, of the buyer rejecting a tender of the goods. A number of authorities would allow the seller in this case to make a second tender.[331] Because of the uncertainty

---

[330] (1878) 4 QBD 500.
[331] *The Kanchenjunga* [1990] 1 Lloyd's Rep. 391, 399 (Lord Goff); *Ashmore & Son* v. *C. S. Cox & Co.* [1899] 1 QB 436, 440–1; *E. E. & Brian Smith (1928) Ltd* v. *Wheatsheaf Mills Ltd* [1939] 1 KB 302, 314; *McDougall* v. *Aeromarine of Emsworth Ltd* [1958] 3 All ER 431; *Empresa*

generated by the first defective tender, the seller may have to move expeditiously to make a second tender prior to the expiry of a delivery period.[332]

The *Borrowman* case was decided before the development of the modern practice of issuing notices of appropriation before the tendering of the documents. Such a notice was rejected by the buyers in *Getreide Import Gesellschaft mbH* v. *Itoh & Co. (America) Inc.*[333] but, since it was thereby rendered ineffectual, the sellers were able to give a later, valid notice.[334] A similar approach is evident in f.o.b. contracts where the buyer is required to nominate a ship a stipulated number of days in advance of its expected arrival. This is tantamount to offering to tender the nominated ship so that, if the seller turns down the original advance notice because it is too short, and another ship can be nominated to arrive within the shipment period, the seller will be bound to accept it.[335] A buyer nominating a ship close to the end of the shipment period may find, if the original ship unexpectedly cannot arrive within that period, that there is insufficient time to give the seller the requisite number of days' advance notice. A separate advance notice is required of the substitute ship; the buyer cannot build upon the original advance notice. For example, suppose a buyer nominates the *m.v. Chalmers* for an August shipment, and gives on 16 August the stipulated ten days' notice of its expected arrival on 26 August. The ship founders on 23 August before arriving at the loading port. The buyer has run out of time to give ten days' notice of the arrival of the substitute vessel, the *m.v. Blackburn*, so that it will arrive in time for an August shipment.[336]

The above authorites support cure only to the limited extent of correcting a defective tender, not a defective delivery.[337] This limited view was taken in early editions of *Benjamin*: 'But an appropriation and

Exportadora de Azucar v. *Industria Azucarera Nacional SA (The Playa Larga)* [1983] 2 Lloyd's Rep. 171, 186; *SIAT di del Ferro* v. *Tradax Overseas SA* [1980] 1 Lloyd's Rep. 53, 62–3 (shipping documents, where a buyer's rejection rights operate only at the tender stage).

[332] Cf. *Ashmore & Son* v. *C. S. Cox & Co.* n. 331 above, 440–1.

[333] [1979] 1 Lloyd's Rep. 592.

[334] *Quaere* the buyer who accepts a notice in the expectation that the seller will not be able to make subsequently a proper tender? Is this a waiver? Cf. the odd case of *Waren Import Gesellschaft* v. *Alfred C. Toepfer* [1975] 1 Lloyd's Rep. 322 (buyer not entitled to reject notice formally valid on its face but pointing to future non-performance).

[335] See *Bremer Handelsgesellschaft mbH* v. *J. H. Rayner & Co. Ltd* [1979] AC 216. In *Agricultores Federados Argentinos Soc. Lda* v. *Ampro SA* [1965] 2 Lloyd's Rep. 157, the buyer was not bound to nominate in advance, so the seller could not take objection to the retraction of a voluntary nomination and the substitution of another ship expected to arrive within the shipment period.

[336] See *Cargill UK Ltd* v. *Continental UK Ltd* [1989] 2 Lloyd's Rep. 290; H. Bennett [1990] *LMCLQ* 466. A number of modern sales forms give the buyer some latitude in these circumstances.

[337] Note how UCC 2–508, the cure provision, refers to the buyer's rejection of a 'tender or delivery'.

tender of goods, not in accordance with the contract, and in consequence rejected by the purchaser, is revocable, and the seller may afterwards, within the contract time, appropriate and tender other goods
which are according to the contract.'[338] Although the Law Commission
decided against statutory reform, cure, whether taking the form of substitute goods or repaired or adjusted goods, is common enough in count-
less unlitigated examples of contracting parties settling their differences.

A broad statement of cure has been proposed for adoption in the various provinces of Canada.[339] This would allow cure of any 'type' that is
'reasonable in the circumstances', if supplied within a reasonable time
'whether before or after the time for performance has expired'. This is
subject to the cure not causing 'unreasonable prejudice or inconvenience' to the buyer. This is a broad formula whose meaning would take
shape in litigation. An extensive cure provision is enacted in the United
Nations Convention on Contracts for the International Sale of Goods
1980. Article 48[340] allows the seller to cure after the delivery date if this
can be done 'without unreasonable delay and without causing the buyer
unreasonable inconvenience or uncertainty of reimbursement by the
seller of expenses advanced by the buyer'. This provision does not specify the form of cure.[341] Article 48 exists in a system that generally eschews
strict termination (or avoidance) rights,[342] whose approach to time
breaches is not easy to discern. In particular, the relationship of cure to
fundamental breach is not spelt out; it is also not easy to see how a time
breach can be 'cured'. A breach that does not give rise to the buyer's right
to avoid the contract may not, by the expedient of the buyer demanding
a cure in the form of substitute goods, be converted into a fundamental
breach.[343]

---

[338] 6th edn, 402. See how this statement was pushed beyond its limits in *Scythes & Co.* v.
Dods Knitting Co. (1922) 52 OLR 475 (Can.). The appropriation referred to here would
appear to be the seller's, the buyer's rejection of which prevents it from becoming consensual with the consequences dealt with above.

[339] Uniform Sale of Goods Act 1981, s. 73. See also Ontario Law Reform Commission,
Report on Sale of Goods, (1979), ii, 444–67; Alberta Institute of Law Research and Reform,
The Uniform Sale of Goods Act (Report no. 38, 1982), 184–97.

[340] Art. 37 deals with cases where the goods are delivered before the delivery date.

[341] Art. 37 refers to the delivery of missing goods, parts and substitute goods, and also to
'remedy[ing] any lack of conformity in the goods delivered'.

[342] See Art. 25 (fundamental breach).   [343] Art. 46(2).

6

Delivery, Acceptance, and Payment

The seller is required to deliver the goods to the buyer[1] at the time and in the mode and quantity required by the contract. The buyer is bound to accept and pay for the goods,[2] the presumption being that delivery and payment are mutual and concurrent conditions.[3]

THE SELLER'S DUTY TO DELIVER

Meaning of Delivery and Acceptance

In common speech, delivery suggests the active transportation of the goods to the buyer. That is not the meaning it has in sales law, presumptive or otherwise. According to section 61(1), '"delivery" means voluntary transfer of possession from one person to another'.[4] In the law of personal property, possession is the relationship between a person and a chattel based upon both the fact and intention of excluding all others from effective control of the chattel.[5] The scope of the control needed for this purpose depends upon the size, shape, and location of the chattel.[6] When the seller transfers possession of goods to the buyer, this entails yielding effective control over them to the buyer coupled with the abandonment by the seller of an intention to exercise effective control and the simultaneous assertion of such an intention by the buyer. It is not enough for the seller to tender the goods to the buyer; the latter must also receive them.[7] Where delivery is to be made at the buyer's premises, it will be effective if the seller without negligence hands over the goods to someone apparently having authority to receive them.[8]

---

[1] S. 27.   [2] *Ibid.*   [3] S. 28.

[4] The meaning of delivery is extended, in certain cases where the buyer acquires an undivided interest in goods pursuant to the Sale of Goods (Amendment) Act 1995, to include the passing of property in goods to the buyer. See s. 2(b) of the 1995 Act, explained in the notes to ss. 20A(5) and 20B(1) of the draft bill contained in Law Commission, *Sale of Goods Forming Part of a Bulk* (Law Com. No. 215), 39.

[5] F. Pollock and R. Wright, *An Essay on Possession in the Common Law* (1888); Harris, 'The Concept of Possession in English Law', in A. G. Guest (ed.), *Oxford Essays in Jurisprudence* (1961); M. G. Bridge, *Personal Property Law* (2nd edn., 1996), ch. 2.

[6] *The Tubantia* [1924] P 78; *Young* v. *Hitchens* (1844) 6 QB 606.

[7] See *Caradoc Nurseries Ltd* v. *Marsh* (1959) 19 DLR (2d) 491.

[8] *Galbraith and Grant Ltd* v. *Block* [1922] 2 KB 155.

Besides a physical tender and receipt of the goods, possession may be transferred to effectuate delivery in various ways. It is possible for a seller to deliver the goods without surrendering possession. This will occur where the seller assumes the character of bailee holding the goods on behalf of the buyer.[9] Delivery may occur symbolically, where a portion of the goods is handed over as representative of the whole,[10] or constructively, where the buyer is given the only effective means[11] of access to the goods, such as a warehouse key.[12] Another constructive delivery takes place where the seller transfers to the buyer an on board bill of lading, which is a common law document of title,[13] for in such a case the bailee in possession is bound to deliver the goods to the holder of the document even before attorning to the holder. The transfer of a document that meets the wider definition of a document of title under the Factors Act 1889 and the Sale of Goods Act[14] would not be a constructive delivery of the goods. In such a case, constructive delivery would occur only when the bailee attorns to the buyer, for the bailee would not be under an obligation to the buyer to deliver until doing so.[15]

According to section 32(1), delivery *prima facie* occurs where goods are handed over by the seller to an independent carrier[16] for the purpose of transmission to the buyer.[17] The reason for this is that the carrier is presumptively the buyer's agent.[18] The *prima facie* rule in section 32(1) applies even if the carrier is not nominated by the buyer; it is not uncommon for an f.o.b. seller, whose duty to deliver consists of placing the goods free on board a ship, to negotiate a contract of carriage as agent for

[9] *Castle* v. *Sworder* (1861) 6 H & N 828; *Elmore* v. *Stone* (1809) 1 Taunt. 458; *Dublin City Distillery Co.* v. *Doherty* [1914] AC 823, 844.
[10] *Dixon* v. *Yates* (1833) 5 B & Ad. 313; *Kemp* v. *Falk* (1882) 7 App. Cas. 573, *per* Lord Blackburn.
[11] For the requirement of exclusive access, see *Dublin City Distillery Co.* v. *Doherty*, n. 9 above, 843–4.
[12] *Ellis* v. *Hunt* (1789) 3 TR 464; *Wrightson* v. *McArthur and Hutchinsons (1919) Ltd* [1921] 2 KB 807, where the court preferred to conclude that there had been a true delivery rather than a constructive delivery.
[13] *Lickbarrow* v. *Mason* (1794) 5 TR 683. But note the wider definition in certain local Acts: e.g. the Port of London Act 1968, s. 183.
[14] Ch. 9 below.
[15] S. 29(4); *Laurie and Morewood* v. *Dudin and Sons* [1926] 1 KB 223; *Farina* v. *Home* (1846) 16 M & W 119; *Dublin City Distillery Ltd* v. *Doherty*, n. 9 above, 847–8; *Lackington* v. *Atherton* (1844) 7 Man. & Gr. 360; *M'Ewan* v. *Smith* (1849) 2 HLC 309; *Wardar's (Import & Export) Co. Ltd* v. *W. Norwood & Sons Ltd* [1968] 2 QB 663. Cf. *Salter* v. *Woollams* (1841) 2 Man. & Gr. 650; *Poulton & Son* v. *Anglo-American Oil Co.* (1911) 27 TLR 216.
[16] Not an employee: *Galbraith and Grant Ltd* v. *Block*, n. 8 above; *Caradoc Nurseries Ltd* v. *Marsh*, n. 7 above.
[17] Sale of Goods Act, s. 32(1); *Wait* v. *Baker* (1848) 2 Ex. 1; *Badische Anilin und Soda Fabrik* v. *Basle Chemical Works* [1898] AC 200; *Dutton* v. *Solomonson* (1803) 3 B & P 582; *Dunlop* v. *Lambert* (1839) 6 Cl. & Fin. 600, 620–1; *Calcutta & Burmah Steam Navigation Co. Ltd* v. *De Mattos* (1863) 31 LJ QB 322, 328; *Ex p. Pearson* (1868) 3 Ch. App 443.
[18] *Wait* v. *Baker*, n. 17 above.

the buyer.[19] The rule in section 32(1) should be displaced where goods are deliverable under a non-negotiable waybill to a named consignee but the seller consigning the goods has reserved, under the contract of carriage, the right to alter delivery instructions. Section 32(1) is also ousted in those cases where delivery to the carrier is not intended by the seller to be delivery to the buyer. This will be so where the seller retains the right of disposal under section 19,[20] where delivery will take place constructively on the exchange of documents between seller and buyer.[21] The rule in section 32(1) will therefore be displaced for c.i.f. (cost, insurance, and freight) sales. Indeed, the goods may already be afloat before the contract of sale is concluded or before a particular cargo is appropriated to the contract, so that it is impossible to treat the carrier retrospectively as the agent for the buyer.[22] In c.i.f. contracts, the seller's delivery obligation is commuted into an obligation to transfer shipping documents[23] and the buyer obtains the benefit of the contract of affreightment on the documentary exchange.[24] The section 32(1) rule will also be displaced in *ex* ship contracts, where delivery is effected when the goods are discharged from the ship.[25]

The ambiguity of acceptance across sales law was noted in an earlier chapter. Here it means the co-operative acts that the buyer must perform in order to enable the seller to make delivery as above defined. The seller cannot deliver unless the buyer voluntarily receives the goods.[26] Where delivery occurs constructively by means of a bill of lading, the transfer of that document, effective to give the buyer constructive possession of the goods, will not occur until the buyer takes delivery of the bill. In cases

---

[19] See s. 32(2); *Cork Distilleries Co.* v. *Great Southern and Western Railway Co.* (1874) LR 7 HL 266, 277; *Pyrene Co. Ltd* v. *Scindia Navigation Ltd* [1954] 2 QB 402, 423; *The Albazero* [1977] AC 774, 785–6, 841–2. The issue is complicated by the question of who has standing to sue the carrier for damage done in transit: Ch. 4 above; *The Albazero*, above; *Leigh and Sillavan Ltd* v. *Aliakmon Shipping Ltd* [1986] AC 785. If the seller were able to sue, it would be because he was still the owner of the goods or (less likely) bore the risk, and thus could be said to contract with the carrier as principal: *The Albazero*, above, 844–5. For a description of the seller's dealings with the carrier in f.o.b. contracts, see *Pyrene Co. Ltd* v. *Scindia Navigation Ltd*, above.

[20] *Wait* v. *Baker*, n. 17 above, 8. *Quaere* the buyer as named consignee in the bill of lading retained by the seller until payment? See *Moakes* v. *Nicholson* (1865) 19 CB(NS) 290 (no delivery).

[21] *E. Clemens Horst Co.* v. *Biddell Bros.* [1912] AC 18, 22–3.

[22] *Keighley, Maxsted & Co.* v. *Durant* [1901] AC 240.

[23] See *Manbre Saccharine Co. Ltd* v. *Corn Products Co. Ltd* [1919] 1 KB 198, 202; *Comptoir d'Achat et du Boerenbond Belge SA* v. *Luis de Ridder Lda* [1949] AC 293, 312. Discussed in the text accompanying nn. 320 ff. below.

[24] This can be accomplished under the Carriage of Goods by Sea Act 1992, s. 2(1), by means of a wider range of documents than the negotiable bill of lading, to which the Bills of Lading Act 1855 limited the potentiality of assignment of the contract of affreightment.

[25] Cf. *Beaver Specialty Ltd* v. *Donald H. Bain Ltd* [1974] SCR 903.

[26] S. 61(1) ('delivery').

where constructive delivery depends upon the presentation of a delivery order or warrant, and the contract expressly or impliedly provides for the buyer to present this document to the bailee, the buyer's duty of acceptance requires that he receive this document and that he present it to the bailee in order to procure the necessary attornment. Where the bailee attorns to the buyer when required to do so by the seller, acceptance by the buyer is a purely passive matter.

In numerous cases, a seller will be unable to make delivery until the buyer performs a preliminary act. For example, a seller may require a statement of the buyer's specifications[27] or, if needing to obtain an export licence before shipping the goods, may require from the buyer information concerning the ultimate destination of the goods.[28] A contract for delivery 'as required' by the buyer[29] or at buyer's call[30] will bind the buyer to give delivery instructions to the seller. An f.o.b. buyer is under a presumptive duty to nominate a ship so that the seller can effect delivery on board.[31]

Place of Delivery

The principal rules concerning the place of delivery are laid down in section 29 of the Act. Sub-section (1) begins by stating that it depends upon the express and implied provisions of the contract whether the seller has to send the goods to the buyer or the buyer has to come and take possession of them. In the absence of any contractual indication to this effect,[32] the presumptive rule in sub-section (2), in all cases bar one, is that delivery occurs at the seller's place of business (or residence if there is no place of business). The buyer will have an implied licence to enter the seller's premises to receive the goods, which, if growing crops, may need to be severed.[33] Sub-section (2) also states the exceptional case to which the above presumptive rule does not apply. Where the contract is for specific goods, the location of the goods, if known to the parties at the contract date, is presumptively the place of delivery.[34] In the great majority of cases involving specific goods, however, the goods are likely to be on the seller's premises. Further, if the seller knows the whereabouts of the

[27] *Kidston and Co.* v. *Monceau Ironworks Co.* (1902) 7 Com. Cas. 82.
[28] *Kyprianou* v. *Cyprus Textiles Ltd* [1958] 2 Lloyd's Rep. 60.
[29] *Jones* v. *Gibbons* (1853) 8 Ex. 920.
[30] *Tradax-Export SA* v. *Italgrani di Francesco Ambrosia* [1986] 1 Lloyd's Rep. 112; *Bunge* v. *Tradax England* [1975] 2 Lloyd's Rep. 235.
[31] *Cargill UK Ltd* v. *Continental UK Ltd* [1989] 2 Lloyd's Rep. 290; *Richco International* v. *Bunge* [1991] 2 Lloyd's Rep. 92; *Colley* v. *Overseas Exporters* [1921] 3 KB 302
[32] An Australian court interpreted the buyer's request 'please supply us' as requiring delivery at the buyer's premises: *Wiskin* v. *Terdich Bros. Pty. Ltd* [1928] VLR 387.
[33] *James Jones & Sons Ltd* v. *Earl of Tankerville* [1909] 2 Ch. 440, 442.
[34] *Salter* v. *Woollams*, n. 15 above.

goods and the buyer does not, it is quite possible that special transport arrangements will be made.[35]

The rules in section 29(2) are ill-suited to constructive delivery. Where there is an attornment by a bailee, delivery will occur as and where the attornment takes place.[36] In the case of shipping documents, as used in c.i.f. contracts for example, it has been said that, in the absence of proven trade usage or an express or implied term based upon prior business dealings, it is doubtful that the seller has to tender documents at the buyer's premises.[37] On the other hand, in *Johnson* v. *Taylor Bros. and Co. Ltd*,[38] where the c.i.f. buyer had to show a breach of contract committed within the jurisdiction in order to effect service abroad, it was held 'without hesitation' that the failure to tender documents to the English buyer, concerning goods shipped in Sweden, had taken place in England.[39] The case involved a requirements contract between a Swedish manufacturer of pig iron and an English industrialist purchasing the iron in order to manufacture axles. The buyer clearly needed the bill of lading to receive the goods from the carrier in England. Where commodities are sold, and the buyer is a trader who has no such physical use for the goods, or where the goods are not sold on credit, the same conclusion is not so compelling. According to Brandon J in *The Albazero*, shipping documents 'would normally be sent to the seller's agent for presentation to the buyer, or delivered to a banker against a confirmed credit, leaving the banker to forward them to his agent at the place of payment for collection of the price'.[40] The place of delivery would therefore be wherever the seller's agent has to present the documents to obtain payment. It is unlikely to be important in practical terms at what precise point in the inter-bank system the documents are exchanged against payment.

The method of delivery, often designated by the use of trade terms, frequently indicates the place of delivery. A sale *ex* factory or works accords with the main presumptive rule in section 29(2). Under an f.a.s. contract, the seller is required to lay the goods free alongside the ship[41] after they have been cleared by customs.[42] Where the sale is on *ex* ship terms, delivery will take place once the goods have been landed at the port of discharge. In the absence of contractual provision, the actual location within the port will depend upon what is usual or customary in that

[35] See *Varley* v. *Whipp* [1900] 1 QB 513.
[36] This should be the place of receipt by the buyer.
[37] *Stein, Forbes & Co.* v. *County Tailoring Co.* (1916) 88 LJ KB 448 (Atkin J). But see *Johnson* v. *Taylor Bros. and Co. Ltd* [1920] AC 144, 156.
[38] N. 37 above.
[39] The court relied upon Kennedy LJ in *Biddell Bros.* v. *E. Clemens Horst Co.* [1911] 1 KB 934, 962. See also *The Albazero*, n. 19 above, 800 (Brandon J), 810 (Roskill LJ).
[40] [1977] AC 774, 800.
[41] *Nippon Yusen Kaisha* v. *Ramjiban Serowgee* [1938] AC 429.
[42] *A. V. Pound & Co. Ltd* v. *M. W. Hardy & Co. Inc.* [1956] AC 588.

port.[43] An f.o.b. sale requires the seller to place the goods on board a ship.[44] Where there is a choice or range of ports, it is presumptively the buyer who chooses,[45] which accords with the buyer's presumptive duty to select the ship, but sometimes the choice is explicitly given to the seller.[46] The seller may under the contract have the choice of different berths in the port.[47] The f.o.b. shipment term binds both parties. The seller may not unilaterally alter the port[48] and the buyer may not unilaterally require delivery on shore before shipment if unable to nominate a ship.[49]

Certain incidental matters may arise in connection with delivery under an f.o.b. contract. According to section 29(6), the expenses of and incidental to putting the goods in a deliverable state are presumptively borne by the seller.[50] Hence the f.o.b. seller bears the cost of putting the goods on board.[51] Although entry into the contract of affreightment with the carrier is the responsibility of the buyer under the so-called 'classic' f.o.b. contract,[52] it is common for this responsibility to be placed upon the seller,[53] who will carry it out as agent for the buyer.[54]

Time of Delivery and Acceptance

If the contract mentions a precise delivery date, the seller will be bound to deliver and the buyer to accept on that date, which will not be interpreted as a mere target date to be met only if the seller has goods to hand.[55] Nor will the contract be interpreted as permitting delivery on a prior date[56] in the absence of a contrary usage.[57] On the day of delivery

---

[43] *Yangtse Insurance Association* v. *Lukmanjee* [1938] AC 429.

[44] *Pyrene Co. Ltd* v. *Scindia Navigation Ltd* [1954] 2 QB 402.

[45] *David T. Boyd & Co. Ltd* v. *Louis Louca* [1973] 1 Lloyd's Rep. 209.

[46] *Gill & Duffus* v. *Soc. pour l'Exportation des Sucres* [1985] 1 Lloyd's Rep. 621.

[47] *Miserocchi* v. *Agricultores Federados Argentinos* [1982] 1 Lloyd's Rep. 202.

[48] *Petrograde Inc* v *Stinnes Handels GmbH* [1995] 1 Lloyd's Rep. 142.

[49] *Maine Shipping Co.* v *Sutcliffe* (1918) 87 LJ KB 382. Cf. *Cohen & Co.* v. *Ockerby & Co. Ltd* (1917) 24 CLR 288, 299.

[50] See also Incoterms 1990, FOB Rules, para. A6 (costs to ship's rail borne by seller).

[51] *Attorney-General* v. *Leopold Walford (London) Ltd* (1923) 14 Ll. LR 359.

[52] *Pyrene Co. Ltd* v. *Scindia Navigation Ltd*, n. 44 above, 402. See the criticism in *H. D. Bain* v. *Field & Co. (Fruit Merchants)* (1920) 3 Ll. LR 26, affd. (1920) 5 Ll. LR 16. A buyer will often employ the services of a freight forwarding agent.

[53] *Pyrene Co. Ltd* v. *Scindia Navigation Ltd*, n. 44 above.

[54] See s. 32(2); *Cork Distilleries Co.* v. *Great Southern and Western Railway Co.* (1874) LR 7 HL 266, 277; *Pyrene Co. Ltd* v. *Scindia Navigation Ltd*, n. 44 above, 423; *The Albazero*, n. 40 above, 785–6 (Brandon J), 841–2 (Lord Diplock).

[55] *Raineri* v. *Miles* [1981] AC 1050 (sale of land). But a seller may undertake only 'best endeavours' to deliver by a stated date: *Hartwell's of Oxford Ltd* v. *British Motor Trade Association Ltd* [1951] Ch. 50; *Monkland* v. *Jack Barclay Ltd* [1951] 2 KB 252.

[56] *Bowes* v. *Shand* (1877) 2 App. Cas. 455.

[57] *Imperial Grain & Milling Co.* v. *Slobinsky Bros.* (1922) 69 DLR 258.

itself, a demand or tender of delivery may be rendered ineffectual under section 29(5) unless made at a reasonable hour.[58]

Should the contract contain no fixed or determinable delivery date, section 29(3) provides that a seller who has to send the goods to the buyer must do so within a reasonable time. A similar implied term would certainly apply to other types of delivery. A reasonable time, as a question of fact,[59] will be influenced by the nature of the goods so that a shorter period should apply to perishable goods[60] or to fashion items than to durable goods. It may also prevent the seller from making premature delivery, as in the case of seasonal goods where to the seller's knowledge the buyer has no storage facilities.[61] Account should be taken of the position of the parties at the contract date in determining a reasonable time,[62] but this should not preclude a reference to post-contractual circumstances, too, when these, outside the seller's control, delay delivery.[63] In certain contracts, however, the seller may assume responsibility for delays attributable to a third party, as in one case where a carrier's negligent navigation delayed the transfer of cottonseed, shipped in Karachi, from the carrier's vessel to the buyer's craft in Hull.[64] Where in one case a c.i.f seller was entitled to substitute a vessel if the named ship was unavailable, this right of substitution could only be exercised once the named ship remained unavailable after the post-contract reasonable period had expired.[65]

Express Delivery Terms

Express terms concerning the time of delivery sometimes call for interpretation. To deliver 'as soon as possible' means to do so at the earliest date within a reasonable range. Bramwell LJ once said: 'To do a thing as soon as possible means to do it within a reasonable time with an undertaking to do it in the shortest possible time.'[66] The buyer's expectations in this respect might have to take a reasonable account of the seller's obligations to other buyers,[67] which does not mean that a seller may

---

[58] *Startup* v. *Macdonald* (1843) 6 Man. & Gr. 593.

[59] S. 59; *Hick* v. *Raymond & Reid* [1893] AC 22, 29 (Lord Herschell).

[60] Market usage may require an untimed delivery to be 'immediate', interpreted as 72 hours in a case dealing with the sale of potatoes: *F. C. Bradley & Sons* v. *Colonial Continental Trading Co.* (1964) 108 SJ 599.

[61] *Dauphin Consumers Cooperative Ltd* v. *Puchalski* (1984) 26 Man. R (2d) 179 (Can.) (fertilizer).

[62] *Ellis* v. *Thompson* (1838) 3 M & W 445, 456–7.

[63] *Monkland* v. *Jack Barclay Ltd* [1951] 2 KB 252; *Hick* v. *Raymond & Reid* [1893] AC 22 (strike).

[64] *Re A. H. Craven & Co. and E. D. Sassoon & Co.* (1911) 17 Com. Cas. 59.

[65] *Thomas Borthwick (Glasgow) Ltd* v. *Bunge & Co. Ltd* [1969] 1 Lloyd's Rep. 17.

[66] *Hydraulic Engineering Co.* v. *McHaffie* (1878) 4 QBD 670, 673. See also *Attwood* v. *Emery* (1856) 26 LJ CP 73; *Cote* v. *Briggs* [1953] 4 DLR 527.

[67] *Bonner-Worth Co.* v. *Geddes Bros.* (1921) 50 OLR 257, 263 (Can.).

divert scarce goods from a buyer, who has ordered them on forward delivery terms, to later buyers prepared to pay higher spot prices.[68]

Problems of interpretation sometimes arise where a delivery period is stipulated. In *Coddington* v. *Paleologo*,[69] the contract called for 900 lengths of cloth, which the buyer intended to bleach for resale, 'delivering on April 17, complete 8 May'. A falling market prompted the question whether, under this severable contract, the seller had to deliver at least some of the goods on 17 April itself, or whether it was sufficient that the cloth be delivered in instalments within the delivery range. The seller argued that the date of commencement was fixed in his interest, while the date of completion was fixed in the buyer's interest. With the Court of Exchequer equally divided, the lower court prevailed in its holding that the seller did not have to commence delivery on the first day.[70] The alternative view would have been difficult to justify in view of the failure of the contract to stipulate the size of the first instalment.[71]

A number of contracts oblige the seller to supply goods 'as required' by the buyer. Where a contract calls for delivery of a stated quantity, the term 'as required' will not mean that the buyer's duty of acceptance is conditional upon actually needing the goods.[72] In the co-operative climate of delivery on 'as required' terms, the buyer's demand must be made in such a way as to afford the seller a reasonable opportunity to provide the goods. A sensible approach, if the contract fails to state a delivery range, would be to require the buyer to make his demand within a reasonable time[73] and the seller to respond to the demand within a reasonable time, with the reasonableness of each party's action assessed in the light of his knowledge of the circumstances of the other. Particular circumstances may require a more immediate response from the seller, especially where there is a delivery range. In *Cie Commerciale Sucres et Denrées* v. *Czarnikow Ltd*,[74] the House of Lords held that the term, 'the seller shall have the sugar ready to be delivered' when the ship presented itself for loading, in a contract for the sale of 12,000 tonnes of sugar f.o.b. Dunkirk, meant that 'the seller shall have the sugar called forward available for loading without delay or interruption as soon as the vessel is ready to load the cargo in question.' According to Sir Michael Kerr in the court below:

---

[68] *Madden* v. *McCallum* [1923] 3 DLR 41.   [69] (1867) LR 2 Ex. 193.

[70] For the buyer, Martin B said: 'I think it better that a shabby defence should prevail, than a loose construction be put upon a mercantile contact, the inevitable consequence of which is uncertainty, litigation and expense': *ibid.* 198.

[71] *Ibid.* 199 (Pigott B).

[72] *Wingold* v. *William Looser & Co. Ltd* [1951] 1 DLR 429. See generally M. Howard (1973) 19 *McGill LJ* 224.

[73] *Wingold* v. *William Looser & Co. Ltd*, n. 72 above.

[74] *The Naxos* [1990] 3 All ER 641.

'[R]eady to be delivered' . . . does not mean that [the sugar] must be physically stacked on the quay when the vessel comes alongside. It means that it must then be available for loading without delay or interruption in the event that the vessel is able to start loading at once and to continue to load without interruption.[75]

In congested port conditions, it is undesirable and expensive to keep a ship tied up waiting for cargo. A buyer chartering a ship to lift a cargo would also run the risk of having to pay the shipowner substantial sums in demurrage payments during this period.

Abandonment

Particular difficulties arise with 'as required' delivery terms in instalment contracts. Sometimes, such contracts have been satisfied only in part, with the balance of delivery being overlooked until the buyer recovers his memory on a rising market. On the face of it, it seems unfair to permit a buyer to make a demand out of time binding on the seller. Nevertheless, if the contract has not yet been terminated for the buyer's breach, assuming the buyer to be in breach and the breach to be a discharging breach,[76] which may not be the case, the seller is in difficulties. Indeed, the rule has been laid down that the seller, prior to terminating for a fail-ure to state requirements, must first give the buyer notice to state those requirements within a reasonable time,[77] seemingly a form of making time of the essence. Section 37(1) imposes a damages liability on a buyer who fails within a reasonable time to take delivery of the goods in response to a request of the seller, but sub-section (2) makes it plain that the remedy in sub-section (1) is without prejudice to any right the seller might otherwise have to terminate the contract for breach.

The seller's difficulties have been surmounted by inferring a mutual intention of both parties to abandon the contract, so far as it relates to undelivered instalments, in the wake of a protracted or 'inordinate' delay. In *Pearl Mill Co. Ltd* v. *Ivy Tannery Co. Ltd*,[78] the contract was for fifty dozen roller skins 'as required'. Between November 1913 and September 1914, twenty dozen skins were delivered, but thereafter the buyers (as well as the sellers) appeared to forget about the order until the buyers demanded delivery of the remaining skins in July 1917. Between September 1914 and July 1917, the buyers turned down various propos-als by the sellers to supply skins on the same terms under a new contract, gave an order to another supplier in July 1915 for fifty dozen skins and informed the sellers that all of their 1916 requirements had been met. It was held that the contract, so far as it related to the undelivered balance of thirty dozen skins, had been abandoned, as each party was entitled to

---

[75] [1989] 2 Lloyd's Rep. 462, 468.   [76] Ch. 5 above.
[77] *Jones* v. *Gibbons* (1853) 8 Ex. 920.   [78] [1919] 1 KB 78.

infer this from the other's inactivity.[79] Although the result suppresses opportunistic behaviour by the buyer, the basis of abandonment requires further elaboration.

The best starting point is that the buyer is under a duty to request delivery within a reasonable time; a failure to do so may amount to a repudiatory breach that may be accepted by the seller without communication.[80] Other approaches are to rationalize abandonment as a contract to abandon the balance of an agreement,[81] based upon mutual uncommunicated promises by the parties; or as the outcome of an implied term in the contract that a delivery lapse if not called for within a reasonable time,[82] or as based upon a representation or an estoppel that becomes binding upon the inactive buyer when the seller relies upon it or alters his position.[83] The difficulty with a contract to abandon is that it is impossible to see how a contract can be concluded by silent offer and silent acceptance.[84] Offer and acceptance by conduct remains a possibility although hard as a matter of interpretation to infer from mutual inactivity.[85] A similar difficulty of interpretation impedes the inference of a binding estoppel.[86] What is clear is that a contract will not be treated as frustrated simply by mutual inactivity.[87]

Requirements and Instalments

A different problem emerges as a side issue in *Jackson* v. *Rotax Motor and Cycle Co.*,[88] where the sellers, French manufacturers, were to supply more than 600 motor horns 'as required'. The court held that the contract was not entire but instead contemplated delivery on severable instalment terms,[89] so that acceptance of earlier instalments would not prejudice the right to reject later non-conforming instalments. Each delivery was to be treated as a separate contract.[90] Suppose, however, that the buyer demanded delivery in one instalment. It is by no means

---

[79] McCardie J adds further that the buyers were estopped from demanding more deliveries.

[80] See *The Splendid Sun* [1981] QB 694, 704 (Denning MR); *The Leonidas D* [1985] 1 WLR 925, 928. In the latter case, Robert Goff LJ, 939, thought this the explanation of the *Pearl Mill* case but it is difficult to see support for this view in the judgments in that case.

[81] *Moore* v. *Crofton* (1846) 3 Jon. & L 438, 445: 'Abandonment of a contract . . . is a contract in itself.'

[82] See *The Leonidas D*, n. 80 above; *Food Corpn. of India* v. *Antclizo Shipping Corpn.* [1988] 1 WLR 603.

[83] See *Collin* v. *Duke of Westminster* [1985] QB 581, 595 (Oliver LJ); *The Hannah Blumenthal* [1983] AC 854, 914 (Lord Brandon), 915–17 (Lord Diplock).

[84] See *The Leonidas D*, n. 80 above, 936–7 (Robert Goff LJ.).

[85] *Food Corpn. of India* v. *Antclizo Shipping Corpn.*, n. 82 above; *Gebr. van Weelde Scheepvaartkantor BV* v. *Cia Naviera Sea Orient SA* [1987] 2 Lloyd's Rep. 223.

[86] See *The Hannah Blumenthal*, n. 83 above, 924 (Lord Brightman).   [87] *Ibid.*

[88] [1910] 2 KB 937. See also *Tarling* v. *O'Riordan* (1878) 2 LR Ir. 82.

[89] *Ibid.*, Cozens-Hardy MR, 944.   [90] *Ibid.*, Farwell LJ, 948; Kennedy LJ, 949.

clear that, in contracts of this type, this should be disallowed, and certainly no clearer how many or how few[91] requests for delivery the buyers should make under the contract and in what amounts. Such a contract might be construed as an entire one that confers on a buyer the option to have delivery instead in separate instalments. Were attention to be drawn to the seller's prejudice in having to deliver at once all of the agreed goods, one response is that this might suit some sellers; another is that the concept of a reasonable time to meet the buyer's demand is flexible enough to accommodate periods of different length depending upon the quantity of goods demanded. In the case of a buyer purchasing raw materials for the manufacture of goods, a reasonable construction of the agreement might be that it contemplates approximately even quantities at even intervals. A further problem with flexible delivery arrangements of this kind concerns the extent to which, especially if delivery occurs over a prolonged period, the buyer should be allowed to frame his demands according to the movement of the market in volatile trading conditions.[92] The construction of 'as required' contracts will depend upon all the circumstances, including the volume of contract goods and the relationship of this figure to the seller's storage or productive capacity and to the buyer's consumption or resale needs as apparent to both parties at the contract date.

Delivery, Acceptance, and Time of the Essence

A more prominent difficulty arising from the time of delivery is whether timely delivery is of the essence of the contract. Because of the interlocking character of the seller's delivery and the buyer's acceptance duties, it is convenient to treat them together. A minor obstacle to this approach is section 27 which recites 'the *duty* . . . of the buyer to accept and pay for [the goods]'.[93] Notwithstanding this provision, it is better to treat the buyer as having separate primary duties of acceptance and payment, for it should not be assumed that the two duties will always be treated with the same degree of strictness. The Act separates acceptance and payment, in section 28 when making payment of the price and delivery mutual and concurrent conditions, and in section 10, which states that stipulations concerning payment are presumptively not of the essence of the contract. Nevertheless, a buyer on cash terms who declines to pay while expressing a willingness to accept delivery will be open to an action

---

[91] Farwell LJ thought the buyer was entitled to call for delivery of a single horn: *ibid.* 948.
[92] This will have implications for damages assessments for non-delivery. See Ch. 10, below.
[93] Emphasis added.

for damages for non-acceptance. His duty is to accept according to the terms of the contract,[94] and these do not allow for credit.[95]

The basic rules of timely performance[96] are, first, that the time of payment is presumptively not of the essence of the contract,[97] and, secondly, that it depends upon the construction of the contract whether any other term is of the essence.[98] Now, this section[99] makes no explicit mention of the doctrine of conditions and warranties, so dominant elsewhere in the Sale of Goods Act.[100] It also fails to lend support to intermediate stipulations or to failure of consideration and, by dividing time obligations into those that are and are not of the essence of the contract, produces a binary classification of its own on lines similar to condition and warranty. As for the words 'of the essence of the contract', these seem to have originated in conveyancing practice and to have been transplanted into the common law of sale in imitation of equity's treatment of sale of land contracts;[101] in equity, time is presumptively not of the essence of the contract.[102] In drafting the Sale of Goods Act 1893, Chalmers for the most part faithfully followed the antecedent common law. It had in recent memory been firmly laid down by the House of Lords that the time of delivery in mercantile contracts, which comprised the great majority of reported cases before 1893, was of the essence of the contract.[103] On the face of it, section 10 is therefore strangely reticent in leaving the time of performance of non-payment obligations as an open question of contractual construction, unless this can be attributed to uncertainty surrounding the role to be played by equitable ideas of timely performance. Where the contract is silent on the time of performance, which then must take place within a reasonable time,[104] it is unlikely that it will be regarded as of the essence of the contract. A different conclusion might well follow if the parties explicitly stipulate for performance within a reasonable time, especially if a reasonable time is

---

[94] S. 27.

[95] Similarly, a buyer to whom a bailee attorns (thereby effecting delivery by the seller) will be liable for non-acceptance if refusing to pay.

[96] See also ss. 37(1) and 48(3).   [97] S. 10(1).   [98] S. 10(2).

[99] Said by McCardie J to give 'a very slender notion of the existing law': *Hartley* v. *Hymans* [1920] 3 KB 475, 483.

[100] Ch. 5 above.

[101] See *Martindale* v. *Smith* (1841) 1 QB 389. In *United Scientific Holdings Ltd* v. *Burnley Borough Council* [1978] AC 904, 925–6, Lord Diplock spoke of the common law's tendency, in the 19th century, to adopt a more rational scheme for classifying contractual obligations, thereby pre-empting equitable intervention.

[102] *Stickney* v. *Keeble* [1915] AC 386; *United Scientific Holdings*, n. 101 above; *Seton* v. *Slade* (1802) 7 Ves. Jun. 265.

[103] *Bowes* v. *Shand* (1877) 2 App. Cas. 455. See also *Reuter, Hufeland & Co.* v. *Sala & Co.* (1879) 4 CPD 239; *Coddington* v. *Paleologo* (1867) LR 2 Ex. 193.

[104] S. 29(3).

expressed to run from a stated date.[105] But this is no explanation for the silence of section 10, which deals only with time stipulations and not with the larger subject of time of performance.

The cases decided since sale was first codified have generally held that timely delivery and acceptance are of the essence of the contract.[106] They have usually failed to say why this should be so. Even where the issue is dealt with in some detail, discussion is confined to the particular type of contract before the court without canvassing the issue of timely performance in sales law as a whole.[107]

Where time is held not to be of the essence, a problem arises concerning the suitability of introducing intermediate stipulations analysis to permit discharge when the breach goes to the root of the contract. Speaking of an f.o.b. buyer's duty to give notice of readiness to load, Lord Wilberforce has stated that the intermediate stipulation analysis of Diplock LJ in *Hongkong Fir Shipping Co. Ltd* v. *Kawasaki Kisen Kaisha Ltd*[108] is inappropriate, for there is only one kind of breach possible, namely to be late.[109] He appears to mean, however, that a time provision should be examined to see whether it is expressly or impliedly a condition before attention is turned to the question of its breach going to the root of the contract. It cannot be the law that, if a time provision fails to meet the test of a condition, there can never arise from the circumstances of its breach a right to terminate, for otherwise a party might be compelled to wait in a state of perpetual suspense for performance that will or might never arrive. That party must be entitled to assume eventually that late performance has become non-performance. A number of decisions on timely delivery are consistent in result with this approach and Lord Wilberforce's words are best understood as underlining the critical importance of time in f.o.b. shipments such that all relevant terms ought to be classified as conditions.

Timely Delivery

The leading case on the seller's duty of timely delivery is *Bowes* v. *Shand*,[110] where a seller shipped the greater part of a quantity of Madras rice in February when the contract called for shipment 'during the months of March and/or April'. The buyer refused to accept the shipping

---

[105] In *McDougall* v. *Aeromarine of Emsworth Ltd* [1958] 3 All ER 431, 439, Diplock J thought such an obligation a condition. Cf. *DTR Nominees Pty. Ltd* v. *Mona Homes Pty. Ltd* (1978) 138 CLR 423, 430 (Stephen, Mason, and Jacobs JJ): '[W]e fail to see how a stipulation calling for action to be taken expeditiously of itself constitutes an essential term.'

[106] e.g. *Hartley* v. *Hymans* [1920] 3 KB 475.

[107] e.g. *Bunge Corpn.* v. *Tradax Export SA* [1981] 2 All ER 513; *Peter Turnbull & Co. Ltd* v. *Mundus Trading Co. Pty. Ltd* (1954) 90 CLR 235; *Toepfer* v. *Lenersan-Poortman NV* [1980] 1 Lloyd's Rep. 143.

[108] [1962] 2 QB 26.   [109] *Bunge Corpn.* v. *Tradax SA*, n. 107 above, 541.

[110] N. 103 above. See S. Stoljar (1955) 71 *LQR* 527, 533–7.

documents since these included February bills of lading, and the House of Lords held that the seller's action for non-acceptance failed. The seller had not complied with all necessary conditions precedent since the time of shipment was part of the contractual description of the goods.[111]

Bowes v. *Shand* reveals a predisposition to solving problems of termination by contractual construction. This allows standard-form commodities contracts to be treated alike; the loss of flexibility in individual cases is compensated by certainty across the range of such transactions and amongst the various connected contracts in string trading conditions.[112] Apart from the observation that technical excuses may be used to escape from a bad bargain,[113] there is absent from the case any examination of the parties' behaviour in terms of the allocation of the risk of market rise and fall. It is difficult to see the seller's early shipment,[114] a venial transgression that had no effect on the quality of the rice at the port of discharge, as an attempt to speculate in the rice market at the buyer's expense. Further, the buyer's behaviour, apparently not associated with any grievance concerning the quality of the goods, is hard to explain except in terms of a determination to use any available excuse to avoid a falling market. Nor is there any discussion in the case of the hardship a seller might suffer by bringing goods at great expense from a distant location, only to have them rejected by the buyer. The expense of carriage is one that the seller will bear in any event,[115] but the resale of the goods in distress circumstances or in thin trading conditions could mean that the loss suffered by the seller exceeds the market decline that a buyer accepting the goods would have experienced. The approach in *Bowes* v. *Shand* might be admirably suited to ensuring predictability and certainty in a conventional commodities agreement, but it could well cause hardship in other sales contracts.

The consistently strict attitude to time in commodities contracts and the desire to offer certainty to future contracting parties are revealed in *Bunge Corpn.* v. *Tradax SA*.[116] The f.o.b. sellers were required to ship 5,000 tonnes of soya meal in June at a Gulf of Mexico port of their own choice. It was the buyers' duty to nominate an effective ship and to give the sellers fifteen days' notice of readiness to load. The buyers were intermediate parties in a string of connected contracts for June soya meal and

[111] Lord Blackburn. See also *Kwei Tek Chao* v. *British Traders and Shippers Ltd* [1954] 2 QB 459, 480–1; *Finagrain SA Geneva* v. *P. Kruse Hamburg* [1976] 2 Lloyd's Rep. 508, 540–1.

[112] *Bunge Corpn.* v. *Tradax SA*, n. 107 above.

[113] Lord Hatherley, n. 103 above, 476.

[114] Much of the report is taken up with the meaning of 'shipped', interpreted as loaded on board rather than leaving port.

[115] The cost of freight would be reflected in the market price (albeit a falling one) commanded by the goods when sold in the importing country.

[116] N. 107 above. See M. G. Bridge (1983) 28 *McGill LJ* 867.

therefore had to await a notice from the ultimate buyers before passing it on to their own sellers. Delays in the transmission of the notice at various points in the string meant that the buyers were four days late in passing this notice on to their own sellers.[117] The sellers therefore repudiated the contract[118] and sued for damages on a declining market.[119] The entitlement of the sellers to do this depended upon the status of the buyers' duty as a contractual condition, for the sellers did not argue that the buyers' breach in the circumstances went to the root of the contract. In both the Court of Appeal and the House of Lords, the buyers' duty was held to be a condition,[120] though both courts conceded that there was a role in sales law for intermediate stipulations analysis.

Bunge reasserts the line taken in *Bowes* v. *Shand* that the status of a contract term is a question of construction and therefore one of law; trade opinion might well be influential in this inquiry but it would not bind a court of construction.[121] The courts relied upon explicit policy arguments not discussed 100 years before in *Bowes* v. *Shand.* Treating the buyers' duty as a condition freed the sellers from having to make difficult judgements of the degree of prejudice emerging from evolving facts,[122] and avoided the risk of their prematurely, and thus unlawfully, repudiating the contract. Strict termination rights would also spare courts the task of dealing with difficult issues of damages assessment and would tend to avoid protracted trials and the cumbersome procedure of a seller issuing notice making time of the essence of the contract.[123] It was also emphasized that a strict rule of construction would facilitate the administration by commodities traders of complex arrays of continuing contracts and would bring about consistency of result for each contract in a sales string.[124] Furthermore, the rule could not be criticized as unduly pro-seller since one of the characteristics of the commodities trade is that the identities of seller and buyer are interchangeable.[125] The point was also made that any decision treating the buyers' duty as less than a contractual condition would be an 'arrogant and unjustifiable' interference with the parties' own assessment that fifteen days' notice was reasonable, presumably because it would give the buyers more time to perform.[126] The flaw in this argument is that, even if the term were not

---

[117] For the circumstances of the delay, see the judgment of Parker J at [1981] 2 All ER 513.
[118] Rather this particular shipment, treated as a separate contract from the balance of the 15,000 tonnes contract.
[119] The report gives no reason for the sellers' behaviour. Perhaps they were faced with difficulties of transport and storage (assuming they were the shippers) in managing their many contracts; or perhaps the sellers were taking a principled stand on the general importance of timely performance in commodities trading conditions.
[120] See also *Peter Turnbull & Co. Ltd* v. *Mundus Trading Co. Pty. Ltd,* n. 107 above.
[121] [1981] 2 All ER 513, 532 (Megaw LJ), 553 (Lord Roskill).
[122] N. 107 above, 536 (Megaw LJ). See J. A. Weir [1976] CLJ 33.
[123] *Ibid.* 545–6 (Lord Lowry).   [124] *Ibid.*   [125] *Ibid.*   [126] *Ibid.* 532 (Megaw LJ).

a condition, the buyers would still be in breach for giving only eleven days' notice, and it is difficult to see any interference where the parties have refrained from expressly designating a term as a condition.[127]

Finally, the courts involved in the *Bunge* litigation were keen to promote certainty, not merely in the relations of the buyers and sellers *inter se*, but in commodities trading as a whole. The contracts here are invariably standard form and amount in substance to a form of private legislation assented to by those in the trade; it is the form that is being interpreted rather than the particular contract, as shown by the policy arguments relied upon and the deference to antecedent commercial practice and established trade opinion. The demands of certainty also require that the parties' clear designation of a term should be respected, hence the impatience shown for arguments tending to undermine the autonomy of the parties[128] by requiring a particular breach to go in fact to the root of the contract before termination is allowed.[129]

Similar obligations concerning the time of performance in commodities contracts have been treated as contractual conditions.[130] Consistently with the line taken in voyage charter cases,[131] the 'expected ready to load' clause in sale of goods has always been regarded as a contractual condition.[132] It has been held, however, that the duty of the c.i.f. seller seeking to invoke a prohibition clause when exports are prevented or impaired by governmental action is not an implied condition but rather an intermediate stipulation.[133] But the buyer's performance is not affected by the receipt of a timely notice from the seller. Obligations

---

[127] In *Tarrabochia* v. *Hickie* (1856) 1 H & N 183, 188, Bramwell B said: 'No doubt it is competent for the parties, if they think fit, to declare in express terms that any matter shall be a condition precedent, but when they have not so expressed themselves, it is necessary for those who construe the instrument to see whether they intended to do it. Since, however, they could have done it, those who construe the instrument should be chary in doing for them that which they might, but have not done for themselves.'

[128] See *Bettini* v. *Gye* (1876) 1 QBD 183.

[129] See the treatment in *Bunge*, n. 121 above, of the judgment of Diplock LJ in *Hongkong Fir Shipping*, [1962] 2 QB 26.

[130] *Graves* v. *Legg* (1857) 2 H & N 210; *Bowes* v. *Shand* (1877) 2 App. Cas. 455; *Reuter, Hufeland & Co.* v. *Sala & Co.* (1879) 4 CPD 239; *Cie Continentale d'Importation* v. *Handelsvertretung der Union* (1928) 44 TLR 297; *Bremer Handelsgesellschaft mbH* v. *J. H. Rayner & Co. Ltd* [1979] 2 Lloyd's Rep. 216; *Toepfer* v. *Lenersan-Poortman NV* [1980] 1 Lloyd's Rep. 143; *Soc. Italo-Belge* v. *Palm and Veg. Oils Sdn. Bhd.* [1981] 2 Lloyd's Rep. 695; *Bergerco USA* v. *Vegoil Ltd* [1984] 1 Lloyd's Rep. 440; *Tradax Export SA* v. *Italgrani di Francesco Ambrosio* [1983] 2 Lloyd's Rep. 109; *Scandinavian Trading Co. A/B* v. *Zodiac Petroleum SA* [1981] 1 Lloyd's Rep. 81; *Gill & Dufus SA* v. *Soc. pour l'Exportation des Sucres SA* [1986] 1 Lloyd's Rep. 322; *Cie Commerciale Sucres et Denrées* v. *Czarnikow Ltd* [1990] 3 All ER 641. Cf. *Phibro Energy* v. *Nissho* [1991] 1 Lloyd's Rep. 38.

[131] *Behn* v. *Burness* (1863) 3 B & S 751; *Maredelanto Cia Naviera SA* v. *Bergbau-Handels GmbH (The Mihalis Angelos)* [1971] 1 QB 64.

[132] *The Mihalis Angelos*, n. 131 above; *Finnish Govt.* v. *H. Ford & Co.* (1921) 6 Ll. LR 188.

[133] *Bremer Handelsgesellschaft mbH* v. *Vanden-Avenne Izegem PVBA* [1978] 2 Lloyd's Rep. 109; *Bunge SA* v. *Kruse* [1979] 1 Lloyd's Rep. 209.

relating to the timely tender of shipping documents have, however, been regarded as very much of the essence of the contract.[134]

While these commodities decisions bear out with great force the proposition that time is normally of the essence, the strictness they reveal should not unthinkingly be extended to all other mercantile contracts. Suppose a seller has to gather raw materials and over an extended period erect a machine to the buyer's personal specifications. Where buyer and seller are committed to a co-operative enterprise of this kind, where various communications are likely to pass between them before delivery, a punctilious concern for time backed up by draconian termination rights is unlikely to be set out expressly in the contract. All sorts of unpredictable factors may affect the seller's ability to perform on time under a complex contract of this type, and the buyer's concerns can be met by a negotiated liquidated damages or price reduction clause. An application of the *Bunge* reasoning to such a contract would be out of place, especially since no ready market would exist for a custom-built machine unwanted by the buyer, and since a defaulting seller would therefore be excessively prejudiced by termination of the contract[135] and vulnerable to oppressive renegotiation on the part of the buyer. A court, it is submitted, should be unwilling to construe or recognize an implied or express intention to permit termination for late delivery where a buyer of this sort has not suffered a substantial detriment.[136]

In other cases, the contract may point away from time being of the essence, as it did where a cancellation clause permitted termination after a stated period of delay, thereby negativing time being of the essence of the agreed delivery date.[137] The failure of a contract to state a delivery date, so that a reasonable time has to be implied, makes it hard to see that timely performance is a condition since the concept lacks a cutting edge;[138] rather a reasonable time is likely to be assessed commensurately with the attainment by the buyer of his contractual purpose. Time will not normally be of the essence of a contract for the delivery of consumer goods.[139] On the other hand, special factors may point to the time of delivery as essential, as they did in one case where a ring had to be supplied in time for a silver wedding celebration.[140] Furthermore, if the delivery date is far advanced so as to give the seller ample time to perform by the agreed date, time is more likely to be regarded as of the

---

[134] *Toepfer* v. *Lenersan-Poortman NV*, n. 130 above.

[135] See the old inequality of damages argument in *Duke of St Albans* v. *Shore* (1789) 1 H Bl. 270.

[136] See *Paton & Sons* v. *Payne & Co.* (1897) 35 SLR 112.

[137] *Steel Co. of Canada* v. *Dominion Radiator Co. Ltd* (1919) 48 DLR 350.

[138] *DTR Nominees Pty. Ltd* v. *Mona Homes Pty. Ltd* (1978) 138 CLR 423, 430.

[139] *Allen* v. *Danforth Motors Ltd* (1957) 12 DLR (2d) 572.

[140] *Alteen's Jewellers Ltd* v. *Cann* (1980) 40 NSR 504 (Can.).

essence, especially if the buyer announces well in advance that he needs the goods for a particular purpose at that time.[141] By stating a paramount need, the buyer has notified the seller that delayed performance will substantially deprive him of the benefit of the bargain as effectively as if time had expressly been declared to be of the essence of the contract. In cases like the last two, the same result will flow whether time is classified as a condition or as an intermediate stipulation.

Supposing that time is not of the essence of the contract, the next question is whether it can become so by subsequent events. It was an equitable innovation that time, initially at large, could by notice later be made of the essence of the contract.[142] The process, explicable in sale of land agreements where it was difficult to make title, is hardly fitted to commercial contracts,[143] especially those involving goods. Where a notice may be given, there is no need to wait until an undue or improper delay has occurred; the notice may be served as soon as the time for performance has expired.[144] Under existing common law principles, a buyer or seller should not be able to serve a notice making time of the essence if the effect of so doing would produce a unilateral variation of the contract.[145] In the case of a sale of goods contract, therefore, the significance of serving a notice is probably best seen as crystallising the period of delay that will produce a breach going to the root of the contract.[146]

Timely Acceptance

Since a seller cannot deliver unless a buyer actually or constructively accepts the goods, the buyer's duty to accept the goods on time should be treated with the same degree of strictness or leniency, as the case may be, as the seller's duty to deliver. The same reasoning does not apply to duties of the buyer that are anterior to the seller's duty to deliver, though the courts are loth to deny the status of condition to a duty that interlocks with a duty of the seller that is a condition.[147]

---

[141] See *Charles Rickards Ltd* v. *Oppenhaim* [1950] 1 KB 616.

[142] *United Scientific Holdings Ltd* v. *Burnley Borough Council* [1978] AC 904, 928; *Cornwall* v. *Henson* [1900] 2 Ch. 298. For the import of making time of the essence of sale of goods agreements, see *Lambert* v. *Slack* [1924] 2 DLR 166, 170; *Portaria Shipping Co.* v. *Gulf Pacific Navigation Co. Ltd* [1981] 2 Lloyd's Rep. 180, 185; *Charles Rickards Ltd* v. *Oppenhaim*, n. 141 above.

[143] *British and Commonwealth Holdings Plc* v. *Quadrex Holdings Inc.* [1989] QB 842, 856 ff.

[144] *Behzadi* v. *Shaftesbury Hotels Ltd* [1991] 2 All ER 477, disapproving on this point *British and Commonwealth Holdings Plc* v. *Quadrex Holdings Inc.*, n. 143 above.

[145] *Behzadi* v. *Shaftesbury Hotels Ltd*, n. 144 above, 496.

[146] A form of making time of the essence also appears in the United Nations Convention for the International Sale of Goods (Vienna, 1980). The buyer or seller can fix an additional reasonable time for performance and may declare the contract avoided if performance does not occur by that date: Arts. 47, 49(1)(b), 63, 64(1)(b).

[147] *Bunge Corpn.* v. *Tradax SA* [1981] 2 All ER 513.

The rather thin case law on acceptance by the buyer shows that it cannot easily be determined whether time will be of the essence. The approach of the courts is sometimes based upon a construction of the contract, but sometimes, consistently with intermediate stipulations analysis, takes account of the consequences of breach. This latter approach is evident in one case where the buyer was one working day late after declining, for religious reasons, to collect goods from the auctioneer's premises on a Saturday. The seller was not entitled to terminate.[148] Time was also held not to be of the essence in *Kidston & Co.* v. *Monceau Ironworks Co.*,[149] where the buyers were late in furnishing specifications for a quantity of iron to be manufactured by the sellers. The buyers' duty had to be performed before the sellers could ship the goods in May or June as required by the contract, but the court emphasized that the buyers' failure to provide the specifications due at the beginning of May did not impede the sellers' ability to organize their production schedule and arrange for shipment within the contract period. Assuming timely performance by the buyers, the sellers' duty to deliver would probably have been treated as of the essence of the contract, and yet the buyers' anterior duty was dealt with in a way consistent with modern intermediate stipulations analysis. This is at odds with *Bunge*[150] where the buyers' duty to give notice of readiness to load was treated as necessarily a condition because the sellers' ensuing duty of delivery was a condition. But *Bunge* was a commodities case where commercial certainty was advanced by consistent treatment of the standard form throughout the trade and down the contractual string. The contract in *Kidston*, though a commonplace one, was by no means of such a standard type and it did not take place in volatile market conditions. Furthermore, though the point is not raised in *Kidston*, it is not illogical to treat a buyer's duty to give timely specifications as an intermediate stipulation and, to the extent of the buyer's default, allow the seller to use this as a defence if sued for his own forced failure to deliver on time. The buyer's breach could operate so as to suspend the seller's duty of timely delivery where the buyer's delinquency eats into the time reasonably available to the seller to perform.

Time was, however, treated as of the essence in a 'spot' transaction for the sale of ten bales of Hessian bags, cash payment against a delivery order on or before 19 September. The sellers were responsible for storage and insurance up to that date and the clearly expeditious character of the c.o.d transaction supported the court's conclusion that time was of the essence of the buyers' duty to take delivery.[151] According to Sankey J:

[148] *Woolfe* v. *Horne* (1877) 2 QBD 355.   [149] (1902) 7 Com. Cas. 82.
[150] N. 147 above.
[151] *Thames Sack and Bag Co. Ltd* v. *Knowles & Co. Ltd* (1918) 88 LJ KB 585.

'[T]he whole object of the contract was to make a bargain that should be completed by the buyers at least by September 19'.[152] Time was also held to be of the essence in a case involving the sale of potatoes to be shipped by canal before Christmas, emphasis being laid upon the perishable nature of the goods.[153]

Equitable Ideas

Any treatment of the strictness of timely delivery and acceptance would be incomplete if it failed to take account of attempts made over the years to introduce equitable ideas to counter the strictness of the common law's approach to timely performance. The fusion in 1873 of the courts of equity and common law, with the consequent administration of principles of equity and common law in the same judicial system, led to the enactment of a rule[154] modified in 1925[155] to read as follows: 'Stipulations in a contract, as to time or otherwise, which according to rules of equity are not deemed to be or to have become of the essence of the contract, are also to be construed and have effect in law in accordance with the same rules.' In *Reuter, Hufeland & Co.* v. *Sala & Co.*,[156] a case of a c.i.f. contract for the sale of twenty-five tons of Penang pepper, one of the issues concerned the sellers' duty to tender properly dated bills of lading, which was held to a condition of the contract. Cotton LJ said:

It was argued that the rules of equity are now to be regarded in all courts, and that equity enforced contracts though the time fixed therein for completion had passed. This was in cases of contracts such as purchases and sales of land, where, unless a contrary intention could be collected from the contract, the Court presumed that time was not an essential condition. To apply this to mercantile contracts would be dangerous and unreasonable . . . [T]he decisions in equity, on which reliance is placed, do not apply.[157]

The same view was stated in *Stickney* v. *Keeble*,[158] where it was asserted that the equitable view on time was a component of the doctrine of specific performance and applied only to the type of contract falling within the jurisdiction to grant that remedy. A provision like section 41 of the Law of Property Act should not therefore be understood as allowing the infiltration of equitable ideas throughout the whole law of contract but should be confined to the types of contract, linked to the doctrine of specific performance, that preoccupied equity before fusion. Since equity's concern with sale of goods contracts was minimal, and specific performance rarely granted, it would follow that section 41 should have little, if

---

[152] *Ibid.* 587.
[153] *Sharp* v. *Christmas* (1892) 8 TLR 687.
[154] Supreme Court of Judicature Act 1873, s. 25(7).
[155] Law of Property Act 1925, s. 41.
[156] (1879) 4 CPD 239.
[157] *Ibid.* 249.
[158] [1915] AC 386.

any, impact upon the law of sale of goods. Some uncertainty stems from the House of Lords decision in *United Scientific Holdings Ltd* v. *Burnley Borough Council*,[159] which concerned a rent review clause in a long-term lease of commercial premises. Opinions were expressed that equity should not be frozen in its pre-fusion boundaries but should be free to expand or retract as the case may be.[160] If such a resurgent equity were to be allowed into commercial sale of goods agreements, it would be destructive of the certainty and forward-planning valued so highly by the House of Lords in *Bunge Corpn.* v *Tradax SA.*[161] Concessions were, however, made in *United Scientific Holdings* that the time of delivery remained of the essence in commercial sale of goods agreements. It cannot be said that the position will never change, but the entitlement of parties to designate a term as a contractual condition,[162] and the general rule that time of delivery is of the essence of commercial sales contracts, have both survived attempts made to undermine them by praying in aid equitable principles.

The Seller's Duty to Deliver the Agreed Quantity

The Sale of Goods Act is strict in the duty it lays on the seller to deliver the agreed quantity, for the buyer is entitled to reject the goods if the seller tenders more,[163] or fewer,[164] goods than the agreed amount. In non-consumer cases, the buyer no longer has the right to reject goods where, since the Sale and Supply of Goods Act 1994, the excess or shortfall is so slight that rejection would be unreasonable.[165] No guidance is given as to what is a slight excess or shortage. In particular, it cannot be said that the reasonableness of the buyer's behaviour depends upon whether the seller is willing to impose no charge for an excess.[166] The buyer's right to reject is lost, not when the quantitative difference is slight *and* it would be unreasonable to reject, but when it is so slight *that* it would be unreasonable to reject. The burden of showing a slight departure from the agreed quantity and the unreasonableness of the buyer's behaviour rests upon the seller.[167] The above provisions in section 30 are all subject to any trade usage, special agreement, or course of dealing between the parties.[168]

---

[159] N. 142 above.

[160] *Ibid.* 924–8 (Lord Diplock); 940–7 (Lord Simon); 957–8 (Lord Fraser).

[161] N. 147 above.

[162] *Bunge Corpn.* v. *Tradax SA*, n. 147 above, clearly shows this to have survived *United Scientific Holdings.*

[163] S. 30(2).   [164] S. 30(1).

[165] S. 30(2A). See the discussion of the companion provision, s. 15A, in Ch. 5 above.

[166] If there is a shortfall, s. 30(1) already reduces the price by requiring the buyer to pay at the contract rate. Where the buyer freely elects to accept more goods, payment is to be made at the contract rate: s. 30(3).

[167] S. 30(2B).   [168] S. 30(5).

Section 30(1), which allows a buyer to reject a short delivery, should be read in conjunction with section 31(1), which states that in the absence of a contrary agreement a buyer is not bound to accept delivery by instalments. If the parties have not agreed to severable delivery, the seller may not deliver some of the goods on account.[169]

Entire or Severable?

Some contracts raise difficult questions of construction as to whether severable (or instalment) delivery is permitted. For example, a contract calling for delivery 'as required' might, as seen above, be interpreted in various ways. Commodities contracts present difficulties too, largely because of the mismatch between the language of the standard form and the expectations generated by a particular contractual adventure, but also because of the modern practice of bulk shipments. In *Cobec Brazilian Trading and Warehousing Corpn.* v. *Alfred C. Toepfer*,[170] a c. & f. contract for the sale of 25,000 tonnes of Argentinian soya beans incorporated the terms of the FOSFA 22 form, which contained the usual provision that each shipment, if more than one were made, should be regarded as a separate contract. Of the 25,000 tonnes, it was agreed that about 19,000 tonnes should be discharged in Santander and about 6,000 tonnes in Seville. The contract called for shipment between 25 June and 10 July. More than 18,000 tonnes were shipped before 10 July; the rest were shipped on 14 July and the ship sailed on the following day. The buyers were held entitled to reject the entire shipment. The contract created an indivisible duty to ship by 10 July, and did not call for delivery in two instalments for Santander and for Seville. Had this been the case, the timely bills could have been applied to the Santander goods and the buyers could have been required to accept them. Separate bills of lading had been issued, a factor favouring divisibility, but other factors tilted the balance in favour of indivisibility. The loading schedule and storage plan of the vessel revealed that, on the sellers' construction, the so-called Santander cargo, despite having to be discharged earlier, was overstowed by the Seville cargo. The FOSFA 22 form was designed to cover a broad range of contractual expectations and a reference to the possibility of separate shipments did not create such a right on the present occasion.

The *Cobec* case shows why sellers should be keen to argue for the severability of the contract. If the contract falls to be disposed of under the repudiatory breach regime of section 31(2), or the common law equivalent, so that the buyer is entitled to terminate only if the breach goes to the root of the contract, this is more tolerant of the seller's quantitative

---

[169] *Reuter, Hufeland & Co.* v. *Sala & Co.* (1879) 4 CPD 239.
[170] [1982] 1 Lloyd's Rep. 528, affd. [1983] 2 Lloyd's Rep. 386.

and temporal failings than is section 30(1). In *Reuter, Hufeland & Co.* v. *Sala & Co.*,[171] the contract was for the sale of twenty-five tons of Penang pepper 'October and/or November shipment . . . per sailing vessel or vessels . . . [t]he name of the vessel or vessels . . . to be declared . . . within sixty days from date of bill of lading'. The seller appropriated to the contract three parcels of pepper shipped on the same vessel. The bill of lading for one of these parcels (five tons) was dated outside the shipment period in December. The buyers asserted they could reject all the bills of lading, even the two representing the twenty tons shipped in time. The Court of Appeal nevertheless held that the seller's delivery obligation was indivisible. Thesiger LJ interpreted the contract as conferring on the seller an election to make divisible or indivisible delivery[172] which, by appropriating three parcels on the same vessel, the sellers had irrevocably exercised in favour of indivisibility so as to fall foul of section 30(1). The same view appears to have been taken by the other majority judge, Cotton LJ, who stated that the severability option could only have been exercised by shipment on board more than one vessel.[173]

Instalments and Quantity

Even if a contract allows for instalment delivery, the conjunction of sections 30 and 31 prompts the question whether a seller may call upon the buyer to accept any instalments at all if it is plain that the seller will be unable to tender the whole of the contractually agreed amount by the end of the delivery period, because, for example, the right to tender one or more instalments has lapsed. Section 31(2) refers to 'defective' deliveries by the seller, which might imply that matters of quantity are dealt with by section 30. There is furthermore a mirror problem, that of the buyer who in similar circumstances has failed to accept delivery. While there is an argument that section 30(1) could apply to the seller's short delivery, it is not in its terms capable of applying to the non-accepting buyer. It would obviously be unreasonable to treat these two cases with differing degrees of severity. In addition, the language of section 31(2) is more apt to cover the defaulting buyer.[174]

In *Regent OHG Aisenstadt und Barig* v. *Francesco of Jermyn Street Ltd*,[175] the court had to deal with the conflict between sections 30(1) and 31(2) and with the need to subordinate one to the other in instalment contracts.[176] It also observed that the latter provision was more consistent with the modern emphasis in contractual termination on intermediate stipulation analysis, and that 'the business sense of a contract of

---

[171] (1879) 4 CPD 239.   [172] *Ibid.* 246–7.   [173] *Ibid.* 250–1.
[174] '[T]he buyer neglects or refuses to take delivery of or pay for one or more instalments.'
[175] [1981] 3 All ER 327.   [176] *Ibid.* 334.

sale requires the more flexible provisions of s. 31(2) to be applied in preference to those of s. 30(1)'.[177] The contract was for the sale of sixty-two
men's suits and forty-eight jackets for delivery in instalments at the sellers' discretion over a three-month period. The buyers unlawfully repudiated the contract before the sellers, in accordance with their plan to
dispatch the goods in five consignments, tendered the first three of these
to the buyers, who refused them all. The sellers then informed the buyers
that, owing to a shortage of cloth, they would be unable to tender one of
the suits they had planned to ship in the fourth consignment; this was
confirmed by the invoice sent with that consignment. The buyers refused
this consignment as well as the fifth, which confirmed the overall shortfall of one suit. Sued for damages for non-acceptance, the buyers' technical defence was that the sellers' failure to tender the missing suit
vitiated all the tenders under section 30(1). Although the defence would
have been sound if the contract had been indivisible,[178] the court held
that the contract was for delivery by instalments. Hence the issue was
governed by section 31(2)[179] and the breach did not go to the root of the
contract.

In an earlier chapter,[180] a number of instalment delivery cases were
discussed that revealed a stricter attitude to breaches occurring on the
delivery of the first instalment. This differentiation between instalment
breaches does not readily accord with the repudiatory breach test laid
down in section 31(2), first enacted after these cases were decided.
Moreover, to the extent that these cases suggest in matters of quantity a
preference for the stricter standard of section 30(1) when the contract is
still at the executory stage, they are also hard to reconcile with the *Regent*
case and so are unlikely to represent the modern law.

A final point emerging from *Regent* concerns a buyer's right to reject
individual instalments even though the contract as a whole may not be
terminated because the breach does not go the root of the contract.
Although there is little authority, it seems to be the law that the rejection
of an individual instalment is governed by the principles of termination
of indivisible contracts,[181] at least if the breach concerns quality or time.
There seems no reason to exclude the same approach for quantitative
lapses. In cases where the instalments are stated in precise quantities
and the timetabling rigid, this will no doubt result in the lapse of the

---

[177] *Ibid.*   [178] *Ibid.* 334. Section 30(2A) was not then in force.
[179] Although a divisible contract, it is not properly speaking governed by s. 31(2), which
applies to delivery by 'stated' instalments, but rather by an identical common law principle.
[180] Ch. 5 above.
[181] This is now recognized by implication in s. 35A(2). It is also reinforced in international sale contracts containing an express clause that each shipment is to be treated as a
separate contract.

buyer's obligations regarding the goods covered by the rejected instalment.[182] But a seller with the latitude given by the contract in *Regent* could organize his tenders in such a way as to minimize the damage that would be caused by the rejection of an instalment and defer the deficiency until all the clothing bar the missing suit has been tendered and accepted.

Indivisible (or Entire) Contracts and Short Delivery

Where the contract is indivisible, section 30(1) is given free rein. The buyer is entitled to reject the short delivery but, if accepting it, must pay at the contract rate.[183] As for the nature of the quantitative standard in section 30(1), the cases show that even a minor lapse will not be excused,[184] even if the seller has no intention of pursuing the buyer for that part of the price referable to the missing goods. There is no room for the application of a substantial compliance doctrine[185] which would allow the seller to claim the price subject to a damages counterclaim, or simply sue for damages for non-acceptance.[186] In some contracts, the quantity stated is merely a conditional or benchmark figure, the seller undertaking to supply up to a certain amount or no more than a certain amount according to availability. A delivery short of this figure does not infringe section 30(1).[187]

Section 30(1) is illustrated by *Behrend & Co.* v. *Produce Brokers Co.*,[188] a case concerning two contracts for the sale of 176 and 400 tons of cotton seed on *ex* ship London terms, delivery to occur on discharge into the buyers' craft alongside the ship. Because of the way the goods had been stowed, the carrier was able to discharge only fifteen tons of one contractual parcel and twenty-two tons of the other. The remaining quantities were stowed under other cargo that had first to be discharged in Hull before the vessel returned to London two weeks later to discharge the balance of the contract goods. Prior to the vessel's return, the buyers notified the sellers that they would not accept the balance of the goods. They were held entitled to do this; it mattered not that the problem was

---

[182] See also the discussion of *Pearl Mill Co. Ltd* v. *Ivy Tannery Co. Ltd* [1919] 1 KB 78.

[183] Whether the seller may retender the correct quantity is a matter of cure, discussed in Ch. 5 above.

[184] *Harland and Wolff Ltd* v. *J Burstall & Co.* (1901) 84 LT 324 (470 instead of 500 loads of timber); *Regent OHG Aisenstadt und Barig* v. *Francesco of Jermyn Street Ltd*, n. 175 above, 334 (if the contract had been indivisible, the absence of one suit from a tender of 62 suits and 48 jackets would have been fatal).

[185] See *H. Dakin & Co. Ltd* v. *Lee* [1916] 1 KB 566; *Hoenig* v. *Isaacs* [1952] 2 All ER 176.

[186] *Arcos Ltd* v. *E. A. Ronaasen & Son* [1933] AC 470.

[187] *Goldsborough Mort & Co. Ltd* v. *Carter* (1914) 19 CLR 429; *Symes* v. *Hutley* (1860) 2 LT 509; *Arbuthnot* v. *Streckeisen* (1866) 35 LJCP 305.

[188] [1920] 3 KB 530. See also *Oxendale* v. *Wetherell* (1829) 9 B & C 386; *Morgan* v. *Gath* (1865) 3 H & C 748.

caused by the way the carrier stowed the cargo. Had the contract been on f.o.b. instead of *ex* ship terms, delivery would have occurred as the goods were received on board and the buyers would have borne the risk of the carrier's stowage plan.[189]

If the carrier in *Behrend* had discharged the whole of its cargo in one continuous process, it should not have mattered if the buyers' goods had come out in irregular intervals punctuated by goods destined for other consignees. In a similar spirit, the courts will tolerate microscopic (but not minor)[190] deviations from the contractual amount falling within the maxim *de minimis non curat lex*,[191] though there is a dearth of authority showing the successful application of this maxim in cases of short as opposed to long delivery.[192] It is uncertain what the new section 30(2A) adds to the *de minimis* maxim; it prevents the rejection of a short tender by a non-consumer buyer where the shortfall is slight and rejection would be unreasonable. It must add something since, unlike the *de minimis* maxim, it does not apply to consumer buyers, but it is unlikely to add very much.

Section 30(1) also provides that a buyer accepting the lesser quantity tendered must pay for them at the contract rate,[193] though it will be open to the parties to agree a fair value instead, a suitable approach where the shortfall upsets unit price calculations. If the buyer accepts the shortfall, it seems correct to regard this as entry into a new contract[194] for the following reasons. First, even before the introduction of the new right of partial rejection,[195] a buyer accepting a shortfall under an entire contract was surely entitled to refuse a tender of the balance by the seller at a later date. Secondly, where a portion of the agreed goods is removed by the buyer from a contractual parcel of whose quantitative deficiency he is justifiably ignorant, the buyer will be bound to pay only for the goods actually removed. He will not be bound to bear the risk of shrinkage in the diminished parcel occurring after delivery.[196] Thirdly, a buyer who accepts a shortfall having already paid is entitled to sue for the balance of

---

[189] Similarly, if the goods are sold on c.i.f. terms and the seller delivers the correct amount to the carrier, the buyer will not be able to reject the goods for bad stowage—established by implication in *Berger & Co. Inc.* v. *Gill and Duffus SA* [1984] AC 382.

[190] N. 184 above.

[191] *Margaronis Navigation Agency Ltd* v. *Henry W. Peabody & Co. Ltd* [1965] 2 QB 430 (obligation to load full and complete cargo under charterparty: 12,588.2 tons instead of 12,600 tons).

[192] The resistance of the *de minimis* maxim in matters of description may be seen in cases such as *Arcos Ltd* v. *E. A. Ronaasen & Son* [1933] AC 470; *Rapalli* v. *K. L. Take Ltd* [1958] 2 Lloyd's Rep. 469; *Wilensko Slaski Towarzystwo Drewno* v. *Fenwick & Co. (West Hartlepool) Ltd* [1938] 3 All ER 429.

[193] *Shipton* v. *Casson* (1826) 5 B & C 378 (action by buyer and set-off by seller of value of delivered goods).

[194] Whether implied in fact or on a restitutionary basis. [195] Cf. s. 35A.

[196] See *Barrow, Lane & Ballard Ltd* v. *Phillip Phillips & Co. Ltd* [1929] 1 KB 574.

the price as on a failure of consideration,[197] which is difficult to explain where the buyer has obtained a benefit under the original contract. But the result is acceptable if the buyer's partial recovery of the price paid is seen as a recovery in full of the price paid under the original contract subject to a set-off of the lesser price owed to the seller for the goods accepted under the new contract. The new contract will not as such expunge the original one. The mere acceptance of a shortfall under a new contract should not estop the buyer from claiming damages for non-delivery under the original contract.[198]

Long Delivery

In the case of long delivery, section 30(2) permits the buyer to reject or accept the whole of the goods or accept just the contract quantity.[199] If the buyer accepts the whole delivery, he must pay for the goods at the contract rate. Where section 30(2) departs from section 30(1) is in the buyer's right to remove from the delivery the excess quantity; in the case of a short tender, the buyer may not accept some goods and reject the rest. The difference is easily defensible since, in the case of long delivery, the buyer is merely appropriating the agreed amount to the contract; no such justification could be made for a buyer abstracting a lesser amount from a short delivery.[200]

As in the case of short delivery, the *de minimis* maxim has a part to play. In *Shipton, Anderson & Co.* v. *Weil Bros & Co.*,[201] the seller, whose delivery obligation had a minimum to maximum range, exceeded the maximum of 4,950 tons by a margin of fifty-five lbs. or 0.0005%, which was held to be *de minimis*. Further, section 30(2A) prevents a non-consumer buyer from rejecting the goods where the surplus where it is slight and rejection would be unreasonable. As in the case of short delivery, it is unclear what this provision adds to the *de minimis* maxim.

[197] *Behrend & Co. Ltd* v. *Produce Brokers Co*, n. 188 above; *Ebrahim Dawood Ltd* v. *Heath Ltd* [1961] 2 Lloyd's Rep. 512; *Biggerstaff* v. *Rowatt's Wharf Ltd* [1896] 2 Ch. 93. On the need to show a total failure of consideration before recovering money, see however *The Trident Beauty* [1994] 1 WLR 161, 164–5 (Lord Goff); H. Beale (1996) 112 *LQR* 205, 208.

[198] See *Household Machines Ltd* v. *Cosmos Exporters Ltd* [1947] KB 217 (loss of profits on resale and indemnities owed to sub-buyers).

[199] See *Cunliffe* v. *Harrison* (1851) 6 Ex. 903 (15 hogsheads of claret instead of 10), *per* Parke B, 906: '[T]he person to whom they are sent cannot tell which are the ten that are to be his; and it is no answer to the objection to say, that he may choose which ten he likes, for that would be to force a new contract upon him.' Against this, it might be argued that the inconvenience suffered by the buyer in selecting the contract quantity would be minimal, especially since the buyer's duties in respect of rejected goods are so modest (see s. 36). See also *Tamvaco* v. *Lucas* (1859) 1 E & E 581; *Payne & Routh* v. *V. Lillico & Sons* (1920) 36 TLR 569 (exceeding the 2% allowance).

[200] This is not a case of partial acceptance, the subject of the new s. 35A (see Ch. 5 above), which applies in the case of title, quality, fitness, and description, and not quantity.

[201] [1912] 1 KB 574.

Estimated Quantities

A matter common to both sub-sections(1) and (2) of section 30 concerns the use of words estimating the amount of a specific batch of goods whose exact quantity is unknown. It is settled that, in such cases, the failure to deliver the amount corresponding to the estimate will not infringe section 30 and consequently the buyer must accept delivery. The words, however, must be truly words of estimate and the parties must have agreed that the buyer shall take the whole batch. In *Re Harrison and Micks, Lambert & Co.*,[202] the contract was for the remainder of a cargo of wheat 'more or less about 5400 quarters'. The word 'about' in the contract signified a range of plus or minus 5 per cent and the remainder of the cargo amounted to 5,974 quarters, which fell outside the 5 per cent range. Nevertheless, the effect of adding the words 'more or less' was to convert the contract quantity into words of estimate so that, as agreed, the buyers had to accept the whole of the remainder of the cargo.[203]

Words of estimate may also qualify the seller's delivery duty in respect of unascertained and future goods. Where sellers agreed to supply the whole of the buyers' steel requirements for the construction of the Forth Bridge, estimated at '30,000 tons more or less', the buyer could not turn to an alternative source of supply for steel in excess of the 30,000 tons.[204] A less tolerant view is likely to be taken of quantifying words such as 'about' and 'more or less' where the seller does not need to make an estimate, being in a position to state the quantity of future goods with some precision and unreasonably falling short or long. In the Canadian case of *Canada Law Book Co.* v. *Boston Book Co.*,[205] a contract for the exclusive distribution rights in Canada of the English Reports Reprint (150 volumes more or less 'of about' 1,500 pages each) did not permit the tender of about 190 volumes, most of which fell short of the 1,500 page mark. It was known in advance what was to be reprinted and the work that had to be done could be calculated within narrow limits; hence, only a slight increase over 150 volumes could be tolerated. There will be even less reason to interpret in a slack fashion words such as 'about' and 'more or less' where the contract is an ordinary one for the sale of unascertained goods from no unusually restricted source.

---

[202] [1917] 1 KB 755.
[203] See also *Levi Guano Co. Ltd* v. *Berk & Co.* (1886) 2 TLR 898; *Borrowman* v. *Drayton* (1876) 2 Ex D 15; *McLay & Co.* v. *Perry & Co.* (1881) 44 LT 152; *Macdonald* v. *Longbottom* (1860) 1 E & E 987; *McConnel* v. *Murphy* (1873) LR 5 PC 203. A seller might, however, warrant that all due care has been taken in giving the estimate: see *Esso Petroleum Co. Ltd* v. *Mardon* [1976] QB 801. Rescission for misrepresentation is also a possibility: *Re Harrison and Micks*, n. 202 above, 761 (Atkin J).
[204] *Tancred, Arrol & Co.* v. *Steel Co. of Scotland Ltd* (1890) 15 App. Cas. 125.
[205] (1922) 64 SCR 182.

The Seller's Documentary Delivery Obligations

In international sales, the seller is commonly under a duty to supply documents to the buyer. In the case, of an f.o.b. contract, the seller may[206] have to tender a bill of lading in addition to performing the physical duty of shipment. The seller may also have other duties to perform, such as supplying a certificate of origin of the goods[207] and, if arranging shipment, giving notice of it to the buyer.[208] Where the contract is entered into on c.i.f. (cost, insurance, and freight) terms, the seller's physical duty to deliver is displaced by documentary obligations, for the contract is properly characterized as a documentary sale.[209] The seller has to enter into or procure proper contracts of affreightment and insurance in respect of goods shipped that, in terms of description, quantity, and quality of the goods, conform to the c.i.f. contract, and transfer to the buyer the benefit of these contracts. The carrier is not the agent of the buyer in taking delivery of the goods on shipment,[210] and it is not a necessary part of the c.i.f. contract that the goods actually be discharged at the named port of destination.[211] The c.i.f. buyer is presumptively[212] under a duty to pay against a tender of shipping documents,[213] which will include a bill of lading (or other transport document), an insurance document and an invoice.[214]

Trade terms such as c.i.f., c. & f.[215] and f.o.b. are shorthand descriptions of particular delivery obligations. It is a characteristic of such contracts that the obligations of the parties, particularly as they relate to documents and time, are strict.[216] The meaning and significance of trade terms are largely to be gathered from commercial custom and usage as

---

[206] It will depend upon the type of f.o.b. contract: see *Pyrene Co. Ltd* v. *Scindia Navigation Ltd* [1954] 2 QB 402.

[207] A common express term in f.o.b. contracts.

[208] *Wimble Sons & Co.* v. *Rosenberg & Sons* [1913] 3 KB 743.

[209] See *Manbre Saccharine Co. Ltd* v. *Corn Products Co. Ltd* [1919] 1 KB 198, 202; *Comptoir d'Achat et du Boerenbond Belge SA* v. *Luis de Ridder Lda* [1949] AC 293, 312.

[210] See the text accompanying n. 22 above.

[211] *Congimex Cia Geral de Comercio SARL* v. *Tradax Export SA* [1983] 1 Lloyd's Rep. 250. It is enough that the contract of affreightment requires the carrier to take them there.

[212] See s. 28.

[213] *E. Clemens Horst & Co.* v. *Biddell Bros.* [1911] 1 KB 934 (Kennedy LJ).

[214] The precise documents and their variants and additions will be discussed in the text accompanying nn. 320 ff. below.

[215] This differs from a c.i.f. contract only in that the buyer remains responsible for insurance: *Norsk Bjergningskompagni A/S* v. *Owners of the Steamship Pantanassa* [1970] 1 All ER 848.

[216] See *SIAT di del Ferro* v. *Tradax Overseas SA* [1980] 1 Lloyd's Rep. 53 (attempted use of 'Tradax documents clause' to dilute seller's documentary responsibilities); *Bunge Corpn.* v. *Tradax SA* [1981] 2 All ER 513; *Toepfer* v. *Lenersan-Poortman NV* [1980] 1 Lloyd's Rep. 143.

amplified by judicial interpretation from time to time.[217] In this regard, the standard terms (Incoterms) issued by the International Chamber of Commerce and revised from time to time[218] are most useful in guiding contractual draftsmanship and in assisting contractual interpretation. They are by no means so deeply rooted in international trade practice as to constitute binding custom or usage that need not be expressly incorporated in a contract.[219] Indeed, they are rarely to be found applying to international commodity sales governed by English law. Delivery terms may be found in various gradations stretching from the seller's to the buyer's premises. Commercial ingenuity sometimes prompts their emergence in hybrid forms.[220]

C.i.f. Contracts

The c.i.f. contract is in frequent use in international sales. Its use may have declined in certain areas of international trade in recent times but it remains very popular indeed in the international commodities markets. The contract developed in the middle years of the nineteenth century but it was not until the period around the First World War that a series of important cases laid down its principal features. Some of these cases arose out of the war itself; the Second World War was responsible for a flurry of later activity.

The duties of a c.i.f. seller[221] have been stated authoritatively on a number of occasions.[222] First, the seller must enter into a contract of affreightment with a carrier[223] requiring the carrier to carry the goods to the named port of discharge. Secondly, the seller must take out insurance on the terms current in the trade[224] unless the contract otherwise provides. Thirdly, goods answering to the contract must actually be

---

[217] Usage settled by prior decisions need not be the subject of fresh evidence: *Brandao* v. *Barnett* (1846) 12 Cl. & Fin. 786 (Lord Campbell). But the meaning of certain provisions may change over time: *C. Groom Ltd* v. *Barber* [1915] 1 KB 316.

[218] Last issued in 1990.

[219] The ICC-sponsored Uniform Customs and Practice for Documentary Credits (UCP 1993) are much more widely used and will apply unless excluded by the parties.

[220] e.g. *The Parchim* [1918] AC 157; *Comptoir d'Achat et du Boerenbond Belge SA* v. *Luis de Ridder Lda*, n. 209 above. In *The Albazero* [1977] AC 774, 809, Roskill LJ drew attention to the care needed in interpreting certain contracts where letters such as c.i.f. and f.o.b. are mistakenly understood by contracting parties. See also Ontario Law Reform Commission, *Report on Sale of Goods* (1979), ii, 347. Incoterms 1990 advises the 'greatest caution' when adding further obligations to the known obligations of the c.i.f. seller: Introduction, para. 12.

[221] It is assumed in the following discussion that the seller is the shipper. Frequently, however, the seller is an intermediate party in a sales string to whom the goods have been sold on c.i.f terms by a previous seller.

[222] *Ireland* v. *Livingstone* (1872) LR 5 HL 395; *Biddell Bros.* v. *E. Clemens Horst Co.* [1914] 1 KB 214 (Hamilton J); *Johnson* v. *Taylor Bros. & Co. Ltd* [1920] AC 144 (Lord Atkinson); *Ross T. Smyth & Co. Ltd* v. *Bailey Son & Co.* [1940] 3 All ER 60 (Lord Wright).

[223] Or the seller may charter a ship.   [224] *C. Groom Ltd* v. *Barber*, n. 217 above.

shipped, and from the named port of shipment if one is named. Fourthly, the seller must make out an invoice for the goods. Fifthly, the seller must tender to the buyer the invoice, the insurance policy, and the bill of lading.[225] Where the buyer pays by means of a banker's letter of credit, the documents that the seller, as beneficiary of the letter of credit, must tender to the bank in order to enforce the bank's promise to pay will be spelt out in the letter of credit. The documentary duties of the seller under the c.i.f. contract will either be restated in or superseded by these documentary requirements in the letter of credit. Cases on the strictness of documentary compliance under letters of credit and c.i.f. contracts are therefore, to all intents and purposes, interchangeable. Whether or not the buyer pays under a letter of credit, the documentary tender by the seller will commonly occur through the agency of a bank and must take place on the agreed date[226] or, if no date is agreed, with all reasonable dispatch.[227] There is no need for the documents to reach the buyer before the ship arrives at the port of discharge[228] but the parties may establish a timetable that requires documentary tender and payment before the arrival of the ship.[229]

A c.i.f. tender therefore involves principally an invoice, an insurance policy, and a bill of lading. The content of the invoice will obviously depend upon the express terms of the contract but, assuming the contract to be silent, it is as a matter of custom and usage sufficient if the invoice is reasonably referable to the consignment appropriated to the contract. Certainly, the practice of shipment in bulk under indivisible bills of lading, with separation only on discharge,[230] is common enough for the invoice not to have to identify the very goods appropriated to the contract.

One purpose of the invoice is to permit the buyer to ascertain which portion of the price refers to the cost of the goods themselves and which to the freight and insurance. It is the seller who absorbs the risk of a rise and fall freight rates and insurance premiums between the contract date and performance.[231] When Blackburn J described the practice in *Ireland* v. *Livingstone*,[232] the buyer would pay the cost of freight on

---

[225] Modern contracts frequently provide for different forms of insurance and transport documents.

[226] *Toepfer* v. *Lenersan-Poortman NV*, n. 216 above.

[227] *Johnson* v. *Taylor Bros. & Co. Ltd* [1920] AC 144; *C. Sharpe & Co. Ltd* v. *Nosawa* [1917] 2 KB 814 (where the date when the goods should have arrived was taken as the basis for calculating damages).

[228] *Sanders Bros.* v. *Maclean & Co.* (1883) 11 QBD 327.

[229] *Toepfer* v. *Lenersan-Poortman NV*, n. 216 above.

[230] See, e.g., *Re Wait* [1927] 1 Ch. 606; *Karlhamns Oljefabriker* v. *Eastport Navigation Corpn. (The Elafi)* [1982] 1 All ER 208.

[231] *Ireland* v. *Livingstone*, n. 222 above, 407; *Blyth & Co.* v. *Richards, Turpin & Co.* (1916) 114 LT 753.   [232] *Ibid.*

discharge and this item would be credited to him against the overall c.i.f. price in the invoice; nowadays, it is common for the freight to be paid in advance by the seller.[233]

Insurance Documents

The seller's duty regarding insurance documents has caused some difficulties in practice. The classic view is that the seller must tender the policy of insurance itself and not a mere certificate of insurance. In *Diamond Alkali Export Corpn.* v. *Fl. Bourgeois*,[234] a quantity of soda ash was shipped from an American port and the seller, in accordance with a growing American practice, tendered a certificate of insurance which in its own words 'represents and takes the place of the policy and conveys all the rights of the signed policy holder . . . as fully as if the property was covered by a special policy direct to the holder of this certificate'. Unable to see a prior course of dealing between the parties or an established trade usage to justify a tender of the certificate, McCardie J held the tender was bad. It was plain in the learned judge's view that the certificate had been issued under a floating policy and the awkwardness of analysing the buyer's position as assignee under the master policy was reason enough to maintain the orthodox position that a tender of the policy was necessary.[235] The proliferation of floating policies and the acceptability of certificates under modern standard-form contracts[236] has probably changed the law in this area. But it is an axiom of c.i.f. sales that, besides acquiring direct rights against the insurer, the buyer should be aware from the document tendered what are the terms of insurance in order to determine whether these accord with the cover that the c.i.f seller should procure.[237]

Where tender of a certificate is allowed or waived, the c.i.f. seller warrants to the buyer that statements in it are true.[238] The seller is also

---

[233] For a discussion of 'freight prepaid' and 'freight collect' bills, see *Soproma SpA* v. *Marine and Animal By-Products Corpn.* [1966] 1 Lloyd's Rep. 367; *Norsk Bjergningskompagni A/S* v. *Owners of the Steamship Pantanassa*, n. 215 above. In a 'freight collect' case, the buyer deducts the cost of freight from the c.i.f. price.

[234] [1923] 3 KB 443.

[235] *A fortiori* a broker's cover note will not be a satisfactory document: *Wilson, Holgate & Co.* v. *Belgian Grain & Produce Co.* [1920] 2 KB 1, 7. A certificate has also been held to be a bad tender under a banker's letter of credit calling for 'an approved policy': *Donald H. Scott & Co.* v. *Barclays Bank Ltd* [1923] 2 KB 1.

[236] See also Incoterms CIF Rules, para. A.3(b) ('insurance policy or other evidence of contract cover').

[237] See *Donald H. Scott & Co.* v. *Barclays Bank Ltd*, n. 235 above, 15 (Scrutton LJ); *Malmberg* v. *Evans* (1924) 30 Com. Cas. 107. A certificate could, if properly framed, meet this standard, a point left open: *Donald H. Scott, ibid.* 17 (Atkin LJ). See also *Promos* v. *European Grain* [1979] 1 Lloyd's Rep. 375 (certificate).

[238] *A. C. Harper & Co. Ltd* v. *Mackechnie & Co.* [1925] 2 KB 423. See also *Comptoir d'Achat et du Boerenbond Belge SA* v. *Luis de Ridder Lda*, n. 220 above.

bound to maintain insurance for the whole of the transit. In *Orient Co. Ltd* v. *Brekke & Howlid*,[239] the contract was for twenty cases of French walnuts c.i.f. Hull. Payment was to be made thirty days after delivery of the documents. These, when tendered, did not include a policy of insurance, for the seller had not insured the goods at all. When the seller sued for the price, the court held that it was a condition of the buyer's duty to pay that an insurance policy be tendered. It did not avail the seller to show that the goods had arrived safely. The report does not show whether they had arrived before the documentary tender, but it should not have mattered either way since a c.i.f. seller may not unilaterally vary the contract and deliver landed goods. Similarly, it should not have made a difference if the seller had reduced the price to take account of the savings on insurance.

Bill of Lading

Of the three principal shipping documents, by far the greatest volume of litigation has concerned the bill of lading, which performs three principal functions. First, it is evidence of the contract of carriage;[240] secondly, it is a receipt for the goods issued by the carrier;[241] and thirdly, it is a document of title. The former two functions, concerning as they do the contractual and bailment responsibilities of the carrier, may be left to texts dealing with carriage.[242] The third function concerns the transferability to the buyer of the seller's rights against the carrier and will be considered further here.

The significance of a bill of lading in negotiable form[243] is that its transfer from seller to buyer effects a constructive delivery of the goods. Subject to the carrier's lien for unpaid freight, the buyer may demand the goods at discharge without the carrier's attornment. Whether the buyer is named from the outset as the consignee, which will not happen in string sales, or has the bill of lading indorsed and delivered to him, he will need to present it to the carrier to demand the goods, for the carrier is both bound and entitled to surrender the goods only to the holder of the bill.[244] Apart from constructive delivery, the bill of lading is also commonly used to effect the passing of the property in the goods to the buyer.

---

[239] [1913] 1 KB 532. See also *A. C. Harper & Co. Ltd* v. *Mackechnie & Co*, n. 238 above.

[240] *The Ardennes* [1951] 1 KB 55; *Sewell* v. *Burdick* (1884) 10 App. Cas. 74.

[241] It also affords evidence, sometimes conclusive, of the condition of the goods on shipment: see *J. Aron & Co. Inc.* v. *Comptoir Wegimont* [1921] 3 KB 435; Hague-Visby Rules, Art. III.

[242] e.g. J. Wilson, *Carriage of Goods by Sea* (2nd edn., Pitman, London, 1993).

[243] The following discussion does not apply to waybills, where the function of the document, which need not be presented by the buyer, is to identify the person to whom the carrier is to deliver the goods.

[244] *The Stettin* (1889) 14 PD 142; *Sze Hai Tong Bank* v. *Rambler Cycle Co.* [1959] AC 576.

The transfer of the bill need not have that consequence; it depends upon the accompanying intention.[245] The passing of the property in association with the bill was, before the Carriage of Goods by Sea Act 1992, of critical importance in determining whether the buyer could sue the carrier upon the contract of affreightment. The constructive delivery of the goods did not alone produce this result.[246] According to the now-repealed section 1 of the Bills of Lading Act 1855, the property in the goods had to pass 'upon or by reason of the indorsement of the bill of lading', which meant that the indorsement of the bill had to play an essential causal part in the passing of property.[247] Since the Carriage of Goods by Sea Act 1992, the passing of property is no longer relevant in determining whether the buyer acquires rights against the carrier. A buyer now acquires rights as the lawful holder of a bill of lading, whether of the 'on board' or 'received for shipment' kind; as the person to whom delivery is to be made under a ship's delivery order; and as the person to whom the carrier is to make delivery under a waybill.[248]

The next question concerns the c.i.f. seller's contractual duty to tender a bill of lading to the buyer. The starting point is the contract.[249] Modern commodities contracts[250] permit either an on-board bill of lading or a negotiable ship's delivery order. The virtue of the former document, as opposed to a received-for-shipment document, is that the holder of the bill of lading receives the assurance that the goods are locked up in the 'floating warehouse' and covered by insurance. A ship's delivery order, if addressed by the carrier to the buyer at destination, will give the buyer holding it the right to demand the goods from the carrier without further attornment. In the absence of such contractual provision, it remains a vexed question what type of transport document the seller must tender to the buyer. It is certainly the case that the seller must tender a document of title. There may no longer be a need for such a document to confer on the buyer direct contractual rights against the carrier,[251] but the buyer will still need a document that entitles him to delivery without

---

[245] *Sewell* v. *Burdick*, n. 240 above; *Leigh and Sillavan Ltd* v. *Aliakmon Shipping Ltd* [1986] AC 785. The transfer of the bill, even with an intention to pass the property, will not have that effect if the goods remain unascertained in the hold: s. 16. It may now serve to pass an undivided share in an ascertained bulk under the Sale of Goods (Amendment) Act 1995 (Ch. 5 above). Nor will the transfer of the bill of lading be effective if the property in the goods has already been transferred to a third party: *The Future Express* [1992] 2 Lloyd's Rep. 79, affd. [1993] 2 Lloyd's Rep. 542.

[246] *Thompson* v. *Dominy* (1845) 14 M & W 403.

[247] *The Delfini* [1990] 1 Lloyd's Rep. 202 (Mustill LJ).

[248] 1992 Act, ss. 1, 2(1). For the incurring of liabilities to the carrier, see s. 3.

[249] If the contract calls for a bill of lading, a delivery order obviously will not do: *Forbes* v. *Pelling* (1921) 9 Ll. LR 202.

[250] e.g. GAFTA 100.

[251] Carriage of Goods by Sea Act 1992, s. 2(1).

attornment, and a document of title is also useful as a pledge for raising finance from a bank.[252]

According to McCardie J after a careful review of the earlier authorities in *Diamond Alkali Export Corpn.* v. *Fl. Bourgeois*,[253] only the on-board bill of lading in negotiable form fell within the mercantile custom, proved in *Lickbarrow* v. *Mason*,[254] as satisfying the definition of a document of title at common law. It was noteworthy that the Bills of Lading Act 1855 recited this very custom in the preamble.[255] The c.i.f. seller therefore had to tender such a bill and not a received for shipment bill. A contrary view, that a received for shipment bill of lading was a document of title, had earlier been expressed by the Privy Council in *The Marlborough Hill*.[256] The court referred to the practice, different from bulk shipments, of small parcels being taken in hand by the carrier and shipped only in the event of a final stowage plan for the cargo as a whole.[257] That case, however, concerned admiralty jurisdiction to entertain claims by holders of bills of lading against a carrier for damage to goods. Despite the headnote, it does not hold that a received for shipment bill of lading is a bill of lading for the purpose of the Bills of Lading Act 1855.[258] Moreover, no effort was made to prove a mercantile custom to this effect.[259] A document of title can be found to be such by virtue of local custom, but it has been emphasized that the proof required is rigorous and that stamping the document 'non-negotiable' defeats the custom.[260] The role of custom cannot be supplanted by contractual language in determining the status of a document of title: the status of a document as one of title has an impact upon the liabilities of third parties such as carriers.[261] In *Ishag* v. *Allied Bank International*,[262] the court held that a document referring to goods 'intended to be shipped' was a document of title since it was tantamount to the received-for-shipment bill found to be a document of title in *The Marlborough Hill*. But *Ishag* does not mention on-board bills or the *Diamond Alkali* case.

It is submitted that a received-for-shipment bill of lading is not a document of title at common law. No custom to such effect has ever been

---

[252] *Sewell* v. *Burdick*, n. 240 above; *The Albazero* [1977] AC 774 (Brandon J); *Ross T. Smyth & Co. Ltd* v. *Bailey Son & Co.* [1940] 3 All ER 60; *The Future Express* [1993] 2 Lloyd's Rep. 542; M. G. Bridge [1993] *JBL* 379–83.

[253] N. 234 above. [254] (1794) 5 TR 683.

[255] *Diamond Alkali Export Corpn.* v. *Fl. Bourgeois* [1923] 3 KB 443, 450.

[256] [1921] 1 AC 444. [257] *Ibid.* 451.

[258] Strictly speaking, it was never necessary for s. 1 of the 1855 Act to operate to transfer rights and duties that a bill of lading be a document of title. The property in goods covered by a bill of lading could pass without transferring the bill: *The Future Express*, n. 251 above.

[259] *Pace Ishag* v. *Allied Bank International* [1981] 1 Lloyd's Rep. 92, 97–8, where a custom was said to have been proved.

[260] *Kum* v. *Wah Tat Bank Ltd* [1971] 1 Lloyd's Rep. 439, 442 ff (mate's receipt).

[261] *The Future Express*, n. 251 above, 95. [262] N. 259 above.

proved. As common as the practice may be to issue such bills, it is always possible for the carrier later to indorse a received-for-shipment bill of lading to show that the goods are now on board,[263] so as to convert it into an on-board bill.[264] Furthermore, a c.i.f. seller is in breach if the goods are never shipped[265] and it is axiomatic that a buyer in documentary sales should be able to see from the documents tendered, and before making payment, that the seller has duly performed the contract. A received-for-shipment bill gives no such assurance. Finally, the chaos caused in matters of title transfer by the circulation at the same time of sets of received-for-shipment bills and on-board bills, dealing with the same goods, favours the taking of a restrictive view of a document of title.

The bill of lading tendered by the c.i.f. seller must be a 'negotiable' one,[266] which means that it may be transferred from one holder to another so as to affect rights in the underlying goods.[267] To say that a bill of lading is negotiable does not mean that the rights of a duly qualified holder override any defect in the title to the goods of the transferor; it is not negotiable in the sense that a bill of exchange is negotiable. Accordingly, for example, a pledgee to whom a bill of lading is transferred cannot, by transferring it to a new holder, confer on that new holder the general property in the goods. The issue and negotiation of a bill of lading will not heal any defects in the title to the goods of the original shipper.[268] To be negotiable, a bill of lading must be made out to a named consignee 'or order', or simply to bearer. It will then be negotiated, in the former case by indorsement and delivery to a named indorsee and, in the latter case, by manual delivery. A holder who is the named indorsee can convert the bill of lading into a bearer bill by the simple expedient of signing it in blank. The main purpose behind the requirement that the bill of lading be negotiable is to permit dealings in goods through the documentary medium: '[T]he object and result of a c.i.f. contract is to enable sellers and buyers to deal with cargoes or parcels afloat and to transfer them freely from hand to hand by giving constructive possession of the goods which are being dealt with.'[269]

---

[263] See the 1980 version of Incoterms CIF Rules A.7.

[264] See *Westpac Banking Corpn.* v. *South Carolina National Bank* [1986] 1 Lloyd's Rep. 311 for the proposition that such a bill is a good on board (or shipped) bill.

[265] *Hindley & Co. Ltd* v. *East India Produce Co. Ltd* [1973] 2 Lloyd's Rep. 515.

[266] *Lickbarrow* v. *Mason*, n. 254 above (coining the expression 'negotiable'); *Diamond Alkali Export Corpn.* v. *Fl. Bourgeois*, n. 255 above; *C. P. Henderson & Co.* v. *Comptoir d'Escompte de Paris* (1873) LR 5 PC 253; *Soproma SpA* v. *Marine and Animal By-Products Corpn.* [1966] 1 Lloyd's Rep. 367.

[267] *Diamond Alkali Export Corpn.* v. *Fl. Bourgeois*, n. 255 above; *Gurney* v. *Behrend* (1854) 3 E & B 622; *Thompson* v. *Dominy* (1845) 14 M & W 403.

[268] In some cases, the holder of a bill of lading will be able, under one of the exceptions to the rule of *nemo dat quod non habet*, to transfer a greater title than his own. See Ch. 9 below.

[269] *Comptoir d'Achat et du Boerenbond Belge SA* v. *Luis de Ridder Lda* [1949] AC 293, *per* Lord Porter, 311–12.

Bills of Lading in Sets

Bills of lading are commonly issued in sets of three (sometimes four) originals, a practice explained by the uncertainties of shipping in the days of sail.[270] Over a century ago, Lord Blackburn said:

> I have never been able to learn why merchants and shipowners continue the practice of working out a bill of lading in parts. I should have thought that, at least since the introduction of quick and regular communication by steamers, and still more since the establishment of the electric telegraph, every purpose would be answered by making one bill of lading only which should be the sole document of title, and taking as many copies, certified by the master to be true copies, as is thought to be convenient.[271]

He nevertheless accurately predicted that the practice would continue since 'merchants dislike to depart from an old custom for fear that the novelty may produce some unforeseen effect'.[272] It is not uncommon nowadays, however, for two or even one original bill to be issued.[273] Frequently, though not in the commodities trade, the carriage of goods takes place under a non-negotiable sea waybill, which has no pretensions to being a document of title and whose purpose is but to identify the person to whom delivery must be made by the carrier. It is not produced by the consignee as a precondition of surrender of the cargo. Furthermore, the impending recourse to electronic 'documentation' heralds the redundancy of the traditional bill of lading.[274]

Where bills of lading are issued in a set, the various originals are identified as 'first', 'second', or 'third', as the case may be.[275] Each one of these bills may be negotiated and each will recite the formula 'the one of which bills being accomplished the others to stand void' or something to similar effect.[276] The meaning of this formula is discussed in cases dealing with the risk of fraud presented by the practice of issuing multiple bills of lading. In *Barber* v. *Meyerstein*,[277] the consignee of goods indorsed the first two bills of lading from a set of three in favour of the plaintiff pledgee and subsequently by fraud obtained advances from the

---

[270] Where the practice is still employed, the various originals will be sent by different routes with the first coming by the fastest route (nowadays by air but formerly by fast passenger steamer: D. Sassoon, *C.I.F. and F.O.B. Contracts* (4th edn., Sweet & Maxwell, London, 1995), §257. The practice is trenchantly criticized in R. Goode, *Proprietary Rights and Insolvency in Sales Transactions* (2nd edn., Sweet & Maxwell, London, 1989), 77–8.

[271] *Glyn Mills, Currie & Co.* v. *East and West India Dock Co.* (1882) 7 App. Cas. 591, 605. See also *Sanders Bros.* v. *Maclean & Co.* (1883) 11 QBD 327, 341–2.

[272] *Ibid.*

[273] Sassoon, n. 270 above, §257.

[274] The implications of such a change affect the contract of carriage more than the contract of sale and so are outside the scope of this book.

[275] *Glyn Mills, Currie & Co.* v. *East and West India Dock Co.*, n. 271 above.

[276] *Ibid.*; *Barber* v. *Meyerstein* (1870) LR 4 HL 317.　　　　　[277] N. 276 above.

defendant broker on the security of the third bill of lading. The goods in question had been landed at a river wharf before either of the above transactions took place. The defendant argued, on the basis of the above-quoted language in the bill of lading, that, despite the landing of the goods, the first two bills had not been 'accomplished' when the third bill was negotiated, since the freight had not yet been paid. In consequence, according to the defendant, 'it simply becomes a matter of expedition and race between the several parties who have taken those different assignments of the bill of lading'[278] with the prize going to the third party himself as the first to obtain actual possession of the goods. The conclusion of the House of Lords, however, was that the first assignee for value of one or more of the bills of lading obtained priority over the other assignees.[279] As Lord Westbury put it:

There can be no doubt . . . that the first person who for value[280] gets the transfer of a bill of lading, though it be only one of a set of three bills, acquires the property; and all subsequent dealings with the other two bills must in law be subordinate to that first one, and for this reason, because the property is in the person who first gets a transfer of the bill of lading.[281]

The practice of issuing bills of lading arose in a more directly contractual context in *Sanders Bros.* v. *Maclean & Co.*,[282] where the seller tendered to the buyer two bills of lading from a set of three and demanded payment; the third bill had been retained by the original shipper who, however, did not use it in any way. When the seller sued for damages for non-acceptance, the court held that the buyer was not justified in rejecting the seller's tender. As Brett MR put it, it would be 'contrary to practice and the known principles of mercantile law with regard to bills of

---

[278] *Ibid.* 326 (Lord Hatherley).
[279] See also *Glyn Mills, Currie & Co.* v. *East and West India Dock Co.*, n. 271 above, *per* Lord Blackburn, 604: '[T]he very object of making a bill of lading in parts would be baffled unless the delivery of one part of the bill of lading, duly assigned, had the same effect as delivery of all the parts would have had.' *Sanders Bros.* v. *Maclean & Co.*, n. 271 above, also notes that the carrier is not liable, for the stipulation in the bill of lading ('the one of which bills being accomplished the others to stand void') exists to permit the master to surrender the goods on the presentment of the first document. If the master has notice of the existence of more than one claimant, then he should interplead, for delivery would otherwise take place at his peril: *Glyn Mills, Currie & Co., ibid.* 613.
[280] A gratuitous transfer will therefore not serve to pass a general or special property. See also *Leask* v. *Scott* (1877) 2 QBD 376 (past consideration and defeat of unpaid seller's right of stoppage in transit) (cf. *Rodger* v. *Comptoir d'Escompte de Paris* (1869) LR 2 PC 393).
[281] N. 276 above, 336. A special property arising from a pledge will not exhaust the whole of the indorser's property, and a second indorsee will therefore obtain the residue of that property. *Barber* v. *Meyerstein* was decided before the enactment in 1877 of the seller in possession exception to the rule of *nemo dat quod non habet*, now contained in s. 24 of the Sale of Goods Act 1979. The impact of that provision in the case of multiple bills will be considered in Ch. 9 below.
[282] N. 271 above.

lading' if the buyer were to be allowed to reject an instrument which 'would pass the property and give the right to possession'[283] merely because the whole set of three was not tendered. Likewise, Bowen LJ asserted that such a strict tender requirement would run counter to mercantile usage, which was concerned far more with the risk of insolvency than with the risk of fraud:

The only possible object of requiring the presentation of the third original must be to prevent the chance, more or less remote, of fraud on the part of the shipper or some previous owner of the goods. But the practice of merchants, it is never superfluous to remark, is not based upon the supposition of possible frauds. The object of mercantile usages is to prevent the risk of insolvency, not of fraud; and any one who attempts to follow and understand the law merchant will soon find himself lost if he begins by assuming that merchants conduct their business on the basis of attempting to insure themselves against fraudulent dealing. The contrary is the case. Credit, not distrust, is the basis of commercial dealings; mercantile genius consists principally in knowing whom to trust and with whom to deal, and commercial intercourse and communication is no more based on the supposition of fraud than it is on the supposition of forgery.[284]

A contract may, however, expressly call for a full set of bills of lading, which is the case with modern commodities forms[285] and with Incoterms.[286] If such is the case, then a seller may not tender an incomplete set coupled with a letter of indemnity.[287] If the bill of lading is not available for tender when the ship arrives, commodities forms will require the seller also to provide the buyer with an indemnity for the carrier so that the carrier will surrender the goods.[288]

Contents of Bill of Lading

A number of issues arise out of the contents of the bill of lading. The bill must evidence that the seller has procured or adopted a proper contract of affreightment with the carrier.[289] More particularly, the buyer should be able to determine that the goods are being carried to the right destination and that the terms of the contract of affreightment accord with the seller's c.i.f. responsibilities. In *SIAT di dal Ferro* v. *Tradax Overseas*

---

[283] N. 271 above 335.   [284] *Ibid.* 343.

[285] e.g. GAFTA 100, cl. 14 (which permits an alternative tender of ship's delivery orders, needed where the contract goods are shipped as part of a larger bulk).

[286] Incoterms 1990, CIF Rules, para. A8.

[287] *Donald H. Scott & Co. Ltd* v. *Barclays Bank Ltd* [1923] 2 KB 1, 11 (Bankes LJ) and 16 (Scrutton LJ) (a documentary credit case but the principle is the same). UCC, Art. 2–323(2) enacts a presumptive rule that only one original need be tendered for overseas sales and, even if the contract requires a full set, permits a seller to tender an incomplete set coupled with a letter of indemnity.

[288] e.g. GAFTA 100, cl. 11.

[289] *Soon Hua Seng Co. Ltd* v. *Glencore Grain Ltd* [1996] 1 Lloyd's Rep. 398.

SA,[290] certain bills of lading for a bulk cargo of soya bean meal c.i.f. Venice stated the destination 'as per charterparty' and others as 'Ancona/Ravenna'. The tender was bad: the first bills were insufficiently informative and the latter evidenced that the sellers had not fulfilled their c.i.f. responsibilities. In *Finska Cellulosa Föreningen* v. *Westfield Paper Co.*,[291] the bill of lading contained the following clause: 'All conditions and exceptions as per charterparty dated [blank].' Responding to the question whether the seller had to tender the original of the charterparty, the court answered no: it was not on the list of documents that the c.i.f. seller had to tender to the buyer. It seems, however, that from previous dealings the buyer was acquainted with the standard form of charterparty used. The real issue in a case of this kind is whether the buyer is given or has access to sufficient information about the contract of affreightment. The need to inform is one of the reasons for the traditional rule that a c.i.f. seller must tender the policy of insurance. The terms of the contract of affreightment cannot be divined from the clause quoted above. If the contract is governed by Incoterms and the bill of lading contains a reference to a charterparty, then the seller must tender a copy of the charterparty.[292] It is submitted that the c.i.f. seller should as a general rule have to give the buyer access to the terms of the contract of affreightment if these are not set out in full in the bill of lading. This might be done by supplying a copy of the charterparty or by referring the buyer to a well-known charterparty form.[293] If the bill of lading is tendered to the buyer under a contract not involving the assignment of rights and liabilities under the contract of affreightment, as where the goods are sold landed in the country of destination,[294] there is no reason why the buyer, who needs the bill to collect the goods, should be informed of the terms of the contract of affreightment.

The bill of lading must be 'clean',[295] which means that it must not qualify the goods or the packing as other than in good order and condition on receipt by the carrier.[296] The abiding principle is that the buyer is entitled to documents that can be disposed of in trade without disponees being put off by questions raised about the goods on the face of the documents. Where a bill of lading is 'claused', that is, annotated to show that

---

[290] [1980] 1 Lloyd's Rep. 53. See also *Lecky & Co. Ltd* v. *Ogilvy, Gilanders & Co.* (1897) 3 Com. Cas. 29.

[291] [1940] 4 All ER 473.   [292] Incoterms 1990, CIF Rules, para. A8.

[293] See *Burstall* v. *Grimsdale* (1906) 11 Com. Cas. 280.

[294] See *Holland Colombo Trading Soc.* v. *Alawdeen* [1954] 2 Lloyd's Rep. 45.

[295] *Cremer* v. *General Carriers SA* [1974] 1 WLR 341; *British Imex Industries Ltd* v. *Midland Bank Ltd* [1958] 1 QB 542. It is usually in such letters of credit cases that the issue arises. The 1980 Incoterms explicitly required 'clean' bills of lading and documents: Foreword, para. 9; FOB Rules, para. A.7; C&F Rules, para. A.6; CIF Rules, para. A.7. The 1990 Incoterms have dropped the reference to 'clean'.

[296] *British Imex Industries Ltd* v. *Midland Bank Ltd* [1958] 1 QB 542, 551.

the goods are not in good order and condition, the documents may be rejected even if the underlying defect in the goods is not so serious as to justify a rejection of the goods themselves.[297] There is an exception to the requirement of a clean bill; it concerns a bill that is claused to show that damage has occurred to the goods after the risk has been transferred to the buyer.[298] If the buyer were able to reject the documents, this would subvert the allocation of risk between the parties. In *M. Golodetz & Co. Inc* v. *Czarnikow-Rionda Co. Inc.*,[299] sugar was in the process of being loaded under a c. & f. contract when a fire broke out on board ship destroying 200 tons that had already been loaded. The standard form bill of lading attested to the good order and condition of the sugar, but a typed addition dealt with the condition of the sugar after the fire. It was held that this addition did not vitiate the requirement that the bill of lading be clean since it referred to the condition of the sugar after shipment, when the risk had passed to the buyer.[300]

Bills of Lading and Letters of Credit

If payment is to be made pursuant to a banker's letter of credit, the seller must comply with the documentary requirements of the letter if he wishes to enforce payment according to its terms. Further, to the extent that the letter of credit restates or supersedes the c.i.f. documentary obligations of the seller, then compliance with its requirements is tantamount to the performance by the seller of his documentary duties under the contract of sale. In commercial matters generally, one expects a strict standard of contractual performance for the sake of certainty and confidence as to one's legal position in fast-moving markets, but the compliance standard for letters of credit is especially strict for the additional reason that bankers are not as well informed as buyers of the underlying business. They cannot inquire into the concrete transaction and will need to know for sure that they are properly making payment according to the terms of the letter of credit, which payment will then be recoverable from the buyer.[301] Referring to shipping documents generally, Lord Sumner once said:

---

[297] *Cehave NV* v. *Bremer Handelsgesellschaft mbH* [1976] QB 44.

[298] In c.i.f. contracts, risk is transferred as from shipment: *Comptoir d'Achat et du Boerenbond Belge* v. *Luis de Ridder Lda* [1949] AC 293.

[299] [1980] 1 WLR 495.

[300] See *Comptoir d'Achat et du Boerenbond Belge* v. *Luis de Ridder Lda*, n. 298 above, and Ch. 4 above.

[301] *J. H. Rayner & Co. Ltd* v. *Hambro's Bank Ltd* [1943] 1 KB 37. At common law, the terms of the contract between the bank and the applicant for the credit (the buyer) require strict scrutiny of the shipping documents by the bank: *Midland Bank Ltd* v. *Seymour* [1955] 2 Lloyd's Rep. 147. The UCP Rules are more lenient in requiring the bank to exercise 'reasonable care' in applying the standard of 'international banking practice' to determine whether the documents conform: Art. 13a.

These documents have to be handled by banks, they have to be taken up or rejected promptly and without any opportunity for prolonged inquiry, they have to be such as can be re-tendered to sub-purchasers, [This underlines the strictness of compliance between buyer and seller.] and it is essential that they should so conform to the accustomed shipping documents as to be reasonably and readily fit to pass current in commerce.[302]

The standard of compliance is both exacting and exact;[303] there is no room to apply the maxim *de minimis non curat lex*.[304] A letter of credit calling for bills of lading to be marked 'freight prepaid' need not be honoured if the seller tenders bills marked 'freight collect'.[305] Another example is *J. H. Rayner & Co. Ltd* v. *Hambro's Bank Ltd*,[306] where a letter of credit requirement that the goods be 'Coromandel groundnuts' was not met by the tender of a bill of lading referring to 'machine shelled groundnut kernels'; it did not matter that it was well understood in the trade that the latter expression meant Coromandel groundnuts, since the bank could not be expected to possess an informed understanding of the trade.

Some relaxation of the strictness of the above standard is evident in *Soproma SpA* v. *Marine and Animal By-Products Corpn.*,[307] where the letter of credit specified shipping documents for 'CHILEAN FISH FULLMEAL, 70% Protein'. The bill of lading, however, referred to 'Chilean Fishmeal' while the commercial invoices described the shipment as 'CHILEAN FISH FULLMEAL 70% protein'. Further slight deviations were to be found in certificates of quality and analysis; the former mentioned a protein count of '67% minimum' and the latter 'protein 69.7%'. McNair J held that the description of the goods in the invoices was accurate and the bare statement in the bill of lading was adequate (despite the conflated reference to fishmeal instead of fish full meal) but that the discrepancies in protein count in both quality and analysis certificates rendered them invalid. According to Article 37c of the Uniform Customs and Practice for Documentary Credits (the UCP Rules, an earlier version of which was relied upon by McNair J), '[t]he description of the goods in the commercial invoice must correspond with the description in the Credit'[308] while '[i]n all other documents, the goods may be described in general terms not inconsistent

---

[302] *Hansson* v. *Hamel and Horley Ltd* [1922] 2 AC 36, 46.

[303] *English, Scottish and Australasian Bank Ltd* (1922) 13 Ll. LR 21; *Equitable Trust Co. of New York* v. *Dawson Partners Ltd* (1927) 27 Ll. LR 49, 52; *Seaconsar Far East Ltd* v. *Bank Markhazi Jomhouri* [1993] 1 Lloyd's Rep. 236; *Banque de l'Indochine SA* v. *J. H. Rayner (Mincing Lane) Ltd* [1983] QB 711.

[304] *Soproma SpA* v. *Marine and Animal By-Products Corpn.* [1966] 1 Lloyd's Rep. 367.

[305] *Ibid.*   [306] N. 301 above.   [307] N. 304 above.

[308] For a standard of exact compliance in the invoice, see *Moralice (London) Ltd* v. *E. D. & F. Man* [1954] 2 Lloyd's Rep. 526.

with the description of the goods in the Credit'.[309] This rule is likely to reflect the present position, whether under the letter of credit or the contract of sale, either because of the incorporation of the UCP Rules or because Article 37c is in harmony with a tendency to relax punctilious standards in unimportant details.[310] Where the UCP Rules apply, the seller is given a quantitative leeway of 5 per cent more or less, which, more generous than the position under section 30 of the Sale of Goods Act, will be recorded in the invoice.[311]

Time Obligations and Shipping Documents

Once the goods have been delivered to the carrier and shipping documents issued, it is the seller's duty to forward them with all reasonable dispatch to the buyer or the buyer's bank for the documentary exchange.[312] It has long been settled that there is no necessary requirement that the documents reach the buyer before the arrival of the ship in the port of discharge.[313] In modern conditions, a combination of speedy shipping and slow postal services has made this a common event. It is of course open to the parties to agree expressly or by implication that the documents must arrive before the arrival of the ship, as happened in one case[314] where payment was due on arrival of the ship or twenty days after the bill of lading date, whichever was earlier. Since nothing had displaced the rule that payment was to occur against a tender of documents, the seller was in breach for not tendering the documents when the twenty days had elapsed and the ship had not yet arrived. Timely performance is a strict condition, breach of which entitles the buyer to terminate the contract.[315]

The seller must also tender a bill of lading that has been issued on shipment. This does not mean that the bill of lading must be signed contemporaneously with the goods being put on board,[316] since it is common practice for the bills to be signed after loading has been completed and indeed after the ship has sailed; a reasonable margin of tolerance is permitted.[317] Nevertheless, it has been held that a bill issued 'thirteen days

---

[309] This rule was not incorporated in the letter of credit in *J. H. Rayner & Co. Ltd* v. *Hambro's Bank Ltd*, n. 301 above.

[310] e.g. *Bremer Handelsgesellschaft mbH* v. *Toepfer* [1980] 2 Lloyd's Rep. 43.

[311] UCP 500, Art. 39b.

[312] *Johnson* v. *Taylor Bros. & Co. Ltd* [1920] AC 144; *C. Sharpe & Co. Ltd* v. *Nosawa* [1917] 2 KB 814 (where the date when the documents should have arrived was taken as the basis for calculating damages, on which point see also *Aruna Mills Ltd* v. *Gobindram* [1968] 1 QB 655).

[313] *Sanders Bros.* v. *Maclean & Co.* (1883) 11 QBD 327.

[314] *Toepfer* v. *Lenersan-Poortman NV* [1980] 1 Lloyd's Rep. 143.   [315] *Ibid.*

[316] *Westpac Banking Corpn.* v. *South Carolina National Bank* [1986] 1 Lloyd's Rep. 311, 316.

[317] *Hansson* v. *Hamel and Horley Ltd*, n. 302 above, 47 (Lord Sumner). This is particularly likely in transhipment cases.

after the original shipment, at another port in another country many hundreds of miles away, is not duly procured "on shipment" '.[318] A bill of lading was also held to be irregular in another case where it was issued seven weeks after the loading, between which dates the ship visited other ports before returning to the loading port.[319]

Besides attesting to timely shipment of the goods, the bill of lading must be dated accurately as of the time when the goods are actually loaded.[320] If the contract gives the seller the option of tendering a received for shipment bill, or indifferently states the goods are received or shipped and then recites a date that does not discriminate between the two, then the buyer may not complain if the bill is dated from the receipt.[321]

Continuous Documentary Coverage

The reason for the requirement that the bill of lading be issued promptly on or after shipment is that the buyer on c.i.f. or similar terms is entitled to continuous documentary coverage.[322] This has emerged as a particular problem in transhipment cases where prior parts of the carriage process may have occurred before the part for which the seller tenders a bill of lading. Transhipment also raises problems concerning responsibility to the transferee buyer where more than one carrier is employed.

In *Landauer & Co.* v *Craven & Speeding Bros.*,[323] a c.i.f. contract for the sale of 400 bales of hemp called for shipment from Hong Kong or from a Philippines port by steamer or steamers direct or indirect to London, with the bill of lading dated between 1 October and 31 December. The contract therefore permitted transhipment. The sellers elected to ship from Manila and obtained a bill of lading dated 28 December. The ship, however, was going no further than Hong Kong, so the sellers forwarded the bill of lading to their Hong Kong agent with instructions to find London shipping space forthwith. The agent was unable to enter into a contract of affreightment until long after the ship had left Manila, and the goods were transhipped from Hong Kong under fresh bills of lading dated 25 March. The second bill of lading for the Hong Kong to London leg was tendered to the buyers, the first bill not having arrived in London, and the buyers accepted the documents under protest. It was the normal

---

[318] *Ibid.*   [319] *Foreman and Ellams Ltd* v. *Blackburn* [1928] 2 KB 60.

[320] Hence, even if the shipment occurs within the shipment period, the seller will be in breach if the bill of lading is falsely dated. This point was not contested by the seller on appeal in *Procter & Gamble Corpn.* v. *Becher* [1988] 2 Lloyd's Rep. 88.

[321] *Weis* v *Produce Brokers' Co.* (1920) 7 Ll. LR 211; *United Baltic Corpn.* v. *Burgett & Newsam* (1921) 8 Ll. LR 190.

[322] *Hansson* v. *Hamel and Horley Ltd*, n. 302 above; *Holland Colombo Trading Soc.* v. *Alawdeen* [1954] 2 Lloyd's Rep. 45.

[323] [1912] 2 KB 95.

course of business for goods shipped at Manila to be transhipped at Hong Kong, but nevertheless shipped under a through bill of lading covering the entire voyage. Scrutton J held that the documentary tender was bad for two reasons. First, when the goods were originally shipped, a contract for the second leg of the voyage had not been entered into. Consequently, the second leg of the voyage was out of time. Secondly, the sellers' tender did not include the first bill of lading, and thus the buyers were not put in possession of any document that permitted them to launch an action against the first carrier should this have become necessary.

The second ground for the decision in *Landauer* was confirmed by the House of Lords in *Hansson* v. *Hamel and Horley Ltd*,[324] which concerned a quantity of guano sold c.i.f. Yokohama and shipped at Braatvag, a Norwegian port. The Japanese carrier did not call at Braatvag so it was necessary to tranship at Hamburg. When the goods were transhipped on to the Japanese ship at Hamburg, the bills of lading were signed on 5 May and stipulated that the goods had been shipped in good order and condition from Braatvag on 22 April. In the judgment of the House of Lords, these bills were not true through bills since, though speaking to the condition of the goods in Braatvag, they gave the buyers no contractual recourse against the first carrier. Moreover, the Japanese carrier did not accept responsibility for the goods prior to their arrival in Hamburg. As Lord Sumner put it: 'When documents are to be taken up the buyer is entitled to documents which substantially confer protective rights throughout. He is not buying a litigation'.[325] Had the ship foundered off the Norwegian coast, the buyers would have had no rights against the Japanese carrier since no contract with that carrier would ever have been forthcoming.[326] In Lord Sumner's view, the sellers should either have tendered a bill of lading authorizing transhipment and signed by the Japanese carrier's agent at Braatvag, or should have forwarded the goods on their own account to Hamburg and shipped them from that port to Yokohama.[327] It is submitted that the tender of two bills of lading, one issued by the local carrier for the Braatvag to Hamburg leg and the other by the Japanese carrier for the Hamburg to Yokohama leg, would not have been good. Having two carriers blaming each other in the event of damage to the goods would be tantamount to 'buying a litigation'.

These cases show that it is possible to effect a documentary exchange in transhipment cases if the correct procedures are used. The buyer is entitled above all to continuous documentary coverage and does not get it if the carrier disclaims all responsibility before[328] or after[329] the point

---

[324] [1922] 2 AC 36.   [325] *Ibid.* 46.   [326] *Ibid.* 47.   [327] *Ibid.* 49.
[328] *Hansson* v. *Hamel and Horley Ltd*, n. 324 above.
[329] *Holland Colombo Trading Soc.* v. *Alawdeen*, n. 322 above, 53 (a non-c.i.f. contract requiring a documentary tender).

of transhipment, but is not deprived of it merely because the bill of lading gives the carrier a liberty to tranship on such terms and this liberty is not in fact exercised.[330] Continuous documentary coverage requires the continuance of a claim against the carrier. *Colin & Shields* v. *W Weddel & Co. Ltd*[331] concerned the tender of a delivery order instead of a bill of lading. The contract called for discharge[332] in Liverpool but the goods were shipped on a vessel bound for Manchester that did not call in at Liverpool. The sellers were in breach on the ground that there was no bill of lading evidencing a proper contract of affreightment of the goods to Liverpool. Furthermore, they were also in breach in that the delivery order they tendered was not properly drawn. The goods had been transhipped at Manchester on a barge and the order tendered by the sellers was addressed, not to the carrier, but to a master porter at one of the berths in the Liverpool docks. This was by no means as effective as a bill of lading in giving the buyers recourse against the carrier. What is ordinarily needed is a document drawn on the carrier in which the carrier attorns to the buyer.[333] In this case, the contract expressly demanded that the delivery order 'be countersigned by a banker, shipbroker, captain or mate if so required' and that the buyers were to be 'put in the same position as if they had been in possession of' a bill of lading. On neither account, had the sellers made a good tender.

Delivery Orders

The above discussion recounts the documentary obligations of a c.i.f. seller and, where relevant, those of c. & f. and f.o.b. sellers where a documentary exchange is envisaged. The common practice of shipping commodities in bulk has led to an increasing number of cases in which the seller pursuant to the contract tenders a delivery order drawn on the ship instead of a bill of lading.[334] Such delivery orders will not permit symbolic dealings with the general property in the goods as would a bill of lading for they are not documents of title.[335] Increasingly, international

---

[330] *Soproma SpA* v. *Marine and Animal By-Products Corpn.* [1966] 1 Lloyd's Rep. 367.

[331] [1952] 2 All ER 237. [332] It was not a pure c.i.f. contract.

[333] See also *Waren Import Gesellschaft Krohn & Co.* v. *International Graanhandel Thegra NV* [1975] 1 Lloyd's Rep. 146.

[334] See *Re Wait* [1927] 1 Ch. 606; *Comptoir d'Achat et du Boerenbond Belge* v. *Luis de Ridder Lda* [1949] AC 293; *Colin & Shields* v. *W. Weddel & Co. Ltd*, n. 331 above; *Cremer* v. *General Carriers SA* [1974] 1 WLR 341. If it is not drawn on the person in possession of the goods, the documentary tender will be invalid: *Waren Import Gesellschaft Krohn & Co.* v. *International Graanhandel Thegra NV*, n. 333 above.

[335] *Margarine Union GmbH* v. *Cambay Prince Steamship Co.* [1969] 1 QB 219; *Comptoir d'Achat et du Boerenbond Belge* v. *Luis de Ridder Lda*, n. 334 above. Nor is a mate's receipt a document of title, though its holder is *prima facie* entitled to the issue of a bill of lading: *Nippon Yusen Kaisha* v. *Ramjiban Serowgee* [1938] AC 429. The issue of mate's receipts is not now a common practice since forwarding agents frequently arrange for shipping space

sales contracts (outside the area of commodities) will permit the tender of a received for shipment bill of lading instead of an on board bill.[336] Furthermore, the accelerating practice in certain trade sectors of substituting, for negotiable bills of lading, non-negotiable documents such as waybills, freight receipts and multimodal transport documents combining terrestrial and maritime transport[337] impedes symbolic dealings with the goods in transit[338] and has ramifications for the carrier's liability and insurance coverage. It is probably too early to assess the implications, for the well-worked out positions of buyer and seller under a documentary sale, of the issuance of shipping documents by electronic means.[339]

Import and Export Licences

International sales frequently require the issue of a licence if goods are to be exported and imported. Two fundamental questions are raised at this point. First, which party is responsible for applying for the licence? Secondly, is the applicant under an obligation to use due diligence in applying for a licence or is the burden a stricter one?[340] In deciding who has the duty to apply for a licence it is convenient to distinguish between export and import licences. Furthermore, one must distinguish the various contracts, which fall into two principal groupings: there are f.o.b. and similar contracts, such as the f.a.s. (free alongside) contract, where the seller's delivery obligations are accomplished at the port of loading, and there are c.i.f. and similar contracts, such as the c. & f. contract, where the goods will have left the loading port before the seller's docu-

with loading brokers: Sassoon, *C.I.F. and F.O.B. Contracts* (4th edn., 1995), §133; *Heskell* v. *Continental Express Ltd* [1950] 1 All ER 1033.

[336] See Incoterms 1990, Introduction, para. 16 (nowadays goods are usually delivered by seller to carrier before shipment on board takes place).

[337] See Incoterms 1990, Introduction, para. 19. For a useful description of modern documentary practice superseding the ocean bill of lading, see R. M Goode, *Proprietary Rights and Insolvency in Sales Transactions* (2nd edn., Sweet & Maxwell, London, 1989), 78–84.

[338] Commonly such documents are used because there is no intention of dealing with the goods in transit.

[339] See the passing reference to EDI procedures in Incoterms 1990, Introduction, para. 18. On electronic systems generally, see R. M. Goode (ed.), *Electronic Banking[:]The Legal Implications* (Institute of Bankers, London, 1985), ch. 10: 'The Electronic Transfer and Presentation of Shipping Documents' (A. Urbach), ch. 11: 'International Trade Data Interchange Systems' (B. Wheble); P. Todd, *Modern Bills of Lading* (2nd edn., Blackwell, Oxford, 1990), ch. 17; Kozolchyk, 'Evolution and Present State of the Ocean Bill of Lading from a Banking Law Perspective' (1992) 23 *J of Maritime Law and Commerce* 161, 196–245; K. Gronfors, *Cargo Key Receipt and Transport Document Replacement* (Gothenburg Maritime Law Association, Gothenburg, 1982); C. Reed, *Electronic Finance Law* (1991), ch. 8: 'International Trade Transactions and Electronic Data Interchange'; Toh See Kiat, *Paperless International Trade: Law of Telematic Data Interchange* (Butterworths Asia, Singapore, 1992), ch. 5: 'Paperless International Trade'.

[340] A related issue to the strictness of the duty is its relationship to an express force majeure or prohibition of export clause.

mentary obligations are performed and, in some cases, before the contract is concluded.

The starting point is that the identity of the applicant is a question of contractual construction. This is not evident, however, if one looks at Incoterms, which state that the seller must '[o]btain at his own risk and expense any export licence or other official authorisation'.[341] In the case of f.a.s. delivery, the assumption is that the buyer applies for the export licence; the seller's duty is only to '[r]ender the buyer, at the latter's request, risk and expense, every assistance in obtaining any export licence'.[342] In neither case, can the Incoterms be said to represent the case law. In *H. O. Brandt & Co.* v. *H. N. Morris & Co. Ltd*,[343] a contract was concluded in time of war between two Manchester merchants for the sale of a quantity of aniline oil f.o.b. Manchester in circumstances showing that the goods were destined for an American recipient. During most of the shipment period, an export licence system, introduced after the contract date and sensitive to the destination of the goods, was in force. The court held that responsibility for the licence rested on the buyers.[344] Scrutton LJ put it in terms of the f.o.b. buyer's duty to provide an effective (in this instance, a legal) ship,[345] an overstatement of the position. But the result in the case can be supported on the ground that the sellers were no better placed than the buyers to apply for a licence and, furthermore, the buyers knew the identity of the American recipient. There will be cases where it makes more sense to put the duty to apply on the seller, for example, where the seller resides in the country of export and the buyer does not. Such a case-by-case approach may lack the simplicity (or dogmatism) of Incoterms, which give a clear guide to merchants, but it is commendably flexible.

The most important feature of the House of Lords decision in *A. V. Pound & Co. Ltd* v. *M. W. Hardy & Co. Inc.*[346] lies in its conclusion that there is no general rule governing the duty to apply for a licence, the matter being one of contractual construction. A contract was made in England between English sellers and the English branch office of an American company for the sale of a quantity of Portuguese turpentine on f.a.s. Lisbon terms. The sellers knew that the turpentine was destined for an East German port but, since they (and the buyers for that matter too) were not registered with the Portuguese authorities, they could not apply for an export licence. But the sellers' supplier, whose identity was kept carefully concealed from the buyers,[347] did apply for a licence to export the turpentine to East Germany, which was refused. The goods had to

---

[341] Incoterms 1990, FOB Rules, para. A2. The seller is bound to pay for export costs incurred before the goods cross the ship's rail: *ibid.*, para. A6.

[342] FAS Rules, para. A2.   [343] [1917] 2 KB 784.   [344] *Ibid.* 795 and 798.

[345] *Ibid.*   [346] [1956] AC 588.   [347] *Ibid.* 604.

clear Portuguese customs before they could be laid up alongside the ship. The sellers contended that the buyers were bound to give fresh delivery instructions while the buyers, initially, counterclaimed damages for non-delivery. The House of Lords concluded that the buyers in the present case were under no duty to apply for the licence; the abandonment of the buyers' counterclaim meant that they did not examine the nature of the duty that rested upon the sellers.[348] The court's refusal to lay down general or unnecessary rules was most clearly stated by Lord Somervell:

> I think this is an area in which it is impossible to lay down general rules. There might be a licence system based not on destination but on the proportion of a manufacturer's product to be sent out of the country. In such a case the facts necessary to be stated would be known to the producer and not to the buyer. It would seem obvious that in such a case it would be for the seller to apply. There may well be cases in which each party must be ready and willing to co-operate. If, in the present case, the sellers had written to the buyers; told them of the licensing system; told them of the suppliers' names and asked them to give the name of the destination and the ship, there might well have been an obligation on the buyers to do these things. . . . There can be no general rule.[349]

This passage usefully emphasizes that applying for a licence often calls for co-operative behaviour between seller and buyer, which could be implied in contracts as a matter of business efficacy. Problems of the kind in this case cannot be resolved by easy assertions that in f.o.b. contracts it is the buyer's duty to nominate an effective ship, for it could just as easily be said in opposition that f.o.b. and f.a.s. sellers are under a duty to deliver 'effective goods', that is, goods that may be lawfully carried to their destination.[350] As for import licences, their acquisition is collateral to the performance of such contracts and concern the factual expectations of the buyer. When Incoterms put the duty on the buyer,[351] they are providing the importing buyer with a checklist of things to do rather than laying down the legal characteristics of f.o.b. and f.a.s. contracts.

In the case of c.i.f. contracts, Incoterms squarely put on the seller the duty to apply for an export licence[352] and on the buyer the duty to apply for an import licence.[353] Nevertheless, although the general approach of the *Pound* case is just as applicable here too, the case law does not depart radically from Incoterms, subject to the following discussion. It is not easy to contemplate a case where the c.i.f. buyer has the duty to apply for an export licence, especially since the goods may be afloat before they are appropriated to the contract. As regards import licences, in *Mitchell*

---

[348] [1956] AC 612–13.   [349] *Ibid.* 611.   [350] *Ibid.* 607–8.
[351] FAS Rules B2; FOB Rules B2.
[352] CIF Rules, para. A2; CFR (namely, c.& f.) Rules, para. A2.
[353] CIF Rules, para. B2; CFR Rules, para. B2.

Cotts & Co. v. *Hairco Ltd*,[354] the c.i.f. London buyer of Sudanese goat hair was bound under the contract to pay for the goods after they had been landed in England. The English buyers, already in possession of the shipping documents, had not applied for an import licence and the customs authorities confiscated the cargo when it arrived. The Sudanese sellers successfully sued for the price of the goods. This c.i.f. contract clearly contemplated the landing of the goods in England, but it should not be assumed that c.i.f contracts will always require the goods to be landed in the country of the destination port. In *Congimex* v. *Tradax Export*[355] the buyer of c.i.f. Lisbon soya bean meal, denied an import licence by the Portuguese authorities, claimed that the contract had been frustrated. It was held, nevertheless, that the goods did not have to be landed in Portugal for the contract to be performed; they could be transhipped or oncarried by the same ship to a French destination.[356]

Where the contract is on *ex* ship or *ex* quay terms, it seems as a matter of construction likely that the seller will bear the burden of applying for both export and import licences (though the buyer may have co-operative duties to perform). Yet Incoterms puts the duty on the buyer in the case of an *ex* ship contract[357] and on the buyer in the case of *ex* quay terms.[358]

The question of how strict is the duty to apply for a licence is again one of contractual construction.[359] The applicant may guarantee or be strictly liable for its procurement, or undertake only to use due diligence. In the absence of contrary indications in the contract, the test of business efficacy for the implication of contractual terms supplies a duty of due diligence.[360] A seller faced with a supervening export prohibition or quota restriction may be liable for the lack of due diligence where it cannot demonstrate that with energy it could have avoided the difficulty[361] or where its difficulties are self-imposed.[362] In applying for a licence, the applicant is entitled to any necessary co-operation from the other contracting party.[363]

---

[354] [1943] 2 All ER 552.   [355] [1983] 1 Lloyd's Rep. 250.

[356] Lisbon is an unlikely port for traffic of this kind. But it is common to ship bulk commodities to ARA ports (Amsterdam/Rotterdam/Antwerp) and then to tranship parcels to further destinations.

[357] DES (namely, *ex* ship) Rules, para. B2.   [358] DEQ (namely, *ex* quay) Rules, para. A2.

[359] For a difficult case, see *Czarnikow Ltd* v. *Rolimpex* [1979] AC 351. The language of Incoterms ('obtain') is too terse to reveal an intention to impose a stricter standard than one of due diligence; an English court interpreting a contract incorporating Incoterms would be likely to require due diligence.

[360] *Re Anglo-Russian Merchant Traders Ltd* [1917] 2 KB 79; *Coloniale Import-Export* v. *Loumidis* [1978] 2 Lloyd's Rep. 60; *Brauer & Co.* v. *James Clark Ltd* [1952] 2 All ER 497; *Peter Cassidy Seed* v. *Osuustukkukauppa* [1957] 1 WLR 273.

[361] *Agroexport State Enterprise* v. *Cie Européenne de Céréales* [1974] 1 Lloyd's Rep. 499.

[362] *K. C. Sethia Ltd* v. *Partabmull Rameshwar* [1950] 1 All ER 51.

[363] *Kyprianou* v. *Cyprus Textiles Ltd* [1958] 2 Lloyd's Rep. 60.

There are cases where the applicant has impliedly undertaken a stricter responsibility. In *Peter Cassidy Seed* v *Osuustukkukauppa*,[364] the Finnish sellers of a quantity of Finnish ant eggs assured the buyer that the procurement of an export licence was a mere formality despite having no grounds for making such a statement. In the circumstances they were held to have guaranteed the licence. In *Pagnan SpA* v *Tradax Ocean Transportation*,[365] the contract was for the sale of Thai tapioca pellets to Italian buyers. No export market for this commodity existed apart from an artificial one subsidized by the EC for limited imports into the EC. The contract stated that the seller 'would provide for [an] export certificate', which was a precondition to the grant of import permission by the EC. There was at all material times a quota export system between Thailand and the EC. Since export certificates for the shipment period had already been allocated in full before the present shipment, the Thai authorities refused one to the sellers. The sellers were held to have undertaken an absolute duty to procure a certificate. They had a more substantial business presence in Thailand than the buyers and were better able to assess the risk of failure to obtain a certificate. Moreover, the goods were no use at all to the buyer if they could not be imported into the EC. Nevertheless, the sellers' absolute duty only went so far as 'oversight, error, mishap, bureaucratic inefficiency or delay, and probably also if the certificate was not provided for simply because the Thai authorities failed to issue it'. The sellers were not so liable where the grant of certificates was 'entirely abrogated or suspended by governmental decree', which had occurred in the present case.

THE BUYER'S DUTY TO PAY

A contract of sale involves the payment by the buyer of 'a money consideration, called the price'[366] and section 27 of the Sale of Goods Act recites the buyer's duty to pay the price. Nothing in the Act, however, deals with the form in which this money consideration has to be paid and there are no rules concerning the place of payment that correspond to the delivery rules in section 29. The contract may state the form of payment. International sales often specify 'net cash against shipping documents' or call for the acceptance by the buyer of a draft bill of exchange which the seller may then discount before its maturity. Where the contract is silent, the common law rule is that payment must be made in legal tender, that is, in coin or bank notes.[367]

---

[364] N. 360 above.   [365] [1987] 2 Lloyd's Rep. 342.
[366] S. 2 of the Sale of Goods Act. See Ch. 2 above.
[367] *Gordon* v. *Strange* (1847) 1 Ex. 477. See Ch. 2 above.

Despite the legal tender rule, payment is commonly made by cheque. At the very least, this practice establishes that legal tender is commonly waived by sellers; it may also show that in certain trades payment by cheque has become a customarily acceptable form of payment. Canadian reform proposals, in recognition of this, would allow payment 'when made by any means and in any manner current in the ordinary course of business';[368] the seller's residual entitlement to legal tender is nevertheless retained by his right to insist on legal tender provided he gives the buyer an extension that is 'reasonably necessary to procure it'.[369] Where the buyer does pay by cheque, and this is accepted by the seller, payment is treated in the absence of a contrary intention as having been made conditionally[370] on the cheque not being subsequently dishonoured by the bank on which it is drawn. In some cases, the seller will announce in advance that payment can be made by means falling outside the legal tender rule. This is commonly seen in cases where the symbol of a credit card is displayed. Payment by credit card is regarded as absolute payment, the merchant having no recourse against the card-holder in the event of default by the credit card company.[371] This is to be contrasted with the ordinary case of payment by cheque as well as with payment pursuant to a banker's letter of credit, where the buyer's duty to pay is suspended and not substituted by the bank's promise to pay.[372]

Unless the contract specifies otherwise, the rule is that the debtor should seek out the creditor.[373] Consequently, unless the parties otherwise agree,[374] in the case of sale and other contracts money payable must be paid at the payee's place of business.[375] This complements the presumptive rule that delivery takes place at the seller's place of business. Where delivery is to occur at some other place, and the presumptive rule that delivery and payment are mutual and concurrent[376] is not

---

[368] Ontario, Draft Sale of Goods Bill 1979, s. 7.2; Uniform Sale of Goods Act 1981, s. 76(2).

[369] *Ibid.*

[370] Sale of Goods Act, s. 38(1)(b); *Currie* v. *Misa* (1875) LR 10 Ex. 153, affd. (1876) 1 App. Cas. 554; *Re Romer and Haslam* [1893] 2 QB 286; *Gunn* v. *Bolckow, Vaughan & Co.* (1875) LR 10 Ch. App. 491; *Bolt and Nut Co. (Tipton) Ltd* v. *Rowlands Nicholls & Co. Ltd* [1964] 2 QB 10. It should make no difference that the cheque is supported by a bank guarantee card: *Re Charge Card Services Ltd* [1987] Ch. 150 (Millett J).

[371] *Re Charge Card Services Ltd* [1989] Ch. 497.

[372] *W. J. Alan & Co.* v. *El Nasr Export and Import Co.* [1972] 2 QB 189; *Maran Road Saw Mill* v. *Austin Taylor & Co. Ltd* [1975] 1 Lloyd's Rep. 156; *E. D. & F. Man Ltd* v. *Nigerian Sweets & Confectionery Co. Ltd* [1977] 2 Lloyd's Rep. 50.

[373] *Drexel* v. *Drexel* [1916] 1 Ch. 251, 259–60; *Fowler* v. *Midland Electric Corpn. Ltd* [1917] 1 Ch. 656; *The Eider* [1891] P 119, 131. There is an exception where the contract is governed by English law and the payee is abroad: *Korner* v. *Witkowitzer* [1950] 2 KB 128, 159.

[374] *Comber* v. *Leyland* [1898] AC 524; *Thorn* v. *City Rice Mills* (1889) 40 Ch. D 357.

[375] *Rein* v. *Stein* [1892] 1 QB 753, 758; *Robey & Co.* v. *Snaefell Mining Co. Ltd* (1887) 20 QBD 152; *Bremer Öltransport GmbH* v. *Drewry* [1933] 1 KB 753, 765–6; *Thompson* v. *Palmer* [1893] 2 QB 80, 84; *Charles Duval & Co. Ltd* v. *Gans* [1904] 2 KB 685, 692.

[376] S. 28.

displaced, this may give rise to an implied intention that payment is to occur at the stipulated place of delivery.

In documentary sales, where the parties are physically separate and the duration of the transit makes it practical and economical to deal in the goods through their documentary expression, it is common for both place and means of payment to depart from the general rule. The separation of buyer and seller creates two major problems for the seller. First of all, once the seller has delivered the goods to the carrier and until payment is received, his capital is tied up in the cargo and does not produce income. Secondly, unless the seller takes preventive measures, after abandoning control of the goods he courts the risk of non-payment by the buyer. This event may arise for various reasons, but notably because of the buyer's insolvency. The key to the resolution of these problems is for the seller to control the goods until payment through the medium of the shipping documents.[377]

The liquidity problem is resolved in part by the ability of the seller, pending the documentary exchange, to pledge the bill of lading with the bank so as to raise bridging finance.[378] But unless the buyer pays cash or its equivalent on the documentary exchange, the seller will find himself extending credit to the buyer and he may not wish to do that. Furthermore, the seller may also run the risk of non-payment by the buyer and to avoid this may wish to retain a property interest in the goods and their proceeds[379] or to obtain a guarantee of payment by the buyer from a third party whose credit is solid. The virtue of the latter step is that it covers the risk of a seller incurring expenses in preparing for performance before the buyer repudiates or otherwise fails to perform the contract.

Letters of Credit

One method of securing most of the seller's objectives, not so commonly employed nowadays but in frequent use in the last century,[380] is for the parties to proceed on a 'documents on acceptance' basis. The seller ships the goods and draws on the buyer for the price. This draft,[381] which may

[377] Some protection is afforded the seller in the case of buyer insolvency by the right of stoppage in transit, but it is a right rarely exercised in modern conditions: Ch. 10 below.

[378] *Sewell* v. *Burdick* (1884) 10 App. Cas. 74; *The Albazero* [1977] AC 774 (Brandon J); *Ross T. Smyth & Co. Ltd* v. *Bailey Son & Co.* [1940] 3 All ER 60; *The Future Express* [1993] 2 Lloyd's Rep. 542.

[379] See Ch. 3 above.

[380] The practice is dealt with in s. 19(3) of the Sale of Goods Act. For a description, see *Guaranty Trust Co. of New York* v. *Hannay & Co.* [1918] 2 KB 623, 659–60 (Scrutton LJ).

[381] It is common to prepare more than one draft ('the first of exchange', 'the second of exchange' etc.) to accompany the separate bills of lading sent by different routes to the buyer.

be payable on sight or at an interval,[382] can be discounted by the seller with a bank, which receives also the shipping documents and presents the draft to the buyer for acceptance.[383] When the buyer accepts the draft, the shipping documents are released to him. Although the bill of lading itself is a useful medium for reserving the right of disposal, the seller's bank may not wish to become involved with a buyer of unknown credit and may well prefer to have dealings with another bank standing behind the buyer. Moreover, the buyer's acceptance of the draft is in itself no guarantee that the buyer will ultimately honour the draft when it is presented for payment. The seller remains vulnerable to a recourse action by his bank if such dishonour by the buyer occurs.

The drawbacks to the documents on acceptance approach are resolved by the system of bankers' letters of credit.[384] The system works in the following way.[385] The buyer (the applicant) persuades a bank, usually in his own country, to issue a letter of credit in favour of a named beneficiary, the seller. This issuing bank corresponds with an advising (or corresponding) bank, usually in the seller's country, which advises the seller of the credit and acts as the issuing bank's agent in effecting payment under the letter of credit. The advising bank may add its own promise to that of the issuing bank, in which event it acts as a confirming bank. Once assured of the promise of payment according to the tenor of the letter of credit, the seller then ships the goods and forwards the requested shipping documents to the advising bank. Payment may take the form of cash. Alternatively, the seller may draw on the issuing or confirming bank for the price, or may draw directly on the buyer, negotiating the draft to the issuing or confirming bank. The issuing bank turns over the shipping documents to the buyer, who will subsequently present the bill of lading to the carrier when the goods are ready for collection. A continuing security in the form of a trust receipt may be taken by the issuing bank, pending repayment of the moneys forwarded to the seller, over the goods and their proceeds.[386] The terms of the contract between the buyer and the issuing bank will govern the reimbursement of the latter.

[382] Or 'usance'.

[383] The seller's bank may act as a 'remitting bank' and send the documents to a 'presenting bank' near the buyer.

[384] They are sometimes referred to as documentary credits or commercial credits. See generally H. C. Gutteridge and M. Megrah, *The Law of Bankers' Commercial Credits* (7th edn., Europa, London, 1984); E. P. Ellinger, *Documentary Letters of Credit* (University of Singapore Press, Singapore, 1970); R. Jack, *Documentary Credits* (2nd edn., Butterworths, London, 1993).

[385] See *W. J. Alan & Co. v. El Nasr Export and Import Co.* [1972] 2 QB 189 (Denning MR).

[386] *North Western Bank Ltd v. Poynter, Son and Macdonalds* [1895] AC 56 (a continuing pledge despite the release of the documents); *Re David Allester Ltd* [1922] 2 Ch. 211; *Lloyds Bank Ltd v. Bank of America National Trust and Savings Assn.* [1938] 2 KB 146.

A number of distinctions may be made between different types of credit. First of all, they may be confirmed or unconfirmed; in the former case, the advising bank adds its own undertaking to the seller that payment will be made. Credits may also be revocable or irrevocable. If the credit is revocable, the seller cannot prepare the goods for shipment with the assurance that payment will be made on the documentary tender.[387] A revocable credit may be cancelled at any time without liability on the part of the bank.[388] A distinction also exists between transferable and non-transferable credits.[389] In the former case, the benefit of a letter of credit may be transferred by the named beneficiary through intermediate sellers to the head seller in a sales string.[390]

Once the letter of credit has been opened, a binding contract between the seller and the issuing bank is constituted[391] in which, it seems plain, technical difficulties posed by the doctrine of consideration[392] will not be permitted to impede commercial expediency.[393] If the letter of credit is irrevocable, then, in the absence of fraud, the obligation of the issuing bank to pay is absolute and may not be qualified by the state of the underlying contract of sale.[394] Although buyer and seller are perfectly free to stipulate that the seller shall look to a third party for payment without recourse against the buyer,[395] this interpretation will not in the absence of express language be drawn to meet the rare case of an issuing bank defaulting on a letter of credit.[396]

Timely Payment

Given its importance, there is surprisingly little authority dealing with the time of payment by the buyer. One reason is that payment is com-

---

[387] Departing from previous editions of the UCP Rules, the current 1993 edition (UCP 500) stipulates that a credit is irrevocable unless otherwise stated: Art. 6c. On the former Art. 7(1)(c) in the 1983 edn., see E. P. Ellinger [1984] *LMCLQ* 578.

[388] UCP 500, Art. 8a.   [389] UCP 500, Art. 48.

[390] See *W. J. Alan & Co.* v. *El Nasr Export and Import Co*, n. 385 above; *Ian Stach Co. Ltd* v. *Baker Bosley Ltd* [1958] 2 QB 130.

[391] *Urquart, Lindsay & Co. Ltd* v. *Eastern Bank Ltd* [1922] 1 KB 318; *Hamzeh Malas & Sons* v. *British Imex Industries Ltd* [1958] 2 QB 127.

[392] The seller may not yet have performed the act requested in the letter of credit by shipping the goods.

[393] Clarke [1974] *CLJ* 260.

[394] *Offshore International SA* v. *Banco Central SA* [1977] 1 WLR 399, 401 ('absolute obligation to pay irrespective of any dispute' in the underlying contract); *United City Merchants (Investments) Ltd* v. *Royal Bank of Canada* [1983] 1 AC 168, 183 ('an assured right to be paid'); *Trendtex Trading Corpn.* v. *Central Bank of Nigeria* [1977] QB 529, 552 ('completely separate from the contract of sale').

[395] *Harrison* v. *Luke* (1845) 14 M & W 139; *Re Charge Card Services Ltd* [1988] 3 All ER 702.

[396] *W. J. Alan & Co.* v. *El Nasr Export and Import Co*, n. 385 above, 210 (Denning MR), disapproving *Soproma SpA* v. *Marine and Animal By-Products Corpn.* [1966] 1 Lloyd's Rep. 367, 385–6.

monly conditioned by the seller's delivery and that uncertainty in the contractual timetable is played out through cases dealing with timely delivery. Section 10(1) of the Sale of Goods Act firmly states that the time of payment is presumptively not of the essence of the contract, thereby legislating the result in *Martindale* v. *Smith*.[397] In that case, the seller contracted to sell to the buyer six stacks of oats on terms giving the buyer liberty to let the oats stand on the seller's land until the middle of August but requiring payment by 16 July. The contract thus separated the buyer's duties of acceptance and payment. The seller repudiated the contract when the buyer defaulted in making timely payment, having warned the buyer in early July that this would happen. The seller subsequently refused two later tenders of the price and declined to allow the buyer to remove the stacks in mid-August.

The seller's repudiation of the contract was held unlawful on two grounds. First, it seems, the goods being specific and the property having passed to the buyer at the contract date, any contractual right of the seller to refuse later payment and retain the goods involved a rescission of the contract that was no longer possible.[398] The other reason was expressed by the court in these terms: 'In a sale of chattels, time is not of the essence of the contract, unless it is made so by express agreement, than which nothing can be more easy, by introducing conventional words into the bargain.'[399] This reasoning appears to be derived from the practice of the Court of Chancery where the presumption that time is not of the essence was commonly countered by the insertion in the agreement of sale of a time of the essence clause.[400] The practice of certain conveyancers in adopting clauses of this type did not make its way into the much less formal world of sale of goods agreements.

Despite the language of *Martindale* v. *Smith* and section 10(1), it is relatively easy in practice to displace the presumption, especially where payment and acceptance are coincidental.[401] Where the buyer has an option that has to be exercised and followed by payment on a certain date, the accepted position that compliance with the terms of an option is strictly required[402] will colour the strictness of the duty to pay on time and be more than a match for any presumption in section 10(1).[403] Moreover, a contract calling for part payment of the price by way of deposit 'as security for the correct fulfilment of this contract' will be interpreted as making time of the essence.[404] The reason given in this

---

[397] (1841) 1 QB 389. [398] See M. G. Bridge (1983) 28 *McGill LJ* 867, 917–18.
[399] N. 387 above, 395. [400] Sanctioned by *Seton* v. *Slade* (1802) 7 Ves. Jun. 265.
[401] See *Mooney* v. *Lipka* [1926] 4 DLR 647.
[402] *Holwell Securities Ltd* v. *Hughes* [1974] 1 WLR 155.
[403] Cf. *Hare* v. *Nicol* [1966] 2 QB 130 (speculative shares and fluctuating markets).
[404] *Portaria Shipping Co. Ltd* v. *Gulf Pacific Navigation Co. Ltd* [1981] 2 Lloyd's Rep. 180 (sale of ship).

case for regarding timely payment as of the essence was that the seller needed the security of a forfeitable deposit in hand before proceeding with further contractual performance.[405] Unless the market in second-hand ships were as volatile as the market in freight rates, it would make more sense, instead of permitting the outright termination of the contract, to allow the seller to suspend further performance of the contract until the deposit is paid.[406] Declining to treat timely payment as a contractual condition is not tantamount to affording the buyer an infinitely elastic time in which too pay, for eventually the failure to pay will go to the root of the contract.[407] Treating timely payment as of the essence in some cases is in tune with the general trend of asserting in commercial matters the importance of timely performance.[408] In international documentary sales, the seller's delivery duty is normally conditional upon performance by the buyer of his payment duty and *vice versa*.[409] The failure by the buyer to pay in these circumstances will be treated as a breach of condition.[410] It is also established that the letter of credit must conform strictly to the contract of sale,[411] and that a failure to provide such a letter of credit is also a discharging breach of contract.[412]

Opening Letters of Credit

Letters of credit act as an assurance to the seller that he can make preparations for the performance of the contract.[413] Where the contract fails to stipulate the date on which or the time within which the credit must be opened, this raises problems of interpretation that are difficult to resolve. Starting with c.i.f. contracts, in *Pavia & Co. SpA* v. *Thurmann-Nielsen*,[414] a contract concluded on 20 January for the c.i.f. Genoa sale of Brazilian groundnuts called for payment by confirmed, irrevocable

---

[405] *Portaria Shipping Co. Ltd* v. *Gulf Pacific Navigation Co. Ltd* [1981] 2 Lloyd's Rep. 185.

[406] On the question of suspension, see the discussion of s. 28, below.

[407] *Decro-Wall International SA* v. *Practitioners in Marketing Ltd* [1971] 1 WLR 361; *Lambert* v. *Slack* [1926] 2 DLR 166, 170.

[408] *Bunge Corpn.* v. *Tradax Export SA* [1981] 2 All ER 513.

[409] See *Shepherd* v. *Harrison* (1871) LR 5 HL 116, 132; *Dix* v. *Granger* (1922) 10 Ll. LR 496; *Cohen & Co.* v. *Ockerby & Co. Ltd* (1917) 24 CLR 288.

[410] *Berger & Co. Inc.* v. *Gill and Duffus SA* [1984] AC 382, 391 (Lord Diplock); *Nichimen Corpn.* v. *Gatoil Overseas Inc.* [1987] 2 Lloyd's Rep. 46.

[411] *Enrico Furst & Co.* v. *W. E. Fisher Ltd* [1960] 2 Lloyd's Rep. 340 (confirming bank's credit had to be irrevocable too); *Wahbe Tamari & Sons Ltd* v. *Colprogeca Sociedade Geral de Fibras Lda* [1969] 2 Lloyd's Rep. 18 (credit not confirmed where bank retained right of recourse against seller).

[412] *Ibid.* But a non-conforming letter of credit may be cured in time: *Kronman & Co.* v. *Steinberger* (1922) 10 Ll. LR 39.

[413] *United City Merchants (Investments) Ltd* v. *Royal Bank of Canada* [1983] 1 AC 168, 183.

[414] [1952] 2 QB 84.

credit and permitted the sellers to ship half of the goods between 1 February and 30 April and the remaining half between 1 March and 31 May. The sellers contended that the credit should have been made available throughout the shipment period (that is, from 1 February onwards) or, alternatively, as soon as possible, or within a reasonable time, from the beginning of the shipment period. In the judgment of the Court of Appeal, the first of these two contentions was accurate. As Denning LJ expressed it:

In the absence of express stipulation, I think the credit must be made available to the seller at the beginning of the shipment period. The reason is because the seller is entitled, before he ships the goods to be assured that, on shipment, he will be paid. . . . [W]henever he does ship the goods, he must be able to draw on the credit. He may ship on the very first day of the shipment period.[415]

Since it is the c.i.f. seller who controls the timetable, and should therefore be able to make preparations to ship on the first day of the shipment period secure in the knowledge that he will be paid, Denning LJ's own observations show that the date of opening the credit should be even earlier than the first shipment date. The buyer should have to furnish the credit within a reasonable time before the commencement of the shipment period or, more exactly, by such a date as would afford the seller the chance to ship on the first date if the seller so chose. The pre-shipment period will obviously have to be squeezed, however, to afford the buyer time to open the credit where the contract, as was the case in *Pavia* itself, is concluded close to the commencement of the shipment period.

The conclusion of the court in *Pavia* may have been influenced by the limited way in which the sellers put their case. In *Sinaison-Teicher Inter-American Grain Corpn.* v. *Oilcakes and Oilseed Trading Co. Ltd*,[416] a case involving not a letter of credit but a functionally similar bank guarantee, a c.i.f. Antwerp/Hamburg contract for the sale of Canadian grain concluded on 11 August called for October/November shipment and for payment in London net cash against shipping documents. On 10 September, the sellers repudiated the contract, not having received the guarantee by that date, and refused to relent when, later that day, a guarantee of payment was issued. The Court of Appeal confirmed the ruling of an arbitration appeal committee that the buyers had to provide the guarantee within a reasonable time before the commencement of the shipment period and had in fact done so. The court pointed out that the buyers were engaged in a 'switch transaction', buying in dollars and reselling in sterling, a procedure that in those days of exchange control required the consent of the Bank of England. The buyers' position was known to the sellers and governed the application of the reasonable time

---

[415] *Ibid.* 88.   [416] [1954] 1 WLR 1394.

test. In applying the test, a court should take care that a reasonable time before shipment does not become a reasonable time after the conclusion of the contract.

In the case of f.o.b. contracts, it has been held that, where the goods are to be shipped on a certain date, the credit should be made available a reasonable time before this date,[417] an unexceptionable holding. Where the f.o.b. contract provides for a shipment period, however, the conclusion is not so obvious. It is generally the buyer's duty to nominate an effective ship[418] and therefore the buyer who controls the shipping timetable, in contrast with c.i.f. contracts, where it is the seller who controls the timetable. This would suggest a duty on the buyer to open a credit when the ship is named, since in the absence of a stated period of notice the buyer must notify the seller of the ship in such time as to give the seller a reasonable time to get the cargo to the shipment port. Nevertheless, a different view was taken in *Ian Stach Co. Ltd* v. *Baker Bosley Ltd.*[419] That case concerned an f.o.b contract for the sale of ship plates, shipment to occur August/September. Both contracting parties were in the middle of a sales string and the buyers never did succeed in opening a credit within the shipment period. In a damages action by the sellers, the court held that it was the buyers' duty to open the credit by 1 August at the latest. Striving to avoid uncertainty, Diplock J had this to say:

It seems to me that, particularly in a trade of this kind, where, as is known to all parties participating, that there may well be a string of contracts all of which are financed by, and can only be financed by, the credit opened by the ultimate user which goes down the string, getting less and less until it comes to the ultimate supplier, the business sense of the arrangement requires that by the time the shipping period starts each of the sellers should receive the assurance from the banker that if he performs his part of the contract he will receive payment. That seems to me at least to have the advantage of providing a definite date by which the parties know that they have to fulfil the obligation of opening a credit.[420]

The best way to dissipate uncertainty is to have a definite date in the contract for the opening of the credit. Furthermore, the above rule gives an illusory air of certainty if it were to be confined to certain string contracts, not operating as a general rule for all f.o.b. contracts. In a simple f.o.b. case where there is only one buyer, it is not easy to see why the buyer should have to open a credit on the first day of the shipment

---

[417] *Plasticmoda SpA* v. *Davidson's (Manchester) Ltd* [1952] 1 Lloyd's Rep. 527.
[418] *Ibid.*
[419] [1958] 2 QB 130. If the credit has to be opened 'immediately', the buyer may not wait until the beginning of the shipment period: *State Trading Corpn. of India Ltd* v. *Cie Française d'Importation et de Distribution* [1983] 2 Lloyd's Rep. 679.
[420] N. 419 above, 143

period. Moreover, the first day of that period will not be sufficient notice if the buyer proposes shipment on that same day.[421] Even in string trading conditions, the above rule is not self-evidently a just one. A parallel case is the nomination of a ship in f.o.b. string trading conditions. The nomination will have to come from the end buyer, and each buyer will have to give his seller timely notice of the ship for every contract in the string. Obviously, the longer the string, the more likely it is that the first buyer will not give the head seller enough notice of the arrival of the ship. The problem becomes, not so much one of timely notice, but rather one of timely relay of a notice originating with the end buyer. The same could be said for relying advice of a transferable credit in the perhaps rare case[422] of the same credit being used at all stages in the string. The head seller should certainly have reasonable notice of the opening of a credit in order to prepare for shipment. The end buyer should also give sufficient notice of the credit to enable it to be relayed with proper dispatch up a sales string to reach the head seller in time for shipment to be prepared. The difficulty is that the end buyer may not realize there is a sales string or, if asked to open a transferable credit extendable to multiple beneficiaries, may not realize the length of the sales string. The approach favoured by Diplock J has the drawback of being fashioned for an apparently unusual case. In many sales strings, different (back-to-back) credits may be opened by different buyers; the length of the sales string should have therefore no effect upon the notice that an individual buyer should give. It is submitted that a preferable approach to the one favoured by Diplock J is for the buyer to give the seller notice of the credit a reasonable time before shipment. If the buyer realizes there is a string, whether or not advised of the length of the string, the extent of the buyer's knowledge that the notice has to be passed on can be factored into the length of a reasonable time.

Payment and Examination

In a previous chapter,[423] consideration was given to the place of examination as it affected the buyer's right to reject non-conforming goods. Examination also poses the question whether the buyer may decline to pay the price until he has exercised his right to examine the goods.[424] In the case of c.i.f. contracts, it is clearly settled that the buyer is under a duty to pay the price on the documentary transfer and may not defer this

---

[421] If a reasonable time before the commencement of the shipment period were to be required, Diplock J's certainty would be lost.

[422] According to UCP 500, Art. 48g, a transferable credit can only be transferred once unless otherwise stated in the credit.

[423] Ch. 5 above.   [424] Ss. 28 and 34(2) of the Sale of Goods Act.

duty until the goods have been landed and examined.[425] Though the place of shipment may once in f.o.b. contracts have been *prima facie* the place where the buyer should examine,[426] this rule has frequently been displaced in the interest of preserving the buyer's right of rejection,[427] so that now there may be no presumptive rule at all, the place of examination depending upon the construction of the particular contract.[428]

Postponing examination, however, will not necessarily mean that the buyer's duty to pay the price is correspondingly deferred.[429] Where an f.o.b. contract calls payment against documents, examination to take place at the port of discharge, the buyer will be bound to pay when the documents are tendered and may not claim to delay this duty.[430] It should not matter that the goods have arrived in port before the documentary exchange because the bill of lading will still be necessary for access to the goods. Support for this position comes from section 28 of the Sale of Goods Act which presumptively requires payment on delivery. Delivery to the carrier is presumptively delivery to the buyer under an f.o.b. contract[431] so that the duty to pay would arise at that point unless it were deferred until documents were presented by the seller.[432] If the contract permits the buyer to examine at the port of shipment, the exercise of this right would spare the buyer the trouble of pursuing a defaulting seller to recover the price. In other cases, where the carriage of goods is required but payment is to take place after the goods arrive at their destination,[433] it will depend upon the construction of the contract when exactly payment must be made, but it is likely that the buyer will first have the right to examine the goods.

---

[425] *Polenghi Bros.* v. *Dried Milk Co. Ltd* (1904) 10 Com. Cas. 42; *E. Clemens Horst & Co.* v. *Biddell Bros.* [1911] 1 KB 934 (Kennedy LJ); *Berger & Co. Inc.* v. *Gill and Duffus SA* [1984] AC 382.

[426] *Perkins* v. *Bell* [1893] 1 QB 193.

[427] *Molling & Co.* v. *Dean & Sons Ltd* (1901) 18 TLR 217; *A. J. Frank & Sons Ltd* v. *Northern Peat Co.* [1963] 2 OR 415 (Can.); *Hammer and Barrow* v. *Coca-Cola* [1962] NZLR 723. See now s. 35(6)(b) of the Sale of Goods Act (as amended in 1994).

[428] *J. W. Schofield & Sons* v. *Rownson, Drew and Clydesdale Ltd* (1922) 10 Ll. LR 480, 482.

[429] Sassoon, *C.I.F. and F.O.B. Contracts* (4th edn., Sweet & Maxwell, London, 1995), §§626–7, *pace* S. Williston, *The Law Governing Sales of Goods at Common Law and under the Uniform Sales Act* (rev. edn., Baker Voorhis, New York, 1948), §448a.

[430] *Morrison* v. *Morrow* (1916) 36 OLR 400 (Can.).

[431] S. 32(1); *Wimble Sons & Co.* v. *Rosenberg & Sons* [1913] 3 KB 743; *Wait* v. *Baker* (1848) 2 Ex. 1; *Badische Anilin und Soda Fabrik* v. *Basle Chemical Works* [1898] AC 200; *Dutton* v. *Solomonson* (1803) 3 B & P 582; *Dunlop* v. *Lambert* (1839) 6 Cl. & Fin. 600, 620–1; *Calcutta & Burmah Steam Navigation Co. Ltd* v. *De Mattos* (1863) 32 LJ QB 322, 328; *Ex p. Pearson* (1868) 3 Ch. App 443.

[432] In an f.o.b. contract, these would consist principally of bill of lading and invoice. Where the bill of lading never comes into the seller's hands (see *Pyrene Co. Ltd* v. *Scindia Navigation Ltd* [1954] 2 QB 402) the contract is likely to require payment against the invoice and a mate's receipt. See *F. E. Napier* v. *Dexter's Ltd* (1926) 26 Ll. LR 62.

[433] S. 28 thus being displaced.

Where the buyer is bound by the contract to pay before examining the goods, attempts are sometimes made to free the buyer from this duty, especially where payment is to be effected through a banker's irrevocable letter of credit. In such cases, the question is not merely whether the buyer may resist payment but whether an issuing or confirming bank may be restrained from honouring its promise to pay the seller. The very reliability of the binding letter of credit may encourage dubious sales practices and put the buyer in the position of having to sue a remote foreign seller in an unfriendly forum. The bank's obligation to the buyer is to pay against a transfer of documents that on their face are conforming;[434] it would inhibit the free flow of international documentary transactions if the bank were required or permitted to penetrate the documents and look to the condition of the underlying goods.[435] For a similar reason, although the buyer has a reasonable time to reject non-conforming documents, the bank is not permitted to give the buyer time to scrutinize the documents.[436] Nevertheless, the possibility of going behind the documents emerges in a number of cases where the seller, the beneficiary of credit, has been guilty of fraud.

Fraud and Letters of Credit

The rule is that, where the seller is guilty of fraud, the bank is both entitled under the letter of credit undertaking to the seller and bound under its contract with the buyer to refuse payment. In other words, the two contracts between the bank and the seller beneficiary, and between the bank and the buyer applicant, contain matching obligations on the part of the bank.[437] The stage at which the seller's fraud is usually material is where the buyer is seeking to enjoin the bank from making payment.[438] The courts have been alive to the damage that too free an exercise of their discretion to enjoin payment might have on the relations *inter se* of the various banks in the system.[439] A rigorous standard of proof is required, the court being satisfied only with 'clear' evidence[440] of a high

---

[434] *Urquart, Lindsay & Co. Ltd* v. *Eastern Bank Ltd* [1922] 1 KB 318, 323; *Westpac Banking Corpn.* v. *South Carolina National Bank* [1986] 1 Lloyd's Rep. 311.

[435] UCP 500, Art. 4: all parties to credit operations deal in documents and not in goods and services.   [436] *Bankers Trust Co.* v. *State Bank of India* [1991] 2 Lloyd's Rep. 443.

[437] See *United City Merchants (Investments) Ltd* v. *Royal Bank of Canada* [1983] 1 AC 168, 185.

[438] *Edward Owen Ltd* v. *Barclays Bank* [1978] QB 159; *Rafsanjani Producers Co-operative Co.* v. *Bank Lenmi (UK) Plc* [1992] 1 Lloyd's Rep. 513.

[439] *Ibid.*; *Discount Records Ltd* v. *Barclays Bank* [1975] 1 WLR 315. But for the view that this can sometimes be overstated, see *United Trading Corpn. SA* v. *Allied Arab Bank Ltd* (1984) [1985] 2 Lloyd's Rep. 554 (note).

[440] *Ibid.*; *Edward Owen Ltd* v. *Barclays Bank*, n. 438 above; *Tukan Timber Ltd* v. *Barclays Bank Plc* [1987] 1 FTLR 154; *Bank of Nova Scotia* v. *Angelica-Whitewear Ltd* (1987) 36 DLR (4th) 161.

standard[441] of which the bank has notice.[442] The mere allegation of fraud is not sufficient[443] but it is overstating the case to say that the evidence must exclude any possibility of an innocent explanation.[444] Nevertheless, it is remarkably difficult to prove fraud so as to persuade the court to order the bank not to pay.[445]

The definition of fraud has at times been elusive.[446] Fraud is far from being established just because the conduct of the seller is 'suspicious' and suggests 'the possibility of sharp practice'.[447] The buyer must show that 'the documents . . . contain, expressly or by implication, material representations that to [the seller's] knowledge are untrue'.[448] Since the bank has not yet paid, the reliance that is normally part of fraud is to be found in the bank's potential reliance.[449] The court interferes because the seller is not allowed to take advantage of his own wrongdoing.[450] It follows that the seller must be a party to the fraud: payment will not be enjoined because of the fraud of a third party, which occurred in *United City Merchants*[451] where the seller was not privy to the falsification of the date of the bill of lading by a ship's loading broker. The court in that case left open the question whether the bank could be enjoined from paying if, apart from the fraud exception as thus defined, a document were a nullity. In that case, the falsely dated bill of lading was nonetheless a valid bill of lading and not, as a forged document would be, a nullity.

Concurrence of Payment and Delivery

A final difficulty arising from the buyer's payment duty is presented by section 28 of the Sale of Goods Act,[452] which states that, unless otherwise agreed,[453] delivery and payment are concurrent conditions. Why, if time of payment is presumptively not of the essence of contracts of sale,[454] and time of delivery is presumptively of the essence of commercial con-

---

[441] *Rafsanjani Producers Co-operative Co.* v. *Bank Leumi (UK) Plc*, n. 438 above.

[442] *Edward Owen Ltd* v. *Barclays Bank*, n. 438 above.

[443] *Bolivinter Oil SA* v. *Chase Manhattan Bank SA* [1984] 1 Lloyd's Rep. 251, 257; *Discount Records Ltd* v. *Barclays Bank* [1975] 1 WLR 315.

[444] *United Trading Corpn. SA* v. *Allied Arab Bank Ltd*, n. 439 above.

[445] In *Sztejn* v. *J. Henry Schroder Banking Corpn.* (1941) 31 NYS (2d) 31, the genesis of the fraud exception to the payment rule, fraud was assumed in an action on a preliminary point of law.

[446] It is not defined in *Sztejn* v. *J Henry Schroder Banking Corpn.*, n. 445 above.

[447] *Edward Owen Ltd* v. *Barclays Bank*, n. 438 above (Geoffrey Lane LJ).

[448] *United City Merchants (Investments) Ltd* v. *Royal Bank of Canada*, n. 437 above, 183.

[449] *Edward Owen Ltd* v. *Barclays Bank*, n. 438 above.   [450] *Ibid.* 184.

[451] N. 437 above.

[452] Stating the pre-Act common law: *Morton* v. *Lamb* (1797) 7 TR 125.

[453] As it frequently is in commercial sales where 30–day credit and more is commonplace.

[454] Sale of Goods, s. 10(1).

tracts[455] and an open question of construction in other cases,[456] is it possible to say that the duties of payment and delivery are concurrent, which is a clear statement of their equality? One critic has asked: 'Why . . . should the buyer be entitled to repudiate the bargain when the seller is unpunctual, but not the seller when the buyer is at fault?'[457]

One way to resolve the conflict is to assert that the law governing the seller's duty to deliver and the buyer's duty to pay did not develop evenly and the Act captured the law at a time of lop-sided development. Consequently, taking the view that the strictness of the buyer's duty is understated, the conclusion is that the buyer's duty to pay is of the essence whenever the seller's duty is of the essence.[458] This view prefers section 28 in the event of conflict with section 10(1). Another approach would be to modulate the language of section 10(1) by accepting that, while the time of payment may be presumptively not of the essence of all contracts, yet it is presumptively of the essence for that sub-class known as commercial sales agreements. The difficulty with this view is that the law was originally codified on the back of commercial contracts. One writer has stated that the seller's right under section 48(3) to resell the goods if the buyer does not pay within a reasonable time blunts the impact of section 10(1) and helps to reduce the conflict between it and section 28 to minor proportions.[459]

Another approach is to separate the buyer's duties of payment and acceptance and stress the absence of any reference to the latter in section 10(1); the buyer's duty of acceptance and the seller's duty of delivery could then be equalized. Sales practice allows the separation of the buyer's two duties. If a buyer is allowed to take delivery before payment, this effectuates the parties' intention that the buyer is to have credit. In such a case, it may be quite proper to conclude that the delinquent buyer's breach is not of a term that is of the essence of the contract; The seller has already surrendered his lien[460] and the difference between, for example, an agreed thirty days' credit and the thirty-one or more days taken by the buyer may not be essential. But if the terms of the contract require payment on delivery, the laying of emphasis upon the buyer's failure to take delivery in the manner required by the contract, that is, accompanied by payment,[461] brings out the critical point that it is the intention of the parties that the buyer is to receive no credit. As practically sensible as this approach is, it is hobbled by the failure of section 28 to make any reference to the buyer's duty of acceptance: it is the duty to pay that is said to be correlative with the seller's duty to deliver.

---

[455] *Bunge Corpn. v. Tradax Export SA* [1981] 2 All ER 513.   [456] S. 10(2).
[457] S. Stoljar (1955) 71 *LQR* 527, 538.   [458] See *Mooney* v. *Lipka* [1926] 4 DLR 647.
[459] P. S. Atiyah, *The Sale of Goods* (9th edn., Pitman, London, 1995 by J. N. Adams), 262.
[460] S. 43(1).   [461] S. 27.

The most elegant solution to this difficulty, and it is submitted the best one, is to accept that sections 10(1) and 28 both accurately reflect the law but to assert that a critical distinction exists between the order of performance of contractual obligations and the termination of contracts. Section 28 deals with the former and section 10(1) with the latter. A buyer unable or failing to pay where payment and delivery are concurrent could not call upon the seller to deliver since he has failed to perform a condition precedent to delivery, but this would not necessarily mean that the seller might terminate the contract on the day payment failed to materialize. If time of payment were not of the essence, the seller would in effect be entitled to suspend his own delivery obligation, citing in defence the buyer's non-payment, but would only be allowed to terminate the contract when the buyer's breach over time went to the root of the contract. Where the default is on the seller's side and time is of the essence of the seller's performance, the buyer would not have to wait but could terminate immediately upon the seller's breach. This solution accommodates the differing failure of consideration and dependent promises principles[462] and the contrasting cases of *Hongkong Fir Shipping Co. Ltd* v. *Kawasaki Kisen Kaisha Ltd*[463] and *Bunge Corpn.* v. *Tradax Export SA.*[464]

WAIVER OF DELIVERY AND PAYMENT OBLIGATIONS

Few words in contract law can be surrounded by so much terminological confusion as 'waiver'. First of all, it can refer to cases where a party (the waivor) excuses another (the waivee) from performing an obligation in full or in the manner or by the date required by the contract. In this sense, waiver operates to prevent the waivor from refusing modified performance from the waivee and from terminating the contract because the modified performance departs from the original contract standard; it also precludes a damages action for breach of contract brought by the waivor. Even here, waiver needs to be distinguished from rescission, variation, and promissory estoppel which, in pursuit of the same goals, have developed along different lines, largely because of difficulties posed by the old writing requirement for sale of goods and by the doctrine of consideration.[465] Secondly, waiver is used more loosely to connote an election between inconsistent rights, such that, the waivor having chosen one right, he is thereafter prevented from changing his mind and pursuing the other. If the waivor prevaricates, however, his decision may

---

[462] Ch. 5 above.   [463] [1962] 2 QB 26.   [464] N. 455 above.
[465] S. Stoljar (1957) 35 *Can. Bar Rev.* 485; G. H. Treitel, *The Law of Contract* (9th edn., Sweet & Maxwell, London, 1995), 725–9.

be made for him by the law.[466] Waiver in this second sense is dealt with explicitly in section 11(2) of the Sale of Goods Act, which states that the buyer, faced with a breach of condition by the seller, 'may elect to elect the breach of condition as a breach of warranty and not as a ground for treating the contract as repudiated'. Section 35 then puts such a waiver in the context of the buyer accepting the goods so as to lose the right to reject them and terminate the contract.[467] In this case, however, the buyer's right to damages for breach of contract is not extinguished.

It has been proposed that the above two meanings should be distinguished by referring to the first as 'total waiver' and the second as 'waiver in the sense of election'.[468] Both types of waiver demand a clear[469] representation by words or conduct emanating from the waivor,[470] but there are differences. Total waiver requires prejudicial reliance by the waivee on the representation, or such other alteration of position as would make it unfair or inequitable for the waivor to retract the representation.[471] Election waiver, however, imposes no such requirement[472] and is best seen as promoting the interests of certainty and constancy in contractual dealings: having approbated, the waivor may not reprobate.[473] In the case of total waiver, the requirement of a clear representation does not necessitate that the waivor knew the consequences of what he was doing or was aware of the legal significance of the step he was taking.[474] But since election waiver is based, not upon the reasonable interpretation by the waivee of the waivor's conduct, but rather upon the choice by the waivor between inconsistent rights, this choice needs to be an informed one.[475] How informed the choice must be is a difficult question: at one

---

[466] *The Kanchenjunga* [1990] 1 Lloyd's Rep. 391, 398 (Lord Goff).

[467] *Ibid.* [468] Treitel, n. 465 above.

[469] *Bunge SA* v. *Cie Européenne de Céréales* [1982] 2 Lloyd's Rep. 306; *Société Italo-Belge pour le Commerce et l'Industrie* v. *Palm and Vegetable Oils (Malaysia) Sdn. Bhd.* [1981] 2 Lloyd's Rep. 695.

[470] Other examples are: *Finagrain SA Geneva* v. *P. Kruse Hamburg* [1976] 2 Lloyd's Rep. 508; *Edm. J. M. Mertens & Co. PVBA* v. *Veevoder Import Export Vimex BV* [1979] 2 Lloyd's Rep. 372; *Peter Cremer* v. *Granaria BV* [1981] 2 Lloyd's Rep. 583; *Bunge SA* v. *Schleswig-Holsteinische Hauptgenossenschaft GmbH* [1978] 1 Lloyd's Rep. 480; *Bremer Handels GmbH* v. *Bunge Corpn.* [1983] 1 Lloyd's Rep. 476; *Bremer Handels GmbH* v. *Deutsche-Conti Handels GmbH* [1983] 2 Lloyd's Rep. 45; *Bremer Handels GmbH* v. *Raiffeisen EG* [1982] 1 Lloyd's Rep. 599; *Cobec Brazilian Trading and Warehousing Corpn.* v. *Alfred C. Toepfer* [1983] 2 Lloyd's Rep. 386.

[471] *Société Italo-Belge pour le Commerce et l'Industrie* v. *Palm and Vegetable Oils (Malaysia) Sdn. Bhd.*, n. 469 above.

[472] *Peyman* v. *Lanjani* [1985] Ch. 457.

[473] *Scarf* v. *Jardine* (1882) 7 App. Cas. 345; *Craine* v. *Colonial Mutual Fire Insurance Co.* (1920) 28 CLR 305, 326–7; *Clough* v. *LNWR Co.* (1871) LR 7 Ex. 26; *China National Foreign Trade Corpn.* v. *Evlogia Shipping* [1979] 1 WLR 1018; *Peyman* v. *Lanjani*, n. 472 above.

[474] *Peyman* v. *Lanjani*, n. 472 above, 189; *Panchaud Frères SA* v. *Ets. General Grain Co.* [1970] 1 Lloyd's Rep. 53; *The Kanchenjunga*, n. 466 above, 398–9.

[475] *Peyman* v. *Lanjani*, n. 472 above. This case shows that election may fail for want of knowledge but that the same conduct may give rise to a binding estoppel. Since the facts

end of the spectrum is the view that the waivor must know the facts supporting his right to choose without being aware of the legal significance of his choice,[476] or even that there is a right to choose,[477] while at the other end knowledge of the legal right to choose between inconsistent rights is necessary.[478] As pure as the latter approach may be, it does condone ignorance of the law. Moreover, if applied relentlessly in practice, it is doubtful that there could ever be a binding election. In the case where election is most likely to be of practical significance, namely, where the buyer wishes to reject the goods and terminate the contract, the acceptance rules of section 35 of the Sale of Goods Act create a special regime of election that excludes the issue of knowledge.

The factual difficulty of separating these two principal meanings of waiver is borne out by an examination of *Panoutsos* v. *Raymond Hadley Corpn. of New York.*[479] A divisible contract for the sale of 4,000 tons of flour provided that the buyer should pay for each shipment by means of a confirmed credit. The seller made a number of shipments before declining to make more on the ground that the credit opened by the buyer at the beginning of the shipment period was not a confirmed credit. The question was whether the seller, having taken no objection to the unconfirmed credit in the past, could cancel the contract without notice in respect of outstanding shipments. The answer was that the seller could not, but that his conduct in drawing knowingly on an unconfirmed credit would not prevent him from giving for the future reasonable notice that a confirmed credit be opened.

As regards past shipments, the conduct of the seller in shipping the goods might be seen as an election to affirm the contract, reserving any entitlement to claim damages; but each such act of condonation might also be seen as a representation by way of total waiver to the buyer that he could continue to make the unconfirmed credit available for future shipments. What makes it hard to separate the two waivers is that breaches of contract of this kind may not yield a provable damages claim, so that one distinguishing feature of the two waivers[480] is empirically

---

may support election and total waiver in close proximity, the confusion between the two waivers is hardly surprising: *Bremer Handels GmbH* v. *C. Mackprang Jr.* [1979] 1 Lloyds's Rep. 221.

[476] *Cerealgamani* v. *Toepfer* [1981] 1 Lloyd's Rep. 337.

[477] *Kammins Ballroom Co. Ltd* v. *Zenith Investments Ltd* [1971] AC 850, 863 (Lord Diplock).

[478] *Peyman* v. *Lanjani*, n. 472 above, 188. This view received a cool reception from Lord Goff in *The Kanchenjunga*, n. 466 above, 398–9. *Peyman* asserts also that the elector need not know that his choice is irrevocable (at 180) or understand the legal consequences of his choice.

[479] [1917] 1 KB 767.

[480] *Ets. Soules & Cie* v. *International Trade Development Co.* [1979] 1 Lloyd's Rep. 122, 133, affd. on this point [1980] 1 Lloyd's Rep. 129.

absent. In addition, the divisibility of the contract means that any election by the seller relates only to the particular shipment, a state of affairs which, again empirically, is hard to distinguish from the freedom given to a total waivor in contracts involving continual or protracted performance to retract the waiver upon reasonable notice to the waivee. By stating that the seller could reinstate the need for a confirmed credit upon reasonable notice to the buyer, the court would seem to have applied a version of total waiver.[481] But this does not mean that the history of the transaction to date could not be explained in terms of election waiver; indeed, the seller's action in making the *first* shipment against the unconfirmed credit, no prior material representation having been made to the buyer, could only be explained as election waiver in relation to that shipment.

The need to distinguish the two types of waiver is also evident in *Panchaud Frères SA* v. *Ets. General Grain Co.*,[482] which concerned a contract for the sale of 5,500 tonnes of Brazilian yellow maize c.i.f. Antwerp, shipment June/July. The sellers tendered a bill of lading relating to one shipment for 200 tonnes dated 31 July but an accompanying inspection certificate clearly showed that shipment had occurred around 10 to 12 August.[483] When the documents were tendered, the buyers paid without objection and, raising the issue of late shipment some two years after the dispute with the sellers arose, were held to have lost the right to reject the goods on that ground. Lord Denning explained the result in terms of total waiver or, as he preferred to call it, estoppel by conduct,[484] since the seller had been led to believe that strict rejection rights for late shipment would not be enforced.[485] Yet he confused the picture by introducing as an example of such an estoppel the acceptance rules in section 35 of the Sale of Goods Act. These have nothing to do with total waiver;[486] they amount to a statutorily modified version of election waiver that leaves intact the buyer's right to claim damages, a right that would disappear in the case of total waiver and its cognates, such as estoppel by conduct and promissory estoppel. Winn LJ also thought in terms of total waiver

---

[481] By way of contrast, a court's conclusion that the acceptance of non-conforming performance in the past under a divisible contract is no representation that similar performance will be accepted in the future seems more in line with election waiver. See, e.g., *Jackson* v. *Rotax Motor and Cycle Co.* [1910] 2 KB 937; *Finagrain SA Geneva* v. *P. Kruse Hamburg*, n. 470 above.

[482] N. 473 above. It was applied in *Bunge GmbH* v. *Alfred C. Toepfer* [1978] 1 Lloyd's Rep. 506 and distinguished in *V. Berg & Son Ltd* v. *Vanden-Avenne Izegem PVBA* [1977] 1 Lloyd's Rep. 499.

[483] In any conflict of dates between the two documents, the date in the certificate is to be preferred because an independent inspector has no reason to falsify the date, whereas bills of lading are notoriously dated on that most elastic of dates, the last of the month.

[484] See also *Intertradex SA* v. *Lesieur Tourteaux SARL* [1978] 2 Lloyd's Rep. 509.

[485] N. 474 above, 57.

[486] See *BP Exploration Co. (Libya) Ltd* v. *Hunt* [1979] 1 WLR 783, 810–12 (Robert Goff LJ).

though he preferred to reword it as a requirement of fair conduct between the parties.[487] Yet he too introduced confusion with election waiver by going on to say that '[t]here may be an inchoate doctrine stemming from the manifest convenience of consistency in pragmatic affairs, negativing any liberty to blow hot and cold in commercial conduct'.[488]

Given the above lack of clarity in the law, it was no great surprise that the claim was made by a seller in a subsequent case[489] that the buyers' taking up of manifestly non-conforming documents amounted also to a representation that they would not pursue a damages claim against the seller; the court, however, found no sufficiently clear representation to this effect.[490] The problem is compounded by the fusion of total waiver, exercised in the past by common law courts in respect of the manner and time of payment and delivery, but not the substance of those obligations, and promissory estoppel,[491] which has been applied to alter with permanent effect the substance of contractual obligations. Since promissory estoppel is capable of having such permanent characteristics, it becomes all the more important not to confuse it with election waiver.

As stated above, total waiver has been preoccupied in the past with the modalities as opposed to the substance of contractual performance. For example, in *Hartley* v. *Hymans*[492] a contract for the sale of 11,000 pounds of cotton yarn required delivery at the rate of 1,100 pounds a week. The buyers could have terminated for the various delays of the sellers in making deliveries, but their demand for better deliveries induced the sellers to believe that the contract was still on foot. Without giving the sellers notice that outstanding deliveries should be made within a reasonable time, the buyers peremptorily repudiated the contract. McCardie J held that the conduct of the buyers in pressing the sellers for further deliveries implied a new agreement that these deliveries could be made in an extended, reasonable period to be defined by the buyers. But the buyers

---

[487] N. 474 above, 59. For the view that the *Panchaud* principle should be applied with 'robustness' and that grain traders are not 'fragile characters wilting under the ups and downs of international trade', see *V. Berg & Son Ltd* v. *Vanden-Avenne Izegem PVBA*, n. 482 above, 505 (Lawton LJ).

[488] N. 474 above, 59. In *BP Exploration Co. (Libya) Ltd* v. *Hunt*, n. 486 above, 810–12, Robert Goff LJ is under no doubt that the root of *Panchaud Frères* is election waiver: 'The decision stems from the need for finality in commercial transactions. . . . [It] does not depend in any way on the representee having relied upon any representation by the buyer'.

[489] *Ets. Soules & Cie* v. *International Trade Development Co.* [1980] 1 Lloyd's Rep. 129.

[490] See too *Cook Industries Inc.* v. *Meuneries Liégeoises SA* [1981] 1 Lloyd's Rep. 359; *Bunge SA* v. *Cie Européenne de Céréales* [1982] 2 Lloyd's Rep. 306; *Bremer Handels GmbH* v. *Finagrain Cie Commerciale Agricole et Financière SA* [1981] 2 Lloyd's Rep. 259. See also Robert Goff LJ in *Ets. Soules & Cie*, n. 489 above, 133: 'Now there is no question of the buyers being deprived of their right to claim damages by any application of the doctrine of election. The sellers recognize that what they must do is to invoke the principle of equitable estoppel'.

[491] *Charles Rickards Ltd* v. *Oppenhaim* [1950] 1 KB 616.   [492] [1920] 3 KB 475.

never did define this further period and were liable in damages for non-acceptance when not honouring their undertaking to accept the outstanding deliveries.

The place of delivery was the subject of a waiver in another case[493] where the goods were to be shipped through Ostend but the sellers rerouted them through Rotterdam.[494] The buyer made no objection when the sellers announced this was to happen. The ship carrying the rerouted goods was stranded and the goods lost. Since the buyer by his conduct had waived the sellers' obligation to ship *via* Ostend, it meant that the risk had passed to the buyer who therefore was liable to pay the price.

A waiver of the due delivery date arose in *Charles Rickards Ltd* v. *Oppenhaim*[495] where a contract for the sale of a coach-built car required delivery at the latest within seven months. When the car was not delivered on time, the buyer continued to press for delivery; he had thus elected not to terminate and had represented to the seller that he would accept a late delivery. After further delays, the buyer informed the seller that he would not accept the car after a stated future date, which the seller was again unable to meet. The seller argued that the buyer's waiver of the original delivery date, which was of the essence of the contract, meant that time was now at large. Delivery thereafter had to be made within a reasonable time, a formula that should take account of the seller's material and labour difficulties. The court, however, found for the buyer who was entitled by a proper notice to make time of the essence again.[496] In this sense, the buyer's waiver was revocable on reasonable notice, but a seller irrevocably relying upon a buyer's waiver, such as the seller shipping through Rotterdam instead of Ostend, should fear no such change of mind by the buyer.

---

[493] *Leather-Cloth Co.* v. *Hieronimus* (1875) LR 10 QB 140.

[494] In fact Ostend had been initially chosen over Rotterdam only because the latter had earlier been ice-bound.

[495] N. 491 above.

[496] No notice would be required if a specific extension period is given and lapses: *Nichimen Corpn.* v. *Gatoil Overseas Inc.* [1987] 2 Lloyd' Rep. 46.

7

The Implied Terms of Description, Fitness, and Quality

This Chapter deals with terms concerning the description, fitness, and quality of the contract goods that are implied by statute into the contract[1] unless the parties have excluded them within the limits permitted by the law.[2] An examination of the general law of contract shows that it is not easy to pin down the nature of implied contractual terms. Expressed as a crude dichotomy, they come in two different versions: first, terms agreed in fact by the parties that are either so obvious that they do not need to be stated[3] or that the parties have not troubled to record in writing;[4] and secondly, those terms implied by law into contracts to give them a minimum of business efficacy,[5] doubtless in accordance with the paramount intention of the parties to create a workable contractual agreement.[6] One explanation of certain implied terms is that initially they express the actual agreement of contracting parties but that, under the weight of case law and inherited assumptions, they become over time automatic accessories of particular contract types.[7] The final stages in the development of an implied term may then be seen in its incorporation in a statute that codifies the common law and in subsequent attempts by common law and statutory means to prevent its exclusion. It

---

[1] In so far as certain statutory changes made to the original Act of 1893 affect the substance of the terms, note should be taken of the implementation dates of these changes: see Sale of Goods Act 1979, Sched. 1 for the position before and after the Supply of Goods (Implied Terms) Act 1973. (References hereinafter to the law before and after 1973 are to the passing of this Act.) See also the Sale and Supply of Goods Act 1994 for the position after 2 Jan. 1995.

[2] On exclusion and similar clauses, see Ch. 8 below.

[3] *Shirlaw* v. *Southern Foundries (1926) Ltd* [1939] 2 KB 206; *Trollope and Colls Ltd* v. *North West Regional Hospital Board* [1973] 1 WLR 601.

[4] *Liverpool City Council* v. *Irwin* [1977] AC 239.

[5] *The Moorcock* (1889) 14 PD 64; *Lister* v. *Romford Ice Co. Ltd* [1957] AC 555.

[6] Cf. Lord Tomlin in *Hillas & Co. Ltd* v. *Arcos* [1932] All ER 494, 499: '[T]he problem for a court of construction must always be so to balance matters that, without violation of essential principle, the dealings of men may so far as possible be treated as effective, and that the law may not incur the reproach of being the destroyer of bargains.'

[7] Cf. Lord Radcliffe in *Lister* v. *Romford Ice Co. Ltd* [1957] AC 555, 591–2: '[T]he common law is a body of law which develops in process of time in response to the developments of society in which it rules. Its movement may not be perceptible at any distinct point of time, nor can we always see how it gets from one point to another; but I do not think that, for all that, we need abandon the conviction of Galileo that somehow, by some means, there is a movement.'

is arguable that this has been the history of implied terms the subject of this Chapter. Nevertheless, there is a powerful and compelling contrary argument that the nineteenth-century cases laid down in an interventionist way these implied terms from the outset as rules of law.[8]

Whatever may be the origin of the implied terms, section 14(1) of the Sale of Goods Act states that no other implied terms of fitness and quality exist in a contract of sale[9] apart from those laid down in section 14,[10] thereby declaring that section 14 is a complete code of implied fitness and quality. This provision, it is submitted, ought not to be read as ousting a term that can genuinely be implied in fact,[11] though one should not underestimate the flexibility and range of the statutory implied terms. The statutory scheme of implied terms may be seen as a device that pre-empts much litigation about quality and fitness, setting a standard against which the parties can define their contractual rights and duties.

The implied terms provide buyers with a healthy measure of protection against defective, disappointing, and substandard goods.[12] Yet it is surprising how ill-informed is the population at large on this matter and how beguiling are the adverse beliefs that manufacturers and not retailers are liable for defective goods, and that buyers may freely return goods to retail sellers for no other reason than a change of mind. Inside this stew of adages and attitudes, one finds the maxim *caveat emptor*. It lingers in section 14(1) but its pedigree and meaning are both obscure. Translated literally, it subjunctively exhorts buyers to beware, and buyers exhibit proper caution who examine goods carefully before they purchase them or secure from the seller an express warranty. As a general bar to recovery, *caveat emptor* belongs to a primitive economy of specific goods and concrete transactions. Even at its height, it never condoned fraud and other unscrupulous practices; if it has a meaning today, the maxim does not instruct buyers that they contract at their own risk but that they should take sensible precautions. *Caveat emptor* has been severely criticized for its spurious Roman pretensions and its incompatibility with mediaeval and religious notions of sellers' obligations for the quality of their wares. It has been described as a nineteenth-century invention that 'sharpened wits, taught self-reliance, [and] made a man—an economic man—out of the buyer'.[13] The lingering presence of *caveat emptor* in section 14(1) is rendered insignificant by the extensive

---

[8] See B. Nicholas, 'Fault and Breach of Contract', in J. Beatson and D. Friedmann (eds.), *Good Faith and Fault in Contract Law* (OUP, London, 1995). Support for this view comes from the language of the judgment of Best CJ in *Jones* v. *Bright* (1829) 5 Bing. 533.

[9] See *McDonald* v. *Empire Garage (Blackburn) Ltd*, *The Times*, 8 Oct. 1975.

[10] And s. 15 for sales by sample.

[11] S. 62(2) permits the incorporation of supplementary common law.

[12] As for express guarantees and warranties, see Ch. 8 above.

[13] W. H. Hamilton, 'The Ancient Maxim Caveat Emptor' (1928) 40 *Yale LJ* 1133, 1186.

protection afforded to buyers by the implied terms in that section as well as by guarantees and product liability provisions.[14]

According to section 13(1) of the Sale of Goods Act,[15] it is an implied term of the contract that the goods shall correspond with their description where the contract is for the sale of goods by description. This term has the status of a condition. This provision prompts two principal questions.[16] First, when does a sale of goods agreement take place by description, and secondly, which words used constitute that description? The words of section 13(1) afford no help in answering either question but some assistance is given in answering the first question by section 13(3), which states that exposing goods for sale or hire does not prevent a sale of goods from being a sale by description. As for the second question, section 13(2) makes it clear that, in the case of a sale by sample, the compliance of the goods with the sample does not dispense with the need to comply also with the description.[17]

Description and Satisfactory Quality

A long-standing difficulty with the description condition has been its relationship over the years with the merchantable (now satisfactory) quality condition. Formerly,[18] in order for the merchantable quality condition to apply, the goods had to be 'bought by description from a seller who deals in goods of that description'; section 13 therefore operated as a gateway into the merchantable quality condition in section 14(2). The tendency in some older authorities to assert that a sale of specific goods is not a sale by description[19] is a clear example of *caveat emptor* thinking. Denying the application of section 13 served to exclude merchantable quality and meant that a buyer, unless able to rely upon the fitness for purpose condition, had to protect himself either by a careful pre-examination of the goods or by bargaining with the seller for an express warranty. The enactment of the Sale of Goods Act in 1893 changed the law by providing that the opportunity to examine goods did not as such rule out

---

[14] Ch. 8 below.

[15] As modified by the Sale and Supply of Goods Act 1994, Sched. 2.

[16] There is a confusing tendency in the cases to conflate them. See, e.g., *Harlingdon and Leinster Enterprises Ltd* v. *Christopher Hull Fine Art Ltd* [1991] 1 QB 564 (Nourse LJ).

[17] For the pre-statutory position, see *Nichol* v. *Godts* (1854) 10 Ex. 191; *Azémar* v. *Casella* (1867) LR 2 CP 431; *Josling* v. *Kingsford* (1863) 13 CBNS 447.

[18] Before 1973.   [19] Discussed in the text accompanying nn. 27 ff. below.

merchantable quality;[20] rather, it was excluded only by an actual examination and then to the extent only of 'defects which such examination ought to have revealed'.[21] Now, since goods available for pre-contractual examination had to be specific goods or part of a specific bulk, this meant that the merchantable quality condition could, despite the *caveat emptor* maxim, apply to specific goods;[22] it meant also that the sales of some specific goods at least had to be sales by description.

The intimate connection between description and merchantable quality is also revealed by the difficulty of distinguishing them in the early cases. For example, in *Gardiner* v. *Gray*,[23] Lord Ellenborough said of a contract for the sale of twelve bags of waste silk:

[T]he purchaser has a right to expect a saleable article answering the description in the contract. Without any particular warranty, this is an implied term in every such contract. Where there is no opportunity to inspect the commodity, the maxim *caveat emptor* does not apply. He cannot without a warranty insist that it shall be of any particular quality or fineness, but the intention of both parties must be taken to be, that it shall be saleable in the market under the denomination mentioned in the contract between them. The purchaser cannot be supposed to buy goods to lay them on a dunghill.

Later cases, however, showed there was more to merchantable quality than saleability under the contract description. Goods might satisfy the contract description and yet be unmerchantable;[24] it was never likely that goods could be of merchantable quality without complying with their description.

Lord Ellenborough's words are useful in positing a distinction, not between specific and unascertained goods as such, but between goods that could and goods that could not have been examined before the contract. As will be seen, this has had an impact not just on the presence of the description condition but also on its range in a given case. The early existence of a description requirement in at least some specific goods cases is also apparent in the way that description can apply to a sale by sample[25] for, in effect, the buyer is being offered an implicit assurance that he will receive the specific goods, or that the goods supplied will come from the specific bulk, from which the sample is drawn. Yet the belief, once entertained, that specific goods are sold as such and not by description has been responsible for difficulties, experienced into the

---

[20] Cf. *Jones* v. *Just* (1868) LR 3 QB 197, where examination precluded protection even against latent, undiscoverable defects. The law was otherwise in the case of latent misdescription: *Josling* v. *Kingsford*, n. 17 above.

[21] S. 14(2) of the 1893 Act.   [22] *Taylor* v. *Combined Buyers Ltd* [1924] NZLR 627, 635.

[23] (1815) 4 Camp. 144, 145. See also *Wieler* v. *Schilizzi* (1856) 17 CB 619; *Mody* v. *Gregson* (1868) LR 4 Ex. 49.

[24] *Jones* v. *Just*, n. 20 above, and cases discussed below.

[25] Referred to in the text accompanying n. 17 above.

twentieth century, about whether a sale can take place otherwise than by description. It seems also to be what lies at the root of statements made in certain cases[26] that descriptive language used with regard to specific goods is not promissory but amounts to a non-promissory condition precedent that the seller must meet for the buyer to be required to take delivery of the goods.

Sale by Description

As stated above, section 13(1) is of no help in showing when a sale takes place by description. The issue here is not how far the range of description goes in a given case but whether there is any description at all. The presence of at least some descriptive language is needed before section 13(1) can apply to a particular contract; the range of the description then determines whether section 13(1) has been infringed. Section 13(3)[27] provides: 'A sale of goods is not prevented from being a sale by description by reason only that, being exposed for sale or hire, they are selected by the buyer.' Because this provision again does not cover the range of description, its enactment was probably unnecessary since, at the same time, the merchantable quality condition was amended so as to remove any need for the sale to take place by description. Be that as it may, this provision removed any lingering doubt that the selection of goods by a buyer from a shelf in a retail store prevented a sale from taking place by description;[28] it did not, however, assert that such a sale necessarily did take place by description, or that all sales were in one degree or another sales by description.

Where the contract is for unascertained goods, it is beyond controversy that the sale must be by description since the buyer must have some means of knowing whether the goods tendered by the seller are the goods called for by the contract. More difficult in such a case is the range of the description and, in particular, the difference between words that identify goods and those that denote the quality of goods.[29] Specific goods, on the other hand, have been identified and agreed upon at the contract date. Where the buyer has seen the goods,[30] he may not need words from the seller to recognize them when they are delivered at a later

---

[26] *Bannerman* v. *White* (1861) 10 CB(NS) 844; *Taylor* v. *Combined Buyers Ltd*, n. 22 above; *Wallis, Son and Wells* v. *Pratt & Haynes* [1910] 2 KB 1003, 1018 (Farwell LJ); *Chanter* v. *Hopkins* (1838) 4 M & W 399 (supporting the view that the seller's liability is for failure to deliver and not for the breach of a description term).

[27] Dating from 1973 with minor changes made in 1979.

[28] See *Wren* v. *Holt* [1903] 1 KB 610, 615.

[29] Discussed in the text accompanying nn. 40 ff. below.

[30] In some cases of specific goods, the buyer will not have seen them, e.g., *Varley* v. *Whipp* [1900] 1 QB 513.

date, but does this mean that such a sale does not take place by description?

In *Taylor* v. *Combined Buyers Ltd*, Salmond J said:

> In the case of specific articles . . . it is possible to sell them without any description at all. The article sold may conceivably be identified merely by its presence and sold *tale quale* without any description of its nature whatever, the buyer taking the chance, for example, as to whether the artice submitted to him is a diamond or a piece of glass. In practice, however, even specific articles are generally sold by description in some sense. They are sold as being of some specified or disclosed nature. An animal is sold as a horse, or as a cow. A precious stone is sold as being a diamond or a ruby.[31]

In other words, specific goods are, apart from exceptional cases, sold by description.[32] In *Grant* v. *Australian Knitting Mills Ltd*, Lord Wright made it clear that the sale of items in a retail store took place by description:[33]

> It may be pointed out that there is a sale by description even though the buyer is buying something displayed before him on the counter: a thing is sold by description, though it is specific, so long as it is not sold merely as the specific thing but as a thing corresponding to a description, e.g., woollen undergarments, a hot-water bottle, a second-hand reaping machine, to select a few obvious examples.[34]

To make sense of it all, it should be understood that words of description need not take a written or oral form; they can be circumstantial. It is not for nothing that section 13 deals with the *implied* condition of correspondence with description. Beyond the proposition that a seller may employ words of description and yet not give an express warranty, a nineteenth-century truth that seems outmoded in modern times, the language of section 13(1) also underlines that description is coloured by place and conduct. To revert to Salmond J's example in *Taylor* v. *Combined Buyers Ltd*,[35] a buyer may take the chance of an item proffered being either diamond or glass, but it would be a most unusual contract. Expensive jewellery stores sell gems, not pieces of glass, and the price demanded of the buyer will be the price commanded by a gem and not a

---

[31] N. 22 above, 633–4. See also *ibid.*, 635–6: '[T]he mere fact that a sale is a sale of a specific chattel is not conclusive to show that it is not a sale by description'.

[32] [1936] AC 85, 100.

[33] A proposition more tentatively expressed in the later s. 13(3).

[34] See also *Thornett* v. *Fehr & Beers* [1919] 1 KB 486, 488–9; *David Jones Ltd* v. *Willis* (1934) 52 CLR 110; *Godley* v. *Perry* [1960] 1 WLR 9; *Beale* v. *Taylor* [1967] 1 WLR 1193; *Morelli* v. *Fitch and Gibbons* [1928] 2 KB 636; *Yelland* v. *National Cafe* (1955) 16 WWR 529. Cf. Vaughan Williams LJ in *Wren* v. *Holt*, n. 28 above. Opinion was divided in *Wallis* v. *Russell* [1902] 2 IR 585.

[35] N. 22 above.

piece of glass. In such circumstances, even if the word diamond is not used, the sale of an item got up to look like a diamond and priced like a diamond will be a sale by description of a diamond; the quality of the diamond, however, will be a different matter. Similarly, if a customer picks up in a supermarket a banana that turns out to be made of wax, it will not avail the seller to argue that the customer bought the specific article *tale quale*, taking the chance of it being real or waxen. The contract would be for the sale of a banana.

Since description and merchantable quality have now been separated by legislative means, and since the seller's liability under section 13(1) depends upon the range of the contractual description, the way seems clear for asserting that all sales are sales by description, albeit in varying degrees. If a buyer and seller agree on 'that thing' out of two similar-looking items, the seller may deliver only the item that he and the buyer have identified by words and gesture. Likewise, the identification of 'that thing' when gesture can refer only to one item would not allow the seller to deliver a quite different item. In all sale of goods contracts, the seller is bound to deliver the agreed goods; even in the most barebones contract, this delivery obligation has to be attachable to some goods and, to the extent that it is so attached, expresses a description requirement, even one so rudimentary as merely to restate the delivery duty in section 27.[36] It is entirely possible that a sale of goods, not known to be diamond or glass, might take place as a sale of 'that thing'[37] but even such limited words are descriptive. Nevertheless, as stated above, the context of the sale may extend the range of the description beyond this modest content. The contract may allocate the risk of the item being either diamond or glass to the buyer, but where the context points to diamond the seller may fall foul of the various rules governing exclusion clauses, including those in the Unfair Contract Terms Act 1977.[38] The line between defining an obligation and excluding it can be a very difficult one to draw, especially the closer one gets to the rudimentary descriptive core of an item. It should not be forgotten that a contract may give the seller the right to tender peas or beans;[39] but the description would still be 'peas or beans' and the seller could not tender cabbages.

[36] Consistent with this approach is the sale by sample case of *Mody* v. *Gregson* (1868) LR 4 Ex. 49.

[37] *Wood* v. *Boynton* (1885) 25 NW 42 (US).   [38] Ch. 8 below.

[39] See the extrajudicial example given by Lord Devlin [1966] *CLJ* 192, 212 (a contract for peas, beans or something else satisfied by delivery of peas, beans or something *eiusdem generis*).

Words of Description

In the modern law, the most important issue is the range of the contractual description, the chief difficulty being the separation of words of description and of quality. Another important theme, bulking increasingly large nowadays, is the relationship of description to the law governing express warranties and misrepresentations.[40] The issue of the range of description has arisen in a number of practical settings, such as the application of an exclusion clause,[41] the scope of the merchantable quality condition,[42] the acceptance rules in sections 11 and 35[43] and the extent of a private seller's liability under section 13(1).[44]

To understand the modern law, it is first necessary to consider the development of description through some of the earlier cases. Those decided prior to *Varley* v. *Whipp*[45] fail to reveal a clear distinction between specific and unascertained goods; what seems to be critical was whether the buyer had the opportunity to examine the goods before the contract was concluded. A number of unascertained goods cases at that time required the seller to deliver goods that conformed to the identity of those agreed upon at the contract date, as opposed to any collateral attributes they might have been represented as having. Thus a seller was held in breach who supplied 'Western Madras' cotton, an inferior type, instead of the 'Long-staple Salem' cotton called for by the contract;[46] likewise another who supplied 'scarlet cuttings' with an adulterative addition of serge so that the goods did not conform to the market understanding of 'scarlet cuttings'.[47]

In *Chanter* v. *Hopkins*,[48] the seller installed in the buyer's brewery a 'Chanter's smoke-consuming furnace' that failed to do the job for which it was required. The case turned primarily upon whether the seller was liable for the machine's failure, but it raises two points of interest for the purposes of description. First, the machine was treated by the court as more akin to specific than to ascertained goods, since the subject matter of the contract was a 'defined and well-known machine' of which the seller was known to hold the patent, clearly an assumption that the attributes of mass-produced articles do not vary in the way that they do for natural commodities. Secondly, Abinger CB made it plain in a well-known passage that a failure by the seller to comply with the contractual

---

[40] Discussed in the text accompanying nn. 107 ff. above.
[41] See, e.g. *Nichol* v. *Godts* (1854) 10 Ex. 191; *Azémar* v. *Casella* (1867) LR 2 CP 431; *Josling* v. *Kingsford* (1863) 13 CB(NS) 447; *Shepherd* v. *Kain* (1821) 5 B & Ald. 240 ('copper-fastened vessel' taken 'with all faults'). See too *Viger Bros.* v. *Sanderson Bros.* [1901] 1 KB 508.
[42] Discussed below. 　　　　　　　　　　　[43] *Varley* v. *Whipp*, n. 30 above.
[44] *Beale* v. *Taylor*, n. 34 above. A private seller incurs no liability under s. 14.
[45] N. 30 above. 　　　　　　　　　　　　　[46] *Azémar* v. *Casella*, n. 17 above.
[47] *Bridge* v. *Wain* (1816) 1 Stark. 504. 　　[48] (1838) 4 M & W 399.

description meant that he had not delivered the contract goods at all, rather than that he had delivered non-conforming goods:

A warranty is an express or implied statement of something which a party undertakes shall be part of a contract, and though part of the contract, collateral to the express object of it. But in many of the cases, the circumstance of a party selling a particular thing by its proper description has been called a warranty, and the breach of such a contract a breach of warranty; but it would be better to distinguish such cases as a non-compliance with a contract which a party has engaged to fulfil; as if a man offers to buy peas of another and he sends him beans, he does not perform his contract; but that is not a warranty; there is no warranty that he should sell him peas, the contract is to sell peas, and if he sells him anything else in their stead, it is a non-performance of it.[49]

This passage has had a substantial impact on the law governing exclusion clauses as well as on the pre-1967 law concerning the buyer's right to reject specific goods where the seller was in breach of his description obligation.[50] It is consistent, too, with a narrow range being given to description, to which end a better example than a contract to supply peas instead of beans could hardly have been chosen.

In a number of nineteenth-century cases, description was held to have been infringed in the case of specific goods unseen by the buyer prior to the contract. Thus the seller on c.i.f. terms of a specific cargo afloat, described as 'Calcutta linseed, *tale quale*', was held to be in breach of contract when the cargo turned out to be heavily adulterated with rape and mustard seed.[51] Similarly, a seller by sample of 'foreign refined rape oil' that was adulterated with hemp oil was unable to sue the buyer for damages for non-acceptance since the goods were not those called for by the contract.[52] In the case of a sale of a specific ship that, unknown to the parties, had gone aground in the Gulf of St Lawrence at the contract date, the question was whether the goods could still be described as a 'ship'; inclement weather and the remoteness of the location greatly reduced the chances of getting the ship off the rock that would have existed closer to England.[53] Even in the case of specific goods examined before the contract, the description obligation could still be infringed where the examination did not and could not have discovered a latent misdescription, as where the substantial admixture of Epsom salts could not be detected by the naked eye in a quantity of oxalic acid.[54]

[49] (1838) 4 M & W 404.   [50] *Varley* v. *Whipp*, n. 30 above.
[51] *Wieler* v. *Schilizzi*, n. 23 above. The cargo was only about 85% pure, instead of the 97–98% which the commodity was capable of attaining.
[52] *Nichol* v. *Godts*, n. 17 above.
[53] *Barr* v. *Gibson* (1838) 3 M & W 390. The case was sent for retrial since the court refused to admit in the definition of a 'ship' any geographical diversity.
[54] *Josling* v. *Kingsford*, n. 17 above.

Deficient as the above cases were in any philosophical discussion of the distinction between essence and attributes, they are generally quite consistent with description being limited to the essential nature or identity of the contract goods.[55] An expansion of the range of description is, however, evident in *Bowes* v. *Shand*,[56] where it was invoked to justify a strict approach to timely shipment of an agreed quantity of unascertained goods and is apparent too in *Varley* v. *Whipp*.[57] The latter contract was for the sale of 'a second-hand self-binder reaping machine . . . new the previous year, and only . . . used to cut fifty or sixty acres'. The seller delivered the reaper free on rail and the buyer returned it to the seller after some unsatisfactory correspondence. At no time prior to the contract had the buyer seen the machine;[58] indeed, it was owned by a third party until bought by the seller after he had entered into a binding contract with the buyer.[59] The machine turned out to be an old, heavily used, mended machine. The Divisional Court found a breach of section 13. Bucknill J was clearly of the view that all of the above-quoted words went to description;[60] Channell J gave no ruling as such but cited as examples of a breach an agreement to supply the 4-year-old horse in the last stall of a stable, which contained instead a cow or a horse of a different age.[61] Channell J also went on to say that there would be a breach of a 'collateral warranty'[62] if a horse stated to be sound proved not to be so. If these examples are a sure guide, both judges would probably agree that the words 'second-hand self-binder reaping machine . . . new the previous year' went to description; there might have been disagreement over the words 'at Upton' and there could well have been disagreement over the words 'only . . . used to cut fifty or sixty acres'.[63]

The drawing of the line between description and incidental quality was explored further by Bailhache J in *T. & J. Harrison* v. *Knowles &*

---

[55] Perhaps surprisingly, there appears at this stage of development no explicit link with the authorities on common law mistake, such as *Kennedy* v. *Australia, New Zealand and Panama Royal Mail Co.* (1867) LR 2 QB 580, restated in *Bell* v. *Lever Bros. Ltd* [1932] AC 161.

[56] (1877) 2 App. Cas. 455. The effects of this are still to be seen: *Coastal (Bermuda) Petroleum Ltd* v. *VTT Vulcan Petroleum SA (The Marine Star)* [1994] CLC 1019 (date of shipment); *Petrograde Inc.* v. *Stinnes Handels GmbH* [1995] 1 Lloyd's Rep. 142 (port of shipment).

[57] [1900] 1 QB 513.   [58] But it was still a contract for specific goods.

[59] The goods were future goods (s. 5(1)) as well as specific goods.

[60] N. 57 above, 517.

[61] *Ibid.* 516. Somewhat elliptically, he locates his discussion of description in the passage dealing with the passing of property.

[62] N. 57 above, 516, showing the influence of Abinger CB in *Chanter* v. *Hopkins*, n. 48 above.

[63] The case has been criticized in the Commonwealth: *Taylor* v. *Combined Buyers Ltd* [1924] NZLR 627, 643 (Salmond J: 'difficult and unsatisfactory'); *New Hamburg Manufacturing Co.* v. *Webb* (1911) 23 OLR 44, 54 (Riddell J: 'going to the very verge (some will say going beyond)').

Foster[64] where the judge was at pains to say that his observations were confined to 'the sale of an existing specific chattel'.[65] The contract concerned two sister ships[66] stated by the seller to have a dead-weight capacity of 460 tons. After taking delivery of the ships, the buyer's examination of one of them showed that its deadweight capacity came to only 360 tons. This made the ships useless for the purpose the buyers had in mind, namely, plying for cargo between West African rivers and the ocean, a purpose they had not disclosed to the sellers. In discussing whether the words about the ships' capacity went to contractual description or collateral warranty, Bailhache put the matter in terms of the difference between condition and warranty,[67] the merit of which is that it aligns the law of description and of express warranty and limits the divergence of the general law of contract and the special law of sale. Concluding that the words of capacity amounted to a warranty, Bailhache J made it clear that 'the absence of such quality or the possession of it to a smaller extent [did not make] the thing sold different in kind from the thing described in the contract'.[68] The difference between the two tonnage figures was 'essentially one of degree and not of kind'.[69]

Specific and Unascertained Goods

The decisions in *Varley* and *T. & J. Harrison* were carefully considered by Salmond J in *Taylor* v. *Combined Buyers Ltd*[70] when proposing a sharp division between the range of description for both specific and for unascertained goods. In the case of unascertained goods, he asserted:

The description defines the contractual obligation of the vendor. He has promised to deliver under his contract goods of a certain number, quality, kind, state, quantity, condition, or other attributes. If he subsequently delivers goods which in any respect whatever fail to conform to this contractual description of them he has broken his contract, and the buyer is not bound to accept the goods. The statutory implied condition of correspondence with the description means in the case of unascertained goods that a buyer is not bound to accept in performance of the contract a delivery of goods different in any respect whatever from this which the vendor promised to supply him.[71]

---

[64] [1917] 2 KB 606, affd. other grounds [1918] 1 KB 608.
[65] *Ibid.* 610. It was not clear that the buyers saw the goods before the contract but quite probable that they did not.
[66] One of which was later named 'The Mafia'.
[67] See also *Abel* v. *Hannay* (1956) 19 WWR 453; *Hart-Parr Co.* v. *Wells* (1918) 40 DLR 169.
[68] N. 64 above, 610.   [69] *Ibid.*   [70] N. 63 above.
[71] *Ibid.* 636, citing only *Bowes* v. *Shand* (1877) 2 App. Cas. 455. For a similar approach by Canadian authorities on unascertained goods, see *Burlington Canning Co.* v. *Campbell* (1908) 7 WLR 544; *Alabastine Co. of Paris Ltd* v. *Canadian Producer Co. Ltd* (1914) 30 OLR 394; *Hart-Parr Co.* v. *Wells* (1918) 40 DLR 169; *Renewo Products Ltd* v. *Macdonald & Wilson Ltd* [1938] 3 WWR 418.

For specific goods, however, Salmond J thought the position different in at least two respects. First, drawing on common law decisions concerning agreements that are invalid because of the shared mistake of the parties, description went, not to the obligation of the seller to deliver conforming goods, but to the very 'validity'[72] of the contract.[73] This points to the seller not being liable in damages for failing to comply with his description obligation, an unlikely construction to put on any contract of sale[74] unless the seller were liable for non-delivery under section 27. Secondly, as regards the range of description, statements made about specific goods might be mere representations inducing the contract, or mere warranties sounding in damages if breached, or conditions of the validity of the contract.[75] A buyer refusing a tender of the goods would have to show that the descriptive words had been incorporated in the contract at the level of a condition.[76] To do this, the buyer would have to demonstrate that the words went to the 'kind, class, or species to which the article belongs'[77] or, alternatively put, to 'the essential or specific nature of the article sold';[78] words carefully excluded by this analysis were those of 'degree', 'quality', and 'unessential attributes'.[79]

The above distinction, however, is not consistent with the broad range given to description in the case of specific goods unseen by the buyer in *Varley* v. *Whipp*[80] where the outcome is that such goods are assimilated for present purposes to unascertained goods.[81]

The Modern Law

Be that as it may, it remains to be seen whether more recent authorities have maintained the distinction between specific and unascertained goods, and whether the broad range of description in the latter case has been trimmed. Because the difficulties in the modern law have mainly concerned unascertained goods, specific goods will be considered first. In their case, Salmond J's approach appears still to be valid. The description condition was infringed where a 'breeding bull' turned out to be infertile[82] and where semen from a particular Simmental bull was

---

[72] But later he refers to this as a 'condition of the contract': n. 63 above, 638.

[73] *Ibid.* 636–7.

[74] But perhaps a lingering expression of *caveat emptor* reasoning.

[75] N. 63 above, 637.   [76] *Ibid.* 638.   [77] *Ibid.* 639.   [78] *Ibid.*

[79] *Ibid.* 640. For Canadian cases on specific goods taking a similar line, see *Twaites* v. *Morrison* (1918) 43 DLR 73; *New Hamburg Mfg. Co.* v. *Webb*, n. 63 above; *Bailey* v. *Croft* [1932] 1 WWR 106.

[80] [1900] 1 QB 513.

[81] For Canadian cases that do the same thing, see *Bannerman* v. *Barlow* (1908) 7 WLR 859 (facts 'almost identical' to those in *Varley* v. *Whipp*); *Runnymede Iron & Steel Ltd* v. *Rossen Engineering & Construction Co.* [1962] SCR 26.

[82] *Elder Smith Goldsborough Mort Ltd* v. *McBride* [1976] 2 NSWLR 631. See also *Cotter* v. *Luckie* [1918] NZLR 811 ('stud bull').

ordered, but that from a Brown Swiss bull delivered instead.[83] It is a difficult question of degree whether statements concerning the age of goods go to their identity; the degree of divergence from the stated age appears to have a bearing on this. Thus the seller was in breach of section 13(1) in delivering a tower crane, described as 'like new' and just over 2 years old, but which turned out to be 10 years old as well as defective.[84] Similarly, the section was infringed where a car sold as a 1972 model turned out to have a 1969 or 1970 engine,[85] and where a car sold as a 1200 cc model built in 1961 proved to be composed of two parts, one of which was older, and to contain a smaller engine.[86] The age of motor vehicles has also been argued as a matter of express warranty.[87] A buyer able to establish an express warranty but unable or unwilling to reject the goods may not wish to press an additional claim under section 13(1).

Where the goods are unascertained, the broad view of description stated in *Taylor* v. *Combined Buyers Ltd*[88] was applied in a number of cases and indeed held the stage until modern times. The leading case in this area is *Arcos Ltd* v. *E. A. Ronaasen and Son*[89] where the seller agreed to supply a quantity of whitewood and redwood staves to be shipped in the summer of 1930 from Archangel. The contract provided that the wood had to comply with precise measurements of length, breadth, and thickness, but nearly all of the wood strayed in some small measure from these dimensions, though not in a way injurious to the buyers' purpose of making staves for cement barrels.[90] The buyers' rejection of the goods was dictated by nothing more than a desire to repurchase on a falling market but the House of Lords held nevertheless that they were entitled to do so because of the sellers' breach of section 13(1). In so holding, the court made it plain both that physical measurement was a matter of description[91] and that compliance with description meant exact and not approximate compliance, the latter having to be bargained for by a seller who wanted it. As Lord Atkin put it: 'A ton does not mean about a ton, or a yard about a yard. Still less when you descend to minute measurements does ½ inch mean about ½ inch. If a seller wants a margin he must and in

---

[83] *Steele* v. *Maurer* (1976) 73 DLR (3d) 85 (really, unascertained goods from a specific bulk), revd. other grounds (1977) 79 DLR (3d) 764.

[84] *Tower Equipment Rental Ltd* v. *Joint Venture Equipment Sales Ltd* (1975) 9 OR (2d) 453.

[85] *Carr* v. *G. & B. Auto Mart* [1978] 5 WWR 361.

[86] *Beale* v. *Taylor* [1967] 1 WLR 1193.

[87] *Oscar Chess Ltd* v. *Williams* [1957] 1 WLR 325, the buyer failing since the seller's lack of expertise made the statement one of opinion only.

[88] [1924] NZLR 627.   [89] [1933] AC 470.

[90] e.g. of the 28-inch staves, 85.3% were between ½ and ⁹⁄₁₆ inches thick instead of the ½ inch required by the contract; the percentage was 75.3% in the case of 17-inch staves. There was evidence that exposure to rain had affected the thickness of the staves.

[91] See also *Ebrahim Dawood Ltd* v. *Heath Ltd* [1961] 2 Lloyd's Rep. 512.

my experience does stipulate for it.'[92] He did nevertheless concede that trade usage might give a special meaning to particular figures;[93] moreover, descriptive words may acquire a special meaning by usage.[94] A dramatic example of the strictness of description is afforded by *Re Moore & Co. and Landauer & Co.*,[95] where the seller delivered Australian tins of peaches differing from the contractual specification only in that some were packed in cases of twenty-four instead of the thirty tins required by the contract. Though suffering no injury at all and seeking only to escape from a bad bargain, the buyer was allowed to reject the goods.[96]

In *Ashington Piggeries Ltd* v. *Christopher Hill Ltd*,[97] a major decision covering the whole of sections 13 to 14 of the Sale of Goods Act, the range of description for unascertained goods was clearly cut down. The case concerned the supply under two connected contracts of Norwegian herring meal containing a poisonous additive.[98] In one contract, herring meal was one of the ingredients in a mink feed compounded by the sellers according to a recipe provided by the buyers, and the question was whether the mink feed could properly be described as including herring meal when that herring meal contained the poisonous additive. The sellers obtained the herring meal from Norwegian suppliers under the terms of a contract calling for 'NORWEGIAN HERRING MEAL fair average quality of the season, expected to analyse not less than 70% protein, not more than 12% fat and not more than 4% salt.' In the case of this latter contract, the question was how many of the quoted words went to the description of the herring meal and, again, whether the presence of the poisonous additive entailed a breach by the suppliers of their section 13(1) obligation.

In both contracts, the House of Lords found there had not been a breach of section 13(1). Dealing with the first contract for the sale of compounded mink feed, Lord Wilberforce clearly framed description in terms of the essential nature of the goods to be supplied:

Whether in a given case a substance in or upon which there has been produced by chemical interaction some additional substance can properly be described or . . . identified . . . as the original substance qualified by the addition of a past participle such as contaminated or oxidised, or as the original substance plus, or intermixed with, an additional substance, may, if pressed to analysis, be a question of an Aristotelian character. Where does a substance with a quality pass into

---

[92] N. 89 above, 479. For an example of an allowance being stipulated for by words like 'about', see *Vigers Bros.* v. *Sanderson Bros.* [1901] 1 KB 508; Ch. 6 above.

[93] N. 89 above, 479.

[94] *Steels & Busks Ltd* v. *Bleeker Bik & Co. Ltd* [1956] 1 Lloyd's Rep. 228 ('pale crepe rubber'); *Peter Darlington and Partners Ltd* v. *Gosho Co. Ltd* [1964] 1 Lloyd's Rep. 149 ('pure' canary seed); *Grenfell* v. *E. B. Myrowitz Ltd* [1936] 2 All ER 1313 ('safety glass').

[95] [1921] 2 KB 119.   [96] Including the conforming portion of goods: s. 30(3).

[97] [1972] AC 441.   [98] Dimethylnitrosamine, a by-product of the curing process.

an aggregate of substances? . . . The test of description, at least where commodities are concerned, is intended to be a broader, more common sense, test of a mercantile character. The question whether that is what the buyer bargained for has to be answered according to such tests as the men in the market would apply, leaving more delicate questions of condition, or quality, to be determined under other clauses of the contract or sections of the Act.[99]

A distinction was therefore drawn between description and quality. As regards the second contract, Lord Guest was consistent with this approach when rejecting the argument that the words 'fair average quality' and the expected analysis of the goods constituted part of the description for, in his view, 'description implies a specification where the goods can be identified by the buyer'.[100]

Ashington Piggeries therefore removed the collateral attributes of unascertained goods from the range of description.[101] In stressing the role played by identification, however, the case does not reveal whether the range of description is now the same for both specific and unascertained goods, or whether identification and identity (or essence) amount to the same thing. This latter question is dealt with in detail in *Reardon Smith Line Ltd* v. *Yngvar Hansen-Tangen*,[102] a time charterparty case governed by principles akin to sale. The dispute arose from an attempt to finance the building of a number of supertankers by a Japanese ship-building company and to control the market in charter hire. The attempt consisted of creating strings of future time charters and sub-charters entered into in respect of each vessel before it was built. The charter market declined and intermediate charterers in the present case wished to avoid the contract. The contract called for the supply of a 'Newbuilding motor tank vessel called Yard No. 354 at Osaka Zosen'. Because Osaka Zosen (that is, Osaka Shipbuilding) was unable to build a tanker of the required size in its yard, it arranged for a new yard to be built 300 miles away in Oshima.[103] In the books of this new yard, the tanker was numbered 004 though referred to as 354 in the Osaka books.

On the analogy of section 13(1) of the Sale of Goods Act, the charterers contended that the number of the vessel and the building of it in Oshima amounted to a breach of the obligation to tender a vessel answering the

---

[99] N. 97 above, 489. See also Lord Diplock, 503–4: '[U]ltimately the test is whether the buyer could fairly and reasonably refuse to accept the physical goods proffered to him on the ground that their failure to correspond with that part of what was said about them in the contract makes them goods of a different kind from those he had agreed to buy. The key to section 13 is identification.'

[100] N. 97 above, 475. See also *Total International Ltd* v. *Addax BV* [1996] 2 Lloyd's Rep. 333.

[101] Sometimes words of quality may be used to identify the goods: *Baker* v. *Fowkes* (1874) 35 UCQB 302 (Can.: sale of the seller's 'new' hearse as opposed to his 'old' hearse).

[102] [1976] 1 WLR 989. See also *Bakker* v. *Bowness Auto Parts Co. Ltd* (1975) 68 DLR (3d) 173.

[103] It also took a 50% interest in the company incorporated for this purpose.

contract description. Rejecting the charterers' contention, the House of Lords ruled that sale of goods authorities should not be extended to contracts of the present nature and that the disputed words in the contract were never intended to be a matter of fundamental obligation but only a means of identifying the vessel. A conflict thereby emerged with *Ashington Piggeries*, resolved by Lord Wilberforce in these terms:

It is one thing to say of given words that their purpose is to state (identify) an essential part of the description of the goods. It is another to say that they provide one party with a specific indication (identification) of the goods so that he can find them and if he wishes sub-dispose of them. The [charterers] wish to say of words which 'identify' the goods in the second sense, that they describe them in the first.[104]

Although the language is not entirely clear, Lord Wilberforce appears to imply that description goes to the essence or identity of goods in the case of unascertained as well as specific goods. In support of this, he makes it clear that some description decisions stand in need of reappraisal because of their 'excessively technical'[105] aspect. Nevertheless, in another passage, he throws the entire matter into doubt when he says:

Even if a strict and technical view must be taken as regards the description of unascertained future goods (e.g., commodities) as to which each detail of the description must be assumed to be vital, it may be, and in my opinion is, right to treat other contracts of sale of goods in a similar manner to other contracts generally so as to ask whether a particular item in a description constitutes a substantial ingredient of the 'identity' of the thing sold, and only if it does to treat it as a condition.[106]

His Lordship was explicitly concerned to see that the law on description kept in step with the law on express warranties and intermediate stipulations as expounded in *Hongkong Fir Shipping Co. Ltd* v. *Kawasaki Kisen Kaisha Ltd*[107] and *Cehave NV* v. *Bremer Handelsgesellschaft mbH*.[108] This explains what appears to be a two-tiered approach to the construction of descriptive words—a strict approach to words that relate to the 'identity' of the thing sold and a flexible approach to other descriptive words outside the core of identity.[109] As for non-core words that merely 'identify' goods, Lord Wilberforce was of the opinion that they could be 'construed

---

[104] N. 102 above, 999.

[105] *Ibid.* 998. He cites *Re Moore & Co. and Landauer & Co.*, n. 95 above, but, interestingly, not *Arcos Ltd* v. *E. A. Ronaasen and Son*, n. 89 above.

[106] N. 102 above, 998.   [107] [1962] 2 QB 26.   [108] [1976] QB 44.

[109] See *Hopkins* v. *Hitchcock* (1863) 14 CB(NS) 65. The contract called for the supply of 'S & H' stamped iron, Snowdon & Hopkins being the manufacturers. When Snowdon retired from the partnership, Hopkins had the iron stamped 'H & Co'. The sellers were held entitled to stamp the iron in the latter way since the words were concerned with iron of a particular quality rather than iron of a particular brand.

much more liberally than they would have to be construed if they were providing essential elements of the description'.[110] Since *Reardon Smith* itself concerned unascertained future goods, Lord Wilberforce's words concerning the need for strictness should properly be understood as relating to transactions in fast-moving, stratified, and volatile markets such as the world of commodities. In such contracts, words relating to the grading and geographical origin and type of goods, such as 'No 1 Oregon winter wheat' would still be regarded as descriptive and interpreted strictly.[111] Nothing in *Reardon Smith*, however, would suggest that even in such cases words like 'fair average quality' should be treated as part of the description of goods.

The range of description for specific and unascertained goods alike has stabilized around the identity of the goods. But the identity of goods is not a constant thing and will vary from case to case. Where commodities are sold under a wide array of labels, it is only to be expected that identity has a fuller meaning than it has in the case of a sale of a specific horse. This allows the special mention of commodities cases without departing from an identity-based core of description. Similarly, goods unseen by the buyer should have a more extensive identity than goods seen.[112] It therefore seems that the range of description can be extended by the terms of the contract itself.[113]

Description and Reliance

Another attempt to align the law on description with the law on express warranties is present in *Harlingdon and Leinster Enterprises Ltd* v. *Christopher Hull Fine Art Ltd*.[114] One dealer sold to another a painting stated unequivocally by the seller to be the work of a German expressionist artist, Gabriele Münter. The seller relied upon an attribution in an earlier auction catalogue; he was not at all expert in German expressionist art, whereas the buyer was. It was found as a fact at trial that the buyer

---

[110] N. 102 above, 999.

[111] See *Berger and Co. Inc.* v. *Gill & Duffus SA* [1982] AC 382, 394 (Lord Diplock); *Tradax Export SA* v. *European Grain & Shipping Ltd* [1983] 2 Lloyd's Rep. 100 ('maximum 7.5% fibre'); *Toepfer* v. *Warinco AG* [1978] 2 Lloyd's Rep. 569. For a broad view of description, see also *Coastal (Bermuda) Petroleum Ltd* v. *VTT Vulcan Petroleum SA (The Marine Star)* [1994] CLC 1019 (date of shipment); *Petrograde Inc.* v. *Stinnes Handels GmbH* [1995] 1 Lloyd's Rep. 142 (port of shipment). Cf. *Tradax Internacional SA* v. *Goldschmidt SA* [1977] 2 Lloyd's Rep. 604, where it was common ground between the parties that the maximum stated percentage in a cargo of white Syrian barley did not go to description.

[112] See *Berger and Co. Inc.* v. *Gill & Duffus SA*, n. 111 above (the sample example).

[113] But see *Montagu L. Meyer Ltd* v. *Kivisto* (1929) 142 LT 480 where timber had to be 'properly seasoned for shipment' and to be measured as appropriate 'for such description of goods'. The court appears to have held that the parties did not mean description in the technical sense; the goods were the goods 'specified' in the contract.

[114] [1991] 1 QB 564; M. G. Bridge [1990] *LMCLQ* 455.

did not rely upon the seller's statement but upon his own examination of the painting, which turned out to be a forgery. By a majority, the Court of Appeal held the seller was not liable under section 13(1). Of the majority judges, Nourse LJ thought the sale had not taken place by description.[115] Furthermore, for section 13(1) to be breached the seller's statement should have passed the test of a contractual condition, which it failed to do because of the buyer's lack of reliance. The other majority judge, Slade LJ, saw description as depending upon a common contractual intention that the disputed statement be a term of the contract. Reliance was not a necessary requirement of section 13(1) liability but its absence in the present case was enough to disqualify the statement from constituting part of the description. The dissenting judge, Stuart-Smith LJ, saw no role for reliance at all.

The introduction of reliance into description in *Harlingdon and Leinster* is innovative.[116] Reliance is a feature of fitness for purpose under section 14(3), where the buyer must rely upon the seller's skill and judgement for the seller to be liable. But reliance in this sense, as opposed to the buyer's reliance on the painting being by Gabriele Münter, which assists in defining the core of description and the basis of the bargain and was certainly present in the case,[117] has in the past been foreign to section 13(1). Nevertheless, there is high authority for the view that the authorship of a painting is not part of the identity of specific goods for the purpose of common mistake.[118] If the identity of goods in section 13(1) is defined in similar strict terms, which accords with the trend of modern authorities on description, then the decision in *Harlingdon and Leinster* is defensible on this ground. Whichever ground best supports the outcome in *Harlingdon and Leinster*, if the case is successful in integrating description into the law governing express warranties, there seems little point in retaining description and section 13(1) as a separate head of liability.[119]

---

[115] But even if the attribution to Gabriele Münter was not part of the description, this should not mean that the sale did not take place by description. If canvas and rubber boots do not have to be 'waders' for the purpose of s. 13(1) (see *Joseph Travers & Sons Ltd* v. *Longel Ltd* (1948) 44 TLR 150), they should still be made of canvas and rubber if that is the basis upon which they are sold.

[116] The case is also important for the role it implies for reliance in the law of express warranty: Ch. 8 below.

[117] Cf. *Joseph Travers & Sons Ltd* v. *Longel Ltd*, n. 115 above, where the parties introduced the word 'waders' as a convenient way of labelling war surplus goods for which there was no defined market. The buyer did not set out to obtain goods that passed the market test of 'waders'.

[118] *Bell* v. *Lever Bros.* [1932] AC 161 (Lord Atkin); *Leaf* v. *Internationl Galleries* [1950] 2 KB 86 (Denning LJ).

[119] Description was removed from the Canadian Uniform Sale of Goods Act 1981 (not yet in force in any Canadian province), though it remained present in the Ontario Draft Sale of Goods Bill 1979 (s. 5.11) that paved the way for the Uniform Act.

SATISFACTORY QUALITY

According to the current text of section 14(2) of the Sale of Goods Act, there is an implied term that, where the seller sells goods in the course of a business, the goods supplied shall be of satisfactory quality. Unlike section 13(1), this implied term applies only to business and not also to private sellers. Since the enactment of the Sale and Supply of Goods Act 1994, section 14(2) is framed as a 'term', but the new section 14(6) explicitly makes that term a condition. The condition of satisfactory quality was known before the 1994 Act as merchantable quality. Apart from the change of name, a number of alterations were made in that Act to the definition of merchantable quality. The very existence of a definition, now to be found in section 14(2A)(2B) but formerly contained in the old section 14(6) of the Sale of Goods Act, dates, not from the original Act of 1893,[120] but from 1973. In the light of this somewhat complex legislative history of satisfactory quality, the best starting point is to examine the development of merchantable quality before 1973, and then consider merchantable quality in the light of the statutory definition introduced in that year before turning to the new definition of satisfactory quality.[121] The principal features of satisfactory quality will be dealt with in this way before attention is turned to certain of its particular applications. Before this is done, however, it is necessary to consider in further detail the types of seller bound by the satisfactory quality standard in section 14(2).

Sale in the Course of a Business

The requirement in section 14(2) that the seller sell the goods 'in the course of a business' dates from 1973. Before that date, it was necessary to show that the goods were 'bought by description from a seller who deals in goods of that description (whether he be the manufacturer or not)'. Two propositions were embraced in this formula. First, a private seller would in no circumstances be liable under section 14(2). Secondly, a business seller would be liable only in restricted circumstances, bounded by the technicalities of the description doctrine.[122] It has been observed already that, in order to enter section 14(2), the buyer had to go through the gateway of section 13 by showing that the goods had been bought by description. The next question was what was meant by the

---

[120] In *Jones* v. *Just* (1868) LR 3 QB 197, Blackburn J did not feel it necessary to direct the Liverpool jury on the meaning of merchantability: see Roskill LJ in *Cehave NV* v. *Bremer Handelsgesellschaft mbH*, n. 118 above.

[121] See M. G. Bridge [1995] *JBL* 398.

[122] The first of these propositions will be considered further under fitness for purpose below.

seller dealing in goods of that description. Even before the law was changed in 1973, this limitation on the scope of the implied term had in effect been lifted. Lord Wilberforce observed in *Ashington Piggeries Ltd* v. *Christopher Hill Ltd*[123] that it meant only that the seller had to be a dealer in the kinds of goods supplied, and not in goods of the particular description supplied under the contract.[124] Consequently, the character of the seller required to invoke the merchantable quality term was the same as that needed for the fitness for purpose term which, prior to 1973, applied when 'the goods are of a description which it is in the course of the seller's business to supply'.[125] In the same case, Lord Wilberforce went further when he made it plain that the seller could be liable even if this was the first time that the seller had supplied goods of that kind.[126] The mink feed in *Ashington Piggeries* was, it was assumed, sold with Norwegian herring meal as an ingredient for the first time.[127] Lord Wilberforce's words that the implied term in section 14(2) governs 'persons in the way of business, as distinct from private persons'[128] are equivalent to the present wording introduced in 1973 that the seller sell the goods 'in the course of a business'.

An issue that might present a problem concerns the business seller who is not a dealer as such but who from time to time, perhaps at irregular and protracted intervals, disposes of second-hand items of unwanted capital equipment.[129] This raises the question why liability should be visited on business sellers but not on private sellers.[130] It also compels a comparison with a similar formula in the Trade Descriptions Act 1968, a regulatory statute, which in section 1(1) applies to '[a]ny person who, in the course of a trade or business . . . supplies . . . any goods'. In *Davies* v. *Sumner*,[131] the House of Lords, referring to the long title of the 1968 Act,[132] held that the formula 'in the context of an Act having consumer protection as its primary purpose conveys the concept of

---

[123] [1972] AC 441, 494–5.

[124] *Ibid.* 494: '[W]hat the Act had in mind was something quite simple and rational: to limit the implied conditions of fitness and quality to persons in the way of business, as distinct from private persons.' See also *Spencer Trading Co. Ltd* v. *Devon* [1947] 1 All ER 284 (flypaper contained for first time artificial additives instead of natural ingredients).

[125] Lord Wilberforce dealt with this aspect of both implied terms indifferently. See also *Farmer* v. *Canada Packers Ltd* (1956) 6 DLR (2d) 63, 73 (where both terms were held to apply simply where a sale took place in the course of a business); *Buckley* v. *Lever Bros. Ltd* [1953] OR 704 (Can.).

[126] N. 123 above, 494 (if the seller is 'willing to accept orders').

[127] *Ibid.*   [128] *Ibid.*

[129] The Ontario Law Reform Commission was opposed to liability in this case: see *Report on Sale of Goods*, i, 209.

[130] Discussed with fitness for purpose below.

[131] [1984] 1 WLR 1301. See also *Havering London Borough* v. *Stevenson* [1970] 1 WLR 1375.

[132] 'An Act . . . prohibiting certain misdescriptions of goods, services, accommodation and facilities provided in the course of trade'.

some degree of regularity'.[133] The defendant was a courier disposing, by way of trade-in with a car dealer, of a vehicle he used almost exclusively for transporting film and televisual material. The courier fell outside the 1968 Act because he had not built up a practice of disposing of cars. Further, the car was not something he exploited as stock-in-trade. For the purposes of a somewhat different statute, the Unfair Contract Terms Act 1977,[134] the Court of Appeal in *R. & B. Customs Brokers Ltd* v. *United Dominions Trust Ltd*[135] followed the approach of the House of Lords and held that a *buyer* did not purchase in the course of a business[136] where the car purchased was incidental to the buyer's business activity and no pattern of regularity in the purchase of cars had developed to make it integral to the buyer's business. If the approach in these cases were followed in section 14(2), it would require a gloss to be put on the plain language of section 14(2) which, as stated above, enacted in clearer terms a position that was entrenched shortly before the 1973 changes by *Ashington Piggeries Ltd* v. *Christopher Hill Ltd*.[137] It is submitted that no good reason exists for limiting the scope of the section 14(2) wording in the above (somewhat convoluted) way in a statute, the Sale of Goods Act, whose purposes differ from the Trade Descriptions Act 1968 and the Unfair Contract Terms Act 1977.[138]

It was not until 1973 that the Sale of Goods Act (as amended) gave a definition of business. According to section 61(1), ' "business" includes a profession and the activities of any government department . . . or local or public authority'. It is submitted that this definition should be given a broad reading so as to embrace all non-private bodies, such as universities and charities like the National Trust. Private individuals who are not traders operating from business premises or adopting business patterns of behaviour may yet sell in the course of a business if they deal with sufficient regularity and with a view to profit.[139] It is submitted that, in the case of doubt, the application of section 14(2) should go in favour of the

---

[133] N. 131 above, 1305.   [134] See Ch. 8 below.   [135] [1988] 1 WLR 321.

[136] So as to deal as a consumer for the purpose of the 1977 Act, s. 12.

[137] N. 123 above.

[138] Certain Canadian cases put a gloss upon the requirements of the section by requiring that the sale be in the ordinary course of the seller's business. This runs counter to imposing liability where the seller deals in goods of the contract type for the first time (discussed above). So the application of the section was ousted when one farmer sold seed to another as a personal favour (*Buckle* v. *Morrison* [1924] 3 WWR 702) and where a municipality sold grain on credit to an impecunious farmer as a sort of outdoor relief (*Lilldal* v. *Rural Municipality of Meota no 468* [1920] 2 WWR 336). See also *Rahtjen* v. *Stern GMC Trucks (1969) Ltd* (1976) 66 DLR (3d) 566 (no liability where second-hand car dealer supplied trailer on one-off basis). Cf. *Connop* v. *Canadian Car Division Hawker Siddeley Canada Ltd* (1978) 24 OR (2d) 593 (Can.) (manufacturer of insulated lorries and subway carriages liable when defective insulating material was installed as a favour in the buyer's yacht).

[139] Cf. *Stevenson* v. *Beverley Bentinck Ltd* [1976] 1 WLR 483.

buyer to the extent that the buyer is denied information that tends to limit the liability of the seller. The burden should not be put on the buyer of inquiring how and for what purpose the university library is disposing of unwanted books or the National Trust is organizing the sale of multi-coloured sweaters. The same idea is evident in section 14(5), which provides that a sale through an agent acting in the course of a business will be deemed to be in the course of a business of the principal seller, unless either the buyer does know that the seller is not acting in the course of a business or reasonable efforts have been made to bring this to the attention of the buyer.[140]

Development of Merchantable Quality

Merchantable quality, the predecessor of satisfactory quality, developed from its earliest days in close companionship with the concept of description, to the point where it was difficult to see any distinction between them. In a nutshell, goods were regarded in the nineteenth century as of merchantable quality if they were saleable under the contract description. This was not the same as requiring the goods to be free from latent defects, for merchantable quality was based upon the market. All manner of goods may be sold in the market and, depending upon their condition and quality, will be priced accordingly. The history of merchantable quality shows that buyers seeking a guarantee against the presence of latent defects must secure an express warranty. Difficulties posed in modern times by the meaning of merchantable quality evidence a shift in the law. The prevailing policy is to impose strict liability for defective manufactured goods, in other words, to provide a warranty against latent defects.

A convenient starting point in the case law is *Parkinson* v. *Lee*,[141] where the contract was for the sale of five pockets of hops that, unknown to the parties, who were both dealers, had been fraudulently watered by the grower. The watering was not evident from samples previously examined by the buyer or from the bulk of the hops at the time of contracting. The Court of King's Bench held that the seller should not in the absence of fraud be liable for latent defects, unless the buyer secured an express warranty, at least where both parties were equally acquainted with the bargained-for commodity.[142]

The significance of the buyer's opportunity to examine the goods, as ineffectual as it was to discover the latent defect in *Parkinson* v. *Lee*, emerged more clearly in *Gardiner* v. *Gray*,[143] where the contract was for

---

[140] See *Boyter* v. *Thomson* [1995] 3 WLR 36.   [141] (1802) 2 East 314.
[142] *Ibid.* 322. A position well-established for the sale of horses.
[143] (1815) 4 Camp. 144.

the sale of twelve bags of waste silk. A specimen of the silk was produced at the time of the contract but the silk subsequently delivered proved to be much inferior. The sale was not a sale by sample, owing to the absence of a descriptive link between the specimen and the delivered goods. The purpose of the specimen was to allow the buyer to form a reasonable judgement of the unseen goods; the contract provided for the sale of a quantity of waste silk without an accompanying guarantee that the specimen provided was equal to the delivered goods. The court found in favour of the buyer; the goods were so inferior that they could not reasonably be sold in the market as 'waste silk'. The buyer was entitled to expect the goods delivered to answer to this description since the absence of an opportunity to examine ruled out the application of *caveat emptor* reasoning. But the court was adamant that the buyer was not entitled to a particular fineness or quality of goods.

A refinement of the understanding of merchantable quality laid down in *Gardiner* v. *Gray*[144] came in *Jones* v. *Bright*[145] where Best CJ introduced the notion that goods were merchantable if fit for any of the purposes for which such goods were normally required. Referring to the contractual description of goods, it followed that if the goods so described could be used for more than one purpose, and were in fact usable for at least one purpose, they were of merchantable quality. A buyer with a particular purpose in mind would have to communicate this to the seller to secure an implied obligation of fitness for particular purpose.

The next important case in defining merchantable quality[146] was *James Drummond and Sons* v. *E. H. Van Ingen & Co.*,[147] where cloth merchants purchased from cloth manufacturers a quantity of worsted coatings equal in quality and weight to samples previously supplied. As the sellers knew, it was the buyers' intention to resell the cloth ('corkscrew twills') to clothiers or tailors. The cloth suffered from the defect of slippage between the warp and the weft, so that it lacked the cohesion necessary to prevent undue wear. This fault was not apparent on any reasonable examination of the samples supplied, which were likewise affected. The cloth was therefore not fit for any of the purposes for which goods of that same general class had been previously used in the trade. The sellers were held to be in breach of the merchantable quality obligation. The decision of the House of Lords was certainly influenced by the presence of a defect in the goods: it was not a mere characteristic[148] to be expected in a cheaper kind of twill. Furthermore, cloth of the contract

---

[144] (1815) 4 Camp. 144.   [145] (1829) 5 Bing. 333.
[146] The landmark case of *Jones* v. *Just* (1868) LR 3 QB 197 was a masterful summary of antecedent developments.
[147] (1887) 12 App. Cas. 284.   [148] *Ibid.* 292.

type was not ordinarily used in the making of inferior clothing,[149] though it is quite possible that such a market could have been found had it been sold under a description connoting the defect. In short, the standard of merchantable quality was in this case clearly influenced by the notions of defectiveness and ordinary trade user. The cloth was not of merchantable quality merely because it could have been put to profitable use at the right price.

The *Drummond* case shows that, on the eve of the first codification of sale in 1893, *Parkinson* v. *Lee*[150] was still good law in holding that a merchantable quality obligation did not arise when the buyer had the opportunity to discover the fault in the goods before the contract. As we shall see, the law in this respect was changed in 1893. *Drummond* also served notice that merchantable quality could not be understood solely in terms of description and saleability; one had to look too at ordinary purpose and defectiveness, and quite possibly too at price. The Act of 1893 did not define merchantable quality, though it did provide that the quality of the goods included their state or condition. The consequence of this was that a number of judicial attempts were made to clarify merchantable quality in a series of important cases.

Judicial Definitions of Merchantable Quality

In *Bristol Tramways Carriage Co. Ltd* v. *Fiat Motors Ltd*,[151] Farwell LJ defined merchantable quality 'as meaning that the article is of such quality and in such condition that a reasonable man acting reasonably would after a full examination accept it under the circumstances of the case in performance of his offer to buy that article whether he buys for his own use or to sell again'.[152] This test involves a radical departure from the classical criteria of description and saleability. For a descriptive standard of what is commercially passable between buyers and sellers in the particular market, it focuses on the reasonable response of the buyer to the seller's tender. Whereas the market approach was concerned with the minimum standard of saleability that could still pass muster under the contract description, the *Bristol Tramways* test set in train a movement towards treating merchantable quality as imposing a minimum quality standard. Although the test has come in for criticism,[153] it is consistent with the modern law's preoccupation with the goods after they have come into the buyer's hands and with modern attempts to define merchantable quality by statutory means. In particular, the test draws

---

[149] This distinguishes the case from *Jones* v. *Padgett* (1890) 24 QBD 650.
[150] N. 141 above.   [151] [1910] 2 KB 831.   [152] *Ibid.* 841.
[153] See, e.g., Lord Reid in *Henry Kendall & Sons* v. *William Lillico & Sons Ltd* [1969] 2 AC 31, 78–9.

attention to those buyers who do not themselves deal with the goods in trade but instead use and consume them over an extended period.

The *Bristol Tramways* test was criticized by Salmond J in *Taylor* v. *Combined Buyers*[154] for its circularity of reasoning: a reasonable buyer will accept the goods when bound to accept them and is bound to accept them when he will accept them. This judgment asserts uncompromisingly that merchantable quality is not concerned with a disembodied quality standard defined without reference to the contract or the market place:

> [T]he term merchantable does not mean of good, fair, or average quality. Goods may be of inferior or even of bad quality but yet fulfil the legal requirement of merchantable quality. For goods may be in the market in any grade, good, bad, or indifferent, and yet all equally merchantable. On a sale of goods there is no implied condition that they are of any particular grade or standard. If the buyer wishes to guard himself in this respect he must expressly bargain for the particular grade or standard that he requires. If he does not do so, *caveat emptor*, and he must accept the goods, however inferior in quality, so long as they conform to the description under which they are sold and are of merchantable quality.

Although the case itself concerned manufactured goods, Salmond J's observations belong to a world of horse and agricultural produce sales. Merchantable quality has caused trouble in modern conditions because it does not accommodate goods mass-produced to an attainable standard of perfection. Even the cheapest of new cars should not be scratched or suffer from other minor faults that can be banished from the manufacturing process. Agricultural produce, on the other hand, may, in the right kind of market, be sold in a damaged condition, and its characteristics will depend upon climate and other variables in the growing year.[155] This degree of seasonal relativity is not to be found, or at least should not be found, in the case of manufactured goods. The descriptive possibilities for new consumer goods are much narrower than for natural commodities, so that it is easier in the former than in the latter case to infer a breach of section 14(2). Merchantable quality is a subtle and varying standard whose application is clearly influenced by the type of damage caused by defective goods as well as the nature of the goods.

Although Salmond J asserted the importance of description, he was adamant that the conditions of merchantable quality and description were separate;[156] for example, beef and bread might still be describable as beef and bread, though unfit for consumption and therefore unmer-

---

[154] [1924] NZLR 627, 646.

[155] It is common in international sales for merchantable quality to be superseded by an express term in the contract that the goods shall be of fair average quality of the season's shipments or something similar.

[156] N. 154 above, 644.

chantable.[157] Moreover, saleability was no synonym for merchantable quality since few things cannot be disposed of at the right price.[158] In the view of Salmond J, a suitably modified definition of merchantable quality would run as follows:

[G]oods sold by description are merchantable in the legal sense when they are of such quality as to be saleable under that description to a buyer who has full and accurate knowledge of that quality, and who is buying for the ordinary and normal purposes for which goods are bought under that description in the market.[159]

The reference to ordinary purposes incorporates the *Drummond*[160] approach, though that case was not referred to in Salmond J's judgment; the reference to the buyer's knowledge of the actual quality of the goods goes unexplained in the judgment but presumably refers to the notion of acceptable quality laid down in *Bristol Tramways*.[161] Above all, *Taylor* v. *Combined Buyers Ltd* illustrates that merchantable quality cannot be defined in the abstract but must be understood in the context of the specific contract, in particular, of the description given thereunder to the goods.[162] Besides its failure to come to terms with mass-produced goods, *Taylor* also fails to take account of mass-produced contracts whose every characteristic is the same in all cases.

The significance of the price paid for the goods, hinted at in the *Drummond* case, was emphasized by Dixon J in *Australian Knitting Mills Ltd* v. *Grant* when he stated:

[The goods] should be in such an actual state that a buyer fully acquainted with the facts and, therefore, knowing what hidden defects exist and not being limited to their apparent condition would buy them without abatement of the price obtainable for such goods if in reasonable sound order and condition and without special terms.[163]

In effect, the notion of price is here substituted for the ordinary use of goods. Instead of the ordinary use supplementing the contractual description so as to identify the market range in which the parties are dealing, price is called upon to perform that function. The above test refers simply to 'a buyer', who may be any buyer; it is indifferent to the various uses to which goods might be put within the market range. The goods supplied might not be fit for all such uses, and, more particularly, not for the use planned by the actual buyer. Even a reasonable buyer might react differently depending upon the use that that buyer had in mind for the goods. To capture the idea that goods are merchantable if, despite defects in them disqualifying them from one of these uses they

---

[157] *Ibid.*   [158] *Ibid.*   [159] *Ibid.* 645.   [160] N. 147 above.
[161] N. 151 above.   [162] N. 154 above, 646–7.   [163] (1933) 50 CLR 387, 413.

can yet be sold at the same price for another use, Lord Reid proposed the substitution in the above test of 'some buyers' for 'a buyer'.[164]

Another oft-quoted definition is that of Lord Wright in *Cammell Laird & Co. Ltd* v. *Manganese Bronze and Brass Co. Ltd*,[165] where he stated that, for them to be unmerchantable, goods 'in the form in which they are tendered' should be 'of no use for any purpose for which such goods would ordinarily be used and hence . . . not saleable under that description'. As Lord Reid has observed, the words 'such goods' must refer to an ideal tender of the goods conforming to the contractual description, rather than to the disputed actual tender;[166] it makes little sense to define a breach of contract by internal reference to itself rather than to the contract standard. Lord Wright's test is essentially a compound of *Jones* v. *Bright*,[167] *Gardiner* v. *Gray*[168] and *James Drummond and Sons* v. *E. H. Van Ingen & Co.*;[169] it adds nothing new to the discussion.

The various elements of merchantable quality laid out above—description, fitness for purpose, acceptance, saleability, and price—were assessed by Lord Reid in *Henry Kendall & Sons* v. *William Lillico & Sons Ltd*,[170] who laid particular emphasis on commercial saleability. In that case, Brazilian groundnut extract, because of a toxic additive, had poisoned a large number of pheasants. Lord Reid posed the question whether, notwithstanding this, it was commercially saleable according to the terms on which it was sold. In his view, merchantable quality was not to be judged solely by reference to market behaviour at the time of the contract of sale. On close examination, the explanation for his lordship's willingness to extend the date of the inquiry stems from the stitching of protection against latent defects to the classical merchantable quality element of saleability under the contractual description.

Saleability, in Lord Reid's view, could not mean simply that other buyers might have bought the disputed goods on the same terms as the actual buyer, for otherwise there would be no protection against latent defects.[171] In considering whether there was an alternative use for the disputed goods, recognized by the market under the same contractual description at the contract date, it was necessary to impute to a hypothetical alternative buyer knowledge of the toxicity of these goods and then to ask whether that buyer would would have accepted the goods under the contractual description.[172] Nevertheless, this alternative buyer should not react in the same way that the market itself did in the immediate aftermath of the discovery that Brazilian groundnut extract

---

[164] *Henry Kendall & Sons* v. *William Lillico & Sons Ltd*, n. 153 above, 79.
[165] [1934] AC 402, 430.
[166] *Henry Kendall & Sons* v. *William Lillico & Sons Ltd*, n. 153 above, 77.
[167] (1829) 5 Bing. 333.   [168] N. 143 above.   [169] (1887) 12 App. Cas. 284.
[170] N. 153 above.   [171] *Ibid.* 75.   [172] *Ibid.* 75–6.

was toxic, when the extract was 'virtually unsaleable'; rather, the buyer was to react as the market did when it settled down upon discovering that the extract could still be used, although in a more circumspect and limited manner than had previously been the case.[173] Any other approach, in Lord Reid's view, was artificial;[174] moreover, there was evidence in the present case of how the market settled down. This, rather surprisingly, showed that similarly toxic Indian groundnut extract was accepted by trade buyers for compounding into cattle feed. They protested when they discovered the toxicity and requested price rebates but did not press the matter in the face of their sellers' intransigence.[175]

Lord Reid therefore concluded that the goods were of merchantable quality since they were saleable under the contractual description to buyers who had in mind, not the purpose of compounding poultry or pheasant feed, but that of compounding cattle feed.[176] The condition of merchantable quality cut out at the point where fitness for purpose picked up; a buyer seeking coverage for the former purpose would therefore have to notify it to the seller in accordance with section 14(3). It is noteworthy that Lord Reid was guided more by the notion of acceptability of the goods than by their initial saleability. The fact that some buyers might grudgingly retain goods, however, does not mean that they would have bought them on the same terms, or accepted the seller's tender of them, had they known of the defect. Lord Pearce, dissenting, maintained that the behaviour of these alternative buyers, admittedly based on a hypothetical market in which the defect was deemed to be known, had to occur in a market that could plausibly have existed at the date of the actual supply.[177] He did not believe that a buyer could have been found without a price abatement and drove his point home with the example of goods infected by a deadly poison, a simple antidote to which is discovered two years after the date of supply. Although the goods might well be saleable two years down the road, they would be unsaleable at the contract date.[178] It is submitted that Lord Pearce's approach is more in tune with saleability as it has long been understood. One might also ask how Lord Reid would have dealt with the case of a buyer of goods for animal feed who finds that the goods supplied have perished in the interval between the discovery that they are toxic and the discovery that they may, however, be fed to cattle.

In one sense, *Henry Kendall & Sons* v. *William Lillico & Sons Ltd*[179] is in line with merchantable quality authorities in maintaining that the existence of a defect in the goods does not necessarily make them

---

[173] *Ibid.* 75.   [174] *Ibid.*   [175] *Ibid.* 76, 79.   [176] *Ibid.*   [177] *Ibid.* 119.
[178] *Ibid.* Sympathy was expressed for Lord Pearce's view by Lloyd LJ in *M/S Aswan Engineering Establishment Co. Ltd* v. *Lupdine Ltd* [1987] 1 WLR 1, 15.
[179] [1969] 2 AC 31.

unmerchantable. But it is submitted that it takes a wrong turning by looking at the way certain buyers might have behaved upon discovering a defect in the goods after delivery, rather than at the way they would have behaved on entering into the contract in the first place or at the point of tender. This shift of focus would seem to be due to the ambiguity of acceptance, implicity understood in the present case in the special sense given to it by section 35, in connection with the right of rejection, rather than in the sense that it has in section 27, which concerns the buyer's duty to accept the seller's tender of the goods.[180] The real question is whether the seller should have sold, not whether the buyer ought to have accepted (in the sense of not rejecting after delivery). Although a greater preoccupation with protection against latent defects looks to the fate of the goods in the buyer's hands, and should therefore expand the buyer's protection under section 14(2), it paradoxically abridged the buyer's protection in the present case. *Henry Kendall & Sons* is criticized here, not because it held that goods fit for an ordinary purpose within the contract description and price range are of merchantable quality though unfit for another purpose;[181] rather, it is criticized because of its failure to appreciate that markets evolve and that market behaviour should be assessed *then* rather than *now*.

A final authority to consider on the evolving meaning of merchantable quality before the introduction of the statutory definition is *Cehave NV* v. *Bremer Handelsgesellschaft mbH*.[182] The facts were unusual.[183] The buyers' behaviour in repurchasing at a distress sale overheated but usable citrus pulp pellets that they had previously rejected showed they should not fairly have rejected those goods and should have been content with damages. About one-fifth of the market value of the goods had been lost by the overheating and, unlike *Henry Kendall & Sons*,[184] the condition of the cargo was apparent on its receipt by the buyers. There was no evidence that some buyers would have accepted the goods without an abatement of the price; indeed, there was trade evidence of the appropriate price discount for goods in that condition. Permitting the buyer to reject the goods might seem harsh but, on the face of it, an application of the merchantable quality standard should have led to that result. The problem with cases like *Cehave* lies not with the meaning of

---

[180] See Ch. 6 above.

[181] This has been the law since *Jones* v. *Bright*, n. 8 above; *James Drummond and Sons* v. *E. H. Van Ingen & Co*, n. 169 above. More recently, see also *Canada Atlantic Grain Export Co.* v. *Eilers* (1929) 35 Ll. LR 206, 213 (Lord Wright); *M/S Aswan Engineering Establishment Co. Ltd* v. *Lupdine Ltd*, n. 178 above. In this respect, the law appears to have been changed by the Sale and Supply of Goods Act 1994, discussed in the text accompanying nn. 208 ff. above.

[182] [1976] QB 44.   [183] See Ch. 5 above.   [184] N. 179 above.

merchantable quality but with its status as a condition in all cases, which ultimately the Law Commission decided not to overturn.[185]

Lord Denning rehearsed the various elements of merchantable quality but interestingly introduced another—the remaining terms of the contract.[186] Merchantable quality was seen in terms of whether, to a commercial man, the buyers should be permitted to reject the goods and whether that commercial man would be guided by an express price abatement clause in the contract, even if it did not apply to the subject matter of the present dispute. Now, this is extraordinary. Clause 5 of the standard form agreement[187] gave a price allowance for goods adulterated by sand, silica, or castor seed, but made no mention of overheating damage. It might have been better if it had done so, but Lord Denning's approach is open to the criticism that it repairs the deficiency of the form by distorting the interpretation of merchantable quality. If there had not also existed in the contract an express term that the goods had to be shipped in good condition, the above interpretation of merchantable quality would have left the buyers without a remedy at all, even though the damage to the goods eliminated one-fifth of their commercial value. It is hard to imagine that a reasonable seller apprised of the condition of the goods would not have sold them without a qualifying word such as 'overheated' or 'damaged'.[188] There is, however, merit in Lord Denning's view that merchantable quality should be assessed in its contractual context. Account could be taken of trade usages and expectations as well as the express terms of the contract, but it is submitted that Lord Denning's approach goes too far. The attitude of a court to minor defects in new manufactured goods might properly be angled to take account of contractual terms setting out a seller's responsibility for dealing with teething problems, or of the seller's evident willingness to correct minor faults or the effectiveness of the manufacturer's warranty programme.[189] Nevertheless, the Court of Appeal in *Rogers* v. *Parish Motors (Scarborough) Ltd*,[190] perhaps influenced by the history of manufacturers' warranties in curtailing contractual rights, was loth to allow recourse to them in aid of defining the standard of merchantable quality. Moreover, the repudia-

[185] Report on *Sale and Supply of Goods* (Law Com. No. 160, 1987) at para. 4.25, with which contrast its Consultative Document (WP No. 85, 1983) at paras. 2.30–31 and 5.4, where it provisionally concluded that the statutory implied terms in ss. 13–14 should cease to be conditions.
[186] N. 182 above, 63.
[187] Form 100 of the Cattle Food Trade Association, now GAFTA 100.
[188] The judgments of Ormerod and Roskill LJJ appear to overlook the significance of words of description in the contract. The former is concerned to uphold an arbitral finding and the latter appears to equate fitness for purpose and merchantable quality.
[189] This can be inferred from *Bernstein* v. *Pamson Motors (Golders Green) Ltd* [1987] 2 All ER 220.
[190] [1987] 2 All ER 232.

tion of cure as a brake on rejection by the Law Commission[191] will not make it easy to invoke the idea of cure as an aid to interpreting merchantable (now satisfactory) quality.

The 1973 Definition of Merchantable Quality

The first statutory definition of merchantable quality, as introduced in 1973[192] and incorporated in section 14(6) of the Sale of Goods Act 1979, read as follows:

> Goods of any kind are of merchantable quality . . . if they are as fit for the purpose or purposes for which goods of that kind are commonly bought as it is reasonable to expect having regard to any description applied to them, the price (if relevant) and all the other relevant circumstances.

On the face of it, this definition is too bland to solve difficult problems,[193] although routine cases could be disposed of without too minute a parsing of the statutory language. It is a commonplace that judicial passages should not be interpreted with the rigour accorded to a statutory text since they are expounded in a limited factual context and need to be adapted to changing circumstances.[194] The above treatment of merchantable quality is a standard, rather than a hard-and-fast definition. It demands imaginative judicial interpretation, since quality is relative, elusive, and dependent upon the type of goods and market. The danger of restrictive canons of interpretation cramping a statutory standard like that set out above is evident in the way the definition has been criticized.[195] This criticism takes the 1973 definition to task because fitness for purpose bulks too large, thereby suggesting that cosmetic and æsthetic aspects of the goods are less important than whether they do the job assigned to them. Similarly, it is argued that to see fitness through reasonable expectations allows account to be taken of actual manufacturing standards, which may be tolerant of minor defects, rather than attainable excellence. This narrow interpretation of the definition of merchantable quality is a by-product of rendering into a statutory form something that perhaps had best been left to judicial exposition. One way to counter the drift to a form of interpretation that destroys the spirit of a broad-textured idea is to maintain contact with the underlying case law. Unfortunately, it cannot be assumed that the 1973 definition was

---

[191] See Ch. 5 above.   [192] By the Supply of Goods (Implied Terms) Act, s. 3.

[193] But Lord Denning thought it the best definition to date in *Cehave NV* v. *Bremer Handelsgesellschaft mbH*, n. 182 above, 62.

[194] See *Cammell Laird & Co. Ltd* v. *Manganese Bronze and Brass Co. Ltd* [1934] AC 402, 429 (Lord Wright); *Henry Kendall & Sons* v. *William Lillico & Sons Ltd*, n. 179 above, 75 (Lord Reid); *B. S. Brown & Son Ltd* v. *Craiks Ltd* [1970] 1 All ER 823.

[195] See Law Com. WP No. 85, n. 185 above, paras. 2.10–12.

designed merely to codify the earlier cases, and it has predictably been asserted that the 'intricacies' of the earlier decisions should be looked at only in exceptional cases.[196] Opinions may differ about whether the 1973 definition was 'clear and free from technicality'[197] or so vague as to be meaningless, and there is much to be said for the practice of turning to the cases for enlightenment,[198] provided this is not done as a matter of routine in simple matters with the cases themselves recited like the tree of Jesse.

A similar criticism of the 1973 definition[199] is that reasonable fitness is not the same as the reasonable acceptance test first propounded by Farwell LJ in *Bristol Tramways Carriage Co. Ltd* v. *Fiat Motors Ltd*.[200] A reasonable buyer might jib at minor defects that would pass the reasonable fitness test. It was indeed a shortcoming of the 1973 definition that it omitted a reference to reasonable acceptance, and possible to see a pointed omission in the case of a criterion well established in the case law. In its working paper preceding the enactment of the Supply of Goods (Implied Terms) Act 1973, the Law Commission put out for consultation the following definition:

'Merchantable quality' means that the goods tendered in performance of the contract shall be of such type and quality and in such condition that, having regard to all the circumstances, including the price and description under which the goods are sold, a buyer, with full knowledge of the quality and characteristics of the goods including knowledge of any defects, would, acting reasonably, accept the goods in performance of the contract.[201]

An explicit reference to fitness for purpose might usefully have been added, although it is arguably implicit in the notion of acceptance. This definition, however, was criticized as too complex and as circular, since the test of whether a buyer should accept the goods[202] depended upon whether a reasonable buyer would have accepted them. Any definition of merchantable quality is bound to be complex: the concept is a complex one. It is also true that there is an element of circularity in the acceptance test[203] but it is not serious: the reasonable buyer and the actual buyer are not one and the same person.

[196] *Rogers* v. *Parish Motors (Scarborough) Ltd*, n. 189 above, 235 (Mustill LJ). See also *Marimpex Mineralöl Handels GmbH* v. *Louis Dreyfus et Cie GmbH* [1995] 1 Lloyd's Rep. 167, 179.   [197] N. 196 above (Mustill LJ).
[198] See Lloyd LJ in *M/S Aswan Engineering Establishment Co.* v. *Lupdine Ltd*, n. 178 above, 6.
[199] See Ontario Law Reform Commission, *Report on Sale of Goods*, i, pp 212–13.
[200] [1910] 2 KB 831.
[201] Working Paper (No 18, 1968), *Provisional Proposals Relating to Amendments to Ss. 12–15 of the Sale of Goods Act 1893 and Contracting Out of the Conditions and Warranties Implied by those Sections*, para. 23.
[202] That is, not reject them for breach of the merchantable quality condition.
[203] See *Taylor* v. *Combined Buyers Ltd* [1924] NZLR 627, 646.

It remains true, however, that merchantable quality is too difficult and protean for its various applications to be encompassed with ease by a statutory definition. Section 14(2) applies to natural commodities, such as grain,[204] and to complex manufactured goods; it also applies to new and to used goods, and to goods purchased for resale as well as to goods purchased for private consumption. Farwell LJ once observed that '[t]he phrase "merchantable quality" seems more appropriate to a retail purchaser buying fom a wholesale firm than to private buyers, and to natural products, such as grain, wool, or flour, than to a complicated machine, but it is clear that it extends to both'.[205] Continuing discomfort with the statutory definition of merchantable quality led to a restructuring and a renaming of the implied term in the Sale and Supply of Goods Act 1994.[206] The name chosen in the Act was 'satisfactory quality' instead of the Law Commission's recommended 'acceptable quality'. The Law Commission was not attracted by neutral adjectives like 'proper' and 'suitable'[207] and thought that 'acceptable' with its reference to the reasonable buyer would encourage out-of-court settlement.

Satisfactory Quality

The new definition reads as follows:

(2A) [G]oods are of satisfactory quality if they meet the standard that a reasonable person would regard as satisfactory, taking account of any description of the goods, the price (if relevant) and all the other relevant circumstances.

(2B) [T]he quality of goods includes their state and condition and the following (among others) are in appropriate cases aspects of the quality of goods—

(a) fitness for all the purposes for which goods of the kind in question are commonly supplied,
(b) appearance and finish,
(c) freedom from minor defects,
(d) safety, and
(e) durability.

The new sub-section (2A) departs from the old definition of merchantable quality in more than just the name; it also substitutes the response of the reasonable person[208] for the fitness for purpose of the goods. This is just as circular as the Law Commission's tentative 1968 definition of merchantable quality: goods are of satisfactory quality if a reasonable person would regard them as satisfactory. Fitness appears in the new sub-section (2B), alongside a number of newly explicit

---

[204] See *Wallis* v. *Russell* [1902] 2 IR 585 (dressed crab).
[205] *Bristol Tramways Carriage Co. Ltd* v. *Fiat Motors Ltd*, n. 200 above, 840.
[206] See M. G. Bridge [1995] *JBL* 398.   [207] Law Com. No. 160, para. 3.18.
[208] Is there any significance in this not being the reasonable buyer?

references to various practical aspects of satisfactory quality; this can only be beneficial in shedding light on the meaning of the implied term. To supplement the above references to statutory definitions of quality, a treatment of a number of practical aspects of the matter is in order.

Cases like *James Drummond and Sons* v. *E. H. Van Ingen & Co.*[209] and *Henry Kendall & Sons* v. *William Lillico & Sons Ltd*[210] established that multi-purpose goods were of merchantable quality if fit for at least one purpose in the range of ordinary purposes;[211] a buyer seeking added protection therefore had to communicate his particular purpose to the seller to invoke the separate implied term of reasonable fitness. If the purpose of a non-communicating buyer were not satisfied by the goods, it was always a difficult matter to determine whether there were other existing purposes in the range of ordinary purposes, not to mention where the burden of persuasion lay in establishing the range of ordinary purposes. An expensive car could not be said to be of merchantable quality just because it could be sold quite satisfactorily as scrap, for the price and description of the goods would exclude scrap from the range of ordinary purposes. In *Jones* v. *Padgett*[212] a quantity of indigo cloth was sold to a woollen merchant who also carried on business as a tailor. The buyer intended to have the cloth made up for servants' liveries in his tailoring business, but did not inform the seller that this was his purpose or indeed that he intended to deal with the cloth as tailor rather than merchant. Because of a latent defect, the cloth could not be used for making liveries but there was nothing to show that it could not be used for other ordinary purposes. Consequently, the seller was not liable for breach of the merchantable quality term. The later decision in *Henry Kendall & Sons* v. *William Lillico & Sons Ltd*[213] endorsed the outcome of *Jones* v. *Padgett* but went further in applying the reasoning to dangerous goods.[214]

The enactment of the first statutory definition of merchantable quality in 1973 posed the question whether the seller's immunity if the goods were fit for one ordinary purpose had survived. It was argued in *M/S Aswan Engineering Establishment Co.* v. *Lupdine Ltd*[215] that the law had changed because now the goods had to be 'as fit for the purpose or purposes', meaning all the purposes 'for which goods of that kind are commonly bought as it is reasonable to expect'. In that case, sellers of liquid waterproof compound were held liable to the buyers because the plastic containers, when stacked, collapsed in conditions of intense heat and

---

[209] (1887) 12 App. Cas. 284.   [210] [1969] 2 AC 31.

[211] Even if the buyer's purpose, not served by the goods, was the most common purpose: *F. E. Hookway & Co. Ltd* v. *Alfred Isaacs & Sons* [1954] 1 Lloyd's Rep. 491.

[212] (1890) 24 QBD 650.   [213] N. 210 above.

[214] See discussion above and the grounds of Lord Pearce's dissent.

[215] [1987] 1 WLR 1.

pressure when exposed for a lengthy period to the Kuwait sun. The sellers in turn sought to pass on this liability to the manufacturing sellers of the containers, who conceded that the containers had been described in the contract as heavy duty pails for export shipment.[216] If the containers were perfectly suitable for export to Europe, as appeared to be the case, the question was whether the manufacturing sellers could be held liable for the different purpose of export to Kuwait, which was not a purpose disclosed to them at the contract date. The Court of Appeal held that the manufacturing sellers were not in breach of section 14(2). Although he would have wished to look at the work of the Law Commission,[217] which was denied him by counsel for both sides, Lloyd LJ[218] concluded that, if Parliament had wished to change the law in the radical way advocated by the claimants, an explicit reference to all purposes would have been made. Moreover, if the claimants had been right, the distinction between merchantable quality and fitness for purpose would have been largely obliterated.[219]

A point left unsettled by the *Aswan* case was how a purpose or purposes is to be defined. The court treated export to Kuwait and to Europe as separate purposes, but it is arguable that there is but one purpose, packaging sealant for export. If this were so, then the focus would shift to whether the containers were reasonably fit for that one purpose as a whole.[220] If Kuwait and Europe are separate purposes, then why should not further differentiation occur so that different countries in Europe are distinguished, perhaps in different seasons, each with its own peculiar climactic conditions? The need to consider this thorny issue has been obviated by the new definition of satisfactory quality which includes 'in appropriate cases . . . fitness for all the purposes for which goods of the kind in question are commonly supplied'.[221] The Law Commission clearly recommended a change that departed from well-established law, asserting that the buyer was entitled to expect that the goods would be fit for all ordinary purposes as defined by the description and the price paid.[222] The burden would therefore be on the seller to limit the description of the goods in order to keep his liability in check.[223] If indeed the old

---

[216] [1987] 1 WLR 15, 25.

[217] The Law Commission has stated that the 1973 definition of merchantable quality did not change the view taken in *Henry Kendall & Sons* v. *William Lillico & Sons Ltd*, n. 210 above, that goods need only be fit for one of their ordinary purposes: Law Com. No. 160, para. 3.32.

[218] With whom Fox LJ agreed. Nicholls LJ delivered a concurring judgment, observing that it would be unreasonable to impose liability when the containers were perfectly adequate for the job in all but the most unusual conditions.

[219] N. 215 above, 15.   [220] Discussed with s. 14(3) below.

[221] S. 14(2B)(a).   [222] Law Com. No. 160, para. 3.35.

[223] *Quaere* might this be open to challenge as an attempt to exclude liability notwithstanding the controls in the Unfair Contract Terms Act 1977?

law has been turned on its head, this involves the rejection of the principle that a buyer seeking a guarantee of quality has to bargain for an express warranty. It is regrettable that the Law Commission did not explore the matter more fully and, in particular, consider whether the change would be as appropriate for commercial as for consumer transactions. There are signs in its 1987 Report that general sales law is being increasingly moulded by the imperatives of consumer protection, and the time may come when separate commercial and consumer statutes are needed.

Be that as it may, despite the Law Commission's wish for a clear definition that would serve useful practical purposes, some considerable uncertainty remains with the new definition of satisfactory quality. In particular, what are 'appropriate cases' for making the seller liable in respect of all ordinary purposes? It is arguable that the result in the *Aswan* case should stand, given the extremity of the conditions in which the containers collapsed. Furthermore, it is difficult to see why the seller in *Jones* v. *Padgett*[224] should be liable to a woollen broker who does not tell him that he proposes to use cloth for liveries or even that he intends to deal with it as a tailor. It may not be appropriate to permit a buyer to reject unwanted goods for breach of section 14(2) just because they are not fit for an ordinary purpose for which the buyer had no intention to use them. The argument is even stronger if the buyer has positively informed the seller that his purpose is a different one. In addition to this difficulty, one may predict that the battleground will shift from enumerating ordinary purposes to determining the difference between ordinary and special purposes. This will encourage some degree of metaphysical discussion. When does a single ordinary purpose split to become two ordinary purposes? How ordinary must a purpose be in order not to be a special one? The use of the containers in *Aswan*, in extreme conditions of temperature and pressure, is quite arguably special rather than ordinary.

Satisfactory Quality and Price

The impact of the new definition of satisfactory quality has to be considered in the light of the relationship between ordinary purpose and price, discussed in *B. S. Brown & Son Ltd* v. *Craiks Ltd*.[225] The quality of the goods in appropriate cases will include fitness for all purposes, and the satisfactoriness of the quality will require account to be taken of the price paid where this is relevant. In *Brown*, a quantity of 'Fibro Plain Cloth' was

---

[224] N. 212 above. See also *Colyer Watson Pty. Ltd* v. *Riverstone Meat Co. Pty. Ltd* (1944) 46 SR (NSW) 32 (pickled pelts suitable for making leather goods though not for processing into high-grade leather).
[225] [1970] 1 All ER 823.

sold according to detailed technical specifications[226] which did not disclose the precise purpose of the buyers. The agreed price was 36¼ pence
a yard and the buyers, unknown to the sellers, intended to use the cloth
for making dresses. At trial,[227] it was found that the price was low for
dress fabrics but at the top end for industrial fabrics without being
unreasonably high. On appeal,[228] it was further stated that the sellers'
equipment and staff were geared to the production of the coarse and
cheap cloth used for industrial fabrics and that the sellers would never
have accepted the order if informed that the buyers intended to make
dresses. The irregularity of the weaving in the fabric meant that it was not
fit for the making of dresses.

The prudent course would have been for the buyers to disclose to the
sellers that they intended to make dresses. In essence, they were substituting an untenable merchantable quality claim for a fitness claim barred
by the lack of disclosure. Their argument was that the price paid took the
cloth out of the range of industrial wear and limited its ordinary purpose
to dress manufacturing. The buyers were unsuccessful because of the
above finding of fact at trial, that the price paid was still within the range
for industrial fabric. But *Brown* is significant in that the House of Lords did
accept that the price, even in the absence of helpful descriptive language,
might define the range of ordinary purposes for the application of the merchantable quality standard. There was, however, some disagreement
about the amount of price movement needed to affect the application of
the implied term in this way. The sellers had resold some of the cloth at
thirty pence a yard and, assuming the new buyers' purpose to be the making of industrial fabric, Lord Guest believed that the difference between
this price and the price in the disputed contract (36 pence) would have to
be 'substantial' for the aggrieved buyers' claim to be well-founded; moreover, the resale price would have to be in the nature of a 'throw away
price'.[229] Lord Reid, on the other hand, was of the view that the contract
price would have to have been 'substantially higher' than the price paid for
the purchase of industrial fabric if the buyers were to succeed.[230] There
was no disagreement, however, over the conclusion that the buyers fell
well short of making their case that the price paid excluded the ordinary
use of industrial fabric. Whichever view is adopted, it seems that Dixon J's
view on price abatement, expressed in *Australian Knitting Mills Ltd* v.
Grant,[231] would have to be moderated in a case of this kind.

---

[226] [1970] 1 All ER 829: ' "49" No. 1717 Fibro 22x22, 2/9s, 2/8s; all viscose yarns, 4½ denier, 6
"staple" '.

[227] 1969 SLT 107, 109.   [228] 1969 SLT 357.

[229] N. 225 above, 828. This part of the judgment is somewhat unclear. Presumably he
does not mean, by 'throw away', a nominal price but rather a price that, in comparison with
the original contract price, is greatly reduced.

[230] *Ibid.* 825.   [231] (1933) 50 CLR 387, 413.

B. S. Brown & Son Ltd v. *Craiks Ltd*[232] therefore stands in the long line of cases holding that the presence of a defect in goods does not of itself render them unmerchantable. The same result should follow from the satisfactory quality term. Subject to the goods now having to fit all ordinary purposes, the implied term of satisfactory quality is concerned only with the minimum level of quality that is saleable under the contract description. In one case,[233] the buyers of a quantity of beetroot canned in vinegar failed in their merchantable quality claim when they could establish only that its shelf life of one year would have been longer if the beetroot had been canned in brine. Again, the same result should be reached in the case of satisfactory quality.

Minor Faults

Suppose, however, that the goods supplied suffer from a minor blemish or fault, perhaps one that can be corrected quickly and inexpensively. Modern manufactured goods are marketed and sold against a background of high expectations and quality control procedures. This undoubtedly has influenced the standard to be expected from the application of section 14(2). Nevertheless, it is a common experience in the case of complex goods, particularly cars, that they suffer from initial problems. Conflicting views have been expressed whether account should be taken of this and of a manufacturer's warranty programme in moderating the quality standard,[234] but the established view is that it should not. This would rule out an application of Lord Denning's opinion in *Cehave NV* v. *Bremer Handelsgesellschaft mbH*[235] that the quality term might be considered in the light of the remaining terms of the contract, for example, any provision made for the return of the goods for adjustment and repair under the terms of a warranty programme. In its report on *Sale and Supply of Goods*,[236] the Law Commission expressed concern that the concentration of the merchantable quality definition upon fitness for purpose might encourage the view that manufacturing blemishes should be condoned if the goods work well enough.[237] There is no good reason why the æsthetic appearance of goods and their freedom from annoying minor defects should not, as well as their function, be seen as part of the buyer's purpose, but there is some little evidence for the Law Commission's concerns.[238] The Law Commission's preoccupation with this problem, together with the concern expressed

---

[232] N. 225 above.   [233] *Geo. Wills & Co. Ltd* v. *Daniels Pty. Ltd* (1957) 98 CLR 77.
[234] See discussion in the text accompanying nn. 189–90 above.
[235] [1976] QB 44.   [236] Law Com. No. 160, 1987.
[237] *Ibid.* paras. 2.11 ff.
[238] See *Millars of Falkirk Ltd* v. *Turpie*, 1976 SLT (Notes) 66.

throughout its Report with consumer protection and the ensuing reference in section 14(2B)(b)(c) to 'appearance and finish' and 'freedom
from minor defects', would suggest that the standard of satisfactory
quality will be a demanding one in its application to new goods.[239] This
is not to say that the appearance and finish of a car at the bottom end of
the price range should be comparable to that of a luxury car. A difficult
case mentioned by the Law Commission[240] is that of the sale of earthenware, where minor imperfections cannot be banished from the manufacturing process. Account should be taken of this in the application of
section 14(2B), but the existence of a separate market in 'seconds' will
prevent any dilution of the standard for earthenware and similar products not sold under the description of 'seconds'.

There already exists authority predating any statutory definition of the
quality standard showing the strictness of the implied term in section
14(2). In *International Business Machines Co.* v. *Shcherban*,[241] a computing scale sold for $295 was shipped by post to a buyer. The buyer rejected
it because a small piece of glass protecting the dial, costing 30 cents to
replace, had been broken. Applying the reasonable acceptance test in
Bristol Tramways Carriage Co. Ltd v. *Fiat Motors Ltd*,[242] the court held
the scale to be unmerchantable. The maxim *de minimis non curat lex* did
not apply: the buyer could not be made to accept damaged goods, even
if the damage was slight.[243] If the result appears harsh, this was the
seller's second attempt to make a conforming tender. The buyer had
already shipped back to Toronto a defective machine. Moreover, there
was no assurance of a swift repair, since the buyer lived in a small town
some distance from the seller's provincial office in Saskatoon.

A similar approach is evident in *Jackson* v. *Rotax Motor & Cycle Co.*,[244]
where a Paris manufacturer sold to an English buyer a large number of
motor horns, many of which had become dented or scratched because of
inadequate packing. It seemed, according to the referee, that the horns
could have been made merchantable at slight cost; he was prepared to
make an allowance of £35 on the purchase price of £450. Yet the price
allowance does not seem slight, there was no indication of who was to
make the horns merchantable, and the sellers were some considerable
distance away. The buyers were in the market for unmarked horns, not
marked horns plus a price allowance. Moreover, the status of merchantable quality as a condition should not have permitted a result

---

[239] Second-hand goods are of course a different matter.
[240] Law Com. No. 160, para. 3.40.
[241] [1925] 1 WWR 405. See also *Winsley Bros.* v. *Woodfield Importing Co.* [1929] NZLR 480.
[242] [1910] 2 KB 831.
[243] For a different result where a missing minor part prevented a second-hand engine
from working, see *Robinson* v. *Burgeson* [1918] 2 WWR 879.
[244] [1910] 2 KB 937.

whereby the buyers had to keep the horns but were granted an allowance. Reversing the referee and the court below, the Court of Appeal was surely correct in holding that the horns were unmerchantable.

Second-hand Goods

The same strict standard of freedom from minor defects cannot be expected for second-hand goods. There is surprisingly little case law on the subject,[245] and the issue has not troubled the Law Commission, which may explain the absence of any explicit reference to second-hand goods in the definition of satisfactory quality. The standard required of the seller depends upon what the reasonable person may expect, in the light of the description and the price, the latter surely being especially relevant in the sale of second-hand goods. Specific disclosures made by the seller about the condition of the goods should be considered under the heading of 'other relevant circumstances' in section 14(2A); such statements assist in defining satisfactory quality in a given case and ought not to be treated as exclusion clauses ousting or limiting the seller's liability under section 14(2). Cars, whether of the same or different ages, are expected to be of variable quality. They may have different mileage figures, which should be reflected in the price. They may have been well or ill-used by previous owners. They may be sold as needing mechanical attention. These variables will affect the extent to which the seller may dispose of defective goods without attracting liability under section 14(2). Unless qualifying language is used, a second-hand car must at least be roadworthy and capable of being safely driven.[246] Lord Denning once said in a second-hand goods case that the standard of liability for merchantable quality was less strict than for fitness for purpose,[247] and the seller's obligations in respect of second-hand goods will be discussed in more detail under that head.

Durability

Durability is a feature of satisfactory quality that has attracted specific mention in section 14(2B). It might have been tidier for it to be regarded as an aspect of fitness for purpose. The merchantable quality standard— and there is nothing to suggest that satisfactory quality is different—

[245] *Bartlett* v. *Sidney Marcus Ltd* [1965] 1 WLR 1013; *Lee* v. *York Coach and Marine* [1977] RTR 35; *Shine* v. *General Guaarantee* [1988] 1 All ER 911; *Business Applications* v. *Nationwide Credit*
[246] See *Lee* v. *York Coach and Marine,* n. 245 above, 42.
[247] *Bartlett* v. *Sidney Marcus Ltd,* n. 245 above, 1016. The liability of the seller in *Crowther* v. *Shannon Motors Ltd* [1975] 1 WLR 30 was dealt with solely in terms of fitness for purpose.

spoke to the character and condition of the goods at the moment of delivery.[248] Fitness for purpose, on the other hand, invites an inquiry into the fate of the goods in the buyer's hands as they are applied to the buyer's purpose,[249] which will be a protracted one for the consumer buyer. Be that as it may, the Law Commission recommended the reference to durability in the definition of satisfactory quality after rejecting proposals to lay down specific periods of durability and to incorporate industry codes of practice.[250] Durability will depend very much on the particular facts and, as a factor of fading strength, will become increasingly difficult to handle with the passage of time. The longer the buyer retains the goods, the more scope there is for argument that the goods have lasted long enough; the more the buyer's own treatment of the goods will bulk large; and the more difficult the buyer will find it to trace the breakdown of the goods to their condition at the date of delivery.

Resale

The existence of defects in the goods may pose a particular difficulty when it bears upon the buyer's prospects of reselling the goods. Two cases may be contrasted. First, in *Niblett* v. *Confectioners' Materials Co. Ltd*[251] the buyers were supplied with a substantial quantity of condensed milk infringing a well-known trade mark. The goods could only be released from the customs shed upon an undertaking by the buyers to destroy the labels, which meant that they could be sold only at a distress price. No buyer aware of the defect in the goods would have bought them on terms similar to those on which they were bought by the actual buyers;[252] the buyers were left with a law suit or a costly embarrassment.

On the other hand, in *Sumner Permain & Co. Ltd* v. *Webb & Co. Ltd*,[253] the decision went in favour of the sellers, who had sold to English buyers on f.o.b. an English port terms a quantity of 'Webb's Indian Tonic'. This tonic contained salicylic acid, an illegal ingredient in the domestic Argentinian market to which the sellers knew the goods were bound. There was no liability in respect of the fitness for purpose term,[254] since the buyers rather than the sellers knew the Argentinian market.

---

[248] See *Bernstein* v. *Pamson Motors (Golders Green) Ltd* [1987] 2 All ER 220, 226; *Lee* v. *York Coach and Marine*, n. 245 above, 42, 43; *Henry Kendall & Sons* v. *William Lillico & Sons Ltd* [1969] 2 AC 31, 118. See also Law Com. No. 160, paras. 3.53–54 (date of supply). The relevant date was said in *R. & B. Customs Brokers Ltd* v. *United Dominions Trust Ltd* [1988] 1 WLR 321, 326, to be the date of the contract, but delivery had already occurred before the contract date. Fitness for purpose cases will be discussed below.

[249] *Lambert* v. *Lewis* [1982] AC 225, 276 (Lord Diplock: 'the goods will continue to be fit . . . for a reasonable time after delivery').

[250] Law Com. No. 160, para. 3.49–50. See also Ontario Law Reform Commission, *Report on Sale of Goods*, i, 215–16.

[251] [1921] 3 KB 387.   [252] *Ibid*.   [253] [1922] 1 KB 55.   [254] *Ibid*. 57n.

Moreover, for the purpose of section 14(2), there was nothing to show that the tonic might not have been sold in other export markets or in the domestic market. It was therefore perfectly possible that other buyers, knowing of the salicylic acid, would have bought the tonic on the same terms as the actual buyers. The court made it plain that the buyers were not entitled to a guarantee that the goods could be resold in all circumstances, a perfectly sensible result. If the tonic had not been saleable in England, but saleable in a number of other export markets, then its sale on export terms should also have resulted in no liability. Conversely, if it had not been saleable in England and had not been sold on export terms, liability should have issued on the ground that no other ordinary purpose existed for the goods in the light of the contractual terms. The definition of satisfactory quality, with its criterion in section 14(2B) of 'fitness for all the purposes for which goods of the kind in question are commonly supplied', could well reverse the outcome of cases like *Sumner Permain*. This would hardly be a sensible reform and it may be that any possible excesses in the statutory changes will be toned down by the qualifying statement that fitness for all purposes will be demanded only in appropriate cases,[255] as well as by a restricted reading of what constitutes an ordinary purpose. If goods can be exported to scores of countries, but the buyer chooses one unfamiliar to the seller, the purpose would appear sufficiently special to require the buyer to satisfy the demands of the fitness for purpose term.

Dangerous Goods

In cases where goods are dangerously defective, especially where they pose a risk of personal injury to human consumers, it is almost axiomatic that they will be held unsatisfactory.[256] It proved not to be too difficult to establish a breach of section 14(2) in cases where beer contained too much arsenic,[257] a loaf of bread contained particles of glass,[258] chocolate milk contained shards of glass,[259] a consignment of proprietary fuel contained an explosive fragment,[260] and a stone in a bun was discovered dentally by the buyer.[261] The courts in the relevant cases did not ask themselves whether a buyer apprised of the adulterant in the goods and

[255] S. 14(2B).
[256] See *Bernstein* v. *Pamson Motors (Golders Green) Ltd*, n. 248 above, 226: '[I]t would be only in the most exceptional case (of which for the moment I cannot imagine an example) that a new car which on delivery was incapable of being driven in safety could ever be classed as being of merchantable quality.'
[257] *Wren* v. *Holt* [1903] 1 KB 610.
[258] *Arendale* v. *Canada Bread Co. Ltd* [1941] 2 DLR 41.
[259] *Shandloff* v. *City Dairy Ltd* [1936] OR 579 (Can.).
[260] *Wilson* v. *Rickett Cockerell & Co. Ltd* [1954] 1 QB 598.
[261] *Chaproniere* v. *Mason* (1905) 21 TLR 633.

314 The Sale of Goods

able to remove it would still have bought the goods without a price abatement.

Where goods are produced for animal consumption, a breach of section 14(2) follows almost as a matter of course if the defect renders the goods unsafe to use at any price or for any purpose. Hence, animal bones improperly cooked by the seller, and so retaining bacteria that killed animals consuming feed made with the bones, were held to be unmerchantable.[262] The same result followed in a case where antarctic whale meat was infected with an undiscoverable botulin toxin.[263] But decisions like *Henry Kendall & Sons* v. *William Lillico & Sons Ltd*[264] show that the mere presence of a defect causing extensive consequential damage will not establish a breach of section 14(2) if the goods could have been purchased on the same terms and applied without causing harm to another ordinary purpose.[265]

Examination

It was stated earlier that case law preceding the first codification of sale in 1893 retained *caveat emptor* to the extent that no warranty of merchantable quality existed for goods that the buyer could have examined before the contract of sale.[266] In that year, the law was changed when the Act provided that the merchantable quality condition was excepted in respect of examination only 'if the buyer has examined the goods' and 'as regards defects that such examination ought to have revealed'. This exception was plainly confined to specific goods or at least a specific bulk. The examination was one conducted before the contract of sale;[267] it was not the post-contract examination upon which hinged the buyer's right to reject the goods and terminate the contract. This point emerged more explicitly when the provision was amended in the 1979 Act to provide that the section 14(2) condition was excepted 'if the buyer examines the goods before the contract is made, as regards defects which that examination ought to reveal'.[268] This stance is continued in the present section 14(2C)(b) which excepts liability for 'any matter making the quality of goods unsatisfactory . . . where the buyer examines the goods before the contract is made, which that examination ought to reveal'.

It seems on the face of it strange that a feckless buyer who conducts no

---

[262] *Feed-Rite Mills (1962) Ltd* v. *East-West Packers Ltd* (1975) 65 DLR (3d) 175.
[263] *Farmer* v. *Canada Packers Ltd* [1956] OR 657 (Can.). [264] N. 248 above.
[265] In *Ashington Piggeries Ltd* v. *Christopher Hill Ltd* [1972] AC 441, the sellers were unable to demonstrate that the goods could safely have been fed to animals other than mink. The 1994 changes would anyway render such efforts unavailing.
[266] See *Jones* v. *Just* (1868) LR 3 QB 197, 202–3 (first and fifth propositions)—even as regards latent defects, at least where the seller was not the manufacturer or the grower.
[267] *Taylor* v. *Combined Buyers Ltd* [1924] NZLR 627, 635. [268] S. 14(2)(b).

examination at all, even if the chance to examine has been offered, should be better off than a more prudent buyer whose examination is negligently conducted.[269] It may be, nevertheless, that a buyer may decide not to examine in order to avoid limiting the seller's responsibilities under section 14(2). The above contradiction emerged in a pointed manner in *Thornett & Fehr* v. *Beers & Son*,[270] where the representatives of the buyer, in a hurry because of their lateness for the appointment, conducted a cursory examination of the outside of barrels of vegetable glue. They did not open up the barrels to discover the evident defect in the glue. The court held that the examination exception applied. There had in fact been an examination which, if conducted properly, would have revealed the defect.[271] It did not matter that no examination of just the outside of the barrels would have disclosed the defect. The decision has attracted criticism but is defensible in that the sellers' careful arrangements for an examination, to which the buyers agreed, indicated a clear intention to avoid liability for any evident defects; the buyers were 'willing to take the risk, the price being so low'.[272] Since 1973, the word 'that' has taken the place of 'such' in the phrase 'such examination'. It has been cautiously suggested that this change might have overturned the *Thornett* decision,[273] but this argument relies upon a degree of finesse not usually dislayed in the armoury of the modern Parliamentary draftsman. The change of wording would, however, give the courts an opportunity to wipe the slate clean if they wished. The examination conducted by the buyer must amount to more than a sighting or even a touching of the goods;[274] a threshold should be crossed before the examination exception begins to operate.

The type of examination that the buyer does conduct need only be a reasonable one; the seller's liability is not excepted because a latent defect in the goods could have been detected by an exhaustive examination. Merely drawing back the elastic was a reasonable examination for a retailer to conduct when purchasing a consignment of plastic catapults; it was not sufficient to reveal a flaw in the plastic.[275] Likewise, the consumer buyer's examination of beer was not capable of detecting an excess of arsenic[276] and the buyer of a yacht that he had seen at a trade

---

[269] The provision was criticized as too generous to buyers by the Law Reform Commission of New South Wales in *Working Paper on The Sale of Goods: Warranties, Remedies, Frustration and Other Matters* (1975), paras. 8.59 ff.

[270] [1919] 1 KB 486.

[271] Cf. *Frank* v. *Grosvenor Motor Auctions Pty. Ltd* [1960] VR 607.   [272] *Ibid.* 489.

[273] *Benjamin's Sale of Goods* (5th edn., 1997 by A. G. Guest and others), §11–055.

[274] The best explanation for the view that the buyer of a car who merely sits in it prior to the contract of sale yet retains the benefit of s. 14(2): see *Frank* v. *Grosvenor Motors Ltd* [1960] VR 607, 609.

[275] *Godley* v. *Perry* [1960] 1 WLR 9, 15.

[276] *Wren* v. *Holt*, n. 257 above, 616, expressed wrongly in terms of an opportunity to examine.

show could not be expected to retain the services of a consulting chemist to discover the latent fault that subsequently produced 'blistering' of the hull.[277]

A difficult issue arising out of the time of the examination occurred in *R. & B. Customs Brokers Ltd* v. *United Dominions Trust Ltd*,[278] where prospective buyers on conditional sale terms were allowed the use of a car before their proposal was accepted by the finance company sellers. They discovered a leak in the roof of the car before they signed the agreement. Because of the buyers' continuing reliance on the skill or judgement of the sellers' agent, the dealer,[279] the Court of Appeal was spared the need to reach a conclusion on the question whether the buyers were prevented from invoking section 14(2) when their pre-contractual use of the car revealed its leaking roof. It is difficult to see why the examination exception should not apply to the advantage of the seller in such a case, though sellers would presumably waive their rights under the exception if they or their agents undertook that the defect would be corrected.

The examination exception was expanded in 1973 so as to provide that the seller was not responsible 'as regards defects specifically drawn to the buyer's attention before the contract was made'. The current text (section 14(2C)(a)) substitutes for the expression 'as regards defects' the words 'any matter making the quality of goods unsatisfactory', which is not a change of any substance. The requirement that the defect or matter be referred to specifically is designed to prevent sellers from excluding their liability under section 14(2) in the guise of a blanket statement designed to take advantage of the exception in section 14(2C)(a). It should be noted that the defect need not be one pointed out by the seller.

REASONABLE FITNESS FOR PURPOSE

Section 14(3) of the Sale of Goods Act states, in brief, that the goods supplied by a seller in the course of a business must be reasonably fit for any particular purpose of the buyer when this is expressly or impliedly made known to the seller and the buyer relies upon the seller's skill or judgement.[280] In the 1893 Act, the fitness term preceded merchantable quality

---

[277] *Canadian Yacht Sales* v. *MacDonald* [1977] 2 Lloyd's Rep. 298 (Can.). See also *John Macdonald & Co. Ltd* v. *Princess Manufacturing Co. Ltd* [1926] SCR 472 ('reasonable inspection').

[278] [1988] 1 WLR 321.   [279] So that the sellers were liable under s. 14(3).

[280] According to s. 14(3):

    'Where the seller sells goods in the course of a business and the buyer, expressly or by implication, makes known—
        (a) to the seller, or
        (b) where the purchase price or part of it is payable by instalments and the goods were previously sold by a credit-broker to the seller, to that credit-broker, any

as section 14(1) in the body of the Act, and in the years thereafter, for reasons discussed below, it proved a more effective source of protection for the disappointed buyer than the merchantable quality term. Reforms of the latter, starting in 1973, have rid it of some difficult aspects, yet it is questionable whether the requirement of satisfactory quality will be any easier to apply than its predecessor, merchantable quality, which lost ground to fitness for purpose because of the latter's greater ease of application. Lord Reid once said that the judicial tendency to limit the scope of merchantable quality had been balanced by a countervailing tendency to give an expansive reading to fitness for purpose.[281] Fitness for purpose was of general application, capable of embracing all sales, whether or not descriptive words were used or the goods were specific. Before 1973, merchantable quality on the other hand was confined to sales by description, which would largely have excluded sales of specific goods as the law was understood in 1893. The technical limits of description on section 14(2) had been eased even before 1973, but fitness for purpose developed apace as it was applied to commonplace as well as esoteric purposes and as the trade name proviso[282] became largely redundant fifty years before its formal abolition in 1973. Fitness for purpose occupies a crucial strategic position. A given set of facts will frequently permit multiple claims to branch off into express warranty, fitness for purpose, negligence (failure to warn) and negligent misstatement, and misrepresentation.

The implied term of fitness for purpose has over the years diminished the impact in sales law of the restrictive express warranty decision of the House of Lords in *Heilbut, Symons & Co.* v. *Buckleton*,[283] which imposed the requirement that a statement had to be made with contractual intention to constitute an express warranty. Although it is easier in modern times to infer an express warranty,[284] a buyer's ability to seek recourse under the fitness term when impliedly or expressly disclosing his purpose to the seller has ensured that there is only a small number of reported decisions on express warranty in sales law.[285]

---

particular purpose for which the goods are being bought, there is an implied condition that the goods supplied under the contract are reasonably fit for that purpose, whether or not that is a purpose for which such goods are commonly supplied, except where the circumstances show that the buyer does not rely, or that it is unreasonable for him to rely, on the skill or judgment of the seller or credit-broker.'

[281] *Henry Kendall & Sons* v. *William Lillico & Sons Ltd* [1969] 2 AC 31, 79.
[282] See discussion in the text accompanying nn. 402 ff. below.
[283] [1913] AC 30.   [284] See Ch. 8 below.
[285] The doctrine of privity of contract is responsible for a number of cases since express warranty bridges the gap separating the buyer from a manufacturer or from a dealer whose contract of sale is with a finance company.

Development of Fitness for Purpose

The cases preceding the 1893 Act do not always draw a consistent distinction between the fitness for purpose and merchantable quality terms.[286] A discernible fitness for purpose strand emerges in *Jones* v. *Bright*[287] where sheets of copper sold for sheathing a barque became perforated in use, lasting for one four-month trip instead of the normal four years. Despite the selection of the (apparently) specific goods by the buyer, the seller was liable in an action on the case in damages. The judgment of Best CJ is important for two reasons. First, it separates merchantable quality from fitness, the former requiring the goods to be fit for some purpose and the latter for a particular purpose when sold for that purpose.[288] Secondly, in a way wholly distant from the spirit of *laissez faire* and *caveat emptor*, it candidly asserts that it is the business of the courts to promote quality control in the manufacture of goods since they should 'make it the interest of manufacturers and those who sell, to furnish the best article that can be supplied'.[289] Furthermore, 'the case is of great importance . . . because it will teach manufacturers that they must not aim at underselling each other by producing goods of inferior quality, and that the law will protect purchasers who are necessarily ignorant of the commodity sold'.[290]

The fitness for purpose obligation was extended in *Brown* v. *Edgington*[291] to a non-manufacturing seller who supplied a hoisting rope that snapped to a buyer who requested it for raising pipes of wine from a cellar. The court declined to distinguish between manufacturers and those who undertook to get articles made. The seller had told the buyer that the rope would be specially made and had left the impression with the buyer that he would be making it.

The development of this head of liability was stemmed by the Court of Exchequer in *Chanter* v. *Hopkins*[292] where the buyer purchased a furnace from the seller, the patentee of 'Chanter's smoke-consuming furnace'. Although the furnace was useless when installed in the buyer's brewery, the court held the seller not liable for the breach of an implied fitness warranty, since the buyer had purchased 'a defined and well-known machine'. There was nothing, like the undertaking[293] in *Brown* v. *Edgington* flowing from the supply of custom-built goods for the buyer's

---

[286] See *Jones* v. *Just* (1868) LR 3 QB 197; *Shepherd* v. *Pybus* (1842) 3 Man. & Gr. 868; *James Drummond and Sons* v. *E. H. Van Ingen & Co.* (1887) 12 App. Cas. 284.

[287] (1829) 5 Bing. 533. See also *Gray* v. *Cox* (1825) 4 B & C 108; *Bluett* v. *Osborne* (1816) 1 Stark. 384.

[288] A distinction set aside by the 1994 changes to satisfactory quality discussed above.

[289] N. 287 above, 543.   [290] *Ibid.* 546.   [291] (1841) 2 Man. & Gr. 279.

[292] (1838) 4 M & W 399.

[293] By this date, the liability of sellers had migrated from case to special *assumpsit*.

purpose, to indicate that the seller had accepted responsibility for the furnace to work in the buyer's brewery. The furnace had well-known properties and was just like any other object of its kind. Consequently, the buyer should trust his own judgement.

The idea of an undertaking was taken further in *Shepherd* v. *Pybus*[294] when the buyer purchased a barge lying at the seller's wharf in order to carry cement. The barge leaked in a way that would not have been discoverable on inspection and the Court of Common Pleas ordered a new trial on the ground that the jury's verdict in favour of the buyer had to be supported by more than just the seller's knowledge of the buyer's special purpose. The buyer also had to give a 'distinct notice . . . or declaration'[295] so as, it would seem, to engage an implied undertaking issuing from the seller that the barge would be fit for that special purpose. Had the barge been purchased only for general use as a barge, it seems that an implied disclosure by the buyer would have been adequate.[296]

It was subsequently confirmed that the *caveat emptor* rule continued to govern sales of specific goods.[297] The Sale of Goods Act 1893, in an earlier draft, would have ruled out a fitness for purpose term where the buyer had the opportunity to examine the goods. The fitness term would thus have been excepted in most cases of specific goods. But the only significance of pre-contractual examination in the modern law is that it may tend against reliance on the seller's skill or judgement. Shortly before the first codification of sale, it was firmly laid down in *Randell* v. *Newson*[298] that the liability of the seller was strict in that there was no exception based upon latent, undiscoverable defects. On the eve of the 1893 Act, it was possible to see the broad outline of the fitness for purpose term.[299] It applied to intermediate as well as to manufacturing sellers; the more general the purpose, the more likely the seller's undertaking would be inferred; liability was more likely to attach to custom-built than to mass-produced items; the seller was strictly liable, even if his skill or judgement could never have revealed a latent defect; and finally, inspection would tend against liability except that, it seems, a buyer would not be expected to find undiscoverable latent defects, just as the seller would be liable despite an inability to find them.

---

[294] N. 286 above.   [295] *Ibid.* 881.

[296] This would involve a departure from *Chanter* v. *Hopkins*, n. 292 above.

[297] *Emmerton* v. *Mathews* (1862) 7 H & N 586 (buyer a meat retailer purchasing from a market trader). See also *Turner* v. *Mucklow* (1862) 6 LT 690.

[298] (1877) 2 QBD 102.

[299] The original s. 14(1) was described as a 'crystallization of the common law' in *Randall* v. *Sawyer-Massey Co.* (1918) 43 OLR 602, 607 (Can.).

Sale in the Course of a Business

As with the satisfactory quality term, the fitness term applies only if the seller sells goods in the course of a business.[300] The development of fitness for purpose liability had nothing to do with status: sellers were adjudged liable not because they were in business, but because they had a skill or judgement that was denied to the buyer. The most obvious example of such skill was the seller who was the manufacturer of the goods and so knew of their properties or was in a position to guard against the emergence of defects in the manufacturing process.[301] Further examples of skill or judgement concerned wholesalers or retailers who selected goods for distribution to buyers.[302] The law developed so as to visit liability on such sellers even if they could not by taking all due care have avoided injury to the buyer. To the extent that their liability became strict, it made sense to say that business sellers as a class were susceptible to liability under section 14(3). The reference in the pre-1973 fitness term to the business seller being liable, whether he was the manufacturer or not, was designed to show that wholesalers and retailers could be liable; it did not mean that liability was confined to manufactured products and excluded natural products. Nevertheless, counsel for the buyer in *Jones* v. *Bright*[303] argued a difference between the two: the reason for this suggested distinction was to establish that the *caveat emptor* immunities of a horse seller should not be extended to a copper manufacturer, since it was only in the former case that 'the seller has no more means than the buyer of guarding against or knowing intrinsic or hidden defects'.[304] Once liability extended beyond manufacturing sellers, the distinction between manufactured and natural products had to collapse.

Since private sellers do not sell new goods, it is hardly surprising that the extension of liability beyond manufacturers did not reach as far as them, given the uncertain nature in the nineteenth century of the liability of all sellers of natural products. The mass production of consumer goods is a post-1893 phenomenon, likewise the disposal of second-hand consumer durables. The private seller of a second-hand car knows a great deal about its history and characteristics, so to this extent there is no shortage of skill or judgement. The immunity of private sellers, however, may be defended on a different ground. Unlike the civil law,[305] the

[300] In this respect, the s. 14(2) discussion above applies here.
[301] See, e.g., *Jones* v. *Bright*, n. 287 above.
[302] See, e.g., *Preist* v. *Last* [1903] 2 KB 148.   [303] N. 287 above.
[304] *Ibid.* 536. According to K. Llewellyn, 'Of Warranty of Quality and Society' (1936) 36 *Col LR* 699, 711: 'Warranty, 1780–1850, divides conveniently in England, and indeed in several of the United States, into horse and non-horse.'
[305] See, e.g., the French Code Civil, Arts. 1641, 1644–5.

common law of sale has declined to sever the two issues of contractual termination and liability in damages.[306] Unless insurance against consequential losses became popular, it would be hard to justify imposing a damages liability on private sellers with no ability to spread the loss or write it off for tax purposes.[307] To permit a buyer to return goods to a private seller or to recover a price abatement would incur no such reproach, but there is no sanction for this in the Sale of Goods Act or the common law of contract.

A further reason for drawing a distinction between business and private sellers is this. The modern law of fitness for purpose shows a degree of strictness in its application to retailers and wholesalers that is clearly actuated by a desire, where goods are defective, to move liability up the chain to the source of the defect, namely the manufacturer or producer.[308] Private sellers, who usually dispose of second-hand goods, are not in the same position as business sellers to remit liability since the second-hand goods they sell are not the new goods that were sold to them.

Strict Liability

Liability under section 14(3) is strict but strangely hybrid in nature. The seller's duty is an absolute one, to see to it not that the goods are absolutely fit for the buyer's purpose, but that they are reasonably fit. This gives the subsection a measure of flexibility that can in certain instances dilute the seller's responsibility. It permits a distinction to be made between new and second-hand goods, the buyer's reasonable expectations being lower for the latter. It permits also a distinction to be made between unsuitability and defectiveness, and between defects that are irritants and defects that are dangerous. Section 14(3) does not as such demand that the goods be defective,[309] though goods that are defective are the more likely to be held unfit for purpose. Paradoxically, even though reasonable fitness gives rise to a dilution of liability in some

---

[306] The Ontario Law Reform Commission, *Report on Sale of Goods* (1979), i, 209, notes a 'persuasive argument' in favour of allowing a price reduction action (Cf. CISG (the Vienna Convention on International Sale of Goods 1980), Art. 50) against a private seller but stops short of a recommendation.

[307] The Ontario Law Reform Commission was not persuaded that the express warranty damages liability of a private seller should be restricted by statute: i, 140–41. But the Uniform Act sponsored by the Uniform Law Conference of Canada would allow in such cases a reduction in damages (s. 114).

[308] See, e.g., *Ashington Piggeries Ltd* v. *Christopher Hill Ltd* [1972] AC 441; *Henry Kendall & Sons* v. *William Lillico & Sons Ltd* [1969] 2 AC 31; *Young & Marten Ltd* v. *McManus Childs Ltd* [1969] 1 AC 454 (Lord Upjohn: 'the ultimate culprit, the manufacturer').

[309] See, e.g., *Macfarlane* v. *Taylor* (1868) LR 1 HL (Sc. & D) 245 (whisky for the West African market, coloured with logwood to resemble rum, produced alarming red secretions in its consumers).

cases, the very flexibility of fitness and its emancipation from defectiveness allows, as will be seen, a very strict form of product liability in other cases.

Although section 14(3) is brought into play by the buyer's reliance on the seller's skill or judgement, liability may exist even if no degree of skill or judgement on the part of the seller could have detected a hidden defect, such as a flaw in a carriage pole[310] or typhoid germs in milk.[311] A retail seller who sells sealed goods that are impossible to examine without breaking the seal is no less liable under section 14(3).[312] Yet the seller must be given a chance to exercise skill or judgement; hence the buyer must state his purpose expressly or impliedly.[313] Lord Reid has remarked upon the relationship between strict liability and skill or judgement:

> If the law were always logical one would suppose that a buyer, who has obtained a right to rely on the seller's skill or judgment, would only obtain thereby an assurance that proper skill and judgment had been exercised, and would only be entitled to a remedy if a defect in goods was due to failure to exercise such skill and judgment. But the law has always gone further than this. By getting the seller to use his skill and judgment the buyer gets under [section 14(3)] an assurance that the goods will be reasonably fit for his purpose and that covers not only defects that the seller ought to have detected but also defects which are latent in the sense that even the utmost skill and judgment on the part of the seller would not have detected them.[314]

As strict as lability is, the impact of it cannot be fully understood without regard to the degree of disclosure that the buyer must make and to the definition of 'particular purpose'. Initially, fitness for purpose evolved to satisfy special or esoteric purposes that the buyer had in mind. Thus the question in *Jones* v. *Bright*[315] was whether sheets of copper, which might have been used for any one of a number of different purposes, were impliedly warranted as fit for the special purpose of sheathing a vessel. But doubts about the extent of liability for merchantable quality led to the application of section 14(3) in cases where the goods had only one purpose and a common one at that. Thus in *Preist* v. *Last*,[316] the seller of a rubber hot water bottle was liable in damages under section 14(3) when it burst and injured the buyer's wife.

---

[310] *Randell* v. *Newson*, n. 298 above

[311] *Frost* v. *Aylesbury Dairy Co. Ltd* [1905] 1 KB 608.

[312] *Bigge* v. *Parkinson* (1862) 7 H & N 955.

[313] This explains the partial dissent of Lord Diplock in *Ashington Piggeries Ltd* v. *Christopher Hill Ltd*, n. 308 above.

[314] *Henry Kendall & Sons* v. *William Lillico & Sons Ltd*, n. 308 above, 84.

[315] (1829) 5 Bing. 533.

[316] N. 302 above. See also *Grant* v. *Australian Knitting Mills Ltd* [1936] AC 85; *Frost* v. *Aylesbury Dairy Co. Ltd*, n. 311 above.

Disclosure and Purpose

The expansion of section 14(3) from esoteric to commonplace purposes obviously had an impact upon the degree of disclosure a buyer had to make to invoke the seller's responsibility.[317] An esoteric purpose will clearly have to be brought home to the seller for most practical purposes by explicit notification, unless for example the buyer's identity and activities make that purpose a notorious one. A commonplace purpose, on the other hand, need not be expressly communicated to the seller,[318] who is likely to assume that that is the buyer's purpose anyway unless informed to the contrary. Thus the buyer in *Preist* v. *Last*[319] did not have to say that the water bottle was needed to warm the bed, nor the doctor in *Grant* v. *Australian Knitting Mills*[320] that the woollen undergarments were designed to bridge the gap between birthday suit and business suit. As a matter of fact, as opposed to law, any evidentiary need for the buyer explicitly to inform the seller will be directly proportional to the speciality of purpose for which the goods are needed. The expansion of section 14(3) into commonplace purposes benefited the consumer buyers of finished, single-purpose goods; it did nothing for the trade buyer of goods who might use them for any one of a number of different purposes.[321]

Once it became established that a seller could incur liability under section 14(3) in respect of commonplace purposes, difficult taxonomic questions were later posed concerning the relationship between commonplace purposes liability and esoteric purposes liability. In particular, what was the commonplace (or even *a* commonplace) purpose of certain goods, and when was that purpose so far from the norm that it had to be treated as a special purpose? A further question concerned goods that proved to be unfit for an undisclosed esoteric purpose, but that would also have proved unfit if applied to the commonplace purpose served by the goods.

The above questions are best answered through a review of two House of Lords decisions. In the first of these, *Henry Kendall & Sons* v. *William Lillico & Sons Ltd,*[322] a quantity of Brazilian groundnut extract had been sold by one dealer in animal feedstuffs (Kendall) to another (Grimsdale); at the next stage in the distribution chain, the extract was compounded

---

[317] S. 14(3) allows disclosure to be made to a credit-broker, defined in s. 61(1), where the price or part of it is payable on instalment terms.

[318] *Ibid.* No difficulty is posed by the parol evidence rule in the workings of fitness for purpose liability: *Bristol Tramways Carriage Co. Ltd* v. *Fiat Motors Ltd* [1910] 2 KB 831; *Cammell Laird & Co. Ltd* v. *Manganese Bronze and Brass Co. Ltd* [1934] AC 402.

[319] N. 302 above.   [320] N. 316 above.

[321] But it did lay the foundation of the developments in *Ashington Piggeries Ltd* v. *Christopher Hill Ltd*, n. 308 above, discussed below.

[322] N. 308 above.

by Grimsdale's buyer into poultry feed and it was then sold to a game farm. When fed to the game farm's breeding pheasants, the feed killed a large number of them because the groundnut extract was contaminated by aflatoxin, the poisonous product of a mould caused by a fungus growing on the groundnuts. At the time of the contract, Kendall knew that the extract that it was selling to Grimsdale would be resold to compounders of animal feed; it did not know whether the extract would ultimately be compounded into cattle feed or poultry feed. In a general sense, the groundnut extract was unfit because it was toxic in varying degrees to cattle and poultry. Furthermore, Kendall could hardly complain of Grimsdale's failure to warn it that the extract would be compounded into poultry feed since its own ignorance of the toxicity of the goods and the varying vulnerability of cattle and poultry meant that the sale would have gone through in any event. Kendall was therefore not deprived of any opportunity to exercise its skill or judgement by the absence of information from Grimsdale and so was held liable in damages under section 14(3).

The House of Lords was at pains, nevertheless, to show that its decision was confined to market conditions prevailing at the date of the contract.[323] It later became known that even toxic groundnut extract could be fed to cattle, though in modest proportions smaller than those used in compounding poultry feed in the instant case. The extract remained unfit, however, for poultry even if used in modest proportions.[324] Thus in the animal feed market, after it became known that Brazilian groundnut extract was contaminated by aflatoxin, and was therefore lethal to poultry and safe for cattle only if used in small quantitites, no market at all existed for the goods in the compounding of poultry feed, while a market continued to exist for cattle feed. In order for a seller to be liable under subsequent contracts for harm done to poultry, a basic question raised in *Henry Kendall & Sons* was whether that seller might merely be informed that the extract was needed for animal feed or whether the buyer had to make it known that it was destined for poultry. Lord Reid doubted that liability should exist in the former case,[325] which is consistent with the tenor of the case as a whole. The resale of the goods for compounding into animal feed would no longer be sufficient to engage a seller's responsibility for all types of animal feed. The buyer would have to be more explicit.

The major lesson to be learned from *Henry Kendall & Sons* is that 'par-

---

[323] N. 308 above 116, *per* Lord Pearce ('according to current standards'); 84, *per* Lord Reid.

[324] *Ibid.* 117 (no need for compounder to use 'abnormally small' proportions to remove lethal effect).

[325] *Ibid.* 84.

ticular purpose' is not a static idea but is to be understood by reference to informed market activity. Goods may pass muster under section 14(3), even though defective, provided there is an attainable purpose to which they can be applied. Increasing knowledge of the properties of goods will therefore modify the market over time and thus the application of section 14(3). For example, while groundnut extract contaminated by aflatoxin might suitably be fed to cattle, a subsequent discovery that beef cattle fed in his way could not be slaughtered for human consumption because of the carcinogenic quality of the meat would change the picture again. If a market still existed for cattle other than beef cattle, then a buyer purchasing goods for beef cattle should have to inform the seller of this to engage the seller's liability under section 14(3) for harm done to beef cattle.

The inference from *Henry Kendall & Sons*, that a buyer of groundnut extract, purchasing for resale to compounders of animal feed, would in future have to inform the seller if the feed were ultimately to be fed to poultry, has to be modified to take account of the House of Lords decision in *Ashington Piggeries Ltd* v. *Christopher Hill Ltd*.[326] In that case, Norwegian producers sold a quantity of herring meal to English compounders of animal feed; the Norwegian producers were not informed of the ultimate destination of the goods. In fact, the meal was used in compounding mink feed according to an original recipe supplied by the sub-buyers, English mink breeders. The herring meal was contaminated by the presence of dimethylnitrosamine (DMNA), a by-product of the preserving process adopted by the Norwegian producers, and a large number of the sub-buyers' mink died. A successful fitness for purpose claim was brought by the sub-buyers against the buyer, who now claimed over against the sellers, the Norwegian producers.

As the complex evidence showed, it was not known at any relevant time that the method of preservation used could bring about DMNA poisoning. Mink were specially vulnerable to this toxic additive, which attacked the liver, but it was never shown how, if at all, the contaminated herring meal might be fed to other animals. When the herring meal was supplied by the Norwegian producers, they knew that herring meal had been fed in the past to Norwegian mink, a practice that at that date had not emerged in England; they also knew of the mysterious deaths in recent years of Norwegian mink but were unaware of any connection between this and herring meal.

The Norwegian producers were held liable in damages under section 14(3) although they did not know—and it was unlikely that they actually contemplated—that the herring meal would eventually be fed to mink. It

---

[326] N. 308 above.

was enough for the buyers to establish that herring meal was generally unfit for compounding into animal feed[327] and that, in accordance with the contractual remoteness of damage rule, had the Norwegian producers contemplated the matter at the contract date, they would have realized it was not unlikely that the herring meal would be fed to mink. *Ashington Piggeries* involves an expansion of section 14(3) liability, as expounded in *Henry Kendall & Sons*, in that it boosts the evidentiary position of the buyer. To establish general unsuitability, a buyer need not show that goods of the same type have actually injured animals other than mink in the range covered by animal feed in general, nor even that, if fed to any of those animals, such as pigs, chickens, cattle, and sheep, the herring meal would cause injury. Rather, the presence of toxicity would raise an evidentiary inference of unfitness across the range.[328] The burden would then fall on the seller to show that the contaminated meal could be fed to other animals in the range,[329] so that the special vulnerability of mink would be seen as an idiosyncracy peculiar to them and falling within the buyer's area of responsibility.[330] Obviously, it would be at least as hard for the seller to prove this as for the buyer to prove the opposite.

Interesting, too, is the court's use of the remoteness of damage rule. The heart of the buyer's case is that the seller commits a breach of contract when the buyer receives, before putting to use, goods that in general terms are unfit across the broad range of the buyer's purpose (selling to an animal feed compounder). It therefore follows that any actual loss incurred by a seller in respect of herring meal compounded into mink feed, in excess of what would have been incurred if the meal had found its way into sheep or cattle feed, is recoverable subject to the remoteness rule.[331] This rule seems to have been quite leniently applied in favour of buyers in *Ashington Piggeries*.[332] The Norwegian producers were held liable in an amount that could well have exceeded any sums they might

---

[327] N. 308 above 492–3, 497–8 (Lord Wilberforce).

[328] *Ibid., per* Lord Wilberforce at 492: '[N]ot only mink have livers'.

[329] *Quaere* how many species? In principle, one ought to suffice. Another point is that such species should be safely fed the herring meal compounded in sensible, rather than microscopic, proportions: see Lord Pearce in *Henry Kendall & Sons v. William Lillico & Sons Ltd* [1969] 2 AC 31, 117.

[330] The subject of divided responsibility is considered below.

[331] This rule in principle requires the type of loss rather than its quantum to be within the reasonable contemplation of the parties at the contract date: *Wroth* v. *Tyler* [1974] Ch. 30. Notwithstanding principle, however, the courts *de facto* seem to require some degree of foresight of quantum when a claim is made for lost profits: *Victoria Laundry (Windsor) Ltd* v. *Newman Industries Ltd* [1949] 2 KB 528 and *Horne* v. *Midland Railway Co.* (1873) LR 8 CP 131 (refusal to award damages for especially lucrative profits).

[332] From the Norwegian producers' point of view, the chances of the herring meal being fed to mink must have been quite slender. Cf. *Koufos* v. *C. Czarnikow Ltd (The Heron II)* [1969] 1 AC 350.

have had to pay if the herring meal had been fed to any other animal species. In the light of the facts as they emerged in the case, a subsequent seller of herring meal might, even if a preserving process not posing the risk of DMNA poisoning is used, well be chary, in view of the particular vulnerability of mink, of supplying such goods to a buyer who intends either to use them for mink feed or to sell them to a sub-buyer with such a use in mind. That seller might wish to recommend a less risky ingredient or decline to sell to a buyer with such a sensitive use in mind. The very success of the the buyers in their action against the Norwegian producers might bring about market conditions in which the trade would view a general disclosure of animal feed compounding or selling to feed compounders as insufficient to cover loss caused to mink.

A similar point to the above emerges in the vigorous dissent of Lord Diplock in *Ashington Piggeries* on the matter of the Norwegian producers' liability.[333] The core of this speech is that a buyer who acquaints the seller merely with a broadly defined purpose, not all the sub-categories of which are best suited by goods possessing identical characteristics, fails to give the seller a proper opportunity to exercise skill or judgement. Lord Diplock would therefore have read the words 'particular purpose' in section 14(3) more restrictively than the majority of the court and would have dispensed with the remoteness of damage approach by requiring knowledge, not foresight, of the sub-category that the buyer had in mind. It was possible that the Norwegian producers might, if given the chance, have recommended against the purchase of herring meal for mink feed for reasons quite unconnected with DMNA poisoning, for example its high fat content.[334]

There is much in Lord Diplock's dissent. Since liability is strict and independent of any knowledge of latent defects, it might be thought that sellers should be given a fair chance to minimise their liability. On the other hand, the decision against the Norwegian producers is consistent with the modern trend for the implied terms in section 14 to operate as guarantees against latent defects, applied in such a way as to push liability up the distribution chain to the point where the defect was created. Lord Diplock's approach could not readily be applied in the case of a buyer purchasing feedstuffs on a general basis, who might at the time of the contract not know the identity and particular purpose of the sub-buyer. The decision of the majority in *Ashington Piggeries* against the Norwegian producers appears to have settled the law, sanctioning a form of strict product liability implemented by means of linked indemnity actions connecting the last buyer to the manufacturer or producer of defective goods.[335]

---

[333] [1972] AC 441, 509–13.   [334] *Ibid.* 510–11.   [335] See Ch. 8 below.

328   *The Sale of Goods*

In *Henry Kendall & Sons*, Lord Pearce observed that the more circumscribed the purpose of the buyer, the narrower the range of goods from which the seller might select in fulfilment of the contract.[336] This would appear to encourage buyers to inform sellers as closely as possible of their needs, not merely for the obvious reason that this encourages sellers to deliver goods that best correspond to buyer' needs, but also because buyers are thus bargaining for stricter seller liability.[337] Yet, if Lord Diplock's criticism in *Ashington Piggeries* is accurate, the decision, in some cases at least, does not encourage buyers to describe in detail the destination of the goods. *Ashington Piggeries*, however, does not abridge the right of sellers to exclude or limit their liability under section 14(3) to the extent that this is permitted by law[338] or to require of their buyers a clear statement of purpose.

Hypersensitive Buyers

The decision in *Ashingon Piggeries* has implications for the position of the hypersensitive buyer. Goods supplied have to be reasonably fit for the buyer's purpose; they do not have to satisfy the scrutiny of a hypercritical buyer. Another way of putting this is to say that a buyer, apparently purchasing goods to perform the same task for which they would be required by any other buyer, should inform the seller of any special sensitivity on his part if the seller's liability under section 14(3) is to be engaged. The best example of this is *Griffiths* v. *Peter Conway Ltd*,[339] where a woman bought a Harris Tweed coat, fit for wear by ordinary individuals, without informing the sellers that she had abnormally sensitive skin. She contracted dermatitis and failed in her action against the seller.[340] The plaintiff, like the mink in *Ashington Piggeries*, was more sensitive than other consumers of the goods. Nevertheless, Harris Tweed, unlike the effect of contaminated herring meal on other animals, does not harm other human beings. Suppose, however, that the coat sold had been made of such a coarse fabric that it would have made any

---

[336] N. 329 above, 115. See also *Bristol Tramways Carriage Co. Ltd* v. *Fiat Motors Ltd*, n. 318 above.

[337] See also the remoteness of damage authorities echoing the same theme: e.g. *Diamond* v. *Campbell-Jones* [1961] Ch. 22; *British Columbia and Vancouver's Island Spar, Lumber and Sawmill Co. Ltd* v. *Nettleship* (1868) LR 3 CP 499; *Horne* v. *Midland Railway Co.*, n. 331 above.

[338] See the discussion of exclusion clauses in Ch. 8 below. The ability of a future defendant to exclude liability may be seen as a corrective to the (sometimes) generous application of the remoteness of damage rule in favour of the plaintiff.

[339] [1939] 1 All ER 685. See also *Slater* v. *Finning Ltd* [1996] 3 WLR 190.

[340] A similar result was reached in *Ingham* v. *Emes* [1955] 2 All ER 740. Cases of this kind raise problems of contributory negligence, which is not as such offset against strict liability. See M. G. Bridge (1982) 6 *Can. Bus. LJ* 184 and Ch. 10 below.

wearer, or a substantial number of wearers, uncomfortable. It would be strange if this made a difference to the outcome of the plaintiff's case, especially if any other Harris Tweed coat would have induced in her the same physical reaction to the fabric. On one reading of *Ashington Piggeries*, the coarse fabric would be generally unsuitable for human wear, and it might be in the reasonable contemplation of the seller that some sensitive wearers would be not unlikely to react especially severely because of that unsuitability. This reading, surely too broad, could be checked if the notion of unsuitability across the range, coupled with acute unsuitability within a narrow part of that range,[341] were confined to cases where the goods generally cause physical harm and not mere discomfort across the range.[342] Confining *Ashington Piggeries* in this way would conform to the idea of reasonable fitness in section 14(3).[343]

Reasonable Fitness

The idea that goods need only be reasonably fit under section 14(3) appears in a number of forms. A vivid illustration is given by Lord Pearce in *Henry Kendall & Sons*[344] in the context of broad fitness requirements presented by the buyer. Supposing a car were sold in England for general touring purposes, section 14(3) would not be breached merely because the car was not 'well adapted for . . . a heat wave'. It seems that what Lord Pearce had in mind was discomfort, because of poor air circulation for instance, and possibly starting and stalling problems. Persistent rainfall being more common in this country, Lord Pearce was disposed to believe that a car was unfit if it did not cope adequately with rain.[345] But it was not just a question of the frequency with which problems arose when goods were applied to a single but versatile purpose; account should also be taken of the quality of harm ensuing, so that goods could be unfit even if they only rarely 'developed some lethal or dangerous trick'.[346]

　Lord Pearce's views encourage the belief that goods may still be reasonably fit for the buyer's purpose even when suffering from a minor defect. The stringency of section 14(3), which operates as a contractual condition, might encourage courts to find the absence of a breach of section 14(3) in the case of complex manufactured goods. The difficulty with

---

[341] Or, though it is more likely in a case of poisonous contaminants, an evidentiary inference thereof.

[342] For a decision on the facts that uncomfortable clothes are not unfit, see *Gordon Campbell Ltd* v. *Metro Transit Operating Co.* (1983) 23 BLR 177 (Can.).

[343] The idea of divided responsibility, discussed in the text accompanying nn. 390 ff. below, also supports this.

[344] N. 329 above, 115.　　　　　　　　　　　　　　　　　　　　　[345] *Ibid.*

[346] *Ibid.* An example would be the engine cutting out in a heat wave when the car is in motion.

this position is that it would compel a buyer of new goods to put up with defects or repair them at his own expense; it also fails to take account of the common, even universal, practice of selling expensive consumer goods with an express manufacturer's guarantee, so that the dealer, acting for the manufacturer, cures the defective part,[347] or replaces it or the goods themselves. The absence of case law could be due in no small part to this practice. The controls now in existence preventing rejection and termination for slight breach[348] should encourage courts to find a breach in the case of non-consumer goods where goods suffer from minor defects, though they might baulk at the same conclusion in consumer cases. An intellectually satisfying way of dealing with the small defect problem is to say that the buyer of complex goods is buying more than just the goods, for he is acquiring also an after-sales service and a guarantee. Goods may therefore be reasonably fit for the buyer's purpose if minor problems can and will be put right with little inconvenience to the buyer and in such a way that the buyer cannot legitimately doubt their future reliability. This use of cure to pre-empt a breach of section 14(3) is not, however, easy to reconcile with the Law Commission's rejection of cure.[349] Moreover, the idea that the buyer acquires not just the goods but also a guarantee package was rejected by the Court of Appeal in a merchantable quality case.[350] The position therefore remains uncertain.

Second-hand Goods

The notion of reasonable fitness helps to explain the diluted application of section 14(3) to second-hand goods. Just as the satisfactory quality term in section 14(2) must take account of varying goods and standards in the market,[351] so section 14(3) bears the mark of differential application as it embraces new and second-hand goods alike. It would be quite unreasonable for the buyer of second-hand goods to receive the same implied guarantee of fitness as the buyer of new goods, but entirely appropriate that the former buyer have some fitness rights. As a working rule, it may be said that the reasonable fitness standard will be graded according to what is reasonable in the circumstances; it will therefore take account of the age of and price paid for the goods, and of descriptive language used concerning the goods. If a car is sold as a car, and not as a broken-down vehicle fit only for scrap and the salvage of spare parts, then, no matter how old it is or how little the buyer paid for it, the buyer

---

[347] See the discussion of cure, Ch. 5 above.
[348] Discussed Ch. 5 above.   [349] Law Com. No. 160, paras. 4.13 ff; Ch. 5 above.
[350] *Rogers* v. *Parish Motors (Scarborough) Ltd* [1987] 2 All ER 232. But support for the idea may be inferred from *Bernstein* v. *Pamson Motors (Golders Green) Ltd* [1987] 2 All ER 220.
[351] See discussion in the text accompanying n. 154 above.

should receive a car that is fit to be driven in safety on the road and that will give fair warning before it has to be taken into a garage for necessary repairs (however expensive these may be). But if the buyer is advised at the time of the contract that certain repairs or changes will need to be carried out to render the car roadworthy, the buyer will not be able to complain of a breach of section 14(3) just because these matters have to be taken in hand. By the use of qualifying or descriptive language, the seller is not excluding liability under section 14(3), which would attract the provisions of the Unfair Contract Terms Act 1977,[352] but is rather defining the circumstances in which the differential standard is to be applied. Whether the goods are reasonably fit for the buyer's purpose involves questions of fact and degree, and the seller is thus filling out the factual background.

The question of the fitness of second-hand goods arose in *Bartlett* v. *Sidney Marcus Ltd*,[353] where a Jaguar car was sold in 1964 for £950. At the time of the contract, the sellers mentioned an oil pressure problem concerning the clutch that could be rectified, depending upon the nature of the problem, either by bleeding the clutch or (more expensively) by repairing a leak between the principal and slave cylinders. The buyer was offered a choice of taking the car with the problem or paying an extra £25 to have the problem rectified by the sellers. The buyer took the car with the problem[354] but felt aggrieved when two weeks later the clutch and oil pressure began to cause trouble, and two weeks after that he was told by a garage that the clutch needed to be replaced for £45. The Court of Appeal held that the seller was not in breach of section 14(3). In the words of Lord Denning MR, a second-hand car was reasonably fit for purpose if 'in a roadworthy condition, fit to be driven along the road in safety, even though not as perfect as a new car'.[355] As plain as it is that section 14(3) was not breached in *Bartlett*, Lord Denning's words come perilously close to a minimal and uniform standard for all second-hand cars,[356] whereas the standard should vary according to age and price. The buyer in *Bartlett* paid a considerable sum for the car, which was at the upper end of the second-hand car market, and should therefore, for example, have felt rightly aggrieved if the engine had needed to be replaced after six months or even a year.

[352] Discussed Ch. 8 below.

[353] [1965] 1 WLR 1013. The report fails to state the age of the car, important in applying the differential standard. See also the s. 14(2) cases, n. 245 above.

[354] The memorandum of sale, though not mentioning the possibility that repair might be required, did say: 'Clutch to be bled. At client's expense.'

[355] N. 353 above, 1017.

[356] *A fortiori*, Salmon LJ, *ibid*. Another example of a second-hand car is *Crowther* v. *Shannon Motor Co.* [1975] 1 WLR 30.

Durability

This survey of second-hand goods shows just how much the issue of durability is integral to the reasonable fitness standard. We saw earlier that durability has been treated in the past as an aspect of merchantable quality and indeed is now to be seen as a factor mentioned explicitly in the statutory definition of satisfactory quality. Satisfactory quality speaks to the condition of goods at the date of delivery[357] or sale,[358] whereas fitness for purpose invites an inquiry into the subsequent history of the goods as they are applied to the buyer's purpose,[359] which may be a protracted one in the case of a consuming buyer. This makes fitness for purpose a more natural carrier for durability.[360] In principle, section 14(3) ought, forensically speaking, to be more helpful to a buyer, who should not be compelled, if the goods break down after delivery, to show a causal link between the breakdown and their condition on delivery. Satisfactory quality, at least in its former identity as merchantable quality, was strictly concerned with the saleability of goods as between seller and buyer, and the moment of sale was the obvious time to assess the matter of saleability. On the other hand, goods are not fit for the buyer's purpose if they are fit only at the moment of sale, because it is not the buyer's purpose to have them only fit at that time. Whatever the principle of the matter, nevertheless, Lord Denning MR in *Crowther* v. *Shannon Motor Co.*[361] asserted that the relevant date for assessing the fitness of goods is the time of sale and not the date of the subsequent breakdown of the goods, although he conceded that the breakdown could be evidence of the condition of the goods at the date of the sale. In practical terms, the issue is reduced to who has the burden of explaining whether the breakdown is due to the seller's breach of section 14(3) or to the buyer's mistreatment of the goods. Perhaps, a flexible evidentiary approach is best that increases the burden on the buyer to lead evidence the longer the goods are in the buyer's possession.[362]

One element of the durability of goods is their fitness to withstand carriage. In an earlier chapter,[363] the seller's liability for entering into an unreasonable contract of carriage was discussed, as well as the reconciliation of the presumptive rule that the buyer bears the risk of deterioration to the goods once these have been delivered to the carrier, on the

---

[357] *Bernstein* v. *Pamson Motors (Golders Green) Ltd*, n. 350 above, 226.
[358] Which commonly takes place on delivery.
[359] *Lambert* v. *Lewis* [1982] AC 225, 276.
[360] Cf. Law Com. No. 160, paras. 3.47 ff.; Ontario Law Reform Commission, *Report on Sale of Goods* (1979), i, 214–15, which does not consider assigning durabilty to s. 14(3).
[361] N. 356 above, 33.
[362] See *Phillips* v. *Chrysler Corpn. of Canada Ltd* [1962] OR 375 (Can.).
[363] Ch. 6 above.

one hand, and the implied conditions of satisfactory quality and fitness, on the other. The conclusion there reached was that goods would not be reasonably fit on shipment unless they were capable of withstanding the rigours of a normal journey. If they were, their subsequent fate would be a matter for the doctrine of risk. If the journey were an exceptionally long or arduous one, a court would probably require cogent evidence of an implied undertaking by the seller to be answerable under section 14(3) for their durability in such a case. Another way of putting it is that it would have to be reasonable for the buyer to rely upon the seller's skill or judgement in the particular circumstances.

Another issue arising out of the durability of manufactured goods is the continuing availability of repair facilities and spare parts. If goods priced for a lengthy life become unusable because, for example, they have been superseded by a later model and vital parts cannot be had, a buyer may rightly feel aggrieved. The argument was advanced earlier, in connection with the minor defects problem, that the sale of such goods could be seen as an integrated whole embracing repair facilities, express warranties, and implied obligations. For a seller to be made liable under existing law for a failure to supply spare parts or an after-sales service, an argument would have to be developed along these lines. A seller might be required to guarantee that these facilities would be reasonably available somewhere, not necessarily at the seller's establishment. As the law stands, it seems unlikely that a seller should incur general liability under section 14 in respect of these matters. To place on retail sellers responsibility for a manufacturer's production policies seems unduly onerous. Furthermore, to require sellers to maintain substantial stocks of parts would be costly. Yet there could be exceptional cases of liability. For example, a seller failing to disclose the imminent obsolescence of goods needing routine supplementary parts that will thereafter become unobtainable—a special type of bag for a vacuum cleaner, for example—may well incur liability under section 14(3).

The Law Commission was firmly of the view that the law should not be changed to require sellers to guarantee the availability of spare parts and repair facilities and noted the absence of any support for such a proposal.[364] It also favoured leaving the matter to manufacturers' codes of practice devised under the auspices of the Office of Fair Trading.[365] Indeed, it is the commitment of the law to privity of contract that conceals the point that it is obviously the manufacturer who should bear any responsibility that exists for repairs and spare parts. It is possible that a manufacturer could incur warranty liability to consumer buyers on the basis of advertising or the content of express guarantees.[366] Finally, it

---

[364] Law Com. No. 160, para. 3.66.   [365] *Ibid.*   [366] See Ch. 8 below.

should, nevertheless, be noted that the liability of the seller in respect of spare parts and repair facilities is a feature of certain Canadian consumer product legislation[367] and has long been part of special legislation dealing with the sale of farm implements,[368] explicable in the latter case by the fragility of distribution networks in a large country with remote farm settlements.

Reliance

It is not sufficient for the buyer to establish disclosure of purpose and the lack of fitness of the goods. The buyer must also rely on the seller's skill or judgement. The matter of reliance raises a number of issues. First of all, actual reliance is a question of fact 'to be answered by examining all that was said and done with regard to the proposed transaction on either side from its first inception to the conclusion of the agreement'.[369] Under the Sale of Goods Act 1893, the burden of proof of reliance was on the buyer. It was often established as a matter of inference.[370] The wording of the present section 14(3) appears to create a presumption of reliance since liability is negatived 'where the circumstances show that the buyer does not rely, or that it is unreasonable for him to rely, on the skill or judgment of the seller'. A higher court, disinclined to interfere with a finding of actual reliance, may be more willing to intervene on the question of whether the buyer's reliance was reasonable.

Reliance may be inferred in appropriate cases under the present wording of section 14(3).[371] There is no provision equivalent to section 14(2C)(b), which excludes liability for unsatisfactory goods as regards matters that an examination conducted by the buyer ought to have revealed. Where the buyer examines the goods, however, the circumstances of an examination may also negative reliance on the seller for the purpose of section 14(3).

A more difficult question relates to the seller's response to the buyer's disclosure of purpose. The 1893 Act required the disclosure to be such

[367] The Consumer Products Warranties Act, RSS, ch. C–30 (Saskatchewan), s. 11.8. The Ontario Law Reform Commission recommended a duty, in the case of new goods, to make spare parts and repair facilities available for a reasonable period: *Report on Sale of Goods* (1979), i, 216.

[368] See M. G. Bridge, *Sale of Goods* (Butterworths, Toronto, 1988), 520–3.

[369] *Medway Oil & Storage Co. Ltd* v. *Silica Gel Corpn.* (1928) 33 Com. Cas. 195, 196, *per* Lord Sumner. See also *Preload Co. of Canada Ltd* v. *City of Regina* [1959] SCR 801; *Laminated Structures & Holdings Ltd* v. *Eastern Woodworkers Ltd* [1962] SCR 160.

[370] This is laid down in numerous cases. See in particular *Grant* v. *Australian Knitting Mills Ltd* [1936 AC 85, 99, *per* Lord Wright; *Manchester Liners Ltd* v. *Rea* [1922] 2 AC 74, 81, *per* Viscount Dunedin; *Ashford Shire Council* v. *Dependable Motors Pty. Ltd* [1961] AC 336, 351, *per* Lord Reid.

[371] *M/S Aswan Engineering Establishment Co.* v. *Lupdine Ltd* [1987] 1 WLR 1, 17, *per* Lloyd LJ.

that the seller 'realised or ought to have realised that the buyer was rely-ing on his skill or judgment'. This wording brought out the important theme that the seller impliedly undertook to hold himself responsible if the buyer's purpose was not satisfied.[372] In the words of Lord Wright in *Cammell Laird & Co. Ltd* v. *Manganese Bronze and Brass Co. Ltd*: '[T]he buyer must bring home to the mind of the seller that he is relying on him in such a way that the seller can be said to have contracted on that foot-ing. The reliance is to be the basis of a contractual obligation.'[373] Although the relevant words are no longer to be found in the text of sec-tion 14(3), it is submitted that this approach is still a useful basis for find-ing the presence (or absence) of reliance by the buyer.

It follows from the above that mere tentative discussions between buyer and seller, grounded in no particular expertise of, or profession of expertise by, the seller, should not produce the requisite reliance of the buyer. This limitation is to be understood as confined to special pur-poses rather than to the general purpose that forms the basis of liability for faulty goods; the latter needs no explicit disclosure at all.[374] Goods may be free from defect and yet not suit the buyer's purpose at all; alternatively, they may suffer from a latent fault not shared by otherwise identical goods produced by the same manufacturing process. This dis-tinction should be understood when considering *M/S Aswan Engineering Establishment Co.* v. *Lupdine Ltd*.[375] In that case, the buyers sought pails strong enough to be used for waterproofing compound sent overseas. They selected a certain type of pail from a catalogue and obtained a sam-ple from the manufacturing sellers before putting in an order. The pails proved unequal to the task of withstanding extreme conditions of tem-perature and pressure, not disclosed to the sellers, so the buyers' claim under section 14(3) failed on that ground. Although Lloyd LJ[376] also con-cluded on the above facts that reliance by the buyer was absent, it is sub-mitted that the following distinction needs to be drawn. The buyers' behaviour may have shown an absence of reliance in respect of the type of pail, but they certainly would have relied upon the sellers not to select defective pails from stock.[377] In another respect, Lloyd LJ's remarks may have been perhaps too robust, taking insufficient account of the possi-bility that reliance may be partial, which is recognized by Nicholls LJ in the same case.[378] It has been authoritatively stated that reliance need not

---

[372] *James Drummond and Sons* v. *E. H. Van Ingen & Co. Ltd* (1887) 12 App. Cas. 284 (Lord Macnaghten); *Manchester Liners Ltd* v. *Rea*, n. 370 above (Lord Buckmaster); *Cammell Laird & Co. Ltd* v. *Manganese Bronze and Brass Co. Ltd* [1934] AC 402 (Lord Wright).

[373] *Ibid.*

[374] See *Preist* v. *Last* [1903] 2 KB 148.   [375] N. 371 above.

[376] *Ibid.* 17. Fox LJ concurred.

[377] See *Marshall* v. *Ryan Motors Ltd* [1922] 1 WWR 364; *Grant* v. *Australian Knitting Mills Ltd*, n. 370 above, 99.   [378] *Ibid.* 27.

be 'exclusive'.[379] Lord Reid has observed that it will be rare for a buyer not to rely at least in part on a manufacturing seller.[380] Lord Sumner has also stated that reliance amounting to a 'substantial and effective inducement' to the buyer's entry into the contract will suffice.[381]

Viewing the reliance issue against the backdrop of the seller's undertaking shows that the buyer may not engage the seller's responsibility by an extravagantly stated purpose. Even before the present text of section 14(3) explicitly required reasonable reliance, this requirement was most probably the law. A mere statement by the buyer that he expects to be perfectly satisfied, or that the goods will never display in their working life even the smallest difficulties, should not render the seller liable in the absence of supporting factors including the nature of the market, the precision that the manufacturing process is capable of achieving and the price paid. To obtain such an undertaking on the part of the seller would probably require an express assumption of responsibility. A case that seems to go very close to the margin of the realistic and fair range of the seller's skill or judgement, quite possibly requiring reconsideration in the light of the amended text of section 14(3), is *Manchester Liners Ltd v. Rea.*[382]

The buyers, Manchester shipowners, ordered from the sellers, Liverpool coal merchants, 500 tons of South Wales bunker coal, stating the coal was needed for their ship, the *Manchester Importer*. Both parties knew that, in the post-war regulated market, access to South Wales bunker coal was limited to supplies currently on the high seas. These supplies were reduced by a railway strike that prevented more coal from being shipped. The coal supplied to the buyers came from a vessel at sea that had been diverted to Manchester. This coal turned out to be unsuitable as bunker fuel in the buyers' ship, but it might have been suitable for other ships. The buyers knew the coal was to come from the diverted ship but they had not agreed to take that coal, however fit or unfit it proved for the *Manchester Importer*. The sellers were held liable under section 14(3) since 'it must . . . be assumed that the [sellers] knew the nature of her furnaces and the character of the coal she used, for it was this coal that [they] contracted to supply'.[383]

The *Manchester Importer* may well have been an ordinary type of Manchester vessel handled by an ordinary and competent Manchester crew,[384] but it is close to the line to say that the mere disclosure of a nar-

---

[379] *Cammell Laird & Co. Ltd* v. *Manganese Bronze and Brass Co. Ltd*, n. 372 above, 427 (Lord Wright).

[380] *Henry Kendall & Sons* v. *William Lillico & Sons Ltd* [1969] 2 AC 31, 82–3.

[381] *Medway Oil & Storage Co. Ltd* v. *Silica Gel Corpn.*, n. 369 above; *McNeil* v. *Village Locksmith Ltd* (1981) 35 OR (2d) 59 (Can.). Cf. the test for an actionable misrepresentation.

[382] N. 372 above.   [383] *Ibid.* 79 (Lord Buckmaster).   [384] *Ibid.* 88 (Lord Atkinson).

row purpose may amount to sufficient evidence of reliance on the seller's skill or judgement,[385] especially where the potentially suitable goods are in very short supply. Nevertheless, the sellers, as coal merchants, must have known or ought to have known that the bunker fuel on the diverted vessel might not have suited the buyers' vessel, and yet did nothing to disclaim responsibility in such an event. In *Teheran-Europe Co. Ltd* v. *S. T. Belton (Tractors) Ltd*,[386] the buyers, an Iranian Company, bought air compressors from English sellers through an English intermediary. The sellers knew that the goods were destined for resale in Iran.[387] When it transpired that under Iranian law the goods could not be resold as 'new and unused', the court gave short shrift to the buyers' argument that the sellers were liable, for the buyers knew all and the sellers nothing about the Iranian market.

Where the seller is no more expert than the buyer, it might be thought that there exists no disparity of skill or judgement between buyer and seller to justify liability under section 14(3). This fails to take account of the product liability policy that those responsible for defects in goods should ultimately be made liable by means of the indemnity chain. In *Henry Kendall & Sons* v. *William Lillico & Sons Ltd*,[388] the toxic Brazilian groundut extract had been supplied towards the head of the distribution chain by one dealer to another, both members of the London Cattle Food Traders' Association and interchangeable as buyer and seller in their mutual dealings. Lord Reid was prepared to conclude that a normal sale of goods from a familiar source between these parties would not attract liability (surely questionable if is the particular goods and not their product type that are defective). Nevertheless, he held with three colleagues[389] that, since these goods came from a new source, the sellers were exercising skill or judgment in putting them on the market, thus vouching that goods of this type were generally fit.

Partial Reliance

As stated above, partial reliance ought to be sufficient to make the seller liable. It is also a feature of those cases where seller and buyer apportion responsibility according to a division of skill or judgement. In *Cammell Laird & Co. Ltd* v. *Manganese Bronze and Brass Co. Ltd*,[390] a shipbuilder

---

[385] *Ibid.* 89 (Lord Dunedin).

[386] [1968] 2 QB 545. See also *Corbett Construction Ltd* v. *Simplot Chemical Co. Ltd* [1971] 2 WWR 332, where the sellers, informed by the buyers that they intended to use ammonium nitrate pellets in blasting operations, informed the buyers that they did not manufacture 'explosive fertilizer'.

[387] *Ibid.* 554 (Denning MR).

[388] N. 380 above. The facts are stated in the text accompanying nn. 170 ff.

[389] Lord Guest dissenting.   [390] [1934] AC 402.

ordered a ship's propellor from a sub-contractor and gave detailed specifications of the power, pitch, diameter, materials, and finishing. Certain details of the thickness of the blades were left to the sub-contractor and, because the propellor proved excessively noisy for reasons linked to the sub-contractor's area of responsibility, liability in damages was imposed pursuant to section 14(3). Similarly, in *Ashington Piggeries Ltd* v. *Christopher Hill Ltd*,[391] the sellers of mink feed were held liable because one of the ingredients they supplied was toxic; if injury to the mink had been caused by the recipe supplied by the buyers, there would have been no liability under section 14(3).

The apportionment of responsibility also arises where products have to be treated in a particular way by the buyer prior to their use. Hence damages will not be awarded to a buyer who fails to take the elementary precaution of cooking meats long enough to kill parasites naturally or notoriously present in it.[392] Unless put on notice of the buyer's unfamiliarity with what is needed, the seller is entitled to expect the buyer to take elementary precautions.[393] Apportioned responsibility is also relevant to those cases of hypersensitive or allergic buyers. The decision against the buyer in *Griffiths* v. *Peter Conway Ltd*,[394] at some risk because of the reasoning in *Ashington Piggeries*, may still be justified on the ground that the buyer retained responsibility for her personal needs since she had failed to enlarge the sellers' responsibility by putting them on notice that she expected something more than a coat that would not cause dermatitis in the general population. The same could be said of *Ingham* v. *Emes*,[395] where a customer in a hair salon did not disclose that she had on a previous occasion reacted adversely to a proprietary hair dye. And yet this same decision raises questions of contributory negligence on the part of the buyer, as well as of the scope of a duty of care in negligence on the part of sellers to warn buyers that they might be hypersensitive or that they should take care to ensure that they are not.[396] In addition, the circumstances in which the skin sensitivity test was applied in *Ingham* v. *Emes* raise doubts about the correctness of the decision. Although the plaintiff knew of her past adverse reaction to the hair dye, instructions on the bottle read out to her contained a statement by the manufacturer that the skin test, which was administered to her, would reveal any predisposition to skin trouble. This should, at least, have raised a serious

---

[391] [1972] AC 441. See also *Venus Electric Ltd* v. *Brevel Products Ltd* (1978) 85 DLR (3d) 282; *Hunter Engineering Co. Inc.* v. *Syncrude Canada Ltd* [1989] 1 SCR 426 (Can.).

[392] *Heil* v. *Hedges* [1951] 1 TLR 512; *Yachetti* v. *John Duff & Sons Ltd* [1942] OR 682 (Can.).

[393] *Heil* v. *Hedges*, n. 392 above.

[394] [1939] 1 All ER 685.   [395] [1955] 2 All ER 740.

[396] The manufacturer may well have such a tortious duty: *O'Fallon* v. *Inecto Rapid (Canada) Ltd* [1940] 4 DLR 276.

question as to whether the range of the seller's skill or judgement was thereby being enlarged.

Negligent Buyers

The question of the buyer's reasonable reliance also prompts consideration of a buyer's contributory negligence. An apportionment of liability cannot be made between a seller's strict liability under section 14(3) and a buyer's negligence, for the seller's behaviour cannot be treated as a tort for purposes of apportionment under the Law Reform (Contributory Negligence) Act 1945.[397] The matter has to be treated in all-or-nothing terms. In *Lambert* v. *Lewis*,[398] a buyer was negligent in continuing to use a defective towing hitch which caused a serious road accident. There does not appear to have been a finding of fact that the buyer knew of the damage,[399] though the buyer failed to take any steps to maintain or inspect the hitch. The Court of Appeal found the sellers liable, since the buyer's conduct was not so unreasonable as to break the chain of causation between the sellers' breach (of the fitness and merchantable quality terms) and the accident. The result did not depend upon whether the defect in the hitch was patent or latent at that time.[400] But the House of Lords, treating the buyer as aware of the defect,[401] reversed the judgment below. The buyer was entitled to invoke the fitness term only until it became 'apparent' that the hitch was broken. To make the sellers liable after that time would be tantamount to the finding that the sellers undertook—which plainly they did not—that the buyer could safely use an obviously damaged hitch on a highway. This approach is not dissimilar to treating any continuing reliance by the buyer after that time as unreasonable.

Trade Name

A final point concerning reliance deserves mention. Prior to the Supply of Goods (Implied Terms) Act 1973, the seller's fitness liability did not extend to 'the sale of a specified[402] article under its patent or other trade

---

[397] See G. H. Treitel, *The Law of Contract* (9th edn., Sweet & Maxwell, London, 1995), 886–91; *Forsikringsaktieselskapet Vesta* v. *Butcher* [1989] AC 852, 856 (CA); *Barclays Bank plc* v. *Fairclough Building Ltd* [1995] QB 214. Cf. M. G. Bridge (1982) 6 *Can. Bus. LJ* 184; Law Commission, *Contributory Negligence as a Defence in Contract* (Law Com. No. 219, 1993).

[398] [1982] AC 225.

[399] But the trial judge refers to it as 'plainly' and 'manifestly' damaged: [1979] RTR 61, 87.

[400] [1980] 2 WLR 299, 317. For a similar approach, see *Mowbray* v. *Merryweather* [1895] 2 QB 640.

[401] N. 398 above.

[402] Not specific. This provision was capable of applying to contracts for unascertained goods.

name'. It embodied the decision of the Court of Exchequer in *Chanter* v. *Hopkins*,[403] where a manufacturer sold the buyer one of his proprietary furnaces. The buyer's action failed since, by purchasing an established product whose properties were well-known and no different from any other example of the genre, the buyer was not calling upon the skill or judgement of the seller to respond to his specific need that the furnace work in his brewery. This reasoning does not appear to support a universal exception of liability where goods are ordered under a trade name, and in particular does not embrace defective examples of goods within the genre where the buyer trusts the seller to select a sound example of the genre.[404] No one can better be relied upon to make such a selection than a seller who is also the manufacturer. Lord Wright once said that the fitness for purpose section laid down a 'canon of construction' rather than 'peremptory law'.[405] This approach to the old section probably best explains the leading case of *Baldry* v. *Marshall*,[406] concerning the sale of a Bugatti car for touring purposes, where the court held that the seller could not escape from liability where there had in fact been reliance by the buyer. This decision substantially undermined the seller's dispensation from liability in trade name cases even before it was repealed in 1973.[407]

Negligence and the Seller

A final matter to consider under section 14(3) is the relationship between the seller's strict liability for unfit goods and negligence. The seller's duty under section 14(3) has been applied, not just to the goods sold, but also to ancillary packages or containers supplied with the goods, whether returnable or not.[408] A more difficult question emerges in the case of goods that can only properly be put to use if the buyer acts in accordance with the seller's instructions. The existence of a contract between seller and buyer does not prevent the seller from owing a duty in the tort of negligence to warn the buyer of dangers associated with the goods;[409] tortious and contractual duties can coexist. The difficulty about any duty

[403] (1838) 4 M & W 399.
[404] See discussion of reliance in the text accompanying nn. 375 ff. above.
[405] *Cammell Laird & Co. Ltd* v. *Manganese Bronze and Brass Co. Ltd*, n. 390 above, 429.
[406] [1925] 1 KB 260. See *Bristol Tramways Carriage Co. Ltd* v. *Fiat Motors Ltd* [1910] 2 KB 831.
[407] But see *Daniels* v. *White* [1938] 4 All ER 258; *Wilson* v. *Rickett Cockerell & Co. Ltd* [1954] 1 QB 598.
[408] *Gedding* v. *Marsh* [1920] 1 KB 668; *Marleau* v. *People's Gas Supply Co.* [1940] SCR 708 (Can.). See also *Wilson* v. *Rickett Cockerell & Co. Ltd*, n. 407 above (exploding substance in fuel), rejecting the conclusion in *Duke* v. *Wilson*, 1921 SC 362 (detonator in coal) that the fitness of goods is a question apart from the presence of a severable additive.
[409] *Clarke* v. *Army & Navy Co-operative Society Ltd* [1903] 1 KB 155.

on the seller's part to advise or warn is whether it should sound at the level of negligence or is so much a component of the goods themselves as to attract strict liability under section 14(3). It is also questionable whether goods can be separated from instructions if they can be used only in accordance with instructions.[410] These issues have been canvassed in a few cases.

In *Lem* v. *Barotto Sports Ltd*,[411] the buyer, experienced with guns, bought a machine for the reloading of spent casings. If operated according to the manufacturer's instructions, the machine would produce shells of factory-made quality. The buyer, injured when the machine was charged with too much powder and shot, complained that the instructions failed to stress the importance of compliance. The court treated the matter as one concerning the duty to warn, and not fitness liability; in the circumstances the warning and instructions had been adequate. A decison like this prevents a buyer from subverting the principles of the tort of negligence, especially the rule of apportionment where the plaintiff has been guilty of contributory negligence, by artificially extending the boundary of the fitness term. It should not be assumed, however, that a warning only ever goes to negligence liability. In *Vacwell Engineering Co. Ltd* v. *BDH Chemicals Ltd*,[412] an explosion fatally injured the buyers' employee. It was caused by water coming into contact with the contents (boron tribromide) of cracked ampoules, caused when the employee washed off warning labels adverting to the risk of vapours but not of explosions. The trial judge found both a breach of the fitness term and negligence on the part of the sellers. In his view, there was no contributory negligence on the part of the buyers or their deceased employee. On appeal, the Court of Appeal noted with approval the terms of a settlement based upon the negligence of the sellers and a 20 per cent deduction against a damages award to be later assessed.[413] The case therefore appears to support attempts to rein in section 14(3) when otherwise it would subvert contributory negligence.

Nevertheless, a manufacturer's instructions were dealt with under section 14(3) in *Wormell* v. *RHM Agriculture (East) Ltd*.[414] A farmer bought a herbicide to kill wild oats threatening his winter wheat crop. Poor weather delayed the spraying of the crop, but the farmer decided to risk a late application despite the warning in the manufacturer's instructions that this might damage the crop. The instructions failed to warn,[415] however, that a late application might prove wholly inefficacious. This

---

[410] Cf. the discussion of computer software as 'goods' in Ch. 2 above.
[411] (1976) 69 DLR (3d) 276.   [412] [1969] 3 All ER 1681.
[413] [1970] 3 All ER 553.   [414] [1986] 1 WLR 336.
[415] And therefore the sellers too. The court also declined to find that the buyer had relied upon the manufacturer's skill or judgement rather than the sellers'.

proved to be the case and the sellers were held liable under section 14(3) at trial on the ground that the instructions were as much an integral part of the goods as the packaging. But the decision was overturned on appeal because the warning was deemed adequate in the circumstances.[416]

Too much should not be made of the difference beteen fitness and negligence. In the case of aberrant products coming off the assembly line, the tort of negligence is often applied in a way hard to distinguish from strict liability.[417] Furthermore, the presence of reasonableness in the definition of fitness encourages an accommodation between the two heads of liability. Even in a case like *Lem* v. *Barotto Sports Ltd*,[418] harmony between these two heads can be arrived at by maintaining that a buyer minded to use a product in a negligent manner may only rely upon the seller's skill or judgement if this is brought to the attention of the seller and elicits a clear (and unlikely) undertaking by the seller.[419] Intractable problems are likely to remain, nevertheless, in the case of goods that amount to reified information, such as computer software. In such a case, the inquiry is likely to be pushed back one stage to pose the question whether the agreement is truly one of sale of goods at all or whether the seller is really dispensing mass-produced advice.[420] Obviously, in the case of software as of a book, a distinction is there to be drawn between packaging[421] and contents. Unless it is desired to extend strict liability into the giving of advice, which could have profound implications for publishers and booksellers, the sound conclusion in such cases would be to subject the seller of books and software only to negligence liability in respect of contents. It is after all only in modern times that the negligent giver of advice has been subject to liability at all.[422]

TERMS IMPLIED IN A SALE BY SAMPLE

It was noted above that under section 13(2) a seller had to comply with the requirements of the description condition even if the goods were sold by sample as well as by description. The governing provision on sales by sample is section 15, which was the subject of a number of consequential amendments under the Sale and Supply of Goods Act 1994.[423] Although little turns nowadays on the distinction between sales by sample and

---

[416] [1987] 1 WLR 1091.   [417] See Ch. 8 above.   [418] N. 411 above.
[419] Cf. *Lambert* v. *Lewis* [1982] AC 225.
[420] See Ch. 2 above; cf. *Lee* v. *Griffin* (1861) 1 B & S 27.
[421] Does the binding of the book come away? Are there blank pages?
[422] *Hedley, Byrne & Co. Ltd* v. *Heller & Partners Ltd* [1964] AC 465.
[423] e.g. the buyer's right to compare the bulk with the sample has now been written into s. 34, the main text dealing with examination.

ordinary sales,[424] a sale by sample should be defined. There is no statutory definition and the starting point is the classic statement of Lord Macnaghten in *James Drummond and Sons* v. *E. H. Van Ingen & Co. Ltd*: 'The office of a sample is to present to the eye the real meaning and intention of the parties with regard to the subject-matter of the contract, which, owing to the imperfections of language, it may be difficult or impossible to express in words.'[425] The proffering of a sample therefore amounts to a non-verbal demonstration of the goods that the buyer may expect to receive; it mutely describes them.[426] It is not every time that a sample is displayed that the contract takes place under section 15. The seller must expressly or impliedly undertake[427] that the bulk will relate to the sample in the way provided for in section 15. Consequently, a sale by sample takes place where there is an express or implied term of the contract to that effect.[428] Lord Ellenborough concluded in *Gardiner* v. *Gray* that the sale did not take place by sample because the 'sample was not produced as a warranty that the bulk correspond with it but to enable the purchaser to form a reasonable judgment of the commodity'.[429] It is inherently more likely that a sale by sample will be inferred where the seller already has the bulk in stock than, for example, where he is a manufacturer proffering specimens of the goods. In modern commodities trading, goods are more likely to be sold according to grades based upon analysis and protein content, and laid down by inspection agencies, than by sample. The detailed cloth specification in *B. S. Brown & Son Ltd* v. *Craiks Ltd*[430] obviated the need to display a sample, for the sample binds as to the bulk only in respect of the normal trade examination, which is usually a visual or rudimentarily tactile one.[431] It is possible to find a hybrid transaction that is located between a sale by grade and a sale by sample. This was the case where shellac had to be supplied in accordance with a sample kept in London and not physically produced before the contract.[432] Devlin J concluded[433] that principles 'analogous' to

---

[424] J. R. Murdoch (1981) 44 *MLR* 388.   [425] (1887) 12 App. Cas. 284.

[426] S. Williston, *Sales* (rev. edn., 1948), para. 250. The meaning of s. 13(2) is therefore that the description of goods may be found in both the sample and in accompanying language. *Quaere* an inconsistency between the sample and the descriptive language?

[427] Sometimes a sale by sample will be implied by trade usage: *Syers* v. *Jonas* (1848) 2 Ex. 111 (tobacco trade).

[428] S. 15(1).

[429] (1815) 4 Camp. 144, 145. A provision to this effect in the Sale of Goods Bill of 1892 was deleted. See also *Re Faulckners Ltd* (1917) 38 DLR 84 (not a sale by sample but a 'sale from samples'); *East Asiatic Co. Inc.* v. *Canadian Rice Mills Ltd (No. 1)* [1939] 3 WWR 180. Cf. *Dawson* v. *Collis* (1851) 10 CB 523.

[430] [1970] 1 All ER 823.   [431] Discussed in the text acompanying nn. 438–40 below.

[432] *F. E. Hookway & Co. Ltd* v. *Alfred Isaacs & Sons* [1954] 1 Lloyd's Rep. 491. A sample may also be used to clarify descriptive language: *R. W. Cameron & Co.* v. *L. Slutskin Pty. Ltd* (1923) 32 CLR 81.

[433] In the *Hookway* case, n. 432 above.

those in section 15 should be applied, an approach diminishing the importance of the section and the concept of a sale by sample.

Once the sale is by sample, the bulk must correspond with the sample in quality.[434] This is a question of fact, easier to resolve than the test of satisfactory quality; there is little case law directly on the issue of compliance. Compliance with sample sometimes arises collaterally to other issues. Thus in *Champanhac & Co. Ltd* v. *Waller & Co. Ltd*,[435] a quantity of surplus government balloons had been sold with 'all faults and imperfections', a phrase apt to exclude merchantable quality[436] but not the seller's separate duty to tender a bulk consistent in quality with the sample.

Compliance with sample has emerged in a more direct way where the buyer is demanding, over and above description and merchantable quality obligations, that the bulk contain enhancing qualities present in the sample but not detectable on an ordinary examination. Lord Macnaghten once said that:

The sample speaks for itself. But it cannot be treated as saying more than such a sample would tell a merchant of the class to which the buyer belongs, using due care and diligence, and appealing to it in the ordinary way and with the knowledge possessed by merchants of that class at the time. No doubt the sample might be made to say a great deal more. Pulled to pieces and examined by unusual tests which curiosity and suspicion might suggest, it would doubtless reveal every secret of its construction. But that is not the way business is done in this country.[437]

In *F. E. Hookway & Co. Ltd* v. *Alfred Isaacs & Sons*,[438] the buyer of shellac for the manufacture of gramophone records was aggrieved when the shellac turned out to be unfit for this purpose (not disclosed to the seller) since it lacked the 'flow' possessed by the standard sample in London. Recovery was denied in that case because the flow of the shellac delivered could only be discovered on an analysis exceeding the standard of the ordinary trade examination of the sample. Similarly, in *Steels & Busks Ltd* v. *Bleeker Bik & Co.*,[439] a quantity of pale crepe rubber was supplied that, because of a preservative added in the course of its manufacture, stained materials with which it came into contact. The preservative was not present in the sample but, because its absence from the bulk could only have been verified by an extraordinary examination, the seller was

---

[434] S. 15(2)(a). See *Russell* v. *Nicolopulo* (1860) 8 CB(NS) 362; *Carter* v. *Crick* (1859) 4 H & N 412; *E. and S. Ruben Ltd* v. *Faire Brothers Ltd* [1949] 1 KB 254 (ease of buyer correcting fault no defence).

[435] [1948] 2 All ER 724. See also *Parker* v. *Palmer* (1821) 4 B & Ald. 387.

[436] Now satisfactory quality in s. 15(2)(c).

[437] *James Drummond and Sons* v. *E. H. Van Ingen & Co. Ltd*, n. 425 above, 297.

[438] N. 432 above.   [439] [1956] 1 Lloyd's Rep. 228.

not in breach of section 15(2)(a). A seller may undertake expressly to reproduce in the bulk qualities not detectable in the sample by ordinary trade methods, as where a sample of guano was offered along with a detailed chemical analysis of the ammonium content.[440]

The requirement that the goods supplied be of satisfactory quality is no different from the obligation of the seller in other types of sale contract, with this difference. Whereas, in the latter case, the seller's satisfactory quality obligation does not extend to defects that an *actual* examination of the goods before the contact should have revealed, the satisfactory quality obligation in a sale by sample is excluded in respect of defects that are 'apparent on reasonable examination of the sample', regardless of whether such examination was in fact carried out. This suggests that sales by sample cannot be collapsed into the general law of sales, but one should not make too much of this difference. A buyer by sample will by definition usually have the sample to hand before the contract[441] and will in the great majority of cases have carried out an actual examination. Moreover, the proffering of the sample may be seen as merely one instance in which the satisfactory quality obligations of the seller might be modified in relation to examination.[442]

As regards the nature of the buyer's examination, the buyer of shoes destined for the French army in the Franco-Prussian War could not be expected to rip open the shoes, which was the only way of discovering the unmerchantable presence of paper in the soles.[443] Likewise an ordinary examination of shirtings would not have revealed the presence of china clay added only to bring the cloth up to contract weight;[444] the tender of an unhelpfully small sample of Brazilian coffee beans was insufficient to show that the bulk of the coffee was unsound;[445] and the examination of a sample of flax seeds would not reveal the presence of 'exceedingly small' wild mustard seeds.[446] The examination of the sample for defects under section 15(2)(c) therefore accords with the examination of the sample under section 15(2)(a) for qualities that should be present in both sample and bulk.

It is hard to justify the continuing existence of a separate sale by

---

[440] *Towerson* v. *Aspatria Agricultural Co-operative Society Ltd* (1872) 27 LT 276.

[441] But not in a sample case like *F. E. Hookway & Co. Ltd* v. *Alfred Isaacs & Sons*, n. 432 above. Why should there be an examination difference in such a case?

[442] See *Thornett & Fehr* v. *Beers & Son* [1919] 1 KB 486.

[443] *Heilbutt* v. *Hickson* (1872) LR 7 CP 438. See also *Godley* v. *Perry* [1960] 1 WLR 9, where drawing back the elastic of a plastic catapult was held a sufficient examination by a retailer. The same examination sufficed between importer and wholesaler who had done business together before.

[444] *Mody* v. *Gregson* (1868) LR 4 Ex. 49.

[445] *Jurgenson* v. *F. E. Hookway & Co. Ltd* [1951] 2 Lloyd's Rep. 129.

[446] *Carlstadt Development Co.* v. *Alberta Pacific Elevator Co.* (1912) 4 AR 366 (Can.).

sample.[447] The rules concerning such sales are petrified incidents in the evolution of modern sales law. Sale by sample rules should not be allowed to impede the natural development of sales law. Fitness for purpose had not evolved into its modern form by the time the sale by sample rules crystallized, and perhaps in consequence fitness for purpose is not listed as one of the seller's obligations in section 15(2). But this should not prevent the owing of a fitness obligation by the seller under section 14(3).

OTHER IMPLIED TERMS

Section 14(4) provides for the annexation by 'usage' of implied terms of quality or fitness. These are not designated as conditions or warranties.[448] This trade usage provision, of little importance in the modern law because of the extensive scope of the implied terms of fitness and satisfactory quality in sections 14(2) and (3),[449] was more important in the nineteenth century when the other implied terms were in an evolutionary state and where trade usage was something of a last resort for those challenging the rigours of *caveat emptor*. In *Jones* v. *Bowden*,[450] it was the custom in auction sales of drugs to describe them as sea-damaged if this had occurred. A seller who repacked a quantity of pimentos damaged at sea without noting this in the broker's catalogue was therefore liable in damages to the buyer.

Section 14(1) proscribes the implication of fitness and quality terms other than those set out in the remainder of the section. There is, however, well-established authority that manufacturers selling goods, of the type they manufacture themselves, undertake that these goods are of their own manufacture.[451] This term concerns description rather than quality, and therefore should not be caught by the proscription in section 14(1).[452]

---

[447] In Art. 2 of the Uniform Commercial Code, the compliance of the bulk with a sample is relegated to an instance of express warranty: Art. 2–313(1)(c).

[448] S. 14(6).

[449] But see *Steele* v. *Maurer* (1976) 73 DLR (3d) 85; *Banks* v. *Biensch* (1977) 5 AR 83 (Can.).

[450] (1813) 4 Taunt. 847.

[451] *Johnson* v. *Raylton, Dickson & Co.* (1881) 7 QBD 438; *Randall* v. *Sawyer-Massey & Co.* (1918) 43 OLR 602 (Can.).

[452] For other cases falling outside s. 14(1), see *Scaliaris* v. *E. Ofverberg & Co.* (1921) 37 TLR 307; *Harris & Sons* v. *Plymouth Varnish & Colour Co. Ltd* (1933) 49 TLR 521.

TERMS IN TRANSACTIONS SIMILAR TO SALE

Even before the passing of the Supply of Goods and Services Act 1982, there was a developed judicial trend to treat contracts akin to sales as though they were sales for the purpose of implying terms of quality and fitness.[453] The contracts in question include work and materials, barter, and chattel leases. To take work and materials as one example, according to Lord Upjohn,[454] it would be 'most unsatisfactory, illogical, and indeed a severe blow to any idea of a coherent system of law' not to subject the supply of roofing tiles by a sub-contractor under a work and materials contract to implied terms like those in the Sale of Goods Act.[455] Similarly, a veterinary surgeon was held strictly liable for a latent defect in serum used to inoculate the plaintiff's cattle.[456]

The 1982 Act[457] now lays down the implied terms in contracts 'for the transfer of goods', defined in section 1(1) as contracts under which the property in goods is transferred or agreed to be transferred. A number of such transactions are excepted from the Act.[458] They include transactions for which pre-existing statute provides implied terms,[459] security agreements, under which the security will be redeemed once the loan advanced is repaid, and transactions under seal not otherwise supported by consideration. For practical purposes, section 1(1) therefore concerns work and materials and barter agreements.[460] To the extent that they are supplied pursuant to contract,[461] goods supplied under manufacturers' and similar promotional schemes should also be caught by the provision.[462] The implied terms in question concern title[463] as well as description, fitness for purpose, satisfactory quality, and equality to sample. Apart from necessary minor modifications, these are identical to the terms laid down for sale of goods agreements. The drafting technique used to attain this result,

---

[453] See, e.g., *Young & Marten Ltd* v. *McManus Childs Ltd* [1969] 1 AC 454; *Samuels* v. *Davis* [1943] 1 KB 526; *Dodds* v. *Wilson* [1946] 2 All ER 691; *G. H. Myers & Co.* v. *Brent Cross Service Co.* [1934] 1 KB 46.

[454] In *Young & Marten Ltd* v. *McManus Childs Ltd*, n. 453 above, 473.

[455] See also *A. G. Canada* v. *Eastern Woodworkers Ltd* [1962] SCR 160; *Helicopter Sales (Australia) Pty. Ltd* v. *Motor Works Pty. Ltd* (1974) 132 CLR 1; *Gloucestershire CC* v. *Richardson* [1969] 1 AC 480; *Watson* v. *Buckley, Osbourne, Garrett & Co. Ltd* [1940] 1 All ER 174; *Star Express Manufacturing Co. Pty. Ltd* v. *VG McGrath Pty. Ltd* [1959] VR 443.

[456] *Dodds* v. *Wilson*, n. 453 above.

[457] See Law Commission, *Law of Contract[:] Implied Terms in Contracts for the Supply of Goods* (Law Com. No. 95, 1979).

[458] S. 1(2).

[459] e.g. goods supplied against the redemption of trading stamps (see the Trading Stamps Act 1964 as amended) and hire purchase (see below).

[460] Barter agreements can in many cases be rationalized as back-to-back sales: Ch. 2 above. A provision in the 1892 Bill would have applied the Act to barter agreements.

[461] See *Esso Petroleum Ltd* v. *Commissioners of Customs and Excise* [1976] 1 All ER 117.

[462] See *Buckley* v. *Lever Bros. Ltd* [1953] OR 704 (Can.).   [463] See Ch. 9 below.

however, is in one respect indirect in its operation. In Schedule 2 of the Sale and Supply of Goods Act 1994, the definition of satisfactory quality in paragraph 6 is the former definition of merchantable quality with 'satisfactory' substituted for 'merchantable'. But in paragraph 10, fitness for all common purposes, together with safety, durability, freedom from minor defects, and appearance and finish are brought into the definition of 'quality'. The result is a definition for transfer contracts of satisfactory quality that tracks the definition for sale of goods.

The provision of services does not prevent a work and materials contract from being a contract transferring goods under the 1982 Act.[464] Further, the standard of liability for services (or work) is the negligence standard of section 13,[465] not the strict liability standard for the goods themselves. In such cases, there may exist two standards of liability under the contract. The Act gives no guidance on the separation of work and materials; the preceding case law appears still to be valid. It shows the distinction to be no easy one to draw. Where work is clearly ancillary to the supply of goods, for example, the garage fitting a new part to the buyer's car, liability should be strict for the goods and fault-based for the labour. It may be difficult, however, to determine whether an accident is caused by defective parts or ineffective work and a court may not be astute to determine that it was the latter. Strict liability and fault-based liability will yield the same result in many cases.

A case that blurs the distinction between fault and strict liability is *Stewart* v. *Reavell's Garage*,[466] where a garage relining the brakes of a Bentley used a liner that was unsuitable for the car's brake drums. The welded, instead of seamless, liner used came away from the brake drums causing the car to crash. Strict liability clearly existed in that the brake liner was unfit for the buyer's purpose, but the issues were clouded by a statement of the supplier's obligation as being 'to provide good workmanship, materials of good quality and a braking system reasonably fit for its purpose'.[467] To require the whole system to be fit for the buyer's purpose appears to challenge basic principle for it would subject to strict liability a supplier who incompetently attached the correct type of liner to the brake drums.

Less controversial instances of strict liability exist where work and materials are integrated in the manufacture of a new product distinguishable from its materials.[468] The manufacturer of custom-built goods for a buyer should be treated as a seller under the Sale of Goods Act, but even where such a contract has been treated as work and materials liability for the goods supplied has been strict. In *Samuels* v. *Davis*,[469] den-

---

[464] S. 1(3).
[465] See also *Kimber* v. *William Willett Ltd* [1947] 1 All ER 61.
[466] [1952] 2 QB 545.
[467] *Ibid.* 551 (Sellers J).
[468] A case of *specificatio*.
[469] [1943] 1 KB 526.

tures made by a dentist were required to be fit for the patient's purpose. But fault should be the standard for the fitting of the completed denture to the patient's mouth, though difficult factual distinctions might have to be made if the dentist had to make a number of trial fittings and adjustments.

The principle applied in *Samuels* v. *Davis* has been taken a step further to support strict liability against a firm of engineers providing only a design and no materials of any kind. In *Greaves & Co. (Contractors) Ltd* v. *Baynham Meikle and Partners*,[470] building contractors had been held liable to the owner of a warehouse when the floor cracked under the movements of fork lift trucks. The contractors in turn claimed over against the defendants, structural engineers, who had designed the warehouse. Conceding that professionals normally owe a duty of reasonable care and skill, the court nevertheless concluded on the particular facts, but without explaining why, that the engineers had undertaken to design a warehouse fit for its purpose. Some light can be thrown on the case if we consider the hypothetical case of a buyer entrusting the design of a complex machine to a designer acting in concert with a manufacturer. Suppose the machine is unfit for the buyer's purpose because of the design, executed with due care and skill, and not because of the materials or their assembly. The buyer would be without a remedy: the designer would not be at fault and the buyer would not have relied upon the manufacturer's skill and judgement in respect of the design. If the functions of designer and manufacturer had been united in the same person, however, then liability for the fitness of the machine supplied would have been strict. The above division of function should not be troublesome in practice, because a court might well infer negligence in the design. Should such a finding not be possible, a potential line of development, perhaps difficult to reconcile with the fault standard for services laid down in section 13 the 1982 Act, would be the ready inference of implied strict liability undertakings for design functions closely allied to manufacture.

Hire purchase contracts are not within the 1982 Act. After a dubious authority applying the implied terms provisions of the Sale of Goods Act to hire purchase contracts,[471] the problem was largely resolved by case law developments.[472] In addition, for contracts within the statutory financial limits, there were implied terms in the Hire Purchase Act 1938 and subsequent hire purchase legislation. Since the Supply of Goods (Implied Terms) Act 1973, all hire purchase contracts contain these

---

[470] [1975] 3 All ER 99.
[471] *Felston Tile Co. Ltd* v. *Winget Ltd* [1936] 3 All ER 473.
[472] e.g. *Karsales (Harrow) Ltd* v. *Wallis* [1956] 2 All ER 866; *Astley Industrial Trust Ltd* v. *Grimley* [1963] 2 All ER 33; *Yeoman Credit Ltd* v. *Apps* [1962] 2 QB 508.

implied terms. For practical purposes, the title,[473] description, fitness, satisfactory quality and equality to sample[474] terms are the same as those for sale of goods agreements. They come into effect when goods are 'bailed', that is supplied.

Contracts of hire (or leasing) attract separate treatment, not only from hire purchase but also from proprietary transfer contracts in the Supply of Goods and Services Act 1982. The scope of implied terms of description, satisfactory quality, fitness for purpose, and equality to sample[475] is the same as for proprietary transfer contracts under the 1982 Act.[476]

[473] For additional common law developments, see Ch. 9 below.
[474] Are hire purchase goods really supplied by sample or is the draftsman being tidy?
[475] 1982 Act, ss. 8–10.
[476] Discussed in the text accompanying nn. 457 ff. above. For a discussion of the evolving common law concerning contracts of hire, see M. G. Bridge, *Sale of Goods* (Butterworths, Toronto, 1988), 528–32.

8

Statements, Liability of Remote Sellers, and Exclusion Clauses

This Chapter deals with a number of issues falling largely or wholly outside the Sale of Goods Act. Although they cannot be covered to the extent of their treatment in specialist tort and contract texts, they exercise such a powerful influence on the bilateral relationship of buyer and seller that they command inclusion in a sale of goods book.

CONTRACTUAL TERMS AND STATEMENTS

The plethora of rules and remedies arising out of false and misleading statements, made in and around the conclusion of a contract, has been cogently criticized as 'an area of law in which the courts have significantly failed to create a coherent body of rules to deal with what is basically a simple situation'.[1] This state of affairs has not been improved by a statutory overlay on the efforts of the courts.

History of Express Warranty

In common with innocent misrepresentation, deceit, and negligent misstatement, there is no definition of express warranty in the Sale of Goods Act.[2] The Act does define 'warranty',[3] but just to mean a term of the contract whose breach sounds only in damages.[4] This definition does not signify a term of the contract, as opposed to a mere representation that induces the contract, which is the meaning given to 'warranty' in this Chapter. Warranty is intimately connected to the implied terms of description, fitness, and satisfactory quality.[5] It is so marked by the hand of history that some attempt should be made to trace its evolution prior

---

[1] D. Greig (1971) 87 *LQR* 179, 211.

[2] See however Williston's definition in the American Uniform Sales Act 1906, s. 12.

[3] A word with numerous senses. See *Chalmers' Sale of Goods Act 1979 Including the Factors Acts 1889 & 1890* (18th edn., Butterworths, London, 1981, by M. Mark), App. II, for the history and examples of warranty.

[4] If the term is a condition, any breach permits the injured party to terminate the contract: Ch. 5, below.

[5] Ch. 7, above.

to the House of Lords decision of 1913 that established the framework of the modern law.[6]

Though plainly an aspect of contract in the modern law, warranty emerged from the action on the case for deceit. Thus in *Chandelor* v. *Lopus*[7] the buyer was unsuccessful in his action on the case for the seller's affirmation that he was selling a bezar stone. To succeed, the buyer would have had to establish either knowledge by the seller that the affirmation was false or the warranting of the stone as a bezar stone. In the latter case, the deceptiveness of the warranty would lie in its disarming the buyer from making further inquiry.[8] It seems that it was necessary for the formal language of warranty to be uttered,[9] and it was certainly necessary as a pleading matter that the plaintiff recite explicitly in his declaration the giving of the warranty.[10]

Subsequently, however, an action on the case was allowed for the false affirmation that two oxen belonged to the seller; it was no defence that the buyer failed to declare that the seller warranted his ownership or knew of a third party's superior title.[11] Where this case differed from earlier authorities was that the buyer had no means of discovering the falsity of the seller's statement. Liability for affirmation of ownership was later said to lie in all cases where the seller was in possession of the goods.[12]

Somewhat surprisingly, there is a dearth of eighteenth century warranty cases, particularly noticeable in matters of quality. Consequently, no rule of liability had emerged for bare affirmations inducing reasonable reliance by the time that warranty migrated from the action on the case to special assumpsit. From its first reported instance in assumpsit in 1778,[13] warranty became increasingly pleaded in this way until it became compulsory to do so in 1841.[14] The consequence of this was that warranty came to be seen as a contractual promise and as requiring consideration from the promisee to be enforceable.[15] This process may also explain why courts became more willing to depart from matters of fact and find warranty in statements of opinion; it certainly explains the assimilation by warranty of statements of intention. Because the action

---

[6] *Heilbut, Symons & Co. Ltd* v. *Buckleton* [1913] AC 30.   [7] (1603) Cro. Jac. 4.

[8] *Williamson* v. *Allison* (1802) 2 East 446, 451.

[9] *Chandelor* v. *Lopus*, n. 7 above. See S. Williston, *The Law Governing Sales of Goods at Common Law and under the Uniform Sales Act* (rev. edn., Baker Voorhis, New York, 1948), §§ 183, 195.

[10] Williston, *ibid.*, §195.

[11] *Crosse* v. *Gardner* (1688) Carth. 90, 3 Mod. 261 (*sub. nom. Cross* v. *Garret*).

[12] *Medina* v. *Stoughton* (1699) 1 Salk. 210, 1 Ld. Raym. 593.

[13] *Stuart* v. *Wilkins* (1778) 1 Dougl. 18.

[14] *Brown* v. *Edgington* (1841) 2 Man. & Gr. 279.

[15] *Roscorla* v. *Thomas* (1842) 3 QB 234. Cf. *Butterfield* v. *Burroughs* (1706) 1 Salk. 211. This movement untimately produced a veritable jungle of collateral terms, collateral contracts, the Statute of Frauds 1679 and the parol evidence rule.

on the case required the defendant's statement to be one of fact, a jury in one old case[16] was directed that the attribution of paintings to Claude and Teniers could only be a matter of opinion since the artists had been dead for 100 years and the paintings could not be traced back to an authentic source. The buyer was expected to exercise his own judgement. The court may, however, have been influenced by the sharp conflict of expert evidence. In a later case,[17] the trial judge was held not to have misdirected the jury when allowing it to decide (as it did) that the attribution of a painting to Canaletto was a warranty.

Later developments included the tightening up of the requirement of fraud in the action for deceit,[18] which thereafter could not accommodate the overflow from the increasing contractualization of warranty. Equity gave relief in some cases where factual misrepresentations induced the making of a contract,[19] but the remedy was rescission and not damages, and rescission was denied if the contract was too far advanced in performance. The characterization of warranty as contractual led in time to the House of Lords decision in *Heilbut, Symons & Co.* v. *Buckleton*[20] which firmly established that an affirmation amounted to a warranty only when made with contractual intention, doubtless as perceived by the objective bystander[21] or the reasonable co-contractant. The court found dubious support for this view in pre-assumpsit authority,[22] best explained as showing intention to be useful in distinguishing statements of fact and opinion, not statements of fact and contractual undertakings.[23]

The legacy of this course of development was that statements were treated as warranties only with difficulty when not made in close contemporaneity with the contract,[24] or when made informally and not included in a later written document.[25] The refusal to contemplate damages for a mere representation falling short of warranty, evidenced also by the tightened definition of fraud, meant that innocent misrepresentation bore an increasing burden.[26] It still laboured under the limitations on rescission and could not, until its statutory reform in 1967, provide a

---

[16] *Jendwine* v. *Slade* (1797) 2 Esp. 572.

[17] *Power* v. *Barham* (1835) 7 C & P 356, affd. (1836) 4 Ad. & E 473.

[18] *Derry* v. *Peek* (1889) 14 App. Cas. 337. But the movement dates from about 1850: Greig, n. 1 above. See the criticisms of S. Williston (1911) 24 *Harv. LR* 415.

[19] Discussed in the text accompanying nn. 76 ff. below.

[20] N. 6 above, criticized by S. Williston (1913) 27 *Harv. LR* 1.

[21] *Dick Bentley Productions Ltd* v. *Harold Smith (Motors) Ltd* [1965] 1 WLR 623.

[22] *Pasley* v. *Freeman* (1789) 3 TR 51. [23] D. Greig (1971) 87 *LQR* 179, 182.

[24] But see *Schawel* v. *Reade* [1913] 2 IR 64.

[25] This used to pose difficulties with the parol evidence rule.

[26] It was extended to cases where the contract had been executed: *Leaf* v. *International Galleries* [1950] 2 KB 86; *Redgrave* v. *Hurd* (1881) 20 Ch. D 1; *MacKenzie* v. *Royal Bank of Canada* [1934] AC 468; *Solle* v. *Butcher* [1950] 1 KB 671; *Lever Bros.* v. *Bell* [1931] 1 KB 557, 588; *Senanayake* v. *King* [1966] AC 63.

remedy in damages.[27] Meanwhile, liability in tort for negligent misstatements opened up in the 1960s[28] at the same time as the warranty test of contractual intention began to be liberalized in practice. Furthermore, the development of the implied description and fitness for purpose conditions[29] owes something to the barriers placed in the way of treating sellers' statements as express warranties.[30]

Modern Law of Express Warranty

A contractual intention to warrant is inferred from the 'totality of the evidence' surrounding the making of a statement; there are no 'secondary principles' that are 'universally true'.[31] Despite occasional observations that the matter is one of fact for a jury to decide,[32] it is better to say that the presence of an intention to warrant, like any other question of contractual intention, is ultimately one of law: there will have to be a sufficiency of evidence to justify any finding of a warranty. The importance of infinitely variable fact, however, means that no single test of warranty suffices[33] and that the *indicia* of intention may work in different combinations from case to case. Furthermore, abiding by such a test may conceal over the years *de facto* changes in the law. The test for a warranty laid down in *Heilbut, Symons* has remained unchanged, apart from a tendency to take account of reliance,[34] but without any doubt a modern court is more ready to infer a warranty than its counterpart of eighty years ago.[35]

In principle, the law still maintains that mere language of commendation or puffery does not constitute warranty, but attitudes have changed. While statements that a reaper was ' a very good second hand' model

---

[27] Discussed in the text accompanying nn. 119 ff. below.
[28] *Hedley Byrne & Co. Ltd* v. *Heller & Partners Ltd* [1964] AC 465. See B. S. Markesinis and S. F. Deakin, *Tort Law* (3rd edn., OUP, London, 1994), 86–95.
[29] Ch. 7 above.
[30] Description is treated as part of express warranty in UCC, Art. 2–313(1)(b) (*aliter* Uniform Sales Act 1906, s. 14.).
[31] *Heilbut, Symons & Co. Ltd* v. *Buckleton* [1913] AC 30, 50. See also *Howard Marine & Dredging Co. Ltd* v. *A. Ogden & Sons (Excavations) Ltd* [1978] QB 574, 595.
[32] e.g. *DeWynter* v. *Fulton* (1915) 7 WWR 1361. The modern practice of a judge sitting without a jury shows the futility of trying to separate fact and law in this area. *Heilbut Symons* should leave no doubt about judicial determination to control the inference of warranty, complementing the takeover of former jury questions concerning the classification of contractual terms and the remoteness of damage.
[33] *Heilbut Symons*, n. 31 above.
[34] *Lambert* v. *Lewis* [1982] AC 225. Note also the implications for express warranty of the Court of Appeal decision in *Harlingdon and Leinster Enterprises Ltd* v. *Christopher Hull Fine Art Ltd* [1991] 1 QB 564, which introduced reliance into contractual description in the cause of aligning description and express warranty: Ch. 7 above.
[35] *Howard Marine & Dredging Co. Ltd* v. *A. Ogden & Sons (Excavations) Ltd*, n. 31 above, 590–1.

which will 'cut ... grain crop[s] efficiently'[36] may have been mere puffery a century ago, identifying puffery in the consumerist conditions of today is practically impossible when a car dealer can be liable for describing a car as a 'good little bus' on which he would stake his life,[37] and a grain dealer for asserting that his goods will fatten poultry at least as well as his competitors' products.[38] Even if a statement is one of opinion, this is no longer conclusive against the plaintiff[39] if the court finds an implied assertion of underlying fact.[40] In *Esso Petroleum Co. Ltd* v. *Mardon*,[41] a statement about the through-put potential of a filling station was held not to guarantee a particular volume of trade: it did, however, imply a warranty that care had been taken in predicting the volume of business. Damages were therefore awarded to put the tenant of the filling station back in the precontractual position;[42] he did not receive an expectation award based upon the accuracy of the prediction. *Esso Petroleum* clearly shows the recent inroad of tort into precontractual relationships.

A review of the cases decided since *Heilbut, Symons* suggests various 'criteria of value' for discovering an intention to warrant. Perhaps the most important of these is the making of a statement 'during and as part of the negotiations for a contract'.[43] The closer the statement to the conclusion of a contract, the more likely it is to be a warranty.[44] But even a statement made some weeks before the contract, if sufficiently powerful, may be a warranty,[45] while a statement made on the eve of a contract might not be.[46]

The manifest importance to the recipient of a statement is influential in the inference of a warranty, as where a buyer let it be known that he

---

[36] *Chalmers* v. *Harding* (1868) 17 LT 571. Cf. *Osborne* v. *Hart* (1871) 23 LT 851 ('superior old port').

[37] *Andrews* v. *Hopkinson* [1957] 1 QB 229; *Uhle* v. *Kroeker* [1927] 3 WWR 636.

[38] *Quaker Oats Co.* v. *Kitzul* (1965) 53 DLR (2d) 630.

[39] But for cases where the plaintiff failed for this reason, see *Oscar Chess Ltd* v. *Williams* [1957] 1 WLR 370; *Savage and Sons Pty. Ltd* v. *Blakney* (1970) 119 CLR 435 (see also trial judgment at [1973] VLR 385); *Uhle* v. *Kroeker*, n. 37 above (assurance that seed flax would plough).

[40] *Esso Petroleum Co. Ltd* v. *Mardon* [1976] QB 801. The same technique can sometimes convert a statement of opinion into a fraudulent misrepresentation of existing fact for 'the state of a man's mind is as much a fact as the state of his digestion': *Edgington* v. *Fitzmaurice* (1885) 29 Ch. D 459, 482.

[41] N. 40 above.

[42] For similar reasoning, see *Perry* v. *Sidney Phillips & Son* [1982] 1 WLR 1297.

[43] *Hudson-Mettagami Exploration Mining Co. Ltd* v. *Wettlaufer Bros. Ltd* (1928) 62 OLR 387 (Can.). See also *Dick Bentley Productions Ltd* v. *Harold Smith (Motors) Ltd* [1965] 1 WLR 623; *Murray* v. *Sperry Rand Corpn.* (1979) 23 OR (2d) 456.

[44] *Couchman* v. *Hill* [1947] KB 554; *Harling* v. *Eddy* [1951] 2 KB 739.

[45] *Howard Marine & Dredging Co. Ltd* v. *A. Ogden & Sons (Excavations) Ltd*, n. 31 above (three months before); *Schawel* v. *Reade* [1913] 2 IR 64.

[46] *Hopkins* v. *Tanqueray* (1854) 15 CB 130 (would not be decided the same way today but still exhumed on ceremonial occasions).

would not even bid for a heifer unless assured that it was not in calf.[47] Between parties of equal bargaining power, their failure to incorporate an assurance in a later written contract will tell against a warranty.[48] Where the maker of a statement assumes responsibility for the accuracy of it, a court is likely to infer a warranty. Thus a seller's assurance that a horse was sound, which dissuaded the buyer from continuing with his examination, was held to be a warranty even though made some weeks before the contract of sale.[49] Conversely, if the seller makes it plain that the buyer should obtain independent corroboration of the truth of his statement, he is negativing any intention to be bound.[50] Expressed in the language of tort, it would not be reasonable for this buyer to rely upon the seller. The reliance factor becomes particularly important when the statement is made by an earlier seller in the distribution chain, such as a producer,[51] for the buyer must show that he entered the main contract of sale on the faith of that statement.[52] Although such reliance should readily be found if the statement is made in persuasive promotional literature,[53] it has been unconvincingly said that a buyer might rely instead upon a producer's reputation as opposed to promotional utterances.[54]

One of the most cogent *indicia* of warranty is the balance of skill, knowledge, and experience between the maker of the statement and its recipient.[55] In encouraging analysis along the lines of reasonable reliance, which brings out the tortious origins of warranty, this accords with the parallel development of liability in tort for negligent misstatement. An attempt was made in *De Lassalle* v. *Guildford* to lay down the test for warranty as follows:[56]

> [A] decisive test is whether the vendor assumes to assert a fact of which the buyer is ignorant, or merely states an opinion or judgment upon a matter of which the vendor has no special knowledge, and on which the buyer may also be expected to have an opinion and to exercise his judgment.

---

[47] *Couchman* v. *Hill*, n. 44 above; *Bannerman* v. *White* (1861) 10 CN (NS) 844. Cf. *Oscar Chess Ltd* v. *Williams*, n. 39 above (consumer 'seller' in trade-in with dealer).

[48] *Howard Marine & Dredging Co. Ltd* v. *A. Ogden & Sons (Excavations) Ltd*, n. 31 above; *Routledge* v. *McKay* [1954] 1 All ER 855. Cf. *Birch* v. *Paramount Estates Ltd* (1956) 167 EG 396.

[49] *Schawel* v. *Reade*, n. 45 above.

[50] *Ecay* v. *Godfrey* (1947) 80 Ll. LR 286; likewise, if an independent survey is normally expected (*Howard Marine & Dredging Co. Ltd* v. *A. Ogden & Sons (Excavations) Ltd*, n. 31 above), a powerful reason for the resilience of *caveat emptor* reasoning in sale of land contracts (see M. G. Bridge (1986) 20 *UBC LR* 53).

[51] A term used herein instead of manufacturer.

[52] *Lambert* v. *Lewis*, n. 34 above; *Murray* v. *Sperry Rand Corpn.*, n. 43 above; *Wells (Merstham) Ltd* v. *Buckland Sand & Silica Co. Ltd* [1965] 2 QB 170; *Shanklin Pier* v. *Detel Products Ltd* [1951] 2 KB 854.

[53] *Murray* v. *Sperry Rand Corpn*, n. 43 above.

[54] *Lambert* v. *Lewis* [1979] RTR 61, 94, *per* Stocker J at trial.

[55] Discussed immediately below.   [56] [1910] 2 KB 215, 221.

In *Heilbut, Symons*,[57] this statement was disapproved for substituting a definitive test for a broad test based upon all the evidence and administered by the jury. The absence of juries in modern civil trials has done away with the need for circumspect directions to be made to them and has encouraged harder-edged judicial statements. Decisions of the last forty years are consistent with the test in *De Lassalle* if the change of substituting 'very persuasive' for 'decisive' is made.

In *Oscar Chess Ltd* v. *Williams*,[58] a private seller trading in a car adopted the statement of its age in the registration document. Since he plainly had no means of verifying the statement, while the trade buyer had, the court held it was one of opinion only. In contrast, a different result was reached in *Dick Bentley Productions Ltd* v. *Harold Smith (Motors) Ltd*,[59] where the trade seller of a car incorrectly told the private buyer that it had been driven only 20,000 miles after being fitted with a replacement engine and gearbox. The court saw no reason for overturning the evidentiary presumption that a statement made to induce entry into a contract was a warranty.[60] Unlike the seller in *Oscar Chess*, the seller in *Dick Bentley* had the means of discovering the truth and his statement lacked all reasonable foundation. Negligence of the maker of a statement and reasonable reliance by the other party have become motive forces in the inference of warranty,[61] though a breach of warranty may yet occur where all due care has been taken.[62] To the extent that negligence and warranty are in the process of fusion, or are so in a given case, it must be asked whether the law should protect the contractual expectation interest or indemnify on a tortious basis. The difference in practice between the two approaches, however, ought not to be overstated.

Deceit

Though once invoked more freely than it is nowadays,[63] it was settled over a century ago that common law fraud, conduct of the most reprehensible kind, was not akin to carelessness and did not assume a constructive form. Courts are intolerant of slack and unfounded allegations

---

[57] [1913] AC 30.   [58] N. 39 above.   [59] N. 43 above.

[60] Though a factor in favour of warranty, it was perhaps novel to put it in terms of an evidentiary presumption.

[61] See also *McRae* v. *Commonwealth Disposals Commission* (1950) 84 CLR 377 (Aust. HC).

[62] But cf. *Harlingdon and Leinster Enterprises Ltd* v. *Christopher Hull Fine Art. Ltd* [1991] 1 QB 564.

[63] See as the evidence of this the Statute of Frauds (Amendment) Act 1828 (Lord Tenterden's Act), 9 Geo. 4, cap. 14.

of fraud[64] and treat such behaviour as professionally improper to be penalized in costs.[65] Equity, however, views fraud more expansively as a species of conduct where one party unconscientiously takes advantage of another, permitting the rescission of certain transactions that do not include arm's length sales.[66]

Fraud was defined in *Derry* v. *Peak*[67] by Lord Herschell as making a false representation '(1) knowingly, or (2) without belief in its truth, or (3) recklessly, careless whether it be true or false'. The lowest common denominator of fraud is thus the making of a statement, which happens to be false, without believing it to be true. The motive of the maker of the statement, including any intention or not to injure the other person, is irrelevant.[68] Thus confined, fraud has played little part in the development of contract and sales law. If pleaded successfully, the plaintiff benefits from having the rescission bars applied more leniently.[69] Fraud also gives rise to damages in the tort of deceit, the plaintiff recovering for losses flowing directly from the fraud.[70] Although put back in the pre-contractual position,[71] the plaintiff is in principle entitled to the benefit of alternative opportunities forgone when contracting with the defendant. In certain cases, the difference between a contractual expectation award, as would be available for a breach of contract, and an indemnification for tortious injury, may therefore not be great.[72]

Innocent Misrepresentation

Innocent misrepresentation developed in equity to redress the rigours of the common law embodied in the strictness of its definition of fraud and in the early reluctance to infer warranty. From contracts habitually within the jurisdiction of courts of equity, such as agreements for the sale of land, innocent misrepresentation spread in time to common law contracts for the sale of goods.[73] Furthermore, though the point was dis-

---

[64] Salmon LJ, *Some Thoughts on the Tradition of the English Bar*, Middle Temple, 25 June 1964: 'To make an allegation of fraud . . . without proper material is an abuse of the process of the Court as a potent form of blackmail.'

[65] For provisions on costs, see RSC Ord. 62.

[66] *Nocton* v. *Lord Ashburton* [1914] AC 932, 953–5; *Morrison* v. *Coast Finance Ltd* (1965) 55 DLR (2d) 710; *Knupp* v. *Bell* (1968) 67 DLR (2d) 256; *Harry* v. *Kreutziger* (1978) 95 DLR (3d) 231.

[67] (1889) 14 App. Cas. 337, 374.   [68] *Ibid.*

[69] *Erlanger* v. *New Sombrero Phosphate Co.* (1878) 3 App. Cas. 1218; *Spence* v. *Crawford* [1939] 3 All ER 271; *Hughes* v. *Clewley* [1996] 1 Lloyd's Rep. 35, 63.

[70] *Doyle* v. *Olby (Ironmongers) Ltd* [1969] 2 QB 158, 167; *East* v. *Maurer* [1991] 1 WLR 461; *Archer* v. *Brown* [1985] QB 401 (including losses occurring after the rescission of the contract.

[71] *Hughes* v. *Clewley*, n. 69 above, 62–3.   [72] See *East* v. *Maurer*, n. 70 above.

[73] Ch. 5, above.

puted in Australasian authority,[74] it has never been seriously doubted in English law that the doctrine of innocent misrepresentation can apply to a sale of goods contract notwithstanding the failure of the Sale of Goods Act expressly to provide for its preservation in such cases.

Before the enactment of the Misrepresentation Act 1967, the only remedy for an innocent misrepresentation was not damages but rescission *ab initio*, which bears a superficial resemblance to the common law remedy of contractual discharge or termination, granted where there has been a breach of a condition or of a lesser term going to the root of the contract.[75] Given the similarity of remedial outcome between rescission and termination, difficult questions arise as to the compatibility of these equitable and common law remedies, where on the facts the plaintiff may choose between them, especially in a sale of goods setting.

In equity, for a misrepresentation to give rise to a right to rescind the contract there has to be a false statement of material fact that induces, at least in part, entry into the contract.[76] As with warranty, fact is capable of embracing opinion statements if they contain an implied assertion that care has been taken in formulating them.[77] It can also embrace statements of future intention so that a misrepresentation is made if the maker of a statement has no present intention of acting in accordance with his declared intention.[78] A statement is material in so far as it would have influenced a reasonable person in the position of the one to whom the statement was made.[79] It may be relied upon even if an inquiry would have revealed its falsity.[80] Once it is shown that a misrepresentation was material and that at a later date the plaintiff entered the contract, a court may fairly infer from those facts alone that the plaintiff did in fact rely upon the misrepresentation.[81] This is not quite the same as saying that the burden is on the defendant to show a lack of reliance[82] since a judge

---

[74] *Riddiford* v. *Warren* (1901) 20 NZLR 572; *Watt* v. *Westhoven* [1933] VLR 458.

[75] Ch. 5 above.

[76] *Redgrave* v. *Hurd* (1881) 20 Ch. D 1; G. Spencer Bower and A. K. Turner, *The Law of Actionable Misrepresentation* (3rd edn., Butterworths, London, 1974). Although it is sometimes said that the maker of the statement must intend to induce a contract, (e.g., Spencer Bower and Turner, *ibid.*, §117), proof goes by the board in the majority of cases (*ibid.*, §118) and there is a shortage of authority for a proposition that threatens to obliterate the distinction between misrepresentation and warranty.

[77] *Smith* v. *Land and House Property Corpn.* (1884) 28 Ch. D 7.

[78] *Edgington* v. *Fitzmaurice* (1885) 29 Ch. D 459, 482.

[79] *Smith* v. *Chadwick* (1882) 20 Ch. D 27, affd. (1884) 9 App. Cas. 187. Other inducing factors may influence the judgment of the person to whom the misrepresentation is made: *Edgington* v. *Fitzmaurice*, n. 78 above.

[80] *Redgrave* v. *Hurd*, n. 76 above. An ineffectual verification of the misrepresentation may, however, show an absence of reliance on the statement: *Attwood* v. *Small* (1838) 6 Cl. & F 232.

[81] *Smith* v. *Chadwick*, n. 79 above (Lord Blackburn). The case concerned fraudulent misrepresentation.

[82] See *Arkwright* v. *Newbold* (1881) 17 Ch. D 201, where all three members of the Court

as finder of fact is not bound to find reliance in those circumstances. Furthermore, the best way for a plaintiff to show materiality is probably to demonstrate that he in fact did reasonably rely upon the statement.[83]

Rescission *ab initio* is a drastic remedy that survives the incorporation of a misrepresentation as a term in the contract.[84] This duality of a statement as both an inducing misrepresentation and as a contractual term creates significant difficulties in co-ordinating the remedies available for each.[85] In particular, the right to rescind, a self-executing remedy,[86] may be lost in circumstances where a right to reject goods and terminate the contract for breach may yet endure. The right to rescind is lost in four separate cases: (1) where the plaintiff affirms the contract;[87] or (2) delays too long in rescinding;[88] or where (3) the subject matter of the contract cannot be restored in its original state;[89] or (4) third party purchasers have acquired in the interim property rights in the subject matter.[90] Prior to the Misrepresentation Act 1967, there was no right to damages for innocent misrepresentation. Consequently, the loss of the right to rescind left without a remedy a plaintiff unable to demonstrate fraud, the incorporation of the statement as a term of the contract or the inducement of an operative mistake by the statement.

Innocent misrepresentation is far more liberal in its grant of rescission rights than is the common law when allowing contractual release in the event of an operative mistake[91]or a discharging breach of contract.[92] This imbalance lies at the heart of the difficulty of reconciling innocent misrepresentation with the governing principles of sales law.[93] The test of innocent misrepresentation is easier to satisfy than the test for express warranty, and even when the latter is established the remedy may well be damages without contractual termination rights. It therefore seems hard in some cases to justify the drastic remedy of rescission when the

of Appeal stated that the plaintiff had the burden of proving that a fraudulent misrepresentation induced entry into the contract. Cf. G. H. Treitel, *The Law of Contract* (9th edn., Sweet & Maxwell, 1995), 318.

[83] Pleading precedents, for example *Atkin's Court Forms* (2nd edn., Butterworths, London, 1984) (Title: 'Misrepresentation and Fraud'), set out actual reliance in statements of claim.

[84] Misrepresentation Act 1967, s. 1(a). For the position in Commonwealth countries, see M. G. Bridge (1986) 20 *UBC LR* 53.

[85] See Ch. 5 above.

[86] *Abram Steamship Co.* v. *Westville Shipping Co. Ltd* [1923] AC 773; *Reese River Silver Mining Co.* v. *Smith* (1869) LR 4 HL 64, 73.

[87] *United Shoe Machinery Co. of Canada* v. *Brunet* [1909] AC 330.

[88] *Leaf* v. *International Galleries Ltd* [1950] 2 KB 86.

[89] *Clarke* v. *Dickson* (1858) EB & E 148, 155.

[90] *Clough* v. *North Western Railway Co.* (1871) LR 7 Ex. 26, 35; *Car & Universal Finance Co. Ltd* v. *Caldwell* [1965] 1 QB 525.

[91] *Kennedy* v. *Panama, New Zealand and Australia Royal Mail Co.* (1867) LR 2 QB 580; *Bell* v. *Lever Bros.* [1932] AC 161.

[92] Ch. 5 above.

[93] Bridge, n. 84 above.

common law remedy may be a lesser one or even non-existent. To a degree such criticism is deflected by the argument that common law and equitable concerns are not in *pari materia*. Whereas the common law is preoccupied with crystallizing the bargain struck between the parties, equity is concerned to suppress a broad range of unconscientious conduct encapsulated in the notion of equitable fraud.[94] As expressed in innocent misrepresentation, equitable fraud, not to be confused with common law fraud,[95] deems it unconscientious for the maker of a statement to insist on retaining the benefits of a contract once apprised that that his innocent but false statement induced the other party's entry into the contract.[96] In the time-honoured tradition of equitable entitlement, equity does not deny the maker's common law rights but binds his conscience not to exercise them.

Misrepresentation and Insolvency

Innocent misrepresentation poses a particular difficulty when the property in goods or money is transferred to the maker of a misrepresentation who later becomes insolvent. Should the transferor have the first call on the assets of the transferee ahead of the latter's other creditors? If the transferor had merely common law rights of termination, then his only claim would be for the usual meagre insolvency dividend since the property in goods delivered to the buyer will not revest in the seller after termination.[97] But if rescission *ab initio* were to be applied literally, the transferor would recover the subject matter of the contract if it remained identifiable. The incorporation of a misrepresentation as a term of the contract should not prevent the transferor from invoking his right to rescind.[98] Yet equitable fraud in the unjust retention of the fruits of a misrepresentation, however useful in reconciling discord in the past between common law and equity, seems a rather fragile principle to justify preferring the transferor in the transferee's insolvency, especially if the inducement was only a partial one. There is little evidence of transferors in the past asserting the right to rescind and recover property on an insolvency. One of the normal rescission bars is the acquisition by third parties of rights in the subject matter prior to rescission. Although the estate of a bankrupt vests in the trustee in bankruptcy,[99] trustees in bankruptcy are not third parties, for they stand in the shoes of the insolvent transferee and their consciences are burdened accordingly.[100]

---

[94] See the authorities cited in n. 66 above.

[95] *Derry* v. *Peek* (1889) 14 App. Cas. 337; *Le Lievre* v. *Gould* [1893] 1 QB 491, 498 (denial by Esher MR of the very existence of equitable fraud).

[96] *Redgrave* v. *Hurd* (1881) 20 Ch. D 1.   [97] *R. V. Ward Ltd* v. *Bignall* [1967] 1 QB 534.

[98] Misrepresentation Act 1967, s. 1(a).   [99] Insolvency Act, s. 306.

[100] *McEntire* v. *Crossley Bros.* [1895] AC 457, 461; *Madell* v. *Thomas* [1891] 2 QB 230, 238; *Re Eastgate* [1905] 1 KB 465; Spencer Bower and Turner, *The Law of Actionable Misrepresentation* (3rd edn., Butterworths, London, 1974), §278.

Company liquidators differ from trustees in the following respect. The property of the company does not automatically vest in them, though provision is made in the Insolvency Act for the liquidator in a compulsory winding-up to apply for a vesting order.[101] Upon a winding-up, a trust of sorts settles upon the property of the company for the benefit of its creditors,[102] though the beneficial interest is held in suspense pending the ascertainment of the various claims against the company.[103] It cannot therefore be said that the creditors are third parties acquiring an interest in the property before the rescission.[104] The two processes of bankruptcy and winding-up closely resemble each other and amount to 'a statutable execution for the benefit of all creditors'.[105] All of this suggests that no distinction should exist between bankruptcy and liquidation for the purpose of rescission *ab initio*. There is nevertheless firm authority[106] that a contract for the allotment of shares may not be rescinded after the commencement of the winding-up, except where, before the start of the winding-up, the allottee has renounced the contract and has taken steps towards having his name removed from the company register. The reason is that other shareholders and creditors may have entered into dealings with the company on the faith of the allottee's name being upon the register.[107] This reasoning does not extend to a supplier of goods seeking the rescission of a contract for misrepresentation, and the recovery of goods supplied, after the commencement of a winding-up.

There is authority for the recovery of goods by rescission upon a bankruptcy in the case of common law fraud,[108] and it is difficult to see why any distinction should be drawn for present purposes between fraudulent and innocent misrepresentation, since both render the contract voidable.[109] The Privy Council, however, in *Re Goldcorp Exchange Ltd*[110]

---

[101] S. 145. Rarely exercised: R. Pennington, *Company Law* (5th edn., Butterworths, London, 1985), 913–14. In any winding-up, the liquidator is empowered to deal with the property of the company and does not need a vesting order to do so: Insolvency Act 1986, Sched. 4 para. 6.

[102] *Re M. C. Bacon Ltd* [1991] Ch. 127.

[103] *Pritchard* v. *M. H. Builders (Wilmslow) Ltd* [1969] 2 All ER 670; *Ayerst* v. *C. & K. Construction Ltd* [1976] AC 167.

[104] Still less third-party purchasers, for they will have provided no further consideration.

[105] *Oakes* v. *Turquand* (1867) LR 2 HL 325. Execution creditors are not purchasers for value: Spencer Bower and Turner, n. 100 above.

[106] *Oakes* v. *Turquand*, n. 105 above; *Re Scottish Petroleum* (1883) 13 Ch. D 413. See D. L. McConnell and J. G. Monroe, *Kerr on the Law of Fraud and Mistake* (7th edn., Sweet & Maxwell, London, 1952), 514–17.

[107] And of the amount of uncalled capital.

[108] *Re Eastgate*, n. 100; above *Tilley* v. *Bowman Ltd* [1910] 1 KB 745.

[109] *Clough* v. *London and North Western Railway Co.* (1871) LR 7 Ex. 26, 34.

[110] [1995] 1 AC 74.

gave short shrift to a misrepresentation claim[111] for the recovery of money.[112] In so far as particular funds could not be identified *in specie*, then the claim in that case for the recovery of the same sum could only be treated as unsecured. The Privy Council, however, appeared to go further and say that money always vests outright in the transferee and that the transferor, upon a later rescission, has only an *in personam* claim for the repayment of an equivalent sum.[113] This would make the transferor just another unsecured creditor. Furthermore, if goods or money were transferred and the transferee had already given a creditor a floating charge over after-acquired assets, then the assets would be encumbered by the charge at the moment of their acquisition by the transferee and the chargee's interest would prevail once the charge crystallized.[114] The intervention of the third-party creditor's rights would therefore suffice to bar a later attempt to rescind.

There yet remains the possibility that the recovery of goods might be permitted after an innocent or fraudulent misrepresentation despite the insolvency of the transferee, which was not ruled out by the Privy Council. The existing law of misrepresentation appears not to debar such a claim, despite the weakness of the distinction between the claimant and other creditors of the insolvent. It is questionable whether the law should be prepared to sanction such *in rem* claims that shrink the size of an insolvent's distributable estate. Although the claim may defeat the transferee's unsecured creditors, its effect upon secured creditors demands further consideration. Since the matter goes to equity's auxiliary jurisdiction, it would seem that, once the transferor declares the contract rescinded, the equitable property in the goods will revest in the transferor and the transferee will later be required by the court to reconvey the legal property in the goods to the transferor.[115] The transferor should certainly defeat a floating charge crystallizing after the declaration of rescission[116] but should lose to a purchaser of the legal estate taking without notice before the court orders the reconveyance in law of the goods.[117] If the charge has already crystallized, however, then the fixed interest of the chargee ought to defeat the later fixed interest of the transferor.[118]

---

[111] It is not made clear whether the misrepresentation was innocent or fraudulent: '[T]he misrepresentations . . . were presumably that (in fact) the company intended to carry out the collateral promise to establish a separate stock and also that (in law) if this promise was performed the customer would obtain a title to the bullion': *ibid.* 220.

[112] Such restitution claims for the recovery of money are treated as personal claims: A. S. Burrows, *The Law of Restitution* (Butterworths, London, 1993), 29.

[113] *Ibid.*   [114] *Ibid.*   [115] *Quaere* when does this occur in the case of fraud?

[116] See *Re Castell & Brown Ltd* [1898] 1 Ch. 315.

[117] See *Pilcher* v. *Rawlins* (1871) LR 7 Ch. App. 259, 269; *Macmillan Inc.* v. *Bishopsgate Trust (No. 3)* [1995] 1 WLR 978, 999–1001.

[118] *Qui prior est tempore, potior est jure.*

A final point is whether the transferor might be faced with a claim by the transferee's trustee or liquidator, defending or taking proceedings in the name of the transferee, that the contract be declared subsisting under section 2(2) of the 1967 Act. The result would be that the transferor would have a claim for damages that could not be collected from the insolvent transferee's estate. It is questionable whether a court would apply this provision, framed in terms of the interests of the immediate contracting parties, so as to embrace the interests of third-party creditors.

Damages

The law on innocent misrepresentation was heavily amended by the Misrepresentation Act 1967, which is by no means a codification of the law on the subject. The Act introduced a damages remedy for a negligent misrepresentation[119] and conferred a discretion on the court to award damages in lieu of rescission in those cases where rescission would be too harsh a remedy.[120] In the ensuing case law, difficulties emerged as to the measure of damages in both these cases and as to whether damages might be awarded in the latter case despite the loss of the right to rescind in the circumstances set out above.

According to section 2(1) of the 1967 Act, where the maker of a misrepresentation that induces entry into a contract is unable to discharge the burden of proving that he had reasonable grounds for believing in its truth, he shall pay damages to the other party, provided that he 'would be liable to damages . . . had the misrepresentation been made fraudulently'. If this proviso is met, then the maker of the statement shall be 'so liable'. The comparison with fraud, both as to liability and (apparently) the measure of damages,[121] is opaque and unnecessarily convoluted. One very plausible view, that the reference to fraud was designed rhetorically to stress the repudiation of the old cry of no damages for innocent misrepresentation, has not found favour with the courts. Instead, it has been accepted that the measure of damages in section 2(1) is the tortious as opposed to the contractual one,[122] and more specifically that the rules relating to damages in the tort of deceit are thus incorporated in the sub-

---

[119] S. 2(1).

[120] S. 2(2). It does not apply to non-disclosure cases: *Banque Kayser Ullmann SA* v. *Skandia (UK) Insurance Ltd* [1990] 1 QB 665.

[121] The words 'so liable'.

[122] *Sharneyford Supplies Ltd* v. *Edge* [1985] 3 WLR 1, 15–16; *F. & B. Entertainments Ltd* v. *Leisure Enterprises Ltd* (1976) 240 EG 455, 460–1; *André et Cie SA* v. *Ets. Michel Blanc et Fils* [1977] 2 Lloyd's Rep. 166, 181; *Naughton* v. *O'Callaghan* [1990] 3 All ER 191. For the contractual approach, see *Watts* v. *Spence* [1976] Ch. 165; *Jarvis* v. *Swans Tours Ltd* [1973] 1 QB 233, 237.

section[123] with the result that the maker of the statement is liable for losses directly flowing from the misrepresentation.[124]

Section 2(2) of the 1967 Act permits a court to award damages 'in lieu' of rescission.[125] The first problem in section 2(2) is whether damages may be awarded if rescission is no longer available. The authors are divided on this question.[126] Having laboured so mightily to confer a fault-based right to damages in section 2(1), it is difficult to see why Parliament should then have gone on to create a very similar general entitlement to damages in section 2(2) for non-negligent misrepresentation. Moreover, the language of section 2(2) is that of damages as an alternative to rescission[127] and the exercise of a judicial choice on equitable grounds having regard to the losses caused to the two parties by upholding or reversing rescission as the case may be. The sounder view is that damages may be awarded only if rescission is a live remedy but the case law seems to be going in favour of damages where the right to rescind has been lost.[128] This view makes neither historical nor literal sense: how can a discretion to award damages be exercised 'in lieu' of a defunct remedy? A final point is that the court's discretion may be exercised whether the party to whom the misrepresentation has been made has already rescinded the contract without the help of the court or is seeking assistance to effect a return of the parties to the pre-contractual position. The court may declare the contract subsisting or revived as it awards damages to the victim of the misrepresentation. Presumably, it might enforce the contract by an award of specific performance if in other respects the case fell within the jurisdiction for that remedy: there is nothing in section 2(2) to enlarge that jurisdiction.

The second problem concerns the measure of damages,[129] for which the subsection provides no guidance. In that the misrepresentation is not as such a term of the contract, there is no obvious reason to award contractual damages. Similarly, there is no legislative sanction for the stringent fraud rule, now established for section 2(1), in all cases where

[123] *Royscot Trust Ltd* v. *Rogerson* [1991] 2 QB 297 and the cases in n. 70 above.

[124] *Doyle* v. *Olby (Ironmongers)Ltd* [1969] 2 QB 158.

[125] The burden of persuading the court to exercise its discretion in favour of damages is on the party seeking to avoid rescission: *British & Commonwealth Holdings Plc* v. *Quadrex Holdings Plc* [1995] CLC 1169, 1199–1200.

[126] *Pro*, *Chitty on Contracts* (27th edn., Sweet & Maxwell, London, 1994 by A. G. Guest and others), §6–058; *contra*, Treitel, *The Law of Contract* (9th edn., Sweet & Maxwell, London, 1995), 332–3 and *Benjamin's Sale of Goods* (4th edn. 1992 by A. G. Guest and others), §12–010.

[127] See also the Tenth Report of the Law Reform Committee on *Innocent Misrepresentation* (HMSO, London, 1962, Cmnd. 1782), para. 27(3).

[128] *Thomas Witter Ltd* v. *TBP Industries Ltd* [1996] 2 All ER 573 (Jacob J), who discusses the matter at length and derives support from *Hansard*. Cf. *Atlantic Lines & Navigation Co. Inc.* v. *Hallam Ltd (The Lucy)* [1983] 1 Lloyd's Rep. 388 (Mustill J).

[129] There are other damages issues too, such as the relevant rule of remoteness.

section 2(2) applies. But the court may declare a contract subsisting where the plaintiff seeking rescission might have elected instead to claim damages for breach of contract or damages for negligent misrepresentation. In the former of these cases, the court should be at liberty[130] to award contractual damages, and in the latter damages in accordance with section 2(1), which would bring in the fraud rule. Where the misrepresentation is both wholly innocent (non-negligent) and non-contractual, damages should be at large, guided by the court's discretionary decision to avoid the hardship that would accrue to the maker of the statement if rescission were to be allowed.[131] In financial terms, the party seeking rescission might be no worse off for being confined to damages while the other party might be spared losses consequent upon a rescission. If the accent is therefore placed upon the avoidance of disproportionate loss, the court should be at liberty to adjust the award according to the particular circumstances. It might, for example, be appropriate to make a restitutionary award if the maker of the false statement has been unjustly enriched as a result of it. Or the award might take account of the better terms that the other party might have negotiated but for the misrepresentation, in which case it would be in the nature of an adjustment of the contract price. Whatever approach is adopted, care should be taken to avoid double compensation where a claim to rescind has been combined with a claim for damages under section 2(1).

Criminal Offences

The Trade Descriptions Act 1968[132] and the Consumer Protection Act 1987 lay down a series of offences concerning certain abuses connected with the distribution of goods and with consumer safety. For present civil purposes, such criminal legislation is relevant in so far as the courts are empowered under the Powers of Criminal Courts Act 1973 to make compensation orders in favour of those suffering 'personal injury, loss or damage' as a result of a criminal offence.[133] This formula does not look a promising one for those who claim they have suffered economic loss as a result of paying an inflated price for goods. If this were correct, it would not include commonplace trade descriptions issues arising out of the

---

[130] Subject to any pleading difficulties that might arise.

[131] The decision to exercise the discretion may be taken precisely because the misrepresentation causes no loss: *Bank Negara Indonesia 1946* v. *Taylor* [1995] CLC 255.

[132] As amended by the Consumer Protection Act 1987, ss. 20 ff. See G. G. Howells and S. Weatherill, *Consumer Protection Law* (Dartmouth, Aldershot, 1995), ch. 10; R. Bragg, *Trade Descriptions* (Clarendon, Oxford, 1991). See also the Food Safety Act 1990 for various offences concerning the sale of food not of the nature, substance or quality demanded, and the false description or presentation of food (ss. 14–15).

[133] S. 35(1).

falsification of car odometer readings. Nevertheless, awards have been made in respect of disappointing holidays,[134] though it is improbable that an economic loss award would be made if a defendant seriously contesting the propriety of such a compensation order.[135] It is unlikely that the tort of breach of statutory duty could be invoked to provide a civil remedy under the Trade Descriptions Act. Such an intention on the part of Parliament appears to be impliedly negatived by section 35, which states that the commission of an offence does not render a contract void or unenforceable.

Trade Descriptions

Subject to the above reservations about the civil scope of the legislation, a number of provisions of the Trade Descriptions Act are material for present purposes. On the part of persons acting in the course of a trade or business, the Act prohibits the following: applying a false trade description to goods,[136] or supplying or offering to supply goods to which a false trade description is applied;[137] the giving of a false indication that goods or services supplied are of a kind supplied to any person;[138] and recklessly or knowingly making false statements about services, accommodation, and facilities.[139]

A seller may act in the course of a trade or business[140] even if the seller's business does not consist primarily of selling. Consequently, a car rental firm selling off cars at intervals as part of its normal business practice does so in the course of a business.[141] A person who in his spare time buys and sells cars after renovating them has been held not to act in the course of a trade or business.[142] The issue was further explored in *Davies* v. *Sumner*,[143] where the defendant used a car almost exclusively for the purpose of his business as a self-employed courier before he traded it in with a dealer in part-exchange for a new car. He failed to disclose that the odometer reading of 18,100 miles did not record the previous 100,000 miles driven. Since the Act had 'consumer protection as its primary purpose', it was necessary for there to be 'some degree of regularity' for conduct to occur in the course of a trade or purpose, which was absent in the

---

[134] *R.* v. *Thomson Holidays Ltd* [1974] QB 592.

[135] See e.g. *R.* v. *Broughton* (1986) 8 Cr. App. R (S) 379; *R.* v. *Holden* [1985] Crim. LR 397. See also the Criminal Law Revision Committee, *Theft and Related Offences* (Eighth Report, HMSO, London, 1966, Cmnd. 2977), 76–9 (restitution and compensation).

[136] S. 1(1)(a).   [137] S. 1(1)(b).   [138] S. 13.   [139] S. 14.

[140] This has a very broad meaning: *Corfield* v. *Sevenways Garage Ltd* [1985] RTR 109, 117.

[141] *Havering London Borough Council* v. *Stevenson* [1971] RTR 58. See also *Corfield* v. *Sevenways Garage Ltd*, n. 140 above, and cf. the scope of s. 14 of the Sale of Goods Act, Ch. 7 above.

[142] *Blakemoor* v. *Bellamy* [1983] RTR 303. Cf. the position of trade or finance purchasers under Part III of the Hire Purchase Act 1964, Ch. 9 below.

[143] [1984] 1 WLR 1301.

present case.[144] Subsequent conduct may be taken into acount in determining whether an earlier transaction took place in the course of a trade
or business.[145] It should be noted that someone not acting in the course
of a trade or business may commit an offence under the Act if the offence
of someone else who is so acting 'is due to' the act or default of the former person.[146]

A trade description is defined[147] so as to embrace a wide range of
attributes of goods, including their composition, method of manufacture, performance, fitness for purpose, physical characteristics, and history. If a car is described as 'beautiful', this will be understood as
referring to the way it performs.[148] It depends upon 'the impression or
impact likely to be made on the mind of the ordinary man', a question of
fact for the trial judge.[149] In appropriate cases, statements should be
interpreted in the context of the type and age of the goods.[150] A statement that a 10-year-old car performs well should not be interpreted with
the same rigour as the same statement made in relation to a 2-year-old
car. A similar point could be made about like statements concerning cars
at different ends of the quality market. A car may not be described as
'new' if it has already been the subject of a retail sale, if its frame or chas-
sis has been distorted in an accident or if the mileage on it significantly
exceeds the usual figure incidental on delivery to a dealer.[151] But the
word does not mean that the buyer will necessarily be the first registered
owner.[152] A number of cases deal with false odometer readings,[153] a category of statements that should leave no room for contextual relativity.
Where dealers in such a position do not wish to vouch for the correctness
of an odometer reading, they should issue disclaimers by 'positive and
effective steps'.[154] But they may not issue disclaimers where they themselves have falsified the readings.[155]

[144] Cf. the position under the Unfair Contract Terms Act 1977 in the text accompanying
nn. 279–81 below, and the status of a mercantile agent, Ch. 9 below.
[145] *Devlin* v. *Hall* [1990] RTR 320.
[146] *Olgeirsson* v. *Kitching* [1986] RTR 129, applying s. 23.
[147] S. 2. It may be implied: *Cottee* v. *Douglas Seaton Ltd* [1972] 1 WLR 1408 (covering up
of repairs).
[148] *Robertson* v. *Dicicco* [1972] RTR 431.
[149] *Kensington and Chelsea (Royal) London Borough* v. *Riley* [1973] RTR 122.
[150] *Chidwick* v. *Beer* [1974] RTR 415.   [151] *R.* v. *Ford Motor Co. Ltd* [1974] RTR 509.
[152] *R.* v. *Anderson* [1988] RTR 260 (manufacturers' sales figures inflated by the practice of
registering cars in dealers' names).
[153] e.g. *Havering London Borough Council* v. *Stevenson*, n. 141 above; *Tarleton
Engineering* v. *Nattrass* [1973] RTR 435; *Taylor* v. *Smith* [1974] RTR 190; *Norman* v. *Bennett*
[1974] 1 WLR 1229; *R.* v. *Hammerton's Cars Ltd* [1976] 1 WLR 1243; *Davies* v. *Sumner*, n. 143
above; *Olgeirsson* v. *Kitching*, n. 146 above; *R.* v. *Southwood* [1987] RTR 273. See also
Holloway v. *Cross* [1981] 1 All ER 1012 (estimation of mileage).
[154] *R.* v. *Hammerton's Cars Ltd*, n. 153 above. See also *Norman* v. *Bennett*, n. 153 above
(disclaimer to be 'as bold, precise and compelling as the trade description itself').
[155] *R.* v. *Southwood*, n. 153 above.

The offence under section 1 is committed where the trade description is 'false'. Section 3 requires falsity to be present 'to a material degree', which convicting magistrates rightly held absent in a case where a 'de luxe' badge had been fitted to a standard car in which most of the requirements of a de luxe car had been fitted.[156] A trade description can be false where, though literally true, it is misleading.[157] The words 'one owner' were held capable of amounting to a false trade description where the one owner in question was a car hire company.[158] For the offence to be committed, the false trade description should be connected with the sale or supply of goods.[159] An offence was committed where a service book with false entries was supplied fifty-six days after delivery, because of an inference drawn that the buyer was pressing for it at the time of the sale.[160] But no offence was committed in a case where forty days after the sale an unnconnected statement was made that 'nothing was wrong' with a car.[161] An offence can be committed where a *buyer* makes a false statement in the course of a trade or businees, as where a dealer said that a trade-in vehicle as scrap.[162] Third parties can also be liable.[163]

The Trade Descriptions Act also prohibits the giving of a false indication that goods or services supplied are of a kind supplied to any person,[164] and recklessly or knowingly making false statements about services, accommodation, and facilities.[165] Where a dealer advertised a video recorder as 'free', without revealing that the customer's trade-in valuation was commensurately reduced, no offence was committed under section 14 since the supply of the recorder did not fall within 'services' or 'facilities' in section 14.[166] An offence was, however, committed where a seller said that 'guaranteed' in relation to a car meant that it could be returned within a stated period for repairs, and yet declined to repair the car when the buyer later brought it in.[167]

There are defences to liability under the Act where the defendant took 'all reasonable precautions and exercised all due diligence' and the offence was due to a mistake or to reliance on information supplied by someone else.[168] It has also been said, in the case of a section 1(1)(b)

---

[156] *Simmons* v. *Ravenhill* [1984] RTR 412.   [157] S. 3(2).
[158] *R.* v. *Inner London Justices, ex p. Wandsworth London Borough Council* [1983] RTR 425.
[159] See *Wycombe Marsh Garages Ltd* v. *Fowler* [1972] 3 All ER 248, where a service was performed incidentally in relation to goods (refusal for wrong reasons of an MOT certificate).
[160] *R.* v. *Haesler* [1973] RTR 487.
[161] *Hall* v. *Wickens Motors (Gloucester) Ltd* [1972] 1 WLR 1418.
[162] *Fletcher* v. *Budgen* [1974] 2 All ER 1243.
[163] *Fletcher* v. *Sledmore* [1973] RTR 371.   [164] S. 13.   [165] S. 14.
[166] *Newell* v. *Hicks* [1984] RTR 135.
[167] *Bambury* v. *Hownslow London Borough Council* [1971] RTR 1.
[168] S. 23. See also the odometer disclaimers, above.

offence, that the absence of reliance by the party to whom the false trade description is made is not an offence but may be a mitigating factor in relation to the penalty.[169] In such a case, it is submitted, a court should not exercise any discretion it might have to make a civil compensation order. Where there is no reliance, a court might in certain cases hold that a statement is not false to a material degree[170] or misleading.[171]

A compensation order might also be sought under the Consumer Protection Act 1987. As for the tort of breach of statutory duty, section 41(1) provides that a breach of safety regulations made by the Secretary of State may be the subject of a civil action. But breaches of the the Act itself are not so actionable. Section 10 lays down the offence of supplying consumer goods that are not reasonably safe with regard to various factors such as get-up, and sections 11 to 12 make provision for offences concerning specific safety requirements laid down by regulation. There is a defence based upon the supplier's due diligence, which would include third party interference with the goods.[172]

THE LIABILITY OF REMOTE SELLERS

Under this heading, we may group a number of parties in the distribution chain, such as producers,[173] importers, and wholesalers, who are not privy to the final contract between the consumer buyer of new goods and his immediate seller.[174] Landmark decisions on the implied terms of satisfactory quality and fitness for purpose have been actuated by the judicial policy of pushing responsibility for defective goods back up the distribution chain to the responsible source.[175] This will be the producer or, if the producer is abroad and unamenable to suit, the importer. Nevertheless, the proper plaintiff in each case is the immediate buyer, though related actions by each buyer in the distribution chain, which ranges from the producer to the consumer buyer, may be conjoined or consolidated in one set of proceedings. Apart from actions on the implied terms in the Sale of Goods Act, a remote seller, such as the producer, may incur liability on an express warranty or guarantee forming part of a contract collateral to the contract of sale. In addition, there may

---

[169] *Chidwick* v. *Beer*, n. 150 above.   [170] S. 3(1).   [171] S. 3(2).   [172] S. 39.
[173] A term used here to include manufacturers.
[174] W. L. Prosser (1960) 69 *Yale LJ* 1099; *ibid.* (1966) 50 *Minn LR* 791; C. J. Miller and P. Lovell, *Product Liability* (Butterworths, London, 1977); Law Commission, *Liability for Defective Products* (Law Com. No. 82, 1977); Ontario Law Reform Commission, *Report on Products Liability* (1979): J. Stapleton, *Product Liability* (Butterworths, London, 1994); G. G. Howells, *Comparative Product Liability* (Dartmouth, Aldershot, 1993).
[175] *Ashington Piggeries Ltd* v. *Christopher Hill Ltd* [1972] AC 441; *Young & Marten Ltd* v. *McManus Childs Ltd* [1969] 1 AC 454.

be liability in the tort of negligence for personal injury and property damage, and liability under the Consumer Protection Act 1987. There are also proposals afoot to affirm, in so far as it needs to be affirmed, the liability of a producer on a guarantee and to make the producer liable directly to the consumer buyer in respect of the implied term of satisfactory quality in the Sale of Goods Act.

The Indemnity Chain

To understand the difficulties facing a buyer in mounting a claim for defective goods against a party other than the immediate seller, the starting point is the doctrine of privity of contract whereby only parties to the contract may derive rights and liabilities from it.[176] In products liability jargon, 'vertical privity' prevents a buyer from suing on a warranty[177] in a contract further up the chain, between, for example, the wholesaler and retailer. 'Horizontal privity' prevents persons altogether outside the distribution chain, such as a non-purchasing user of the goods[178] or an outsider injured by goods under the control of the buyer or a user, from moving laterally into the buyer's shoes to launch against his seller a warranty action. Were outsiders able to overcome the horizontal privity obstacle, they would still have to deal with vertical privity in pursuing sellers further up the chain.

The privity doctrine is closely associated with the rule that consideration must move from the promisee,[179] and emerged when distribution chains were rudimentary, and a contract formed directly between producer and consumer buyer not at all uncommon.[180] The later development of lengthier distribution chains, before the tort of negligence had expanded to give consumer buyers and users some recourse against producers, served to insulate producers from consumer grievances and stimulated the growth of strict warranty liability against retail sellers, even when those sellers had resold packaged goods they could not have examined.[181]

Strict though the liability of the immediate seller is, and sympathetic as courts are to the pushing of liability up the distribution chain, this process of indemnification, based upon a system of third-party

---

[176] *Dunlop Pneumatic Tyre Co. Ltd* v. *Selfridge & Co. Ltd* [1915] AC 847, 853.

[177] For simplicity, 'warranty' will be used to embrace express and implied warranties and conditions.

[178] A borrower or donee.

[179] *Price* v. *Easton* (1833) 4 B & Ad. 433; *Tweddle* v. *Atkinson* (1861) 1 B & S 393; *Coulls* v. *Bagot's Executor and Trustee Co. Ltd* (1967) 119 CLR 460; B. Coote [1978] *CLJ* 301.

[180] Sutton (1969) 7 *Alta LR* 130, 173.

[181] See, e.g., *Bigge* v. *Parkinson* (1862) 7 H & N 955.

notices,[182] can break down for a number of reasons at some point in the chain.[183] There might, for example, be an intervening bankruptcy,[184] or an exemption clause in one of the contracts may bring liability to a halt, or the disclosure of one of the buyer's purposes may not be precise enough to allow indemnification,[185] or one of the buyers may have difficulty identifying his seller,[186] or a limitation period may toll so as to arrest the process of indemnification.[187]

Negligence

Where a buyer suffers personal injury or property damage, a claim in negligence may be launched directly against the producer.[188] In the case of design faults, it may be difficult to establish negligence in fact[189] but aberrant products fresh from the assembly line so loudly bespeak negligence, once fault by the buyer and anyone else between him and the producer has been eliminated, that one may as well speak of an evidentiary presumption of negligence, of whatever strength, on the part of the producer.[190] Some goods are not so much defective as suitable for use only if the producer issues an adequate warning or instructions about their proper use: a failure to issue such a warning will be treated as negligence.[191] Similarly, an immediate seller may also incur liability in negligence for a failure to warn or instruct, the existence of a contract of sale being no bar to such a tort action.[192]

With respect to economic loss caused by defective goods, exemplified by loss of profits attributable to inefficiency in the goods, the cost of repairing them, or an inherent loss of value, the courts have generally held fast against an extension of negligence liability.[193] But some exceptions have emerged. Recovery is likely to be permitted where the buyer expends money on the goods in order to avert the risk of physical loss

---

[182] *Young & Marten,* n. 175 above.   [183] S. Schwartz (1979) 11 *Ottawa LR* 583.
[184] *Muirhead* v. *Industrial Tank Specialties Ltd* [1986] QB 507.
[185] But see attempts to minimize this difficulty in *Ashington Piggeries,* n. 175 above.
[186] *Lambert* v. *Lewis* [1982] AC 225.   [187] *Young & Marten,* n. 175 above.
[188] *George* v. *Skivington* (1869) LR 5 Ex. 1; *Donoghue* v. *Stevenson* [1932] AC 562; *Grant* v. *Australian Knitting Mills Ltd* [1936] AC 85.
[189] *Wyngrove's Curator Bonis* v. *Scottish Omnibuses Ltd,* 1966 SC (HL) 47; *Davie* v. *New Merton Board Mills Ltd* [1959] AC 604.
[190] *Grant* v. *Australian Knitting Mills Ltd,* n. 188 above. But see *Daniels* v. *White & Sons Ltd* [1938] 4 All ER 258.
[191] *Lambert* v. *Lastoplex Chemicals Co. Ltd* [1972] SCR 569 (Can.); *Buchan* v. *Ortho (Pharmaceutical) Canada Ltd* (1986) 25 DLR (4th) 658.
[192] *Clarke* v. *Army and Navy Co-operative Society Ltd* [1903] 1 KB 155.
[193] *Young & Marten,* n. 175 above; *Rivtow Marine Ltd* v. *Washington Iron Works* [1974] SCR 1189 (Can.); *Dutton* v. *Bognor Regis UDC* [1972] 1 QB 372 (Stamp LJ). Cf. *Junior Books Ltd* v. *Veitchi Co. Ltd* [1982] 1 AC 520.

posed by a defect.[194] In addition, where the buyer suffers physical loss, recovery will be allowed in respect of economic loss consequent upon that physical loss.[195] The House of Lords decision in *Junior Books Ltd* v. *Veitchi Co. Ltd*,[196] marooned by recent decisions of the same court drawing back the tide of economic loss liability in negligence, allowed a privity-vaulting factory owner to recover directly from a flooring sub-contractor the cost of prematurely having to replace a defective floor. No explanation was given for why the factory owner chose not to sue the main contractor.[197] In *Lambert* v. *Lewis*,[198] the House of Lords stated its willingness to allow the retail seller of a defective towing hitch to recover the damages liability it owed to the buyer, not from the wholesaler, who could not be identified, but directly from the producer. Since the retail seller was held not liable, however, the claim did not in the end have to be pressed. It is by no means certain that a court would now be so sympathetic to the buyer.

It would be wrong to see in the above developments an opening up of liability for economic loss that would make deep inroads ino the privity of contract doctrine. The recent retrenchment of liability for economic loss[199] has occurred hand in hand with the direction that plaintiffs should protect themselves from loss by contract and seek recourse against their contractual partners.[200] This accords with buyers pursuing their sellers rather than producers. One obvious objection to extending the liability in negligence of the producer is that it outflanks a producer's attempt to limit or exclude contractual liability by a clause to that effect in the contract with the immediate buyer. After initially being attracted to the idea,[201] the House of Lords now prefers to deny recovery altogether than to mould the content of any negligence duty, sounding in economic loss and owed, for example, by a producer to a consumer buyer, to fit the contractual duty of the producer at the top of the distribution chain.[202] Since producers can be reached by way of the indemnity

[194] *D. & F. Estates* v. *Church of England Commissioners* [1989] AC 177. In the case of complex products, a difficult question is whether damage caused by a component to the rest of the product is physical or economic loss. See the views of Lords Bridge and Oliver: *ibid.*

[195] See *Muirhead*, n. 184 above, where on the facts the distinction between recoverable and irrecoverable losses is not clearly drawn. Profits from the sale of lobsters killed in a tank as a result of a defective pump should be allowed, but not profits that would have been made if further lobsters had been put into a properly functioning tank.

[196] N. 193 above; D. Cohen (1984) 18 *UBC LR* 289.

[197] The building industry is however particularly prone to the risk of insolvency.

[198] N. 186 above.

[199] e.g. *Candlewood Navigation Corpn. Ltd* v. *Mitsui OSK Lines Ltd* [1985] 2 All ER 935; *Leigh and Sillavan Ltd* v. *Aliakmon Shipping Co. Ltd* [1986] AC 785; *Muirhead*, n. 184 above; *Murphy* v. *Brentwood District Council* [1991] AC 398 (overruling *Anns* v. *Merton London Borough Council* [1978] AC 728).

[200] *Aliakmon Shipping*, n. 199 above.   [201] *Junior Books*, n.193 above.

[202] See *Aliakmon Shipping*, n. 199 above.

process, it seems a somewhat technical defence to allow them to invoke privity when they are not sheltering behind a wall of limited or excluded liability contained in the immediate purchase contract.

Express Warranty and Guarantee

If producers choose to promote their products and stimulate sales at the retail level so as to feed commercial activity further down the distribution chain, a strong case can be made for making them liable to the consumer buyer. Unlike their American counterparts, English courts have not been prepared to give such buyers extended implied warranty rights against producers. Nevertheless, there is the possibility of express warranty liability arising out of advertising and of rights promised in producers' guarantees addressed to the consumer buyer.

Although it has been established for over 100 years that a producer reaching out to a consumer can incur liability on a collateral contract,[203] reported instances of such liability are rare and tend not to involve mass advertising[204] Where a statement is made by a third party to a consumer contract of sale,[205] the tortious characteristics of warranty are heightened. Suppose that A, a producer, makes a statement to B, a consumer buyer, who then purchases goods from C, a retail seller. According to collateral contract analysis, A, to be liable, should bargain for B's entry into the contract with C, and B should do so in a way suggestive of accepting an offer of liability from A if the statement turns out to be incorrect. Courts are rarely so pedantic as to observe the niceties of these legal steps in actual decision-making. What appears to count is B's reliance upon the statement.[206] Where a retailer sued a producer on a statement that its towing hitch needed no maintenance and was fool-proof, however, the Court of Appeal showed a surprising reluctance to infer a contractual intention on the part of a producer in respect of the contents of its sales literature.[207] The trial judge[208] showed a corresponding readiness to believe that the retailer relied upon the producer's reputation rather than its statements, as though any neat separation could be made between the two.

Whether the looser approach to analysing the steps in a collateral contract is adopted, or a rigorous analysis preferred, many producers'

---

[203] *Carlill* v. *Carbolic Smoke Ball Co.* [1893] 1 QB 256. On collateral contracts generally, see K. W. Wedderburn [1959] *CLJ* 58.

[204] *Shanklin Pier* v. *Detel Products Ltd* [1951] 2 KB 854; *Wells (Merstham) Ltd* v. *Buckland Sand & Silica Co. Ltd* [1965] 2 QB 170.

[205] Car dealers may be liable for warranty statements that are collateral to a finance contract such as hire purchase: *Andrews* v. *Hopkinson* [1957] 1 QB 229; *Webster* v. *Higgin* [1948] 2 All ER 127.

[206] *Lambert* v. *Lewis* [1982] AC 225; *Wells (Merstham) Ltd*, n. 204 above.

[207] *Lambert* v. *Lewis*, n. 206 above, 262.   [208] [1979] RTR 61, 94.

guarantees fall outside a collateral contract since they come too late to affect the consumer buyer's decision to enter into the contract with the retail seller. A good example of this is the guarantee that is to be found inside the packaged goods once purchased.[209]

The inference of warranty on the part of a third party such as a producer is commonly a device that serves to prevent the doctrine of privity of contract from diluting contractual responsibility.[210] Statements from a producer may appease a buyer who then desists from securing a corresponding warranty from the retail seller or from displaying his reliance upon the skill and judgement of that seller. The collateral contract breaks down the insulation of the producer from that retail contract. Though Lord Moulton said over eighty years ago that the incidence of collateral contracts was rare,[211] his words do not accurately record the modern tolerance of collateral warranties. With the disappearance of the parol evidence rule,[212] it is somewhat incongruous to speak of two contracts between the same parties arising out of the same contractual adventure, as opposed to the one contract that is a blend of writing and informal collateral warranty.[213] Nevertheless, Lord Moulton's words may still retain some vitality. In *Lambert* v. *Lewis*,[214] the Court of Appeal indicated that the requirement of contractual intention was harder to satisfy where the alleged collateral warranty came from a third party to the supply contract.[215]

Doubts as to the legal liability of a producer on a guarantee have been addressed by the Department of Trade and Industry in a consultative paper,[216] which canvasses the possibility of making guarantees civilly enforceable by statutory means. The Department has also sought guidance on the appropriate measure of damages (tort or contract?) and has at this stage ruled out prescriptive measures to determine the scope and duration of any guarantee that a producer chooses to give. A further question being asked is whether the retailer should be jointly and

---

[209] Though it would be forensically difficult to establish, a buyer of goods on repeated occasions might be able to establish a warranty on the basis of previous transactions, provided the warranty statement is contained in the packaging on the instant occasion.

[210] See *Shanklin Pier* v. *Detel Products Ltd*, n. 204 above; *Wells (Merstham) Ltd*, n. 204 above.

[211] *Heilbut, Symons & Co.* v. *Buckleton* [1913] AC 30, 47.

[212] Law Commission, *Law of Contract [:] The Parol Evidence Rule* (No. 154, HMSO, London, 1986, Cmnd. 9700). Older authorities supporting the rule are *Morgan* v. *Griffith* (1871) LR 6 Ex. 70; *Erskine* v. *Adeane* (1873) LR 8 Ch. App. 756; *Henderson* v. *Arthur* [1907] 1 KB 10. But see now *City and Westminster Properties (1934) Ltd* v. *Mudd* [1959] Ch. 129; *Brikom Investments Ltd* v. *Carr* [1979] QB 467.

[213] See *J. Evans & Son (Portsmouth) Ltd* v. *Andrea Merzario Ltd* [1976] 1 WLR 1078.

[214] N. 206 above

[215] *Ibid.* 262. The third party was the producer and the supply contract was between wholesaler and retailer.

[216] *Consumer Guarantees*, Feb. 1992.

severally liable with the producer on the latter's guarantees. This initiative seems to have been overtaken for practical purposes by a European Commission green paper[217] which, in the context of exploring a unified European approach, is seeking reactions to a range of solutions to the problem of 'commercial' guarantees. These would range from compulsory to voluntary schemes of regulation,[218] and from the enforcement of guarantees only in the country where they are given to their portability throughout the countries of the European Union.

A final point arising from producers' guarantees concerns their use as a medium for conveying a clause exempting the producer from liability at common law for negligence. Apart from any difficulty the producer might have at common law in inferring consent to the exemption from a consumer's acceptance of the guarantee, the Unfair Contract Terms Act 1977 denies legal effect to such exemptions. First of all, liability for death or personal injury may not by 'any contract term or . . . notice' be excluded or restricted.[219] Secondly, 'the negligence of a person concerned in the manufacture or distribution of goods' may not be excluded or restricted by a contract term or notice contained in or referring to a guarantee, where goods ordinarily supplied for private use or consumption turn out to be defective when in consumer use.[220] Goods are treated as being in consumer use whenever they are not used exclusively in the course of a business.[221]

Product Liability and Extended Warranty

In the common law world, many attempts have been made in the courts and legislatures to confer rights against distributors outside the consumer sale contract. These distributors are usually producers and importers, and those whom it is sought to benefit are consumer users and buyers and other persons injured by defective goods. The avenues of recourse to the outside distributor include strict liability in tort and extended warranty rights. An extended warranty liability would arise if the consumer buyer, for example, were given the benefit of a contractual warranty in the contract between, for example, the producer and wholesaler. A theoretical alternative to this type of extended warranty would be

---

[217] *Green Paper on Guarantees for Consumer Goods and After-Sales Services,* COM(93)509, 15 Nov. 1993.

[218] Dealing with the legal enforceability of commercial guarantees, the circumstances governing their presentation, advertising that mentions them, their relationship with 'legal' guarantees arising under the sale contract etc.

[219] Unfair Contract Terms Act 1977, s. 2(1). It is also an offence for a guarantee to suggest that it supersedes the buyer's statutory implied term rights: Consumer Transactions (Restrictions on Statements) Order 1976, SI No. 1813.

[220] Unfair Contract Terms Act 1977, s. 5.   [221] *Ibid.* s. 5(2)(a).

the imposition of the warranty liability of the retail seller, under the consumer sale, on parties such as the producer further up the distribution chain. The fountain head of these initiatives in tort and extended warranty is the United States.

In that country, liability has attached to producers and distributors of defective products for the injuries of a victim not privy to any contract with them on two bases: extended warranty and strict product liability. In the case of extended warranty,[222] the liability of producers to ultimate product users has been justified on the ground that the producer, of an automobile for instance, puts the product 'in the stream of trade and promotes its purchase by the public',[223] and it is reasonably to be contemplated that the injured user may not be the buyer.[224] It was observed in one case, where the consumer buyer of a carpet sued the producer directly, that the intermediate seller was 'simply a way station, a conduit on [the carpet's] trip from manufacturer to consumer'.[225] Furthermore, it was said that the indemnification process based upon privity encouraged circuity[226] of actions and placed an improper burden on the consumer buyer, where the dealer, for one reason or another, was not amenable to suit.[227]

The implied warranty owed by a producer to his immediate buyer has been extended down the distribution chain by various devices, including the idea that it runs with products like a covenant runs with land; that it extends, by way of exception to privity, to anyone who can be identified as a third party beneficiary; that public policy demands the producer's liability; and that warranties are effectively writ large in producers' advertising.[228] In a number of American jurisdictions, this liability has extended to cases where the buyer's loss is economic in the sense that there is no physical or personal injury, but just a buyer's disappointment that the product is as a result of defects not worth the price paid for it.[229] Article 2 of the Uniform Commercial Code contains three optional provisions on extended warranty liability for adoption by individual

---

[222] *Henningsen* v. *Bloomfield Motors Inc.* (1960) 161 A 2d 69; *Spence* v. *Three Rivers Builders & Masonry Supply Inc.* (1958) 90 NW 2d 873.

[223] *Henningsen*, n. 220 above, 84 (overcoming vertical privity).

[224] *Ibid.*, 99–100 (overcoming horizontal privity).

[225] *Santor* v. *Karagheuzian Inc.* (1965) 207 A 2d 305, 309. This cannot be true of all products and all industries.

[226] Multiplicity?   [227] N. 225 above.

[228] *Santor*, n. 225 above. See also *Nobility Homes of Texas In.c* v. *Shivers* (1977) 557 SW 2d 77, which articulates the fear of intermediate 'collapsible corporations' in the distribution chain.

[229] e.g. *Santor*, n. 224 above; *Nobility Homes*, n. 228 above; *Morrow* v. *New Moon Homes Inc.* (1976) 548 P 2d 279. *Contra*, see, e.g., *State of Oregon* v. *Campbell* (1968) 448 P 2d 215; *John R. Dudley Construction Inc.* v. *Drott Manufacturing Co.* (1979) 412 NYS 2d 512: *Williams* v. *General Motors Corpn* (1973) 198 SE 2d 766.

states,[230] only one of which is open to the reasonable interpretation that it covers economic loss.

Tort

A number of states, reflecting a view promoted by section 402A of the Restatement Second on Torts, favour making the producer of defective products strictly liable in tort for distributing hazardous products. One advantage of this approach is that it more readily than warranty accommodates victims, such as users and outsiders, standing outside the distribution chain and, furthermore, is not radically divergent in effect from the way that the tort of negligence is often applied in the case of aberrant products.[231] Although strict liability in tort does not seem the obvious way to accommodate an economic loss claim for a disappointing bargain, a number of courts have permitted this.[232] The California courts, on the other hand, have strongly taken the position that contract law, not tort law, is the proper vehicle for vindicating bargain claims.[233] There is much to commend this view though its conceptual purity strikes an odd note in a body of law dominated by pragmatic considerations.

Reform

A number of Canadian jurisdictions have consumer legislation that incorporates extended warranty rights.[234] Extended warranty liability for personal injury and property damage was recommended in 1972 by the Ontario Law Reform Commission.[235] The Commission's 1979 report on *Sale of Goods*[236] favoured extended warranty protection for buyers. Although this proposal was largely actuated by economic loss claims, including inherent loss of value, it was wide enough to extend also to personal injury and property damage.

Despite being unpersuaded by them, the Ontario Law Reform Commission rehearsed the various arguments justifying the exclusion of liability for economic loss to remote buyers as follows.[237] First, there is not the same case for deterrence in economic loss vindication as there is for physical loss. Secondly, it would be anomalous to grant recovery in economic loss against a manufacturer for breach of a strict warranty

---

[230] UCC Art. 2–318.   [231] See *Grant* v. *Australian Knitting Mills Ltd* [1936] AC 85.
[232] The alternative holding in *Santor*, n. 224 above. See also *Mead Corpn.* v. *Allendale Mutual Insurance Co.* (1979) 465 F Supp. 355.
[233] *Seely* v. *White Motor Co.* (1965) 403 P 2d 145.
[234] Notably Saskatchewan and New Brunswick. See M. G. Bridge, *Sale of Goods* (Butterworths, Toronto, 1988), 540–2. There is also farm implement legislation of long standing that makes interesting inroads into the doctrine of privity: *ibid.* 539–40.
[235] *Report on Consumer Warranties and Guarantees in the Sale of Goods.*
[236] See also the *Report on Products Liability* (1979).
[237] *Report on Sale of Goods* (1979), i, 245–7.

when the tort of negligence is ungenerous in compensating such loss. Thirdly, commercial buyers at least ought to be able to protect their interests by private bargain. And fourthly, economic loss liability would increase a manufacturer's enterprise risks and make it difficult to plan future costs and secure insurance cover. Dismissing these arguments, the Commission was persuaded by other reasons for extending economic loss liability, namely, that manufacturers reach out to the consuming public and the line between express and implied warranties is commonly thin; that it is often a matter of mere chance whether a defective product causes physical or economic injury; that the manufacturer's economic loss liability is a known risk since it is already borne in respect of the immediate buyer; that an intervening bankruptcy in the distribution chain might exclude a deserving warranty claimant; and that extended warranty recourse might cut out wasteful indemnity actions. A modified version of the proposed provision was adopted as uniform law but has never been enacted.[238]

The Department of Trade and Industry, in a consultative paper,[239] has launched a tentative proposal that producers (and where relevant importers) should be liable along with the retail seller for the satisfactory quality of the goods. The proposal is a vague one. It seems not to extend to the fitness-for-purpose implied term in the consumer sale contract. What is clearer, however, is that the producer would be bound by the retail sale contract; the proposal is not that the consumer buyer would derive rights from the sale contract to which the producer is a party. It is therefore a case of extended liability rather than extended warranty. The consultative paper advises that caution may be needed in that the producer would not normally control the price of the goods paid by the consumer buyer or the description of the goods by the retail seller, both important elements in the present statutory definition of satisfactory quality. It would seem that the producer could not shelter behind any exclusion clauses in its contract of sale with the wholesaler or retailer as the case may be. It may be that the liability of producer and retailer would be joint and several but the proposal does not say. Nor is the proposal informative about the mechanics of rejection of the goods and contractual termination.

A similar proposal is to be found in a green paper issued by the European Commission,[240] which mentions the illogicality of having a

---

[238] Uniform Sale of Goods Act 1981, s. 50. See Alberta Institute of Law Research and Reform, *The Uniform Sale of Goods Act* (Report No. 38, 1982), 125–6; Manitoba Law Reform Commission, *Uniform Sale of Goods Act* (Report No. 57, 1983).

[239] *Consumer Guarantees*, Feb. 1992, 8–9.

[240] *Green Paper on Guarantees for Consumer Goods and After-Sales Services*, n. 217 above, 86–8. See S. Weatherill (1994) 110 *LQR* 545.

consumer buyer seek recourse only against a retailer, who has no influence on the production process. The Commission is also struck by the 'counter-intuitive' nature of a producer's liability for physical injury to the person and property of individuals[241] and immunity from claims that the product is economically disappointing. The liability proposed, a joint one with the seller of defective goods, would be of a 'quasi-subsidiary' nature, in that the producer would be brought in only if it is impossible or onerous to sue the seller. Moreover, the contract of sale would not as such be terminated *qua* the producer, who could nevertheless be called upon to cure the seller's defective performance and to answer for the buyer's 'direct losses'.

The Consumer Protection Act 1987

Pursuant to a European directive,[242] the Consumer Protection Act was passed in 1987. The origin of the directive lies in the need to standardize the liability of producers so as to bring about level competitive conditions within the European Union, though there are other influencing considerations, such as the perceived incongruity of buyers and non-buyers having different legal rights, and of a consumer having recourse only against a retail seller when defects in the goods are the responsibility of the producer. The Act imposes a form of strict tortious liability on producers to those injured by defective products.

Liability under the Act arises in respect of a 'product', which includes goods (as well as their components and raw materials) and electricity.[243] 'Goods' are then defined to include 'substances', which themselves include liquids, vapours and gases, and crops and fixtures.[244] Overall, products for the purposes of the 1987 Act are broader than the Sale of Goods Act definition of goods.[245] Section 2 of the Act makes liable the 'producer',[246] who is defined as the manufacturer or the person who won, abstracted, or processed the product. The extension beyond manufacturers is clearly needed to bring in those producing minerals and forms of energy. The word 'producer' also includes importers and those who attach their own brands to a product,[247] such as a supermarket chain. It excludes the suppliers of game and agricultural produce that have not yet undergone an industrial process,[248] as well as those who do not supply in the course of a business.[249] There is also a provision

---

[241] See Product Liability Directive 85/374 [1985] OJ L210/29 and the Consumer Protection Act 1987.

[242] 85/374/EEC [1985] OJ L210/29. See J. Stapleton, 'Three Problems with the New Product Liability' in P. Cane and J. Stapleton (eds.), *Essays for Patrick Atiyah* (OUP, London, 1991).

[243] S. 1(2). [244] S. 45(1). [245] See Ch. 2 above. [246] S. 2(2)(a).
[247] S. 2(2)(b)(c). [248] S. 2(4). [249] S. 4(1)(c).

designed to ensure that intermediate sellers co-operate in passing on the names of producers where a request is made within a reasonable time by injured persons who cannot practicably identify the producers themselves.[250] Those sellers are themselves deemed to be producers if they do not supply the information sought or the names of their immediate sellers (to whom the injured person might then make a further inquiry).

On the face of it, a producer's liability is strict. It exists where 'any damage is caused wholly or partly by a defect in a product'.[251] There is no reference to a fault standard. Nevertheless, a 'defect' exists if 'the safety of the product is not such as persons generally are entitled to expect',[252] which appears to give some considerable latitude to the sellers of detonators, which cannot be expected to be as safe as marshmallows, and cigarettes, whose inherent dangers are notorious. The language of section 3(1) thus contains the seeds of a state of the art (or development risks) defence, repeated in explicit terms in section 4(1)(e) as arising where 'the state of scientific and technical knowledge at the relevant time' was such that producers of such products could not have been expected to discover in them the alleged defect. This appears to come close to ruling out strict liability in the case of those, such as drug companies, who manufacture innovative products. Yet liability under the Act is quite different from negligence, in that the burden of raising the defence, which does not look easy to discharge, rests upon the producer.[253] The notion of 'defect' is not on the face of the Act differentially interpreted according to whether the injury caused by the product arises out of defective design, defective manufacture, or defective instructions or warnings accompanying the product. The state of the art defence, however, is peculiarly apt in matters of design.

The damage for which a producer may be liable is 'death or personal injury or any loss of or damage to any property (including land)',[254] which does not include damage done by the product to itself,[255] in reality a form of economic loss. The claim is that value for money is not received when a product does not last as long as it ought to have done. If a claim is made for damage to other property of the claimant, this has to belong to the claimant and be property 'ordinarily intended for private use, occupation or consumption'.[256] To prevent trivial claims from being advanced, the Act does not rely only upon the usual cost deterrent to

---

[250] S. 2(3).
[251] S. 2(1). For a failure to prove cause, see *Loveday* v. *Renton* (pertussis vaccine) *The Times*, 31 Mar. 1988.
[252] S. 3(1). See C. Newdick [1988] *CLJ* 455.
[253] Note that the Act permits the defence of contributory negligence to be raised by the defendant producer against the claimant: s. 6(4).
[254] S. 5(1).   [255] S. 5(2).   [256] S. 5(3).

small-scale litigation: it disallows the award of damages in property cases where the amount recoverable would not exceed £275.

Rather surprisingly, the Act does not explicitly state who may bring an action against the producer. It must necessarily be someone who suffers injury as defined by the Act, an injury caused by a defect in the product. Section 7 refers in general terms, for the purpose of preventing the disclaimer of a producer's liability under the Act by notice or contractual clause, to 'a person who has suffered damage'. There is no reason to exclude anyone who suffers the relevant injury, for example a motorist injured as a result of the defective steering on another motorist's car. There would appear to be no need that the plaintiff be a buyer or a member of the buyer's family.

UNFAIR CONTRACT TERMS

At common law, exemption clauses are controlled principally by the tests of incorporation and construction.[257] The first, based upon fact, poses the question whether an exemption clause has been included in a contract. It is difficult, but by no means impossible, to rule out on this ground a clause in a signed document but there are numerous examples of unincorporated clauses contained in obscure or ill-placed notices or in documents that arrive too late. Even if a clause passes this factual incorporation test, it may yet fail to cover the plaintiff's claim if, as a matter of law, its language is inadequate. In scrutinizing the language of clauses for this purpose,[258] the courts apply a *contra proferentem* rule of construction. For example, a seller giving 'no warranty express or implied' does not thereby exclude a condition.[259] A clause excluding liability for breach of implied terms does not exclude liability for breach of express terms.[260] Again, a clause referring to 'goods delivered' does not protect the seller when he is sued by the buyer for non-delivery of goods.[261] Perhaps more artificial in its approach to the language of exemption clauses is the 'negligence only' rule by which general words of exclusion, not explicitly mentioning negligence but capable of extending to it, will so apply only if negligence is the only plausible head of liability.[262] So, in *White* v. *John*

---

[257] See Treitel, *The Law of Contract* (9th edn., Sweet & Maxwell, London, 1995), 197–224.
[258] A question of law, like all issues of contractual interpretation.
[259] *Wallis Son & Wells* v. *Pratt & Haynes* [1911] AC 394.
[260] *Andrews Bros.* v. *Singer and Co.* [1934] 1 KB 17.
[261] *Beck & Co.* v. *Szymanowski* [1924] AC 43.
[262] In *Hollier* v. *Rambler Motors (AMC) Ltd* [1972] 2 QB 71, the plausible alternative, strict liability for fire damage to customers' cars, existed only in the minds of uninformed members of the public, where it had been placed by Salmon LJ.

Warwick & Co. Ltd,[263] a contract for the hire of a cycle provided that 'nothing in this agreement shall render the owner liable for any personal injuries'. The defective saddle injured the hirer and the owner was held liable for breach of its duty to take care in supplying a safe cycle. A plausible stricter form of liability, arising from the breach of an implied duty to supply a cycle fit for its purpose, was covered by the clause and therefore ousted negligence from it. Cases like those discussed above simply encourage the drafting of exclusions of all liability, whether for breach of warranty or condition, express or implied, negligence or otherwise.

More recently, the House of Lords has signalled a desire to avoid strained results and return to more straightforward canons of construction, at least where the parties are of equal bargaining power.[264] The danger with the previous approach was that it was capable of striking down freely agreed clauses supported by sensible business reasons, such as the allocation of a particular risk to the least-cost insurer. The House of Lords felt able to take this step because of the enactment of the Unfair Contract Terms Act 1977, which firmly controls the abuse of exemption clauses. This Act cuts across the dichotomy of fact and law established by the previous tests of incorporation and construction. These tests continue to apply, though it would hardly be sensible to take up forensic time discussing the meaning of a clause that is plainly invalidated under the Act.

Implied Terms and Exclusion

Besides new material, the Act contains provisions drawn from the Supply of Goods (Implied Terms) Act 1973 and amends the Misrepresentation Act 1967. Far from being a comprehensive treatment of unfair contract terms, an expression that appears only in the title, it deals with certain exclusion, limitation, and indemnity clauses.[265] In its particular application to sale of goods contracts,[266] the Act deals with the exclusion of the statutory implied terms in commercial and consumer contracts. First of all, the seller's obligations in section 12 of the Sale of Goods Act may not be excluded or restricted at all, regardless of the nature of the contract.[267] With regard to the other implied terms of description, satisfactory quality, fitness for purpose, and equality to sample, a basic distinction is drawn between cases where the buyer is and is not dealing as a consumer. Where the buyer deals as a consumer, liability under these

---

[263] [1953] 1 WLR 1285.
[264] *Photo Production Ltd* v. *Securicor Transport Ltd* [1980] AC 827.
[265] It also deals with non-contractual notices excluding tortious liability.
[266] For a general treatment of the Act, see the standard contract texts.
[267] S. 6(1)(a).

implied terms may not be restricted or excluded at all.[268] This will not be narrowly interpreted. A car dealer's attempt to sell goods 'as seen and inspected' was stated to be an invalid attempt to cut down the scope of his description duty in *Hughes* v. *Hall*.[269] A clause in the contract requiring a consumer buyer to elect in favour of accepting unsatisfactory or unfit goods with a price allowance, rather than rejecting them and recovering the price, should also be seen as 'restricting' liability and hence void under the Act.[270] Where the buyer does not deal as a consumer, the clause will have effect only to the extent it passes the test of reasonableness,[271] according to criteria laid down in Schedule 2 of the Act. In the case of misrepresentation, section 3 of the Misrepresentation Act[272] subjects all clauses excluding or restricting liability or the availability of remedies to the standard of reasonableness laid down in the Unfair Contract Terms Act.[273] It is not clear why consumer and non-consumer contracts should in this one respect be treated alike.

Dealing as a Consumer

The deceptively simple notion of dealing as a consumer in fact comprises three elements: first, the buyer must not contract in the course of a business or hold himself out as doing so; secondly, the seller must be acting in the course of a business; and thirdly, the goods must be of a type ordinarily supplied for private use or consumption.[274] There is also a rebuttable presumption that a buyer deals as a consumer.[275] Business is defined as including 'a profession and the activities of any government department or local or public authority'.[276]

The question whether the buyer was purchasing in the course of a business arose in *R. & B. Customs Brokers Co. Ltd* v. *United Dominions Trust Ltd*.[277] The buyer was a private company in business as a shipping

---

[268] S. 6(2)(a).   [269] [1981] RTR 430.

[270] There is a difficulty. In the very similar case of a buyer signing a delivery note containing small print expressing satisfaction with the goods, the Law Commission proposed additional legislation (in Law Com. No. 160, *Sale and Supply of Goods*) whose effect is to provide that the buyer is deemed not to have accepted the goods prior to an opportunity to examine them. This legislation became s. 35(2),(3) of the Sale of Goods Act as amended by the Sale and Supply of Goods Act 1994.

[271] S. 6(3).   [272] As amended by the Unfair Contract Terms Act.

[273] The general standard in s. 11(1) as opposed to Sched. 2.

[274] S. 12(1). Consequently, a private seller, since he is not in business, may exclude the description condition, subject to reasonableness, regardless of the identity and purpose of the buyer. The Act also provides by way of override that buyers at auction never purchase as consumers: s. 12(2).

[275] S. 12(3).

[276] S. 14, which suggests a broad view should be taken of the activities of universities, whether ancient, old or new.

[277] [1988] 1 All ER 847.

broker and the car was bought for the personal and business use of two directors. The argument (not advanced) that a buyer does not purchase in the course of a business where the purpose is not wholly a business one would have been difficult to resist.[278] The court, however, reached the same result by holding that, since this purchase was only incidental to the buyer's business, the buyer did not purchase vehicles sufficiently regularly[279] for this transaction to have been conducted in the course of that business. In reaching this conclusion, the court relied upon case law arising out of a similarly worded provision in the Trade Descriptions Act 1968.[280] It is not easy, apart from the authority of the House of Lords, to see why business should be so intimately tied to regularity.[281] Nor is it a matter of identifying cases where the buyer needs protection and cases where the buyer does not, since both categories of buyer obtain protection under the Act, albeit in varying degrees.[282] A better approach would be to take account of the lack of business experience and bargaining power that goes with intermittent dealings by factoring these matters into the treatment of reasonableness.

Where the buyer does not deal as a consumer, the criteria of reasonableness are to be found in Schedule 2. These include the strength of the parties' bargaining power and the buyer's ability to acquire the goods elsewhere, the existence of an inducement to the buyer to accept the exemption clause,[283] whether the buyer should have known of the term,[284] the reasonableness of complying with a condition that would have suspended the exemption clause,[285] and the production of goods for the buyer's special needs. Obviously, since these are guidelines, they are only illustrative and other sensible criteria should not be excluded.[286] For example, it might make perfect commercial sense for the parties to agree that defects be put right under the terms of the manufacturer's (satisfactory) guarantee scheme. The reasonableness of a clause might also depend upon its cumulative effect with other clauses in the

---

[278] See Dillon LJ, *ibid.* 855. But the directors' personal use may well be the company's business use, and the company is the buyer: *ibid.* 853.

[279] This was only the second or third vehicle acquired on credit terms.

[280] *Davies* v. *Sumner* [1984] 1 WLR 1301 (HL).

[281] What about the seller disposing of equipment surplus to his business requirements at irregular and infrequent intervals? Are these sales in the course of a business for the purpose of s. 14 of the Sale of Goods Act? See Ch. 7, below.

[282] See Dillon LJ, n. 277 above, 853 ('two classes of innocent contracting parties . . . for whom differing degrees of protection against unfair contract terms are afforded').

[283] A lower price would be such an inducement.

[284] *AEG (UK) Ltd* v. *Logic Resources Ltd* [1996] CLC 265. See also the above discussion of incorporation.

[285] This would include, e.g., a requirement that defects be notified to the seller within a given time.

[286] S. 11(2) declares them to be of 'particular' relevance.

contract.[287] As for monetary limitation clauses, section 11(4) adds the further criteria of the resources of the *proferens* and the insurability of the liability risk. It is not clear why the size of the money sum does not receive mention and why these factors are not also made specifically relevant in the case of other types of clause.

Where the buyer does not deal as a consumer, section 6(3) states that liability can be restricted or excluded 'but only in so far as the term satisfies the requirement of reasonableness'. This suggests that some degree of severance is permissible. If severance consists of deleting sub-clauses, this should fall within the spirit and letter of section 6(3).[288] More difficult is the case where a blue pencil has to be applied within the body of a provision. It is submitted that the balance of the clause should be allowed to go forward if it is reasonable and makes linguistic sense. This leaves the clause that would have to be rewritten in order to conform to the requirement of reasonableness. It is not easy to see, with reference to the criteria in Schedule 2 and section 11(4), how this could be done without rewriting the contract, which neither court nor *proferens* should be at liberty to do.

The European Directive

The implementation of the European Directive dealing with unfair terms in consumer contracts was put out for consultation by the Department of Trade and Industry[289] and the directive brought into effect by statutory instrument.[290] The directive has no specific application to sale of goods contracts, except in so far as the preamble recites the need to assist the sale of goods by stimulating competition and to provide effective consumer protection by rendering European sales law uniform, and points to consumers' ignorance of sales law in other member states of the European Union.[291] The directive and the Unfair Contract Terms Act will operate in parallel. It should be noted that the Act applies to both consumer and non-consumer contracts, and renders particular clauses void whereas the directive consigns a number of clauses to an indicative (or 'grey') list. The effect of a clause amounting to an unfair term under

---

[287] *AEG (UK) Ltd* v. *Logic Resources Ltd*, n. 284 above.

[288] Cf. *R. W. Green Ltd* v. *Cade Bros. Farm* [1978] 1 Lloyd's Rep. 602.

[289] Implementation of the EC Directive on Unfair Terms in Consumer Contracts (93/13/EEC) [1993] OJ L95/29.

[290] The Unfair Terms in Consumer Contracts Regulations SI 1994 No. 3159, effective 1 July 1995. See generally N. M. Padfield (1995) 10 *JIBL* 175; H. Beale, 'Legislative Control of Fairness: The Directive on Unfair Terms in Consumer Contracts', in J. Beatson and D. Friedmann (eds.), *Good Faith and Fault in Contract Law* (OUP, London, 1995).

[291] How does the directive serve to educate consumers?

the directive is that it is not binding on the consumer; the contract minus the term remains in force if 'it is capable of continuing in existence' without the term.[292]

[292] Art. 6.

9

The Seller's Duty and Power to Transfer Title

This Chapter is divided into two parts. First, it deals with the contractual relations of seller and buyer and the scope of the title to the goods that under section 12 of the Sale of Goods Act the seller is obliged to invest in the buyer. Secondly, it deals with the various circumstances in which a seller of goods, lacking the right to sell them to the buyer, has yet the power to override the superior title of a third party by the act of transferring the goods to the buyer. The disparate circumstances in which a seller can achieve this amount to a substantial inroad into the rule of *nemo dat quod non habet* that no one can transfer a better title than the one that he himself possesses.

THE SELLER'S DUTY TO TRANSFER TITLE

Section 12 contains a number of implied terms, the most important of which is the condition[1] that, in the case of a sale, the seller has the right to sell the goods, and that in the case of an agreement to sell he will have such a right at the time when the property is to pass. A contract of sale is an agreement to sell until the property passes, whereupon it becomes a sale, except where the passing of property at the contract date meant that it always was a sale.[2] Section 12(1) imposes two obligations on the seller where the property does not pass at the contract date: first, a promise that the seller will have the right to sell at a future date; and secondly, a promise springing at that future date that the seller does have the right to sell. Even if only the latter obligation had been spelt out in section 12(1), the doctrine of anticipatory repudiation would have supplied also the equivalent of the first. Under the doctrine of anticipatory repudiation, a seller clearly unable to transfer title at an agreed future date might be said to be in present breach of the latter obligation.[3] Nevertheless, where a seller has the capacity and the will to buy out the true owner, and thus transfer good title to the buyer at the agreed future date, it is difficult to

---

[1] Prior to the implementation of the Supply of Goods (Implied Terms) Act 1994, the status of this term was in s. 12(1) itself. The 1994 Act introduced the cosmetic change locating the status of the term in s. 12(5A).

[2] S. 2(4)–(6). Ch. 2 above.

[3] For prospective incapacity as repudiation, see Ch. 6 above.

see that a breach of section 12(1) has occurred. If the contract of sale is a conditional sale, and the buyer must in the meantime pay instalments to the seller, this places the buyer in an invidious position.

In *Barber* v. *NWS Bank plc*,[4] an express term, that 'the property in the Goods shall pass to the Customer' upon payment in full, was conceded by the seller to amount to an express term that the seller was the owner of the goods at the contract date. This concession was regarded by the Court of Appeal as 'both correct and unavoidable'.[5] By any standard of construction, this conclusion is extraordinary, confusing as it does the seller's title obligations under section 12 and the passing of property between seller and buyer. It does, however, possess the merit of plugging the gap in the statutory coverage of the seller's title obligations. The express term was treated as a condition of the contract, rather than an intermediate stipulation, on the ground that without it the agreement would not work. This draws attention to the failure of section 12(1) expressly to provide that a conditional seller should have the right to sell the goods at the contract date. If the Court of Appeal is correct, a conditional sale lacking an express title term is unworkable.

Section 12(1) states blandly that the seller must have a right to sell. It does not state that the seller must transfer ownership or title, nor that the seller must pass the property in the way and at the time provided for in the Act.[6] Ownership is not mentioned at all in the Act and title, apart from a mention in the marginal note to section 12, is dealt with in the sections on the *nemo dat* rule. Property is defined in section 61(1) as the general property and not a mere special property. A special property is a possessory interest of a type claimed by bailees and pledgees,[7] so that the general property refers to the whole of the seller's interest in goods without any reservation of reversionary rights of the kind made by bailor or pledgor. A contract in which the whole of a transferor's proprietary interest in goods is exchanged for a money consideration is therefore a contract of sale to which the passing of property rules in sections 16 to 19 apply.

In defining the scope of section 12(1), there is no need to gauge how far the general property exceeds in scope the special property; it is a provision dealing with contractual undertakings, not conveyancing. The provision speaks of a right to sell and refrains from using terms like ownership, title, or property. It records the seller's undertaking to transfer at the agreed time the best possessory entitlement in the world. It is

---

[4] [1996] 1 All ER 906. [5] *Ibid.* 910.
[6] On terminology and concepts, see A. Kiralfy (1949) 12 *MLR* 424; G. Battersby and A. D. Preston (1972) 35 *MLR* 268.
[7] *Donald* v. *Suckling* (1866) LR 1 QB 585; *Nyberg* v. *Handelaar* [1892] 2 QB 202; O. W. Holmes, *The Common Law* (1881), 242. See *The Odessa* [1916] 1 AC 145, 155–9 (disapproval of special property terminology).

hard to speak of the ownership of goods in the sense of an absolute right, good against the world. A strong argument can be made that there is no such thing as a law of property in goods:[8] proprietary entitlement is resolved through tortious actions, principally conversion and trespass *de bonis asportatis*, in which standing to sue is based upon possession or the right to immediate possession[9] rather than upon anything called ownership; the remedy is nearly always damages rather than specific delivery of the goods;[10] and a plaintiff is successful who demonstrates a superior possessory entitlement to that of the defendant.[11] This point is weakened, however, by the Torts (Interference with Goods) Act 1977,[12] which seeks to reduce overcompensation and to encourage all interested parties to join in the litigation.[13] Subject to this, ownership is relative rather than absolute.[14] It is unusual for documents to be kept recording changes of ownership of goods, and the common law does not lend itself to the view that restrictive covenants and encumbrances can attach themselves to goods[15] so as to follow them through changes of ownership.[16]

Early cases on the inference of express warranty[17] show the courts have long found contractual promises in representations of ownership made by sellers. Nevertheless, some resistance to the universal inference of an implied undertaking, arising from the mere fact of sale, survived until well into the nineteenth century. This resistance seems to have been fuelled by *caveat emptor* thinking, the idea being that the buyer should secure an express undertaking, and was expressed at length by Baron Parke in *Morley* v. *Attenborough*.[18] A pawnbroker was held not to

---

[8] Kiralfy, n. 6 above.

[9] E. H. Warren (1936) 49 *Harv. LR* 1084; *Jeffries* v. *Great Western Railway Co.* (1856) 5 E & B 802; F. Pollock and R. Wright, *An Essay on Possession in the Common Law* (OUP, London, 1888), 5; M. G. Bridge, *Personal Property Law* (Blackstone, London, 1992), 49–55.

[10] Specific delivery was introduced by the Common Law Procedure Act 1854, s. 78. The remedy is rarely awarded: *General and Finance Facilities Ltd* v. *Cook's Cars (Romford) Ltd* [1963] 1 WLR 644; *Howard Perry & Co.* v. *British Railways Board* [1980] 1 WLR 1375 (interlocutory relief).

[11] Public policy apart (see *Parker* v. *British Airways Board* [1982] QB 1004), a thief would be able to sue an person unlawfully interfering with his possession: see *Buckley* v. *Gross* (1863) 3 B & S 566; *Bird* v. *Town of Fort Frances* [1949] OR 292.

[12] Ss. 5(4), 7–8.

[13] The now-repealed market overt exception to the rule of *nemo dat quod non habet* in the text accompanying nn. 143–4 below, created the nearest thing to an absolute title in effacing all earlier titles.

[14] See also Rules of the Supreme Court, Ord. 15, r. 10A; County Court Rules, Ord. 15, r. 4.

[15] Kiralfy, n. 6 above.

[16] Mortgage and conditional sale are both based upon the notion of undivided ownership, transferred in the first case and retained in the second. Of course, this notion is qualified by equitable ideas, which also support charges on personalty.

[17] *Crosse* v. *Gardner* (1688) Carth. 90, *sub nom. Cross* v. *Garret* at 3 Mod. 261; *Medina* v. *Stoughton* (1699) 1 Salk. 210, 1 Ld. Raym. 593.

[18] (1849) 3 Ex. 500.

have undertaken to transfer outright ownership when selling an unre-
deemed pledge, a result that might also be reached today.[19] According to
Parke B, the seller of unascertained goods gave such an undertaking, but
a seller of specific goods did so only in two cases: first, where trade custom required it and, secondly, where it could readily be inferred from the
nature of the seller's business, such as that of retail shopkeeper.[20] The
reason for the absence of a general undertaking for specific goods was
that, formerly, such sales had occurred in market overt, where the
buyer's acquisition of clear title meant that no such undertaking was
needed.[21] Later authorities, however, thought the exceptions had consumed the general rule[22] and this was the position first codified in 1893.

Title and Failure of Consideration

While section 12(1) formally states the seller's undertaking that he has a
right to sell as a condition, also the case for fitness and satisfactory quality in section 14, this undertaking is in some ways treated as a matter of
fundamental obligation transcending even a contractual condition. In
Rowland v. *Divall*,[23] the defendant seller sold a car to the plaintiff dealer,
who paid cash, repainted the car, and drove it from Sussex to Dorset. He
exhibited it in his showroom for two months and then sold it to a local
buyer, who in turn used it for two months before it was repossessed by
the police as a stolen car. The dealer reimbursed the buyer and brought
the present action to recover from the defendant, not damages, but his
own purchase money as on a total failure of consideration.[24] The defendant pleaded that the dealer's intermediate enjoyment of the car over the
four month period amounted to the receipt of a benefit precluding any
rescission of the contract *ab initio*, a necessary precondition to a failure
of consideration action.[25] The court, nevertheless, found a failure of

---

[19] S. 12(3).   [20] N. 18 above, 509 ff.   [21] *Ibid.* 511.
[22] *Sims* v. *Marryat* (1851) 17 QB 281; J. P. Benjamin, *A Treatise on the Sale of Personal Property* (2nd American edn., Sweet & Maxwell, London, 1873), 522–3. See also *Eicholz* v. *Bannister* (1864) 17 CB(NS) 708.
[23] [1923] 2 KB 500. See G. H. Treitel (1967) 30 *MLR* 139, 146–9; M. G. Bridge, 'The Title Obligations of the Seller of Goods', in N. Palmer and E. McKendrick (eds.), *Interests in Goods* (Lloyds of London Press, London, 2nd edn., 1998); Lord Goff of Chieveley and G. Jones, *The Law of Restitution* (4th edn., Sweet & Maxwell, London, 1993), 421–4.
[24] Such a claim, sanctioned by s. 54, is to a degree independent of an action for breach of the undertaking in s. 12(1) and has links with standard common law mistake authorities like *Kennedy* v. *Panama, New Zealand and Australian Royal Mail Co.* (1867) LR 2 QB 580; *Gompertz* v. *Bartlett* (1853) 2 E & B 849; and *Gurney* v. *Womersley* (1854) 4 E & B 133. This type of action in title cases was sanctioned by Erle CJ in *Eicholz* v. *Bannister*, n. 22 above. See also *Australian Credit Corpn.* v. *Ross* [1983] 2 VLR 319.
[25] *Weston* v. *Downes* (1778) 1 Dougl. 23; *Towers* v. *Barrett* (1786) 1 TR 133; *Hunt* v. *Silk* (1804) 5 East 449.

consideration.[26] Rejecting the seller's assertion that a benefit, even if not the one bargained for, could preclude rescission and thus the failure of consideration action,[27] the court equated enjoyment with lawful enjoyment.[28] Consequently, the buyer's precarious and unlawful possession was no impediment to the action.[29]

The court's decision amounts to treating wasting assets as bought for the abstract enjoyment of title rather than for consumption—a dubious proposition—for that is all that separates lawful enjoyment from unlawful enjoyment. The reasoning proves too much. It could not tenably be argued to similar effect that goods are bought only so that they can be enjoyed as fit for the buyer's purpose or as of satisfactory quality. *Rowland* v. *Divall* may thus be seen as the other side of the coin to the now-repealed rule preventing the buyer of specific goods from rejecting them and terminating the contract once the property has passed.[30] Just as the passing of property no longer prevents the rejection of specific goods, so the seller's failure to vest a lawful title in the buyer should no longer be treated as a total failure of consideration if there has in fact been a clear enjoyment derived from the goods. This is not to deny that there may be cases where the buyer obtains no benefit, as where the seller is unable to transfer even possession to a prepaying buyer. The receipt of any benefit broadly of the kind bargained for ought to preclude an action for the recovery of the price if the goods have been accepted.[31] *Rowland* v. *Divall* sidesteps the acceptance and *ex post facto* warranty rules in the Sale of Goods Act,[32] when the better solution would have been to remit the buyer to a damages claim amounting to the price paid minus the benefit.[33]

Rowland v. *Divall* is also a troublesome case for the way that failure of consideration arguments become confused with the issue whether the buyer was precluded from rejecting the goods for a breach of condition

[26] N. 23 above, 523–4 (Bankes LJ in particular). Curiously, s. 54 is not mentioned in the case.

[27] *Taylor* v. *Hare* (1805) 1 B & PNR 260.

[28] See also *Rover International Ltd* v. *Cannon Film Sales Ltd* [1989] 1 WLR 912, 925; *David Securities Pty. Ltd* v. *Commonwealth Bank of Australia* (1992) 175 CLR 353, 381–83; *Baltic Exchange Co.* v. *Dixon* (1993) 176 CLR 344, 351.

[29] Atkin LJ added an estoppel argument that the seller could not plead the buyer's enjoyment of a benefit: n. 23 above, 507.

[30] Ch. 5 above.

[31] See *Taylor* v. *Hare*, n. 27 above; *Linz* v. *Electric Wire Co. of Palestine* [1948] AC 371 (shares); *Lawes* v. *Purser* (1856) 6 E & B 930 (patent). There is also the possibility that it would be inequitable for a seller, having changed his position, to return the money (see *Lipkin, Gorman* v. *Karpnale Ltd* [1991] 2 AC 548). This argument was summarily rejected in *Barber* v. *NWS Bank plc* [1996] 1 All ER 906, where the defendant conditional seller had paid money received for the contract goods to its own supplier.

[32] Ch. 5 above.

[33] There may in some cases be a damages claim for the loss of resale profit and for the cost of defending an action in conversion by the true owner.

after accepting them, together with the related issue of whether a buyer could reject goods if unable to place them at the disposal of the seller. An undiscoverable latent defect of title should be no more potent than a latent defect of quality in prolonging the buyer's rejection period.[34] Scrutton LJ chose to dispose of the seller's objection, so far as it related to rejection as opposed to rescission *ab initio*, by asserting that it hardly lay in the seller's mouth to complain of the buyer's inability to return the goods when this very inability stemmed from the seller's breach of section 12(1).[35] Atkin LJ conjured up a section 11(4) implied agreement ousting the acceptance rules in section 35 and also asserted that 'there can be no sale of goods at all which the seller has no right to sell',[36] thus ousting the very applicability of those acceptance rules. This latter expedient is unfortunate, for what is surely significant in the characterization of contracts of sale is what the seller promised to do rather than succeeded in doing. A pursuit of the latter approach would find in the very breach of section 12(1) the circumstances of its own exclusion.[37] The seller intended to divest himself totally of his interest in the goods and successfully accomplished this.

The major drawback to *Rowland* v. *Divall*, whether rationalized as a failure of consideration leading to rescission *ab initio* or as a belated and irregular rejection for breach of condition, is that the buyer obtains an unpaid-for benefit, a result stigmatized as unjust.[38] On the facts of the case itself, rough justice may have been done, since the buyer did not pursue a damages claim, whether for loss of profit or for damage to his business reputation arising from the sale of a stolen car. Further, he had bought out the true owner for an undisclosed amount.[39] But an application of the reasoning in *Rowland* v. *Divall* has led to buyers in later cases receiving free and lengthy periods of beneficial use.[40] Any objection that the possession of such buyers is precarious and that they are at risk of being sued in conversion can be met by factoring any loss thereby suffered into a damages claim against the seller.[41]

---

[34] See Ch. 5 above.   [35] N. 23 above, 505–6.

[36] *Ibid.* 507. He added an estoppel argument, that the seller could not plead the buyer's enjoyment of a benefit: *ibid.*

[37] Although this approach undermines a damages claim on the contract, it does not have the same effect on a failure of consideraton action.

[38] Law Reform Committee, *Twelfth Report (Transfer of Title to Chattels)* (HMSO, London, 1966, Cmnd. 2958), 15.

[39] Bankes LJ considered this irrelevant: see the report at [1923] All ER 270, 272.

[40] *Butterworth* v. *Kingsway Motors Ltd* [1954] 1 WLR 1086 (10½ months); *McNeill* v. *Associated Car Markets Ltd* (1962) 35 DLR (2d) 581 (nearly 20 months); *Barber* v. *NWS Bank plc*, n. 31 above (22 months).

[41] Canadian cases have offset against successful claims for the recovery of money on a failure of consideration amounts representing the benefit obtained by the buyer from the use of the goods: *F. & B. Transport Ltd* v. *White Truck Sales Manitoba Ltd* (1964) 47 DLR (2d) 419, affd. (1965) 49 DLR (2d) 670; *Wiebe* v. *Butchart's Motors Ltd* [1949] 4 DLR 838.

A flaw in the failure of consideration argument in *Rowland* v. *Divall* is that it draws from an outmoded view of rescission *ab initio* as a necessary complement to a price recovery action, otherwise now refuted in the law of restitution.[42] This view highlights a logical inconsistency in combining a claim, denying the existence of the contract, for the return of the price with an action for damages on the contract. A buyer terminating a contract in the orthodox way may recover the price paid as part of a rolled-up damages award that adjusts the consequence of termination.[43] If the doctrine of failure of consideration is denied application, on the ground that the Sale of Goods Act adequately protects the buyer's position by means of section 12(1) and the damages and rejection remedies associated with it,[44] the problem of the buyer's free benefit[45] could then be resolved by confining the buyer who has accepted the goods to an appropriate award of damages.

Even here, nevertheless, the notion of unlawful enjoyment should not be allowed to distort the assessment of damages. Yet in the hire purchase case of *Warman* v. *Southern Counties Car Finance Corpn.*[46] this is what happened. A hirer, who had plainly elected to sue the finance company for damages, for breach of an *ex post facto* implied warranty that it had title to the goods, was allowed to recover as damages the sum of all instalments paid, on the ground that his option to purchase the goods was valueless.[47] This approach should be resisted. In favour of the application of section 35 in the normal way, remitting the buyer to a damages action in section 12(1) where a benefit has been enjoyed, is the absence of a particular problem evident in other cases of non-conforming goods. Unlike goods that are unfit, section 12(1) cases do not face having to decide which of the parties should have the burden of dealing with unwanted goods. The goods may function perfectly adequately but have been repossessed by the true owner. *Rowland* v. *Divall* represents the pathological survival of archaic ideas in a contract law that has witnessed in modern times the establishment of contractual termination on a firm, prospective basis.[48]

The response of law reform agencies is interesting to a problem that is now too entrenched to be resolved other than by statutory means. In a

---

[42] *Fibrosa Spolka Akcyjna* v. *Fairbairn Lawson Combe Barbour Ltd* [1943] AC 32, overruling *Chandler* v. *Webster* [1904] 1 KB 493.

[43] In effect, this happened in *Mason* v. *Burningham* [1949] 2 KB 545.

[44] But see *Northwest Co. Ltd* v. *Merland Oil Co. of Canada Ltd* [1936] 2 WWR 577.

[45] Unlikely to arise where the buyer is still within the s. 35 acceptance period.

[46] [1949] 2 KB 576.

[47] The same approach is taken in *Australian Credit Corpn.* v. *Ross* [1983] 2 VLR 319; *Shoard* v. *Palmer* (1989) 98 FLR 402.

[48] *Photo Production Ltd* v. *Securicor Transport Ltd* [1980] AC 827; *Johnson* v. *Agnew* [1980] AC 367.

1968 working paper,[49] the Law Commission recommended the implementation of the Law Reform Committee's earlier recommendation that the buyer give credit for any benefit received.[50] The final report, however, recommended that a study of the law of restitution be done before any amendment to section 12.[51] A 1975 working paper on restitution recommended reform subject to resolving a number of ensuing practical problems.[52] The 1983 report that followed, however, decided to defer a final recommendation on section 12 until further work on sale reform had been done.[53] The working paper on sale in the same year provisionally recommended that a buyer's recovery of the full price should be subject to a judicial discretion where there had been a significant use of the goods.[54] But the tide favouring reform turned with the final report of the Law Commission on *Sale and Supply of Goods*[55] which recommended that nothing be done. First of all, any reform would be procedurally difficult to implement where there was a chain of transactions.[56] Secondly, the Law Commission could not see why the buyer should pay the seller for the use of someone else's goods. One response to this is to point to the outcome in *Butterworth* v. *Kingsway Motors Ltd.*[57] Another is that the contract is still a sale of goods contract under which the seller has transferred the general property to the buyer. It is not to the point that the buyer proves to the hilt a breach of contract. This of itself does not justify displacing the normal rules on rejection of the goods and damages. *Rowland* v. *Divall*, however, treats this contract for practical purposes as a nullity.[58]

Further difficulties in the application of section 12(1) to a chain of transactions have been presented by *Butterworth* v. *Kingsway Motors Ltd.*[59] A car, subject to a hire purchase agreement, was unlawfully sold by the hirer (the fifth party) to a car dealer (the fourth party) for £1,000. The dealer in turn sold it for £1,015 to the third party, who then sold it for

---

[49] Law Com. Working Paper No. 18, *Provisional Proposals Relating to Amendments to Sections 12–15 of the Sale of Goods Act 1893 etc.*

[50] N. 38 above, 15.

[51] Law Com. No. 24, *First Report on Exemption Clauses in Contract*, para. 12.

[52] Law Com. Working Paper No. 65, *Law of Contract[:]Pecuniary Restitution on Breach of Contract*, paras. 57–58.

[53] Law Com. No. 121, *Law of Contract[:]Pecuniary Restitution on Breach of Contract*, para. 1.12.

[54] Law Com. Working Paper No. 85, *Sale and Supply of Goods*, para. 6.7.

[55] Law Com. No. 160 (1987), paras. 6.1–5.

[56] For a summary and criticism of these difficulties, see M. G. Bridge, 'The Title Obligations of the Seller of Goods', in N. Palmer and E. McKendrick (eds.), *Interests in Goods* (Lloyds of London Press, London, 2nd edn., 1998), 325–7.

[57] [1954] 1 WLR 1286. Discussed in the text accompanying nn. 59 ff. below.

[58] For an explicit holding to this effect, see *H. W. West Ltd* v. *McBlain* [1950] NI 144.

[59] N. 57 above. See also *Patten* v. *Thomas* (1965) 66 SR (NSW) 458; *Lucas* v. *Dixon* [1926] VLR 400.

£1,030 to the defendant sellers, who finally sold it for £1,275 to the plaintiff. The four sales were all for cash and followed each other in rapid succession. After the plaintiff had had the use and enjoyment of the car for 10½ months, he received a letter from the finance company owner demanding possession of the car, but also giving him the option of paying off the hirer's hire purchase debt of £175 and keeping the car. The plaintiff then wrote a solicitor's letter to the defendant sellers clearly electing to put an end to the contract and demanding the return of his purchase money. About a week later, the plaintiff was informed by the finance company that the hirer had paid off the debt and that it would release the car. Nevertheless, the plaintiff continued to press the defendant sellers for the return of his money and requested instructions for the disposal of the car, which the defendants did not provide. At the date the plaintiff put an end to the contract, the car had fallen in value to £800; this figure had fallen further to £450 by the time of the action in the present case. When the plaintiff sued for the return of the price, the defendant sellers apparently claimed over in damages for breach of section 12(1) against the third party,[60] and similar claims were made by the third party against the fourth party and by the latter against the fifth party hirer at the head of the distribution chain. The final result was that the plaintiff buyer had the free use of the car for nearly a year, during which time it depreciated from £1,275 to £800.

This is quite unconscionable and argument enough that the transfer of ownership, as important as it is, is not the sole object of a sale of goods agreement.[61] The defendant sellers then had to absorb the car's depreciation from the date of the buyer's rescission to the trial, a matter of £350. This was treated as an incident, not so much of mitigation of damages, as of the defendants' ownership of the car. The remaining depreciation of £475, occurring during the plaintiff's possession of the car, was then transmitted as a section 12(1) *ex post facto* warranty claim back up the chain to the fifth party hirer. On any view of the matter, the overall result is less than satisfactory.

In deciding that the plaintiff buyer was entitled to the return of his money, Pearson J applied the rescission and failure of consideration analysis adopted in particular by Bankes LJ in *Rowland* v. *Divall*,[62] though he stated that the result would have been the same if the matter had been treated as one of fundamental breach entitling the buyer to treat the contract as repudiated. With respect, this understates the role

---

[60] This was the explanation given in *Patten* v. *Thomas*, n. 59 above, 464.
[61] Long-term financial leases attest to the significance of beneficial use whilst demystifying title.
[62] [1923] 2 KB 500, 523–4.

that the acceptance rules in section 35 could play.[63] If the contract had not been terminated, a claim only for damages could hardly justify the return of the price in full, for reasons stated above. A rescission *ab initio* having been promptly and already self-executed by the buyer through his solicitor's letter, it was not relevant to his claim that the titles of all the sellers in the distribution chain were 'fed' (or cured) as far as the defendant sellers when the hirer later paid off the hire purchase debt and acquired the general property in the car. It was unnecessary to say whether the buyer's rescission could have been prevented if the hirer's title had been fed before this happened, and since it seemed that all other buyers had elected to pursue a damages claim, seeking neither to rescind *ab initio* nor to terminate for breach. While reluctant to express a firm opinion on the matter, Pearson J felt it would be 'extraordinary' for the buyer in such a case to rescind for a failure of consideration.[64]

Since a failure of consideration claim looks to what in fact has been received under an extant contract, it seems right to rule out the action if the seller's title is fed before the rescission of the contract.[65] A claim that the contract has been terminated, allowing the buyer to recover the price as part of a post-termination damages adjustment, is a different matter. Section 12(1) recites 'an implied condition . . . that in the case of a sale [the seller] has a right to sell the goods'. Leaving aside Atkin LJ's difficulty whether they could properly be characterized as sales of goods at all, the sales in *Butterworth* were all present sales and the sellers all committed a discharging breach of condition at the moment of sale. No later feeding of title erases this breach of condition and prevents a buyer from terminating the contract, subject to section 35 and acceptance. Nevertheless, the act inconsistent with the seller's ownership[66] that all sellers in the chain performed when reselling the goods would bulk large and preserve the effect of a feeding of title. This argument probably renders unnecessary any attempt to argue the existence in this corner of sales law of a doctrine of cure that prevents the buyer from exercising rights of contractual termination.[67]

A final difficulty arising from the feeding of title concerns the seller with a defective title who makes two purported proprietary transfers and then subsequently acquires title to the goods. The question is how prior-

---

[63] *Pace* the reasoning of Atkin LJ that the acceptance rules are ousted in *Rowland* v. *Divall*, n. 62 above, 507.

[64] N. 57 above, 1295. Cf. *Lucas* v. *Dixon*, n. 59 above; *H. W. West Ltd* v. *McBlain*, n. 58 above. The issue was left open by Winn LJ in *Bennett* v. *Griffin Finance Ltd* [1967] 2 QB 46. Feeding title may be relevant outside sale in other proprietary transfers. In support of feeding, see the pledge cases of *Whitehorn Bros.* v. *Davison* [1911] 1 KB 463, 475; *Blundell-Leigh* v. *Attenborough* [1921] 3 KB 235.

[65] See E. P. Ellinger (1969) 5 *VUW LR* 168, 173.   [66] S. 35: Ch. 5 above.

[67] See Ch. 5 above.

ity between the two earlier transferees is to be determined. In *Patten* v. *Thomas*,[68] the hirer of a hire purchase car unlawfully sold the car and created a distribution chain like the one in *Butterworth*. The hirer subsequently paid off the finance company, but did so with moneys obtained by mortgaging the same car. At the time of this mortgage, the hirer had no title to convey to the mortgagee, but paying off the finance company appeared to feed both the mortgage and the series of sales transactions. Plainly it could not do both and the question was whether title to the car was now in the mortgagee or in the ultimate buyer. The court decided that the ultimate buyer prevailed on temporal grounds, since the sale chain was created before the mortgage. A later Queensland case[69] supports this result. The hirer of goods had unlawfully sold them to two buyers and the court, applying the equitable rule that a purported present sale of future property amounts to a covenant to convey that creates an equitable interest as soon as the property comes into existence,[70] concluded that, as between the equitable interests of the two buyers, the first in time should prevail.[71]

Limited Title Sales and Exclusion Clauses

According to section 6(1)(a) of the Unfair Contract Terms Act 1977, the seller's liability in respect of the implied terms in section 12 of the Sale of Goods Act may be not be excluded or limited. This prohibition extends to all contracts of sale and not just consumer transactions. Nevertheless, it is one thing to exclude or limit liability, and another for the parties to agree that 'the seller should transfer only such title as he or a third person may have'.[72] The line between a prohibited exclusion and a limited title sale is a peculiarly elusive one to draw. Before this is done, it should be asked what lies behind the outright ban on exclusion clauses under section 12 when this ban applies only to consumer transactions for the other implied terms in sections 13 to 15 of the Sale of Goods Act.

The Law Commission's extensive discussion of implied terms and exclusion clauses[73] is concerned only with the implied terms in sections 13 to 15. There is only the following statement made about section 12: 'We see no justification for varying or excluding the implied conditions and warranties imposed by section 12, save where it is clear that the

---

[68] N. 59 above.

[69] *Denis Geary Motors Pty. Ltd* v. *Hunter Street Finance Ltd* [1979] Qd. R 207.

[70] *Tailby* v. *Official Receiver* (1888) 13 App. Cas. 523.

[71] In such a case, the superior title of the first buyer may be defeated by an application of the *nemo dat* exception in s. 24 of the Sale of Goods Act, discussed in the text accompanying nn. 395 ff. below, if the seller remains in possession at the time of the second purported sale.

[72] S. 12(3).   [73] In Law Com. No. 24, n. 51 above.

seller is purporting to sell only a limited title.'[74] It is likely that this dog-matic view arose out of the title fundamentalism that inspired *Rowland v. Divall*, especially the view of Atkin LJ that '[t]here can be no sale at all of goods which the seller has no right to sell'.[75] The literature predating the 1969 report[76] certainly was inspired by the idea that a breach of the terms in section 12 was a fundamental breach of contract, which at the time could not as a matter of substantive law be excluded. Largely because of the success of the Unfair Contract Terms Act 1977 in control-ling certain abuses, the courts may now afford to take a more flexible view of exclusion and similar clauses, recognizing that in certain cases they play a fair role in defining the terms of the bargain and identifying the least cost insurer.[77] Indeed, it has long been recognized that exclu-sion clauses are central features of the contractual bargain and not merely forensic appendages brought into play when a contractual dis-pute is resolved.[78] This principle, that clauses defining obligations and clauses excluding obligations cannot properly be distinguished, is breached by section 12(3) of the Sale of Goods Act, which attempts to do precisely that in defining limited title sales.

As difficult as it is to separate limited title sales and exclusions, it must be done. Perhaps the most obvious case of a limited title sale, which need not be expressed to be so in the contract but may be inferred from the cir-cumstances, is a sale by sheriffs and bailiffs pursuant to their office,[79] where there has long been a desire to protect such officers in the exercise of their functions.[80] The common law development of the section 12 implied terms was retarded largely by such transactions. The law has also been sympathetic to secured creditors exercising powers of sale upon the debtor's default[81] and to auctioneers acting on behalf of unnamed prin-cipals.[82]

Another pointer to a limited title sale is the presence of circumstances

---

[74] *Ibid.*, para. 17. The Law Reform Committee, in *Transfer of Title to Chattels* (Cmnd. 2958, HMSO, London, 1966), had earlier seen no reason to distinguish sale and hire pur-chase, where a ban on exclusion already existed: para. 38.

[75] [1923] 2 KB 500, 506–7.

[76] A. Hudson (1957) 20 *MLR* 236; *ibid.*, (1961) 24 *MLR* 690; A. G. Guest (1961) 77 *LQR* 98, 100.

[77] *Photo Production Ltd* v. *Securicor Transport Ltd* [1980] AC 827.

[78] B. Coote, *Exception Clauses* (Sweet & Maxwell, London, 1970), 17. Cf. *'Istros' (Owners)* v. *F. W. Dahlstrom & Co.* [1931] 1 KB 247.

[79] *Peto* v. *Blades* (1814) 5 Taunt. 657; *Chapman* v. *Speller* (1850) 14 QB 621; *Niblett Ltd* v. *Confectioners' Materials Co. Ltd* [1921] 3 KB 387, 401; *Payne* v. *Elsden* (1900) 17 TLR 161.

[80] *Peto* v. *Blades*, n. 79 above. On the protection of sheriffs and other officers, see County Courts Act 1984, s. 98 (as amended by Insolvency Act 1986, s. 183); Supreme Court Act 1981, s. 138B (see *Supreme Court Practice*, Sweet & Maxwell, London, 1997, 47/6/4).

[81] *Morley* v. *Attenborough* (1849) 3 Ex. 500 (pawnbroker).

[82] *Wood* v. *Baxter* (1883) 49 LT 45 (personal liability of auctioneer acting for unnamed principal limited to existence of his authority).

where the buyer is or should be aware of a cloud on the seller's title.[83] An example of an implied limited title sale is where the seller functions almost as a buying agent, acquiring the goods to order and turning them over rapidly to the buyer.[84] In *Warming's Used Cars Ltd* v. *Tucker*,[85] a used-car dealer gave a small deposit on a car to a seller and then got in touch with the sub-buyer, who he knew was interested in buying a car of this type. The sub-buyer drew a cheque for the balance of the price in favour of the seller and allowed a profit on the sale to the buyer, the dealer, as part of a periodical settlement of a running account between them. At all material times, the car remained on the premises of the seller before being taken to the sub-buyer's trade premises. The car turned out to be stolen and the sub-buyer's action against the dealer for breach of section 12(1)[86] was unsuccessful. The circumstances of the sale were held to negative the section 12 undertakings by the dealer.

The facts as presented might well have justified the conclusion that the dealer was in reality an agent purchasing on commission, leaving the field clear for an action by the 'sub-buyer' directly against the seller. Accepting that the court's characterization of the transaction was accurate, however, one objection to the outcome of the case is that a too-ready inference of a limited title sale in such circumstances runs counter to the policy of encouraging liability to pass up a distribution chain to the source of the fault in the goods. In section 12(1) cases, this will be the first unlawful seller or, if the seller is a rogue or a man of straw, the buyer who trusted that seller. An interesting question is whether the buyer under a limited title sale, who discovers that someone other than his seller was the true owner, has any recourse at all against his seller outside section 12(1). This buyer has plainly obtained nothing of value from the contract[87] so the question arises whether he can claim the recovery of any price paid, or resist paying it, on the ground that there has been a total failure of consideration. It is submitted that, in limited title sales, the buyer takes the risk of paying for something that is of no value, so that an action of this kind could not be sustained.[88]

The above decisions deal with cases where an implied limited title would be inferred. What of express contractual clauses to this effect? Clearly, in cases where an implied intention of a limited title sale would probably be inferred even without the clause, an express clause would be

---

[83] *Page* v. *Cowasjee Eduljee* (1866) LR 1 PC 127 (no liability on sale of stranded vessel by ship's master); *Northwest Co. Ltd* v. *Merland Oil Co. of Canada Ltd* [1936] 2 WWR 577.

[84] See *Clark* v. *England* (1916) 10 WWR 1056.

[85] [1956] SASR 249.   [86] Also for the implied warranty of quiet possession.

[87] Assuming that he has not had the use and enjoyment of the goods.

[88] An obvious exception to this would be where the seller was seeking to retain the price paid by two buyers: see *Chapman* v. *Speller*, n. 79 above; *Northwest Co. Ltd* v. *Merland Oil Co. of Canada Ltd* [1936] 2 WWR 577.

unlikely to be struck down as an exclusion clause. Any clause of general application in a standard form, or inserted in a contract of sale just because it might for unimaginable reasons turn out to be useful, would surely be classed as an exclusion clause. A difficult case is the car dealer with a large turnover and time only to consult the standard sources of information, sometimes fallible, concerning encumbrances of one kind or another on vehicles that are traded in. It is not at all clear that such a dealer could by standard clauses protect himself, or whether other factors could be taken into consideration, such as the consumer status of his purchaser, or the existence of any warning or explanation to the purchaser. The distinction between limited title clauses and exclusion clauses is very unsatisfactory but there is no evidence that it has caused much trouble in practice.

Range of Section 12(1)

The seller's liability under section 12(1), based on the 'right to sell', extends beyond matters of title. In *Niblett Ltd* v. *Confectioners' Materials Co. Ltd*,[89] the sellers agreed to sell 3,000 cases of tinned milk bearing one or more of three brand names, including 'Nissly', a name that infringed the trade mark of a well-known manufacturer. One third of the tins delivered bore the offending mark, and for this reason were detained by customs officials when they arrived in this country. The buyer had to remove the labels from the tins to secure their release, which greatly reduced their value. Scrutton LJ took a literal view of section 12(1): 'If a vendor can be stopped by process of law from selling he has not the right to sell.'[90] Similarly, the provision has been held to be breached where goods failed to comply with mandatory food[91] and electrical safety[92] standards. It would therefore seem generally that section 12(1) is infringed when the sale of goods amounts to a criminal offence or can be restrained by injunction.[93]

   Section 12(1) might be taken further. Suppose a seller agrees to sell specific goods to a buyer and, before the property in them passes to that buyer, agrees to sell them to a second buyer. The second buyer in such circumstances might reasonably wish not to take delivery of or retain the

---

[89] [1921] 3 KB 387.

[90] Scrutton LJ had some doubt whether a limited title sale might have been intended if the contract had called only for the supply of 'Nissly' cans, *sed quaere*?

[91] *Egekvist Bakeries Inc.* v. *Tizel* [1950] 1 DLR 585.

[92] *J. Barry Winsor & Associates Ltd* v. *Belgo-Canadian Manufacturing Co. Ltd* (1976) 76 DLR (3d) 685.

[93] In *Microbeads AG* v. *Vinhurst Road Markings Ltd* [1975] 1 WLR 218, 221–2, Denning MR said: 'The words "a right to sell the goods" mean not only a right to pass the property . . . to the buyer, but also to confer on the buyer the undisturbed possession of the goods.'

goods, given the possibility of becoming embroiled in a dispute with the first buyer, which might take the form of an action for interference with contractual relations. The second buyer, it is submitted, should be able to invoke section 12(1). The warranty of quiet possession in section 12(2)(b) might not afford sufficient protection. First it is only a warranty; this limitation would be particularly apparent to someone wishing not to take delivery of the goods in the first place. Secondly, the first buyer's action in tort might not amount to an interference with the second buyer's possession.

A further aspect of the seller's 'right' to sell concerns the seller who unlawfully disposes of goods, thereby committing the tort of conversion as against the true owner, but who does so under an exception to the rule of *nemo dat quod non habet*[94] so that the buyer obtains a title that overrides that of the true owner. The buyer, especially if purchasing goods (like cars) that are the subject of earlier recorded hire purchase or similar agreements, may find it in practical terms impossible to dispose of the goods by way of resale. Even if the buyer's quiet possession is not impaired by the finance company that retained title to the goods,[95] such a buyer has plainly suffered a loss. Moreover, while the right to sell term is a condition, the quiet possession term is a mere warranty. It is more than a little difficult to see how such a seller, committing the tort of conversion, can be said to have a 'right' to sell, as opposed to a power.

The little authority that there is, however, points to the seller's freedom from liability. In *Karlhamns Oljefabriker* v. *Eastport Navigation Corpn.*,[96] the court considered a contract for the sale of a quantity of goods in a larger commingled mass. Such a contract might be an intermediate contract in a sales string, in respect of which contract the seller never acquires the property in the goods because the quantity in this contract, as opposed to the end contract in the string, is at no time ascertained. In the opinion of Mustill J, intermediate sellers in this position were not in breach of section 12(1) since that provision 'involves no promise about the seller's proprietary rights, only that he will be able to create the appropriate rights in the buyer'.[97] Neither this case, nor the others cited in favour of the seller, directly address the question of the *nemo dat* exception under discussion. The problem that concerned Mustill J, even

---

[94] Discussed in the text accompanying nn. 138 ff. below.

[95] Atkin LJ said in *Niblett Ltd* v. *Confectioners' Materials Co. Ltd*, n. 89 above, 403: 'It may be that possession would not be disturbed if the only cause of complaint was that the buyer could not dispose of the goods'.

[96] [1982] 1 All ER 208. See also *Niblett Ltd* v. *Confectioners' Materials Co. Ltd*, n. 89 above, 401 (Atkin LJ); *R.* v. *Wheeler* (1991) 92 Cr. App. R 279 (noted by I. Brown (1992) 108 *LQR* 229) (rescission for misrepresentation refused since a buyer in these circumstances did not suffer a loss); *Benjamin's Sale of Goods* (5th edn., 1997 by A. G. Guest and others), §4.004.

[97] N. 96 above, 215.

if not resolved after the Sale of Goods (Amendment) Act 1995,[98] can be dealt with satisfactorily by different means. A seller of bulk commodities surely licenses buyers and sub-buyers to agree to sell parcels from the bulk, a very common occurrence, in circumstances where that seller retains title to that bulk. In that sense, each intermediate seller has a right to sell. Furthermore, each of these intermediate contracts surely features a limited title sale that modifies anyway the effect of section 12(1). It is submitted that, because of the very real loss that a buyer might suffer when acquiring goods under the terms of a *nemo dat* exception, there is no case for putting a gloss on the language of section 12(1). The words should be given their literal meaning and the seller made liable.[99]

As stated above, the language of section 12(1) is broad enough to embrace agreements to sell, an example of which is conditional sales under which the property passes once the buyer has paid all of the stipulated instalments of the price.[100] The seller undertakes that he will have a right to sell 'at the time when the property is to pass'. An interesting question concerns the buyer who is faced with a demand for the goods by a third party who has a superior title to that of the seller. As we shall see, the buyer's quiet possession is thus impaired but, unless the seller thereby commits an anticipatory repudiation of the above obligation in section 12(1), the buyer may not terminate the contract. If the buyer is unable to do so, then in principle the buyer must continue paying instalments as they fall due. There is in English law no broad entitlement for a party to demand that the other provide 'adequate assurance of due performance'[101] or to suspend contractual performance.[102] If the third party displaces the buyer from possession, the seller will surely have committed an anticipatory repudiation of section 12(1), although there may be cases where the seller can credibly point to negotiations with the third party likely to lead to the acquisition of that third party's rights, and

---

[98] On paying his seller, each intermediate seller would acquire and be able to transmit an undivided share of the bulk: Ch. 3 above.

[99] In *Barber* v. *NWS Bank plc* [1996] 1 All ER 906, a seller in a position to pass a good title to the conditional buyer under Part III of the Hire Purchase Act 1964 (discussed in the text accompanying nn. 544 ff. below) was held nevertheless to be in breach of an express title condition of the contract. The court, however, relied upon the language of the statute (s. 27(6)—*sed quaere?*) and not upon the argument advanced in this text, for which see also R. M. Goode, *Commercial Law* (2nd edn., Penguin, London, 1995), 298.

[100] See *McNeill* v. *Associated Car Markets Ltd* (1962) 35 DLR (2d) 581; *Barber* v. *NWS Bank plc*, n. 31 above (express clause).

[101] UCC, Art. 2–609 (each contracting party guarantees that the other's performance expectation will not be impaired). Where a party reasonably feels insecure, he may suspend performance until the other provides adequate assurance that performance will be duly forthcoming and treat any failure to do so within a reasonable time as a contractual repudiation.

[102] See J. Carter, 'Suspending Contract Performance for Breach', in J. Beatson and D. Friedmann (eds.), *Good Faith and Fault in Contract Law* (OUP, London, 1995).

hence pointing to the seller's ability to comply with section 12(1) by the time the buyer pays the last instalment. The effect of a buyer's action, taking advantage of any contractual right to accelerate payment by paying off all future instalments,[103] is hard to assess but it could accelerate a present breach of the implied condition in section 12(1) before the seller has time to pay off the third party.

Non-sale Contracts

Section 12(1) does not extend to contracts of hire and hire purchase. In the latter case, the sale that usually occurs at the end of the period of hire does so pursuant to an option that the hirer is not bound to exercise.[104] There is only a slight body of case law on the subject of a finance company's title obligations under a hire purchase agreement. Sometimes an agreement will contain an express undertaking that the finance company is the owner.[105] The importance of such an express undertaking will lead to its being treated as a contractual condition.[106] The functional equivalence of a hire purchase to sale has resulted in the hirer not being estopped in the same way as an ordinary bailee from denying the bailor's title.[107] There is also common law authority that the finance company is the owner at the date of the contract.[108] A better moment, if the agreement is executed before delivery, might be the date of the delivery itself.[109]

Legislation, of general application to hire purchase contracts,[110] provides for the title obligation to spring at the moment the property is to pass under the agreement. If this legislation stood alone, without the common law authorities, it would put hirers in an intolerable predicament, not knowing whether they dare continue making payments in the hope that the finance company's title would be cleansed in due course, or even whether they might bring on the crisis by tendering all future instalments, thus bringing forward the operative date of the finance company's obligation. The combination of case law and statute, not incompatible, would appear to give the hirer the choice of dates of obligation.[111]

---

[103] Cf. *Warman* v. *Southern Counties Car Finance Corpn.* [1949] 2 KB 576.

[104] *Lee* v. *Butler* [1893] 2 QB 318; *Helby* v. *Matthews* [1895] AC 471; *Belsize Motor Supply Co.* v. *Cox* [1914] 1 KB 244.

[105] As was conceded and approved by the court in *Barber* v. *NWS Bank plc*, n. 99 above.

[106] *Ibid*; *Karflex Ltd* v. *Poole* [1933] 2 KB 251; *Warman* v. *Southern Counties Car Finance Corpn.* n. 103 above.

[107] *Karflex Ltd* v. *Poole*, n. 106 above.

[108] *Ibid.*; *Warman* v. *Southern Counties Car Finance Corpn.*, n. 103 above.

[109] *Mercantile Union Guarantee Corpn.* v. *Wheatley* [1938] 1 KB 490.

[110] Supply of Goods (Implied Terms) Act 1973, s. 8(1)(a).

[111] A. Diamond, *Introduction to Hire Purchase Law* (2nd edn., Butterworths, London, 1971), 54.

The obligations under a hiring agreement are established by section 7 of the Supply of Goods and Services Act 1982. The bailor does not, of course, undertake that he will have a right to sell at the moment the property is to pass, because the property does not pass, unless the parties at the end of the term agree on the sale of the goods, in which case the rules in section 12 of the Sale of Goods Act will apply. The bailor's corresponding obligation is the implied condition that he has a right to transfer possession of the goods by way of hire; alternatively, he undertakes that he will have the right to transfer possession in the case of an agreement to hire. These obligations are quite distinct from the quiet possession obligations, also owed, which protects the possession of the hirer when it is acquired.[112]

Section 12 Warranties

Section 12(2) of the Sale of Goods Act recites two further implied terms, this time warranties. First, there is the implied warranty that the goods are and will remain free from encumbrances before the property is to pass. This duty is subject to charges and encumbrances known or disclosed to the buyer before the date of the contract.[113] In a limited title sale, the seller further warrants that all charges or encumbrances known to him have been disclosed to the buyer before the date of the contract.[114] Secondly, there is the warranty that the buyer shall have quiet possession of the goods with the exception of disturbance arising out of such charges or encumbrances.[115] The quiet possession warranty of the seller under a limited title sale still applies to interference by the seller, by a third party whose limited title is being passed on by the seller, and by anyone claiming through the seller or such third party (apart from those claiming under a charge or encumbrance disclosed or known to the buyer at the contract date).[116] The case law on the quiet possession warranty is meagre and that on the encumbrance warranty more meagre still.

It is practically impossible to envisage a case that falls within the encumbrance warranty but not within section 12(1) or the quiet

---

[112] S. 7(2) of the 1982 Act.

[113] S. 12(2)(a). For very similar implied terms in other types of contract, see Supply of Goods (Implied Terms) Act 1973, s. 8(1)(b)(i) (hire purchase); Supply of Goods and Services Act 1982, s. 2(2)(a) (other contracts for the transfer of goods). Canadian case law has held that the registration of an encumbrance under personal property security legislation does satisfy the test of disclosure or knowledge: *Zuker* v. *Paul* (1982) 37 OR (2d) 161.

[114] S. 12(4). For very similar implied terms in other types of contract, see Supply of Goods (Implied Terms) Act 1973, s. 8(1)(b)(i) (hire purchase); Supply of Goods and Services Act 1982, ss. 2(2)(a) (other contracts for the transfer of goods) and 7(2) (hire—quiet possession only).

[115] S. 12(2)(b).

[116] S. 12(5).

possession warranty. For that reason alone, it is likely that the repeal of section 12(2)(a) would yield no practical consequences. It is not easy to envisage encumbrances against goods. The common law has traditionally been unreceptive to the notion of covenants running with chattels.[117] Charges could include legal or equitable mortgages as well as equitable charges.

Quiet Possession

A number of quite taxing problems arise in the case of the quiet possession warranty. First, can the seller be liable if, at the contract date, even at the date that property passes, there does not exist a cloud on the seller's title, but a third party later interferes legitimately with the buyer's possession? Secondly, for how long after the buyer acquires possession does the seller's guarantee last? Thirdly, how far does the seller's liability extend, and in particular is the seller liable for all third-party interferences with the buyer's possession?

The first question involves rights of a third party against the contract goods springing into existence after the contract of sale. *Microbeads AG v. Vinhurst Road Markings Ltd*[118] concerned the sale of a number of items of road marking equipment by a Swiss seller to an English buyer. The process of invention and application for letters patent being a confidential one, neither party knew that another English company had filed an application for a patent three years earlier and the complete specification itself two years earlier. The completed specification was not published, and thus brought to the attention of the outside world, until several months after the equipment had been sold and delivered to the buyer.[119] At that time, the third party acquired patent rights to the invention. There was no doubt that the seller had complied with the condition in section 12(1), which was to be judged when the property passed. This occurred before the publication of the specification. The Court of Appeal held that the seller bore the burden of the retrospective application of the patent for the purpose of section 12(2)(b). The warranty guaranteed the buyer's quiet possession in the future when the third party could, by taking legal action, prevent the buyer from using the equipment. As

---

[117] *Port Line Ltd* v. *Ben Line Steamers* [1958] 2 QB 146, distinguishing *Lord Strathcona Steamship Co.* v. *Dominion Coal Co.* [1926] AC 108; *Swiss Bank Corpn.* v. *Lloyds Bank Ltd* [1982] AC 584. Cf. *Law Debenture Trust Corpn.* v. *Ural Caspian Oil Corpn.* [1993] 1 WLR 138, 143.

[118] [1975] 1 WLR 218.

[119] In *Gencab of Canada Ltd* v. *Murray-Jensen Manufacturing Ltd* (1980) 29 OR (2d) 552, the letters patent had been granted long before the contract of sale and the seller could have discovered their existence. The buyer's quiet possession was infringed when the buyer was warned of the patent rights and even before the patent holder began proceedings.

between an innocent buyer and an innocent seller, the loss should fall on the latter. It is a close call, but the decision seems unexceptionable; liability under section 12 is strict.[120]

The future character of section 12(2)(b) invites the second question: how far into the future might the seller be liable? Compared to other obligations under the Sale of Goods Act, the quiet possession warranty is unique in that it cannot be determined at the date of delivery whether the seller is in breach or ever will be in breach. No duration of the warranty is stated in its text and the presumption must be that the seller guarantees the buyer's possession as long as the buyer retains an interest in the goods. Individual acts of interference would be subject to the usual six-year limitation period[121] but, as long as the buyer retains a possessory interest in the goods,[122] a claim should arise in respect of each interference, even if it is the same third party who interferes on each occasion. Ackner LJ, in *The Playa Larga*,[123] was concerned about the prospect of endless liability on the part of sellers. In that case, the sellers sought to confine their exposure to a latent defect in their performance and to 'the time of performance', contrary to the *Microbeads* case where the interference took place seven to ten months after the various dates of delivery and sale. Ackner LJ, however, gave some comfort to the notion that a seller should only be liable if the buyer had not accepted the goods under section 35.[124] This restriction, justified by expediency rather than by logic, would certainly cramp section 12(2)(b). The quiet possession warranty is precisely that—a warranty—and the acceptance period, often of short duration and difficult to protect, has nothing to do with the case. In the absence of qualifying legislation, there is no time limit on the seller's exposure apart from the limitation period running from the fact of interference.[125]

The exposure of the seller will cease to exist if the goods themselves cease to exist. If the buyer disposes of them to a sub-buyer, the seller's liability should also cease. The seller does not protect the sub-buyer's quiet possession, and the quiet possession of the buyer cannot be

[120] What about the supply of equipment whose use is later made unlawful under secondary legislation dealing with health and safety? Would it depend upon whether the parent legislation had been enacted at the date of the sale? Or a report recommending its enactment had been published?

[121] Limitation Act 1980, s. 5.

[122] What about the buyer who has only a right to immediate possession?

[123] *Empresa Exportadora de Azucar* v. *Industria Azucarera Nacional SA* [1983] 2 Lloyd's Rep. 171.

[124] But the buyers in *Microbeads*, n. 118 above, had almost certainly accepted the equipment.

[125] *Quaere* liability only so long as durability demands that the goods remain fit for the buyer's purpose or of satisfactory quality under s. 14?

infringed after the buyer has delivered the goods to the sub-buyer.[126] If the sub-buyer is able to sue the buyer for breach of the quiet possession warranty, the odd result is that the buyer will be unable to seek an indemnity from the seller unless able to point to another implied term in section 12 that has been breached. On the facts in *Microbeads*, if the defendant sellers had bought the road marking equipment from head sellers, they would have been unable to pass on their liability to these head sellers.

The third problem includes an assessment of action on the seller's part that could make him liable for breach of the warranty. In *The Playa Larga*,[127] the seller was liable for colluding with a third party who interfered with the buyer's quiet possession. The seller participated in discussions with the Cuban Government, the consequence of which was the withdrawal from a Chilean harbour of a ship bearing a c. & f. cargo already paid for by the Chilean buyer. It would seem that the buyer's constructive possession of the cargo[128] was thus being interfered with by the seller and the Cuban Government.

A further aspect of this problem is the identity of the person interfering with the buyer's possession. The section 12(2)(b) warranty appears to be modelled upon its sale of land equivalent, the covenant of quiet enjoyment of land.[129] The circumstances of a sale of land, including the investigation of title by the buyer, deprive the buyer of protection if he is evicted by title paramount, confining an action on the covenant to interferences by the seller. Opinions have been expressed that the quiet possession warranty in sale of goods should similarly be confined,[130] but it is settled that the very different circumstances of a sale of goods justify the imposition of liability for third-party interference.[131] A seller will be liable if, as a result of his default, a third party lawfully interferes with the

[126] A buyer out of possession, able to resist a prior owner's claim in conversion by raising a *nemo dat* exception by way of defence, would have no s. 12(2)(b) claim against the seller and, as seen above, might have no s. 12(1) claim either.

[127] N. 123 above. For further instances of seller interference, see *Healing (Sales) Pty. Ltd* v. *Inglis Electrix Ltd* (1968) 121 CLR 584; *Gatoil International Inc.* v. *Tradax Petroleum Ltd* [1985] 1 Lloyd's Rep. 350, 360–1 (unjustified exercise of lien).

[128] As (*semble*) the holder of the bill of lading transferred on payment. The fact of interference with quiet possession had earlier been conceded. See also *Gatoil International Inc.* v. *Tradax Petroleum Ltd*, n. 127 above, where a breach of s. 12(2)(b) appears to have been found in the conduct of the sellers, also the sub-charterers of the ship, in giving orders to the ship not to release the cargo at a time when the bills of lading had not come into the buyers' hands. If correct, this should be confined to interferences with a buyer's factual expectation of obtaining possession from a third party, or else the seller will be in breach whenever he is late in delivering the goods.

[129] *Niblett Ltd* v. *Confectioners' Materials Co. Ltd* [1921] 3 KB 387, 403.

[130] *Bergfeldt* v. *Markell* [1921] 1 WWR 453, applying *Monforts* v. *Marsden* (1895) 12 RPC 266, itself disapproved in *Niblett*, n. 129 above.

[131] *Mason* v. *Burningham* [1949] 2 KB 545; *Microbeads AG* v. *Vinhurst Road Markings Ltd* [1975] 1 WLR 218; *The Playa Larga*, n. 123 above.

buyer's possession,[132] but not where the third party is 'totally uncon-nected with the seller',[133] otherwise the seller would be guaranteeing the buyer against burglaries and thefts, or where the claim is not a 'lawful' one.[134] Short of such extreme cases is the third party with the arguable claim, for example, the owner defeated by a *nemo dat* exception or the *Romalpa*[135] seller who mistakenly believes that the clause permits the contract goods to be repossessed from a sub-buyer. If such interference is not unreasonable, it is submitted that the seller should be liable for the third party interference. Furthermore, if the seller is aware of the prospect of unreasonable interference by a particular claimant, and fails to warn the buyer of this or negotiate a limited title sale,[136] there is a good case for the application of section 12(2)(b).[137] An example would be the sale of jewellery by a family member who knows of the risk that another member will make an unreasonable claim against the buyer.

THE *NEMO DAT* RULE AND ITS EXCEPTIONS

A legal system concerned with the protection of private property, and not open to any countervailing policies, would assert with unabated vigour the maxim *nemo dat quod non habet*,[138] by which the transferee's title could never exceed the title of the transferor and would always be vul-nerable to a superior title. If, on the other hand, a legal system pursued to the same degree a policy of facilitating transactions, again without coun-tervailing policies, it would maintain that a transferee could trust in the appearance of ownership created by possession of goods in the hands of the transferor. The common law takes an intermediate position, starting from the *nemo dat* maxim and grafting on a number of exceptions. A number of these are statutory ones enacted in response to the needs of the commercial community.[139] This pragmatic resolution of the irrecon-cilable demands of private property protection and the facilitation of transactions is expressed by Denning LJ as follows:[140]

---

[132] *Gatoil International Inc.* v. *Tradax Petroleum Ltd*, n. 127 above (shipowner exercising lien over cargo against seller as sub-charterer of ship).

[133] *The Playa Larga*, n. 123 above, 178.

[134] *Niblett Ltd* v. *Confectioners' Materials Co. Ltd*, n. 129 above, 403.

[135] *Aluminium Industrie Vaasen BV* v. *Romalpa Aluminium Ltd* [1976] 1 WLR 676.

[136] The scope of a limited title sale here may be limited by the language of s. 12(5)(c), and there is the further difficulty that a limited title sale appears to be confined to cases where the seller's title is indeed limited, which is not the case here.

[137] *Pace* the confinement in *Niblett*, n. 129 above, to 'lawful' claims.

[138] Restated in s. 21(1) of the Sale of Goods Act.

[139] R. S. T. Chorley (1932) 48 *LQR* 51.

[140] *Bishopsgate Motor Finance Corpn.* v. *Transport Brakes Ltd* [1949] AC 322, 336–7.

In the development of our law, two principle have striven for mastery. The first is the protection of private property: no one can give a better title than he himself possesses. The second is for the protection of commercial transactions: the person who takes in good faith and for value without notice should get a good title. The first principle has held sway for a long time, but has been modified by the common law itself and by statute so as to meet the needs of our own times.

It would be more accurate to say that the various statutory exceptions to *nemo dat* were designed to maintain a balance between these two principles rather than redress it in favour of the facilitation of transactions. Nevertheless, the above passage reveals a conflict going far beyond the resolution of individual disputes. The clash of opposing principle should be borne in mind, even though individual cases often reveal internal inconsistency and illogicality.

Title chains may be of variable length, but they can be simplified to three principal actors. First, there is the owner of goods. Secondly, there is the rogue[141] who unlawfully either acquires or disposes of the goods. Thirdly, there is the innocent purchaser who acquired the goods from the rogue in good faith. The rogue disappears or is not worth suing so, as between the dispossessed owner and the transferee who has paid the rogue, the common judicial *cri de cœur* is which of these two innocent persons should suffer the consequences of the rogue's dishonesty.

The exceptions of common law origin to the *nemo dat* rule are as follows. First, there is the voidable title rule by which a party to whom the transferor's title has defeasibly passed may in turn pass on that title to a *bona fide* purchaser.[142] This can be accomplished indefeasibly provided it is done before the first transaction is rescinded by the transferor. Secondly, until the repeal of the rule by the Sale of Goods (Amendment) Act 1995, a seller of goods in market overt could effectively transfer title to a *bona fide* purchaser.[143] The theoretical importance of this exception was that it was the only exception, of common law or statutory origin, that treated as irrelevant the details of the transaction between owner and rogue in the simplified title chain above. This exception could launder doubtful titles and created the nearest thing to absolute ownership recognized by the common law.[144] The third of these exceptions is the doctrine of apparent authority.[145] It applies where the third-party

---

[141] A title of convenience. The 'rogue' is usually dishonest but sometimes acts mistakenly and in good faith.

[142] This has been codified as s. 23 where the second transaction is a sale. The common law governs if it is a pledge or other disposition.

[143] S. 22 of the Sale of Goods Act 1979.

[144] For details of the market overt rule, see M. G. Bridge, *Sale of Goods* (Butterworths, Toronto, 1988), 584–9.

[145] Codified in s. 21(1) where the second transaction is a sale. Generally, see F. Reynolds and B. Davenport (eds.), *Bowstead on Agency* (16th edn., Sweet & Maxwell, London, 1996).

purchaser reasonably but incorrectly apprehends that an agent has the owner's permission to sell. Apparent authority is not to be confused with implied authority, where an agent has an actual but unexpressed authority to act. Similar to apparent authority, and commonly confused with it, is the doctrine of apparent ownership, where in limited circumstances a purchaser may reasonably equate possession in the hands of a transferor with ownership. A purchaser may often be incurious as to whether someone is in possession of goods as agent or owner.

There exist also a number of statutory exceptions to the *nemo dat* rule, all inspired by notions of apparent authority or ownership, though they are legislative extensions of a common law that inadequately protects good faith purchasers. These exceptions concern dispositions by mercantile agents in possession of goods, or of documents of title, with the owner's consent,[146] as well as dispositions by sellers[147] and buyers[148] in possession. All of the *nemo dat* exceptions that are located or partly codified in the Sale of Goods Act are circumstantially related to a contract of sale, whether because the contract between owner and rogue is one of sale or because the transfer from the rogue to the innocent purchaser takes the form of a sale. This amounts to less than a full legislative treatment of all the exceptions to the *nemo dat* rule. Indeed, it is by no means obvious that the Sale of Goods Act was and is the proper place to deal with title disputes: there is much to be said for a separate and comprehensive statute.

Outside the Act lies the transfer of money and negotiable instruments, for these are not goods.[149] Title to money is transferred once it passes in currency to a good faith purchaser.[150] Negotiable instruments resemble money, in that their transfer for value, by indorsement and delivery or just delivery, as the case may be, creates in the transferee an unencumbered title, subject to a few exceptions. Negotiable documents of title are treated somewhat differently. Their negotiability consists of the freedom with which they may be transferred so as to endow the current holder with a direct right to call on a bailee to surrender the goods they represent.[151] But they are also significant, whether as common law or statutory documents of title,[152] in that their transfer may affect title to the underlying goods. Transferability and true negotiability should be distinguished since documents of title never have the currency of money. They lack its intrinsic value and their issue does not as such affect the antecedent title chain to the goods they represent.

---

[146] Factors Act 1889, s. 2.　　　　[147] Factors Act, s. 8; Sale of Goods Act, s. 24.
[148] Factors Act, s. 9; Sale of Goods Act, s. 25(1).　　　　[149] Ch. 2 above.
[150] *Miller* v. *Race* (1758) 1 Burr. 452.
[151] M. G. Bridge, *Personal Property Law* (Blackstone, London, 2nd edn., 1996), 137–40.
[152] Discussed in the text accompanying nn. 353 ff. below.

Sales under a Voidable Title

Under section 23, a good faith purchaser of goods to which the seller's title is voidable acquires a 'good title'[153] if, at the time of the sale, the seller's title has not yet been avoided.[154] The section makes no reference to the rogue obtaining possession of the goods, nor to the purchaser obtaining possession from the rogue. Nor does the sale have to comply with an ordinary course of business test. In such an unlikely transaction, however, serious questions would arise in respect of the purchaser's good faith and absence of notice.

In determining the applicability of the section, the question usually asked is whether the contract under which the seller acquired title is void because of a fundamental mistake as to the rogue's identity, or whether it is merely voidable because the rogue's fraud[155] induced in the mind of the owner a lesser mistake as to the rogue's attributes, notably credit-worthiness. A rogue acquires no title at all under a void contract.[156] The leading, but now embattled, authority is *Cundy* v. *Lindsay*[157] where a rogue called Alfred Blenkarn rented premises at No. 37 Wood Street and No. 5 Little Love Lane. A well-established firm called W. Blenkiron and Son traded from No. 123 Wood Street. The rogue sent letters to the plaintiffs, Belfast linen manufacturers, ordering a large quantity of hand-kerchiefs, giving his address as '37, Wood Street . . . entrance, second door in Little Love Lane'. He signed the letters 'A. Blenkarn & Co.' but in such a misleading way that the plaintiffs read the signature as 'A. Blenkiron & Co'. The plaintiffs, knowing W. Blenkiron and Son to be a reputable firm, dispatched the handkerchiefs to Blenkarn on credit terms. He decamped with the proceeds after selling the handkerchiefs to the innocent defendants.

Blackburn J's decision in favour of the defendants at first instance was overturned by the Court of Appeal; the ensuing appeal was dismissed by the House of Lords. In Lord Cairns's view, no contract existed between the plaintiffs and Alfred Blenkarn because the plaintiffs, knowing

---

[153] This can be transferred in the normal way to a sub-purchaser even if that sub-purchaser at the time had notice of the circumstances in which the purchaser acquired title: *Peirce* v. *London Horse and Carriage Repository Ltd* [1922] WN 170.

[154] A similar common law principle will apply where the rogue's disposition takes the form of a pledge instead of a sale: *Whitehorn Bros.* v. *Davison* [1911] 1 KB 463; *Babcock* v. *Lawson* (1880) 5 QBD 284. But no title at all is transferred for present purposes under a sale or return: *Truman* v. *Attenborough* (1910) 26 TLR 601.

[155] An innocent misrepresentation would suffice.

[156] The criminal law once drew a distinction between false pretences and larceny by a trick, the latter offence corresponding to cases where any supposed contract between owner and rogue was void. See *Heap* v. *Motorists' Advisory Agency Ltd* [1923] 1 KB 577; *Lake* v. *Simmons* [1927] AC 487; *Whitehorn Bros.* v. *Davison*, n. 154 above.

[157] (1878) 3 App. Cas. 459.

nothing of the existence of an Alfred Blenkarn,[158] intended to deal only with the 'well-known and solvent house of Blenkiron & Co'. It was all tantamount to a forgery of this firm's signature by the rogue and a later interception by the rogue of the goods sent to the firm.[159] The decision of the House of Lords appears to be based on an inference from the uncontested factual record of the case. One might well wonder how such an inference could be drawn when neither the proper name nor the proper address of the genuine firm was used by either the rogue or the plaintiffs. One might wonder, too, what the result would have been if the plaintiffs had been confused by a genuine signature from the rogue. A rule of law is out of the question, since it is in practical terms impossible to formulate, except to say that contractual offers and acceptances are enforceable only by the person to whom they are addressed, which carries the matter hardly any further. *Cundy* v. *Lindsay* would appear to be confined to cases where contracting parties deal with each other at a distance. Even here, it was not followed in one case where the rogue gave himself a bogus corporate identity and branch offices,[160] for how could an intention to deal with a non-existent entity be inferred.

Transactions between rogues and owners *inter praesentes* are more likely to be held to be voidable. In *Phillips* v. *Brooks Ltd*,[161] a rogue claiming to be Sir George Bullough, a man of substance whose existence was known to the plaintiff jeweller, bought a ring from the jeweller and paid for it with a worthless cheque. He later pledged it with the innocent defendants. The jeweller was held to have intended to deal with the person physically present,[162] so the rogue was able to pass a valid possessory title to the defendants. It was said in the later case of *Ingram* v. *Little*[163] that parties *inter praesentes* presumptively intend to deal with each other and that the presumption can be shifted only with difficulty. The majority found in that case that the presumption had been displaced on facts justifying little more than sympathy for the plight of the unworldly owners deceived by the rogue.[164] Claiming to be a certain P. G. M.

---

[158] 'Of him they knew nothing, and of him they never thought': n. 157 above, 465.

[159] Lord Cairns, *ibid.* 464.

[160] *King's Norton Metal Co. Ltd* v. *Edridge, Merrit & Co. Ltd* (1897) 14 TLR 98, changing the emphasis from the absence of an intention to deal with the rogue to the existence of an intention to deal with some other person.

[161] [1919] 2 KB 253. See *Terry* v. *Vancouver Motors U-Drive Ltd* [1942] 1 WWR 503 (affirmed [1942] SCR 391), *per* McDonald CJBC (commenting on the difficulty of distinguishing *Cundy* v. *Lindsay* and the unsatisfactory distinction between contracts *inter praesentes* and *inter absentes*).

[162] See E. C. S. Wade (1922) 38 *LQR* 201, arguing that the property had already passed in the ring (specific goods) before the rogue announced his identity. See also *Ingram* v. *Little* [1961] QB 31, 51, 60.

[163] N. 162 above.

[164] See Phillimore LJ in *Lewis* v. *Averay* [1972] 1 QB 198, 208 ('the very special and unusual facts of the case').

Hutchinson of Stanstead House, Caterham, the rogue was allowed by its Bournemouth owners to take away a car in return for a worthless cheque. The owners had never heard of Hutchinson, but released the car after one of them discreetly verified his existence in a telephone directory. The court finding that the owners did not intend to deal with the person physically present, the loss fell on a Blackpool car dealer who had bought the car from the rogue and who in all probability could more easily afford the loss than the owners.

Devlin LJ, the dissenting judge, agreed that the presumption could be displaced, citing the case of the transaction concluded on the premises of a reputable company with someone who appeared to be representing the company but who was in fact an unauthorized rogue.[165] Nevertheless, in Devlin LJ's view, the owners' behaviour in *Ingram* v. *Little* revealed little more than a concern for the creditworthiness of the buyer, a matter of attributes rather than identity, and the extent to which they had been duped did not affect the issue.[166] This sounder approach to the facts of the case was later vindicated by the Court of Appeal in *Lewis* v. *Averay*.[167]

In that case, a rogue obtained possession of a car under a contract of sale in return for a worthless cheque, representing himself as an actor famous for playing the television role of Robin Hood.[168] The rogue was held to have acquired a voidable title on the sale, which was transmitted to the defendant on the resale. Although Lord Denning was prepared to hold that a mistake as to identity can never render a contract void,[169] the majority of the court held that the presumption of an intention by the plaintiff to deal with the person opposite had not been displaced, a conclusion almost certain to be followed in similar cases.

In these cases, the purchaser's legal position is determined by the contract between owner and rogue of which he knows nothing. Devlin LJ in *Ingram* v. *Little* asked: 'Why should the question whether the defendant should or should not pay the plaintiff damages for conversion depend upon voidness or voidability, and upon inferences to be drawn from a conversion in which the defendant took no part?'[170] He would have preferred a scheme of even apportionment between owner and purchaser in the case of pure misfortune, adjusted where one or the other had been guilty of negligence.[171] Nevertheless, all of the statutory extensions to apparent authority[172] turn upon the details of a relationship between

---

[165] *Hardman* v. *Booth* (1863) 1 H & C 803. Cf. *Boulton* v. *Jones* (1859) 2 H & N 564.
[166] N. 162 above, 67, 69.   [167] N. 164 above.
[168] The actor's name on the cheque was misspelt: Richard Green(e).
[169] See UCC, Art. 2–403(1); Law Reform Committee, *Twelfth Report (Transfer of Title to Chattels)*, Cmnd. 2958 (HMSO, London, 1966), para. 15.
[170] N. 162 above, 73.   [171] *Ibid.* 73–4.
[172] Mercantile agency and sellers and buyers in possession.

owner and rogue unknown to the purchaser. Such illogicality would seem to be the natural product of the irreconcilable clash between the protection of private property and the facilitation of transactions. *Ingram* v. *Little* was interpreted by Megaw LJ in *Lewis* v. *Averay* as requiring the issue of void or voidable to turn on the rogue's apprehension of whether the owner's offer was being made to him or someone else.[173] This is a perfectly acceptable rendering of the principle of objectivity in contract formation,[174] though Megaw LJ thought it wrong that the purchaser's protection should hinge upon the rogue's apprehension.[175]

Rescission

Section 23 does not say how the owner might avoid the contract of sale before the rogue resells the goods to the innocent purchaser. The problem is a difficult one, since rogues put themselves beyond the reach of owners. If, exceptionally, the owner is able to confront the rogue, any behaviour of the owner evincing an intention to disaffirm the contract should suffice.[176] It is not clear whether the avoidance contemplated by section 23 takes place at common law or in equity. Equitable rescission *ab initio* does not in principle require judicial intervention,[177] though the court's assistance may be needed to work out its remedial consequences. Prior to the fusion of the courts of common law and equity, the common law had developed a remedy amounting to rescission *ab initio* in cases of fraud.[178] Further, whilst at common law rescission *ab initio* is no longer a permissible outcome of termination for breach,[179] the property in goods could revest in a seller by virtue of an implied resolutive condition,[180] producing the same result as in equitable rescission.

An owner's rescission of the contract depends upon an election to avoid the contract, which requires clear and positive evidence that the elector has chosen a particular remedy.[181] It may be that the

---

[173] N. 164 above, 208. Cf. A. Goodhart (1941) 57 *LQR* 228, 240.

[174] *Smith* v. *Hughes* (1871) LR 6 QB 597; *Tilden Rent-A-Car* v. *Clendenning* (1978) 83 DLR (3d) 400; *Harris* v. *Great Western Railway Co.* (1876) 1 QBD 515; *UGS Finance Ltd* v. *National Mortgage Bank of Greece* [1964] 1 Lloyd's Rep. 446.

[175] N. 164 above, 208.

[176] The contract was affirmed where the owner said at a police station that all he wanted was his money: *Jim Spicer Chev. Olds. Ltd* v. *Kinniburgh* [1978] 1 WWR 253.

[177] *Abram Steamship Co. Ltd* v. *Westville Shipping Co. Ltd* [1923] AC 773; *Car and Universal Finance Co. Ltd* v. *Caldwell* [1965] 1 QB 525; *Bevan* v. *Anderson* (1957) 23 WWR 508. But note that the right to rescind may be removed under s. 2(2) of the Misrepresentation Act 1967.

[178] *Clarke* v. *Dickson* (1858) E B & E 148; *Clough* v. *London and North Western Railway Co.* (1871) LR 7 Ex. 26.

[179] *Johnson* v. *Agnew* [1980] AC 367; *Photo Production Ltd* v. *Securicor Transport Ltd* [1980] AC 827.

[180] *R. V. Ward Ltd* v. *Bignall* [1967] 1 QB 534.

[181] *Reese Silver Mining Co.* v. *Smith* (1869) LR 4 HL 64, 74 (Lord Hatherley LC). See also Denning MR, at first instance, in *Car and Universal Finance Co.* v. *Caldwell*, n. 177 above,

circumstances will demand as clear evidence of the elector's choice a communication to the other party. Communication is obviously necessary too where the elector may choose to sue one of two parties but not both.[182] The elector may also have to communicate a choice of remedies if the contract fairly implies that this should occur to save the other party from detrimental action. Communication, in the form of rejection, is also necessitated by section 35 of the Sale of Goods Act if the buyer does not want his retention of the goods to be seen as an acceptance of them.[183] But there are cases where the elector's choice is so vividly clear that no communication is required. One example of this is the recaption of goods;[184] another occurs in *Car and Universal Finance Co.* v. *Caldwell*,[185] where the disappearing rogue was in no position to demand that the owner's election to avoid the contract be communicated to him.

As between owner and rogue, the above statement appears uncontroversial, but the later involvement of an innocent purchaser raises the question whether the owner should be allowed thus to rescind when the rogue is on the loose with possession of the goods and the semblance of ownership. One response to this is that the mere investiture of the rogue with possession of the goods is not tantamount to an appearance of ownership or authority to dispose of goods. *Car and Universal Finance* does show, however, that the process of avoidance is coloured by some concern for the predicament of purchasers. In that case, as soon as the rogue's cheque was seen to be worthless, the owner notified the police and a motoring organization. A number of dubious transactions were launched in respect of the car, but the owner's action occurred before the arrival of the first good faith purchaser. Conceding that an election to rescind should normally be communicated to the other party, the court held it did not apply in the present case since the rogue had put it out of the owner's power to communicate with him. The owner's behaviour was 'the best other means possible' to an actual communication.[186] While the court was explicitly indifferent to the purchaser in working out the contractual position between owner and rogue, it is hard to believe

---

532. The disagreement between Lord Denning and the Court of Appeal, *ibid.*, about the need to communicate the election may be reconciled, it is submitted, by the immediately ensuing arguments in this text. Davies LJ is equivocal on the need to communicate. On the question of the elector's knowledge of the choice being made, see *Peyman* v. *Lanjani* [1985] Ch. 457 and Ch. 6 above.

[182] *Scarf* v. *Jardine* (1882) 7 App. Cas. 345.

[183] Cf. s. 48(3),(4) inferentially supporting the absence of a need to communicate in certain cases of resale.

[184] *Re Eastgate* [1905] 1 KB 465; *Car and Universal Finance Co.* v. *Caldwell*, n. 177 above, 558 (Davies LJ).

[185] N. 184 above. See also *Newton's of Wembley Ltd* v. *Williams* [1965] 1 QB 560.

[186] N. 177 above, 558 (Davies LJ).

that the same conclusion would have been reached if the owner had merely stated his position in a letter to his solicitor.

In 1966, the Law Reform Committee stated[187] that the decision in *Car and Universal Finance* had largely destroyed the value of the section 23 exception for innocent purchasers. Without weighing up the various arguments or putting section 23 into the wider context of the *nemo dat* rule with its various exceptions, the Committee recommended simply that the owner should have to communicate his rescission to the rogue, which would in most cases render inefficacious the owner's right to rescind.

Burden of Proof

Section 23 does not state whether owner or purchaser bears the burden of proof of good faith or its absence. Since the voidable title rule is an exception to *nemo dat*, one might expect the purchaser should have to show his own good faith. This seems a reasonable inference from section 23 itself: it does not refer to bad faith and it is contrary to sensible forensic practice to require the owner to prove a negative, namely, the purchaser's want of good faith.[188] Nevertheless, the Court of Appeal in *Whitehorn Bros.* v. *Davison*[189] held that the burden lay on the plaintiff owner seeking to recover goods from the defendant, since the plaintiff 'comes to displace another from the enjoyment of property'.[190] This reasoning would fall short of the owner who had already recapted the goods or sought them in interpleader proceedings.[191] It is submitted that the burden should in all cases fall on the purchaser.[192] This would be consistent with other exceptions to *nemo dat*. The purchaser, moreover, is better placed to relate the circumstances of the transaction than the owner, and the rogue is rarely to be found.

Apparent Authority and Apparent Ownership

The governing provision is section 21(1), which states an exception to the *nemo dat* rule where goods are sold by someone who is neither the owner nor the owner's authorized agent and 'the owner of the goods is by his conduct precluded from denying the seller's authority to sell'. This may

---

[187] Cmnd. 2958, para. 16.

[188] On the difficulties of a party coming to court 'blindfold', see *Fowler* v. *Lanning* [1959] 1 QB 426.

[189] [1911] 1 KB 463. The Court of Appeal considered itself bound by the *Whitehorn* rule in *Thomas* v. *Heelas* 27 Nov. 1986 (CAT no. 1065).

[190] N. 189, 481 (Buckley LJ). See also Vaughan Williams LJ at 478.

[191] But see Kennedy LJ, *ibid.*, 487, for whom the burden falls on anyone 'who comes forward to deprive another of his title to property', a proposition that should apply equally to a purchaser seeking to deprive the owner.

[192] See to this effect the Law Reform Committee, n. 187 above, para. 25.

be taken loosely to encapsulate both apparent authority and apparent ownership. It should be noted at the outset that the goods must be 'sold' by the apparent owner or agent. Consequently, if the property does not pass under the contract of sale concluded by that person, no title will be transmitted to the purchaser. This was the result in *Shaw* v. *Commissioner of Police of the Metropolis*,[193] where the owner of a car gave possession of it to a rogue on unusual agency terms, taking a post-dated cheque for a substantial sum that was subsequently dishonoured. The rogue agreed to sell the car to the plaintiff purchaser from whom he received a banker's draft in the agreed amount, the third party 'rightly' conceding in the present case[194] that the property in the car was not to pass until the rogue received payment under the draft. The rogue attempted to present the draft for payment to a bank where he had shortly before opened an account, but that bank declined to pay cash against the draft and the rogue disappeared. It was most unlikely that the rogue would ever attempt to recover payment against the draft, so it was an 'extremely remote' possibility that the indemnity the plaintiff offered his own bank, which had issued the draft and had reimbursed the plaintiff the amount he had paid for it, would be called in. The plaintiff's only loss, therefore, was the loss of bargain. It would have been extraordinary if the plaintiff had been held entitled to retain a valuable car for nothing, and the court recoiled from a result that would have offended its sense of justice.

Apparent authority exists whenever one person is precluded by his words or conduct from denying that another is his agent and authorized to transact certain business with third parties.[195] A person will be so precluded if he creates the appearance that an agent with limited authority has more authority than in fact he possesses, but the doctrine can equally apply where no actual relationship of agency exists at all.[196] The third party must prove that he entered into dealings with the agent on the faith of an appearance created by the principal and not the agent.[197] Apparent authority is thus a particular manifestation of estoppel.[198] It is a matter of debate whether an agent with actual but not apparent authority does indeed consummate a contractual relationship directly between principal and third party, as opposed to a state of affairs that

---

[193] [1987] 3 All ER 405.   [194] *Sed quaere?*

[195] *Pickering* v. *Busk* (1812) 15 East 38; *Freeman & Lockyer* v. *Buckhurst Park Properties (Mangal) Ltd* [1964] 2 QB 480; *Hely-Hutchinson* v. *Brayhead Ltd* [1968] 1 QB 549; *Canadian Laboratory Supplies Ltd* v. *Engelhard Industries Ltd* [1980] 2 SCR 450, revg. in part (1977) 78 DLR (3d) 232.

[196] *Bowstead on Agency* (16th edn., Sweet & Maxwell, London, 1996 by F. M. B. Reynolds), §8–027.

[197] *Colonial Bank* v. *Cady* (1890) 15 App. Cas. 257.

[198] *Bowstead*, n. 196 above, §8–029.

estops a principal from denying such a contractual relationship.[199] The latter would appear correct but does not explain why the apparent agent or owner is able to transfer a real title and not just its procedural simulacrum.[200]

Apparent authority may arise actively where a principal voluntarily[201] represents to the third party the existence of authority in the agent, but commonly arises in a more passive form where the agent is placed by the principal in a position that usually carries with it a certain degree of authority.[202] This will be so where the agent is put in a nominate position that, in the experience of the commercial world, is invested with a known authority. This usual authority would be an implied, actual authority if the principal did not in his dealings with the agent abridge it. But if this authority is limited and third parties not duly notified, the usual authority that extends beyond the undisclosed abridgment of authority will be an apparent authority that binds the principal.[203]

Estoppel by Representation

Most sale of goods cases have concerned apparent owners or agents of a class who sometimes deal on their own account and sometimes for an undisclosed or unnamed principal. The estoppel may take the form of a representation (words) or conduct; references are sometimes made to negligence as though it were separate from words and conduct. It is possible, however, that an owner's negligence may be used, not to destroy his title as such, but to found a counterclaim by a purchaser sued for conversion of the goods. A clear example of an estoppel by representation is *Eastern Distributors Ltd* v. *Goldring*.[204] The owner of a van wished to purchase a car but had insufficient money for a deposit. When the dealer suggested that a deposit could be procured on the security of the van, owner and dealer colluded in a scheme that led a finance company to believe that the dealer was the owner of the van as well as of the desired car, and that a deposit had been put down on both vehicles. The true owner signed in blank a hire purchase proposal form and a memorandum of agreement concerning the van, as well as a note certifying that he had taken delivery of the van. The finance company accepted this

---

[199] *Ibid.* [200] *Eastern Distributors Ltd* v. *Goldring* [1957] 2 QB 600.
[201] *Debs* v. *Sibtec Developments Ltd* [1990] RTR 91 (robber procured representation by duress).
[202] A. Hornby [1961] *CLJ* 238. [203] *Bowstead*, n. 196 above, §§8–018, 8–026.
[204] N. 200 above. For a similar case where the true owner holds out the car dealer to a finance company as the owner, see *Stoneleigh Finance Ltd* v. *Phillips* [1964] 2 QB 539. See also *NZ Securities & Finance Ltd* v. *Wrightcars Ltd* [1976] 1 NZLR 77 (car said by owner to be 'paid for'); *Big Rock Pty. Ltd* v. *Esanda Finance Corpn. Ltd* (1992) 10 WAR 259 (mortgagee's letter stated (erroneously) that the mortgage payments had all been made); *Shaw* v. *Commissioner of Police of the Metropolis* [1987] 3 All ER 405 (owner signed a letter certifying car as sold).

proposal but rejected the one concerning the car. In breach of his authority from the owner of the van, the dealer went ahead and sold the van to the finance company. Informed that the car proposal had fallen through, the owner of the van sold it to the present defendant.

The issue of title to the van was resolved in favour of the finance company plaintiff since, by signing the documents in blank, the owner had knowingly armed the dealer with the means to deceive the finance company and was privy to the representation of ownership made by the dealer. A problem not confronted in the case is the following. How does the owner's statement cause the purchaser to be misled if the purchaser would just as much have been misled by the dealer forging the owner's signature to the documents? The finance company did not so much rely upon the owner as upon the established figure of the dealer. The doctrine of estoppel by representation is not, however, pitched at this level of scepticism. It is enough that the owner made the statement and that the purchaser believed it, without the purchaser having to believe on independently verifiable grounds that it was the owner who made the statement.

Difficulties may arise as to the meaning of a representation made by the owner. In *Moorgate Mercantile Co. Ltd* v. *Twitchings*,[205] a number of finance companies were members of Hire Purchase Information Ltd, a voluntary title registration service. The finance company claiming title to a car disposed of by a rogue had failed to effect registration of its title. The service's response when the purchaser consulted it was that the car was not covered by a recorded hire purchase agreement. The House of Lords declined to inflate this into a statement that no registrable agreement had been concluded.[206]

Estoppel by Conduct

Estoppel by conduct has caused greater difficulty in the case law than estoppel by representation. The starting point is the proposition that the mere transfer of possession of goods or the indicia of title does not create an estoppel that the person in possession is the owner,[207] for possession is consistent with a range of transactions from bailment to outright sale, not all of which involve the transfer of the general property. In

---

[205] [1977] AC 890.

[206] Cl. 1 of the conditions governing the issue of information slips provided: 'All information is given to the best knowledge and belief of H.P. Information Ltd. according to the information contained in its records.' The service was also held not to be the agent of the finance company in making representations: n. 205 above, 902, 918, 923, 930.

[207] *Johnson* v. *Crédit Lyonnais Co.* (1877) 3 CPD 32; *Central Newbury Car Auctions Ltd* v. *Unity Finance Ltd* [1957] 1 QB 371. For a case that is particularly hard on the purchaser, see *McVicar* v. *Herman* (1958) 13 DLR (2d) 419.

Farquarson Bros. and Co. v. *C. King and Co.*,[208] the plaintiff firm of tim-ber merchants authorized one of its clerks to arrange for timber sales to its known customers, and informed the warehouse holding the timber that the clerk's delivery orders were to be honoured. The warehouse was not told, however, of the limitation on the clerk's authority to issue deliv-ery orders. The clerk therefore had constructive possession of the timber. Over a number of years, the clerk, assuming the identity of 'a phantom broker, an imaginary being [that he] created, associated and worked . . . for his own purposes under the plain and unpretentious name of Brown',[209] sold quantities of timber to the defendants. To effect the sales, he instructed the warehouse to deliver the timber to the order of Brown and, as Brown, indorsed the delivery orders in favour of the defendants. Nothing said or done by the plaintiffs amounted to a representation, to the defendants (as opposed to the warehouse), that the imaginary broker, Brown, whom the defendants never saw or inquired after, had the right to sell timber to the defendants. The plaintiffs and the defendants never came into direct contact with each other, and so the estoppel argument failed.

The estoppel argument succeeded, however, in the Canadian case of *Canadian Laboratory Supplies Ltd* v. *Engelhard Industries Ltd*,[210] where an employee of the plaintiffs, exceeding his actual authority, bought on their behalf ever-increasing amounts of platinum over several years and was able to process payment for it through the plaintiffs' accounts department at approximately sixty-day intervals. Intercepting the plat-inum, the employee sold most of it back to the defendant sellers as waste material, receiving sums close to the original purchase price. The employee purported to resell on behalf of an imaginary person, a scien-tist engaged in a confidential process. For some of the time during which the fraud was carried out, the employee was held to have purchased new platinum with the plaintiffs' authority and to have sold it back as its apparent owner in the form of waste. The dealings of the employee were seen as an integrated whole, the plaintiffs being in the invidious position of seeking to affirm the purchases of platinum but to disaffirm the resales of platinum waste.

Despite a discredited Privy Council decision,[211] the decision in *Farquarson* that the mere transfer of possession or its constructive equivalent does not raise an estoppel also holds true if what is trans-ferred is a document of title or other delivery instrument. The leading case is *Mercantile Bank of India Ltd* v. *Central Bank of India Ltd*[212] where a purchaser of groundnuts, deliverable to the order of the holder of

---

[208] [1902] AC 325.
[209] *Ibid.* 334–5 (Lord Macnaghten).
[210] N. 195 above.
[211] *Commonwealth Trust Ltd* v. *Akotey* [1926] AC 72.
[212] [1938] AC 287.

railway receipts, pledged these receipts with the respondent bank as security for a loan. The bank transmitted the receipts to its own godown[213] keeper who released the receipts to the purchaser for the sole purpose of collecting the groundnuts from the railway, which were then to be deposited in the bank's godown.[214] The purchaser then fraudulently used the same receipts to obtain a second advance from the appellants. The purchaser was held to be able to transfer to the appellants only such title as he had, which was encumbered by the pledge to the respondent bank. The release of the railway receipts did not create an estoppel.[215]

Indicia *of Title*

It has been argued that the estoppel position changes if the owner, instead of transferring just the possession of the goods or delivery documents, transfers also *indicia* of title. The notion of *indicia* of title, a vague expression, emerges in *Central Newbury Car Auctions Ltd* v. *Unity Finance Ltd*.[216] A distinguished-looking rogue visited the plaintiff car dealers to acquire a car[217] and signed the usual hire purchase forms, leaving a car he claimed as his own, but which was the subject of a hire purchase agreement, as a trade-in and deposit. He was allowed to take away the car, as well as the logbook,[218] despite the finance company's instruction that this should not be done before it granted permission. The finance company declined the proposal, believing the prospective bailee to be a rogue. The logbook, a permanent document recording in an officially validated form the identity of the person bound from time to time to pay road tax on the vehicle, had been signed neither by the dealers[219] nor by the previous owner (whose name had been entered in it). Despite its continuity, the fact that owners almost always sign it and the practical difficulties of selling a car without it,[220] the logbook was not a

---

[213] A form of warehouse.

[214] A tightly controlled form of trust receipt, where the bank's possessory interest in the documents by way of pledge is deemed to continue notwithstanding the release of the documents for a limited purpose. See *North Western Bank Ltd* v. *John Poynter, Son & Macdonalds* [1895] AC 56 (cf. *Babcock* v. *Lawson* (1880) 5 QBD 284); *Official Assignee of Madras* v. *Mercantile Bank of India Ltd* [1935] AC 53; *Lloyds Bank Ltd* v. *Bank of America National Trust and Savings Association* [1938] 2 KB 146; *Re David Allester Ltd* [1922] 2 Ch. 211.

[215] Marking the receipts would not have helped the bank to prevent the fraud, for then the rogue might have sold the goods themselves.

[216] N. 207 above.   [217] Valued at £337 10s.

[218] The vehicle registration document.

[219] The dealers were not bound to pay road tax and so their name did not appear in the book.

[220] The logbook warned that the person in whose name the vehicle was registered might not be the owner.

document of title either at common law or under statute.[221] The rogue assumed the identity of the previous owner and signed the logbook in his name before selling the car to a purchaser,[222] who in turn sold it to the defendant finance company, which bailed it on the usual hire purchase terms to the second defendant.

By a majority, the court held that the plaintiffs were not estopped by their conduct from denying the rogue's authority to sell.[223] This was in spite of the plausibility of the rogue and the purchaser's investigation of the files of a service recording the great majority of hire purchase agreements. The defendants' argument that the scales were tipped by a combination of the plaintiffs' negligence and the persuasive character of the logbook was unsuccessful. So far, the decision in *Central Newbury* is just another illustration of the difficulty of maintaining the estoppel argument. But the dissenting judgment of Denning LJ is significant for the bridge it establishes with a series of decisions that are practically impossible to reconcile with estoppel theory.

Denning LJ did not dispute the orthodoxy that mere careless conduct by an owner in the control of goods or their entrustment to another does not estop the owner from contesting a title derived through a rogue.[224] But he believed the situation different where the owner is induced to part with the property in the goods or the power of disposing of them, or behaves as if he had such an intention by arming a rogue with the necessary documents.[225] The owners in the present case may have intended to dispose of their property in favour of the finance company rather than the rogue, but that did not matter. What counted was the combined effect of their intention to dispose of their property and the facility with which the rogue could present himself as the owner when given the unsigned logbook together with the car. Now, this seems to have little to do with any orthodox understanding of estoppel but rather strikes new ground in finding significance in the owner's divesting behaviour *qua* a third party. Nevertheless, the dissent does come close to certain agency authorities that are hard to explain.

Inherent Agency Power

The starting point is the famous case of *Watteau* v. *Fenwick*,[226] where the manager of a beer house had a limited authority to purchase stock-in-

---

[221] See also *Joblin* v. *Watkins & Roseveare (Motors) Ltd* [1949] 1 All ER 47; *Pearson* v. *Rose & Young Ltd* [1951] 1 KB 275; *Shaw* v. *Commissioner of Police of the Metropolis* [1987] 3 All ER 405.

[222] For £20.

[223] Despite the evident ease with which the rogue could reproduce the previous owner's 'signature'.

[224] He therefore accepted decisions like *Farquarson Bros. and Co.* v. *C. King and Co.*, n. 208 above, and *Mercantile Bank of India Ltd* v. *Central Bank of India Ltd*, n. 212 above.

[225] N. 207 above, 381–2.   [226] [1893] 1 QB 346.

trade. It did not extend to the cigars that the manager purchased on credit from the plaintiff. There was nothing to indicate that the manager was not the owner of the beer house; indeed, the licence in his name was prominent over the door. The plaintiff seller believed the manager to be the owner, and the cigars were goods of a type usually dealt with in a beer house. Wills J relied upon the principle of usual authority in holding that the seller was entitled to recover the price of the cigars from the defendant owner of the beer house. A limitation of the authority usually confided to managers would not avail the principal against third parties uninformed of this limitation. Put in the alternative form, that a third party is entitled to rely upon the appearance of authority in a particular class of agent, the following difficulty presents itself: how can a third party rely upon an agent's usual authority when he does not know he is dealing with an agent?

Some help in resolving the difficulty comes from the notion of 'inherent agency power', contained in the Restatement Second on Agency,[227] which exists 'purely as a product of the agency relation'.[228] It does not depend upon authority or estoppel but is *sui generis*, and is similar to the test that a master is liable for torts committed in the course of a servant's employment.[229] The master's vicarious liability does not depend upon whether the victim of the tort is aware of the employment relationship or whether the servant is acting within his authority, which commonly he is not. Inherent agency power has been criticized as so vague that it creates more problems than it resolves,[230] but it has been promoted as consonant with notions of fairness and consistent with the practices of the business world.[231] It has also been said that inherent agency power is justified because the principal has reposed more trust in the agent than has the third party, which is hardly a reason for making the principal liable.[232] Other arguments are that the demands of business do not give the third party time to investigate an agent's authority, met by the response that this is relevant only if he knows he is dealing with an agent; that the principal must take the burden as well as benefit of an agent's activities, greeted by the retort that this can apply to the third party too; and that liability follows control, criticized as begging the question.[233]

On the other hand, *Watteau* v. *Fenwick*, in compelling the principal to accept both benefit and burdens of an agent's activity, prevents him from running what amounts to a limited liability company in disguise.

---

[227] American Law Institute 1957 (Reporter: Seavey), §8A.
[228] *Ibid.*, Comment a.   [229] D. H. Bester (1972) 89 *SALJ* 49, 53.
[230] A. Conant (1968) 47 *Nebraska LR* 678, 686. See also *Bowstead on Agency* (16th edn., Sweet & Maxwell, London, 1996 by F. M. B. Reynolds), §8–078.
[231] Restatement Second on Agency, §§ 8A, Comment a, and 161, Comment a.
[232] J. L. Montrose (1939) 17 *Can. Bar Rev.* 693, 711 ff. (criticizing Seavey).
[233] *Ibid.*

Further, where an agent sells rather than buys, an argument, empirically difficult to demonstrate, is that agents are more likely to exceed a limited selling authority than to arrogate to themselves a selling authority that does not exist at all.[234]

The legal supports for inherent agency power seem somewhat fragile but a number of estoppel authorities are actuated by the notion or something similar. Though by no means the first of these cases, *Lloyds and Scottish Finance Ltd* v. *Williamson*[235] raises the issue squarely. An owner entrusted his car to a dealer and repairer for the purpose of repair and the solicitation of offers to purchase. The dealer exceeded his authority by lending the car to a creditor, saying the car was for sale. The owner later authorized the dealer to sell provided a minimum cash price of £625 were remitted to him, the dealer to retain any surplus as commission. The dealer then sold the car to a friend of his creditor for £625, but the price was paid to the creditor in partial discharge of the dealer's debt. Although this method of payment prevented the dealer from acting in the ordinary course of business of a mercantile agent under section 2 of the Factors Act 1889,[236] it did not impair the estoppel argument of the purchaser since he bought the car in the belief that the dealer was the owner. There is naturally no need for apparent owners to act in the ordinary course of business of a mercantile agent.[237]

The Court of Appeal held that the purchaser had obtained good title to the car. The owner had impliedly authorized the dealer to sell the car as principal and had put him in a position enabling him to do so; hence the owner was estopped[238] from denying the dealer's authority[239] to sell. Now, all of this was unknown to the purchaser from whose vantage point there is no difference in appearance between a dealer with full and a dealer with limited authority to sell. The dealer's fraud, moreover, was in no way facilitated by the owner's conduct in expanding his authority beyond the authority to receive offers. The case is difficult to rationalize[240] but, it is submitted, is best explained as concerned with the

---

[234] The Restatement Second on Agency refers to dispositions of property by agents where the excess of authority is more formal than substantial, as where the agent departs from the authorized mode of sale: §8A, Comment b.

[235] [1965] 1 All ER 641.   [236] See the text accompanying nn. 280 ff. below.

[237] See also *Motor Credits (Hire Finance) Ltd* v. *Pacific Motor Auctions Pty. Ltd* (1963) 109 CLR 87, affd. on different grounds *sub nom. Pacific Motor Auctions Pty. Ltd* v. *Motor Credits (Hire Finance) Ltd* [1965] AC 867.

[238] *Pace* para. 1 of the headnote. Salmon LJ, n. 235 above, 645, denies a 'true estoppel' but he appears to mean that the purchaser's title is real rather than metaphorical: see *Eastern Distributors Ltd* v. *Goldring* [1957] 2 QB 600 (with which cf. *Simm* v. *Anglo-American Telegraph Co.* (1879) 5 QBD 188, 206).

[239] The case does not separate apparent authority and apparent ownership: [1965] 1 All ER 641, 644.

[240] *Bowstead*, n. 230 above, 363, n. 70, attempts to justify it on actual authority grounds.

inherent usual power of a car dealer to sell, the converse of the agent's power to buy in *Watteau* v. *Fenwick*.[241]

Thus rationalized, *Lloyds and Scottish Finance* accords with a number of cases where instruments of title are lodged with an agent who has a limited authority to deal with them but is thus enabled to present himself as their owner.[242] It also helps explain the reasoning of Lord Halsbury in *Henderson & Co.* v. *Williams*,[243] the difficulty of which provoked the same judge to tumescent language in *Farquarson Bros. and Co.* v. *C. King and Co.*[244] In *Henderson*, the owners of a quantity of sugar lying in a warehouse were induced by the fraud of a rogue to believe that he was representing one of their established customers.[245] They instructed the warehouse to transfer the sugar to the order of the rogue who sold the goods to the plaintiff. Before paying the price, the plaintiff secured from the defendant warehouse an undertaking to hold the goods to his order. By thus attorning to the plaintiff, the warehouse incurred personal liability on an estoppel. Although the rogue had concluded no contract with the owners, Lord Halsbury and Lindley LJ[246] both went on to say that the owners had authorized the rogue to dispose of the goods. Indeed they had intended to surrender all title to the sugar but had failed to do so only because the purported contract of sale negotiated by the rogue was a nullity. The argument is the same as the one made by Denning LJ in dissent in *Central Newbury Car Auctions Ltd* v. *Unity Finance Ltd*.[247] Once again, one asks unavailingly how far the dealings between owners and rogue served to mislead the *bona fide* purchaser for value.

The issue was developed further in *Jerome* v. *Bentley*[248] where a rogue called 'Major Tatham' obtained possession of a diamond ring on the ground that he had better social contacts than the owner (a jeweller). He was given a limited authority to hold the ring only for seven days and to sell it for a minimum cash price which was to be remitted to the owner, the rogue to keep any surplus as a commission.[249] In excess of his authority, the rogue sold the ring outside the seven day period for a cash price much lower than the minimum figure. The result in favour of the owner is a perfectly orthodox application of the rule that mere possession does not create the semblance of apparent authority to sell or apparent ownership. But Donovan J went on to consider the principle in *Watteau* v.

---

[241] [1893] 1 QB 436.

[242] *Brocklesby* v. *Temperance Building Society* [1895] AC 173; *Rimmer* v. *Webster* [1902] 2 Ch. 163; *Fry* v. *Smellie* [1912] 3 KB 282; *Abigail* v. *Lapin* [1934] AC 491.

[243] [1895] 1 QB 521.   [244] [1902] AC 325.

[245] Hence the issue of voidable title did not arise. See *Hardman* v. *Booth* (1863) 1 H & C 803.

[246] The latter with some hesitation because of *Kingsford* v. *Merry* (1856) 1 H & N 503.

[247] [1957] 1 QB 371.   [248] [1952] 2 All ER 14.

[249] Similar to the arrangements in *Lloyds and Scottish Finance.*

Fenwick,[250] dismissing it on the ground that it applied to well-known classes of agents (including, one imagines, well-known classes of traders) with a recognized usual authority. As an itinerant socialite, 'Major Tatham' could not be said to have any usual authority. Moreover, unlike the manager in *Watteau* v. *Fenwick*, whose authority was continuing but limited at the time of the purchase, 'Major Tatham's' authority had expired altogether at the end of the seven days, and he was thereafter to be treated as a thief of the ring. The conditions laid down by Donovan J are consistent with those met by the dealer in *Lloyds and Scottish Finance*, and one therefore has to conclude that there is some substance in the notion of inherent agency power. As will be seen, the practical effect of this development is to expand the *nemo dat* exception in section 2 of the Factors Act 1889.

Estoppel by Negligence

Estoppel by conduct and estoppel by negligence are overlapping categories. The central issue presented by the latter is whether the rights of a *bona fide* purchaser should be affected by negligence on the part of the owner which does not add to the rogue's appearance of ownership or authority. The cases show that negligence in this context has to respond to the technical requirements of the tort of that name, that is, there must be a duty of care and a breach of that duty, as well as damage, factually caused by the breach, that does not fall outside the remoteness of damage rule. Arguments in favour of expanding estoppel by negligence have invariably relied upon a battered dictum of Ashhurst J in *Lickbarrow* v. *Mason*[251] that 'whenever one of two innocent persons must suffer by the acts of a third, he who has enabled such third person to occasion the loss must sustain it'. Reliance on this dictum is the badge of a losing cause, for 'enabled' is much too wide.[252] As Lord Lindley once put it, 'every one who has a servant enables him to steal whatever is within his reach'.[253]

Even if the owner has been negligent in safeguarding his interests, the *bona fide* purchaser's cause is not carried much further. As Lord Macnaghten said: '[H]ow can carelessness, however extreme, in the conduct of a man's own business preclude him from recovering his own property which has been stolen from him?'[254] This attitude has also

---

[250] N. 241 above. He also considered *Rimmer* v. *Webster* [1902] 2 Ch. 163.

[251] (1787) 2 TR 63, 70.

[252] *Farquarson Bros. and Co.* v. *C. King and Co.*, n. 244 above, 342 (Lindley LJ); *Central Newbury Car Auctions Ltd* v. *Unity Finance Ltd*, n. 247 above, 388–9 (Hodson LJ).

[253] *Farquarson Bros. and Co*, n. 244 above. The inhospitability of the common law to estoppel by negligence may have been coloured by the widespread employment of domestic servants among the professional and judicial classes.

[254] *Ibid.* 335–6, citing the examples of the owner who loses a valuable dog because it is not properly chained up, and the owner of a watch who carelessly leaves it on a park bench or restaurant table.

coloured the approach taken in cases where an owner negligently entrusts or surrenders possession of goods.[255] The predicament of the *bona fide* purchaser is also compounded if there is an element of carelessness on his own part in dealing with the rogue. Lord Macnaghten put the matter as sharply as it can be put:[256]

If it were permissible it would be interesting to inquire which of the two firms parties to this litigation was the more blameworthy from a moral point of view. The plaintiffs trusted a man whom they had long known and whom they believed to be honest. The defendants trusted a man, whom a breath of suspicion and the most ordinary inquiries would have unmasked.

As inhospitable as the legal landscape is to estoppel by negligence, the idea has excited such interest over the years that it is worth asking how it could be implemented in litigation. One way would be to give the defendant purchaser a defence to an action in conversion brought by the true owner. Unless the defendant can establish a representation, in which case negligence would appear to add nothing to the defence, the defendant is disqualified from raising the owner's negligence as a defence by section 11(1) of the Torts (Interference with Goods) Act 1977, which states that '[c]ontributory negligence is no defence in proceedings founded on conversion, or on intentional trespass to goods'. A different way of formulating the defendant's position, not ruled out by section 11(1), would be to assert that estoppel by negligence amounts to a representation by omission. A negligent failure to contradict a rogue's representation of authority or ownership would itself amount to a representation that the rogue is so authorized.[257] It is hard to resist the conclusion, however, that an owner who is dispossessed by a rogue is not, except in a fictitious way, making any such representation. To condone the defence being framed in these terms, moreover, comes close to flouting section 11(1). Yet another way in which the owner's negligence can be taken into account is to say that the purchaser has no defence to an action in conversion brought by the owner but may assert a counterclaim against a negligent owner for the economic loss caused when the purchaser paid the irrecoverable price to the rogue. If the purchaser has himself been negligent too, the owner would then be able to plead by way of defence to the counterclaim the purchaser's own contributory negligence. This apportionment of loss would consummate by different means the division of loss once recommended by Lord Devlin for

---

[255] See also *Moorgate Mercantile Co. Ltd* v. *Twitchings* [1977] AC 890, 925.
[256] *Farquarson Bros. and Co.* v. *C. King and Co.*, n. 244 above, 335.
[257] P. S. Atiyah, *The Sale of Goods* (9th edn., Pitman, London, 1995 by J. N. Adams), 323.

dividing losses between innocent owners and innocent purchasers.[258] This method of treating the purchaser's invocation of the owner's negligence was left open by Lord Wilberforce *Moorgate Mercantile Credit Co. Ltd* v. *Twitchings*,[259] but it comes very close to flouting the will of Parliament as later expressed in section 11(1). Furthermore, developments in the tort of negligence in the last decade or so make the prospects of success for such an economic loss claim appear most unpromising.[260]

Be that as it may, the concept of estoppel by negligence was accepted by Blackburn J more than 100 years ago when he stated the requirement of 'the neglect of some duty that is owed to the person led into the belief, or . . . to the general public of whom that person is one, and not merely neglect of what would be prudent in respect of the party himself'.[261] In *Central Newbury Car Auctions*, Morris LJ jibbed at the notion of a duty of care owed to the world.[262] But although multiple parties might be involved in the rogue's chain of deception, in the end there is only one sale price or pledge advance secured by the rogue. The liability in negligence of manufacturers of defective goods is a duty owed to the world, though only one consumer will drink the ginger beer containing the decomposing snail.

The difficulty of persuading a sceptical court of the merits of estoppel by negligence is illustrated by *Mercantile Credit Co. Ltd* v. *Hamblin*.[263] The owner of a car, seeking an advance on the security of her car, at the dealer's suggestion signed hire purchase proposal forms in blank in the belief that they were mortgage documents. Unlike mortgage forms, hire purchase forms presented the dealer as the owner of the car. The dealer, outwardly respectable and socially known to the owner, gave her a blank cheque with instructions to fill in the amount of the loan. She later withdrew from the agreement but the hire purchase proposal had already gone through and the dealer paid for the car by the finance company. When the owner refused to pay hire purchase instalments, the finance

---

[258] Rejected by the Law Reform Committee because the procedural complexities of its operation in a title chain: Cmnd. 2958, 15. The present position is complex already: see *Butterworth* v. *Kingsway Motors Ltd* [1954] 1 WLR 1286.

[259] N. 255 above, 906.

[260] e.g. *Leigh and Sillavan Ltd* v. *Aliakmon Shipping Co. Ltd* [1986] AC 785; *Muirhead* v. *Industrial Tank Specialties Ltd* [1986] QB 507.

[261] *Swan* v. *North British Australian Co.* (1863) 2 H & C 175, 182. These words were approved by Lord Sumner in *R. E. Jones Ltd* v. *Waring and Gillow Ltd* [1926] AC 670, 693. The requirement of a duty was emphasized in *Thomas Australia Wholesale Vehicle Trading Co. Ltd* v. *Marac Finance Australia Ltd* [1985] 3 NSWLR 452.

[262] [1957] 1 QB 371, 393. For the difficulties posed by duty of care, see *Mercantile Bank of India Ltd* v. *Central Bank of India Ltd* [1938] AC 287; *Rimmer* v. *Webster* [1902] 2 Ch. 163; *Wilson* v. *Pickering* [1946] KB 422.

[263] [1965] 2 QB 242.

company claimed she was estopped by her negligence from disputing the dealer's title. The Court of Appeal found for the owner, holding that the finance company had failed to show the technical requirements of negligence, in particular, the existence of a duty of care and a breach of that duty.[264] Despite the existence of a duty of care when the owner signed the forms, she was not in breach of that duty. She knew the dealer and, furthermore, the blank cheque disarmed any suspicions that she might have had. Statements were also made that the effective cause of the finance company's loss was the fraud of the dealer rather than the negligence of the owner.[265] But since the dealer's fraud is the very risk posed by the owner's negligence, this approach seems highly dubious.[266] Perhaps the most surprising feature of the case is that, though signing the forms in blank, the owner was not treated as making the statements later inserted by the dealer. Had she been regarded as making those statements, then an inquiry into negligence should not have been required.[267]

The difficulties of estoppel by negligence came to a head in *Moorgate Mercantile Co. Ltd* v. *Twitchings*,[268] shortly before the enactment of section 11(1) of the Torts (Interference with Goods) Act 1977, a case demonstrating 'the perennial failure of English law to develop a proper method of charging moveable property'.[269] It was the contention of the dealer who had purchased a car from a hire purchase bailee[270] after being informed that no hire purchase agreement in respect of it was on file, that the finance company owner was estopped by its negligence in failing to register the hire purchase agreement from denying the bailee's title to sell the car. The voluntary registration scheme run by Hire Purchase Information Ltd recorded about 98 per cent of all hire purchase agreements relating to motor vehicles, and was the only practical means available to dealers buying cars to ascertain whether they were encumbered by a hire purchase agreement. According to a bare majority of the House of Lords, which found in favour of the finance company, the dealer was owed no duty that registrable hire purchase agreements should actually be registered. Lord Edmund-Davies saw no reason why all careless behaviour should be elevated into a tort and no justification

---

[264] [1965] 2 QB 271.   [265] *Ibid.* 266, 275.

[266] See *Moorgate Mercantile Co. Ltd* v. *Twitchings*, n. 255 above, 928; *Stansbie* v. *Troman* [1948] 2 KB 48. On severing the chain of causation in negligence, see *Weld-Blundell* v. *Stephens* [1920] AC 956; *The Oropesa* [1943] P 32; *Home Office* v. *Dorset Yacht Co.* [1970] AC 1004; *Knightley* v. *Johns* [1982] 1 All ER 851.

[267] Cf. the knowledge of the owner of the contents of the forms in *Eastern Distributors Ltd* v. *Goldring* [1957] 2 QB 600.

[268] N. 255 above.   [269] *Ibid.* 905 (Lord Wilberforce).

[270] And thus was not protected by Part III of the Hire Purchase Act 1964, discussed in the text accompanying nn. 544 ff. below.

why non-member finance companies should be compelled by the tort of negligence to join the scheme.[271] It was also thought invidious to distinguish between finance companies that were members and finance companies that were not.[272] Nor did it make any difference that there was a common membership in the scheme of finance companies and car dealers; mere propinquity with a dealer did not impose a duty on a finance company to take care of its own property.[273] Concern was also expressed at the possibility of Hire Purchase Information Ltd, in giving selective information to the public, incurring thus a duty of care.[274] Had there been a duty of care, a failure on the part of the finance company to register would have been held to be a breach of this duty.[275]

Now, the dealer knew in his dealings with the scheme that there was an element of risk. Not all agreements were registered, though the lion's share was. It is scant relief to the dealer to know that mistakes like the present one occurred only rarely and that the coverage of the scheme was close to universal. The presence in life of unavoidable risks does not render any the more acceptable a further layer of avoidable risk created by the negligence of others. The dissenting speeches of Lords Wilberforce and Salmon are compelling. Lord Wilberforce was impressed by the degree of reliance by car dealers on the scheme.[276] The paradox that those joining the scheme might be disadvantaged by the imposition of a duty of care was met by the proper response they would derive countervailing advantages in the form of mutual benefits and lower administration costs.[277] It is unlikely, however, that the position established in *Twitchings* and confirmed in legislation will change in the foreseeable future.

It is interesting to note, nevertheless, a lack of consistency between this area and the law on *non est factum*. *Non est factum* is a plea that the signer of a document may enter when fundamentally mistaken about the nature of the document he signs so that it cannot be said to be his document at all. The resulting document is a nullity. The signature is commonly induced by the fraud of another and often takes the form of a disposition of property. This plea may be defeated by the negligence of a party signing a document,[278] even though the document signed is no less fundamentally different. It looks distinctly odd that an owner carelessly

---

[271] N. 255 above, 919.

[272] *Ibid.* See also Lord Russell, at 930, speaking of the finance company joining the scheme 'putting its head into the noose of an estoppel' if this were to entail liability in negligence.

[273] *Ibid.* 925–6 (Lord Fraser).

[274] *Ibid.* 927 (Lord Fraser).

[275] *Ibid.* 921 (Lord Edmund-Davies), 927 (Lord Fraser).

[276] *Ibid.* 904.

[277] *Ibid.* 906.

[278] *Saunders* v. *Anglia Building Society* [1971] AC 1004; *Marvco Color Research Ltd* v. *Harris* [1982] 2 SCR 774.

signing a document runs a considerable risk of disentitlement while an owner careless in other respects does not.[279]

Mercantile Agency

The doctrine of estoppel does little to assist the *bona fide* purchaser for value. In particular, it is far from any assurance that the purchaser may safely trust to possession as the *indicium* of title. As a result of various statutory exceptions to the *nemo dat* rule, extending the protection afforded by the doctrine of estoppel, however, the purchaser may in certain instances repose confidence in another's possession of goods or documents of title to goods. Besides the separate instances of the seller and the buyer in possession of goods or documents of title, these statutory exceptions include the mercantile agent in possession in section 2 of the Factors Act 1889,[280] the provisions of which legislation are expressly preserved in the Sale of Goods Act alongside the recital of the *nemo dat* rule.[281] Taken together, these exceptions fall short of conferring protection in all cases where persons are entrusted with goods.[282]

Mercantile Agents

The only reference to factors in the Factors Act is in the title; the Act is by no means confined to just that class of agent.[283] According to section 1(1): 'The expression "mercantile agent" shall mean a mercantile agent having in the customary course of his business as such agent authority either to sell goods or to consign goods for the purpose of sale, or to buy goods or to raise money on the security of goods.'[284] This definition

---

[279] See Ontario Law Reform Commission, *Report on Sale of Goods* (1979), ii, 310–11 and the recommendation that an owner owes a duty of care when entrusting goods to others. Although the Commission divided equally on the case of a contributorily negligent purchaser, and so made no recommendation, the Uniform Sale of Goods Act adopted in 1982 by the Uniform Law Conference of Canada would allow apportionment in this case.

[280] This is essentially a consolidation of earlier legislation of 1823, 1825, 1842, and 1877. For a discussion of the history of the legislation, see *Johnson* v. *Crédit Lyonnais Co.* (1877) 3 CPD 32; *Cole* v. *North Western Bank* (1875) LR 10 CP 354 (quoting Lord Tenterden's abstract of the 1823 and 1825 Acts); *Mildred, Goyeneche & Co.* v. *Maspons* (1883) 8 App. Cas. 874; *Kaltenbach* v. *Lewis* (1883) 24 Ch. D 54, 61 (noting the difficulty of coming to terms with evolving commerce).

[281] S. 21(1), (2)(a).

[282] *Cole* v. *North Western Bank*, n. 280 above; *Davey* v. *Paine Bros. (Motors) Ltd* [1954] NZLR 1122.

[283] In the 19th century, a factor was a selling agent entrusted with possession of a principal's goods for that purpose, in contrast with a broker, who might never see the goods at all. Nowadays, a factor is someone who discounts future trade debts and offers a debt management service.

[284] *Heyman* v. *Flewker* (1863) 13 CBNS 519, 527.

excludes servants and employees,[285] carriers,[286] repairers,[287] and warehousemen,[288] all of whom as a class lack such authority in the customary course of their businesses. A seller who remains in possession of goods after a sale is not as such a mercantile agent.[289] The agent, nevertheless, need not fit into a well-established niche in order to be a mercantile agent; the category has in the past evolved to accommodate changing mercantile usage. For example, peripatetic jewellery salesman have been held to be mercantile agents,[290] likewise retail car dealers selling their own stock-in-trade to finance companies and private purchasers,[291] as well as second-hand vehicles entrusted to them by private individuals.[292] But car dealers always selling on their own behalf and never on behalf of a principal will not be mercantile agents.[293]

Pitching mercantile agency at the retail sales level involves extending a mercantile idea to transactions involving buyers who themselves are not merchants and, since retail sales are often conducted in myriad ways, has meant that mercantile agency cannot be confined to a closed, nineteenth-century list of categories of mercantile agents. This extension, together with the practice adopted by certain types of mercantile agents of selling the principal's goods as though they were their own, has made it difficult to see mercantile agency as a mere extension of apparent authority or estoppel. It has also created difficulties in applying the test that the agent must act in the ordinary course of business of a mercantile agent.

It is also clear that a person may be a mercantile agent even though this is the first time he has ever acted as such. Willes J saw no valid reason for distinguishing between the first of such an agent's principals and subsequent principals:[294]

Assuming the case of ten persons who on ten successive days put their property for sale upon commission into the hands of another, who thereupon should

---

[285] *Lamb* v. *Attenborough* (1862) 1 B & S 831; *Fuentes* v. *Montis* (1868) LR 3 CP 268, affd. (1868) LR 4 CP 93.

[286] *Monk* v. *Whittenbury* (1831) 2 B & Ad. 484.

[287] *Forristal* v. *McDonald* (1883) 9 SCR 12, 17 (Can.). See also *Directors etc. of City Bank* v *Barrow* (1880) 5 App. Cas. 664 (tanner).

[288] *Cole* v. *North Western Bank*, n. 280 above; *Schafhauser* v. *Shaffer* [1943] 3 DLR 656.

[289] *Johnson* v. *Crédit Lyonnais Co.* n. 280 above.

[290] *Weiner* v. *Harris* [1910] 1 KB 285.

[291] *Motor Credits (Hire Finance) Ltd* v. *Pacific Motor Auctions Pty. Ltd* (1963) 109 CLR 87; *W. J. Albutt & Co. Ltd* v. *Continental Guaranty Corpn. of Canada Ltd* [1929] 3 WWR 292.

[292] *Folkes* v. *King* [1923] 1 KB 282; *Paris* v. *Goodwin* [1954] NZLR 823; *Stadium Finance Ltd* v. *Robbins* [1962] 2 QB 664; *Lewis* v. *Richardson* [1936] SASR 502; *Davey* v. *Paine Bros. Motors Ltd*, n. 282 above.

[293] *Belvoir Finance Ltd* v. *Harold G. Cole & Co. Ltd* [1969] 1 WLR 1877; *Evans* v. *Ritchie* (1964) 44 DLR (2d) 675.

[294] *Heyman* v. *Flewker*, n. 284 above, 527. See also *Mortgage, Loan & Finance Co. of Australia Ltd* v. *Richards* (1932) 32 SR(NSW) 50.

think it worth his while to set up as commission-agent, it would not be easy to suggest any sound distinction between the cases of the first and the last employer, or between either of them and that of the first customer who arrived after the words 'commission-agent' had been put up over his door.

Similarly, someone may be a mercantile agent though this is the first time he has acted for the particular principal and in this particular fashion in his mercantile dealings. This was the case in *Lowther* v. *Harris*,[295] where an art dealer who had his own antique shop was admitted to the house of his principal for the purpose of showing a collection of furniture and tapestry to prospective purchasers. He was nonetheless a mercantile agent.

Obviously, a combination of the informal behaviour of certain mercantile agents and the extension of the Factors Act to mercantile agents acting as such for the first time comes quite close to the proposition that anyone who receives goods from the owner in the capacity of agent for purposes connected with their sale is a mercantile agent. This step, however, has not been taken.[296] In the final resort, the person receiving the goods must be an agent of an established commercial type.[297] For example, in *Heap* v. *Motorists' Advisory Agency*,[298] the owner of a car entrusted it to a man calling himself Captain the Hon. Roger North for the purpose of driving it to a named friend of North's in Uxbridge looking to purchase a car. Although North later did become a car dealer, the court held that he was not a mercantile agent at the time he obtained possession of the car.[299] Similarly, in the Canadian case of *Bush* v. *Fry*,[300] a piano was delivered to a music teacher, who was known in no other capacity, for the purpose of sale to a particular, named customer. The teacher then shipped the instrument under an assumed name to Toronto, took on that name when he came to Toronto and pledged the piano. The special *ad hoc* agency of the music teacher was held not to be a mercantile agency. Obviously the difference between cases like these and *Lowther* v. *Harris* depends largely on the degree to which courts are prepared to recognize novel examples of mercantile activity for the purpose of section 2 of the Factors Act.

[295] [1927] 1 KB 393; *Thoresen* v. *Capital Credit Corpn.* (1964) 43 DLR (2d) 94.

[296] *Jerome* v. *Bentley* [1952] 2 All ER 114.

[297] *Heyman* v. *Flewker*, n. 284 above; *Directors etc. of City Bank* v *Barrow*, n. 287 above.

[298] [1923] 1 KB 577.

[299] Cf. the question whether a certain 'Major Tatham' could be said to have a usual authority for the purpose of the estoppel doctrine in *Jerome* v. *Bentley*, n. 296 above.

[300] (1887) 15 OR 12.

Receipt as a Mercantile Agent

It is not enough that the agent be a mercantile agent, for he must also receive the goods in his capacity as a mercantile agent. As a Canadian judge once put it:[301]

[N]o case has ever decided that the owner of goods is estopped merely because he has entrusted with the possession of his property a person who, being engaged in a business in the course of which he sells goods of the same kind as those which have been delivered to him as bailee, in breach of his duty, has wrongfully sold the goods of his bailor as his own. If this were so, no man could safely leave his watch with a watchmaker who sells watches, or his carriage with a carriage maker who sells carriages, to be repaired.

This additional requirement is a judicial gloss upon section 2 of the Factors Act. It was introduced on the basis of old factors legislation, which required that the agent be 'intrusted with and in possession of'[302] the goods before the owner could be bound by their 'sale or disposition'. Cases decided under this provision required the agent to be entrusted in his capacity as a mercantile agent.[303] Although the current Factors Act substitutes for the above language a requirement that the mercantile agent obtain 'with the consent of the owner . . . possession of goods or of the documents of title to goods',[304] there still remains the judicially introduced requirement that possession be obtained *qua* mercantile agent.[305] Certain older cases[306] have held not to be a mercantile agent one who is authorised only to relay offers of purchase to the owner and not to enter into any binding contracts of sale. This is inconsistent with other authority[307] and wrong in principle, for what is important is the selling authority usually confided in such agents rather than the actual authority that is restricted between owner and agent in an undisclosed way.

The requirement that the mercantile agent receive *qua* mercantile

[301] *Forristal* v. *McDonald*, n. 287 above, 17. [302] Factors Act 1825, s. 2.

[303] *Hellings* v. *Russell* (1877) 33 LT 380; *Cole* v. *North Western Bank* (1875) LR 10 CP 354; *Monk* v. *Whittenbury*, n. 286 above; *Forristal* v. *McDonald*, n. 287 above; *Directors etc. of City Bank* v. *Barrow*, n. 287 above; *Johnson* v. *Crédit Lyonnais Co*, n. 289 above; *Turner* v. *Sampson* (1911) 27 TLR 200, 202.

[304] S. 2(1). Said to be effectively the same thing as entrustment: *Lake* v. *Simmons* [1927] AC 487, 509–10; *Oppenheimer* v. *Attenborough & Son* [1907] 1 KB 510, 516.

[305] *Astley Industrial Trust Ltd* v. *Miller* [1968] 2 All ER 36; *Belvoir Finance Co. Ltd* v. *Harold G. Cole & Co. Ltd*, n. 293 above; *Staffs Motor Guarantee Co. Ltd* v. *British Wagon Co. Ltd* [1934] 2 KB 305; *Kendrick* v. *Sotheby & Co.* (1967) 111 SJ 470 (statue entrusted for purpose of obtaining a photograph signed by sculptor's widow). Cf. *Moody* v. *Pall Mall Deposit and Forwarding Co. Ltd* (1917) 33 TLR 306; *Cahn* v. *Pockett's Bristol Channel Steam Packet Co. Ltd* [1899] 1 QB 643, 660–1.

[306] *Biggs* v. *Evans* [1894] 1 QB 88 (Wills J—a judgment similar to the one he gave in *Watteau* v. *Fenwick* [1893] 1 QB 346); *Brown and Co.* v. *Bedford Pantechnicon Co. Ltd* (1889) 5 TLR 449.

[307] *Pearson* v. *Rose & Young Ltd* [1951] 1 KB 275, 288; *Lloyds and Scottish Finance Ltd* v. *Williamson* [1965] 1 All ER 641.

agent has meant that section 2 does not apply where a finance company repossesses a vehicle and deposits it with a garage for storage purposes only.[308] Section 2 has also been held not to apply to the acquisition of a car by a car rental company, because receipt for hire does not fall within the usual authority of a mercantile agent as defined in section 1(1) of the Factors Act.[309] A mercantile agent who receives possession of goods under the terms of sale or return or sale on approval agreements obtains them as a potential buyer and not as an agent at all and would, if selling them to an innocent purchaser, be more accurately pictured, as between himself and the owner, as reselling rather than selling the goods.[310] Obviously, it can be a difficult question of interpretation whether the agent has received *qua* agent or *qua* potential buyer.[311] The third-party dimension has ensured that courts do not consider themselves bound by the label chosen by the parties themselves.[312]

Disposing Power of Mercantile Agents

Section 2(1) of the Factors Act states the power of a mercantile agent as follows:

Where a mercantile agent is, with the consent of the owner, in possession of goods or of the documents of title to goods, any sale, pledge or other disposition of the goods, made by him when acting in the ordinary course of business of a mercantile agent, shall, subject to the provisions of this Act, be as valid as if he were expressly authorised by the owner of the goods to make the same; provided that the person taking under the disposition acts in good faith, and has not at the time of the disposition notice that the person making the disposition has not authority to make the same.

This provision raises a number of points. The meaning of 'mercantile agent' and the requirement of receipt in that capacity have already been considered. First of all, though section 2(1) speaks of the 'owner', it does not launder title but rather effaces whatever title, which may be a possessory one, is vested in the party transferring possession to the mercantile agent. A limited possessory title was defeated in *Lloyds Bank Ltd* v. *Bank of America National Trust and Savings Association*[313] where a financing bank released to the buyers of certain goods documents of title relating to them. The buyers took the documents on trust receipt terms and were to keep the goods and their proceeds of sale separate from their other assets. Despite the buyers having the general property in the goods and the bank a possessory interest by way of a deemed continuing pledge that survived the release of the documents, the bank was held to be the

---

[308] *Schafhauser* v. *Shaffer* [1943] 3 DLR 656.
[309] *Astley Industrial Trust Ltd* v. *Miller*, n. 305 above.
[310] *Weiner* v. *Harris* [1910] 1 KB 285.   [311] *Ibid.*   [312] *Ibid.*
[313] [1938] 2 KB 146. See also *Beverley Acceptances Ltd* v. *Oakley* [1982] RTR 417.

owner for the purpose of section 2(1) and the buyers to be mercantile agents receiving them in that capacity. Consequently, an unauthorized but ordinary course pledge of the documents by the buyer was held to override the interest of the bank.

Possession in section 2 has the same meaning as that given to it in other areas of personal property law, that is to say, it is constituted by physical control of the goods complete with an intention to exclude others.[314] In *Lowther* v. *Harris*,[315] the mercantile agent was not in possession of the furniture and tapestry while it remained in Colonel Lowther's house. Admittedly, the agent had the key and had access by permission to certain parts of the house for his personal occupation.[316] But the owner kept a secretary in the house during business hours and the court rightly held that it was not until the agent fraudulently obtained permission to remove the tapestry from the house and did so that he could be said to have acquired possession of it.[317]

The agent's possession of the goods or documents of title must be obtained with the 'consent' of the owner.[318] Fraud alone will not destroy the owner's consent.[319] A particular difficulty that used to arise before the reform of the law of theft in 1967[320] was whether the commission of larceny by a trick[321] by the agent destroyed the consent.[322] The cases initially were divided and contrasting opinions were expressed whether the 'technicalities' of criminal law were to be introduced into commercial law.[323] Even before larceny by a trick was abolished, it was settled, however, that the owner's consent might in fact be given even to an agent who had committed larceny by a trick.[324] Central to the offence of

---

[314] *Cahn* v. *Pockett's Bristol Channel Steam Packet Co. Ltd* [1899] 1 QB 643; M. G. Bridge, *Personal Property Law* (Blackstone, London, 1993), 12–17.

[315] [1927] 1 KB 393.   [316] He was a 'licensee, perhaps caretaker': *ibid.*

[317] See also *Brown and Co.* v. *Bedford Pantechnicon Co. Ltd*, n. 305 above.

[318] The consent is to the agent's possession of goods and is not an intention to pass the property in the goods to the agent: *Cahn*, n. 314 above. It must be given by the owner and not by someone in unlawful possession (*Cook* v. *Rodgers* (1946) 46 SR(NSW) 229; *Brandon* v. *Leckie* (1972) 29 DLR (3d) 633) or by an unauthorized agent (*W. J. Albutt & Co. Ltd* v. *Continental Guaranty Corpn. of Canada Ltd* [1929] 3 WWR 292).

[319] *Cole* v. *North Western Bank*, n. 303 above 393; *Cahn*, n. 314 above, 659.

[320] Theft Act 1967.

[321] Described as 'a most bewildering subject' in *London Jewellers Ltd* v. *Attenborough* [1934] 2 KB 206, 213.

[322] For authority that larceny by a trick destroyed consent, see: *Oppenheimer* v. *Frazer & Wyatt* [1907] 2 KB 50; *Heap* v. *Motorists' Advisory Agency Ltd* [1923] 1 KB 577; *Lake* v. *Simmons* [1926] 2 KB 51 (Atkin LJ).

[323] No: *Folkes* v. *King* [1923] 1 KB 282, 305 (Scrutton LJ). Yes (and they are not technicalities): *Lake* v. *Simmons*, n. 322 above, 71 (Atkin LJ) and [1927] AC 487, 509–10 (Lord Sumner).

[324] *Folkes* v. *King*, n. 323 above (Bankes and Scrutton LJJ); *Paris* v. *Goodwin* [1954] NZLR 823; *Pearson* v. *Rose & Young Ltd*, n. 307 above; *Roache* v. *Australian Mercantile Land & Finance Co. Ltd* (1966) 67 SR(NSW) 54, 66; *London Jewellers Ltd* v. *Attenborough*, n. 321 above. The same holds true for buyers and sellers in possession: *Du Jardin* v. *Beadman Bros. Ltd* [1952] 2 QB 712; *Reed* v. *Motors Ltd* [1926] SASR 128.

The Sale of Goods

larceny by a trick was the absence of the owner's intention to pass the property in the goods, or the power of disposing of the property, to the agent.[325] While larceny by a trick might therefore destroy the voidable title of a rogue under section 23 of the Sale of Goods Act,[326] it did not have the same effect under section 2 of the Factors Act, since the owner never intended to pass the property in the goods to the rogue agent. Indeed, he employed the agent to create an opportunity for the future transfer of the property, and in some cases would actually and genuinely be authorizing the agent to pass the property on limited terms.[327] Accordingly, a preoccupation with larceny by a trick diverted attention from the relevant question in section 2, namely, whether the agent was in fact in possession of the goods with the owner's consent. It added nothing to mercantile agency and its abolition complements the sensible course already taken by the case law under section 2.

To facilitate the forensic task of the innocent purchaser of the goods in a title dispute with the owner, the Factors Act establishes a number of evidentiary presumptions favouring the purchaser. Someone who has the custody of the goods, or who controls someone else who has it, will be deemed to be in possession.[328] Once the mercantile agent is shown to be or to have been in possession of the goods, it will then be presumed in the absence of evidence to the contrary that this was with the owner's consent;[329] the burden of proof of showing this not to be the case is therefore on the owner. Furthermore, any consent given by the owner to the agent's possession of goods or of documents of title to goods is deemed to be given also with respect to documents of title into which those goods or documents of title are translated.[330] Thus a mercantile agent depositing his principal's goods in a warehouse and being issued with a warehouse receipt will be deemed to be in possession of the warehouse receipt with the consent of the owner, and any effective dealings with the warehouse receipt will bind the goods. Likewise, a mercantile agent who exchanges one manufacturer's warehouse receipt for another will obtain the second receipt with the consent of the owner if that was the way the first was obtained.[331] The final, and probably the most important, presumption is contained in section 2(2):

Where a mercantile agent has, with the consent of the owner, been in possession of goods or of documents of title to goods, any sale, pledge, or other disposition, which would have been valid if the consent had continued, shall be valid

---

[325] *Whitehorn Bros.* v. *Davison* [1911] 1 KB 463; *Folkes* v. *King*, n. 323 above; *London Jewellers Ltd* v. *Attenborough*, n. 321 above; *Dennant* v. *Skinner* [1948] 2 KB 164.

[326] Discussed above.

[327] e.g. *Folkes* v. *King*, n. 323 above.　　　　　　　　　　　　　　　[328] S. 1(2).

[329] S. 2(4), discussed in *Fuentes* v. *Montis* (1868) LR 3 CP 831.　　　[330] S. 2(3).

[331] *Ibid.*, overruling *Hatfield* v. *Phillips* (1845) 14 M & W 665.

notwithstanding the termination of the consent: provide that the person taking under the disposition has not at the time thereof notice that the consent has been terminated.[332]

Given the mercurial habits of disappearing rogue agents, this is a presumption that in practical terms is impossible to rebut. Its most significant effect has been in section 25 of the Sale of Goods Act which, as we shall see, by requiring the buyer in possession to act in the same way as a mercantile agent, has imported the relevant provisions of the Factors Act into the interpretation of section 25.

Ordinary Course of Business

Perhaps the most difficult problem posed by section 2(1) concerns the requirement that the agent act in the ordinary course of business of a mercantile agent in selling, pledging, or otherwise disposing of the goods or documents of title. The difficulty is caused by the fact that the innocent purchaser need not realize he is dealing with a mercantile agent.[333] This development appears to stem from the practice of nineteenth-century brokers, acting on behalf of undisclosed principals, of not revealing that they were acting as agents when carrying on a business in which they commonly bought and sold on their own behalf. The leading case on the subject is *Oppenheimer* v. *Attenborough & Son*,[334] where a diamond broker fraudulently pledged some diamonds that he had obtained for the purpose of showing to named potential purchasers. At the trial, it appeared that diamond brokers did not have a usual authority to pledge their principals' diamonds. The broker in question, however, had also transacted business for a number of years as a diamond merchant and in that capacity had pledged diamonds on a number of occasions with the defendants for short-term advances. The issue was whether the diamond broker had to act in the ordinary course of business of a diamond broker when dealing with the defendants, who did not know that the broker was acting in the capacity of a broker.

In finding for the defendant pawnbrokers, the Court of Appeal might have held that it was sufficient for the broker to behave in the ordinary course of business of a diamond merchant, which was evidently what the pawnbrokers believed him to be,[335] but it did not so hold. Instead, the court drew on the difference in language between sections 1(1) and 2(1),

---

[332] This overrules *Fuentes* v. *Montis*, n. 329 above. See now *Folkes* v. *King*, n. 323 above, 301–2; *Pearson* v. *Rose & Young Ltd* [1951] 1 KB 275, 288.

[333] *Oppenheimer* v. *Attenborough & Son* [1908] 1 KB 221. See Buckley LJ's interpretation of s. 4 (at 221) and Kennedy LJ (at 231).

[334] N. 333 above.

[335] The case is not clear on this. See Buckley LJ's assumption, n. 333 above, 230, of the pawnbroker's ignorance of a diamond broker's usual authority (*sed quaere* of a large pawnbroker involved in much litigation in this period?). Kennedy LJ, *ibid.* 231, is clearer on this.

the former requiring an agent to have a minimum usual authority in the course of his business as 'such agent' in order to qualify as a mercantile agent under the Act, and the latter, looking to the transactions entered into by mercantile agents who had passed the threshold test in section 1(1), requiring these transactions to have been entered into in the ordinary course of business of 'a mercantile agent'. Thus stated, the language in section 2(1) is to be seen as colouring the good faith and absence of notice of the purchaser or pledgee: the mercantile agent's ordinary course behaviour is judged by formal and general business criteria, namely, whether he acted 'within business hours, at a proper place of business and in other respects in the ordinary way in which a mercantile agent would act'.[336]

The ordinary course of business is clearly a question of fact[337] and should be interpreted according to the pattern of practice of the particular trade. *Oppenheimer* v. *Attenborough & Son*[338] lays down in very bland terms a formal test of businesslike behaviour, which a diamond broker in one case failed to meet who persuaded a 'friend' to pledge diamonds with a pawnbroker.[339] But even general business behaviour has to be coloured by the context. For example, it may well be in the ordinary course of business for a car dealer to raise money by mortgage financing on existing stock,[340] but the same could hardly be said of an encyclopedia salesman. It would not matter how businesslike and professional that salesman was in approaching the lender. Furthermore, the agent may not act in a way in which no responsible agent would have acted; the innocent purchaser or pledgee may truly believe that he is dealing with an owner, but the agent's behaviour must be objectively consistent with the behaviour of someone who is an agent rather than an owner. Thus section 2(1) will not apply where the agent, instead of receiving payment, permits the sum due to be set off against an indebtedness owed personally by the agent to the purchaser or pledgee.[341] Although at one time the

---

[336] Kennedy LJ, 230–1 (Buckley LJ). See also *Newton's of Wembley Ltd* v. *Williams* [1965] 1 QB 560 (kerbside sale in Warren Street); *People's Credit Jewellers Ltd* v. *Melvin* [1933] 1 DLR 498.

[337] *Jensen* v. *Harrison* [1933] 3 WWR 669.   [338] N. 333 above.

[339] *De Gorter* v. *George Attenborough and Son* (1904) 19 TLR 19. An auction sale was held on the facts not to be in the ordinary course in *Waddington and Sons* v. *Neale and Sons* (1907) 96 LT 786.

[340] *Industrial Acceptance Corpn. Ltd* v. *Whiteshell Finance Corpn. Ltd* (1966) 57 DLR (2d) 670.

[341] *Lloyds and Scottish Finance Ltd* v. *Williamson* [1965] 1 All ER 641; *Biggs* v. *Evans* [1894] 1 QB 88 (payment to agent's judgment creditor). Cf. New Zealand cases where a set-off is regarded as occurring in the ordinary course of business if the purchaser believes he is contracting with someone acting on his own account: *R. and E. Tingey & Co. Ltd* v. *John Chambers & Co. Ltd* [1967] NZLR 785; *Ceres Orchard Partnership* v. *Fiatagri Australia Pty. Ltd* [1995] 1 NZLR 112 (sale in the ordinary course of business not confined to what is ordinarily done in business).

common law did not recognize the usual authority of agents to pledge their principals' property, factors legislation responded[342] to the emergent practice of factors making advances to their principals and keeping themselves in funds by pledging the goods or documents of title until an ensuing sale.[343]

The car trade has been a particularly fruitful source of reported cases on the subject of ordinary course of business. It has been held without any difficulty that dealers act in the ordinary course of business when accepting an exchange or trade-in.[344] In certain circumstances, a dealer will not sell in the ordinary course of business unless the sale is accompanied by the appropriate documents. A number of decisions hold that the car logbook, the forerunner of the present registration document, must accompany the goods if the sale of a second-hand car is to be effective under section 2(1) of the Factors Act.[345] Although the logbook, in common with the modern registration document, was not a document of title[346] and merely designated the person responsible for paying road tax, it was a permanent document lasting for the life of the car and its transfer was in practical terms a necessary incident of any transfer of the vehicle. This was not the case with the sale of a new vehicle,[347] where the registration authority might not yet have issued the logbook. The position would appear to be the same for modern registration documents, although they are not permanent in character and are reissued with each registered change of ownership. In what can only be described as an effort to assist a private owner against an innocent trade purchaser in one case when the owner had been duped by the rogue into parting with possession of the logbook, it was held that, while the logbook may not have been 'goods' within section 1(3) of the Factors Act, the rogue should not have had it, therefore could not be said to have sold the car with it, and so the sale did not take place in the ordinary course of business.[348] The proposition has only to be stated for its logical flaws to be apparent.

Section 2(1) of the Factors Act applies to the 'sale, pledge or other

---

[342] Factors Act 1842, s. 1.

[343] *Fuentes* v. *Montis*, n. 329 above, 277–8; *Roache* v. *Australian Mercantile Land & Finance Ltd*, n. 324 above, 69. See also *Oppenheimer* v. *Attenborough & Son*, n. 333 above; *Janesich* v. *George Attenborough and Son* (1902) 102 LT 605.

[344] *Davey* v. *Paine Bros. (Motors) Ltd* [1954] NZLR 1122; *Lewis* v. *Richardson* [1936] SASR 502.

[345] *Pearson* v. *Rose & Young Ltd*, n. 332 above; *Stadium Finance Ltd* v. *Robbins* [1962] 2 QB 664.

[346] *Central Newbury Car Auctions Ltd* v. *Unity Finance Ltd* [1957] 1 QB 371; *Joblin* v. *Watkins* [1949] 1 All ER 47n; *Pearson* v. *Rose & Young Ltd*, n. 332 above; *J. Sargent (Garages) Ltd* v. *Motor Auctions (West Bromwich) Ltd* [1977] RTR 121; *Beverley Acceptances Ltd* v. *Oakley* [1982] RTR 417.

[347] *Astley Industrial Trust Ltd* v. *Miller* [1968] 2 All ER 36.

[348] *Stadium Finance Ltd* v. *Robbins*, n. 345 above (Ormerod and Dankwerts LJJ). See also *Pearson* v. *Rose & Young Ltd*, n. 332 above.

disposition' of the goods by the mercantile agent. If there is a sale, it must not be an accommodation sale with the agent remaining in possession of the goods at all material times and the expectation being that the agent will buy back at an elevated price reflecting the time value of the money advanced by the purchaser.[349] Auctioneers receiving goods from mercantile agents for the purpose of the sale have unsuccessfully argued that this receipt amounts to a pledge or disposition.[350]Despite the auctioneer in one case making an advance of the contingent sale price to the agent, the relationship between the two was rightly held not to amount to a pledge; the redemption of the goods by the agent was never contemplated by the parties. It has also been held that the transfer by the agent to the auctioneer cannot be treated as a disposition, since this implies a divesting of the general property in the goods in a manner akin to a sale;[351] the agent merely transfers possession to the auctioneer and has no intention of vesting any other property interest in the auctioneer.

It is not clear from a reading of section 2(1) whether possession must necessarily be transferred by the mercantile agent. Obviously it must in the case of a pledge,[352] but the section does not clearly state that it should for a sale or a disposition. It does however refer to a 'taking under' a sale, pledge, or disposition, but this can be understood as a general reference to the nature of the property interest purportedly conferred by the agent on the transferee, which will vary according to whether he is a buyer or a pledgee. It is submitted that, like the voidable title provision of section 23, section 2(1) does not require an actual transfer of possession to the transferee in cases of sales and other dispositions. But the absence of such a transfer might colour other Factors Act questions, such as whether the transaction took place in the ordinary course of business and whether the transferee acted in good faith.

Documents of Title

Section 2(1) applies to dealings in documents of title as well as in goods. If the Act had been confined to the common law understanding of a document of title, which is satisfied only by a negotiable bill of lading,[353] the

---

[349] *Joblin* v. *Watkins*, n. 346 above.

[350] *Waddington and Sons* v. *Neale and Sons*, n. 339 above. For a further discussion of 'disposition' under s. 24 of the Sale of Goods Act, see discussion in the text accompanying nn. 456 ff. below.

[351] *Roache* v. *Australian Mercantile Land & Finance Co. Ltd* (1966) 67 SR(NSW) 54. See also *Suttons Motors (Temora) Pty. Ltd* v. *Hollywood Motors Pty. Ltd* [1971] VR 684.

[352] But see the notional transfer under the second pledge, where the first pledge (redeemable at any time) of a bill of lading had not exhausted the value of the goods, in *Portalis* v. *Tetley* (1867) LR 5 Eq. 140.

[353] Ch. 6 above. See also *Gunn* v. *Bolckow, Vaughan & Co.* (1875) LR 10 Ch. App. 491; *Cole* v. *North Western Bank* (1875) LR 10 CP 354; *Official Assignee of Madras* v. *Mercantile Bank of India Ltd* [1935] AC 53.

purchasers receiving delivery orders and warrants would have obtained singularly little protection. But section 1(4) of the Factors Act gives the following definition:

The expression 'document of title' shall include any bill of lading, dock warrant, warehouse-keeper's certificate, and warrant or order for the delivery of goods, and any other document used in the ordinary course of business as proof of the possession or control of goods, or authorising or purporting to authorise, either by endorsement or by delivery, the possessor of the document to transfer or receive goods thereby represented.

This definition poses the question whether a non-negotiable document, in the form of a sea waybill for example, may be a document of title under section 1(4). This question may be approached from two angles. The first approach is to ask if the document is of a type against which the bailee in possession of goods would be expected in the ordinary course of business to surrender the goods therein represented. Such documents would go beyond a negotiable bill of lading since they would include other negotiable (that is, transferable) documents that do not confer direct rights against the bailee, namely, documents calling for delivery to the holder for the time being or bearer. The second approach assesses the character of the document as affording evidence of ownership or of authority to deal in the underlying goods.

The first approach clearly excludes non-negotiable documents since delivery will be made by the bailee, not against any document as such, but pursuant to instructions given by the bailor. Documents such as a sea waybill will name a consignee, but the bailee may be directed by the consignor to deliver to someone else instead.[354] The treatment of non-negotiable documents under the second approach is less clear. Section 1(4) of the Factors Act appears to contemplate a wider range of documents than those in negotiable form. It does refer to an entitlement to receive goods arising out of indorsement or delivery of a document, a reference to its negotiation.[355] But it also refers to the 'possessor' of a document, instead of the 'holder' we expect to see in the case of negotiable documents, and it refers separately to documents that prove possession or control of goods. On balance, it seems that a party in possession of a non-negotiable document may have a disposing power under section 2(1) of the Factors Act. One example would be an agent, to whom goods are entrusted, who consigns them under the terms of a sea waybill. As long as the goods are at sea and the carrier amenable to a change of delivery instructions, the agent's possession of the waybill would represent 'proof

---

[354] See the indirect recognition of this practice in the wording of s. 2(1)(b) of the Carriage of Goods by Sea Act 1992.
[355] See s. 11 of the Factors Act.

of possession *or control* of goods' (emphasis added). Other examples
would depend upon the particular commercial context.[356]

Whatever may be the scope of section 2 in relation to non-negotiable
documents, it should be noted too that it confers certain powers upon
mercantile agents in relation to negotiable documents that could not be
exercised by the owners themselves. Apart from the case of negotiable
bills of lading, the owner of goods may not by documentary means effect
a pledge of goods held by a third party except by securing from that third
party an attornment in favour of the new bailor;[357] the mere endorsement or delivery of the negotiable document itself to the new holder
would not operate as a pledge. But section 2(1) of the Factors Act[358]
empowers a mercantile agent to make an effective pledge of the goods by
negotiating a document of title[359] even if it is not a bill of lading.[360]

Pledges

The Factors Act contains a number of provisions dealing with pledges.
First of all, section 3 provides that a pledge of documents of title by a
mercantile agent will be deemed to be a pledge of the goods themselves.
Although section 3 does not refer explicitly to mercantile agents, it is contained in a part of the Act bearing the heading 'Dispositions by
Mercantile Agents' and so should be read in that context. Secondly, section 4 limits the effect of certain pledges by providing that, if a pledge of
goods by a mercantile agent secures a debt incurred by the pledgor
before the pledge, the effect of the pledge is confined to whatever interest the pledgor has in the goods. The origins of section 4 lie in an earlier
provision dealing with pledges by factors of goods over which they had a
lien.[361] Section 4 was considered in *Kaltenbach* v. *Lewis*[362] where a commission agent unlawfully pledged bills of lading with produce brokers as
security for a short-term loan. The money was needed to pay the brokers

---

[356] The conclusion that a non-negotiable document falls with s. 2 of the Factors Act is
indirectly borne out by *Mercantile Bank of India Ltd* v. *Central Bank of India Ltd* [1938] AC
287, where the Privy Council, applying s. 178 of the Indian Contracts Act, which treats railway receipts as documents of title, was prepared to say that even a non-negotiable receipt
was a document of title.

[357] See Ch. 6 above.   [358] In combination with s. 3.

[359] As defined in s. 1(4).

[360] See *Official Assignee of Madras* v. *Mercantile Bank of India Ltd*, n. 353 above.

[361] Earlier legislation also provided for the transfer of only this lien interest where the
pledgee had notice that the goods did not belong to the factor. See R. Munday (1977) 6
Anglo-Am LR 221, 246, referring to the fifth edition of *Abbot on Shipping* as cited in *Cole* v.
North Western Bank, n. 353 above, 361–2. The Factors Act, in ss. 4 and 7(1), recognizes that
possessory liens may be transferred or pledged, a relic of the rule that agents acting for
overseas principals did not establish privity between the principal and the third party but
contracted themselves with both parties. There is strong contrary authority at common
law: *Donald* v. *Suckling* (1866) LR 1 QB 585; *Franklin* v. *Neate* (1844) 13 M & W 481.

[362] (1883) 24 Ch. D 54, applying s. 3 of the 1825 Act, the predecessor of the present s. 4.

themselves, on the following day, the price of certain shellac sold to him by the brokers. The brokers did not know that the pledges were unauthorized, and the advance was not made to secure an antecedent debt, since the price of the shellac fell due only on the following day. The reason for the restriction in section 4 is that the owner of goods is prejudiced enough by the mercantile agent's disposing powers under the Act without in effect becoming susceptible to a general lien claimed against the mercantile agent.[363]

The above prohibition on a general lien had posed problems in cases where a mercantile agent pledges his principal's goods or documents of title, together with other goods or documents of title, in return for one consolidated advance. An Australian court has held that the Factors Act protects only specific advances and does not permit a combined pledge for a consolidated amount that might vary from time to time.[364] This appears to be a somewhat drastic result where the amount of the pledge advance could be apportioned so as to cover the proportionate value of the principal's goods or documents of title, and where the balance in a continuing pledge account could be calculated on first in, first out principles if subsequent pledge securities were added.

A different approach was adopted in *Thoreson* v. *Capital Credit Corp. Ltd*,[365] which dealt also with section 12(2) of the Factors Act, which entitles an owner to recover goods from a pledgee on reimbursing the latter the amount of the pledge advance. In that case, the British Columbia court upheld the validity of a pledge of the plaintiff's trailer where a mercantile agent consolidated his pledge account with the pledgee in return for the grant of a fresh advance. The court held that the owner was entitled to redeem his goods, a trailer, only if he paid off the whole advance secured on this and six other trailers, and not merely a rateable proportion of the advance fitting his own trailer. This is tantamount, as against the owner, to allowing the pledgee a general lien, for the amount the pledgee might have advanced on the owner's trailer alone would have fallen well short of the advance actually made. Although this recognition of a consolidated pledge does not overtly affect section 4 of the Factors Act, which declines to recognize pledges for antecedent and not future advances, it involves a departure from the approach taken in *Kaltenbach* v. *Lewis*,[366] as well as that in the Australian case referred to above. Although the matter is not free from doubt, it is unlikely that a pledgee was ever intended to obtain the advantages under sections 4 and 12(2) of the Factors Act that were obtained by the pledgee in *Thoresen*. The better

[363] *Ibid.*
[364] *Re Farmers and Settlers Co-operative Society Ltd* (1908) SR (NSW) 41, applying *Kaltenbach*, n. 362 above.
[365] (1964) 43 DLR (2d) 94.   [366] N. 362 above.

solution, it is submitted, is to apportion the pledge advance to the rate-able value of the owner's goods; it is fair though not easy to do.

Consignments

The oldest provision in the Factors Act is section 7[367] but little is known (or remembered) of it and it attracts little textual analysis. According to section 7(1):

> Where the owner of goods has given possession of the goods to another person for the purpose of consignment or sale, or has shipped the goods in the name of another person, and the consignee of the goods has not had notice that such person is not the owner of the goods, the consignee shall, in respect of advances made to or for the use of such person, have the same lien on the goods as if such person were the owner of the goods, and may transfer any such lien to another person.

Section 7(1) raises a number of obvious difficulties of interpretation. It does not state what is meant by 'consignment', 'advances', or 'lien'. Over a century ago, Lord Blackburn said of its precursor:

> The enactment has never been altered and its provisions have, in practice, been found to work so harmoniously with the practice of merchants that I am not aware that any case has ever arisen requiring a court of law to construe it, which probably is the reason why an Act of such importance is not familiar to every one.[368]

The case in question concerned a cargo of tobacco, owned by a Cuban resident, that had been shipped by a Cuban broker to an English commission agent, on terms requiring the latter to take out marine insurance against a total loss. The question was whether the commission agent had a lien on the insurance moneys, paid upon the loss of the cargo, for the personal indebtedness to him of the Cuban broker under their running account. Lord Blackburn would have held that the commission agent had such a lien under section 7(1),[369] were it not for the fact that he had notice of the existence of the Cuban principal; it was not necessary that the principal's name be known. The reason for the denial of a lien where there was notice that the mercantile agent was not the owner was taken to be a general principle of the common law 'that it was unjust, with knowledge, to take one man's goods to pay another's debt'.[370]

Section 7(1) was also put forward in another case by an auctioneer who had made an advance to a mercantile agent, whom he believed to be the owner of a piano, in contemplation of the sale of that piano.[371] It was said

---

[367] S. 1 of the 1823 Act, devoted exclusively to it.
[368] *Mildred, Goyeneche & Co.* v. *Maspons* (1883) 8 App. Cas. 874, 884.
[369] Lord Fitzgerald doubted it: *ibid.*   [370] *Ibid.* 885.
[371] *Waddington and Sons* v. *Neale and Sons* (1907) 96 LT 786.

abruptly that section 7(1) need not be considered at all, and the reason is apparent. While an auctioneer may have a common law lien on the goods for his commission and sale expenses, he would surely have to bargain expressly for a lien in connection with any money-lending activities. If the word 'lien' were read expansively, section 7(1) would make considerable inroads into the limitations on apparent ownership and would undermine the limitations on the mercantile agent's power in section 2(1), particularly the limitations that the agent receive as a mercantile agent and act in the ordinary course of business of a mercantile agent. The greater scope of a mercantile agent's disposing power under section 7(1) is brought out by sub-section (2), which provides that nothing in sub-section (1) limits or affects sales, pledges, and dispositions by mercantile agents.[372]

Section 7(1) seems to reflect patterns of overseas mercantile activity no longer current today. If the word 'advance' is read liberally so as to cover any disbursement or expenditure, section 7(1) may be seen as protecting the lien rights, special or general, of certain consignees acting as factors,[373] bankers,[374] calico printers,[375] and dyers.[376] A banker, for example, making advances to a consignee on the security of a bill of lading might therefore be able to claim a lien as against an undisclosed owner who is neither the named consignor (perhaps a mere forwarding agent) nor the consignee. A warehouseman might also be able to claim against such an owner in respect of his storage charges,[377] though only if 'advance' is broadly interpreted. These liens could be upheld in circumstances where the lienee's claims might fail under section 2(1).

Good Faith and Notice

Section 2(1) of the Factors Act requires the purchaser or pledgee taking from the mercantile agent to act in good faith and not to have notice of the mercantile agent's lack of authority. The Factors Act does not define 'good faith' but it will certainly be understood in the same way as it is in the Sale of Goods Act,[378] namely to mean honest behaviour. Normally, good faith and notice will coincide,[379] for someone may not claim to be

---

[372] Curiously, it does not mention s. 2(1).
[373] *Cowell* v. *Simpson* (1809) 16 Ves. Jun. 258; *Rolls Razor Ltd* v. *Cox* [1967] 1 QB 552.
[374] *Brandao* v. *Barnett* (1846) 12 Cl. & F 786.
[375] *Weldon* v. *Gould* (1801) 3 Esp. 268.   [376] *Savill* v. *Barchard* (1801) 4 Esp. 53.
[377] There are also common law means for such persons asserting rights against owners who have not bailed goods to them: see *Bowmaker Ltd* v. *Wycombe Motors Ltd* [1946] KB 505; *Tappenden* v. *Artus* [1964] 2 QB 185.
[378] S. 61(3). It is probably best defined as the absence of bad faith: *Mogridge* v. *Clapp* [1892] 3 Ch. 382, 391. Kay LJ, *ibid.* 401, defined good faith as the 'belief that all is being regularly and properly done'.
[379] See, e.g., their synthesized treatment in *Forsyth International (UK) Ltd* v. *Silver Shipping Co. Ltd* [1994] 1 WLR 1332, 1349–51.

acting in good faith when he has notice of the agent's lack of authority. But if notice were to be read in an expansive fashion, a gap would be opened up between it and good faith.

It is rare for purchasers dealing with a mercantile agent to be made explicitly aware that the agent is acting in excess of his authority. A more likely possibility is that purchasers are actually put on notice by the circumstances of the transaction. It has been held that notice of an interest may exist where the transferee is wilfully blind[380] and fails to make even the most rudimentary inquiries dictated by the common sense of the circumstances.[381] Notice may also be inferred from the terms of the transaction between the mercantile agent and the transferee. It has been held that an unusually low price for an automobile could be evidence of notice,[382] especially where the purchaser is 'rather uncomfortable and suspicious',[383] but care should be taken in applying this to goods of elastic value, such as second-hand cars. The opinion has also been expressed that 'an unusual rate of interest' levied by a pledgee might be 'strong evidence' of notice.[384] Finally, where one joint purchaser has notice, this notice is attributed also to the other joint purchaser.[385]

Apart from actual notice, attempts have at various times been made to fix purchasers with constructive notice as a result of failing to inspect a register. The registers relevant for present purposes would be bills of sale registers as well as the national register of company charges, particularly the latter. The common law has long been resistant to constructive notice in dealings with personal property, thus revealing a desire to permit business to be conducted expeditiously without time-consuming enquiries. Lindley LJ once said it was 'extremely important not to encourage the application of the equitable doctrines of constructive notice to honest mercantile transactions'.[386] In the case of corporate assets, such as raw materials, work-in-progress, and stock-in-trade, these would normally be encumbered by a floating charge, under the terms of which the company has an actual right to dispose of the assets in question free of the charge.[387] Consequently, even actual notice of the

---

[380] *Re Gomersall* (1875) 1 Ch. D 137; *Jones* v. *Gordon* (1877) 2 App. Cas. 616.
[381] *Mehta* v. *Sutton* (1913) 10 LT 529.
[382] *Heap* v. *Motorists' Advisory Agency* [1923] 1 KB 577.   [383] *Ibid.* 591.
[384] *Janesich* v. *George Attenborough & Son* (1910) 102 LT 605.
[385] *Oppenheimer* v. *Frazer & Wyatt* [1907] 2 KB 50.
[386] *Kaltenbach* v. *Lewis* (1883) 24 Ch. D 54, 78. See also *Manchester Trust* v. *Furness* [1895] 2 QB 39; *Greer* v. *Downs Supply Co.* [1927] 2 KB 28; *Vowles* v. *Island Finances Ltd* [1940] 4 DLR 357; *Worcester Works Finance Ltd* v. *Cooden Engineering Co. Ltd* [1972] 1 QB 210; *General Motors Acceptance Corpn.* v. *Hubbard* (1978) 87 DLR (3d) 39; *Feuer Leather Corpn.* v. *Frank Johnstone & Sons* [1981] Com. LR 251; *Joseph* v. *Lyons* (1884) 15 QBD 280.
[387] *Re Hamilton's Windsor Ironworks* (1879) 12 Ch. D 707; *Wheatley* v. *Silkstone and Haigh Moor Colliery Co.* (1885) 29 Ch. D 715; *Re Automatic Bottle Makers Ltd* [1926] 1 Ch. 412; *Re Bond Worth Ltd* [1980] Ch. 228. See also *National Mercantile Bank* v. *Hampson* (1880) 5 QBD 177; *Taylor* v. *M'Keand* (1880) 5 CPD 358.

existence of such a charge would not fetter the disposing power of a company.[388] The life blood of a company's business is the turnover of its stock-in-trade and the business would be paralysed if a chargee's interest followed the goods into the hands of the ordinary course purchaser. This would damage the commercial interests of both company and chargee. Constructive notice becomes more of an issue if the assets sold by the company are, like equipment and other permanent assets, the subject of a fixed charge or mortgage.[389] There does exist a doctrine of constructive notice, in respect of the registrable particulars of a company charge,[390] but it would appear to be confined to those who can reasonably be expected to inspect the register of company charges,[391] a category that would include creditors of the company taking security but would exclude those purchasing goods from the company in the ordinary course of business. The common law's long-standing hostility to constructive notice would come to the assistance of such purchasers. Nevertheless, in a case involving share dealings, whose relevance for sale-of-goods transactions in this area is far from clear, it has been said that a form of constructive notice, less rigorous than the doctrine that prevails in transactions involving land, imputes to a purchaser 'notice of such facts as he would have discovered if he had taken proper measures to investigate them'.[392] It is unlikely, even if such a doctrine could apply to sale of goods agreements, that it would have a practical impact on the kinds of informal transactions typically dealt with under the rubric of *nemo dat* transactions.[393]

The burden of proof clearly lies on the purchaser to show he acted in good faith and without notice.[394] Earlier in this Chapter, it was noted that the Court of Appeal placed the burden of proof on the plaintiff in proceedings arising out of the voidable title provision, section 23 of the Sale

---

[388] Cf. s. 13 of the Factors Act: the disposing powers of an agent outside the Act are not to be abridged by anything in the Act.

[389] In so far as the charge or mortgage is equitable, there is of course a general *nemo dat* exception favouring the *bona fide* purchaser of the legal estate: *Pilcher* v. *Rawlins* (1871) LR 7 Ch. App. 259, 269; *Macmillan Inc* v. *Bishopsgate Trust (No. 3)* [1995] 1 WLR 978, 999–1001. In the case of a legal mortgage, the purchaser will have to invoke s. 2(1) of the Factors Act or one of the other recognized common law or statutory *nemo dat* exceptions.

[390] *Wilson* v. *Kelland* [1910] 2 Ch. 306.

[391] R. M. Goode, *Legal Problems of Credit and Security* (2nd edn., 1988), 83–4.

[392] *Macmillan Inc.* v. *Bishopsgate Trust (No. 3)*, n. 389 above, 1000.

[393] A surer guide is *Feuer Leather Corpn.* v. *Frank Johnstone & Sons*, n. 386 above, 253 ('no general duty on a buyer of goods in an ordinary commercial transaction to make inquiries as to the right of the seller to dispose of the goods').

[394] *Oppenheimer* v. *Frazer & Wyatt*, n. 385 above; *Heap* v. *Motorists' Advisory Agency*, n. 382 above; *Stadium Finance Ltd* v. *Robbins* [1962] 2 QB 664; *Suttons Motors (Temora) Pty. Ltd* v. *Hollywood Motors Pty. Ltd* [1971] VR 684; *Buckland* v. *Clarke* [1956] SR (NSW) 185 (an estoppel case); *Newton's of Wembley Ltd* v. *Williams* [1965] 1 QB 560.

of Goods Act. In all other cases of *nemo dat* exceptions, the burden of proof can confidently be said to be on the transferee asserting an interest against the owner.

The Seller in Possession

Prior to the enactment of the Factors Act 1877, the power of a seller, left in possession of the contract goods or of documents of title to those goods, to transfer title to an innocent purchaser or pledgee was determined according to the ordinary principles of estoppel flowing from an appearance of ownership or authority. In that same year, it had been held that a seller, left in possession of goods or of documents of title, was not to be treated as in receipt thereof as a mercantile agent, even if otherwise he occupied the position of a mercantile agent.[395] Responding to this decision, the 1877 Act conferred on sellers in possession of documents of title the power to convey title,[396] and this power was extended to sellers left in possession of the goods themselves in the Factors Act 1889.[397]

Sale of Goods Act and Factors Act

The relevant provision in the Sale of Goods Act is section 24:

Where a person having sold goods continues or is in possession of the goods, or of the documents of title to the goods, the delivery or transfer by that person, or by a mercantile agent acting for him, of the goods or documents of title under any sale, pledge, or other disposition thereof, to any person receiving the same in good faith and without notice of the previous sale, has the same effect as if the person making the delivery or transfer were expressly authorised by the owner of the goods to make the same.

This provision is paralleled by the almost identical section 8 of the Factors Act 1889, which departs from the Sale of Goods Act provision by extending the seller's power to the additional case where the delivery or transfer occurs 'under any *agreement for* sale, pledge, or other disposition' (emphasis added). The significance of this extension will be discussed below.

A general question arising under the relationship between the Factors and Sale of Goods Acts concerns the extent to which provisions in the Factors Act can also be read into the interpretation of the seller and buyer in possession exceptions to *nemo dat* in sections 24 to 25 of the Sale of Goods Act. Although 'the Factors Acts of 1889 and 1890 and the Sale of Goods Act 1893 must for many purposes be treated as one code',[398] it is

---

[395] *Johnson* v. *Crédit Lyonnais Co.* (1877) 3 CPD 32.   [396] S. 3.   [397] S. 8.
[398] *Worcester Works Finance Ltd* v. *Cooden Engineering Co. Ltd* [1972] 1 QB 210, 220.

not clear how far this treatment goes. The Factors Act definition of 'mercantile agent'[399] is repeated with more elaborate punctuation in section 26 of the Sale of Goods Act. Moreover, the definition of 'document of title' in the Sale of Goods Act[400] simply incorporates by reference the Factors Act definition of the same.[401] But there are other matters, such as the method of 'transfer' of documents of title, which are dealt with in the Factors Act[402] but not in the Sale of Goods Act. Furthermore, section 5 of the Factors Act requires consideration to support a sale, pledge, or disposition by a mercantile agent. It is not clear whether this is required also for pledges and dispositions under section 24 of the Sale of Goods Act.

A similar problem relates to the very interpretation of the seller and buyer in possession provisions of the Factors Act itself. To return to section 5, this is to be found in a part of the statute under the heading 'Dispositions by Mercantile Agents'; the seller and buyer in possession sections are contained in another part headed 'Dispositions by Sellers and Buyers of Goods'. This raises the question whether the need for consideration is to be read forward into sections 8 and 9 of the Factors Act, which do not deal with dispositions by mercantile agents. The opinion has been expressed that sections 8 and 9 are not to be read subject to definitional material in the earlier part of the Factors Act.[403] This is contentious, and will be discussed below.[404]

Disposing Power of Seller

The first requirement of section 24 is that the seller has already 'sold' the goods. If there has been merely an agreement to sell to a first buyer, the seller will be able to transmit his title to a second buyer in accordance with normal principles and there should be no need to invoke section 24. The second buyer would in these circumstances not have to comply with section 24 at all, though, if he took with notice that the seller was in breach of the agreement to sell to the first buyer, he might be held liable to the first buyer in the tort of interference with contractual relations. Certainly, if the seller made a gift of the goods to a donee who had no notice of an agreement to sell them, the first buyer could have no complaint against the donee since the seller at all material times had retained the property in the goods.

A more taxing question concerns the first buyer who has acquired an equitable property in or a charge on the goods. Atkin LJ in *Re Wait*[405] was prepared to allow the contracting parties to bargain for such rights,

---

[399] S. 1(1).   [400] S. 61(1).   [401] S. 1(4).   [402] S. 11.
[403] *Inglis* v. *Robertson* [1898] AC 616, 629–30.
[404] The Law Reform Committee in 1966, Cmnd. 2958, recommended without discussion the repeal of ss. 8–9 of the Factors Act.
[405] [1927] 1 Ch. 606.

though the House of Lords has interpreted *Re Wait* somewhat sweep-ingly as an outright denial of equitable proprietary principles in sales law.[406] Assuming that a buyer could acquire an equitable entitlement in goods later made the subject of a second sale, a second buyer for value without notice would override the first seller's equitable interest in any event, on general principles of equity without having to pray in aid sec-tion 24. Where general equitable principles and section 24 part com-pany, however, is in the statutory requirement that the second buyer take delivery of the goods. No such requirement is exacted in equity if a second purchaser of the legal estate is to override the equitable interest of an earlier purchaser.

Since section 24 requires that the seller has 'sold' the goods, it follows that the section will not govern if the first contract is a conditional sale agreement, for until the property passes to the buyer there is no sale.[407] But in *Vowles* v. *Island Finances Ltd*,[408] a car dealer agreed to sell a car on conditional sale terms and then assigned his interest in the car as well as the benefit of the agreement to the defendant finance company. Before the conditional buyer took delivery of the car, the dealer sold the car to the plaintiff, a *bona fide* cash-paying buyer, who did take delivery. While the conditional sale itself was not a sale, the court concluded that the assignment to the finance company amounted to a sale and in conse-quence the *bona fide* purchaser obtained a good title under section 24.

Chattel Mortgages

One question that cannot easily be answered is whether section 24 applies in the case of a seller who has borrowed money on the security of a mortgage of goods. A chattel mortgage is modelled on a sale of the goods by mortgagor to mortgagee, which sale is defeasible by a resolutive condition, namely payment in full of the sum owed.[409] On the face of it, the mortgagor retaining possession after executing a mortgage is a seller in possession. If this view is correct, it would balance the relationship between sections 24 and 25. A financier taking a mortgage interest in a seller's goods would be vulnerable under section 24 to dealings by the seller. If finance were advanced to a borrower on conditional sale terms, the financier would again be vulnerable, but this time under section 25, since the borrower is a buyer in possession.[410] If *bona fide* purchasers dealing with commercial sellers are, as a class, deserving of protection,

---

[406] *Leigh and Sillavan Ltd* v. *Aliakmon Shipping Co. Ltd* [1986] AC 785.
[407] S. 2(4).   [408] [1940] 4 DLR 357.   [409] *Keith* v. *Burrows* (1876) 1 CPD 722.
[410] S. 25(2)(b) excludes from the scope of the section only those conditional sale con-tracts that pass the test of a consumer credit agreement laid down in the Consumer Credit Act 1974, s. 8. It does not exclude commercial contracts of the type under discussion.

they should not be prejudiced by the fact that the seller's goods are financed on mortgage as opposed to conditional sale terms.

An argument against applying section 24 in the case of chattel mortgages arises from section 62(4) of the Sale of Goods Act: 'The provisions of this Act about contracts of sale do not apply to a transaction in the form of a contract of sale which is intended to operate by way of mortgage, pledge, charge, or other security.' On the face of this, chattel mortgages are therefore excluded from section 24. Charges are certainly excluded since they are not modelled on a sale; indeed, the chargor merely encumbers assets without conveying a property interest to the chargee.[411] If mortgages, however, were to be excluded from section 24, it would have been much easier and more natural to provide that the Act *simpliciter*, rather than its contract of sale provisions, does not apply to them. Section 62(4) can be given a coherent meaning if it is read so as to exclude two-party sales issues flowing from the beneficial and absolute passing of property and delivery from seller to buyer. There seems little reason to extend to chattel mortgagees rights concerning the delivery of the goods and their quality characteristics when the goods are never delivered to the mortgagee and the expectation of the parties is that the security will eventually be lifted. On this reading, section 62(4) could be denied application to three-party title problems. Indeed, the *nemo dat* provisions are not naturally housed in a sale of goods statute and could just as easily have been made the subject of a special title transfer statute. Moreover, there is no equivalent to section 62(4) in the Factors Act and therefore nothing to inhibit a straightforward interpretation of section 8, the equivalent of section 24 of the Sale of Goods Act.

The cases do not reveal a concern with the above problem and the reason is not difficult to find. Section 24 could serve a practical purpose only in the case of goods subject to a fixed legal mortgage, for reasons stated above. The law does not recognize mortgages and fixed charges over stock-in-trade in so far as they leave the company free, as for practical reasons they must, to dispose of stock beneficially in the ordinary course of its business.[412] A live problem would present itself if the seller were seeking to dispose of equipment the subject of a legal mortgage. For reasons stated above, it is submitted that a sale of such equipment to a *bona fide* buyer should fall within section 24.

---

[411] *Re Bond Worth Ltd* [1980] Ch. 228; *Carreras Rothmans Ltd* v. *Freeman Mathews Treasure Ltd* [1985] Ch. 207.

[412] The security would be recognized as a floating charge instead. See *Re Yorkshire Woolcombers Association Ltd* [1903] 2 Ch. 284, affd. *sub nom. Illingworth* v. *Houldsworth* [1904] AC 355; *Re Bond Worth Ltd*, n. 411 above. In Canada, mortgages and fixed charges will be recognized as such despite the freedom given to the company to deal with the assets so encumbered in the ordinary course of business: *Dedrick* v. *Ashdown* (1888) 15 SCR 227; *Meen* v. *Realty Development Co. Ltd* [1954] 1 DLR 649.

Constructive Possession

The requirement in section 24 that the seller be in possession of the goods or documents of title will normally be satisfied by the seller having actual possession. Some difficulty arises where the seller's possession is constructive,[413] a bailee holding the goods on his behalf. The purpose behind section 8 of the Factors Act 1889 was to extend the protection, given already in the case of mercantile agents in possession, accorded to *bona fide* purchasers relying on the semblance of ownership or authority reflected by other cases of possession. Like other *nemo dat* exceptions, the seller in possession rule cannot systematically be rationalized in terms of authority or ownership because it may be a matter of pure accident that the *bona fide* purchaser turns out to have been dealing with a seller in possession; the purchaser may have no idea of the seller's identity, so that the latter's power under section 24 may be better explained as stemming from status rather than appearances. But if, given the origin of section 24, sense has to be made as much as possible of its appearances pedigree, it is not easy to see why it should be extended beyond cases where the seller is in actual possession of goods or documents of title. In *Pacific Motor Auctions Pty. Ltd* v. *Motor Credit (Hire Finance) Ltd*,[414] Lord Pearson said: 'The object of the section is to protect an innocent purchaser who is deceived by the vendor's physical possession of goods or documents and who is inevitably unaware of legal rights which fetter the apparent power to dispose.' It must also be remembered that actual possession of documents of title is constructive possession of the underlying goods and that the breadth of the definition of documents of title in sale of goods and factors legislation ensures relatively few cases in which constructive possession through a bailee is evidenced without a document of title.

Be that as it may, section 1(2) of the Factors Act states: 'A person shall be deemed to be in possession of goods or of the documents of title to goods, where the goods or documents are in his actual custody or are held by any other person subject to his control or for him on his behalf.' This provision certainly has a bearing on the interpretation of the seller in possession provision in section 8 since it is contained in a part of the Act headed 'Preliminary', which qualifies the balance of the Act and not just the following part only, which deals with dispositions by mercantile agents. It would be perverse to deny the same interpretation to section 24 of the Sale of Goods Act just because it is not qualified by section 1(2). Sections 8 of the Factors Act and 24 of the Sale of Goods Act would therefore seem to apply where, for example, a seller bails goods to a bailee even without receiving a delivery warrant or an acceptance of a delivery

---

[413] Ch. 6 above.   [414] [1965] AC 867, 886.

order. In *City Fur Manufacturing Co. Ltd* v. *Fureenbond (Brokers) London Ltd*,[415] the owner of certain furs stored in a warehouse sold them to the plaintiffs, promising the latter to apply a portion of the price to the outstanding storage charges and to give them a delivery order. Subsequently, the owner pledged the furs with the defendants for the amount of the storage charges, the defendants drawing a cheque for this amount in favour of the warehouseman and taking physical delivery of the furs. Though the owner was not in actual possession of the goods or the documents of title, the court still held that he was a seller in possession and that possession was to be interpreted in the wide, constructive sense allowed for in section 1(2). More difficult is the case of a bailee who has undertaken to a previous owner to surrender the goods to the seller but, though disposed to deliver the goods to or at the request of the seller, has not given a binding commitment to this effect to the seller. Even this case would appear to fall within the words 'on his behalf' in section 1(2), which, if literally interpreted, is not concerned with the question whether the bailee will respond to the seller's demands.

Quality of Seller's Possession

Although section 24 applies where the seller 'continues or is in possession'[416] of the contract goods or documents of title, it makes no reference to the capacity in which the seller holds them, and, in particular, does not provide that the seller shall hold them as seller instead of, for example, as bailee. The earlier cases carried over from the law on mercantile agency a capacity restriction argument, despite the merely incidental reference to mercantile agency in section 24,[417] and held that the seller should hold *qua* seller.[418] Thus in *Staffs Motor Guarantee Ltd* v. *British Wagon Co. Ltd*,[419] where a motor vehicle dealer raised finance on the security of a lorry by selling it to a finance company and hiring it back on hire purchase terms, the lorry remaining at all times in the dealer's possession. The lorry was later sold fraudulently by the dealer to a *bona fide* purchaser and the court held that the dealer's possession of the lorry was referable to his status as hire purchase bailee rather than as seller.

---

[415] [1937] 1 All ER 799.

[416] The court in *Mercantile Credit Ltd* v. *F. C. Upton & Sons Pty. Ltd* (1974) 48 ALJR 301 held the seller was in sole possession even though the assignee of the buyer's rights had a registered office on the same premises as the seller.

[417] See the respondent's unsuccessful argument in *Pacific Motor Auctions Pty. Ltd* v. *Motor Credit (Hire Finance) Ltd*, n. 414 above.

[418] *Mitchell* v. *Jones* (1905) 24 NZLR 932; *Staffs Motor Guarantee Ltd* v. *British Wagon Co. Ltd* [1934] 2 KB 305; *Olds Discount Co. Ltd* v. *Krett* [1940] 2 KB 117; *Eastern Distributors Ltd* v. *Goldring* [1957] 2 QB 600. The issue did not have to be decided in *Union Transport Finance Ltd* v. *Ballardie* [1937] 1 KB 510, where the dealer retained possession of the car but never attorned to the finance company so as to assume the character of bailee.

[419] N. 418 above.

Consequently, the dealer was unable to pass title to the purchaser. Similarly, in *Ahrens Ltd* v. *George Cohen, Sons & Co. Ltd*,[420] manufacturing sellers produced a number of masters for sound recordings, at the behest of a buyer, and further undertook from time to time to press sound recordings from these masters. The property in the masters passed under the contract to the buyer. Subsequently, the sellers mortgaged their property and assets in favour of a bank and the question arose whether the bank's title overrode that of the buyer under section 24. The court interpreted the mortgage as confined in its sweep to the manufacturers' own assets, but went on to state that, in view of the sellers' manufacturing responsibilities, their continuing possession was not referable to the contract of sale and section 24 therefore did not apply in any event.

These prior authorities were convincingly set aside by the Privy Council in what is now the leading case on section 24, *Pacific Motor Auctions Pty. Ltd* v. *Motor Credits (Hire Finance) Ltd*.[421] In that case, a car dealer entered into a finance agreement in the form of a 'floor plan' with the respondent finance company. Under the terms of this agreement, the finance company was to acquire title to the cars in return for paying the dealer 90 per cent of the price the latter paid its supplier for the cars. Title to the cars would be reconveyed to the dealer on payment back of the 90 per cent advance, together with interest, from the proceeds of sale of the cars to the dealer's customers.[422] Until delivery of these cars to the customers in the dealer's name, the cars remained at all material times in the dealer's possession. Because of the dealer's financial troubles, the respondent withdrew its licence to deal in the cars covered by the 'floor plan'. Subsequently, the dealer sold a number of these cars to another dealer, the appellant company. As the appellant was a creditor of the dealer, the appellant's cheque was endorsed by the dealer in favour of the appellant; the appellant and dealer agreed that the cars in question should be sold back to the dealer if and when the dealer discharged its indebtedness to the appellant.

It was the respondent's contention, *inter alia*, that the dealer was in possession of the cars covered by the 'floor plan' as bailee rather than as seller in possession, but this was rejected by the Privy Council. Counsel for the appellant put this point most neatly in asserting that 'possession' should be viewed in the same manner in which the courts approach an estoppel question, that is to say, by looking at outward appearance rather than the inner fact.[423] Indeed, section 24 was regarded by the Privy Council as extending to purchasers the limited protection afforded by the doctrine of estoppel. It was the Privy Council's view that no decided

---

[420] (1934) 50 TLR 411.   [421] N. 414 above.
[422] Very similar to mortgage financing.   [423] N. 414 above, 876.

case had squarely raised the question of an attornment to the buyer by the seller in possession as bailee so as to change the status of the seller to that of bailee.[424] Since the purpose of section 24 was 'to protect an innocent purchaser who is deceived by the vendor's physical possession of goods or documents and who is inevitably unaware of legal rights which fetter the apparent power to dispose',[425] it should not be restricted in the way contended for by the respondent.[426] In addition, the early confinement of the seller in possession provision to documents of title[427] suggested a straightforward interpretation of section 24 which did not look to the character of possession, since it was not easy to see how this character could change with regard to documents of title. Furthermore the provision of the Factors Act presumptively deeming custody of goods or documents to be possession[428] told also against the respondent's contention.

Another problem dealt with in the *Pacific Motor Auctions* case concerned the continuity of the dealer's possession. Section 24 refers to instances where the seller 'continues or is in possession of the goods'. At first glance, the provision would seem to apply whenever the seller acquires possession, demanding only a unity of two things, namely the seller's identity as someone who has previously sold the goods and his possession of the goods or documents of title. This interpretation would therefore permit the application of section 24 regardless of a break in the continuity of the seller's possession; it should not matter, either, if the seller subsequently recovers possession from someone who did not buy the goods from him, such as a buyer further down the title chain or even a thief. Circumstances in which a seller might conceivably resume an interrupted possession include the following. Goods are redelivered for warehousing to a seller by a finance company repossessing them from a defaulting instalment purchaser.[429] Again, a cash or finance buyer of a car may take it for repairs or servicing into the garage side of the seller's business. While it may no longer be relevant to ask in what capacity the seller receives back the goods, the question that is squarely presented is whether the above illustrations come within the mischief of section 24. It is no help in resolving this question that section 24 has exceeded the scope of estoppel principles so as to take on the characteristics of a provision that depends on the status of the person making the second sale, pledge or other disposition.

[424] *Ibid.* 885.   [425] *Ibid.* 886.

[426] See also *Worcester Works Finance Ltd* v. *Cooden Engineering Co. Ltd* [1972] 1 QB 210; *Mercantile Credits Ltd* v. *F. C. Upton & Sons Pty. Ltd*, n. 416 above. The Privy Council in *Pacific Motor Auctions*, n. 414 above, 888–9, also concluded that the respondent's contention failed *in limine* since the seller retained possession of the car *qua* seller.

[427] S. 3 of the 1877 Act.   [428] S. 1(2).

[429] *Olds Discount Co. Ltd* v. *Krett*, n. 418 above.

In *Mitchell* v. *Jones*,[430] a New Zealand court concluded that, when the seller delivered the goods to the buyer, 'the relationship of buyer and seller between them was at an end'.[431] One might respond to this that the buyer would be quick enough to call on the seller *qua* seller if he wished to assert a warranty claim and return the goods for the requisite repairs or adjustment. The Privy Council in *Pacific Motor Auctions* held nevertheless that *Mitchell* v. *Jones* was correctly decided on this point. In *Mitchell* v. *Jones*, the court observed that the words 'or is in possession' in section 24 countenanced a case where the seller was not in possession of the goods at the time of the sale but subsequently acquired them.[432] This was said in *Pacific Motor Auctions* to be 'plainly right'[433] and nothing further was said on the subject. Nevertheless, it will be relatively rare for seller and first buyer to agree on the passing of property to goods not yet in the seller's possession; the above interpretation seems therefore somewhat strained. On the other hand, some of the more extreme hypotheses concerning the circumstances in which a seller resumes possession argue a need to limit a literal application of section 24. It is noteworthy that section 24 makes no explicit reference to the first buyer's consent to the seller's possession[434] and so, for example, would not appear to require discussion of the authorities dealing with larceny by a trick.

It might well, however, be sensible to permit broken possession to lead to a disposing power under section 24 if this were linked to the idea that certain buyers appreciate more than others the risks of a seller resuming possession. This would apply more to finance companies turning over repossessed goods to a former seller than, for example, to a consumer buyer taking in his car a year later for warranty work or servicing. The one should be aware of the risk while the other might be justifiably ignorant. The claims of a *bona fide* purchaser seem to have some considerable force against the former, and rather less against the latter. In *Pacific Motor Auctions*, the court itself rejected the contention that the seller should be treated as though he were a mercantile agent, but to deny the application of section 24 where a seller resumes possession of repossessed goods is tantamount to requiring the seller to receive them *qua* mercantile agent, as is the case with section 2(1) of the Factors Act.

Despite the considerable authority of the Privy Council, it is therefore submitted that, in cases of broken possession, the character of the seller *qua* seller should play a relevant part. Though the line is not easy to draw, it is submitted that a seller should continue to have disposing power

---

[430] N. 418 above.   [431] *Ibid.* 935.
[432] See also *Worcester Works Finance*, n. 426 above; *Bradshaw* v. *Epp* [1937] 4 DLR 746, 752–3.
[433] N. 414 above, 885.   [434] See *Worcester Works Finance*, n. 426 above.

when it is by virtue of the original sale relationship that he resumes possession.[435] This would be so when an original seller is obliged under the terms of a recourse or similar arrangement with a finance company to assist in the storage or sale or repossession of goods the subject of an agreement on which there has been a default. It would not be so where a buyer adventitiously takes a car for servicing to the garage from which he bought it. More difficult is the case of a consumer buyer taking a car in for warranty repairs, whether by virtue of his Sale of Goods Act rights or by virtue of an extended express warranty given by the manufacturer. This last instance might sensibly be read out of section 24, but the difficulty of doing so with the buyer whose car needs servicing illustrates the agony of the *nemo dat* rule and its exceptions in tight circumstances. If only because of the ignorance of the risk of the consumer buyer in the former instance, it is submitted that section 24 should be interpreted in his favour; careful law reform seems, however, a better alternative. A final argument in favour of extending section 24 to at least some broken possession cases is that the purpose of the provision could easily be frustrated by an almost symbolic possession taken, for example, by the first buyer, a finance company under a stocking plan of the type in *Pacific Motors*, which sends one of its representatives down from time to time to drive cars around the block.

Delivery and Transfer

Another issue raised by section 24 concerns the meaning of 'the delivery or transfer . . . of the goods or documents of title'. At first sight, it might seem that 'delivery' and 'transfer' both equally refer to 'goods' and 'documents of title'. On this interpretation, bearer documents, for example, might be delivered and goods might be transferred by the seller in possession under the second transaction. If this were so, a seller in possession might effectively 'transfer' goods to a second buyer without actually delivering them. The law, however, has read 'transfer' as exclusively referable to 'documents of title' and 'delivery' to 'goods'.[436] In consequence, the second buyer must take delivery if he is to override the title of the first buyer in a case not involving documents of title.[437] The opposite result would not be impracticable since a second buyer who does not take delivery would be vulnerable to a third buyer and so on.

The effect of section 11 of the Factors Act is that documents of title are transferred by delivery in the case of bearer documents and documents

[435] See the similar buyer in possession argument in *Langmead* v. *Thyer Rubber Co. Ltd* [1947] SASR 29.

[436] *Nicholson* v. *Harper* [1895] 2 Ch. 415, 418.

[437] *Kitto* v. *Bilbie, Hobson & Co.* (1895) 72 LT 266 (assignment alone insufficient). See also *Bank of New South Wales* v. *Palmer* [1970] 2 NSWLR 532; *NZ Securities & Finance Ltd* v. *Wrightcars Ltd* [1976] 1 NZLR 77.

indorsed in blank by a named consignee, or by indorsement to a named transferee. Where indorsement occurs, the better view is that a transfer would be completed only when the bill of lading is also delivered to the indorsee.[438] Apart from this detail, section 11 restates the common law. In the case of delivery of goods, the question is whether constructive delivery is permitted. Although it could be invoked in aid of interpreting section 8 of the Factors Act,[439] while section 1(2) states that constructive possession is tantamount to actual possession, it does not refer to delivery as such. The older view is that section 24 requires the second buyer to take actual possession. In *Nicholson* v. *Harper*,[440] the second transaction was a pledge of the goods to a warehouseman who at all times had been in possession of the goods anyway. Even assuming that he could have attorned to himself as the new bailor so as to effect a constructive delivery, the court held that section 24 was not satisfied.[441]

The same result was reached in *Bank of New South Wales* v. *Palmer*,[442] where the property in a boat had passed to the buyer at the relevant stages in its construction before the boat-builder mortgaged it in favour of a bank. Since physical possession had never been transferred to the bank, the court ruled in favour of the buyer. Nor would a seizure of the goods have helped the bank's cause, since delivery is defined in the Sale of Goods Act as 'the voluntary transfer of possession from one person to another'.[443] A delayed voluntary transfer of the goods to the bank ought to enable it to override the interest of the first buyer, for section 24 requires delivery to take place 'under' the sale, pledge, or other disposition, and not necessarily at the same time.

The above section 24 cases, however, have now been undermined by a number of decisions under section 25(1) recognizing that delivery can occur by constructive means. These decisions will be examined below. Since in this respect no distinction is to be drawn between sections 24 and 25(1), the section 24 cases discussed above cannot safely be treated as authoritative on the modern approach to this issue. This assumption, that delivery may occur by constructive means, is helpful in dealing with a problem concerning the transfer of documents of title. Suppose that a seller in possession of goods issues a document of title, for example a

[438] *Sanders* v. *Maclean* (1883) 11 QBD 327 (Bowen LJ).

[439] And not the almost identical s. 24 of the Sale of Goods Act.

[440] N. 436 above, followed in *New Zealand Securities & Finance Ltd* v. *Wrightcars Ltd*, n. 437 above.

[441] The case has been explained as merely holding that a delivery is required in addition to a sale etc: *Gamer's Motor Centre (Newcastle) Pty. Ltd* v. *Natwest Wholesale Australia Pty. Ltd* (1987) 163 CLR 236, 249 (Mason CJ); *Forsyth International (UK) Ltd* v. *Silver Shipping Co. Ltd* [1994] 1 WLR 1334, 1345.

[442] N. 437 above.

[443] See also *Forsyth International (UK) Ltd* v. *Silver Shipping Co. Ltd*, n. 441 above.

delivery warrant, to a second buyer. The goods themselves are not physically delivered; nor is a document of title transferred. Although 'transfer' has been given a loose interpretation, so as to be satisfied where a buyer in possession of a delivery order issued a fresh delivery order to the subbuyer,[444] it could not confidently be predicted that the case mentioned above of the seller issuing a delivery warrant would be treated as a case of transfer. It would therefore be better to find that the seller accepting the status of bailee has constructively delivered the goods.

The Sale of Goods (Amendment) Act 1995

This conclusion leads in to a series of problems arising under the Sale of Goods (Amendment) Act 1995.[445] Suppose that a seller in possession of a bulk has succeeded in passing to a number of prepaying buyers an undivided share in the contract bulk in such a way as to account for the whole bulk. Subsequently, that seller wrongfully sells a portion of the bulk to a later buyer. This gives rise to a number of difficulties. First, if the seller were to issue a document of title to that later buyer so as to effect a constructive delivery, the principle of deemed consent to removals from the bulk in the 1995 Act seems not to extend to such cases of 'over-sales'.[446] The Law Commission was of the view, however, that the later buyer would acquire property rights with the assistance of section 24.[447] Yet it has to be demonstrated that a seller who has succeeded in transferring an undivided interest to earlier buyers has 'sold' goods according to section 24. The definition of 'goods' may have been extended to include an undivided share in goods[448] but nothing has been done to change the definition of 'sale' in the Sale of Goods Act, which requires the transfer of the general property.[449] It would be strange if the buyer obtaining an undivided share were less vulnerable to section 24 than a buyer of ascertained goods who has left the seller in possession. It is submitted therefore that the outright transfer of an undivided share should be seen as the transfer of the general property in that undivided share so as to render applicable section 24. A later buyer receiving the goods themselves rather than a document of title would be in the same position but would

---

[444] *D. F. Mount Ltd* v. *Jay & Jay (Provisions) Ltd* [1960] 1 QB 159, discussed Ch. 10 below.

[445] Discussed Ch. 3 above. References to this Act below will be to the provisions that it introduces into the Sale of Goods Act 1979.

[446] Law Com. No. 215, para. 4.18. Although the deemed consent applies to 'any delivery' to 'any other owner in common of the bulk' (s. 20B(1)(a)), it appears to be confined to owners who acquire rights under s. 20A, a passing-of-property rather than a transfer-of-title provision.

[447] *Ibid.* See R. Bradgate and F. White [1994] *LMCLQ* 315, 321, for criticism of the Law Commission's assumption that problems of this nature can be dealt with routinely under s. 24.

[448] S. 61(1).   [449] S. 2(4)–(6).

not have to deal with issues of constructive delivery and the transfer of documents.

A second group of problems arises out of the rights that a later buyer, obtaining a document of title rather than the goods themselves, acquires at the expense of the earlier co-owning buyers. The Law Commission seems to believe that the later buyer simply joins earlier buyers as a rateable owner of the bulk in the following way.[450] Assuming two earlier buyers have each acquired an entitlement to 30,000 tonnes from a 60,000 tonne bulk, before the seller unlawfully sells 30,000 tonnes in the same bulk to a later buyer, then all three buyers would each have a 20,000 tonne entitlement in the bulk. Now, this offends a principle of title transfer law, which is that losses caused by a rogue are not simply divided between owner and innocent third party.[451] Section 24, which cannot just be impressionistically combined with the 1995 Act as the Law Commission would want, grants rights to the later buyer at the expense of earlier buyers. Consequently, the later buyer should have a 30,000 tonne entitlement and the earlier buyers, whose shares will have commensurately abated, 15,000 tonnes each.[452]

The next issue concerns later shrinkage in the bulk. Unless and until that later buyer's goods have been separated from the bulk, it is submitted that the later buyer's interest amounts to an undivided share of the bulk and is therefore liable to be abated in the usual rateable way. But is that later buyer also vulnerable to removals from the bulk by those co-owners whose shares were earlier reduced by the unlawful sale? Could one of the earlier buyers recover from the bulk his full 30,000 tonnes before the unlawful sale later comes to light, at the expense not only of his co-owner at the time but also of the later buyer? If this were allowed, the effect of the section 24 transaction would be reversed as regards that earlier buyer. The rule of consent to removals from the bulk applies in respect of buyers who obtain an undivided share in the bulk 'by virtue of section 20A'.[453] The difficulty is that the later buyer's rights arise by virtue of section 24 of the Sale of Goods Act, a title transfer provision, together with antecedent case law authority by which the non-ascertainment of goods is no bar to the acquisition of rights by third parties under the transfer of title provisions of the Sale of Goods Act.[454] They do not arise by virtue of section 20A, a passing of property provision. If the later

---

[450] Law Com. No. 215, para. 4.18.

[451] See discussion in the text accompanying nn. 170–1 above.

[452] If it looks perverse to give the later buyer greater rights than the earlier ones, this is consistent with general principles of title transfer dealt with in this Ch.

[453] S. 20B(1).

[454] *Ant Jurgens Margarine-Fabrieken* v. *Louis Dreyfus & Co.* [1914] 3 KB 40; *Capital and Counties Bank Ltd* v. *Warriner* (1896) 12 TLR 216. Discussed in the text accompanying nn. 514–15 below.

buyer's rights are not liable to be defeated by removals from the bulk, however, this gives rise to difficult accounting exercises where multiple dealings occur in a bulk, and is at odds with the evident policy in the 1995 Act of avoiding complex accounting exercises of this nature. But the current statutory provision is not apt to avoid this result.

There also has to be considered the position of the sub-buyer to whom, for example, a co-owning buyer has transferred a delivery warrant issued by the seller. This case is covered by section 20B(1)(b), which provides that the other co-owners are deemed to consent to 'any dealing with or removal or disposal of goods in the bulk' by a co-owning buyer 'in so far as the goods fall within that co-owning owner's undivided share in the bulk'. If shrinkage has already occurred in the bulk before the transfer of the warrant, then the buyer's share will have been reduced and the other co-owning buyers' consent will be limited to that reduced share. There does not appear to be a *nemo dat* exception protecting the sub-buyer from shrinkage. As regards the other co-owning buyers, the buyer is not a seller in possession under section 24 or a buyer in possession under section 25(1). But if the original seller retains a share in the undivided bulk, then the transaction entered into by the buyer could, pursuant to section 25(1), give the sub-buyer protection against shrinkage at the original seller's expense.

A final point concerning the 1995 Act is that the deemed consent of co-owning buyers to removals from the bulk under section 20B(1)(a) appears not to be qualified by notice or good faith requirements. If this is correct, then an unusual exception to the rule of *nemo dat* has been created. A buyer who learns of a shrinkage in the bulk, perhaps of an unlawful sale of an undivided share to a later buyer, has a positive incentive to race to the warehouse and claim his full contractual share.[455] It is more than possible that this apparent departure from basic principle will be trimmed down by restrictive interpretation. It is more than possible, too, that the 1995 Act will give rise to real problems in the years ahead. It was passed with the laudable intention of solving a problem that was a real impediment to international trade in commodities, but an *ad hoc* reform of this nature, bolted on to the Sale of Goods Act, is no substitute for a root-and-branch review of the whole law of passing of property and title transfer.

Dispositions

The transaction entered into by the seller in possession must be a 'sale, pledge or other disposition' if it is to override the first buyer's title to the goods. 'Sale' has the meaning ordinarily given to it in the Sale of Goods

---

[455] Cf. *Barber* v. *Meyerstein* (1870) LR 4 HL 317.

Act and cannot therefore extend to an agreement to sell,[456] such as a conditional sale where instalments remain outstanding. *A fortiori*, a hire purchase agreement is not caught by 'sale' since the bailee never undertakes that he will exercise the option to purchase.[457] When the hire purchase and the conditional sale agreements are fully executed so that a sale is consummated,[458] it still could not be said that the delivery of the goods took place 'under a sale' since in fact it occurred with a view to a future agreed or potential sale. But it is a different question whether transactions like these are covered by 'disposition'.

'Pledge' in s. 25(1) has the meaning ordinarily given to it in personal property law.[459] Delivery under an agreement to pledge would therefore not qualify, though, like an executory sale, it is appropriate to consider whether it is a 'disposition'. One problem concerning the meaning of 'disposition' is whether it catches an outright gift. On the face of it section 24 does not require the disponee to have furnished any consideration but, given the almost grudging nature of the legislative response to the rigours imposed by the *nemo dat* rule, it would be curiously generous to gratuitous disponees to allow them to take the goods clear of the first buyer's title. In the Factors Act, as was observed above, section 5 requires the presence of consideration for the 'validity of a sale, pledge, or other disposition'. This clearly bears upon section 2(1) of the Factors Act since that provision and section 5 are contained in a part of the Act headed 'Dispositions by Mercantile Agents'. It has been stated that this part of the Act should be read independently of those sections in the United Kingdom Act headed 'Dispositions by Buyers and Sellers of Goods'.[460] This view is more troublesome in the case of section 24, since section 25, as we shall see, has been interpreted as requiring the incorporation by reference of the provisions relating to mercantile agents. It is submitted that, regardless of whether section 5 of the Factors Act may be relied upon to assist in the interpretation of section 24 of the Sale of Goods Act,[461] an *eiusdem generis* reading of 'sale, pledge or other disposition' should require consideration to be present for a disposition, as it clearly has to be in the case of sale and pledge because of their very nature.[462]

The meaning of 'disposition' was considered at some length in

---

[456] S. 2(4),(5).

[457] *Lee* v. *Butler* [1893] 2 QB 318; *Helby* v. *Matthews* [1895] AC 471; *Belsize Motor Supply Co.* v. *Cox* [1914] 1 KB 244.

[458] S. 2(6).

[459] M. G. Bridge, *Personal Property Law* (Blackstone, London, 1993), 137–40.

[460] *Inglis* v. *Robertson* [1898] AC 616, 629–30 (Lord Herschell).

[461] See *Worcester Works Finance Ltd* v. *Cooden Engineering Co. Ltd* [1972] 1 QB 210, 220 (Megaw LJ: the provisions of factors and sale of goods legislation to be read 'for many purposes . . . as one code').

[462] *Contra* A. D. Preston (1972) 88 *LQR* 239, 243, relying upon *Kitto* v. *Bilbie, Hobson & Co.* (1895) 72 LT 266.

Worcester Works Finance Ltd v. *Cooden Engineering Co. Ltd.*[463] The respondents owned a car which they sold to Griffiths, who paid for it with a cheque that was dishonoured on each of the three occasions the respondents presented it to the bank. Meanwhile, Griffiths used the car to set up a sham hire purchase transaction with the innocent appellants and a bailee, his confederate Millerick, who signed a delivery receipt but never took delivery of the car from Griffiths. The sham transaction involved a purported sale of the goods to the appellants. Later, the respondents repossessed the car, which was still in Griffiths' possession, apparently with his consent.[464] Griffiths kept up in Millerick's name the payment of the instalments to the appellants, and then stopped payments leaving the appellants and respondents to dispute title to the car. The Court of Appeal held that there had been a 'disposition' by Griffiths, the seller in possession *qua* the appellants, back to the respondents, the original sellers. Lord Denning thought that 'disposition' was 'a very wide word' capable of extending 'to all acts by which a new interest (legal or equitable) in the property is effectually created'.[465] This is plainly too wide, for it would allow a subsequent equitable interest to override a prior legal interest,[466] hardly the result that any court should strive for when legislation does not compel it. Megaw LJ asserted that a disposition had occurred in the present case, for what was required was 'some transfer of an interest in property, in the technical sense of the word "property" as contrasted with mere possession'.[467] Similarly, Phillimore LJ said that 'there must be some disposal of the goods which involved transfer of property'.[468]

The fortunate respondents in *Worcester Works* had the unwitting presence of mind to avoid two possible courses of action, either of which might have proved fatal to their claim under section 24. They might simply have repossessed without the knowledge, leave, or co-operation of Griffiths; there could not then have been a 'disposition' by Griffiths in the absence of some conscious act on his part.[469] The respondents might also have purported unilaterally to avoid the contract of sale, because of

[463] N. 461 above.   [464] *Ibid.* 219.

[465] *Ibid.* 218, quoting *Carter* v. *Carter* [1896] 1 Ch. 62, 67.

[466] Preston, n. 462 above, 244.

[467] N. 461 above, 220 (Megaw LJ). In a buyer-in-possession case, however, it was held that delivery to an auctioneer for the purpose of sale was a 'disposition': *Shenstone & Co.* v. *Hilton* [1894] 2 QB 52. This is plainly wrong and inconsistent with authorities decided under s. 2 of the Factors Act: *Waddington and Sons* v. *Neale and Sons* (1907) 96 LT 786; *Roache* v. *Australian Mercantile Land & Finance Co. Ltd* (1966) 67 SR(NSW) 54, 59 (something in the nature of a sale). See also the buyer in possession case of *Smith* v. *Campbell* (1911) 17 WLR 49 (Can.) (not delivery for storage to warehouse).

[468] N. 461 above, 219.

[469] Or even a 'delivery': see s. 61(1) and *Forsyth International (UK) Ltd* v. *Silver Shipping Co. Ltd* [1994] 1 WLR 1334.

the fraud of Griffiths, after the resale by Griffiths to the appellants.[470] This would have been ineffective under section 23 of the Sale of Goods Act, because his voidable title would already have been transmitted to the appellants. But it might have undermined any later disposition by Griffiths under section 24, because the purported avoidance would have destroyed whatever residual title to the goods that Griffiths might have had. How could Griffiths have transferred any property in the goods, to someone claiming their ownership, over and above possession of them in that event? Whatever puzzling difficulties might be posed in relation to the meaning of disposition in section 24, it is submitted that the word should catch delivery under an executory conditional sale or hire purchase agreement,[471] which compels or permits the eventual purchase of the goods. The buyer or bailee, having paid a deposit, acquires an interest in the goods transcending mere possession that is hard to rationalize in terms of legal and equitable interests but is recognized in various important ways.[472] The argument in favour of the second purchaser is even more clearly made, at least for conditional sales, by the extended language in section 8 of the Factors Act, which protects such a purchaser taking 'under *any agreement* for sale, pledge, or other disposition (emphasis added)'.

Effect of Section 24

Once the seller delivers goods under a sale, pledge, or other disposition, this transaction 'has the same effect as if the person making the delivery or transfer were expressly authorised by the owner of the goods to make the same'. In the case of delivery of goods, the argument has been advanced that section 24 amounts to rather less than an overriding of the first buyer's title for all that it does is to sanction the delivery by the seller in possession, and would therefore only protects the second buyer against a conversion action based on the receipt of (rather than the later refusal to deliver up) the goods.[473] Support for this view is said to lie in 3 of the Factors Act 1877, the forerunner of sections 8 of the Factors Act 1889 and 24 of the Sale of Goods Act. Section 3 only applied to transactions involving delivery of the goods or transfer of documents where the seller had been left in possession of the documents of title.[474] Moreover,

---

[470] At first blush, an avoidance of the contract of sale before the resale by Griffiths to the appellants would have been equally ineffective, for Griffiths would still have had the disposing power of a buyer in possession under s. 25(1) so long as he remained in actual possession. But Griffiths never in fact delivered the car to the appellants, and therefore a recovery of the goods by the respondents before such a delivery would have been effective. Had the appellants beaten the respondents to the goods in Griffiths's hands, and had obtained delivery from him, their title would then have been perfected under s. 25(1).

[471] See *Union Transport Finance Ltd* v. *Ballardie* [1937] 1 KB 510.

[472] Ch. 10 below.   [473] L. A. Rutherford and I. A. Todd [1979] CLJ 346.

[474] Note, not possession of the goods alone.

it provided that such delivery or transfer 'shall be as valid and effectual as if such a vendor or person were an agent or person entrusted with the goods or documents', a formula similar to the one that is present in section 25 (the buyer in possession exception) but not in section 24 of the Sale of Goods Act. Thus the argument is pressed that this evidences a legislative will to give inferior protection to persons taking delivery of goods from sellers left in possession of just the goods.[475]

The cases decided under section 24 are squarely against this view,[476] which, moreover, understates the difficulty of attaining precision in the drafting of legislation in this area. It is hard to see, too, why the legislature should ever have seen fit to confer such minimal protection on buyers from sellers in possession of goods. Moreover, the same heterodoxical argument could be made in the case of transfer of documents of title since their transfer will not necessarily pass the general property in the underlying goods. It depends on the intention of the transferor,[477] and a conservative reading of section 24 would not be satisfied with the provision's failure to state the deemed intention of the owner. In consequence, the argument makes internal linguistic sense but does not speak at all to the evolution of the *nemo dat* exceptions and does not come to terms with commercial reality.

The reference to the 'owner' in section 24 could be useful in solving one acute difficulty. Suppose a seller continues in possession of goods and, prior to his transfer to the second buyer, the first buyer assigns his interest in the contract goods to a sub-buyer. Does the title of the second buyer under section 24 override that of the sub-buyer? Another possibility is that the first buyer has granted a security over his future property in favour of a finance company, and this security attaches at the moment the property passes to the first buyer under the contract of sale. A decision in favour of the sub-buyer, it is submitted, would unduly shrink the protection given to those dealing with sellers in possession and would fail to meet the mischief of the section. The original seller continues in possession at all material times and the transfer to the second buyer is deemed by section 24 to occur with the consent, not of the first buyer, but of the 'owner'. There seems every reason to interpret this as the first buyer or the sub-buyer as the case may be.[478] Where the sub-buyer is a finance company claiming an interest under a future property clause, there is the added reason that its interest, springing on

---

[475] N. 473 above.
[476] See, e.g., *Pacific Motor Auctions Pty. Ltd* v. *Motor Credit (Hire Finance) Ltd* [1965] AC 867.
[477] *Sewell* v. *Burdick* (1884) 10 App. Cas. 74.
[478] A similar problem under s. 25(1) is discussed in the text accompanying nn. 506 ff. below.

attachment, is only an equitable one,[479] and therefore vulnerable to *bona fide* purchasers of the legal estate, who will not therefore need to invoke section 24.

Good Faith and Notice

Section 24 requires that the second buyer act in good faith and without notice, which has the same meaning here[480] as under section 2(1) of the Factors Act. There is, however, no requirement that the seller in possession act in the ordinary course of business; the behaviour of the seller in *Pacific Motor Auctions*[481] in indorsing back the second buyer's cheque is a graphic illustration of this.

The Buyer in Possession

Like the seller in possession section, the buyer in possession provision originated in the Factors Act 1877. The same difficulties arise with respect to parallel provisions in factors and sale-of-goods legislation and to the influence of the former legislation in interpreting the latter, though they are diminished significantly by the explicit incorporation of the mercantile agency standard in section 25(1). Case law decided before 1877 established that a buyer in possession could not without more ado be treated as a mercantile agent.[482] The present provision is section 25(1) of the Sale of Goods Act:

Where a person having bought or agreed to buy goods obtains, with the consent of the seller, possession of the goods or documents of title to the goods, the delivery or transfer by that person, or by a mercantile agent acting for him, of the goods or documents of title, under a sale, pledge, or other disposition thereof, to any person receiving the same in good faith and without notice of any lien or other right of the original seller in respect of the goods, has the same effect as if the person making the delivery or transfer were a mercantile agent in possession of the goods or documents of title with the consent of the owner.

A number of themes, such as the meaning of 'transfer' and 'disposition', are common to section 25(1) and will not be repeated. Notice and good faith have been considered in connection with section 2(1) of the Factors Act. A preliminary question is whether section 25[483] extends beyond sale of goods to catch work-and-materials contracts. Unlike other provisions of the Sale of Goods Act that operate as rules of presumed intention,

---

[479] *Holroyd* v. *Marshall* (1862) 10 HLC 191; *Tailby* v. *Official Receiver* (1888) 13 App. Cas. 523.

[480] *Worcester Works Finance Ltd*, n. 461 above.　　　　　　[481] N. 476 above.

[482] *Jenkyns* v. *Usborne* (1844) 7 M & G 678; *M'Ewan* v. *Smith* (1849) 2 HLC 309; *Cole* v. *North Western Bank* (1875) LR 10 CP 354.

[483] And s. 24, too, although the problem is more likely to arise under s. 25(1).

section 25(1), in common with other statutory exceptions to the *nemo dat* rule, does not codify contractual practice or pre-Act case law. There is authority which seems to exclude it from work and materials contracts,[484] although a plausible argument could be made that the materials under such a transaction are bought or agreed to be bought. Certainly, the mischief of section 25(1) could accommodate its extension to such transactions.[485] If the objection were taken that sections 24 to 25(1) of the Sale of Goods Act may only apply to sale of goods contracts as therein defined, the same cannot be said of their near-identical counterparts, sections 8 to 9 of the Factors Act.

'Bought or Agreed to Buy'

The first difficulty in section 25(1) concerns the meaning of 'bought or agreed to buy' goods. If the buyer has bought the goods so that the general property has vested in him, it is not clear why he should need to be empowered by section 25(1) to transmit title to a second buyer; he should be able to do that on normal title principles. Inserting a reference to 'bought' also raises the troublesome possibility that a second purchaser, apprised of a seller's complaint against the first buyer and therefore affected by notice of it, may be defeated in a title action brought by the seller, even though title would have otherwise passed down the chain according to normal principles. Nevertheless, some limited sense can be made of this provision. If there were any lingering belief that a seller terminating a contract for non-payment by the buyer in possession could revest the property in himself,[486] section 25(1) would come to the assistance of those dealing with the buyer in possession. Furthermore, section 25(1) might need to be understood in terms of the unpaid seller's lien.[487] Although at common law a possessory lien endures only as long as the lienholder retains possession, there is authority for the view that a temporary release of the goods on the agreed terms that the lien shall persist does not destroy a lien.[488] If this were so, it would serve to justify the ability of the buyer in possession to transmit a clear title to a second purchaser taking 'without notice of any lien' attaching to the goods in which the buyer has the general property.[489] Another instance in which

[484] *Dawber Williamson Roofing Ltd* v. *Humberside County Council* (1979) 14 *Build. LR* 70, 77.

[485] The contracts in the building cases of *Archivent Sales & Developments Ltd* v. *Strathclyde Regional Council* (1984) 27 *Build. LR* 98 and *W. Hanson (Harrow) Ltd* v. *Rapid Civil Engineering Ltd* (1987) 38 *Build. LR* 106 were sale of goods contracts.

[486] He cannot: *R. V. Ward Ltd* v. *Bignall* [1967] 1 QB 534.

[487] J. C. Smith (1963) 7 *JSPTL* 225.

[488] *Albemarle Supply Co. Ltd* v. *Hind* [1928] 1 KB 307. See also the trust receipt authorities (pledge surviving release of bill of lading).

[489] Conversely, the buyer to whom the property has passed in goods that are subject to a seller's lien, and who unlawfully removes them from the seller's possession, so that the

The Sale of Goods

the word 'bought' can be said to have a meaning concerns contracts of sale, under which the property has passed to the buyer, that are avoided for the buyer's fraud or misrepresentation. Section 23 of the Sale of Goods Act does not permit the transfer of a voidable title after the seller has publicized an intention to avoid the contract. In contrast, as will be seen below, the power of a buyer to transmit a voidable title under section 25(1) survives even a publicised avoidance of the contract by the seller.

The words 'agreed to buy' in section 25(1) catch the case of a conditional sale.[490] It also applies where the passing of property through a proffered bill of exchange is under section 19(3) conditional upon the buyer's acceptance of the bill.[491] Hire purchase is not included since the bailee does not agree to buy and may not exercise a unilateral option to purchase.[492] Receipt on sale or return on approval terms is also excluded since, again, the recipient has not agreed to buy and holds the goods as a bailee to whom an offer of sale has been addressed.[493]

Consent of the Seller

The buyer in possession must receive the goods or documents of title with the 'consent' of the seller. Larceny by a trick and its effect on consent arise in the same way as they do for mercantile agents and section 2(1) of the Factors Act, and the section 25(1) authorities go the same way.[494] In principle, the authorities on section 25(1) can, and should, take the same broad line as those under section 24 dealing with the question whether the buyer should be in possession of the goods *qua* buyer. In the nature of things, this issue is likely to arise less often in section 25(1), but it did arise in *Langmead* v. *Thyer Rubber Co. Ltd*.[495] In that case, the parties, after bargaining about the price of a car with or without a new coat of paint applied by the seller, agreed that the buyer should be allowed to take the car away to have it painted. The seller had refused to accept the buyer's cheque in payment and it seems that the parties

lien remains intact (see Ch. 10 below), will not be able to transfer title clear of this lien: the seller will not have consented to the buyer's possession.

[490] *Lee* v. *Butler* [1893] 2 QB 318; *General Motors Acceptance Corpn.* v. *Hubbard* (1978) 87 DLR (3d) 39. Cf. *Kozak* v. *Ford Motor Credit Co.* (1971) 18 DLR (3d) 735. Note that s. 25(2) excludes consumer conditional sales (as defined in s. 25(2)(b) and s. 8 of the Consumer Credit Act 1974) from the scope of s. 25(1).

[491] *Cahn* v. *Pockett's Bristol Channel Steam Packet Co. Ltd* [1899] 1 QB 643. See also *Marten* v. *Whale* [1917] 2 KB 480.

[492] *Helby* v. *Matthews* [1895] AC 471.

[493] *Percy Edwards Ltd* v. *Vaughan* (1910) 26 TLR 545.

[494] *Du Jardin* v. *Beadman Bros.* [1952] 2 QB 712; *Reed* v. *Motors Ltd* [1926] SASR 128. It should not matter that the contract is illegal (but see *Belvoir Finance Co. Ltd* v. *Harold G. Cole & Co. Ltd* [1969] 1 WLR 1877). It is also immaterial that the contract is unenforceable for want of compliance with the Consumer Credit Act 1974: *R.* v. *Modupe, The Times*, 27 Feb. 1991.

[495] [1947] SASR 29.

agreed to a presently binding contract of sale defeasible in the event of the buyer being unable to pay, in which event he was to be reimbursed by the seller for the cost of repainting the car. After the buyer had taken the car away, he sold it to a dealer who purchased it in good faith. The South Australian court held that the dealer was protected by section 25(1) on the ground that there had been some degree of causal connection between the buyer's possession and the contract of sale.[496] Thus, one of the judges doubted that section 25(1) would apply to possession given for a 'special and temporary purpose which cannot be related to the contractual intention'.[497] This is similar to the argument made above that section 24 should be applied to certain instances of broken possession by the seller.

Mercantile Agency and Buyer in Possession

Undoubtedly the most difficult issue arising out of section 25(1) concerns the comparison of the sale, pledge, or other disposition to that which would have been made by a mercantile agent in the same situation. The question is whether the buyer has to act in the way that a mercantile agent would have acted, so as to be empowered to transmit a good title to the second buyer, or whether it is sufficient that the buyer should act as a buyer in possession might act, in which case the law gives the same effect to the transaction of the buyer in possession as it gives to a transaction duly accomplished by a mercantile agent in possession.[498] The former view was taken by the Court of Appeal in *Newtons of Wembley Ltd* v. *Williams*,[499] where a dealer sold a car to a rogue, who paid for it with a cheque that was later dishonoured. Property was not to pass until the cheque had been cleared, but the dealer allowed the rogue to take the car away. The rogue sold the car in a London street market to a second buyer who in turn sold it to a third buyer, the present defendant. Before the rogue sold the car to the second buyer, the dealer had taken steps to avoid the contract,[500] so that the rogue was no longer empowered to pass his voidable title under section 23 of the Sale of Goods Act.

According to the court, the transaction between the rogue and the second buyer had to take place in the ordinary course of business of a mer-

---

[496] *Ibid.* 33–4, 41.

[497] *Ibid.* (Napier CJ, citing the case of the seller who allows the buyer to borrow his car in order to fetch a mechanic to the buyer's car, which has just broken down).

[498] See *Gamer's Motor Centre Pty. Ltd* v. *Natwest Wholesale Australia Pty. Ltd* (1987) 163 CLR 236, 259; *Langmead* v. *Thyer Rubber Co. Ltd*, n. 483 above, 39, where Reed J describes s. 25(1) as an 'as if' provision and so selects the second alternative. This view was also favoured in *Forsyth International (UK) Ltd* v. *Silver Shipping Co. Ltd* [1994] 1 WLR 1334, 1351, but the court was bound by the contrary decision in the *Newton's of Wembley* case, discussed in the text accompanying nn. 499 ff. below.

[499] [1965] 1 QB 560. See also *Kozak* v. *Ford Motor Credit Co*, n. 490 above.

[500] *Car and Universal Finance Co. Ltd* v. *Caldwell* [1965] 1 QB 525.

cantile agent if the second buyer, and through him the third buyer, were to be protected by section 25(1). The position was admittedly obscure, but in the opinion of the court no other solution was possible. Sellers LJ emphasized the need to avoid giving an expansive reading to section 25(1) since it abrogated in part the *nemo dat* rule which protects owner-ship.[501] Yet, it should not be forgotten that, as a result of the interpreta-tion of section 2(1) of the Factors Act, the test of the ordinary course of business of a mercantile agent is not at all demanding; it merely requires a general observance of business forms.[502] In consequence, the sale in the London street market was to be regarded as made in the ordinary course of business of a mercantile agent, since, though private sellers went there, it was also a place resorted to by dealers. It is only this laxity of practice that makes the court's invocation of section 2(1) either sensi-ble in determining the scope of section 25(1) or plausible in terms of statutory construction. Had the sale by the buyer in possession taken place away from trade premises, and the sale by the second to the third buyer occurred on trade premises, the result would have been quite dif-ferent, for the demands of section 25(1) are not met by behaviour *qua* a mercantile agent occurring further down the chain.

But it would be a mistake to take the decision in *Newtons of Wembley* completely at face value, for by invoking the mercantile agent test the court saved the day for the second and third buyers. An avoidance of the contract under section 23 of the Sale of Goods Act would have required that same behaviour by the dealer to have been treated as a determina-tion of its consent to the buyer retaining possession of the car. Bringing in the mercantile agent, however, served also to introduce section 2(2) of the Factors Act[503] by which the dealer's initial consent was deemed to continue until the first of alternative events occurred, namely the repos-session of the goods by the dealer or the receipt of notice by the second buyer of the revocation of consent. Neither of these events had occurred in *Newtons of Wembley* by the relevant date.[504] Far from being unfavourable to second buyers, *Newton's of Wembley* in fact gives their interests a boost at the expense of owners.

A–B–C–D Problem

A rather odd problem of interpretation that has emerged under section 25(1)[505] has been the subject of decision first in Canadian and New

---

[501] N. 499 above, 574. [502] *Oppenheimer* v. *Attenborough & Son* [1908] 1 KB 221.

[503] Reversing *Fuentes* v. *Montis* (1868) LR 3 CP 831.

[504] A Canadian court refused to follow *Newton's of Wembley* where there had been no publicized avoidance of the contract by the seller: *General Motors Acceptance Corpn. Ltd* v. *Hubbard*, n. 490 above.

[505] It could also arise under s. 24.

Zealand courts[506] and more recently in the House of Lords.[507] Section 25(1), having referred to the buyer obtaining possession with the consent of the 'seller', then makes the transaction entered into by the buyer turn upon the conduct of a hypothetical mercantile agent in possession with the consent of the 'owner'. Suppose that A, an owner, entrusts goods to B, not a mercantile agent, in circumstances that do not meet the requirements of apparent authority or ownership. B unlawfully sells the goods to C, who in turn resells them to D. Under ordinary *nemo dat* principles, C would be defeated in a title dispute with A. But an argument has been made that C is in possession with the consent of his seller, B, and that C's transaction with D is supported by the deemed consent of the owner, A, to C's possession of the goods. The argument in effect requires a separation of the persons of seller and owner in section 25(1) and, while linguistically ingenious, is quite at odds with *nemo dat* principles and with the way the law has developed in this area. The only *nemo dat* exception that is not concerned with the history of the first flawed transaction in a title chain was the now-repealed market overt rule, and the decisions rejecting the above argument are perfectly sound. Any other result would leave the *nemo dat* rule in shreds and reduce the owner's protection to a conversion action against the rogue and the first innocent purchaser in the chain.

In *National Employers Mutual General Insurance Association Ltd* v. *Jones*,[508] there was a lengthy title chain reducible to the above A–B–C–D model with a thief occupying the position of B. The owner succeeded by a majority in the Court of Appeal.[509] In the House of Lords, Lord Goff delivered the judgment of the court in favour of the owner, and demonstrated, through a review of the emergence of the exceptions to the *nemo dat* rule, especially the factors legislation, that the language of section 25(1) could not be given a literal meaning. The seller- and buyer-in-possession exceptions were added to that of the mercantile agent because sellers and buyers in possession could not be treated as mercantile agents,[510] and were not meant to usher in a change in policy of a

---

[506] *Brandon* v. *Leckie* (1972) 29 DLR (3d) 633; *Elwyn* v. *O'Regan* [1971] NZLR 1124; A. Zysblatt (1974) 9 *UBC LR* 186.

[507] *National Employers Mutual General Insurance Association Ltd* v. *Jones* [1990] 1 AC 24.

[508] N. 507 above.

[509] [1987] 3 All ER 385. Croom Johnson LJ, 399, asserted that s. 25(1) presupposed 'a valid transaction by or on behalf of the true owner at some stage'. May LJ, 396, was of the view that the general property should pass or purportedly pass from B to C which, since B was a thief, it could not. With respect, a thief surrendering the totality of his rights to a buyer is just as much transferring the general property as a true owner selling his goods. The title that the thief transfers, however, is a weak one, but that is a different matter.

[510] See the need for a mercantile agent to be in possession *qua* mercantile agent, discussed in the text accompanying nn. 301 ff. below.

fundamental kind.[511] One might add that Part III of the Hire Purchase Act 1964[512] would make little sense at all if the argument of the second buyer in *Jones* had been upheld.

Lien and Stoppage in Transitu

Besides parallel-buyer and seller-in-possession provisions in sale-of-goods and factors legislation, the same duplication occurs with provisons concerning the loss of the seller's lien and his right of stoppage *in transitu*.[513] This provision allows the above rights to be defeated once the buyer in possession of a document of title lawfully transfers it to a holder providing consideration. It therefore covers some common ground with section 25(1) of the Sale of Goods Act. The difficulties generated by these provisions will be dealt with in the next chapter, but two points may usefully be dealt with here. First, in relation to a document of title, whether it takes the form of a warrant issued by a warehouseman, or an order addressed by a seller to a warehouseman, there is a problem of compatibility between sections 25(1) and 47(2) of the Sale of Goods Act, on the one hand, and section 16 of the same Act, on the other. The question is whether the seller's rights may be defeated by a transfer of a document of title even though the goods that are subject to the document have not been separated from bulk and have not therefore been ascertained so as to permit the property to pass. Existing authority holds that the seller's rights can be defeated,[514] but is hard to justify on anything other than estoppel grounds. With the passing of the Sale of Goods (Amendment) Act 1995, further support for these decisions comes from the seller having an undivided interest by way of tenancy in common in a defined bulk of goods.[515] A sale of an undivided share in goods is now a sale of goods for the purposes of the Sale of Goods Act,[516] including sections 24 and 25(1).[517]

The second point, which may be taken solely as a section 25(1) point, concerns whether a buyer in possession of a bill of lading can be said to 'transfer' a delivery order that he issues under it in order to deal with a parcel of the underlying cargo, when he delivers the order to the subbuyer. It would be unduly technical to deny protection to the second buyer on these facts. Indeed, section 47, depriving the seller of his lien

[511] N. 507 above, 58–60, 62.
[512] Discussed in the text accompanying nn. 544 ff. below.
[513] S. 47 of the Sale of Goods Act and s. 10 of the Factors Act.
[514] *Ant Jurgens Margarine-Fabrieken* v. *Louis Dreyfus & Co.* [1914] 3 KB 40; *Capital and Counties Bank Ltd* v. *Warriner* (1896) 12 TLR 216. But see A. Nicol (1979) 42 *MLR* 129.
[515] See Ch. 3 above.
[516] S. 2(c) of the 1995 Act amending the definition of 'goods' in s. 61(1) of the Sale of Goods Act 1979.
[517] *Quaere* for the purposes of the Factors Act 1889?

where a document has been 'transferred' to a buyer in possession, has been applied to a seller issuing a delivery order to that buyer.[518] Similarly, a transfer has been held to occur when the seller issues a delivery order to a bailee who, on receipt of it, gives a delivery warrant to the buyer who then transfers that warrant to the sub-buyer.[519]

Delivery by Buyer in Possession

The transaction entered into by the buyer in possession must involve either a transfer of documents of title or a delivery of goods. In recent years, it has become clear that such delivery can occur by constructive means.[520] In *Four Point Garage Ltd* v. *Carter*,[521] the sellers, pursuant to directions given by the buyer, delivered a car directly to the sub-buyer in the mistaken belief that the sub-buyer was merely leasing it from the buyer. The sub-buyer paid the buyer and the buyer defaulted on payment to the sellers. It was the sellers' contention that section 25(1) did not apply since the buyer had not delivered the goods, but the court had little difficulty in seeing that the arrangement merely abbreviated delivery to the buyer and redelivery to the sub-buyer. When the sellers responded to the buyer's directions, there occurred a constructive delivery to the buyer coupled with a redelivery by the sellers, acting as the buyer's agent, to the sub-buyer.[522] The result is firmly within the mischief of section 25(1). If a sub-buyer is likely to be misled by the appearance of agency or ownership in a buyer given possession, the likelihood is all the greater if the seller actively assists the buyer in performing the latter's obligations under the sub-sale contract.

Constructive delivery was also recognized as effective in transferring title in *Gamer's Motor Centre (Newcastle) Pty. Ltd* v. *Natwest Wholesale Australia Pty. Ltd*[523] which concerned a 'floor plan' for the financing of a dealer's inventory of second-hand cars similar to the plan in *Pacific Motor Auctions*.[524] Cars in the dealer's inventory were sold to the respondent finance company and bailed back to the dealer without ever leaving the dealer's possession. At issue was the question whether the dealer had delivered the cars to the finance company for the purpose of section 25(1), for the dealer did not have an unfettered title to the vehicles in

---

[518] *Ant Jurgens Margarine-Fabrieken* v. *Louis Dreyfus & Co*, n. 514 above.

[519] *Capital and Counties Bank Ltd* v. *Warriner*, n. 514 above.

[520] Symbolic means should also be effective: *Forsyth International (UK) Ltd* v. *Silver Shipping Ltd* [1994] 1 WLR 1332, 1346 (citing a passage on the meaning of delivery in M. Chalmers, *The Sale of Goods Act, 1893, Including the Factors Acts, 1889 & 1890* (5th edn., Butterworths, London, 1902)).

[521] [1985] 3 All ER 12. See also *Archivent Sales & Development Ltd* v. *Strathclyde Regional Council*, 1985 SLT 154.

[522] See also *E. & S. Ruben Ltd* v. *Faire Bros. & Co. Ltd* [1949] 1 KB 254.

[523] (1987) 163 CLR 236.   [524] [1965] AC 867.

question but had acquired them from the appellant seller under an agreement to sell. In the New South Wales Court of Appeal,[525] the dissenting judge maintained the actual delivery was required if the bank was to override the interest of the respondent seller under section 25.[526] The seller-in-possession authorities took this view of identical language in section 24 and the word 'receiving', present in both subsections, pointed to actual and not constructive delivery.[527] Moreover, the policy of the subsection was to draw title inferences from an actual change in possession manifest to the world at large. The majority, however, was more concerned to point to the way that delivery in sales law was generally taken to connote both actual and constructive delivery,[528] an approach subsequently adopted by the majority of a divided High Court. They noted that 'received' in section 25 could be usefully contrasted with 'actually received' in section 5 of the Sale of Goods Act, the Statute of Frauds provision. Furthermore, they could not see why the *bona fide* purchaser should have to obtain possession of the goods that was demonstrable to the world at large. As McHugh JA put it: 'The problem arises because the original buyer is in possession not because of what the sub-buyer does.'[529] In other words, any failure of the second buyer under section 25 to take actual delivery can only prejudicially affect subsequent, and not prior, buyers, and a second buyer who does not insist on actual delivery takes a risk as regards third buyers and so on.

An extended form of constructive delivery has been created by the Sale of Goods (Amendment) Act 1995. The definition of 'delivery' in section 61(1) of the Sale of Goods Act 1979 has been amended to include contractual appropriations of goods that serve to pass the property in the goods to the buyer under section 20A or section 20B.[530] This means that a buyer in possession of goods or of documents of title to goods has the power to give a good title in an undivided share of bulk goods to a prepaying sub-buyer, even without the removal of the goods, or the transfer of a document of title, or the attornment of the bailee to the sub-buyer. It is not clear why this sub-buyer should succeed under section 25(1) when any other sub-buyer would have to show a delivery or constructive delivery of the goods or a transfer of a document of title.

Even a constructive delivery, however, must be a voluntary one. This point underpins the decision in *Forsyth International (UK) Ltd* v. *Silver Shipping Ltd*,[531] where a tanker had been chartered under a Shelltime 4 charterparty. In time charterparties, possession of the vessel remains at all times with the shipowners, whose servant, the master, is required to

---

[525] [1985] NSWLR 475.   [526] *Ibid.* 479–82 (Kirby P).
[527] See also *Bank of New South Wales* v. *Palmer* [1970] 2 NSWLR 532.
[528] N. 525 above, 487 ff.   [529] *Ibid.* 493.
[530] S. 2(b) of the 1995 Act.   [531] N. 521 above.

respond to the charterers' orders. Upon redelivery of the vessel, the charterers commonly leave it with the same quantity of bunkers as it had on delivery at the commencement of the charter period. In the present case, this was achieved by a sale of existing bunkers to the charterers with provision for a sale back of bunkers on board the vessel when the ship was redelivered. The plaintiffs contracted to sell bunkers to the charterers and had them delivered to the ship. When the shipowners terminated the charterparty contract for non-payment of hire, payment had not yet been made for these bunkers. The shipowners claimed that the buyer in possession, the charterers, had delivered these bunkers to the sub-buyer, the shipowners, under the sale back in the charterparty. This claim was unsuccessful. Although the court was prepared to accept that there could be a constructive delivery under a section 25(1) transaction,[532] it held that the delivery that occurred in the present case did not satisfy the delivery test in section 61(1) of 'a voluntary transfer of possession'. The buyer did not acquiesce in the withdrawal of the ship,[533] which occurred when the shipowners unilaterally exercised their right to terminate the charterparty for breach of contract.

Now this decision presents two difficulties. First, the decision, on its own terms, would have had to go the other way if the charterparty had run its course without the commission of a discharging breach of contract by the charterer. It seems odd that the seller's rights should depend upon whether the charterparty was discharged by breach or by performance. In exercising their right to withdraw the ship and terminate the contract, the shipowners were acting in accordance with rights voluntarily agreed under the contract, even if the bunkers the actual subject of the sale back would not necessarily have been the bunkers left in the vessel had the charterparty run its full course. Secondly, the court held, quite correctly, that the shipowners, who never surrendered possession of the vessel to the charterers, were therefore also in possession of the bunkers.[534] More controversially, however, it also held that the charterers had the right to immediate possession since the shipowners were contractually bound, through the master, to obey the charterers' orders for the employment of the vessel (an activity necessitating the consumption of bunkers). Even if this right to immediate possession were rephrased in terms of constructive possession,[535] it is not easy to see why a charterer has any more of a right to the possession of bunker fuels than

---

[532] It was not critical of the decisions in *Four Point Garage*, n. 521 above, and *Gamer's*, n. 523 above.

[533] Unlike the rogue in *Worcester Works Finance Ltd* v. *Cooden Engineering Co. Ltd* [1972] 1 QB 210, who 'cheerfully hand[ed] over the key'.

[534] Following *The Span Terza (No. 2)* [1984] 1 WLR 27.

[535] The right to immediate possession is the right to demand actual possession at any time, which hardly fits the present case.

a passenger in a London taxicab has of the contents of its fuel tank. The significance of this point is that the court looked for a delivery of the bunkers in terms of the voluntary surrender of this right to immediate possession. If the shipowners had had at all material times possession, unlimited by any such right of the charterers', then delivery would already have occurred and the decision could not have gone against them on the ground that it did. Even if a right to immediate possession is conceded to the charterers, it is arguable that the possession of the shipowners means that delivery was made when the bunkers were put on board.

Section 25(1) requires the second buyer to take delivery of the goods 'under any sale, pledge or other disposition thereof'. Although not a decision on section 25(1), *Shaw* v. *Commissioner of Police of the Metropolis*[536] supports the view that an agreement to sell will not suffice for present purposes.[537] It was held in that case that the rogue and the innocent purchaser did not intend the property to pass to the latter until his bank draft had been honoured. Even allowing for any court's deep reluctance to find such parties intending the property to pass before payment, it is difficult to see how an unpalatable result could be avoided if the property was plainly intended to pass and the purchaser had not yet paid the absconding rogue. A further point concerns additional language in section 9 of the Factors Act which treats as authorized by the owner a delivery of goods 'under *any agreement for* sale, pledge, or other disposition thereof' (emphasis added). This language would have been broad enough to catch the events in *Shaw* if the contract between owner and rogue had been characterized as one of sale rather than agency. It was interpreted in *Re Highway Foods International Ltd*,[538] where both sale and resale contracts contained a retention of title clause and payment had been made under neither contract. The goods, a quantity of meat, were then returned by the sub-buyer to the seller to permit safety checks to be made, and seller and sub-buyer concluded a new contract for a price identical to the one the sub-buyer had earlier agreed to pay the buyer. Receivers acting for the buyer argued that title to the goods had already passed to the sub-buyer under section 9 so that the seller had no right to repossess them and sell them on fresh terms directly to the sub-buyer. It was not clear in the buyer's case how the assertion that the sub-buyer had obtained title was compatible with the buyer's own retention-of-title clause.[539] The buyer failed because, although the sub-

[536] [1987] 3 All ER 405, discussed in the text accompanying nn. 193–4 below.
[537] See also *W. Hanson (Harrow) Ltd* v. *Rapid Civil Engineering Ltd* (1987) 37 *Build. LR* 106.
[538] [1995] BCC 271.
[539] The practical issue at the heart of this case was whether the buyer had a claim to the moneys placed on deposit by the sub-buyer pending resolution of the title dispute between the seller and buyer.

buyer acquired authorized and thus lawful possession under section 9, this was short of the title needed to override the title of the seller. A further and smaller quantity of meat had been processed to such a degree that it lost its original identity. Although the issue would have benefited from a fuller discussion, it seems that title to this meat passed upon its transformation by the sub-buyer by virtue of the rule of law that the operator becomes the owner of new products[540] without any need to invoke sections 9 or 25(1).

Consumer Conditional Sales

It is ironic that consumer conditional sales are removed from section 25(1) because of their kinship with hire purchase transactions, given that one of the reasons for the emergence of hire purchase was the desire to avoid the seller-in-possession exception to the rule of *nemo dat*.[541] Instead of extending section 25(1) to protect those deriving title from hire purchase bailees, section 25(1) was cut down to remove its protection from those deriving title from consumer conditional buyers.[542] Most consumer cases, however, will involve motor vehicles, and special legislation, applicable to both hire purchase and conditional sale transactions, has to some extent reproduced the protection given to innocent purchasers by section 25(1) of the Sale of Goods Act.[543]

Part III of the Hire Purchase Act 1964

Part III of the Hire Purchase Act 1964[544] applies to motor vehicles[545] that are the subject of either conditional sale or hire purchase agreements.[546] It does not apply to sale or return agreements, security bills of sale,[547] or to financial leases, despite the fact that the latter two perform the same economic function as hire purchase and conditional sale agreements. Nor would it apply to a case where a dealer permits a prospective hire

---

[540] See Ch. 3 above.   [541] *Helby* v. *Matthews* [1893] AC 471.

[542] This was effective with the implementation of the 1979 Act but it was foreshadowed by provisions of the Consumer Credit Act 1974 (s. 192(4) and Sched. 4, para. 4) that never came into force.

[543] Hire purchase and conditional sale contracts are defined in identical terms in the Consumer Credit Act 1974, s. 189, and in Part III of the Hire Purchase Act 1964, s. 29(1), as amended by the Consumer Credit Act, Sched, 4, para. 22. Oddly enough, non-consumer conditional sales may be the subject of both a s. 25(1) and a Part III transaction.

[544] As amended by the Consumer Credit Act 1974, Sched. 4, para. 22.

[545] S. 29(1): 'a mechanically propelled vehicle intended or adapted for use on roads to which the public has access'. This could include farm vehicles, although they are by no means exclusively or mainly (words absent from s. 29(1)) used on public roads.

[546] References hereafter to bailees will include both conditional buyers and hire purchase bailees. Part III refers to them compendiously as 'the debtor'.

[547] A point not lost on a South Wales car dealer eager to avoid losing title under Part III: see the *Independent*, 29 Sept. 1989.

purchase bailee to take away a car before the bailee's hire purchase proposal is turned down by the finance company.[548] As a purely pragmatic response to the fact that title problems usually erupt in the case of second-hand cars rather than refrigerators, Part III does not sit easily in anyone's attempt to erect a comprehensive theory of *nemo dat* and its exceptions. The statutory techniques of protecting innocent purchasers are also different from those displayed in the Factors Act and Sale of Goods Act. The limited coverage of Part III makes it a matter of happy accident for those *bona fide* purchasers who, in a subsequent dispute with a finance company owner, discover that they dealt with a bailee rather than a financial lessee.

A disposition made by a bailee to a private purchaser acting in good faith and without notice is deemed to have been made with the owner's title vested in the bailee immediately before the disposition.[549] Curiously, the Act does not begin by deeming that the purchaser acquires a good title from the bailee or that the bailee acts as the authorized agent of the finance company owner.[550] This way of phrasing the matter would protect the purchaser from any possibility of liability in conversion arising from the act of dealing with the bailee. More significantly, it would also mean that the purchaser acquires the motor vehicle on whatever title terms have been agreed with the bailee. In accordance with normal principle, private purchasers who have acquired a good title under Part III will be able to transmit that title clear of the finance company's interest, regardless of the *bona fides* or notice of purchasers who deal with them. The Act defines a private purchaser in negative terms as one who does not carry on the business of a trade or finance purchaser at the time of the disposition.[551] A trade or finance purchaser is defined as one carrying on a business that consists wholly or partly of buying motor vehicles for the purpose of resale or supply on hire purchase or conditional sale terms.[552] The mischief of the legislation is plain enough: trade or finance purchasers have the opportunity to consult registers of hire purchase and conditional sale agreements,[553] whereas private pur-

[548] The position in *Central Newbury Car Auctions Ltd* v. *Unity Finance Ltd* [1957] 1 QB 371.

[549] S. 27(2). If the owner's title is defective, the protection given to private purchasers is commensurately reduced: s. 29(5).

[550] *Quaere* the liability of that bailee under the contract of sale to his purchaser? Could it be said that the bailee has the right to sell under s. 12(1) of the Sale of Goods Act? See discussion of s. 12(1) above.

[551] S. 29(2).

[552] *Ibid.* Again, note the absence of any reference to financial leasing. A finance company whose business in respect of motor vehicles consisted exclusively of financial leases would by definition be a private purchaser (hardly a sensible result), unless its practice of selling vehicles at discounted prices at the end of the term, whether to the lessee or otherwise, made a difference.

[553] Notably the register maintained by Hire Purchase Information Ltd.

chasers do not. In *Stevenson* v. *Beverley Bentinck Ltd*,[554] the plaintiff was a tool inspector who, in his spare time, purchased and renovated vehicles prior to reselling them.[555] He bought for his personal use a car that turned out to be the subject of a hire purchase agreement and the question was whether he could claim the protection of section 27(2). It was held that he could not, since carrying on the business of a trade or finance purchaser was a matter of status rather than of the capacity in which the purchaser was acting at the time of the disposition. The plaintiff carried on a business, even if it was only a part-time one.[556]

Should a trade or finance purchaser acquire the vehicle from the bailee, then title will pass to a private purchaser dealing with the trade or finance purchaser, provided that that private purchaser acted in good faith and without notice.[557] The same result will follow if there is more than one trade or finance purchaser between bailee and the first private purchaser.[558] The technique is to deem that, for the purpose of the disposition to the first private purchaser, title was vested in the bailee immediately before the disposition to the first trade or finance purchaser. This limited deeming provision will therefore leave at risk of liability in conversion any number of trade or finance purchasers in the chain between the bailee and the first private purchaser.[559] The first private purchaser will have a protected statutory title, but not the previous trade or finance purchaser or purchasers. A reading of the above provisions shows that a statutory title passes only if the first private purchaser has acted in good faith and without notice. If the first private purchaser falls short of this standard, then it does not matter how much good faith is mustered among any number of subsequent private purchasers, for they are all damned. If this does not seem an attractive result, it should be recalled that purchasers dealing with mercantile agents or buyers and sellers in possession cannot pass a good title to good faith disponees if they themselves fail to comply with the standard of good faith and absence of notice. Nevertheless, odd results might flow from this limitation in Part III. Suppose, for example, that on a matrimonial break-up a spouse, with or without the consent of the finance company owner,

[554] [1976] 1 WLR 483.

[555] The court counted 37 transactions in the preceding 18 months. Sometimes the plaintiff acted for a principal.

[556] Cf. the matter of dealing as a consumer under the Unfair Contract Terms Act 1977, Ch. 8 above.

[557] S. 27(3).   [558] *Ibid.*

[559] This is confirmed by s. 27(6) which also, for the avoidance of doubt, states that the bailee is not exonerated from any civil or criminal liability by virtue of the provisions of Part III. S. 27(6) applies also to the liability of trade or finance purchasers. It has been held that its effect is to keep alive the contractual liability of a conditional seller under an express term that the seller was the owner of the goods at the contract date: *Barber* v. *NWS Bank plc* [1996] 1 All ER 906.

assumes the burden of paying instalments, but unlawfully disposes of the vehicle before all of the instalments have been paid. The arrangment between the two spouses would probably pass the test of a disposition[560] but, since the spouse agreeing to make the payments clearly has notice of the outstanding hire purchase agreement, it follows that no title could be transmitted under Part III to a subsequent purchaser.

Section 27(4) makes as obscurely as it can an important point about the time when a private purchaser's good faith and absence of notice are to be considered. Where the disposition made to the first private purchaser is a hire purchase agreement, it appears that that private purchaser[561] will acquire a good title if he acted in good faith at the time the vehicle was first acquired on bailment terms. The bailee should thus be at liberty to keep up the hire purchase agreement and exercise an effective option to purchase at the end of the term, even though by that time he has notice of the original owner's title. This provision is not extended to conditional buyers. The reason would appear to be that hire purchase was singled out because of the double disposition factor, namely, the initial acquisition on hire purchase terms and the subsequent sale implemented by the exercise of the option to purchase. Section 27(4) ensures that the bailee is not disqualified as a result of the second disposition. In a conditional sale, there is only the one disposition, made when the goods were acquired on sale terms, since the passing of property is an automatic affair once all the instalments have been paid. Part III makes it plain that a disposition includes a conditional sale agreement and not the acquisition of title under a conditional sale agreement.[562] A conditional buyer's protection will not therefore be lost as a result of discovering the existence of the original owner after the conclusion of the conditional sale contract.[563]

Subject to section 29(4), the question of a bailee's good faith should be determined in the same way as it is for other areas of title transfer. The absence of notice of a pre-existing hire purchase or conditional sale contract, however, also invites consideration of section 29(3), which refers to the absence of 'actual notice that the vehicle is *or was* the subject of any such agreement' (emphasis added). Section 29(3) was considered in

---

[560] In s. 29(1). The first spouse's transfer of the option should be a sale of goods since there is an intention to divest himself of the whole of his interest in the vehicle. In addition, agreeing to make payment to a third party would not detract from the agreement being classified as one of sale.

[561] As well as anyone to whom he transfers his option to purchase: s. 27(4)(b) ('a person claiming under him').

[562] S. 29(1). See also s. 29(3): 'a person becomes a purchaser . . . if, and at the time when, a disposition of the vehicle is made to him'.

[563] S. 29(1) would appear to protect the buyer even before delivery of the goods or before any portion of the price has been paid.

Barker v. *Bell*,[564] where a private purchaser was falsely informed by the bailee that all of the payments had been made. The Court of Appeal held that the purchaser acquired a good title under Part III. The use of the past tense in section 29(3) appeared to deny such a title since the purchaser certainly knew that the vehicle had been the subject of a hire purchase agreement. But this language could sensibly be confined to the case where a hire purchase agreement was automatically terminated according to its own terms at the moment of the unlawful disposition by the bailee. Hence, 'a purchaser is only affected by notice if he has actual notice that the car is on hire-purchase'.[565]

In his forensic tasks, the private purchaser who claims a good title, or any subsequent purchaser claiming through him, is aided by an impressive series of presumptions:[566] that the disposition to the first private purchaser was made directly by the bailee;[567] that if there was no such direct disposition, then the bailee disposed of the goods directly to a different private purchaser, who acted in good faith, and that the present private purchaser can trace his title back to that other private purchaser;[568] and that, if it should be proved that the bailee disposed of the goods directly to a trade or finance purchaser, then the first private purchaser who came along acted in good faith and the present private purchaser can trace his title back to that other private purchaser.[569]

Finally, section 27(5) states that the provisions of the section apply notwithstanding section 21 of the Sale of Goods Act,[570] and without prejudice to the Factors Act 1889 and any other enactment authorizing the apparent owner to dispose of goods as though he were the true owner. They therefore leave unimpaired, for example, the buyer in possession exception in section 25 of the Sale of Goods Act.[571] This means, in the case of a non-consumer conditional sale, that persons dealing, or in a chain originating, with the conditional buyer have the choice of seeking title protection under Part III[572] or section 25[573] of the Sale of Goods Act. The benefits of Part III are that a purchaser can claim protection even though payment has not been made in full or delivery taken before notice of the owner's claim arises. A trade or finance purchaser appearing on the scene before the first private purchaser, on the other hand, would take the section 25 route. A purchaser whose disposition is governed by both sets of provisions does not have to satisfy both. They are facultative provisions which state when a purchaser acquires a good title:

---

[564] [1971] 1 WLR 983.   [565] *Ibid.* 986.
[566] These are rebuttable: see *Soneco Ltd* v. *Barcross Finance Ltd* [1978] RTR 444.
[567] S. 28(1),(2).   [568] S. 28(3).   [569] S. 28(4).
[570] They therefore override the rule of *nemo dat*.   [571] Also s. 8 of the Factors Act.
[572] Which is not confined to consumer transactions.
[573] Which still applies to non-consumer conditional sales.

they do not each say that a purchaser will acquire good title only if he satisfies section 25 or Part III as the case may be.

Other Powers of Sale

Section 21(2)(b) contains a saving provision that the *nemo dat* rule, as formulated in section 21(1), does not affect 'the validity of any contract of sale under any special common law or statutory power of sale or under the order of a court of competent jurisdiction'. The purpose of this provision is tolerably plain as being to preserve the effectiveness of certain titles, conferred under special and statutory powers of sale, but the drafting is quite curious in saving the validity of the 'contract of sale' rather than the title or the 'sale' itself. The contract of sale of goods belonging to another[574] is not an illegal contract at common law or otherwise invalid. Indeed, it generally supports a breach of contract action based on section 12 of the Sale of Goods Act if the seller has not acquired the right to sell at the time when the property is to pass to the buyer. In the event of the exercise of a power of sale, whether at common law or under statute, the question of the purchaser's title is not settled by section 21(2)(b) but by the relevant common law or statutory rules dealing with the power of sale. The aim of section 21(2)(b), however, appears to be to put it beyond doubt that the enactment in section 21(1) of the *nemo dat* rule does not repeal certain common law and statutory powers of title transfer outside the Factors and Sale of Goods Acts. The provision should also reinforce the immunity of sellers from a section 12 action in those cases where an effective title is transferred pursuant to the exercise of the power of sale.

Common law powers of sale include those of pledgees,[575] mortgagees,[576] and agents of necessity.[577] Under statute, bailees may dispose of uncollected goods[578] and confer 'a good title to the purchaser as against the bailor'[579] but not as against the owner.[580] Another example is the unpaid seller who, upon reselling after exercising a right of lien or stoppage in transit, is able to confer a good title on the new buyer as against the original buyer.[581] Other common statutory examples include

---

[574] e.g. *Varley* v. *Whipp* [1900] 1 QB 513.

[575] *Halliday* v. *Holgate* (1868) LR 2 Ex. 299; *Burdick* v. *Sewell* (1884) 13 QBD 159, 174.

[576] *Deverges* v. *Sandeman, Clark & Co. Ltd* [1902] 1 Ch. 579; *Stubbs* v. *Slater* [1910] 1 Ch. 632; *Re Morritt* (1886) 18 QBD 222 (power regulated by the Bills of Sale Act 1878 (Amendment) Act 1882, ss. 7, 13).

[577] *Great Northern Railway Co. Ltd* v. *Swaffield* (1874) LR 9 Ex. 132,138; *Sims & Co. Ltd* v. *Midland Railway Co. Ltd* [1913] 1 KB 103.

[578] Torts (Interference with Goods) Act 1977, ss. 12–13.

[579] *Ibid.*, ss. 12(6), 13(2).   [580] *Ibid.*, s. 12(4).

[581] S. 48(2). Although the modern orthodoxy is to treat title as revesting in the unpaid seller upon contractual termination, this was not always so: see Ch. 10 below.

sales by innkeepers,[582] pawnbrokers,[583] sheriffs,[584] tax collectors,[585] liquidators,[586] company administrators,[587] administrative receivers,[588] distraining landlords[589] and receivers of wrecks[590] and of salved property.[591]

Where a power of sale exists, clarity requires that, in addition to the seller's personal immunity, a good title should flow to the purchaser, but this, regrettably, is frequently left to inference. It seems hardly sensible to confer a power, and thus an immunity, on the seller, the effect of which is to procure the commission of the tort of conversion by the purchaser. The issue was discussed in *Bulbruin Ltd* v. *Romanyszyn*,[592] in connection with a local authority's powers to dispose of abandoned vehicles.[593] The Court of Appeal, on a close reading of the relevant provisions, discerned an intention to give the purchaser a good title against the original owner.[594] Furthermore, there is little point in giving a seller a power to sell, and thus immunity against the owner, if that seller can be sued under section 12 of the Sale of Goods Act by a buyer who does not obtain good title against the owner.[595] Yet this position is clearly contemplated in the case of bailees exercising powers of sale,[596] and the seller can presumably, by entering into a limited title sale, protect himself against a breach of contract action by the disappointed buyer.

---

[582] Innkeepers Act 1878, s. 1.   [583] Consumer Credit Act 1974, s. 121.

[584] Insolvency Act 1986, ss. 183, 184(2), 346; Bankruptcy and Deeds of Arrangement Act 1913, s. 15; *Curtis* v. *Maloney* [1951] 1 KB 736; *Dyal Singh* v. *Kenyan Insurance Co.* [1954] AC 287; Supreme Court Act 1981, s. 138; County Courts Act 1984, ss. 98–99. Special provision used to be made for executing sheriffs in s. 26 of the Sale of Goods Act 1893, not consolidated in and surviving the Sale of Goods Act 1979. The executing sheriff is now dealt with by above provisions of the Supreme Court Act and County Courts Act.

[585] Taxes Management Act 1970, s. 61.   [586] *Ibid.*, s. 234(3),(4).

[587] *Ibid.*, ss. 15, 234(3),(4), Sched. 1, para. 2.

[588] *Ibid.*, ss. 43, 234(3),(4). The statutory power to sell the assets of a company in administrative receivership (Insolvency Act 1986, s. 42(1) and Sched. 1, para. 2), and the powers of a trustee-in-bankruptcy (*ibid.*, s. 314 and Sched. 5, para. 9) and liquidator (*ibid.*, ss. 165(2), 167(1) and Sched. 4, para. 6) to sell assets of the insolvent do not amount to a power of sale of someone else's assets.

[589] Distress for Rent Act 1689, s. 1; Insolvency Act 1986, s. 347.

[590] Merchant Shipping Act 1995, s. 227.

[591] *Ibid.*, ss. 240, 243(2), 244(2) (sale without prejudice to title of third party).

[592] [1994] RTR 273. For the protection of buyers purchasing goods subject to execution, see County Courts Act 1984, s. 98; Supreme Court Act 1981, s. 138B.

[593] Road Traffic Regulations Act 1984, ss. 99, 101, and Removal and Disposal of Vehicles Regulations 1986, reg. 15(1).

[594] It also pointed to cases where it was 'clear' that title passes on sale, namely, sales by distraining landlords (Distress for Rent Act 1689), by innkeepers (Innkeepers Act 1870), and by tax collectors (Taxes Management Act 1970).

[595] *Bulbruin Ltd* v. *Romanyszyn*, n. 592 above, 278.

[596] Torts (Interference with Goods) Act 1977, s. 12(4),(6).

10

The Remedies of the Seller and the Buyer

This Chapter is concerned with the remedies of buyer and seller. In the case of the buyer, a right to damages may arise for non-delivery or for late delivery, or because the goods delivered fail to conform to the standard set by the express or implied terms of the contract. In addition to the normal damages due on such an event, the facts of the case may disclose a claim to special or consequential damages. A buyer who has paid the price for goods that the seller does not deliver, or that are delivered and rightly rejected, will wish to recover the price as on a total failure of consideration. Specific performance is also available in exceptional cases, usually to a buyer in lieu of damages for non-delivery.

The seller has a number of real remedies that can be exercised against the contract goods. An unpaid seller may assert a lien or a right of retention of the goods. Other real rights are the rights of stoppage *in transitu* and resale, triggered respectively by insolvency and discharging breach. The seller may also sue in debt for the price of the goods if the appropriate conditions are met; unlike the buyer's claim to specific performance, the subject of a discretionary award, the seller's claim is granted as of right. Where an action for the price is not available or is waived by the seller, there is instead the seller's action for damages for non-acceptance. There is also an action for special or consequential damages.

This chapter will deal with the general law of contractual remedies only to the extent that it is necessary for an understanding of its particular application to the law of sale,[1] and will not define the proprietary actions in tort by way of trespass or conversion, for these are adequately discussed in textbooks on the law of torts.[2] But the various statutory actions for damages will be shown as anchored in the law of remoteness of damage, laid down in a series of cases beginning with *Hadley* v. *Baxendale*,[3] as well as in the principle of mitigation of damages. The Sale of Goods Act imports explicitly a reference to the market in the sections dealing with non-delivery and non-acceptance, and this will be treated as revealing the statutory choice of a clear-cut rule for the assessment of damages which responds to both remoteness principles and mitigation.

---

[1] Hence the treatment of the rule against penalties, e.g., is left to the standard contract texts.

[2] See also M. G. Bridge, *Personal Property Law* (Blackstone, London, 2nd edn., 1996), Ch. 3.

[3] (1854) 9 Ex. 341.

These are listed in the Sales of Goods Act as the unpaid seller's lien, or right to withhold delivery where the property has not yet passed, the right of stoppage *in transitu*, and the right of resale.[4] These rights accrue to an unpaid seller[5] and are affected by the buyer's insolvency.[6] It is therefore convenient to begin with a definition of 'unpaid seller' and 'insolvency'.

'Unpaid Seller'

As defined by section 38(1) of the Sale of Goods Act, an 'unpaid seller' is one who either has not been paid in full,[7] or who has accepted conditional payment by bill of exchange or other negotiable instrument, and the condition has been defeated by the dishonour of the instrument or otherwise. Payment in full poses a particular difficulty for severable instalment contracts and will be referred to below. In an earlier chapter, it was established that payment by negotiable instrument will normally constitute conditional payment.[8] The significance of this is that a lien lost on conditional payment will revive if the condition is not met.[9]

For the purpose of section 38 and the following sections, a 'seller' is defined to include certain agents occupying the position of seller, such as an agent who is the indorsee of a bill of lading.[10] If, therefore, a principal consigns goods to a buyer and indorses the bill of lading in his agent's favour, the agent, in his dealings with the buyer, will be able to exercise the real rights of the seller.[11] The other example given in section 38 is the 'consignor or agent who has himself paid (or is directly responsible for) the price'. A commission agent purchasing goods on behalf of a principal and paying for them himself will therefore be able, in relation to a principal who fails to repay him, to exercise the rights of an unpaid seller.[12] It is well settled that a buyer rejecting goods has no real rights that he may exercise so as to secure repayment of the price paid.[13]

---

[4] S. 39(1).   [5] S. 38(1).

[6] Insolvency specifically activates the seller's right of stoppage *in transitu*: s. 39(1)(b).

[7] See *Feise* v. *Wray* (1802) 3 East 93.

[8] Ch. 6 above. It may exceptionally amount to absolute payment: Ch. 2 above.

[9] *Valpy* v. *Oakeley* (1851) 16 QB 941; *Griffiths* v. *Perry* (1859) 1 E & E 680 (right akin to stoppage *in transitu*).

[10] S. 38(2).   [11] *Morison* v. *Gray* (1824) 2 Bing. 260.

[12] *Van Casteel* v. *Booker* (1848) 2 Ex. 691; *Feise* v. *Wray*, n. 7 above. See the explanation of this in *Ireland* v. *Livingstone* (1872) LR 5 HL 395, 408–9 (Blackburn J) and in *Cassaboglou* v. *Gibb* (1883) 11 QBD 797, 803–4 (Brett MR), 806–7 (Fry LJ).

[13] *J. L. Lyons & Co.* v. *May and Baker Ltd* [1923] 1 KB 685; *Kwei Tek Chao* v. *British Traders and Shippers Ltd* [1954] 2 QB 459.

Insolvency

The buyer's insolvency is an event that activates the seller's right of stoppage *in transitu*. It may also persuade the seller to exercise a lien or right of retention to guard against non-payment. Section 61(4) of the Sale of Goods Act[14] gives the following definition of insolvency: 'A person shall be deemed to be insolvent within the meaning of this Act if he has either ceased to pay his debts in the ordinary course of business or he cannot pay his debts as they become due'. Provisions in insolvency legislation may render some assistance in interpreting section 61(4). The central feature of the relevant sections is the debtor's inability to pay.[15] A corporate debtor is deemed unable to pay its debts if it fails to pay a debt of at least £750 within three weeks of a written statutory demand being served at the company's registered office.[16] The statutory demand can thus be used also to deal with the debtor who can pay but refuses to do so. For both corporate insolvency and bankruptcy, the failure to satisfy a judgment wholly or in part also amounts to an inability to pay one's debts.[17] In *Re Phoenix Bessemer Steel Co.*,[18] it was held that the buyer had not made a declaration of insolvency when it invited its principal creditors to 'a private meeting of two or three . . . friends'. The buyer was a limited company with a large amount of property and fixed plant and with a very considerable amount of uncalled capital. For about three months after the meeting it carried on business as a solvent concern, meeting its debts as they fell due. The court therefore held that the buyer was not insolvent. On the other hand, the buyer's own statement that he is unable to pay his debts as they fall due will be treated as conclusive evidence of insolvency for present purposes.[19]

The effect of the buyer's insolvency on outstanding contracts must next be considered.[20] First of all, insolvency will not alone amount to an anticipatory breach entitling the seller to terminate the contract.[21] It has been said that the circumstances must show an intention or an inability to perform.[22] A manifest inability to perform with all the goodwill in the

---

[14] As amended by s. 235 and Sched. 10, Part III, of the Insolvency Act 1985.

[15] Insolvency Act 1986, s. 123. Added to this in the case of individual insolvency (bankruptcy) is the lack of reasonable prospect of being able to pay: *ibid.*, s. 267(2)(c).

[16] *Ibid.*, s. 123. No minimum amount is prescribed in s. 268 for bankruptcy.

[17] *Ibid.*, ss. 123(1)(b), 268(1)(b).   [18] (1876) 4 Ch. D 108.

[19] See *Ex p. Chalmers* (1873) 8 Ch. App. 289 (declaration at creditors' meeting).

[20] See F. Oditah (1992) 108 *LQR* 459, 494–6.

[21] *Ex p. Chalmers*, n. 20 above; *Mess* v. *Duffus* (1901) 6 Com. Cas. 165; *Griffiths* v. *Perry* (1859) 1 E & E 680, 688; *Jenning's Trustee* v. *King* [1952] 2 All ER 608; *Re Grainex Canada Ltd* (1987) 34 DLR (4th) 646.

[22] *Mess* v. *Duffus*, n. 21 above.

world may still amount to an anticipatory repudiation.[23] A seller who has difficulties showing a repudiation by the buyer may try an alternative route. A contract still to be performed at least in part may be abandoned by mutual agreement of the parties.[24] In *Morgan* v. *Bain*,[25] deliveries under an instalment contract were due to start two weeks after the buyers filed a liquidation petition. The contract was not mentioned at the creditors' meeting and the buyers did nothing until, six weeks after the date performance had fallen due, they obtained fresh capital and offered cash for the agreed goods on a rising market. The buyers' inaction following upon a declaration of insolvency amounted to a presumptive intention to abandon the contract[26] and the failure of the sellers to deliver at the agreed time constituted evidence of an intention to accept the buyers' offer of abandonment.[27] Apart from repudiation and abandonment, it is open to parties to provide that the contract will be determined in the event of the insolvency of one of them.[28] It is common for commodity contracts[29] to provide that unperformed contracts will be closed out at the market rate then prevailing. This means that the contract is transformed into one for financial differences and a party pays or receives a settlement according to how the market at that date (and not the estimated delivery date) stands in relation to the contract price. In *Shipton, Anderson & Co. (1927) Ltd* v. *Micks, Lambert & Co.*,[30] the provision did not automatically close out the transaction. The buyer took care not to elect to invoke it and was thereby spared having to account under the provision for the gain made when purchasing the goods for a lesser sum on a falling market.

If the contract has not been terminated by mutual abandonment or consequent upon the buyer's repudiation, its fate rests with the trustee-in-bankruptcy or company liquidator who has a statutory power to disclaim onerous property (which includes contracts).[31] In a real sense, once the buyer becomes insolvent, the contract is thereupon frozen so that the question whether the contract is to proceed to performance is

---

[23] *Foran* v. *Wright* (1989) 64 ALJR 1, 9, 17; *British and Beningtons Ltd* v. *North Western Cachar Tea Co. Ltd* [1923] AC 48; *Rawson* v. *Hobbs* (1961) 107 CLR 466; *Universal Cargo Carriers Corpn.* v. *Citati* [1957] 2 QB 401; *Anchor Line Ltd* v. *Keith Rowell Ltd* [1980] 2 Lloyd's Rep. 351. See also *Ex p. Stapleton* (1879) 10 Ch. D 586, 589.

[24] The difficulty of showing rescission by mutual abandonment should not be underestimated: see Ch. 6 above.

[25] (1874) LR 10 CP 15.

[26] *Ibid.* 26 (Brett J, relying upon *Ex p. Chalmers*, n. 20 above). See also *Lawrence* v. *Knowles* (1839) 5 Bing. NC 399.

[27] *Morgan* v. *Bain*, n. 25 above, 28.   [28] Oditah, n. 20 above.

[29] GAFTA and FOSFA contracts contain such provisions.

[30] [1936] 2 All ER 1032.

[31] Insolvency Act 1986, ss. 178, 315. For the general powers of a company administrator, see *ibid.*, s. 14 and Sched. 1.

left to be decided by the trustee or liquidator. In view of the doctrines of repudiation and abandonment, a trustee or liquidator had better decide promptly in favour of continuance.[32] Even if the contract continues, it will not necessarily do so upon the same terms. Contracts that have extended credit to the buyer or have given the buyer the option of paying cash or on deferred payment terms can be enforced only by a trustee or liquidator prepared to pay cash.[33] In *Ex p. Chalmers*, the sellers were held entitled to demand cash to cover, not only the undelivered instalment itself, but also the previous instalment for which payment had not yet been made. This is tantamount to reviving a lost lien in the case of that previous instalment and is hard to justify except as an exercise in impressionistic justice. The above rules relating to the role of the trustee or liquidator apply whether or not the property in the contract goods has passed to the buyer; in other words, they apply where the seller exercises his lien or right to withhold delivery, as well as where the goods are stopped *in transitu*.[34]

The Unpaid Seller's Lien

A lien at common law is a passive right of retention that may be exercised by the members of certain professions or callings against the owner where the lienee acquires possession[35] of goods with the actual or apparent consent[36] of the owner. An unpaid seller has a lien when the property has passed to the buyer but a right of retention if the property has not yet passed.[37] In the latter case, although the permissible conduct of the seller in relation to the goods is otherwise identical, the seller is not exercising any right against the owner, for the seller is the owner.

A common law lien does not come with powers of enjoyment and sale,

---

[32] *Morgan* v. *Bain*, n. 25 above; *Ex p. Stapleton*, n. 23 above; *Ex p. Chalmers*, n. 20 above; *Re Grainex Canada Ltd*, n. 21 above.

[33] *Ex p. Chalmers*, n. 20 above; *Re Grainex Canada Ltd*, n. 21 above; *Morgan* v. *Bain*, n. 25 above.

[34] It has also been asserted that the rights of a trustee-in-bankruptcy may be exercised by a sub-buyer: *Ex p. Stapleton*, n. 23 above, *sed quaere*? This has been explained as turning on the equitable interest (in all sales?) acquired by the sub-buyer in the contract goods: *Kemp* v. *Falk* (1882) 7 App. Cas. 573, 578. This is hard to justify in the light of *Re Wait* [1927] 1 Ch. 606, Ch. 3 above.

[35] In some cases, e.g. the innkeeper and the guest's luggage, the lienee exercises control rather than possession before taking effective action: *Lord's Trustee* v. *Great Eastern Railway Co. Ltd* [1908] 2 KB 54 (Fletcher Moulton LJ).

[36] *Bowmaker Ltd* v. *Wycombe Motors Ltd* [1946] KB 505; *Tappenden* v. *Artus* [1964] 2 QB 185.

[37] The seller's right will be hereafter referred to as a lien unless it needs to be differentiated from the right of retention. In actuality, the right-of-retention language was added for the purpose of enactment in Scotland.

but the unpaid seller has a statutory right of resale.[38] The seller's lien, like other special liens at common law, is coextensive only with the debt. It follows that the lien over the goods is just for the price and not for any sums incurred in storing or maintaining the goods.[39] Expenses exclusively referable to the exercise of a lien by the lienee may not be recovered at all from the lienor,[40] still less be secured by a lien over the goods on which the expenses were incurred. The seller who stores goods may not claim another lien over them as warehouseman, for the reason that at common law a warehouseman does not have a lien for storage charges.[41] The seller's enjoyment of a lien over goods the property in which has passed to the buyer has two significant features for defining his liability: first, it acts as a defence to any action that a buyer might wish to take for the seller's failure to perform his contractual delivery obligation,[42] and secondly, it denies the buyer out of possession that right to the immediate possession of the goods that is necessary to maintain an action in conversion.[43] So long as the lien persists, the seller is entitled to resist performance for his part, and eventually, if payment is not forthcoming, will be able to move to the resale of the goods.[44] The seller exercising a lien has sufficient possession to maintain an action in conversion against a wrongdoer.[45] There is no reason to deny this in cases where the wrongdoer is a buyer to whom the property has passed.

Should the lien be unlawfully exercised by the seller, or the goods unlawfully disposed of,[46] it follows that the seller's defences fall and he becomes vulnerable to an action on the contract for damages for non-delivery, or in conversion.[47] If the buyer has not paid, such a seller will be able to set off the buyer's liability for the price in a tort action brought by the buyer.[48] Damages will therefore be nominal unless there has been a

[38] *Thames Ironworks Co.* v. *Patent Derrick Co.* (1860) 1 J & H 93; *Cowell* v. *Simpson* (1809) 16 Ves. Jun. 275 (difference between passive lien and vendor's lien).

[39] *Somes* v. *British Empire Shipping Co.* (1859) 28 LJQB 220.

[40] *China-Pacific SA* v. *Food Corpn. of India* [1982] AC 939, 962. See N. E. Palmer, *Bailment* (2nd edn., Sweet & Maxwell, London, 1991), 943 ff.

[41] Palmer, *ibid.* 872 ('extremely doubtful'); *Hatton* v. *Car Maintenance Co. Ltd* [1915] 1 Ch. 621.

[42] Ss. 27 and 51 of the Act must therefore be read subject to s. 39.

[43] *Lord* v. *Price* (1874) LR 9 Ex. 54; *McGregor* v. *Whalen* (1914) 31 OLR 543, 555 (Can.).

[44] S. 48.

[45] *Nippon Yusen Kaisha* v. *Ramjiban Serowgee* [1938] AC 429.

[46] Or the seller unlawfully refuses the buyer's tender of the price: *Martindale* v. *Smith* (1841) 1 QB 389. But if the seller has to sue the buyer for the price, his lien will last until judgment for the price is satisfied: s. 43(2), codifying *Scrivener* v. *Great Northern Railway Co.* (1871) 19 WR 388.

[47] *Mulliner* v. *Florence* (1878) 3 QBD 484, 491; *McGregor* v. *Whalen*, n. 43 above.

[48] *Miles* v. *Gorton* (1834) 2 C & M 504; *Chinery* v. *Viall* (1860) 5 H & N 288; *McGregor* v. *Whalen*, n. 43 above. If the buyer is insolvent, the seller may exercise this right of set off against the buyer's insolvency representative: Insolvency Act 1986, s. 323; Insolvency Rules, r. 4.90.

The Sale of Goods

market rise; the remedial outcome will thus be the same as if the buyer had sued in contract for damages for non-delivery.[49]

In addition to the buyer's insolvency, section 41(1) expresses the seller's lien (or right of retention) as arising and subsisting until the price is tendered when the goods have been sold without any stipulation as to credit, or where the goods have been sold on credit but the term of credit has expired. The first of these two cases,[50] a sale not concluded on credit terms, contemplates the presumptive interpretation of contractual performance contained in section 28 of the Sale of Goods Act, by which delivery and payment are mutual and concurrent conditions. Where this rule applies and the buyer is late in tendering payment, the seller has a contractual right to refrain from delivering the goods. If the property has not passed to the buyer, this right of retention cannot truly be regarded as a 'right against the goods'.[51] The right becomes a proprietary right by way of lien when the property in the goods has passed to the buyer. This will be so when the goods are specific and the presumptive rule in section 18, Rule 1, serves to pass the property at the contract date. A lien will also arise in the case of goods initially unascertained if they have been unconditionally appropriated to the contract under section 18, Rule 5.[52] It is increasingly unlikely that the rule for specific goods in section 18, Rule 1, will be applied nowadays. Furthermore, the unconditional appropriation of goods initially unascertained will usually occur when the seller surrenders possession on delivery. Unpaid sellers have also in modern times developed a keen appreciation of the wisdom of inserting retention of title clauses in their standard trading terms. Consequently, the exercise of the seller's lien will be a much rarer event than the exercise of a contractual right of retention.

Credit

The second of the two cases, which turns on the expiry of the credit granted to the buyer, is harder to explain, for the reason that credit is normally granted in the form of allowing the buyer delivery before payment with the period of credit running from delivery. In this case, the grant of credit is tied up with the surrender of possession by the seller and therefore the loss of his lien.[53] In s. 41(1)(b), however, credit appears rather to signify the disconnection of payment and delivery, where the buyer is entitled to call for delivery before payment but is bound to pay within a stated period.[54] Credit would thus mean the seller's agreement not to

---

[49] *Valpy* v. *Oakeley* (1851) 16 QB 941.

[50] *Bloxam* v. *Sanders* (1825) 4 B & C 941; *Miles* v. *Gorton*, n. 48 above.

[51] Part V of the Sale of Goods Act is entitled 'Rights of Unpaid Seller Against the Goods'.

[52] Or the property has passed pursuant to an intention under s. 17.

[53] This may be regarded as a waiver of the seller's lien under s. 43(1)(c).

[54] *Bunney* v. *Poyntz* (1833) 4 B & Ad 568; *New* v. *Swain* (1828) Dan. & Ll. 193.

demand payment as soon as the contract is concluded, even though the goods are specific or ascertained and in a deliverable state, and the buyer is entitled to demand the goods at any time.[55] If the buyer fails for whatever reason to take delivery of the goods before the last date for payment, the lien waived[56] by the seller when granting credit is revived and with it the seller's contractual right under section 28 not to deliver before payment. Some sellers who have granted credit in this way may be fortuitously still in possession of the goods when the buyer becomes insolvent.[57] Even though the period of credit has not expired, they will be able to exercise a lien under section 41(1)(c).

Section 41(2) provides that the seller's lien is not lost merely because the seller attorns to the buyer as bailee or agent.[58] But an unpaid seller granting credit to the buyer, who stores goods for the buyer after an attornment, may exercise a lien after the expiry of the credit period.[59] Case law decided before the Act under section 17 of the Statute of Frauds held that a buyer could be in actual receipt of goods for the purpose of the section if the seller attorned to him as bailee, on the ground that the seller's lien would in such circumstances be lost.[60] It was later held, however, that the insolvency of the buyer would allow the lien to revive where goods were being held by the seller in the capacity of warehouseman.[61] At one stage in its drafting history, section 41(2) was confined to insolvency to reflect the above development but now permits the survival of the lien on the more extended basis stated above.

Loss of Lien

According to section 43(1), the seller's lien is lost in the following three cases: first, when the goods are delivered to a carrier or other bailee for the purpose of transmission to the buyer and the right of disposal has not been reserved; secondly, when the buyer or an agent lawfully obtains possession of the goods; and thirdly, when the seller waives his lien.[62]

The first of these cases is but a particular example of the second, for the carrier is *prima facie* the agent of the buyer,[63] so that delivery and the

---

[55] In *Dixon* v. *Yates* (1833) 5 B & Ad. 313, 340, Parke B explained the passing of property in specific goods at the contract date as turning upon a deemed delivery of them to the buyer. This idea gives some assistance in understanding the sense in which credit is used in s. 41(1)(b).

[56] See s. 43(1)(c); *Poulton and Son* v. *Anglo-American Oil Co. Ltd* (1911) 27 TLR 216, affd. on other grounds (1911) 27 TLR 216.

[57] *Ex p. Chalmers* (1873) 8 Ch. App. 289.

[58] But the facts may show a waiver of the lien under s. 43(1)(c).   [59] S. 41(1)(b).

[60] *Cusack* v. *Robinson* (1861) 1 B & S 299 (Blackburn J).

[61] *Gunn* v. *Bolckow, Vaughan & Co.* (1875) LR 10 Ch. App. 491; *Grice* v. *Richardson* (1877) 3 App. Cas. 319.

[62] These instances are in addition to tender, unlawful disposal and execution of judgment.

[63] Ch. 6 above.

transfer of possession for general sales purposes occur on surrender of the goods to the carrier.[64] This is subject to the seller's right of stoppage *in transitu* which, when validly exercised, revives the seller's lien. If the seller has retained the right of disposal, this negatives delivery to the buyer once the goods are surrendered to the carrier[65] and so, consistently with this, the seller continues to exercise his right to withhold delivery constructively through the shipping documents.[66] In some cases, the waiver of the lien is of finite duration;[67] whether it is capable of being permanent will be determined in accordance with the standard rules on waiver and promissory estoppel.

The transfer of possession by the seller to the buyer or his agent under section 43(1)(b) will not normally be a difficult matter, but occasional problems are presented in drawing inferences from the fact of control over the goods.[68] In one case, timber in the possession of a wharfinger was measured, stamped, and treated by the buyer in accordance with the contract of sale, to such an extent that the court held that possession had been lost by the seller.[69] The case may be better explained as involving an attornment[70] by the wharfinger, for an attornment by a bailee to the buyer will destroy the seller's lien.[71] A mere instruction from the seller to the bailee to hold the goods for the buyer will not amount to the constructive change of possession that is produced by an attornment.[72]

The possession acquired by the buyer under section 43(1)(b) must be a lawful one; a wrongful taking of the goods by the buyer will not destroy the lien.[73] It follows that such a buyer, though having bought the goods, will not have obtained possession of the goods with the consent of the seller for the purpose of section 25(1). Although the property in the goods has passed to the buyer, the title transferred by the buyer to the sub-buyer will therefore be encumbered with the seller's lien.[74] Section 47(1) provides that the seller's lien[75] is not affected by a sub-sale negotiated by the buyer unless the seller assents to it, which is not the case in this instance.[76]

As stated earlier, an assent to a sub-sale may be regarded as an instance of the waiver principle contained in section 43(1)(c). The seller's

---

[64] S. 32(1).   [65] Ch. 3 above.

[66] By reserving the right of disposal, the seller prevents the property from passing.

[67] Where a period of credit is extended to the buyer.

[68] See *Wrightson* v. *McArthur and Hutchinson's (1919) Ltd* [1921] 2 KB 807.

[69] *Cooper* v. *Bill* (1865) 3 H & C 722. See also *McGregor* v. *Whalen* (1914) 31 OLR 543, 555 (Can.).

[70] Attornment is discussed in Ch. 6 above.

[71] *Pooley* v. *Great Eastern Railway Co.* (1876) 34 LT 537.

[72] *Poulton and Son* v. *Anglo-American Oil Co.*, n. 56 above.

[73] *Wallace* v. *Woodgate* (1824) 1 C & P 575.   [74] Ch. 9 above.

[75] And the right of stoppage *in transitu*.

[76] There seems no reason to confine this to a case where the goods at all material times are in the seller's possession.

assent will not be inferred from mere notice of the sub-sale; it has to amount to a renunciation of his rights over the goods and to show the seller's intention for the sub-contract to be performed without regard to the terms of the head contract.[77] The passive receipt by the seller of a delivery order from the sub-buyer, even when coupled with the past practice of delivery pursuant to such orders once the immediate buyer paid for the goods, has been held not be an assent.[78] But in *D. F. Mount Ltd* v. *Jay & Jay (Provisions) Ltd*,[79] the sellers agreed to sell on a falling market a quantity of tinned peaches from a larger bulk lying in their name in a warehouse. It was agreed between sellers and buyers that the price should come from the moneys received by the buyers from their sub-buyers. The sellers issued a delivery order in favour of the buyers, and the buyers in turn issued a delivery order in favour of the sub-buyers. In the sub-sale contract, it was provided that the sub-buyers should resell the goods back to the buyers a week later at a small profit. When, a week later, the sub-buyers duly gave a delivery order in favour of the buyers, receiving a cheque in payment that was later dishonoured, and then claimed the goods, the warehouseman interpleaded between the rival claimants, sellers and sub-buyers. The court held that the sellers had assented to the sub-sale by assuming the risk of the buyers' dishonesty. Besides the sellers' knowledge that the price would come from the sub-sale price, the sellers were aware that the buyers had to issue a delivery order to the sub-buyers in order to secure payment. It did not matter, moreover, that the goods in question had at no material time been ascertained from bulk;[80] the sellers' right to withhold delivery[81] was abated as regards the bulk to the extent of the contract quantity.

Section 47(2) of the Sale of Goods Act also provides that the seller's lien[82] is defeated when a document of title[83] lawfully transferred[84] to the buyer is in turn re-transferred for valuable consideration to a sub-buyer or pledgee acting in good faith. In *D. F. Mount Ltd* v. *Jay & Jay (Provisions) Ltd*,[85] it was held that the requirement of transfer was satisfied even though the seller had issued a delivery order in favour of the buyer, who

---

[77] *Mordaunt Bros.* v. *British Oil and Cake Mills Ltd* [1910] 2 KB 502.

[78] *Ibid.* Note that the requirement of an assent may be easier to infer in a case of specific goods.

[79] [1960] 1 QB 159.

[80] A conclusion easier to reach now that the Sale of Goods (Amendment) Act 1995 has been passed, conferring rights by way of tenancy in common in a defined bulk.

[81] Not a lien: the property had not passed.   [82] And right of stoppage *in transitu*.

[83] Defined by s. 1(4) of the Factors Act 1889 and s. 61(1) of the Sale of Goods Act in more expensive terms than at common law: Ch. 9 above.

[84] If the document is transferred by way of pledge, the owner's rights are defeated only up to the amount of the pledge: *Sewell* v. *Burdick* (1884) 10 App. Cas. 74; Ch. 9 above.

[85] N. 79 above.

in turn issued a fresh delivery order in favour of the sub-buyer.[86] It would have been unduly technical to read the requirement of transfer as including only cases where the same document changes hands twice. A delivery order has also been held to be a document of title under section 47(2) when it is issued against a carrier in respect of part of a bulk shipment, the whole of which is represented by a bill of lading.[87] Like the seller's assent to the sub-sale, this rule is also capable of explanation in terms of waiver.

Waiver may be seen too in section 42, which states that a seller who delivers part of the agreed goods may nevertheless exercise a lien on the remainder of the goods unless the circumstances show an agreement to waive the lien. The principal provision of section 42 comes from case law ruling that part delivery does not amount to a constructive delivery of the whole.[88] But circumstances may show that part delivery is truly intended by the parties to represent the whole.[89] Nevertheless, it is *prima facie* not to be regarded as delivery of the whole.[90]

It is clear that a lien temporarily or conditionally waived, for example, where a period of credit is extended to the buyer or a negotiable instrument is accepted in payment, may revive where the term expires or the instrument is dishonoured.[91] Less clear, however, is the issue whether a lien that has been released unconditionally and irrevocably may revive at a future date. In one old case, it was held that goods returned to a seller solely for the purpose of packing could not be made the subject of an unpaid seller's lien.[92] This could be explained as based on the absence of an intention of buyer and seller that the seller was to have a lien entitlement, and on the seller's repossession of the goods in the capacity of someone other than a seller. As between buyer and seller alone, there seems no reason why the parties might not agree to the revival of an abandoned lien, provided possession is duly resumed by the seller.[93] This view was upheld in one New Zealand case where the goods, a quantity of logs, were at all times present on the seller's land, where a construction project was in progress.[94] But the court went on to say that the seller's lien thus revived was the original lien and not a new lien, with the consequence that it defeated an intervening mechanic's lien pressed by

---

[86] See also *Ant Jurgens Margarine Fabrieken* v. *Louis Dreyfus & Co.* [1914] 3 KB 40. Cf. *Farmeloe* v. *Bain* (1876) 1 CPD 445.

[87] *Ant Jurgens*, n. 86 above.

[88] *Miles* v. *Gorton* (1834) 2 C & M 504; *Dixon* v. *Yates* (1833) 5 B & Ad. 313 (seller refused to give delivery receipt for all the goods). See also *Bunney* v. *Poyntz* (1833) 4 B & Ad. 568.

[89] *Kemp* v. *Falk* (1882) 7 App. Cas. 573 (Lord Blackburn).

[90] *Ex p. Cooper* (1879) 11 Ch. D 68, 73.

[91] *Poulton and Son* v. *Anglo-American Oil Co. Ltd* (1910) 27 TLR 38.]

[92] *Valpy* v. *Gibson* (1847) 4 CB 837.

[93] See *Harris* v. *Tong* (1930) 65 OLR 133, 144 (Can.).

[94] *Bines* v. *Sankey* [1958] NZLR 886.

a third party.[95] It is submitted that a lien might still be a valid lien if taken *de novo*, which avoids the unfairness of permitting it to defeat an intervening security. A later New Zealand case refused to accept the proposition that an abandoned lien could be revived by repossession.[96] On this point, the case appears to go too far, but the result is supportable, because the goods had been returned to the seller only for the purpose of repair, and not so as to permit the seller to reassert the lost lien.

A reading of the Sale of Goods Act and of the antecedent common law supports a strong argument that the seller's lien is superior to any security interest of the buyer's creditors. If the lien can be asserted against purchasers from the buyer, then *a fortiori* it can be asserted against those with a security interest over the buyer's assets, for the buyer's property in the goods is already encumbered to the extent of the lien.

Severable instalment contracts have presented some difficulties in respect of the scope of the seller's lien. In principle, a seller who delivers an instalment on credit terms loses his lien over that instalment, and it does not revive on non-payment. Furthermore, provided the buyer has not committed a discharging breach by failing to pay, the seller may not demand that cash be received against delivery of the next instalment, for the contract, still on foot, provides for the grant of credit to the buyer.[97] The situation is different, however, where the buyer becomes insolvent, and it is only the intervention of the buyer's insolvency representative that prevents the seller from invoking a repudiation of the contract based on the buyer's manifest inability to pay. In such cases, it has been held that the trustee must pay cash for future instalments, and may not demand future instalments even on such terms if he does not also pay for outstanding instalments.[98] Since the trustee does not have to adopt the contract, it has been said that he should take the contract as a whole and not merely the beneficial portion, for it would otherwise be unfair to require the seller to prove in bankruptcy.[99] A final point concerns the buyer's insolvency, which does not justify the seller in refusing to deliver an instalment for which payment actually has been made.[100]

---

[95] *Ibid.* 898.

[96] *United Plastics Ltd* v. *Reliance Electric (NZ) Ltd* [1977] 2 NZLR 125 (where the *Bines* case was not cited in the judgment).

[97] *Steinberger* v. *Atkinson and Co. Ltd* (1914) 31 TLR 110; *Snagproof Ltd* v. *Brody* [1922] 3 WWR 432, 437.

[98] *Ex p. Chalmers* (1873) 8 Ch. App 289; *Re Grainex Canada Ltd* (1987) 34 DLR (4th) 646, 671.

[99] *Re Grainex Canada Ltd*, n. 98 above, 671.

[100] *Merchant Banking Co. of London* v. *Phoenix Bessemer Steel Co.* (1877) 5 Ch. D 205.

The Right of Stoppage *in Transitu*

This is an extraordinary right given to the seller,[101] in the event of the buyer's insolvency, to resume possession of the goods[102] and thereby reassert his lien, notwithstanding that the property in the goods has passed to the buyer and that constructive delivery of the goods to the buyer has already been made on the delivery of the goods to the carrier.[103] It may be asserted at any time before the transit of the goods to their agreed destination has been completed.[104]

The right of stoppage *in transitu* strictly only applies where the property in the goods has passed to the buyer, for if it has not, the seller may instead fall back on his ownership of the goods on the buyer's insolvency.[105] Nevertheless, stoppage decisions and principles may usefully be looked at in such cases, especially in so far as they deal with the rights and duties of seller and carrier *inter se*. Support for this approach comes from section 39(2) of the Sale of Goods Act, which confers on a seller in whom the property in the goods is still vested 'a right of withholding delivery similar to and co-extensive with the rights of lien and stoppage in transit where the property has passed to the buyer'. A seller invoking section 39(2) and claiming rights akin to stoppage will therefore be at least as well placed as a seller invoking stoppage, properly so-called, in resuming possession of the goods. Evidence of the relative unimportance of the distinction between the two cases comes from the extension of stoppage to the case where goods have been rejected by the buyer,[106] so that the property in them revests in the seller.

Reported cases on the subject of stoppage have been exceedingly rare in the last sixty years, and this is not merely attributable to the fact that the law on the subject has been settled. The right of stoppage *in transitu* is predicated upon the lengthy transit of goods that have been shipped on credit terms in which, typically, the seller exchanges the shipping documents against a draft upon the buyer which the buyer accepts. In

---

[101] Or someone in the position of the seller: s. 38(2). See also *The Tigress* (1863) 32 LJ Adm. 97; *Bird* v. *Brown* (1850) 4 Ex. 786. Even before the Sale of Goods (Amendment) Act 1995, a seller could stop *in transitu* even if, for want of ascertainment, the goods had never vested in him: *Jenkyns* v. *Usborne* (1844) 7 M & G 678.

[102] The right of stoppage will extend to the proceeds of sale once a prior-ranking pledge has been satisfied: *Kemp* v. *Falk* (1882) 7 App. Cas. 573. But it does not extend to insurance moneys received after the destruction of or damage done to goods: *Berndtson* v. *Strang* (1886) LR 3 Ch. App. 588, revg. in part (1867) LR 4 Eq. 481. It will extend to the proceeds of sale if there has been a sub-sale: *Ex p. Golding Davis* (1880) 13 Ch. D 628.

[103] The general entitlement is set out in s. 44.   [104] S. 45.

[105] See *Gibson* v. *Carruthers* (1841) 8 M & W 321; *Bolton* v. *Lancashire and Yorkshire Railway Co.* (1866) LR 1 CP 431.

[106] S. 45(4), codifying *Bolton* v. *Lancashire and Yorkshire Railway Co*, n. 105 above.

times of rapid transit,[107] the ability of a seller to issue a stop notice is correspondingly abridged. More importantly, the practice in international sales of sellers reserving the right of disposal after shipment, surrendering this right on the documentary exchange only against payment under a banker's credit, guarantees them the continuing property in the goods and a reliable and solvent paymaster. In either event, such sellers will not need the additional right of stoppage *in transitu* conferred by the Sale of Goods Act.

Seventy years ago, Scrutton J spoke of the right of stoppage as 'a custom . . . which had grown up with no special reference or congruity to the English law' creating 'considerable difficulty in fitting in this international usage and national law'.[108] The sale of goods contract being largely the preserve of common lawyers, there has been a tendency to christen the ill-fitting right of stoppage as an equitable right.[109] Some resemblance between this right and equitable rights emerges in the rule that the right of stoppage is curtailed as soon as the bill of lading is transferred to a *bona fide* purchaser for value.[110] In reality, however, the right of stoppage was taken from the law merchant in the late seventeenth century[111] and for a long time was exercised under the bankruptcy jurisdiction of the Lord Chancellor.[112] It is therefore based upon international commercial custom, though recognized by law and equity[113] and now by statute.

Justification for Right of Stoppage

A more difficult inquiry concerns the justification for giving the seller a preferential right on the buyer's insolvency, for the seller has already parted with the property in and possession of the goods. More than 200 years ago, it was asserted that the seller's goods should not be applied to the payment of the insolvent buyer's debts,[114] but since the property has passed, it can hardly be said that these are still the seller's goods. Moreover, if this explanation still retains its force, it is difficult to see why

---

[107] S. 45(1) of the 1893 Act was confined to land and water transit; these limitations are absent from the 1979 Act. Statutory comprehensiveness? Or may air carriers look forward to dealing with stop notices?

[108] *Booth Steamship Co. Ltd* v. *Cargo Fleet Iron Co. Ltd* [1916] 2 KB 579, 597.

[109] *Kemp* v. *Falk*, n. 102 above; *Ex p. Golding Davis*, n. 102 above; *Nippon Yusen Kaisha* v. *Ramjiban Serowgee* [1938] AC 429.

[110] S. 47(2), discussed above in the text accompanying nn. 82 ff.

[111] *Wiseman* v. *Vandeputt* (1690) 2 Vern. 203.

[112] *Gibson* v. *Carruthers*, n. 105 above; *Booth Steamship*, n. 108 above.

[113] *Kendall* v. *Marshall, Stevens & Co.* (1883) 11 QBD 356, 364. Stoppage was adopted at common law in *Lickbarrow* v. *Mason* (1793) 4 Bro. Parl. Cas. 57, 6 East 22n, reinstating (1787) 2 TR 63, itself revd. by (1790) 1 H Bl. 357. In equity, the right of stoppage was enforced by a bill: *Schotsmans* v. *Lancashire and Yorkshire Railway Co.* (1867) LR 2 Ch. App. 332.

[114] *D'Aquila* v. *Lambert* (1761) 1 Amb. 399, approved in *Booth Steamship*, n. 108 above, 580.

it should not continue to give the seller a bankruptcy preference while the goods remain in an identifiable form in the buyer's possession. As it is, the seller's preference trades on the technicality of the rule that delivery to the carrier is constructive delivery to the buyer and, for the purpose of the extraordinary right of stoppage, deems that delivery does not in fact occur before the transit is over.

A slightly different explanation of the right of stoppage was given in *Bloxam* v. *Sanders*[115] where it was said that the buyer's right to possession of goods, the property in which has passed to him, is defeasible on his insolvency; but nothing is said about why the buyer's property and possession should be defeasible in transit cases. A Canadian judge once referred to the 'persuasive equity' of the stoppage rule, which restored goods to the unpaid seller instead of distributing them among the buyer's creditors.[116] Stoppage *in transitu* has also been explained as introduced for the benefit of trade,[117] which presumably means that sellers are encouraged to surrender goods to a carrier when they know that the goods can be stopped on the buyer's insolvency. The response to this is that sellers can more effectively protect themselves by retaining the right of disposal and stipulating for payment under a banker's letter of credit. Failing this, a seller might contract on retention of title terms. Stoppage *in transitu* therefore seems difficult to reconcile with modern patterns of selling activity. Its continued existence, it is submitted, is best explained by inertia and by the conviction that the buyer's creditors, secured and unsecured, should be denied access to goods that the buyer has never paid for and that have not come into his actual, visible possession.

Duration of Transit

Section 45 deals with the duration of the transit and contains two principal rules for determining the duration of the transit. Sub-section (1) provides that the transit is over when the carrier or other bailee[118] charged with transmitting the goods to the buyer actually delivers them to the buyer or his agent.[119] This rule clearly demonstrates that, for the purpose of stoppage *in transitu*, delivery is essentially based on actual rather than constructive possession by the buyer.[120] The buyer is therefore not in actual possession while the goods are in the hands of the carrier, even if

---

[115] (1825) 4 B & C 941.   [116] *Wiley* v. *Smith* (1876) 1 OAR 179, 217.

[117] *Bohtlingk* v. *Inglis* (1803) 3 East 381; *Berndtson* v. *Strang*, n. 102 above, 490.

[118] *Smith* v. *Goss* (1808) 1 Camp. 282 (wharfinger).

[119] *Dixon* v. *Baldwin* (1804) 5 East 175. Or the buyer's insolvency representative: *Ellis* v. *Hunt* (1789) 3 TR 464.

[120] *Gibson* v. *Carruthers*, n. 105 above; *Berndtson* v. *Strang*, n. 102 above; *Bohtlingk* v. *Inglis*, n. 117 above; *Heninekey* v. *Earle* (1858) 4 E & B 427; *Ex p. Rosevear China Co.* (1879) 11 Ch. D 560.

the carrier is appointed by the buyer,[121] for the carrier's agency to accept delivery on behalf of the buyer, in circumstances whereby the property in the goods vests in the buyer, is not sufficient to defeat the right of stoppage.[122] Indeed, it has been said that the 'essential feature of a stoppage *in transitu* . . . is, that the goods at the time should be in the possession of a middleman'.[123]

Section 45(1) must, however, be read subject to the other principal rule in the section, which is to be found in sub-section(3):

If after the arrival of the goods at the appointed destination the carrier or other bailee or custodier acknowledges to the buyer or his agent that he holds the goods on his behalf and continues in possession of them as bailee or custodier for the buyer or his agent, the transit is at an end, and it is immaterial that a further destination for the goods may have been indicated by the buyer.

Sub-section (3) places pragmatic limits upon a right of stoppage that might otherwise endure for months or even years if the buyer delays in removing the goods from storage at the port of discharge.[124] It recognizes that some buyers may never take actual delivery of the goods but may, instead, choose to deal with them through the medium of warehouse receipts, delivery orders, and the like. In what may be the interests of simplicity, it seems also to formulate a broad rule that the seller is not entitled to trace the goods through too many middlemen involved in the transit of the goods. Because it is sometimes difficult to decide which of the two subsections, sub-section (1) or (3), accounts for a decision, the various instances of the loss of stoppage rights under the two provisions will be considered together.

Actual receipt of the goods will obviously defeat the seller's right of stoppage *in transitu*, but a partial delivery and receipt will do so in principle only in respect of the part delivered.[125] It is possible, however, for the part to be a symbolic delivery of the whole, but the burden of establishing this will rest on the buyer's insolvency representative or on whoever else seeks to overcome the seller's right.[126] The burden might well be discharged if the part delivered were a component of a manufactured machine.[127]

It is clear that constructive possession at the port of discharge, in such a way that the buyer may remove the goods whenever he wishes, defeats the seller's right of stoppage. Thus a buyer who initially refused to accept goods, but then subsequently accepted the key to the warehouse in

---

[121] *Ibid.*　　　[122] *Bethell & Co. v. Clark & Co.* (1888) 20 QBD 615, 617, 619.
[123] *Schotsmans v. Lancashire and Yorkshire Railway Co*, n. 113 above, 338.
[124] *Wiley v. Smith*, n. 116 above.
[125] S. 45(7); *Whitehead v. Anderson* (1842) 9 M & W 518; *Griffith v. Perry* (1859) 1 E & E 680; *Ex p. Cooper* (1879) 11 Ch. D 68.
[126] *Ex p. Cooper*, n. 125 above.　　　[127] *Ibid.*

which they were stored, thereby curtailed the seller's right of stoppage.[128] This would not be the case, however, where a buyer who has declined to accept goods mistakenly takes possession of them, whether personally or through an agent.[129]

It is also clear that delivery of the goods on board a ship that is owned by the buyer will prevent the seller from stopping the goods.[130] The same result should follow where the buyer has chartered the ship by demise,[131] for in such cases the buyer obtains possession of the ship itself. If a buyer merely travels as a passenger on board the ship, this will of course not be sufficient to reduce the goods into his possession.[132] It has on a number of occasions been held that the right of stoppage persists even though it is the buyer who has booked space on the ship[133] or has chartered it for a particular voyage.[134] Furthermore, the transfer to the buyer of the bill of lading will not in itself defeat the seller's right of stoppage.[135] Yet it has been said that the right of stoppage is defeated if the goods are delivered on board a ship that is destined for a 'roving voyage'.[136] The reason for this limitation is hard to see, unless it is based on the need to confine the right of stoppage to relatively narrow temporal limits. Certainly, the right of stoppage persists even though goods are loaded on a ship whose actual destination is unknown to the seller,[137]so this factor probably does not explain the 'roving voyage' limitation.

Certain difficulties are presented in cases of compound transit where, for example, goods are first shipped by road or rail and later transhipped for an ocean voyage. If the seller ships the goods by an inland carrier to a forwarding agent acting for the buyer at the port of overseas shipment and awaiting instructions from the buyer, the transit comes to an end as soon as the goods come into the hands of the forwarding agent;[138] it makes no difference that the seller knows the ultimate destination. If,

---

[128] *Heinekey* v. *Earle*, n. 120 above. See also *Whitehead* v. *Anderson*, n. 125 above (entry on board ship by buyer's assignee in bankruptcy, who touched the goods, did not break transit).

[129] *Bolton* v. *Lancashire and Yorkshire Railway Co.* (1866) LR 1 CP 431.

[130] *Van Casteel* v. *Booker* (1848) 2 Ex. 691; *Schotsmans* v. *Lancashire and Yorkshire Railway Co*, n. 113 above; *Berndtson* v. *Strang* (1867) LR 4 Eq. 481, 489.

[131] S. 45(5) states that it depends upon the circumstances whether the master on a chartered ship has goods in his possession as carrier or as agent for the buyer.

[132] *Lyons* v. *Hoffnung* (1890) 15 App. Cas. 391.

[133] e.g. *Bethell & Co.* v. *Clark & Co.*, n. 122 above; *Ex p. Golding Davis* (1880) 13 Ch. D 628.

[134] *Bohtlingk* v. *Inglis*, n. 117 above; *Berndston* v. *Strang*, n. 130 above; *Ex p. Rosevear China Co*, n. 120 above; *Kemp* v. *Falk* (1882) 7 App. Cas. 573.

[135] e.g. *Schotsmans* v. *Lancashire and Yorkshire Railway Co.* (1867) 2 Ch. App. 332; *Lyons* v. *Hoffnung*, n. 132 above; *The Tigress* (1863) 32 LJ Adm 97.

[136] *Berndtson* v. *Strang*, n. 130 above, 490.

[137] *Ex p. Rosevear China Co.*, n. 120 above. A seller in a hurry can read a shipping register.

[138] *Valpy* v. *Gibson* (1847) 4 CB 837. See also *Ex p. Miles* (1885) 15 QBD 39; *Kendall* v. *Marshall, Stevens & Co.* (1883) 11 QBD 356; *Jobson* v. *Eppenheim* (1905) 21 TLR 468.

however, the goods come into the hands of the ocean carrier in pursuance of an arrangement to that effect between seller and buyer, it is clear that the seller's right of stoppage survives delivery of the goods by the inland to the ocean carrier.[139] It is a question of construction of the contract of sale[140] and of the subsequent conduct of the parties whether such an extended shipment is thus contemplated. Lord Esher once said:

[W]here the transit is a transit which has been caused either by the terms of the contract or by the directions of the purchaser to the vendor, the right of stoppage in transitu exists: but, if the goods are not in the hands of the carrier by means either of the terms of the contract or of the directions of the purchaser to the vendor, but are in transitu afterwards in consequence of fresh directions given by the purchaser for a new transit, then such transit is no part of the original transit, and the right to stop is gone. So also, if the purchaser gives orders that the goods shall be sent to a particular place, these to be kept till he gives fresh orders as to their destination to a new carrier, the original transit is at an end when they have reached that place.[141]

Thus, where a London merchant bought goods from an English manufacturer 150 miles away, and after the contract requested the manufacturer to consign the goods 'to the *Darling Downs*, to Melbourne, loading in the East India Docks', it was held that the transit did not end before the ship reached Melbourne.[142] If, however, the second carrier specially attorns to the buyer, the situation is the same as if the goods had come into the hands of a forwarding agent, and the transit is deemed at an end.[143]

As seen earlier, section 45(3) deems the transit to have ended when the goods arrive at their appointed destination and the carrier or other bailee attorns to the buyer. The application of this rule has not always been straightforward, but the cases support the following propositions. First of all, when the goods have arrived at their destination and the carrier continues to hold them *qua* carrier, the transit will be considered as still continuing.[144] Merely informing the buyer that the goods are ready for collection,[145] or that they will be given up when practical arrangements can be made to that effect,[146] will not in itself amount to an attornment. The rule of attornment is thus applied with some rigour so as to demand distinct evidence of a true undertaking by the carrier to hold the goods

---

[139] *Bethell & Co.* v. *Clark & Co.* (1888) 20 QBD 615; *Kemp* v. *Ismay, Imrie & Co.* (1909) 100 LT 996; *Reddall* v. *Union Castle Mail Steamship Co. Ltd* (1914) 84 LJKB 360.

[140] *Ex p. Watson* (1877) 5 Ch. D 35.

[141] *Bethell & Co.* v. *Clark & Co.*, n. 122 above, 617.   [142] *Ibid.*

[143] *Reddall* v. *Union Castle Mail Steamship Co. Ltd*, n. 139 above.

[144] *Bolton* v. *Lancashire and Yorkshire Railway Co.* (1866) LR 1 CP 431; *Ex p. Barrow* (1877) 6 Ch. D 783 (goods held by carrier's agent).

[145] *Mechan & Sons* v. *North Eastern Railway Co.* 1911 SC 1348.

[146] *Coventry* v. *Gladstone* (1868) LR 6 Eq. 44.

for the buyer, and even an acceptance by the buyer in response to the carrier's undertaking,[147] which may be inferred from the lapse of a reasonable time.[148] By declining to take delivery of the goods, the buyer may prolong the transit to the advantage of the seller.[149] The right of stoppage tends to be construed generously in favour of the seller.[150] If, on arrival at the discharge port, the carrier warehouses the goods on the buyer's instructions, the transit thereupon comes to an end.[151]

Regardless of attornment, the transit will be treated as coming to an end where the buyer pays or tenders the freight, for any subsequent refusal by the carrier to deliver once his lien has thus been lifted will be wrongful.[152] It depends upon the circumstances whether an unpaid carrier with a lien over the goods continues to hold them *qua* carrier[153] or *qua* warehouseman.[154] The right of stoppage will, however, persist, despite a warehousing of the goods by the carrier, if the goods are warehoused in the name of the seller,[155] or even in the name of a bank that has financed the contract of sale.[156]

Section 45(2) provides that the transit is at end if the buyer or an agent obtains delivery of the goods before they have arrived at their appointed destination.[157] It is not clear what the position would be if the buyer were to seize the goods unlawfully in defiance of the carrier's lien but likely that, though this would be a wrong committed against the carrier, it would be effective against the seller.[158] A related matter concerns seizure of the goods in transit by the buyer's insolvency representative or by a sheriff executing a judgment. This should be regarded as terminating the transit.[159]

Notwithstanding the termination of the transit, or the seller's failure to issue a timely stop notice, the buyer and seller may consensually rescind the contract of sale so as to revest the property in the seller, provided this is done before the buyer's insolvency.[160] Similarly, a buyer who rejects

---

[147] *Bolton* v. *Lancashire and Yorkshire Railway Co*, n. 144 above.

[148] *Taylor* v. *Great Eastern Railway Co.* (1901) 17 TLR 394.

[149] *Ex p. Cooper* (1879) 11 Ch. D 68, 73. See also *James* v. *Griffin* (1837) 2 M & W 623 (buyer asked agent to take delivery on behalf of the seller).

[150] *Bethell & Co.* v. *Clark & Co.* (1888) 20 QBD 615, 617.

[151] *Johann Plischke und Sohne GmbH* v. *Allison Bros. Ltd* [1936] 2 All ER 1009.

[152] S. 45(6); *Bird* v. *Brown* (1850) 4 Ex. 786.

[153] *Crawshay* v. *Eades* (1823) 1 B & C 181.

[154] *Kemp* v. *Falk* (1882) 7 App. Cas. 573, 584.

[155] *Lewis* v. *Mason* (1875) 36 UCQB 590 (Can.).

[156] *Re Alcock Ingram & Co. Ltd* [1924] 1 DLR 388.

[157] *Whitehead* v. *Anderson* (1842) 9 M & W 518; *London and North Western Railway Co.* v. *Bartlett* (1861) 7 H & N 400; *Reddall* v. *Union Castle Mail Steamship Co. Ltd*, n. 139 above. But not just because the buyer demands the goods while they are in transit: *Jackson* v. *Nichol* (1839) 5 Bing. NC 50.

[158] *Whitehead* v. *Anderson*, n. 157 above, 534.

[159] *Ellis* v. *Hunt* (1789) 3 TR 464; *Oppenheim* v. *Russell* (1802) 3 B & P 42.

[160] And does not amount to a preference: Insolvency Act 1986, ss. 239, 340.

the contract goods thereby revests the property in the seller and revives a right akin[161] to the right of stoppage.[162] This will be the case even if the seller refuses to take back the goods.[163]

Effect of Stoppage

The mere exercise of a right of stoppage does not as such rescind the contract of sale.[164] Insolvency, as discussed above, does not of itself amount to an anticipatory repudiation of the contract. Rather, a seller who stops the goods[165] is to be treated as having resumed possession of the goods,[166] thereby reasserting the lien he surrendered on delivering the goods to the carrier. In that position, the seller may proceed to a termination of the contract and a resale of the goods in the event of the buyer's insolvency representative failing to adopt the contract of sale.

According to section 47(2), the seller's right of stoppage *in transitu* is defeated in the event of a document of title[167] being lawfully transferred to a *bona fide* purchaser for the value. In the case of a transfer occurring under a sale, the seller's right is defeated altogether,[168] while it is postponed subject to the interest of the pledgee where the transfer occurs under a pledge.[169] The section is applicable even if the buyer has made a subsale prior to receiving the bill of lading.[170] Even if the transfer takes place under a sub-sale, it has been held that the transit continues so long as the sub-buyer has not actually paid for the goods.[171] Since the seller's right of stoppage is curtailed in the interests of *bona fide* purchasers and not of the buyer's creditors, this result seems correct in principle[172] provided the stop notice otherwise arrives in time. A seller may also stop the goods to the prejudice of a sub-buyer who has paid for them and to

---

[161] S. 39(2).

[162] S. 45(4); *Bolton* v. *Lancashire and Yorkshire Railway Co.*, n. 144 above.

[163] *Ibid.*

[164] S. 48(1); *Schotsmans* v. *Lancashire and Yorkshire Railway Co.* (1867) LR 2 Ch. App. 332; *Kemp* v. *Falk*, n. 154 above; *Booth Steamship Co. Ltd* v. *Cargo Fleet Iron Co. Ltd* [1916] 2 KB 579. The question was still thought a doubtful one in *Phelps Stokes & Co.* v. *Comber* (1885) 29 Ch. D 813, 821.

[165] Whether he receives possession or directs the carrier to hold to his order: s. 46(1); *Booth Steamship*, n. 164 above. The carrier's duty is to be found in s. 46(4). See also *Continental Grain Co.* v. *Islamic Republic of Iran Shipping Lines* [1983] 2 Lloyd's Rep. 620.

[166] S. 44.

[167] In the expanded statutory sense of s. 61(1) of the Sale of Goods Act and s. 1(4) of the Factors Act 1889, overruling in this respect *Lackington* v. *Atherton* (1844) 7 M & G 360 where the transfer of a delivery order (not a common law document of title) did not defeat the right of stoppage.

[168] S. 47(2)(a); *Leask* v. *Scott* (1877) 2 QBD 376; *Cahn* v. *Pockett's Bristol Channel Steam Packet Co. Ltd* [1899] 1 QB 643.

[169] S. 47(2)(b); *Kemp* v. *Falk*, n. 154 above.

[170] *Cahn* v. *Pockett's Bristol Channel Steam Packet Co. Ltd*, n. 168 above.

[171] *Ex p. Golding Davis* (1880) 13 Ch. D 628. See also *Ex p. Falk* (1880) 14 Ch. D 446.

[172] See, however, *Kemp* v. *Falk*, n. 154 above.

whom the property has passed, if there has not been a transfer of the document of title.[173]

The seller's stop notice[174] must make plain his intention to resume possession of the goods.[175] It must also identify with sufficient certainty the contract goods: a notice was held not to be sufficient when it failed to indicate to a warehouseman which particular items despatched to a consignee, out of a much larger number held by the warehouseman in the name of the consignee, were subject to the notice.[176] Section 46(2) provides that the 'notice may be given either to the person in actual possession of the goods or to his principal'.[177] Consequently, a notice reaching the ship's master will be sufficient; likewise one to the offices of the carrier, provided it gives the carrier sufficient time to communicate diligently with the master.[178] It is unlikely that a notice issued to the consignee would be adequate.[179]

Once a valid stop notice has been issued to the carrier,[180] the seller is to be regarded as having the right to immediate possession of the goods and can therefore maintain an action in conversion if the carrier declines to surrender the goods or hold them to the seller's order, or persists in delivering the goods to the consignee.[181] If the notice is given to the carrier, the carrier must forward it with reasonable diligence to the master of the ship.[182] The seller, however, is under an obligation to pay the carrier's freight both up to the point of stoppage[183] as well as to the redelivery point,[184] and the carrier has a lien on the cargo for the freight.[185] The carrier has only a special lien for the freight and may not claim under the contract of carriage in respect of any general lien for the whole amount

---

[173] The sub-buyer falls outside the protective language of s. 47. See also *Kemp* v. *Falk*, n. 154 above, from which this may be inferred. *Quaere* the constructive possession of the buyer in possession under s. 25(1)? It would surely strain that provision if a constructive delivery to the sub-buyer could be founded upon the constructive delivery to the buyer that occurred with the start of the transit.

[174] The seller may effectively recover possession without issuing a notice: s. 46(1).

[175] *Phelps Stokes & Co.* v. *Comber*, n. 164 above, 821–2.

[176] *Clementson* v. *Grand Trunk Railway Co.* (1877) 42 UCQB 263 (Can.).

[177] *Whitehead* v. *Anderson* (1842) 9 M & W 518.

[178] S. 46(3); *Kemp* v. *Falk* (1882) 7 App. Cas. 573.

[179] See *Phelps Stokes & Co.* v. *Comber*, n. 164 above, 822 (opinion declined).

[180] The carrier is under no duty to determine if the seller's demand is justified: *The Tigress* (1863) 32 LJ Adm. 97, 101.

[181] *Litt* v. *Cowley* (1816) 7 Taunt. 169; *Thompson* v. *Traill* (1826) 6 B & C 36; *Booth Steamship Co. Ltd* v. *Cargo Fleet Iron Co. Ltd* [1916] 2 KB 579; *The Tigress*, n. 180 above.

[182] *Kemp* v. *Falk*, n. 178 above, 585–6.

[183] *Booth Steamship*, n. 164 above. *Quaere* the seller who is not party to the contract of carriage with the carrier? It is submitted that the seller should pay, for otherwise the seller condemns the carrier to pursue a freight claim against an insolvent buyer and without the benefit of a lien.

[184] S. 46(4).

[185] *Booth Steamship Co. Ltd* v. *Cargo Fleet Iron Co. Ltd* [1916] 2 KB 579.

of the indebtedness of the buyer under a running account.[186] Whether the relationship between carrier and seller is contractual or quasi-contractual[187] is probably of little account, for the above rights and duties are clearly established as a matter of customary mercantile law.

The Right of Resale

The modern understanding of section 48 of the Sale of Goods Act, which deals with the seller's right of resale, is probably further from the intention of the draftsman than is the case with any other section of the Act. To anyone approaching it with the values and principles of contract law in the late twentieth century, section 48 is a mystery. To make sense of the section, it has to be first interpreted in the light of the case law on which it was founded before the modern revisionist view is discussed. The principal difficulties in section 48 lie in sub-sections (3) and (4) and in the relationship between the two provisions:

(3) Where the goods are of a perishable nature, or where the unpaid seller gives notice to the buyer of his intention to re-sell, and the buyer does not within a reasonable time pay or tender the price, the unpaid seller may re-sell the goods and recover from the original buyer damages for any loss occasioned by his breach of contract.

(4) Where the seller expressly reserves the right of resale in case the buyer should make default, and on the buyer making default re-sells the goods, the original contract of sale is rescinded but without prejudice to any claim the seller may have for damages.

Development of Resale Right

The first point to note about these provisions is that, while founded upon a breach of contract by the buyer, they do not expressly demand that the buyer commit a discharging breach of contract. Sub-section (3) refers to the buyer's failure to pay, and sub-section (4) to the more general case of default. As the law was established in *Martindale* v. *Smith*,[188] the buyer's duty of timely payment was not of the essence of the contract, so the absence of any reference to discharge in section 48 is quite understandable. The next point to make is that sub-section (3) was based on case law ruling that the seller could recover from the buyer a loss occasioned by the resale, even if the seller's behaviour was wrongful.[189] This will be explained in due course. The seller's claim, as encapsulated in sub-section (3), consisted in essence of the deficiency between the initial

---

[186] *Booth Steamship*, n. 185 above; *Oppenheim* v. *Russell* (1802) 3 B & P 42; *United States Steel Products Co.* v. *Great Western Railway Co.* [1916] 1 AC 689.
[187] See *The Tigress*, n. 180 above; *Booth Steamship*, n. 185 above.
[188] (1841) 1 QB 389.   [189] *Page* v. *Cowasjee Eduljee* (1866) LR 1 PC 127.

contract price and the resale price. This could be recovered by the seller in the form of an action on the contract for damages for non-acceptance,[190] or possibly in the form of an action for the original contract price,[191] in which latter case it seems to have been assumed that the seller could not reap a windfall by failing to give credit to the buyer for the resale price and for any deposit paid by the buyer.[192] The difference between these two forms of action seems to have been one of pleading only.[193]

In order for the above claim to be made, the contract had to remain 'open', that is to say, unrescinded.[194] An action for damages could not be maintained on a rescinded contract, for the understanding was that rescission operated retrospectively so as to destroy contractual entitlement *ab initio*. Nor could the seller frame an action for the price in the counts of goods bargained and sold or goods sold and delivered, for the passing of property to the buyer was essential for such an action to succeed, and rescission *ab initio* also destroyed the conveyance of the general property in the goods to the buyer. In consequence, the property in the goods was still vested in the buyer at the moment the seller resold the goods and the seller exercised rights midway between those of a lienee and those of an owner;[195] he was to be treated as though he were a pledgee with a right of sale in the event of the pledgor's failure to redeem the pledge. Hence, section 48(3) could be seen as conferring a power of sale that complemented the unpaid seller's lien provided for elsewhere in the Act.[196]

In order for the seller to recover his deficiency, authority existed to the effect that it was not necessary for the resale to be preceded by notice to the buyer of the seller's intention to resell;[197] the specific reference to the

---

[190] *Maclean* v. *Dunn* (1828) 4 Bing. 722.

[191] Tentative support for this is in *Acebal* v. *Levy* (1834) 10 Bing. 376. See also *Page* v. *Cowasjee Eduljee*, n. 189 above, 145–6. The property would have had to pass for this approach to be adopted: s. 49(1). Cf. *Maclean* v. *Dunn*, n. 190 above, 728 (tentative view that the seller could not sue for the price after resale).

[192] *Acebal* v. *Levy*, n. 191 above. Cf. *Lamond* v. *Davall* (1847) 9 QB 1030.

[193] *Acebal* v. *Levy*, n. 191 above, 384. But note the difficulties in *R. V. Ward Ltd* v. *Bignall* [1967] 1 QB 534.

[194] *Maclean* v. *Dunn*, n. 190 above, 728 (the resale did not rescind); *Greaves* v. *Ashlin* (1813) 3 Camp. 426.

[195] Lord Blackburn, *A Treatise on the Effect of the Contract of Sale on the Legal Rights of Property and Possession in Goods, Wares and Merchandise* (2nd edn., 1885, J. Graham), 445–6; *Sawyer* v. *Pringle* (1891) 28 OAR 218, 226, 231 (Can.); *McPherson* v. *United States Fidelity and Guarantee Co.* (1915) 33 OLR 524, 538 (Can.).

[196] *McCowan* v. *Bowes* [1923] 3 DLR 756, 766.

[197] *Maclean* v. *Dunn*, n. 190 above; *Fitt* v. *Cassanet* (1842) 4 M & G 898; *McCowan* v. *Bowes*, n. 196 above, 762–3. A failure to notify where time was not of the essence would make the resale wrongful with the consequences noted below: *Page* v. *Cowasjee Eduljee*, n. 189 above.

perishables in section 48(3) was merely an illustrative case of resale[198] where urgent circumstances dispensed with any need for notice.[199] But notice of resale could be explained in various ways, for example, as the best evidence of the seller's intention not to rescind the contract *ab initio*,[200] or as necessary to make time of the essence of the contract so as to render the resale lawful,[201] or as akin to the procedure to be employed by a pledgee in effecting a lawful[202] sale of the pledged goods.[203] Provided the resale were conducted lawfully, even a buyer to whom the property had passed could not complain, for his failure to perform the contract meant that he lacked the immediate right to possession necessary to maintain an action in conversion.[204]

Suppose, however, that the seller failed to conduct the sale in a lawful manner, assuming that this required a notice to be first issued to the buyer,[205] or even that the seller unlawfully repossessed the goods prior to resale.[206] The effect of this was that the buyer obtained the right to immediate possession and hence title to sue in conversion. But the buyer who had not paid would not recover the full value of the goods;[207] investing the buyer with such an action merely made doubly certain that a seller suing for a deficiency could not reap a windfall, for it prevented a seller from recovering the price without giving credit for the resale price and for any deposit received from the buyer.[208]

The cases underlying section 48(3) seem all to have been decided on the basis of property having passed to and remaining in the buyer,[209] so that section 48(2) became necessary for the protection of the second buyer on the resale. It provides that such a buyer obtains a good title as against the original buyer if the resale occurs after the seller exercises his

---

[198] In *Maclean* v. *Dunn*, n. 190 above, 91, 728, Best CJ said that price volatility made all goods perishables, the rise and fall of the market making a general resale rule expedient.

[199] Cf. agency of necessity: *Pragen* v. *Blatspiel, Stamp and Heacock Ltd* [1924] 1 KB 566.

[200] *Page* v. *Cowasjee Eduljee*, n. 189 above.

[201] *Ibid*. 245. On making time of the essence, see *Cornwall* v. *Henson* [1900] 2 Ch. 298 (land); *Lambert* v. *Slack* [1926] 2 DLR 166, 170.

[202] *Page* v. *Cowasjee Eduljee*, n. 189 above; *Sawyer* v. *Pringle*, n. 195 above; *McPherson* v. *United States Fidelity and Guarantee Co.*, n. 195 above. These cases establish that an unlawful sale may be tortious without rescinding the contract of sale.

[203] *Halliday* v. *Holgate* (1868) LR 3 Ex. 399. This is probably the best explanation of *Ex p. Stapleton* (1879) 10 Ch. D 586.

[204] *Lord* v. *Price* (1874) LR 9 Ex. 54; *Milgate* v. *Kebble* (1841) 3 M & G 100.

[205] *Page* v. *Cowasjee Eduljee*, n. 189 above, 145.   [206] *Ibid*.

[207] See *Chinery* v. *Viall* (1860) 5 H & N 288.

[208] *Page* v. *Cowasjee Eduljee*, n. 189 above; *Stephens* v. *Wilkinson* (1831) 2 B & Ad. 320 (trespass). For the observation that it is curious that a seller repossessing the goods may elect to keep, and not resell, them and also forfeit the buyer's deposit, see *Gallagher* v. *Shilcock* [1949] 2 KB 765.

[209] This seems also to have been true of *Maclean* v. *Dunn*, n. 190 above, though the court makes nothing of it. See *Page* v. *Cowasjee Eduljee*, n. 189 above (though there had been no formal registration of the change of ownership under the relevant shipping legislation).

lien or his right of stoppage *in transitu*. No reference is made to the seller's power of withholding delivery, the counterpart of the unpaid seller's lien where the property has not passed. Furthermore, the index of the seller's real rights in section 39(2), which applies where the property has not passed, does not mention resale; mention of it is however made in the index in section 39(1), which applies where the property has passed. In consequence, the seller's power to transmit title where the property remains vested in him is but a feature of the general law of title transfer.[210] Where the property has passed, section 48(2) comes into play to protect the second buyer. Unlike section 24, it imposes no requirements of continuity of possession, good faith, and delivery, which omission buttresses the argument that the seller is exercising a right of resale[211] akin to that of a pledgee.[212]

Section 48(4) still requires explanation. It is based on the decision in *Lamond* v. *Davall*,[213] which proved hard to assimilate into the remainder of the case law and whose legacy was therefore a separate statutory provision. In *Lamond* v. *Davall*, the contract contained an express right of resale[214] and deficiency entitlement if the buyer failed to pay for the subject matter (shares) by a certain date. The court held that the right of resale rendered conditional a sale that, without it, would have been absolute. By invoking the right and reselling the goods, which occurred at a loss, the seller thereby nullified the earlier sale. It followed that the seller could not claim the price on either of the relevant common counts.[215] Besides, the court assumed that allowing the seller to sue for the price would allow him to retain the resale price as a windfall,[216] which was unfair; moreover, the seller might find it inconvenient to be treated as the buyer's agent for resale purposes. But the seller was allowed to maintain an action for damages for the deficiency and the cost of resale. Although section 48(4), supposedly codifying *Lamond* v. *Davall*, speaks of resale under an express power as rescinding the contract, nothing is said in that case about the contract being rescinded *ab initio*. Rescinding the contract *ab initio* would make it difficult to explain the continuing existence of a damages entitlement under an express provision of that contract as the law then stood. The separate existence of sub-section (4) unduly complicates an already difficult area of law; the

[210] *Wait* v. *Baker* (1848) 2 Ex. 1; *R. V. Ward Ltd* v. *Bignall* [1967] 1 QB 534.

[211] The modern understanding of resale, treating it as the outcome of a contractual termination revesting the property in the seller, empties s. 48(2) of content.

[212] See s. 21(2)(b) of the Sale of Goods Act 1979.   [213] (1847) 9 QB 1030.

[214] The absence of such a clause was said in *Maclean* v. *Dunn* (1828) 4 Bing. 722 not to negative an implied right of resale; the practice of inserting such clauses in East India Company contracts was done *ex abundante cautela*: *ibid*. 728–9.

[215] Goods bargained and sold and goods sold and delivered.

[216] Cf. *Acebal* v. *Levy* (1834) 10 Bing. 376.

decision in *Lamond* v. *Davall* could have been folded into sub-section (3).[217]

Modern Rationalization

Such was the separate evolution of sub-sections (3) and (4) of section 48. Codifying statutes summarize the case law thrown up by the accidents of litigation and do not, unless the product of a severely rational mind, make allowances for gaps in the system to which litigation has not yet responded. The modern contractual orthodoxy of prospective discharge for breach destroyed the foundation of section 48(3) and (4) and, in *R. V. Ward Ltd* v. *Bignall*,[218] created the opportunity for statutory revision.

That case concerned a claim rising out of an entire contract for the sale of two cars. When the buyer refused to take delivery, the sellers wrote a letter asserting that the property had passed to the buyer, that the buyer was liable to pay the price, and that, furthermore, the sellers would dispose of the cars for the best price they could command and look to the buyer for the deficiency if he failed to pay by a stated date. The deficiency claim was expressed by the sellers as a claim for damages. By the time of the trial, only one of the cars had been sold. The court therefore awarded a large sum as deficiency damages, which included a rateable portion of the sale price for the unsold car, and did not make an order for the disposal of the unsold car. Applying, however, the principles underlying the pre-codification cases, the judgment was quite consistent with a conclusion that the contract of sale had never been rescinded, that the property in the unsold car remained vested in the buyer, that the sellers had merely exercised a statutory right of sale annexed to their unpaid seller's lien, and that the unsold car would be released to its owner, the buyer, once the judgment debt was paid in full.[219]

But this was not at all the way that the sellers' claim was rationalized by the Court of Appeal, whose approach was based on the premise that the resale was conducted by the seller *qua* owner, rather than *qua* creditor with a possessory security and right of sale, and that any revesting of the

---

[217] The result in the case is quite consistent with *Maclean* v. *Dunn*, n. 214 above, where the court did not have to consider the locus of property. Williston was not happy with s. 48 and the results of this are in the Uniform Sales Act 1906, s. 60. It differs from s. 48 in the following principal respects: (a) it explicitly allows resale in the additional case where the buyer's failure to pay goes on beyond a reasonable time; (b) it states that notice of the resale is not necessary for its validity, though it may be material in determining whether the buyer's delay is unreasonable; (c) it imposes on the seller a duty of reasonable care and judgement in resale (a matter not broached in the English case law); (d) it makes it plain that the seller does not hold any surplus for the buyer; and (e) it makes no mention of rescission and collapses the distinction between the presence and absence of resale clauses. Rescission itself is dealt with in s. 61.

[218] N. 210 above.

[219] But see the difficulty the court had in following the argument through the pleadings.

property in the sellers[220] had to occur on the basis of a contract that had been discharged for the buyer's breach.[221] As Diplock LJ put it: 'Any act which puts it out of his power to perform thereafter his primary obligations under the contract, if it is an act which he is entitled to do without notice to the party in default, must amount to an election to rescind the contract'.[222] Contractual termination operated prospectively[223] but nevertheless effected a divesting of the buyer's property in the goods. This latter proposition, the mechanics of which were not explained, was regarded as self-evident.[224] The particular virtue of treating the resale as consequent upon the termination of the contract was that it protected the seller from the unnecessary complication of an action by the buyer in conversion or for damages in contract for non-delivery of the goods.[225] This was achieved by interpreting section 48(3) as providing that time was of the essence for all sales of perishables, hence the absence of a need to serve notice on the buyer, as well as for any sale where the seller chose to make it so by serving notice on the buyer.[226] The lack of a reference to rescission in section 48(3), when it was mentioned in section 48(4), was explained away as displaying an intention that the exercise of an express contractual right of resale under the latter provision was not to be treated as an act performed by the seller as agent for the buyer.[227]

R. V. Ward Ltd v. *Bignall* imposes the modern view of contractual discharge on statutory provisions that were actuated by a different philosophy. Despite the confident tone of Diplock LJ's judgment, the decision represents poor legal history, but it does have three compelling merits. First, it avoids the confusion that would inevitably spring up if the section were applied without a thorough understanding of the outmoded principles on which it was based. Secondly, a seller terminating the contract for the buyer's discharging breach will be able to recover damages in the normal way.[228] The seller will be seeking to recover any shortfall between the original contract price and the price recoverable on a resale. If the market rule for the assessment of damages operates, the seller will

---

[220] The court concluded that the passing of property rule in s. 18, Rule 1, had been impliedly ousted by the parties but went on to deal with the case on the assumption it applied.

[221] Hence the overruling of *Gallagher* v. *Shilcock*, n. 208 above.

[222] N. 210 above, 548. Note that Diplock LJ brings s. 48(1) into his analysis as showing that the exercise of a lien or a right of stoppage *in transitu* would not necessarily amount to contractual termination.

[223] This approach would extend also to s. 48(4). For the gradual triumph of prospective termination in sale of land cases, see, e.g., *Harold Wood Brick Ltd* v. *Ferris* [1935] WN 21; *Johnson* v. *Agnew* [1980] AC 367 (overruling *Capital and Suburban Properties Ltd* v. *Swycher* [1976] Ch. 319 and *Horsler* v. *Zorro* [1975] Ch. 302).

[224] *Ibid.* 550 ('of course, well-established'). No cases were cited.

[225] N. 210 above, 550.   [226] *Ibid.* 550.   [227] *Ibid.* 543, 551

[228] See discussion of damages for non-acceptance in the text accompanying nn. 549 ff. below.

in effect have to mitigate his damages by securing the best available resale price. If the resale price itself defines the damages claim, the mitigation rule is introduced in a more overt way. The role of mitigation, though not excluded by the pre-codification cases, was not sanctioned by them either. Thirdly, by introducing contractual discharge, the case avoids the troublesome possibility of the buyer activating the seller's obligation to deliver by tendering the price after the resale. It does, however, leave unexplained quite why, and how, the revesting of property in the seller occurs on prospective contractual discharge.

As a matter of technique, this would clearly have to be done on the basis of an implied resolutive condition, or condition subsequent.[229] If the buyer becomes insolvent before the condition is sprung, this should not of itself prejudice the seller, since the buyer's insolvency representative stands in the buyer's shoes and takes subject to the proprietary claims maintainable against the buyer.[230] So, in a case like *R. V. Ward Ltd* v. *Bignall*, where the seller remains in possession, he would be protected against a solvent or an insolvent buyer alike by virtue of his statutory lien and right of resale. These rights would not, however, avail the seller after he delivers the goods to the buyer or delivers them to a carrier and loses his right of stoppage *in transitu*. The silence of the Sale of Goods Act beyond the point when stoppage *in transitu* might be exercised testifies to a statutory intention that the unpaid seller has no further real rights.[231] Applying the new orthodox approach in *R. V. Ward Ltd* v. *Bignall*, the parties can be treated as impliedly providing for a revesting of the property in the goods in the seller within the same limits of the draftsman's intention. The Sale of Goods Act contains no provisions dealing with the exercise of an express contractual right of repossession, or with the consequences of terminating a contract under which the property remains in the seller but possession is transferred to the buyer, or with the case where the contract expressly springs a revesting of title in the seller. It is clear that a seller surrenders all real rights to the goods when both property and possession are transferred to the buyer. Nevertheless, the effect of *R. V. Ward Ltd* v. *Bignall*, which turns the revesting of property in the seller into a matter of implied contractual intention, is to make it difficult to explain why this should not also happen to a seller who has lost both property and possession. If the contract were to contain a provision allowing the seller, in the event of the buyer's breach, to repossess the goods after property and possession have passed to the buyer, or

---

[229] See *Automatic Fire Sprinklers Pty. Ltd* v. *Watson* (1946) 72 CLR 435, 463–4; *Commission Car Sales (Hastings) Ltd* v. *Saul* [1957] NZLR 144.

[230] Ch. 8 above.

[231] Hence a seizure of the goods by the seller will amount to a conversion: *Page* v. *Cowasjee Eduljee* (1866) LR 1 PC 127.

stipulating for a revesting of the property in the seller in that event, such provisions would be treated as registrable bills of sale or charges under the relevant legislation.

One drawback to the interpretation of section 48(3) adopted by the courts is that it gives no explanation why the sub-section provides only two examples, if they are indeed meant to be examples rather than a *numerus clausus*, of a discharging breach by the buyer. The buyer's failure to accept and pay for the goods may well go to the root of the contract, even in the case of non-perishable goods where the seller has failed to make time of the essence. Again, the buyer's manifest inability to pay may amount to a repudiation of his contractual obligations.[232] Another example is where the contract itself makes time of the essence without requiring the service of notice on the buyer. Section 48(3) cannot therefore, for practical purposes, be seen as an index of the seller's rights to terminate for breach by the buyer, since the general law supports his right to terminate in other instances too.

Another point emerging from *R. V. Ward Ltd* v. *Bignall* concerns the status of section 48(2) as a *nemo dat* exception. It was noted above that the provision was not needed where the property in the goods had never vested in the buyer, for the seller had the power to transmit title in accordance with ordinary property principles. When the property has revested in the seller after a valid termination of the contract, again the seller's power to transmit title is to be justified by ordinary principle rather than by any dispensing power in section 48(2). But the seller may have resold after exercising his lien or right of stoppage *in transitu*, without having complied satisfied section 48(3) in those cases where this provision is needed to effect a valid termination of the contract. The seller, for example, may have failed to issue a notice making time of the essence or may have issued an inadequate notice.[233] Section 48(2), not preconditioned on a valid termination, would empower the seller nevertheless to transmit title to the second buyer. This, of course, leaves unexplained why the seller's power in this instance, which does not depend upon delivery or the buyer's good faith or unbroken possession,[234] should be broader than his section 24 power. The old view that the seller acts rather as a pledgee with a right of sale provides at least a rational explanation of this difference.

Reservation of Title Clauses

A final issue arising out of resale concerns reservation of title clauses where the seller repossesses the goods after the buyer defaults on

---

[232] But see the discussion of insolvency in the text accompanying nn. 14 ff. above.

[233] This assumes that the seller is otherwise entitled to terminate: see discussion in the text accompanying nn. 218 ff. above.

[234] Stoppage *in transitu* effects a resumption of broken possession.

payment of the agreed price. The issue was discussed at some length in *Clough Mill Ltd* v. *Martin*[235] where Robert Goff LJ considered the case of a contract that remained subsisting notwithstanding the seller's resale of the contract goods for which the buyer had not paid. He did not say how or why the contract might have remained on foot after repossession and resale, and did not refer to section 48 or to *R. V. Ward Ltd* v. *Bignall.* It is perfectly possible for a resale to be conducted pursuant to an agreement after the breach by buyer and seller, so the case is no authority on the impact of resale on the contract of sale.

A distinction was drawn by Robert Goff LJ between contracts that had not and contracts that had been terminated before the resale. This was done in order to demonstrate an implied term in the contract in the former case that the seller should account to the buyer for any surplus received from the resale over and above the amount owed by the buyer. This comes close to treating the seller as a pledgee or mortgagee exercising a power of sale over goods belonging to the buyer. The likelihood of any surplus being realized is greater in the case of all moneys clauses than in the case of a clause reserving title only until payment is made for the contract goods. A surplus would also be perfectly possible if sellers were ever able effectively to reserve title to new goods manufactured by the buyer from materials supplied by the seller together with the buyer's labour and possibly materials supplied by other sellers. In the case of a contract that had been terminated, Robert Goff LJ could see no basis for an implied term surviving termination requiring the seller to account for a surplus.[236] It is difficult to see why termination should produce starkly different results in the two cases, and Robert Goff LJ did refer to the buyer in the case of termination having an action for the recovery of money on a failure of consideration.[237] But a buyer recovering money in such an action would be denied any appreciation in the value of the chattel; a seller having to account for a surplus would be required to surrender any appreciation as part of that surplus.

ENFORCING THE PRIMARY OBLIGATIONS OF THE PARTIES

This section of the Chapter is concerned with those personal actions of buyer and seller that require direct performance by the other party of one or more of his primary obligations under the contract, rather than substituted performance in the form of damages. The seller's action for the price will therefore be dealt with; likewise the availability of specific performance and injunctive relief. The latter remedies are usually

---

[235] [1985] 1 WLR 111.　　　　[236] *Sed quaere* if termination operates prospectively?
[237] Discussed in the text accompanying nn. 311 ff. below.

associated with actions brought by buyers, but, on appropriate facts, they may be sought by sellers too. The real counterpart to a buyer's action for specific performance is a seller's action for specific performance,[238] requiring the buyer to take delivery of the goods, possibly, for example, to take them on an instalment basis as they roll off the seller's assembly line.[239] When the seller sues the buyer in debt, as he does when he sues for the price, the judgment rendered is that the buyer shall pay a liquidated sum of money; it does not, without more ado, compel the buyer to take delivery of the goods or to compensate a seller who is left with the inconvenience of unwanted goods on his hands.[240] That it may be to the buyer's clear economic advantage to accept delivery of goods for which he has been made to pay is quite another matter.

The Action for the Price

The Sale of Goods Act lays down two instances where the seller may sue for the price, namely, where the property has passed to the buyer, and where the contract clearly characterizes the duty to pay as an obligation independent of the date of performance of the seller's primary obligations. The first of these instances is dealt with by section 49(1): 'Where, under a contract of sale, the property in the goods has passed to the buyer and he wrongfully neglects or refuses to pay for the goods according to the terms of the contract, the seller may maintain an action against him for the price of the goods'.

Passing of Property

The first feature to note is that the above entitlement to maintain a debt action against the buyer is limited to cases where the property has passed and does not include cases where the buyer's obligation to pay simply falls due.[241] As seen in an earlier chapter,[242] the buyer is bound to pay when so required under the contract, and this obligation matures, subject to contrary agreement, when the seller is ready and willing to deliver the goods according to the terms of the contract. Yet it is well established

---

[238] Cf. Lord Denning in *Attica Sea Carriers Corpn.* v. *Ferrostaal Poseidon Bulk Reederei GmbH (The Puerto Buitrago)* [1976] 1 Lloyd's Rep. 250, 255 (debt claim as specific performance).

[239] A seller may have locked his entire output potential into producing custom-built goods for the buyer's unique needs. Specific performance, or equivalent short-term injunctive relief, may be needed to avert irreparable prejudice.

[240] To sue in debt for the price, the seller must aver compliance with all conditions precedent, namely, in the majority of cases, the transfer of the property in the goods together with a readiness and willingness to effect delivery of the goods. For specific performance, the seller need only be ready and willing to perform a contract that is open for future performance.

[241] Ss. 27–28.   [242] Ch. 6 above.

that the mere tender of delivery does not entitle the seller to sue for the price.[243]

A curious aspect of the case law is that there is no discussion of the merits of permitting sellers to sue in debt rather than for damages, and thus it cannot be said that the present position is explained by a keen judicial sense of the circumstances where sellers should be afforded the procedural[244] and other advantages of suing in debt. Besides the commercial advantages referred to below, a seller suing in debt will not be constrained by the remoteness-of-damage rules. Certain speculative losses, hard to prove in a damages action, will lie concealed in a debt claim. Over and above the debt claim, however, there may be an additional damages claim for injury flowing from delayed performance,[245] and this will be subject to the normal remoteness rules. In principle, the seller suing for the price will not have to mitigate his damages, since mitigation limits the defendant's secondary obligation to pay damages rather than his primary obligation to pay the price.

The essence of a debt action is that the debtor has actually received a *quid pro quo*, an executed consideration,[246] and therefore must account for the debt to his creditor. Before the abolition of the forms of action, the appropriate liquidated money counts were goods bargained and sold and goods sold and delivered, under both of which counts the property had to have passed.[247] These two counts were simplified forms of pleading *indebitatus assumpsit*, which was predicated on a fictitious promise to pay an antecedent debt, and the difficulty of reconciling the buyer's contractual duty to pay with the seller's entitlement to sue in debt may be seen as evidence of the imperfect amalgamation of special *assumpsit* and debt in the modern law of contract.

The most important functional issue posed by the debt action is which of the two parties, seller or buyer, should be the one who is left to dispose of unwanted goods.[248] It has also been said to be economically wasteful to force unwanted goods on a buyer,[249] but, if goods may be consumed by the buyer or disposed of in the market without undue difficulty, there should not be any waste. Moreover, if the goods are custom-built for the buyer's needs, greater economic waste is likely to arise if they are left in

---

[243] *Colley* v. *Overseas Exporters* [1921] 3 KB 302.

[244] For the summary judgment process, see RSC Ord. 14. A plaintiff suing for the price is not constrained by rules of remoteness of damage or mitigation of damages.

[245] *Wadsworth* v. *Lydall* [1981] 1 WLR 598; *International Minerals & Chemical Corpn.* v. *Karl O. Hahn AG* [1986] 1 Lloyd's Rep. 80.

[246] *Martin* v. *Hogan* (1917) 24 CLR 234, 262 (the consideration does not pass until the property passes in sale of goods).

[247] *Atkinson* v. *Bell* (1828) 8 B & C 277; *Colley* v. *Overseas Exporters*, n. 243 above.

[248] Ontario Law Reform Commission, *Report on Sale of Goods* (1979), ii, 416.

[249] *Ibid.*

the seller's hands, good only for their break-up value or for expensive alterations to suit another buyer.

It should not be forgotten that the buyer is amenable to a price action only if he 'wrongfully' withholds payment,[250] and the merits of a seller who is willing to perform and is faced with a contract-breaking buyer ought not to be overlooked.[251] In some cases, it may be difficult indeed for sellers to prove they have actually incurred a loss because of the buyer's breach.[252] Just as difficulties of assessment can be avoided by securing a deposit to be forfeited on breach, or by inserting in the contract a liquidated damages clause, so the right to sue for the price can obviate an intractable damages inquiry. It is not enough simply to ask which party is better able to dispose of the goods if the above considerations are ignored. For one thing, there may be many cases where a buyer can make grudging use of the contract goods. Not every repudiating buyer will be unable to use raw materials for widget-making because he has quit the widget-making business, or be unable to use the seller's widget-making machines because he has filled his factory with someone else's machines. Furthermore, in many instances involving carriage of the goods to a distant place, requiring the seller to dispose of the goods could be unfairly onerous. Without denying the importance of having the law respond to functional issues, it should never be forgotten that commercial certainty is itself one of those issues. There is a great deal to be said for a rule that states precisely when a seller is entitled to sue for the price, especially if the goods are of volatile value or quickly depreciate, just as a regime of strict rejection of non-conforming goods and contractual termination has its commercial attractions. Whether the relatively precise rule that we currently have is located in the right place, however, is a different matter.

Section 49(1) of the Sale of Goods Act was considered at some length in *Colley* v. *Overseas Exporters*,[253] where buyers and sellers were both Sheffield merchants. The contract was for the sale of a quantity of belts on f.o.b. Liverpool terms. It was therefore the sellers' responsibility to get the goods to a ship in Liverpool nominated by the buyers. The ship originally nominated by the buyers was withdrawn by its owners from

---

[250] S. 49(1).

[251] Alberta Institute of Law Research and Reform, *The Uniform Sale of Goods Act* (Report No. 38, 1982), 108.

[252] See the lost volume problem, discussed in the text accompanying nn. 697 ff. below. A liquidated damages clause may close the indemnity gap between remoteness of damage and factual causation. Diplock LJ said in *Robophone Facilities Ltd* v. *Blank* [1966] 1 WLR 1428, 1448, that it constituted disclosure under the second limb of the rule in *Hadley* v. *Baxendale* (1854) 9 Ex. 341.

[253] N. 243 above. A case difficult to reconcile with an orthodox interpretation of s. 49(1) is *Minister for Supply and Development* v. *Servicemen's Co-operative Joinery Manufacturers Ltd* (1951) 82 CLR 621.

service, and, despite repeated efforts, the buyers were unable to nominate another ship. Meanwhile, the goods were packed for export and
sent by the sellers to Liverpool, where they arrived at the offices of the
forwarding agents. At this point, the sellers were faced with an uncertain
quantum of future consequential damages,[254] for items such as the cost
of consigning goods to a different market, possibly with some repacking,
or the cost of keeping the goods in storage until another buyer turned up.
The sellers instead took out a specially indorsed writ leading to summary
judgment for a liquidated amount, arguing that the buyers' failure to
nominate estopped[255] them from denying that the price was due. This
argument was rejected by McCardie J, who held that the property would
not pass until the goods were put on board[256] and that no principle of law
could be invoked to deem that a necessary condition had been fulfilled
when in fact it had not been.[257] If the failure of the sellers to comply with
all necessary conditions were excused in this case, a seller could sue in
debt in all cases where the buyer repudiated,[258] even if the goods were
unascertained at the material time.[259]

Although the property may have passed, the buyer may be sued for the
price only if his refusal to pay is 'wrongful'. A buyer lawfully rejecting
goods, and thereby revesting them in the seller, is not wrongfully refusing to pay.[260] Further, if goods are sold on a 'to arrive' basis and fail to
arrive, the seller may not recover the price even if the property has
passed.[261] Again, if credit has been extended to the buyer and the period

---

[254] Discussed in the text accompanying nn. 622 ff. below.

[255] This claim failed *in limine:* n. 243 above, 311: 'Estoppel is a vague word. It is often
used to support a submission not capable of precise juristic formulation.'

[256] See Ch. 3 above. If the seller reserves the right of disposal, this is treated as preventing the property from passing. See, e.g., *Stein, Forbes & Co.* v. *County Tailoring Co.* (1916) 86
LJKB 448. Atkin J, 448–9, doubted the unconditional appropriation of goods to the contract
where the right of disposal is reserved. Cf. *Napier* v. *Dexters Ltd* (1926) 26 Ll. LR 62, 63–4,
where Roche J says that, since the right of disposal is unilateral, the seller may waive it and
sue for the price.

[257] Distinguishing *Mackay* v. *Dick* (1881) 6 App. Cas. 251 on the ground that it concerned
a resolutive condition (or condition subsequent), namely, the failure of a machine to pass
a test, and that the buyer's failure to co-operate meant that no test, and therefore no divesting of the property that had already passed to the buyer, could take place. While a discharging breach classically waives the injured party's readiness and willingness to perform
for a damages action, it does not have this effect on a debt action. See *Jones* v. *Barkley* (1781)
2 Dougl. 684; *Laird* v. *Pim* (1846) 7 M & W 474.

[258] A repudiation by one party does not permit the other 'to enforce the contract on the
notional footing that he has performed his part of the contract': *Foran* v. *Wright* (1989) 64
ALJR 1, 6 (Mason CJ), citing *Laird* v. *Pim*, n. 257 above.

[259] An f.o.b. seller will commonly reserve the right of disposal, in which case the property
will not pass on shipment (Ch. 3 above) and the seller will not be able to sue for the price.
Such a seller, however, will be in a position to claim the price from a bank issuing or confirming a letter of credit as the means of effecting payment.

[260] *Vidal* v. *Wm Robinson & Co.* [1952] 1 DLR 1001.

[261] *Calcutta and Burmah Steam Navigation Co.* v. *De Mattos* (1863) 30 LJQB 322.

has not yet elapsed, the seller's right to sue for the price will be suspended until the debt falls due. If the seller accepts a bill drawn on a third party as final payment, he may not sue the buyer in debt if that third party defaults.[262] Finally, the meaning of 'wrongfully' should be understood in the context of risk too.[263] If property has passed to the buyer but the risk remains on the seller, it is submitted that the seller will clearly be unable to sue for the price since the concept of risk is to be understood as qualifying the circumstances in which a suit for the price will be allowed.[264] Conversely, where the property remains in the seller but the risk is on the buyer, the seller should be allowed to sue for the price on the theory of all necessary conditions, including the passing of property, being deemed to have been complied with prior to the bringing of the action.[265]

Payment on a 'Day Certain'

The other instance where the Sale of Goods Act explicitly allows an action for the price is to be found in section 49(2):

Where, under a contract of sale, the price is payable on a day certain irrespective of delivery and the buyer wrongfully neglects or refuses to pay such price, the seller may maintain an action for the price, although the property in the goods has not passed and the goods have not been appropriated to the contract.

The genesis of this provision is Rule 1 of Serjeant Williams's notes to *Pordage* v. *Cole*.[266] Under section 49(2), in essence, the dependency between the seller's duty to deliver and the buyer's duty to pay the price, presumptively established by section 28, is severed by the terms of the contract itself. The buyer's duty to pay is consequently 'irrespective of delivery'[267] and the seller's right to call upon the buyer to pay the price matures on the date that payment falls due. That date must be one that is fixed, 'a day certain',[268] for the contract itself would not otherwise provide a precise standard for determining the maturity of the duty to pay. There is no need on the face of section 49(2) for a seller to establish that the buyer's duty to pay is a condition precedent to his own duty to deliver; it is enough that the duties of payment and delivery are independent of each other. Therefore, in section 49(2), the question of the seller's

---

[262] *Harrison* v. *Luke* (1845) 14 M & W 139.   [263] S. 20.   [264] Ch. 4 above.

[265] *Alexander* v. *Gardner* (1835) 1 Bing. NC 671; *Castle* v. *Playford* (1872) LR 7 Ex. 98.

[266] (1669) 1 Wms. Saund. 319 (appointing a day for payment independently of performance by the payee).

[267] *Muller, Maclean & Co.* v. *Leslie and Anderson* [1921] WN 235, decided under s. 49(2), held that payment against documents was not 'irrespective of delivery' under the terms of that subsection.

[268] *Martin* v. *Hogan* (1917) 24 CLR 234, 261 (a day fixed at the contract date and not left to be ascertained later).

own readiness and willingness to perform is not relevant, for the provision reflects an archaic procedural law under which an aggrieved buyer would have to submit to the price action and bring a separate cross action against the seller.[269] The provision harks back to a time predating the modern law of breach of contract[270] and, taken with the debt provision in section 49(1), reveals a curious antique mixture of debt and seventeenth-century *assumpsit*. In sum, section 49, taken as a whole, does not even begin to respond to any of the practical considerations that might be examined to discover whether a plaintiff seller's remedy is more appropriately debt than damages.

An examination of the case law does not throw very much light on the matter. In *Dunlop* v. *Grote*,[271] a contract for the sale of a quantity of iron provided that, if the buyer did call for the iron 'on or before the 30th day of April, 1845, the said iron was to be paid for [on that date]'. The seller was entitled to recover the price once that date arrived because it was a day certain and payment on that date bore no relation to delivery.

A number of difficult cases have claims to be included in section 49(2) or possibly in a common law extension to it.[272] In *Workman Clark & Co.* v. *Lloyd Brazileño*,[273] a shipbuilding contract[274] provided that the first instalment fell due once the ship reached a particular stage in its construction; naturally, this was not expressed to occur on a day certain. If the buyers failed to pay at this stage, one of the avenues open to the sellers was the suspension of future work under the contract until payment was made. The court held that the sellers could sue the buyers for a liquidated sum under the summary judgments procedure. Had this been a severable contract for the supply of goods in instalments, the contract could easily have been structured to provide for a debt action under either sub-section (1) or (2) of section 49. The buyers' duty to pay, nevertheless, could without difficulty be reconciled with the language of Serjeant Williams's first rule. *Dunlop* v. *Grote*[275] was only one example of that rule, but it was the one codified in 1893.

Another case clearly within the letter of Serjeant Williams's first rule but not the letter of section 49(2) is *Minister for Supply and Development* v. *Servicemen's Co-operative Joinery Manufacturers Ltd*,[276] where a contract for the sale of specific machinery provided that the property was not to pass before delivery[277] but that payment was to be 'net cash before delivery'. Payment, therefore, was irrespective of, indeed antecedent to,

---

[269] e.g. *Nichols* v. *Raynbred* (1615) Hob. 88.
[270] M. G. Bridge (1983) 28 *McGill LJ* 867, 873–5.
[271] (1845) 2 Car. & K 153.
[272] Under s. 62(2).
[273] [1908] 1 KB 968.
[274] The court did not actually say that it was governed by the Sale of Goods Act.
[275] N. 271 above.
[276] (1951) 82 CLR 621.
[277] Hence s. 49(1) did not apply.

delivery, and was not to occur on a day certain. Indeed, it was not easy to say when exactly the buyers had to pay, but the Australian High Court held that the buyers came under a duty to pay within a reasonable time.[278] A failure to pay at that time gave rise to a debt, so that the sellers were able to sue for the price without averring that delivery had been made.[279]

In a number of decisions, resistance has met the attempts of sellers to sue for the price in documentary sales where the buyer has refused to take up the documents. In *Stein, Forbes & Co.* v. *County Tailoring Co.*,[280] a contract for the sale of a large quantity of dressed sheepskins called for payment 'net cash against documents on arrival of the steamer'. Atkin J held that the seller could not recover the price when the buyer refused the documents. Clearly, the price was not payable on a day certain, and so the case did not fall within section 49(2). Moreover, payment was not to occur irrespective of delivery,[281] and so could not fall within any common law extension of section 49(2) inspired by Serjeant Williams's first rule.

Reform

The cases decided under section 49(2) or its common law extension, considered as a whole, do not establish a rational and satisfactory line between debt and damages. This matter has not been considered by the Law Commission of this country but it has been reviewed overseas. Although its solution turned upon only one issue—that of who was best able to dispose of unwanted goods—the Ontario Law Reform Commission did look at the substance of the problem. It recommended that an entitlement to recover the price should turn upon the buyer's acceptance of the goods,[282] a test that suffers from being both unduly protracted (and hence unfair to the seller) and unnecessarily vague.[283] The Canadian Uniform Sale of Goods Committee preferred a test that was both easy to administer and established a balance between buyers' and sellers' interests. It preferred delivery as the event permitting a seller

---

[278] N. 276 above, 642.

[279] See, however, *Shell-Mex Ltd* v. *Elton Cop Dyeing Co.* (1928) 34 Com. Cas. 39, where the court declined to read the following clause as entitling the seller to recover the price irrespective of delivery: 'Sellers have the right at any time to invoice the buyers the due quantities of oil not taken up and to demand payment of the invoice amounts, and such quantities . . . shall be at buyers' risk and expense.' Wright J, 44, read 'invoice' as 'invoice and deliver'.

[280] (1916) 86 LJKB 448.

[281] See also *Muller, Maclean & Co.* v. *Leslie and Anderson*, n. 267 above; *Martin* v. *Hogan*, n. 268 above.

[282] *Report on Sale of Goods* (1979), ii, 415–18.

[283] Alberta Institute of Law Research and Reform, *The Uniform Sale of Goods Act* (Report No. 38, 1982), 108.

to sue for the price.[284] In the majority of cases currently governed by section 49, the same result as to price entitlement would be reached through the medium of the passing of property rules,[285] so the actual legal position would change very little in the event of such a reform. This approach, at least, would be more overtly responsive to the practical issues mentioned above and is therefore to be welcomed.

Interest and Foreign Currency

The next question is whether a seller entitled to sue for the price may also recover interest from the buyer for delay in making payment. Any entitlement of the seller that does exist is preserved by section 54, but section 54 does not create any right to interest. The common law rule was that damages could not be awarded for a failure to pay a sum of money; a claim for interest was seen as tantamount to such a damages claim.[286] The contract might, however, make provision for the payment of interest[287] and, in exceptional cases, a claimant kept out of his money might recover as damages the interest he had to pay a third party in consequence of non-payment.[288] Similarly, since inflation and currency devaluation are different sides of the depreciation coin, a claimant may also suffer a recoverable currency loss.[289] Numerous other special instances of interest entitlement existed.[290] Since 1982,[291] it has been possible, in and to the extent of the court's discretion, to recover simple interest at common law, once proceedings have begun, dating back from the time that the cause of action arose.

As stated above, a claimant entitled to recover a sum of money may suffer loss in the event of a currency devaluation prior to payment being made.[292] The contract of sale may, for example, require payment in Swiss francs. Just as in principle a plaintiff's damages are calculated in accord-

[284] Uniform Sale of Goods Act, s. 106(1)(a), (4).   [285] Ch. 3 above.

[286] *London, Chatham and Dover Railway Co.* v. *South Eastern Railway Co.* [1893] AC 429; *Page* v. *Newman* (1829) 9 B & C 378. This position has been confirmed in modern times by the House of Lords: *President of India* v. *La Pintada Cia Navegacion SA* [1985] AC 104.

[287] N. 286 above.

[288] *Wadsworth* v. *Lydall* [1981] 1 WLR 598 (second limb of the rule in *Hadley* v. *Baxendale* (1854) 9 Ex. 341, discussed below); *President of India*, n. 286 above.

[289] *International Minerals and Chemical Corpn.* v. *Karl O. Helm AG* [1986] 1 Lloyd's Rep. 81; *President of India* v. *Lips Maritime Corpn.* [1988] AC 395.

[290] e.g. in Admiralty proceedings (*Tehno-Impex* v. *Gebr. van Weelde Scheepvartkantor BV* [1981] 2 All ER 669) and in equity (*Brown* v. *IRC* [1965] AC 244; *Wallersteiner* v. *Moir (No. 2)* [1975] QB 373; *O'Sullivan* v. *Management Agency & Music Ltd* [1985] QB 429).

[291] The Administration of Justice Act 1982 (s. 15 and Sched. 1), enacting a new s. 35A of the Supreme Court Act 1981. See also County Courts Act 1984, s. 69. For the recommendations of the Law Commission preceding this statutory change, see *Report on Interest* 1978 (Law Com. No. 88).

[292] See H. McGregor, *McGregor on Damages* (16th edn., Sweet & Maxwell, London, 1997), §§622 ff.; *Dicey and Morris's Conflict of Laws* (12th edn., Sweet & Maxwell, London, 1993 by L. Collins), ch. 36.

ance with the position at the date of breach,[293] so the amount owed in Swiss francs was at one time translated into sterling at that same date. If, therefore, sterling devalued against the Swiss franc between the date when the price should have been paid and the date judgment was given in favour of the seller, the seller would suffer a loss in exchanging the sterling award for Swiss francs. This position, based on a philosophy of currency nominalism,[294] was exploded by the emergence of floating exchange rates following upon the collapse of the Bretton Woods agreement and the fixed dollar price for gold. The House of Lords in *Miliangos* v. *George Frank (Textiles) Ltd*[295] ruled that judgment could in future be given in appropriate cases in a foreign currency,[296] a result protecting the Swiss seller entitled under the contract to payment in Swiss francs. This, of course, was the exact equivalent of delaying the date of conversion from the breach date to the judgment date.[297]

Instalment Contracts

Contracts for the payment of the price in instalments have posed problems concerning the seller's right in respect of instalments of the price that have been paid or have accrued due and payable before the contract is terminated for the buyer's breach. It will be considered below to what extent moneys paid by way of deposit or instalment may be recovered by the contract-breaker. This will involve consideration of the action for money had and received on a failure of consideration and of the seller's right in some cases to forfeit prepaid moneys.

It is well established, in the case of hire[298] and hire purchase[299] contracts, that instalments falling due before the contract is terminated for the hirer's breach may be recovered by the supplier by way of debt.[300] This is consistent with the modern orthodoxy that contracts are termi-

---

[293] Discussed in the text accompanying nn. 549 ff. below.

[294] See *Treseder-Griffin* v. *Co-operative Insurance Society* [1956] 2 QB 127, 144: 'Sterling is the constant unit of value by which in the eye of the law everything is measured.'

[295] [1976] AC 443.

[296] For a full discussion of the governing principles and the ensuing case law, see McGregor, n. 292 above.

[297] *Miliangos*, n. 295 above, 501, though, more accurately, the date chosen for conversion was the date the plaintiff was given leave to execute judgment: *Miliangos*, 468–9.

[298] See *Robophone Facilities Ltd* v. *Blank* [1966] 1 WLR 1428; *Interoffice Telephones Ltd* v. *Robert Freeman Co. Ltd* [1958] 1 QB 190.

[299] *Brooks* v. *Beirnstein* [1909] 1 KB 98; *Chatterton* v. *Maclean* [1951] 1 All ER 761; *Yeoman Credit Ltd* v. *Waragowski* [1961] 3 All ER 145 (express clause). See also *National Cash Register Co. Ltd* v. *Stanley* [1921] 3 KB 292 and *Sandford* v. *Dairy Supplies Ltd* [1941] NZLR 141 (duty to pay instalments falling due only after delivery of goods to hirer).

[300] For general authorities supporting the duty to pay sums falling due before termination, see *Hinton* v. *Sparkes* (1868) LR 3 CP 165; *Dewar* v. *Mintoft* [1912] 2 KB 373; *Damon Cia Naviera SA* v. *Hapag-Lloyd International SA* [1983] 2 Lloyd's Rep. 522; *Bank of Boston Connecticut* v. *European Grain and Shipping Ltd (The Dominique)* [1989] AC 1056 (payee in breach).

nated for breach prospectively without affecting vested entitlements under the contract thus truncated.[301] A claim for outstanding instalments may also be coupled with a damages action for any deficiency incurred by the finance company when disposing of the goods.[302] Earlier cases had drawn a distinction between breaches by the hirer that, in going to the root of the contract, were truly repudiatory and breaches that permitted the finance company merely to exercise a right to withdraw from the agreement. In the former instance, damages for the finance company's deficiency were allowed; in the latter, they were denied on the ground that the loss arose from the finance company's exercise of its right of withdrawal.[303] The question here is whether a hirer's failure to comply with a payments clause, when not going to the root of the contract, necessarily amounts to a breach of condition just because the finance company has an express right of withdrawal for non-payment. The application of conventional contract principles should produce an affirmative answer.[304]

If controls have to be placed upon the parties' autonomy in characterizing terms as conditions in respect of trivial breaches, or if the hirer should be given relief against forfeiture of his interest upon termination, then this should be done without distorting principle. It is settled that a breach of condition will be present (and thus a repudiatory breach need not be demonstrated by the finance company) if timely payment is expressly made of the essence in the contract.[305] The uncertain availability of damages can therefore be avoided by simple drafting. A finance company suffering loss needs an action for damages after termination because it may not both repossess the goods and demand the payment of all future instalments.[306]

---

[301] *Heyman* v. *Darwins Ltd* [1941] AC 356; *McDonald* v. *Dennys Lascelles Ltd* (1933) 48 CLR 457; *Johnson* v. *Agnew* [1980] AC 367; *Photo Production Ltd* v. *Securicor Transport Ltd* [1980] AC 827.

[302] *Lombard North Central Finance Co. Ltd* v. *Butterworth* [1987] QB 52; *Robophone Facilities Ltd* v. *Blank*, n. 298 above; *Interoffice Telephones Ltd* v. *Robert Freeman Co. Ltd*, n. 298 above.

[303] *Financings Ltd* v. *Baldock* [1963] 2 QB 104; *Brady* v. *St Margaret Trust* [1963] 2 QB 494. See also *AMEV–UDC Finance Ltd* v. *Austin* (1986) 68 ALR 185 (Aust. HC); *Shevill* v. *Builders' Licensing Board* (1982) 149 CLR 620 (Aust. HC); *Progressive Mailing Houses Pty. Ltd* v. *Tabali* (1985) 157 CLR 17 (Aust. HC).

[304] Cf. G. H. Treitel, *The Law of Contract* (9th edn., 1995), 765–7. The so-called 'condition' in *Wickman Machine Tool Sales Ltd* v. *Schuler AG* [1974] AC 235 was not recognized as such when it surely must have been if the contract had spelt out the manufacturer's right to withdraw from the distributorship on breach of the term by the distributor.

[305] *Lombard North Central Finance Co. Ltd* v. *Butterworth*, n. 302 above. For a case leaving it regrettably unclear how serious must be the hirer's breach for damages to lie after termination, see *Keneric Tractor Sales* v. *Langille* [1987] 2 SCR 440 (Can.), discussed by M. G. Bridge (1989) 2 *Banking & Finance LR* 344.

[306] *Laird* v. *Pim* (1841) 7 M & W 474; *McEntire* v. *Crossley Bros. Ltd* [1895] AC 457, 465.

The position with regard to instalments of the purchase price paid or payable under a contract of sale prior to the termination date has not attracted the same quantity of case law. In *Hyundai Heavy Industries Co. Ltd* v. *Papadopoulos*,[307] the House of Lords distinguished shipbuilding contracts from other contracts of sale when holding that termination in the former case did not affect accrued rights to instalments. In particular, moneys payable before that date remained payable and moneys paid could not be recovered as on a failure of consideration by the defaulting buyer. The earlier case of *Dies* v. *British and International Financing and Mining Corporation Ltd*[308] had allowed the buyer to recover a prepaid instalment of the price where the circumstances did not show a contractual intention that this sum be forfeited[309] in the event of termination for his breach. In such cases, payment under the contract is not absolute but conditional on performance.[310] But the peculiar characteristic of a shipbuilding contract, comparable in this respect to a building contract rather than a contract of sale of goods, was that it required the seller to do work or incur expense on the subject matter of the sale. The shipbuilder thus requiring to be put in funds by the buyer was therefore entitled to accrued instalments needed for disbursements on purchasing materials, paying designers and workmen, and paying fees for inspection. It is well known that the payment schedule in such contracts marches broadly in step with the pattern of these disbursements. This reasoning may not effectively counter the assertion that a seller seeking protection should expressly bargain for forfeiture, in default of so doing remaining entitled nevertheless to recover disbursements by way of damages from the defaulting buyer, but it does set apart shipbuilding contracts from conventional contracts of sale.

Recovery of Money on a Failure of Consideration

It should be realized that the buyer in *Dies* had not taken delivery of the goods. Suppose the contract of sale is concluded on instalment terms and the buyer obtains the use and enjoyment of the goods before paying in full and acquiring the general property in them. Conditional contracts of this sort should be treated in the same way as contracts of hire and hire purchase. The buyer's instalments may not be payable for the use of the goods as such, but a buyer who has enjoyed the goods will be in no position to claim that there has been a total failure of consideration to justify

---

[307] [1980] 1 WLR 1129. See also *Hyundai Heavy Industries Co. Ltd* v. *Pournaras* [1978] 2 Lloyd's Rep. 502.

[308] [1939] 1 KB 724. See also *Palmer* v. *Temple* (1839) 9 A & E 508.

[309] Discussed in the text accompanying nn. 318 ff. below.

[310] *McDonald* v. *Dennys Lascelles Ltd*, n. 301 above; *Palmer* v. *Temple*, n. 308 above; *Dies* v. *British and International Financing and Mining Corporation Ltd*, n. 308 above (described at 744 as the recovery of the buyer's property rather than a failure of consideration action).

the recovery of prepaid moneys. Apart from retaining accrued instalments, the seller who has suffered a deficiency will be entitled to recover
damages on the same principles as those obtaining in the hire purchase
cases. This is consistent with the modern approach of treating resale as
terminating the contract of sale.[311]

The buyer's action to recover money on a failure of consideration, like
any other debt action, is in principle not fettered by remoteness and mitigation limitations. It is expressly preserved by section 54 of the Sale of
Goods Act. As stated above, it may be invoked even by a contract-breaking buyer, subject to any entitlement of the seller to forfeit prepaid moneys. Notice has already been taken of the peculiarly potent nature of this
money action where the seller is wholly unable to convey a valid title to
the buyer.[312] But the action will also be available in other cases, where
the seller fails to deliver or otherwise commits a discharging breach of
contract.[313] In this connection, a failure of consideration refers, not to
the value of the seller's executory promise, but to its value as performed.
The rightful rejection of non-conforming goods will also qualify the
buyer for a price recovery action. Although in principle a buyer may not
combine a damages action on the contract with a claim for money had
and received, since the latter requires first of all the rescission of the contract, the same claim can in substance be made in the form of a combined damages claim. It is therefore unlikely that a pleading technicality
of this kind could successfully be maintained nowadays.

The defaulting buyer will not succeed at common law in recovering
pre-paid money where it is the parties' contractual intention that the
seller should keep the money.[314] This intention will be presumed in the
case of deposits,[315] which, in addition to being affected towards payment
in full, are also designed to serve as earnest money guaranteeing due performance of the contract.[316] As regards instalments, this intention will
have to be shown by the seller.[317]

Equitable Relief against Forfeiture

Failing common law relief, the next issue is whether equity will afford
assistance by way of relief against forfeiture to the defaulting buyer. Four

[311] *R. V. Ward Ltd* v. *Bignall* [1967] 1 QB 534, overruling on this point *Gallagher* v.
Shilcock [1949] 2 KB 764.

[312] See Ch. 9 above.

[313] *Fitt* v. *Cassanet* (1842) 4 M & G 898.　　　　　[314] *Palmer* v. *Temple*, n. 308 above.

[315] *Howe* v. *Smith* (1884) 27 Ch. D 89; *Harrison* v. *Holland and Hannen and Cubitts Ltd*
[1922] 1 KB 211.

[316] *Howe* v. *Smith* (1884) 27 Ch. D 89; *Soper* v. *Arnold* (1889) 14 App. Cas. 429; *Ockenden*
v. *Henley* (1858) 1 EB & E 485; *Waugh* v. *Pioneer Logging Co.* [1949] SCR 299 (Can.).

[317] *Mayson* v. *Clouet* [1924] AC 980, disapproving of *Harrison* v. *Holland and Hannen
and Cubitts Ltd*, n. 315 above, 213 (Bankes LJ); *McDonald* v. *Dennys Lascelles Ltd*, n. 301
above.

questions arise for consideration. First, is equitable relief confined to transactions, like mortgages, sale of land, and leases, that preoccupied equity in the years preceding fusion?[318] Secondly, is relief restricted to buyers ready and willing to perform at the time they seek relief? Thirdly, does relief take the form of granting specific performance to the buyer or an order requiring the seller to return prepaid moneys? Fourthly, does the buyer have to show a proprietary interest in the goods, the subject matter of the contract?

The uncertainty in defining the range of equitable relief against forfeiture lies in pinpointing its position between two equitable doctrines, namely, the doctrine of specific performance and the rule against penalty clauses.[319] The analogy with penalty clauses seems strong when the buyer is simply seeking to recover prepaid money, while specific performance asserts itself when the buyer claims an interest in the contract goods and further time to perform. If specific performance is paramount in the forfeiture doctrine, relief will tend to be confined to contracts of a type amenable to specific performance, which would cramp relief against forfeiture in sale of goods cases. Furthermore, relief would be limited to buyers ready and willing to perform, at least within the further time granted in accordance with equitable views that time is not normally of the essence of the contract.

If, however, the rule against penalties inspires relief against forfeiture, the dominant question is whether a seller, forfeiting prepayments or repossessing the goods as the case may be, is calculated at the outset of the contract to secure a benefit in excess of the actual losses suffered under the contract in consequence of the buyer's breach.[320] This could be the case where the payment schedule is planned to stay ahead of any reasonable assessment of the depreciation of the goods in the buyer's hands.[321]

In *Stockloser* v. *Johnson*,[322] the plaintiff agreed to buy, on conditional sale terms, quarrying machinery that was subject to hiring agreements with a third party, who paid royalties for the use of the machines. These hiring agreements were assigned to the plaintiff, whose plans to pay the purchase instalments out of the royalties received were defeated by the reduction of royalty payments caused by poor weather. Upon late payment, the defendant exercised his contractual right to give notice terminating the conditional sale agreements. The conditional sale agreements, besides reserving title in the defendant seller, also permitted the

---

[318] Cf. *United Scientific Holdings Ltd* v. *Burnley Borough Council* [1978] AC 904.

[319] See generally Law Commission (Working Paper No. 61, 1975), *Penalty Clauses and Forfeiture of Monies Paid.*

[320] On penalty clauses, see Treitel, n. 304 above, 898–902.

[321] Cf. *Robophone Facilities Ltd* v. *Blank* [1966] 1 WLR 1428.   [322] [1954] 1 QB 476.

seller on termination to repossess the machinery and forfeit all moneys paid. In the present action, the plaintiff sought to recover the instalments paid on the ground that their retention amounted to a penalty.

In the result, the plaintiff was unsuccessful. The majority view[323] was that it was not unconscionable for the defendant to forfeit the moneys since the contracts clearly allocated to the plaintiff the risk of a rise and fall in the level of royalty payments received from the hirer. The minority view[324] would also have denied relief on the ground that, the contract having been terminated, there was no room for relief in the absence of fraud, sharp practice, or unconscionable conduct in the formation of the contract.[325] The majority were of the view that in appropriate circumstances an order could be made directing the repayment of forfeited moneys,[326] thus rejecting the role of specific performance. Denning LJ gives the example of the necklace where 90 per cent of the purchase price has already been paid and the buyer has an 'equity of restitution'.[327] The majority judgments also appear to indicate that retention of the moneys would have to be both penal and unconscionable if recovery were to be ordered. Yet unconscionability is not demanded in the case of penalty clauses, and there seems no good reason to require it where the repayment of forfeited moneys is sought just because the claimant is requesting the assistance of the court to recover moneys vested in the defendant. It is noteworthy that clauses permitting the withholding of a portion of the contract price, common in building contracts, are measured by the rule against penalties and not by the principles of relief against forfeiture.[328]

Romer LJ, in the minority, asserted that relief could only take the form of more time being given, prior to the termination of the contract, to a purchaser ready and willing to perform.[329] In his view, therefore, relief was linked to the doctrine of specific performance though he did not relate it to the type of contracts normally amenable to a specific

---

[323] Somervell and Denning LJJ.   [324] Romer LJ.

[325] All vitiating factors giving rise to rescission in equity: see *Galbraith* v. *Mitchenall Estates Ltd* [1965] 2 QB 473, 482. For opposition to the view that courts of equity should 'serve as a general adjuster of men's bargains', see *Bridge* v. *Campbell Discount Co. Ltd* [1962] AC 600, 626 (Lord Radcliffe).

[326] See *Steedman* v. *Drinkle* [1916] AC 275; *Brickles* v. *Snell* [1916] AC 599, 605; *Mussen* v. *Van Diemen's Land Co.* [1938] 2 Ch. 253, 264–6. The majority's interpretation of *Steedman* was criticized by Romer LJ. See also *Galbraith* v. *Mitchenall Estates Ltd*, n. 325 above, 485 (the uncertain state of the law favouring the view of Romer LJ).

[327] N. 322 above, 491.

[328] *Commissioner of Public Works* v. *Hills* [1906] AC 368; *Waugh* v. *Pioneer Logging Co. Ltd* [1949] SCR 299 (Can.); *Gilbert-Ash (Northern) Ltd* v. *Modern Engineering (Bristol) Ltd* [1974] AC 689.

[329] See *Steedman* v. *Drinkle*, n. 326 above; *Re Dagenham (Thames) Dock Co. Ltd* (1873) LR 8 Ch. App. 1022; *Kilmer* v. *B. C. Orchard Lands Ltd* [1913] AC 319; *Brickles* v. *Snell*, n. 326 above; *Stickney* v. *Keeble* [1915] AC 386.

performance decree. This view appears to have prevailed in subsequent case law[330] A number of cases have involved applications for further time to perform,[331] where the principle of commercial certainty has been safeguarded against attempts to withdraw contractual termination rights. These cases are therefore unsympathetic to a buyer seeking further time to perform in the face of a seller who has clear rights of termination.

Consumer cases are a category apart in that statutory provision is made for an extension of time under regulated consumer credit agreements,[332] a category which may include conditional sales and hire purchase[333] as well as hire agreements.[334] Under section 87(1) of the Consumer Credit Act 1974, a default notice must first be served before a regulated agreement can be terminated or goods repossessed. The notice, in the prescribed form, must specify the breach and, alternatively, the action that has to be taken if the agreement is to be reinstated or the amount of compensation to be paid in respect of the breach.[335] The court has a discretion for the party in breach to be given further time to perform.[336] Further, powers exist to order the repayment of hire purchase instalments after repossession of the goods.[337] A finance company also needs the permission of the court when repossessing goods after one-third of the total price of hire purchase or conditional sale goods has been paid.[338]

More recently, the majority view in *Stockloser* v. *Johnson*[339] has been accepted in substance if not in form by the Privy Council in *Workers Trust & Merchant Bank Ltd* v. *Dojap Investments Ltd*[340] where relief against the forfeiture of a 25 per cent 'deposit' in a sale of land agreement was granted on the ground that its retention would amount to a penalty.[341] Such a large payment was not objectively reasonable as earnest money.[342] In declining to recognize that the parties had intended to forfeit prepaid moneys in the first place, the Privy Council did not have to adjudicate between the two views in *Stockloser*.[343] Invoking the penalties

---

[330] *Galbraith* v. *Mitchenall Estates Ltd*, n. 325 above. See also the delphic statement in *Starside Properties Ltd* v. *Mustapha* [1974] 1 WLR 816, 824.

[331] See, e.g., *Sport Internationaal Bussum BV* v. *Inter-Footwear Ltd* [1984] 1 WLR 776; *Barton Thompson & Co. Ltd* v. *Stapling Machines Co.* [1966] Ch. 499; *BICC Plc* v. *Burndy Corpn.* [1985] Ch. 232; *Shiloh Spinners Ltd* v. *Harding* [1973] AC 491; *Afovos Shipping Co. SA* v. *R. Pagnan & Flli* [1983] 1 WLR 195; *Scandinavian Trader Tanker Co. AB* v. *Flota Petrola Ecuatoriana* [1983] 2 AC 694; *Mardorf Peach & Co. Ltd* v. *Attica Sea Carriers Corpn.* [1977] AC 850; *A/S Awilco* v. *Fulvia SpA di Navigazione* [1981] 1 Lloyd's Rep. 371; *Goker* v. *NWS Bank Plc, The Times,* 23 May 1990.

[332] Consumer Credit Act 1974, s. 8(2).   [333] *Ibid.*, ss. 12–13.   [334] *Ibid.*, s. 15.
[335] *Ibid.*, s. 88.   [336] *Ibid.*, ss. 129 ff.   [337] *Ibid.*, s. 132.
[338] *Ibid.*, s. 90.   [339] N. 327 above.   [340] [1993] AC 573.
[341] The court relied upon *Commissioner of Public Works* v. *Hills* [1906] AC 368.
[342] N. 340 above, 579–80.   [343] N. 327 above.

rule would leave no room for any unconscionability criterion. It would also exclude any reference to the doctrine of specific performance and thus be of general application, and would survive a clause making time the essence of payment by a buyer. The approach taken in *Workers Trust* would appear to be just as applicable to an instalment payment plan 'frontloaded' to keep the quantum of payments ahead, at least to an unreasonable degree, of any depreciation suffered by the goods. As matters currently stand, a claim for the repayment of money is more likely to hold promise for instalment purchasers than a claim for more time to perform. The difficulties in estimating the role of equitable relief against forfeiture in the recovery of money have been defused by the invocation in *Workers Trust* of the rule against penalties.

Specific Relief

Specific performance of the contract of sale[344] is dealt with by section 52(1) of the Sale of Goods Act:

In any action for breach of contract to deliver specific or ascertained goods the court may, if it thinks fit, on the plaintiff's application, by its judgment or decree direct that the contract be performed specifically, without giving the defendant the option of retaining the goods on payment of damages.

The section goes on to provide that the application may be made at any time before judgment or decree[345] and that the decree may be unconditional or made on 'such terms and conditions as to damages, payment of the price, and otherwise as seem just to the court'.[346]

Judicial Discretion

The above provision states in statutory form the equitable discretion associated with the award of specific performance. It dates from a statute of 1856[347] which was designed to encourage the more liberal grant of specific performance so as to bring English law into line with Scots law.[348] It has certainly not had that effect, for no discernible increase in

[344] G. H. Treitel [1966] JBL 211; J. Berryman (1985) 17 *Ottawa LR* 295; G. Jones and W. Goodhart, *Specific Performance* (2nd edn., Butterworths, London, 1996); R. Sharpe, *Injunctions and Specific Performance* (1983). For a theoretical discussion of the efficiency of specific relief, see A. Kronman (1978) 45 *U Chi. LR* 351; A. Schwartz (1979) 89 *Yale LJ* 271.

[345] S. 52(2). This accords with *Johnson* v. *Agnew* [1980] AC 367. But an applicant may in some cases make a binding election in favour of damages before this point is reached: *Ming Leong Devlopment Pte. Ltd* v. *JIP Hong Trading Co. Ltd* [1985] AC 511.

[346] S. 52(3). See *Hart* v. *Herwig* (1873) LR 8 Ch. App. 860, 864 (buyer required to make payment into court).

[347] Mercantile Law Amendment Act 1856, 19 & 20 Vict., cap. 97, s. 2, enacting the recommendations of the Second Report of the Mercantile Law Commissioners 1855.

[348] Treitel, n. 344 above; Berryman, n. 344 above.

the award of the decree can be traced to section 52. Indeed, it is inherently unlikely that the equitable discretion, exercised on a case-by-case basis, could be applied more generously in favour of buyers just because the court is statutorily reminded that it has a discretion. There would, as a matter of technique, have to be criteria laid down in the statute giving direction as to the way in which the court might exercise the discretion.[349] In any event, far from section 52 actually expanding the grant of specific performance, it has if anything encouraged its contraction, for the failure of the section to speak to cases other than those concerning specific goods and ascertained goods, combined with the belief that the Sale of Goods Act should as far as possible be regarded as a comprehensive code, has led to the conviction that the remedy cannot lie where there is a contract for the sale of unascertained goods not yet ascertained.[350]

In reality, however, the Act cannot be treated as a comprehensive code for section 52 does not address itself to injunctive relief, whether in interlocutory or permanent form, that in fact serves the same ends as specific performance.[351] Furthermore, the section deals only with buyers' actions against sellers and not with sellers' actions against buyers. There is an uncodified discretion to entertain a specific performance claim in the latter case,[352] although it has been observed that the limits laid down in section 52 should be observed.[353] Since this means that a seller of unascertained goods may not apply for specific performance before the goods are ascertained, it is in practical terms a meaningless restriction. Ascertainment is usually effected by sellers rather than buyers and the seller would only have to ascertain and then seek specific performance.

The meaning of 'specific' and 'ascertained' was discussed in earlier chapters. Although the Sale of Goods Act does not state when goods have become 'ascertained', it is established as taking place when they are earmarked or otherwise identified by the seller as goods he intends to use in fulfilment of the contract.[354] Growing crops and natural products become 'specific or ascertained' once they are severed under a contract of sale.[355] In cases of this nature, it is quite possible that ascertainment

---

[349] Cf. the Canadian Uniform Sale of Goods Act, s. 115 (referring to payment and the buyer's proprietary interest).

[350] *Re Wait* [1927] 1 Ch. 606.

[351] In *Sky Petroleum Ltd* v. *VIP Petroleum Ltd* [1974] 1 WLR 576, Goulding J was aware that an interlocutory injunction amounted to specific performance of a continuing contract for the time being.

[352] *Shell-Mex Ltd* v. *Elton Cop Dyeing Co.* (1928) 34 Com. Cas. 39, 46; *Elliott* v. *Pierson* [1948] 1 All ER 939, 942.

[353] *Shell-Mex*, n. 352 above.

[354] *Re Wait*, n. 350 above; *Thames Sack and Bag Co. Ltd* v. *Knowles & Co. Ltd* (1918) 88 LJ KB 585, 588 ('the indivisibility of the goods must in some way be found out').

[355] *James Jones & Sons Ltd* v. *Earl of Tankerville* [1909] 2 Ch. 440, 445. In *Kursell* v. *Timber*

occurs at the same time as unconditional appropriation for the purpose of passing the property.[356]

A review of the cases shows that the courts have not, in the exercise of their discretion,[357] conceded that it should be moulded by the nature of the question facing them.[358] For example, it cannot be said with any confidence that the judicial discretion will be tilted in one direction, where the seller is insolvent,[359] but in another direction, where the buyer is dependent for his requirements over a long period on the seller. The insolvency difficulties posed when a buyer pays the price before the property in the goods passes were considered in an earlier chapter[360] and will not be re-examined here. It remains to consider the way in which the equitable discretion is exercised in general terms and how it bears upon particular types of goods. A preliminary point to make is that the award of specific performance is governed by the same considerations as apply where a claimant is seeking the specific delivery of goods,[361] formerly in a detinue action but now when suing in conversion.[362] A buyer to whom the property in specific goods has passed, for example, will be no better off in seeking to recover the goods *in specie* by framing an action in conversion for their recovery instead of in contract for specific performance.

Inadequacy of Damages

The foremost consideration in the grant of specific performance is that the remedy is given only where the normal common law remedy of

Operators and Contractors Ltd [1927] 1 KB 298, the entire cut of a Latvian forest complying with stated dimensions was held not to be 'specific' in connection with property and risk. It is difficult to see too that it was ascertained. Whether in such a case specific performance ought to be awarded, and whether this should depend upon whether buyer or seller severs, are different questions.

[356] S. 52 is applied whether or not the property has passed to the buyer: *James Jones & Sons* v. *Tankerville*, n. 355 above, 445. Where the seller refuses to deliver goods the property in which has passed to the buyer, and a specific performance claim is or is likely to be unsuccessful, it would seem that the seller would be a seller in possession under s. 24 for the purpose of title transfer. S. 24 does not require the seller to be in possession with the consent of the buyer.

[357] For a good example of the use of discretionary considerations, see *Butler* v. *Countryside Finance Ltd* [1993] 3 NZLR 623.

[358] Treitel, n. 344 above, 211–12.

[359] But see *Swiss Bank Corpn.* v. *Lloyds Bank Ltd* [1982] AC 584, 595 (Buckley LJ) and *Eximenco Handels AG* v. *Partredereit Oro Chief* [1983] 2 Lloyd's Rep. 509, 521, to the effect that the seller's insolvency should bear upon the discretion being exercised in the buyer's favour. For the view that insolvency makes no difference, see *Anders Utkilens Rederei A/S* v. *O/Y Louisa Stevedoring Co. A/B* [1985] 3 All ER 669, 674.

[360] Ch. 3 above.

[361] *Whiteley* v. *Hilt* [1918] 2 KB 808; *Cohen* v. *Roche* [1927] 1 KB 269; *Asamera Oil Corpn Ltd* v. *Sea Oil & General Corpn.* [1979] 1 SCR 633 (Can.) (undifferentiated treatment of specific performance and specific delivery).

[362] Torts (Interference with Goods) Act 1977, s. 3.

damages is inadequate. In contracts for the sale of goods, this limitation is expressed by the requirement that the goods must be unique or irreplaceable and therefore not to be procured on the market.[363] Nevertheless, the fact that a contract may concern specific goods, so that only these goods and no others, no matter how similar or otherwise identical, may be tendered by the seller in fulfilment of the contract, does not mean that these goods are unique for the purpose of granting specific performance. Specific performance in the sale of goods is very much an exceptional remedy for quite rare circumstances; it is not granted for articles of commerce and trade.[364] Where the article is not to be had upon the open market, it has been said that this demonstrates a *prima facie* case for specific performance.[365] This may be putting the matter too favourably for the buyer, for the remedy can be and is denied even where there is no close equivalent available.[366] Since specific performance is a discretionary remedy which will not readily be scrutinized on appeal,[367] a degree of inconsistency in the cases is only to be expected.

Specific performance or its equivalent has been ordered in a number of instances dealing with unique chattels, such as two jars of 'unusual beauty, variety and distinction',[368] an Adam door,[369] and stone from Old Westminster Bridge.[370] But in one case concerning the sale of Hepplewhite chairs, specific relief was denied because the buyer was an antique dealer purchasing the chairs for resale and so treating them as ordinary articles of commerce.[371] The availability in some cases of damages awards in contract for emotional and similar losses, which recognizes that contracts may be designed to attain expectancies other than

---

[363] *Adderley* v. *Dixon* (1824) 1 Sim. & St. 607, 610. In *Howard E. Perry & Co. Ltd* v. *British Railways Board* [1980] 1 WLR 1375, the court ordered, in interlocutory proceedings under s. 4 of the Torts (Interference with Goods) Act 1977, the delivery up of scarce and irreplaceable goods detained by a tortfeasor. See also *Sky Petroleum Ltd* v. *VIP Petroleum Ltd*, n. 351 above, discussed in the text accompanying nn. 382–3 below.

[364] *Buxton* v. *Lister* (1746) 3 Atk. 383; *Cohen* v. *Roche*, n. 361 above; *Dominion Coal Co. Ltd* v. *Dominion Iron and Steel Co. Ltd* [1909] AC 293.

[365] *Eximenco Handels AG*, n. 359 above, 520.

[366] e.g. *Cohen* v. *Roche*, n. 359 above. In *CN Marine Inc.* v. *Stena Line A/B* [1982] 2 Lloyd's Rep. 336, the court reversed the trial judge's discretion in favour of specific performance, even though the ship had highly individual characteristics.

[367] But see *CN Marine*, n. 366 above.

[368] *Falcke* v. *Gray* (1859) 4 Drew 651, which suggests that courts should scrutinize the sufficiency of the buyer's consideration, not an inquiry normally undertaken. The contract was unusual in the sense that the parties explicitly agreed that the goods were to be sold at an objectively fair valuation.

[369] *Phillips* v. *Lambdin* [1949] 2 KB 33, 41.

[370] *Thorn* v. *Commissioners of Works and Public Buildings* (1863) 32 Beav. 490 (the arch stone, spandrill stone, and Bramley stone) The case does not state why the buyer wanted the stone, and nothing suggests it was for its historical or antique value.

[371] *Cohen* v. *Roche*, n. 361 above.

merely financial ones,[372] ought to lead to a willingness to grant specific performance where a chattel has a certain sentimental value. Damages for intangible losses, often quantified on reflexive and instinctual grounds, are much less likely to attain the true contractual expectancy than performance *in specie*. Nevertheless, if the law were as firmly committed to the expectation interest as is sometimes asserted,[373] one would expect a greater judicial willingness to grant specific performance than is the case.

The remedy of specific performance or an equivalent form of relief has also been granted for more mundane objects which are difficult to acquire because no ready market exists.[374] There has therefore been a tendency to give specific relief in respect of contracts to sell ships.[375] The Australian High Court once granted specific performance of a contract to sell a taxi cab with its attendant licence, because such licences were rare and taxi cabs with licences therefore practically unobtainable.[376] In a Canadian case involving the sale of a Cadillac, which the buyer, an undertaker, initially wished to convert into a hearse, specific performance was allowed because the buyer, despite due diligence, was unable to obtain another car of this type.[377] It did not appear, however, that the buyer had to show that no other type of car would have served the same purpose as well as the Cadillac. A case that can certainly be faulted for the way the discretion was exercised is *Société des Industries Métallurgiques SA* v. *Bronx Engineering Co. Ltd*,[378] where the remedy was denied despite the fact that the buyer of a complex machine to be manufactured by the seller would have to wait a further nine to twelve months for a substitute machine to be supplied by another seller.

Specific performance has been granted because of the impossible task that would have faced the buyer in proving his loss in damages at trial,[379] but if mere difficulty were sufficient,[380] the remedy should have been granted in the *Bronx Engineering* case and also should lie as a matter of

---

[372] M. G. Bridge (1984) 62 *Can. Bar Rev.* 323; D. Harris, A. Ogus, and J. Phillips (1979) 95 *LQR* 581.

[373] See *Harvela Investments Ltd* v. *Royal Trust Co. of Canada* [1986] AC 207, 227, for a statement that specific performance when timeously granted promotes the expectation interest in the way that damages does.

[374] But the willingness of a court to grant the remedy in such cases may be defeated by the vagueness of the description of the goods: *Butler* v. *Countryside Finance Ltd*, n. 357 above.

[375] *Hart* v. *Herwig* (1873) 8 Ch. App. 860 (injunction to prevent German seller from removing ship from English port); *Behnke* v. *Bede Steam Shipping Co. Ltd* [1927] 1 KB 649 (ship of particular value to buyer). But cf. *CN Marine*, n. 366 above.

[376] *Dougan* v. *Ley* (1946) 71 CLR 142.

[377] *Simmons & McBride Ltd* v. *Kirkpatrick* [1945] 4 DLR 134.

[378] [1975] 1 Lloyd's Rep. 465.   [379] e.g. *Hart* v. *Herwig*, n. 375 above, 866.

[380] Denied in the injunction case of *Fothergill* v. *Rowland* (1873) LR 17 Eq. 132.

routine in any long-term delivery contract (which is not the case[381]). Nevertheless, an interim injunction was granted in *Sky Petroleum Ltd* v. *VIP Petroleum Ltd*[382] to prevent future breaches by the seller of a long-term petrol requirements contract. Because of the impossibility of obtaining an alternative source of supply in the over-excited oil market prevailing at that time, there was every reason to believe that the buyer's business might founder without the seller's oil. The court was in no doubt that the grant of this injunction was tantamount to an interim decree of specific performance. Moreover, the decree operated with regard to future supplies of oil, that is, goods not yet ascertained and so not within the terms of the statutory discretion in section 52. The same considerations help to explain why some complex sales agreements, assuming the form, for example, of franchise agreements or exclusive distributorship agreements, become the subject of specific relief.[383] The parties to such contracts become heavily integrated into each other's business and damages will often be a very poor substitute for specific relief in view of the loss of good will and the economic dislocation produced on a peremptory breach.

Prohibitory Injunctions

A question that sometimes arises is whether a prohibitory injunction should issue, restraining the seller from delivering the contract goods to anyone other than the buyer, in circumstances where specific performance would not be available.[384] Such a decree, while not enjoining the seller actually to deliver to the buyer,[385] would in practice amount to the same thing if the seller wished to make any effective use of his assets. Where the contract contains an express negative stipulation to the above effect, the courts have been swayed by the well-known principle in *Doherty* v. *Allman*[386] that an injunction should issue as a matter of course, since the court is merely being requested to sanction something

---

[381] *Dominion Coal Co. Ltd* v. *Dominion Iron & Steel Co. Ltd* [1909] AC 293.

[382] [1974] 1 WLR 576.

[383] *Evans Marshall & Co. Ltd* v. *Bertola SA* [1973] 1 WLR 349; *Baxter Motors Ltd* v. *American Motors (Canada) Ltd* (1973) 40 DLR (3d) 450. In *Evans Marshall*, 380, Sachs LJ referred to 'the creation of certain areas of damage which cannot be taken into monetary account in a common law action for breach of contract: loss of goodwill and trade reputation are examples'. Unlike the remoteness of damage rule, the equitable discretion is not based on the reasonable contemplation of the defendant at the contract date.

[384] See R. Sharpe, *Injunctions and Specific Performance* (Canada Law Book Co., Toronto, 1983), 669–98.

[385] *Metropolitan Supply Co.* v. *Ginder* [1901] 2 Ch. 799. See the practical compulsion of the buyer in *Foley* v. *Classique Coaches Ltd* [1934] 2 KB 1; *Servais Bouchard* v. *Prince's-Hall Restaurant Ltd* (1904) 20 TLR 574. A seller may in some cases be enjoined from preventing the buyer from entering land to sever crops: *James Jones & Sons* v. *Tankerville* [1909] 2 Ch. 440.

[386] (1878) 3 App. Cas. 709, 720.

explicitly agreed upon by the parties.[387] Thus, in *Donnell* v. *Bennett*,[388] a manure manufacturer agreed to purchase all the unwanted fish parts produced by a fish processor for a two-year period, and the latter also explicitly undertook not to sell any such goods to other buyers in that same period. Fry J awarded the remedy sought, though with some considerable misgivings, since it did not actually compel the defendant to deliver the goods to the plaintiff. On the other hand, in *Fothergill* v. *Rowland*,[389] a contract to supply all the coal from a particular colliery seam contained no such express negative covenant. It was admitted by the buyer that specific performance of the contract could not have been obtained, and Jessel MR, despite the revulsion he felt for the defendant's conduct, refused to grant a prohibitory injunction that would have amounted to specific performance by a roundabout method.

The distinction between positive and negative covenants may be somewhat elusive in practice for 'every agreement to do a particular thing in one sense involves . . . the negative of doing that which is inconsistent with the thing you are to do'.[390] In the last resort, the distinction between positive and negative has to be pursued as a matter of substance rather than form,[391] and an implied negative covenant may in a proper case be discerned in a covenant positively worded.[392] That the law may be less than satisfactorily clear in pursuing the negative quality of a covenant is evident in the comparison of an output case, like *Fothergill* v. *Rowland*,[393] where an injunction was denied, with a requirements case, like *Metropolitan Electric Supply Co. Ltd* v. *Ginder*,[394] where an injunction was granted.

Like injunctions, declarations are not mentioned in section 52. They can serve a valuable function in clarifing the position of the parties, especially in long-term contracts, before disagreements come to a head with a refusal to perform.[395]

---

[387] This proves too much for it should support specific performance as the general remedy, subject perhaps to exceptions.

[388] (1883) 22 Ch. D 835. See also *Thomas Borthwick & Sons (Australia) Ltd* v. *South Otago Freezing Co. Ltd* [1978] 1 NZLR 538; *Sanderson Motors (Sales) Pty. Ltd* v. *Yorkstar Motors Pty. Ltd* [1983] 1 NSWLR 513.

[389] N. 380 above.

[390] *Whitwood Chemical Co.* v. *Hardman* [1891] 2 Ch. 416, 426.

[391] *Manchester Ship Canal Co.* v. *Manchester Racecourse Co.* [1901] 2 Ch. 37.

[392] *Metropolitan Supply Co.* v. *Ginder* [1901] 2 Ch. 799; *Bower* v. *Bantam Investments Ltd* [1972] 1 WLR 1120.

[393] N. 380 above.   [394] N. 392 above.

[395] See, e.g., *Spettabile Consorzio Veneziano* v. *Northumberland Shipbuilding Co. Ltd* (1919) 121 LT 628, 635; *Louis Dreyfus & Cie* v. *Parnaso Cia Naviera SA* [1960] QB 49; *J. H. Vantol Ltd* v. *Fairclough, Dodd and Jones* [1955] 1 WLR 642, 648.

THE SECONDARY OBLIGATION TO PAY DAMAGES: COMMON ISSUES

This section of the Chapter deals with damages issues that are common to claims brought by both buyer and seller,[396] though they may arise in a contextually different form in the two instances. The treatment of damages claims in the law of contract inevitably has to start from the postulate that damages are awarded to place the plaintiff in the position he would have occupied had the contract been duly performed by the defendant.[397] This is a contractual application of the principle that the function of damages is to put the injured party in the position he would have been in if the wrong had not been committed.[398] The expectation entitlement, projecting the plaintiff forward to a post-contract position that the defendant's breach prevented him from attaining, is to be distinguished, at least for the purpose of conceptual analysis, from a reliance entitlement, which would be promoted by returning the plaintiff to his pre-contract position.[399]

As helpful as such a distinction is for intellectual purposes, however, its practical significance stands to be overestimated. Admittedly, a reliance claim is usefully made by plaintiffs who are in no position to prove a speculative expectation entitlement, and whose difficulties of proof are to be attributed to the defendant's breach of contract.[400] In such cases, a financial return of the plaintiff to his pre-contract position, coupled with an award of interest to compensate him for being kept out of his money,[401] is an acceptable substitute from the vantage-point of justice, even though risk-taking entrepreneurs are not noted for placing substantial investments in a bank deposit account. If, nevertheless, the defendant is able to demonstrate that the contract was financially a losing one for the plaintiff, the orthodox position is that the expectation

---

[396] McGregor, *McGregor on Damages* (15th edn., 1988); Treitel, *The Law of Contract* (9th edn., 1995), ch. 21; S. M. Waddams, *The Law of Damages* (2nd edn., Canada Law Book Co., Toronto, 1991).

[397] *Robinson* v. *Harman* (1848) 1 Ex. 850, 855; *Wertheim* v. *Chicoutimi Pulp Co.* [1911] AC 301, 307; *British Westinghouse Electric and Manufacturing Co. Ltd* v. *Underground Electric Railways Co. of London Ltd* [1912] AC 673, 689.

[398] See *Livingstone* v. *Rawyard's Coal Co.* (1880) 5 App. Cas. 25, 39; *British & Commonwealth Holdings Plc* v. *Quadrex Holdings Plc* [1995] CLC 1169, 1226.

[399] L. L. Fuller and A. Perdue (1936) 46 *Yale LJ* 52. For the pursuit of the reliance interest where the expectation claim is unprovable, see M. G. Bridge, 'Expectation Damages and Uncertain Future Losses' in J. Beatson and D. Friedmann (eds.), *Good Faith and Fault in Contract Law* (1995).

[400] See, e.g., *Anglia Television Ltd* v. *Reed* [1972] 1 QB 60; *Security Stove & Manufacturing Co.* v. *American Railway Express Co.* (1932) 51 SW 2d 572; *Commonwealth of Australia* v. *Amann Aviation Pty. Ltd* (1991) 66 ALJR 123 (noted by G. H. Treitel (1992) 108 *LQR* 226); Bridge, n. 399 above.

[401] For a discussion of pre-judgment interest, see Waddams, n. 396 above, and McGregor, n. 396 above.

award, that might have been made if the plaintiff had formed his claim in that way, sets the ceiling for any recovery of damages, and so as much of the plaintiff's reliance claim as exceeds this ceiling is irrecoverable.[402]

Apart from this divergence of reliance and expectation, it should be appreciated that an award of reliance damages, in the form of a return of moneys disbursed by the plaintiff as a result of entering into the contract,[403] will not in itself turn back the clock. If the plaintiff is truly to be indemnified, he must have restored to him the time or opportunity value of that award. By entering into a contract with the defendant, the plaintiff may have passed up the opportunity in competitive market conditions of concluding a contract with someone else. An accurate reliance award will compensate the plaintiff for this lost opportunity, and, in the perhaps unlikely case of perfect market conditions, will yield the same figure as an expectation award.[404] As a *prima facie* rule, the Sale of Goods Act gives a buyer as damages, where the seller fails to deliver, the difference between the contract price and the (higher) market price prevailing at the date fixed for delivery. This could be analysed, in competitive market conditions, as the plaintiff's lost expectation or, in reliance terms, as the lost opportunity to secure the goods on the same contract terms from another seller who would have delivered.

A plaintiff's expectation claim, once a breach of contract has been established, has three further hurdles to negotiate. First of all, the plaintiff must prove in fact that it was the breach of contract, rather than some other event or cause, that produced the loss.[405] The effect of the

---

[402] *C. & P. Haulage* v. *Middleton* [1983] 3 All ER 94; *CCC Films (London) Ltd* v. *Impact Quadrant Films Ltd* [1985] QB 16; *McRae* v. *Commonwealth Disposals Commission* (1951) 84 CLR 377; *Bowlay Logging Ltd* v. *Domtar Ltd* [1978] 4 WWR 105. (But see *Dataliner Ltd* v. *Vehicle Builders and Repairers Asscn.*, 27 July 1995 (unreported), where the trial judge's ruling that the burden of proof was on the plaintiff to show that the contract would have been profitable was upheld as the correct approach by the Court of Appeal without consideration of the authorities or the arguments.) It is submitted that a defendant should not be permitted to oppose a restitutionary claim on the ground of a losing contract. There is no reason to let the defendant profit from his own breach, or even to retain benefits received from the plaintiff so as to reduce his own contract losses. The cap placed on the plaintiff's reliance recovery is at the expense of the possibility that the plaintiff might in time have turned round a losing contract; it may also permit the defendant to rely upon the terms of the very contract that he is repudiating. This cap should not be placed on a damages claim where the plaintiff had speculative, even remote and unprovable, gains to be made: *Security Stove*, n. 400 above; *McRae* v. *Commonwealth Disposals Commission*, above; *Amann Aviation*, n. 400 above. See also *Wallington* v. *Townsend* [1939] Ch. 558; *Nurse* v. *Barns* (1664) T Raym. 77.

[403] Such an award is more extensive than the indemnity that accompanies rescission *ab initio*: *Whittington* v. *Seale-Hayne* (1900) 82 LT 49; *Newbigging* v. *Adam* (1886) 34 Ch. D 582.

[404] Fuller and Perdue, n. 399 above; Bridge, n. 399 above. See also *East* v. *Maurer* [1991] 2 All ER 733; *V. K. Mason Construction Ltd* v. *Bank of Nova Scotia* (1985) 16 DLR (4th) 598.

[405] *Quinn* v. *Burch Bros. (Builders) Ltd* [1966] 2 QB 370; *Cia Financiera Soleada SA* v. *Hamoor Tanker Corpn. (The Borag)* [1981] 1 WLR 274. See also *Wertheim* v. *Chicoutimi Pulp Co.*, n. 397 above.

defendant's breach may be erased by subsequent conduct of the plaintiff. In *Beoco Ltd* v. *Alfa Laval Co. Ltd*,[406] the sellers supplied a defective heat exchanger whose replacement, interrupting the buyers' production process, would have entailed a loss of profits. The buyers, however, caused even more disruption to production when their incompetent repair of the exchanger generated an explosion. They were not allowed damages for a notional loss of the profits that would have continued owing to the sellers' breach but for their own intervention.

One explanation of the doctrine of mitigation is that the true cause of the plaintiff's loss is his own failure to take evasive action after the breach,[407] and the same could be said for the denial of damages in certain cases to plaintiffs whose own impecuniosity aggravates any loss attributable to the defendant's breach.[408] Likewise, in cases where a warranty action fails because of the plaintiff's intervening negligence, the denial of damages may be rationalized in terms of factual causation.[409] There is a paucity of case law directly raising the factual causation problem. This is due in part to the plaintiff's right, when confronting an unprovable expectation claim, to elect instead in favour of a reliance claim. An alternative recourse to a plaintiff in difficulties is to seek recovery of damages for the loss of a chance. Recovery for loss of a chance, however, is not freely allowed just because the plantiff cannot prove his expectation loss. The plaintiff must cross a threshold of probability of success before recovering under this head and, it is submitted, the lost chance must constitute the subject matter of the transaction or at least an integral part of it.[410] This latter qualification rules out such damages in conventional market-based sale of goods cases. Recovery for loss of a chance, nevertheless, may be appropriate in the case of profit-earning chattels. But even in such a case, the price the buyer agrees to pay may already have factored into it the chance of profit so that he cannot demonstrate a genuine loss.[411]

The second hurdle mentioned above is that the loss claimed by the plaintiff must be of a type recognized by the law. The financial and physical interests of buyer and seller do not pose a problem in this respect, but a long-standing difficulty has been presented by plaintiffs' claims for

---

[406] [1994] 4 All ER 464, disapproving *Schering Agrochemicals Ltd* v. *Resibel NV SA* (4 June 1991, unreported).

[407] See, e.g., *Payzu Ltd* v. *Saunders* [1919] 2 KB 581; *Sotiros Shipping Inc.* v. *Sameiet Solholt (The Solholt)* [1983] 1 Lloyd's Rep. 605. See discussion below.

[408] *Liesbosch, Dredger* v. *SS Edison* [1933] AC 449; *Freedhof* v. *Pomalift Industries Ltd* (1971) 19 DLR (3d) 153. Cf. *Bacon* v. *Cooper (Metals) Ltd* [1982] 1 All ER 397 (the cost of mitigation, discussed below).

[409] *Lambert* v. *Lewis* [1982] AC 225; *Ingham* v. *Emes* [1955] 2 QB 366.

[410] *Chaplin* v. *Hicks* [1911] 2 KB 786; Bridge, n. 399 above.

[411] *Sapwell* v. *Bass* [1910] 2 KB 486.

intangible losses, relating to disappointment, injured feelings, emotional distress, and similar matters,[412] brought about by a breach of contract. Awards for such losses are usually denied without regard to whether they pass the test of remoteness of damage.[413] But in exceptional cases, the plaintiff's expectation interest[414] is protected by an award, namely, in those cases where enjoyment[415] or the avoidance of distress[416] are central to the purpose of the contract. The majority of sale of goods agreements will fall outside these exceptions because goods are usually purchased for commercial or unsentimental reasons. Nevertheless in *Ruxley Electronics and Constructions Ltd* v. *Forsyth*,[417] a swimming pool was built to afford 'a pleasurable amenity'. When the home owner experienced disappointment because it had not been built to specifications, the trial judge awarded an appreciable sum as damages.[418] The same approach to damages may lie where a yacht builder or coach builder falls short of the contractual standard, but is unlikely where mass-produced goods without distinguishing features are the subject-matter of the contract.

The third hurdle to the plaintiff's recovery is that of legal causation, or remoteness of damage.

The Remoteness of Damage Rule

A wholehearted commitment to the expectation principle would identify compensation with factual causation, but the expectation principle has been described as 'one of those generous aspirations which the law does well to put but sparingly into practice'.[419] The same commentator regards the remoteness-of-damage rule as consonant with the wishes of the business community that a contracting party should not be the insurer of the other's contractual adventure and that a fair apportionment of business risk may be attained with the aid of the remoteness rule. It should not be forgotten that many breaches of contract flow from promises whose performance is strict and take place in circumstances where the party in breach has unavailingly sought with reasonable efforts to avoid this result.

---

[412] M. G. Bridge (1984) 62 *Can. Bar Rev.* 323. There is no similar embargo on physical inconvenience: *Hobbs* v. *London and South Western Railway Co.* (1875) LR 10 QB 111.

[413] See *Hamlin* v. *Great Northern Railway Co.* (1856) 1 H & N 408; *Addis* v. *Gramophone Co.* [1909] AC 488; *Bliss* v. *S. E. Thames Regional Health Authority* [1987] ICR 700; *Watts* v. *Morrow* [1991] 4 All ER 937.

[414] See D. Harris, A. Ogus, and J. Phillips (1979) 95 *LQR* 581.

[415] *Jarvis* v. *Swans Tours* [1973] QB 233.   [416] *Heywood* v. *Wellers* [1976] QB 446.

[417] [1995] 3 WLR 118, discussed further below.

[418] £2,500, which Lord Lloyd thought rather high in the circumstances: n. 417, 139.

[419] G. Washington (1931) 47 *LQR* 345, (1932) 48 *LQR* 90, 107.

Developments prior to the Court of Exchequer decision in *Hadley* v. *Baxendale*[420] saw damages awards given over to the discretion of juries and the acceptability of awards within the tolerance of factual causation. But *Hadley* v. *Baxendale* demonstrated that 'it is not always wise to make the defaulting promisor pay for all the damage which follows as a consequence of his breach'.[421] An analysis of the case and ensuing damages decisions shows how this was achieved, but the cases are rather less revealing on the question why this was done by the courts. In *Hadley* v. *Baxendale* itself, the remoteness rule was expressed by Baron Alderson in the form of two branches or limbs:

> Where two parties have made a contract which one of them has broken, the damages which the other party ought to receive in respect of such breach of contract should be such as may fairly and reasonably be considered either arising naturally, i.e. according to the usual course of things, from such breach of contract itself, or such as may reasonably be supposed to have been in the contemplation of both parties, at the time they made the contract, as the probable result of the breach of it.[422]

As the rule was interpreted over the years,[423] remoteness was a function of two variables, namely, the anticipated[424] probability of the promisee's loss occurring in consequence of the promisor's breach, and the degree of knowledge imputed or specially communicated to the promisor[425] at the date of entry into the contract. Probability was measured in the light of this knowledge.

The rule, as elaborated, therefore created an incentive on promisees to make disclosure by the contract date if they wished promisors to incur a degree of responsibility outside the range of ordinary human contemplation.[426] In response, the promisor might take the opportunity to negotiate contract terms commensurate with this added degree of responsibility or to exclude or limit his liability under the contract. Seen

---

[420] (1854) 9 Ex. 341; J. Danzig (1975) 4 *J Leg. Stud.* 249.

[421] L. L. Fuller and A. Perdue (1936) 6 *Yale LJ* 52, 84.   [422] N. 420 above, 354.

[423] See in particular *British Columbia etc. Saw Mill Co.* v. *Nettleship* (1868) LR 3 CP 499; *Re R. and H. Hall Ltd and W. H. Pim Inc. and Co.'s Arbitration* (1928) 33 Com. Cas. 324; *Victoria Laundry (Windsor) Ltd* v. *Newman Industries Ltd* [1949] 2 KB 528; *Monarch Steamship Co. Ltd* v. *Karlshamns Oljefabriker A/B* [1949] AC 196; *C. Czarnikow Ltd* v. *Koufos (The Heron II)* [1969] 1 AC 350.

[424] Namely, what the defendant could have foreseen if he had directed his mind to a future breach: *Victoria Laundry*, n. 423 above; *H. Parsons (Livestock) Ltd* v. *Uttley, Ingham & Co. Ltd* [1978] QB 791.

[425] It is more accurate to speak of the promisor alone than of promisor and promisee: *Cory* v. *Thames Ironworks and Shipbuilding Co. Ltd* (1868) LR 3 QB 181.

[426] They might not want to. If the buyers in *Cory*, n. 425 above, had disclosed the exceptionally profitable plans they had for the huge hulk, clearly an embarrassment to the sellers after the default of previous buyers (see *Thames Iron Works Co.* v. *Patent Derrick Co.* (1860) 1 J & H 93), the predictable consequence would have been a steep rise in the contract price.

in this way, the increase in liability stemming from disclosure could be justified if the courts permitted arm's-length exclusions of liability and did not invoke unduly rigorous canons of construction in respect of a clause protecting the promisor from the consequences of enhanced disclosure. It was sometimes said that communication of additional information was not in itself enough unless it were also accompanied by an undertaking, implied at least, to bear an added measure of responsibility.[427] This particular gloss may no longer find judicial favour.[428] It may be explained as due to the special contract that a common carrier had to conclude in order to be free of the regime of liability laid down by earlier carriers' legislation for the conduct of what was a common calling.[429] One of the difficulties in assessing the impact of the remoteness rule lies in measuring how much of the inherited law may fairly be said to be special carriers' law rather than general contract law.

In calculating the quantity and the significance of knowledge in a given case, it was sometimes difficult to know where to draw the line between knowledge that should be imputed to the promisor and knowledge that should have been subject of special disclosure if the promisor's ordinary measure of liability were to be increased. This probably best explains the modern fashion of restating the remoteness rule as a consolidated rule rather than as a rule with separate limbs.[430] Carriers, however, could be expected to know rather less of the consignor's and consignee's businesses[431] than sellers of goods would know of their buyers' businesses. As between sellers, some would be more informed than others of the use that buyers would make of their goods. An engineering company selling a surplus boiler that the buyers were to remove to their own laundry,[432] for example, would know less about the way that boiler would work in the buyers' internal economy than would be known by the sellers of a pulverizing plant, who knew how it was to be installed and how it was to be housed and worked in with ancillary machinery.[433] In principle, the remoteness rule would bear upon the different cases with varying degrees of rigour.[434]

[427] *British Columbia etc. Saw Mill Co.* v. *Nettleship*, n. 423 above; *Horne* v. *Midland Railway Co.* (1873) LR 8 CP 131 (and note the sceptically narrow interpretation of the quite extensive information conveyed in that case); *Robophone Facilities Ltd* v. *Blank* [1966] 1 WLR 1428, 1448.

[428] *The Heron II*, n. 423 above, 442.

[429] See the Carriers Act 1830, 1 Will. 4, cap. 68 (though note this statute was concerned with loss rather than delay).

[430] *Victoria Laundry*, n. 423 above; *The Heron II*, n. 423 above.

[431] *Horne* v. *Midland Railway Co.*, n. 427 above; *British Columbia etc. Saw Mill Co.*, n. 423 above.

[432] *Victoria Laundry*, n. 423 above.

[433] *Cullinane* v. *British 'Rema' Manufacturing Co. Ltd* [1954] 1 QB 292.

[434] But see *The Heron II*, n. 423 above where the carrier's liability could not have been any less strict than a seller's would have been in broadly similar circumstances.

The application of the remoteness rule was also influenced by the willingness of courts, even as they admitted that the *quantum* of loss need not be contemplated by the promisor,[435] to separate financial loss into different heads or types.[436] The damage suffered, for example, in one case[437] in repurchasing and reshipping lost machinery parts was different in kind from the loss of profits[438] suffered by the consignee in not being able to run a timber mill until the parts were replaced. Where the damage concerned property or the human person, the same willingness to subdivide the loss was absent and this, more than anything, accounts for the harmony in practice of the tort and contract remoteness rules in cases of overlapping liability, even though the rules are assessed in terms of different levels of probability.[439]

Probability

As for the level of probability in the contract rule, it can probably be said that the amount of judicial ink spilt on the issue has not yielded worthwhile results.[440] Various formulae have been considered, and the choice appears to lie among the following though none of them would appear to command universal support: the loss is recoverable if, within the reasonable contemplation of the parties at the contract date, it is 'liable'[441] to result, or 'not unlikely'[442] to result, or represents a 'serious possibility'[443] or a 'real danger'.[444] It is clear, however, that the loss consequent upon breach may be considerably less than of even probability,[445] and clear too that probability is not to be regarded in the light of neutral observation, even if such were possible, but is coloured by the dictates of justice in a particular case.[446] This is probably best expressed by Lord du Parcq:

---

[435] e.g. *Wroth* v. *Tyler* [1974] Ch. 30.

[436] See, e.g., *Cory* v. *Thames Ironworks and Shipbuilding Co. Ltd*, n. 425 above; *Victoria Laundry*, n. 423 above; *The Heron II*, n. 423 above (separation of market loss and lock-up value claims).

[437] *British Columbia etc. Saw Mill Co.*, n. 423 above.

[438] Given the resistance at the time to lost profits claims, this item was expressed as the lost rental value of the mill as a going concern.

[439] *H. Parsons (Livestock) Ltd*, n. 424 above; *The Heron II*, n. 423 above (the collapsing ceiling illustration).

[440] See in particular *Re R. and H. Hall Ltd*, n. 423 above; *Victoria Laundry*, n. 423 above; *Monarch Steamship*, n. 423 above; *The Heron II*, n. 423 above.

[441] *Victoria Laundry*, n. 423 above; *The Heron II*, n. 423 above, 397, 415.

[442] *Re R. and H. Hall Ltd*, n. 423 above, 333–6; *The Heron II*, n. 423 above, 388, 397.

[443] *Monarch Steamship*, n. 423 above, 233; *The Heron II*, n. 423 above, 415, 425.

[444] *Monarch Steamship*, n. 423 above; *The Heron II*, n. 423 above.

[445] *The Heron II*, n. 423 above.

[446] See Lord Denning's attempt to break away from the differences in terminology between contract and tort rules: *H. Parsons (Livestock) Ltd*, n. 424 above.

Circumstances are so infinitely various that, however carefully general rules are framed, they must be construed with some liberality, and not too rigidly applied. It was necessary to lay down principles lest juries should be persuaded to do injustice by imposing an undue, or perhaps inadequate, liability on a defendant. The court must be careful, however, to see that the principles laid down are never so narrowly interpreted as to prevent a jury, or judge of fact, from doing justice between the parties. So to use them would be to misuse them.[447]

Although the courts are, perhaps, unduly coy in giving voice to the dictates of justice in particular cases, the decisions appear to yield a number of postulates, not all of which could be applied in harmony in the same case, and a number of which, as a matter of legal fashion, have been pursued with varying degrees of enthusiasm at different stages in their history. A consistent theme in the case law is that the defendant should not be called upon to underwrite a plaintiff's speculative venture, especially if it is an unsound one; the contractual expectation of the plaintiff is not that the defendant should become an insurer of his risk.[448] Similar to this approach is the attitude evinced in some decisions that it would be unjust to impose upon the defendant a ruinous form of liability.[449] This attitude is particularly marked in cases where the defendant's contractual remuneration is out of all proportion to the liability the plaintiff is seeking to pin on him, a state of affairs especially likely in the case of carriers who act as peripheral conduits rather than as integral elements in the plaintiff's venture.[450] In the interest of justice, courts will seek to draw the line at the direct financial consequences of a breach, and will not wish to pursue its reverberating and possibly limitless consequences.[451]

On the other hand, a court will be disposed to favour the application of the remoteness rule in the interest of the plaintiff, if otherwise the defendant's breach will go without an effective sanction.[452] If the contractual remuneration is particularly generous[453] or if the terms of the contract

[447] *Monarch Steamship*, n. 423 above, 232, quoted in *The Heron II*, n. 423 above, 397. See also R. Cooke [1978] *CLJ* 288.
[448] *British Columbia etc. Saw Mill Co.* v. *Nettleship* (1868) LR 3 CP 499; *Victoria Laundry (Windsor) Ltd* v. *Newman Industries Ltd* [1949] 2 KB 528 (very lucrative dyeing contracts); *Munroe Equipment Sales Ltd* v. *Canadian Forest Products Ltd* (1961) 29 DLR (2d) 730.
[449] *Victoria Laundry*, n. 448 above ('harsh results'); *Kerr Steamship* v. *Radio Corpn. of America* (1927) 157 NE 140.
[450] *Hadley* v. *Baxendale* (1854) 9 Ex. 341; *British Columbia etc. Saw Mill Co.*, n. 448 above; *Victoria Laundry*, n. 448 above; *Horne* v. *Midland Railway Co.* (1873) LR 8 CP 131. Cf. *The Heron II* [1969] 1 AC 350.
[451] *British Columbia etc. Saw Mill Co*, n. 448 above, 510 (the illustration of the Calcutta barrister); *Freedhof* v. *Pomalift Industries Ltd* (1971) 19 DLR (3d) 153.
[452] *Cory* v. *Thames Ironworks and Shipbuilding Co. Ltd* (1868) LR 3 QB 181. See also the excellent, but unsuccessful, argument of counsel for the carrier in *The Heron II*, n. 450 above.
[453] *Cathcart Inspection Services Ltd* v. *Purolator Courier Ltd* (1982) 39 OR (2d) 656 (Can.).

and the surrounding circumstances demonstrate a sharply defined undertaking to produce a contractual benefit,[454] then the defendant's damages liability will be accordingly expanded.[455] Another likely impulse concerns deliberate, self-enriching breaches by the defendants. Although the defendant carrier in *The Heron II* undertook to carry the plaintiff's sugar to Basrah under the terms of a voyage charterparty, it deliberately and unlawfully denied the plaintiffs the exclusive use of the ship, for which they had paid, when it deviated to various ports in performing additional contractual undertakings.[456] Although the deliberate nature of the breach was not remarked upon expressly by the House of Lords, it is difficult to believe this did not impress their lordships, who gave a reading of the remoteness rule that was generous to the plaintiffs.[457] This approach is not truly punitive, for it operates only in the shortfall between a conventionally applied remoteness rule and the limits of factual causation.[458]

Although the modern fashion is to apply a consolidated rule of remoteness of damage, the lay-out of the relevant sections in the Sale of Goods Act betrays the separate limbs of the rule in *Hadley* v. *Baxendale*.[459] The language of the statutory provisions does not respond exactly to Baron Alderson's famous words in that case, but it is an uncontroversial matter that the Act merely restates the rule.[460] The first limb is to be found in the various sections dealing with damages for non-delivery, non-acceptance, and the delivery of defective goods,[461] while the second limb is to be found in the section dealing with special and consequential damages.[462]

Mitigation[463]

It is a fundamental principle of the law of damages that one injured by the wrong of another may not, if he has the power to take evasive action,

---

[454] *Jarvis* v. *Swans Tours Ltd* [1973] QB 233; *Cathcart Inspection Services*, n. 453 above.

[455] But there is not a special remoteness rule for absolute, as opposed to due care, contractual undertakings: *H. Parsons (Livestock) Ltd* v. *Uttley, Ingham & Co. Ltd* [1978] QB 791, 811–12.

[456] But note the authoritative rejection of the defendant's gain as a measure of contract damages: *County Council of Surrey* v. *Bredero Homes Ltd* [1993] 1 WLR 1361; P. Birks (1993) 109 *LQR* 518; A. S. Burrows [1993] *LMCLQ* 453.

[457] On deliberate breaches, see also *Re R. and H. Hall Ltd and W. H. Pim Inc. and Co.'s Arbitration*, n. 423 above (Lord Blanesburgh).

[458] See the similar approach to the interpretation of clauses as liquidated damages clauses rather than penalties, according to actual rather than recoverable losses: *Robophone Facilities Ltd* v. *Blank* [1966] 1 WLR 1428, 1447–8.

[459] (1854) 9 Ex. 341.

[460] See, e.g., *H. Parsons (Livestock) Ltd*, n. 455 above, 807; *Bostock & Co. Ltd* v. *Nicholson & Sons Ltd* [1904] 1 KB 725, 735.

[461] Ss. 50–51, 53.   [462] S. 54.   [463] M. G. Bridge (1989) 105 *LQR* 398.

remain idle in the face of mounting or threatened prejudice. A contractual claimant who wishes to recover compensatory damages for the loss suffered must bestir himself so that responsibility is not laid at his own door. It is sometimes said that the injured party has a 'duty' to mitigate, but this expression is hardly apt for, if it is a duty at all, it is one that he owes only to himself:[464] he suffers any loss occurring after the time he should have resumed responsibility for his own welfare in the area of the contractual expectancy. This duty to mitigate is accompanied contextually by two other mitigation rules. The first of these is that expenses reasonably incurred in taking steps to minimize the loss may be charged to the account of the contract-breaker. According to the second of these additional rules, any benefits the injured party obtains in taking action that is prompted and occasioned by the breach of contract will, to the extent that it averts a threatened loss, be offset against the liability in damages of the contract breaker. These three mitigation rules, implicitly recognized under the Sale of Goods Act, will now be discussed in turn.

Duty to Mitigate

The first of the above mitigation rules, the duty to mitigate, is most usually attributed to factual causation, in that a claimant who fails to stave off an unavoidable loss cannot claim that the loss was caused by the defendant's breach of contract. As Viscount Haldane put it in *British Westinghouse Electric and Mfg. Co. Ltd* v. *Underground Electric Rys. Co. of London Ltd*,[465] the compensatory principle is qualified by a rule 'which imposes on a plaintiff the duty of taking all reasonable steps to mitigate the loss consequent on the breach, and debars him from claiming any part of the damage which is due to his neglect to take such steps'.[466] This explanation may not be entirely satisfactory since, while the burden of proof rests upon the plaintiff to demonstrate that the injury suffered flows from the defendant's breach of contract, it is for the defendant to prove that losses suffered by the plaintiff could have been avoided by action taken in mitigation.[467] Furthermore, it seems rather arbitrary to assert that the plaintiff's disputed loss has only one effective cause, namely his own inanition rather than the preceding breach of contract by the defendant.

[464] *Darbishire* v. *Warren* [1963] 1 WLR 1067, 1075; *Sotiros Shipping Inc.* v. *Sameiet Solholt (The Solholt)* [1981] 2 Lloyd's Rep. 574, 580 (Staughton J: duty to mitigate 'a condition attached to the right to claim damages'); *Red Deer College* v. *Michaels* [1976] 2 SCR 324, 330–1 (Can.).

[465] [1912] AC 673.

[466] *Ibid.* 689. See also *Jamal* v. *Moolla Dawood Sons and Co.* [1916] 1 AC 175, 179; *Koch Marine Inc.* v. *D'Amica Società Di Navigazione ARL (The Elena d'Amico)* [1980] 1 Lloyd's Rep. 75, 88.

[467] *Roper* v. *Johnson* (1873) LR 8 CP 167, 178, 181–2; *James Finlay & Co.* v. *Kwik Hoo Tong Handel Maatschappij* [1928] 2 KB 604, 614; *Red Deer College* v. *Michaels*, n. 464 above, 331.

Another explanation would be that losses the plaintiff could reasonably have avoided cannot be said to be within the reasonable contemplation of the parties at the contract date as liable to result from the defendant's breach, and thus are too remote.[468] The drawback to this is that mitigation authorities do not usually explore the parties' reasonable contemplation *ex ante*, but rather look to the reasonableness of the plaintiff's behaviour in the face of a prospective or incrementally mounting loss.

The statement of mitigation, as a general rule independent of remoteness, prompts a search for a different explanation. Probably the best explanation is that the expectation interest, though a creature of the contract, is sanctioned by the legal system which, in the interests of justice broadly understood, recoils from unduly prejudicing the defendant by conferring protection to the full extent of factual causation. Just as the remoteness rule is applied so that, in ordinary cases, the defendant is not an insurer of contractual adventures, so the mitigation rule instructs plaintiffs that a contractual promise may not absolve them from responsibility for their own welfare, and that they may in the circumstances now be better placed than the defendant to take steps towards the broad goal contemplated by the contract. Such an approach would involve scrutiny of the defendant's behaviour and position, and an inquiry into the means of the plaintiff and the predicament he was in when the contract was breached.

Mitigation is a question of fact governed by the circumstances of individual cases.[469] The steps the plaintiff ought to take are defined by prudence and reasonableness.[470] In the words of a Canadian judge, the breach of contract releases to the plaintiff a capacity to act which 'becomes an asset in [his] hands . . . and he is held to a reasonable employment of it in the course of events flowing from the breach'.[471] If, for reasons of impecuniosity, the plaintiff is unable to take rapid or effective steps in mitigation, he will not be judged too harshly for this.[472] Where the course of mitigation suggested by the defendant involves complex and risky litigation, the plaintiff will not be faulted for failing to

---

[468] *Cia Naviera Maropan SA* v. *Bowater's Lloyd Pulp and Paper Mill Ltd* [1955] 2 QB 68, 93, 98–9; *Radford* v. *De Froberville* [1977] 1 WLR 1262, 1272–3; *Perry* v. *Sidney Phillips & Son* [1982] 1 All ER 1005, revd. in part on other grounds [1982] 3 All ER 705; *Wingold Construction Co. Ltd* v. *Kramp* [1960] SCR 556 (Can.).

[469] See, e.g., *Payzu Ltd* v. *Saunders* [1919] 2 KB 581.

[470] *Karas* v. *Rowlett* [1944] SCR 1, 8.					[471] *Ibid.*

[472] *Perry* v. *Sidney Phillips & Son*, n. 468 above; *Clippens Oil Co. Ltd* v. *Edinburgh and District Water Trustees* [1907] AC 291, 303; *Trans Trust SPRL* v. *Danubian Trading Co. Ltd* [1952] 2 QB 297, 306; *Radford* v. *De Froberville* [1977] 1 WLR 1262, 1268; *Dodd Properties Ltd* v. *Canterbury City Council* [1980] 1 WLR 433, 453 (plaintiff's financial stringency flowing, as a matter of common sense, from defendant's tort); *Bacon* v. *Cooper (Metals) Ltd* [1982] 1 All ER 397.

pursue it.[473] Nor will a plaintiff buyer be required to impair his commercial reputation by forcing on his sub-buyers non-conforming goods or documents, tendered by the defendant seller.[474]

A buyer of goods will not be required to take extraordinary steps to buy in equivalent goods on the market. In *Lesters Leather & Skin Co. Ltd* v. *Home and Overseas Brokers Ltd*,[475] a seller failed to deliver a conforming quantity of snake skins that were to be shipped from India c.i.f. a United Kingdom port. The Court of Appeal, held, *inter alia*, that it would be unreasonable to expect the seller to order forward the same goods from India, for this would take eight or nine months; as a commercial venture it would be considerably more onerous than expecting a buyer of Bordeaux wines to mitigate by going to Bordeaux.

Illusory Mitigation

Mitigation has posed particular difficulties in sale of goods cases when it involves dealings between the same contracting parties.[476] In *Payzu Ltd* v. *Saunders*,[477] the buyers of a quantity of crêpe de chine to be delivered over a nine month period on thirty-day credit terms failed to pay promptly for the first instalment. Although this was not a discharging breach, the seller repudiated the contract, and was therefore adjudged herself to be in breach. Nevertheless, the same goods were offered for sale again by the seller at the same price but on net cash terms; the buyers declined the offer and accepted the seller's repudiation as terminating the contract. Since, against a rising market, the buyers were unable to obtain better terms than those offered by the seller, and since the seller was not insisting that the buyers forgo their action for damages for breach of contract,[478] the court held that it was unreasonable for the buyers to turn down the offer. In the words of the trial judge, parties involved in a mercantile dispute should not be permitted 'an unhappy indulgence in far-fetched resentment or an undue sensitiveness to slights or unfortunately worded letters'.[479] Scrutton LJ observed that 'in commercial contracts it is generally reasonable to accept an offer from the party in default'.[480]

This approach should be limited to cases where the plaintiff suffers a loss that could have been avoided by mitigating in this way, and where the plaintiff does not have to change his plans regarding the use or disposal of the contract goods. A buyer would not therefore be required to accept a tender of defective goods, for this would be tantamount to

---

[473] *Pilkington* v. *Wood* [1953] Ch. 770.
[474] *James Finlay & Co.* v. *Kwik Hoo Tong Handel Maatschappij* [1929] 1 KB 400. Cf. *Canso Chemicals Ltd* v. *Canadian Westinghouse Ltd* (1974) 10 NSR (2d) 306 (Can.).
[475] [1948] WN 437.   [476] Bridge, n. 463 above.   [477] N. 469 above.
[478] For loss of the credit facility.   [479] N. 469 above, 586.   [480] *Ibid.* 589.

depriving him of the right of rejection,[481] though a buyer might well be required to take up goods previously rejected because the documents were non-complying or the shipment date was wrong.[482] In this latter case, a buyer rejecting documents tendered under a forward contract and now searching for substitute goods on the spot market is unlikely to have good grounds for rejecting the goods, formerly covered by those documents, when of suitable quality.

The problem of the relationship between mitigation of damages and contractual termination rights turns up in other cases too. One of these, *Strutt* v. *Whitnell*,[483] is a sale of land case that states a principle germane also to sale of goods. It concerned the sale of a house with a covenant of vacant possession that was infringed because the tenant had acquired statutory protection against ejection. The question was whether the mitigation rule compelled the purchaser to surrender the house to the vendors and recover his money as opposed to retaining the house and pursuing a claim in damages. In holding that the purchaser could not be faulted for failing to choose the former of two equivalent remedial positions, the court denied the vendors the entitlement to submerge their loss in the diminished capital value of the house instead of suffering it in the form of a damages liability. Had the court ruled otherwise, a litigant might lose completely the right to recover damages if he rejects an offer of settlement that accurately records his injury.[484] *Strutt* v. *Whitnell* therefore demonstrates that the doctrine of mitigation, which some-times has painful remedial consequences, cannot be used to direct the deployment of assets and their monetary equivalents just between the plaintiff and the defendant: there will have to be a genuine loss suffered once the combined assets of plaintiff and defendant are added together before mitigation comes into play.

The above point seems to have been overlooked by the court in *The Solholt*.[485] A ship was sold for $5 million and rejected because of delivery three days late on a rising market[486] when its value had reached $5.5 million. It was subsequently sold for $5.8 million by the sellers. In the view of the court,[487] the buyers were quite entitled to terminate the contract for late delivery, but should then have offered to repurchase the ship from the sellers at the original contract price and without prejudice to

---

[481]	*Heaven & Kesterton Ltd* v. *Ets. François Albiac & Cie* [1956] 2 Lloyd's Rep. 316. Nor would the buyer have to accept any other offer involving a surrender of rights: *Houndsditch Warehouse Co. Ltd* v. *Waltex Ltd* [1944] KB 579.

[482]	*Heaven and Kesterton*, n. 481 above.	[483]	[1975] 1 WLR 870.

[484]	*Ibid.* 873.

[485]	[1981] 2 Lloyd's Rep. 574, affd. [1983] 1 Lloyd's Rep. 605.

[486]	The reason for the buyers' apparently strange behaviour was not established. One possibility was that they were trying to manoeuvre the sellers into a price reduction.

[487]	Following *Payzu Ltd* v. *Saunders*, n. 469 above. Cf. *Strutt* v. *Whitnell*, n. 483 above.

their claim for damages for the three-day delay. Satisfied that the sellers would have agreed to this, the court refused to award damages representing the increased price that the buyers would have had to pay for an equivalent ship. Although troubled by the conclusion that the seller had profited substantially from its own breach, the court was still unable to see the flaw in its decision.

The decision, it is submitted, is for various reasons wrong. First of all, it made the buyers' right of termination an illusory one. The result is exactly the same as if it had been the buyers who had committed the discharging breach and the sellers who had accepted it as terminating the contract. If strict rights of contractual discharge are inappropriate, they should be curtailed directly and not undermined by covert means. Secondly, on the facts, it is difficult to see why the initiative should have come from the buyers and interesting to speculate on how the sellers would have viewed the behaviour and mental state of buyers rejecting a late ship and then asking for it to be delivered after all under a different contract. Thirdly, the doctrine of mitigation should only be applied where the plaintiff suffers an avoidable loss that he wishes to lay at the door of the defendant to that party's detriment. No such loss occurred in *The Solholt*.[488] The so-called loss of the buyers was merely an alternative expression of the sellers' correlative gain, for in the result the sellers were allowed to keep all the post-contract increase in value of the ship. The buyers' loss only became a loss when they were not permitted to recover as damages the increased value of the ship between the contract date and the due delivery date.

Another way of putting this is to say that a buyer's duty to mitigate looks to future events from the point of mitigation, and bears no relation to what has happened in the past. In consequence, the buyers should certainly have recovered the $500,000 increase in value accruing to the due delivery date. As for the subsequent $300,000, accruing up to the date the seller eventually sold the ship, the buyers' failure to take the ship from the sellers might be regarded as a personal speculation concerning the future value of the ship based on the losing assumption that the value of the ship had peaked.[489] They had the use of their money during that period.[490] If indeed the value of the ship had thereafter declined, the buyers would have made a gain, from witholding their money, to which the sellers would have had no claim.

This criticism of *The Solholt*[491] prompts a further look at *Payzu Ltd* v.

---

[488] N. 485 above.
[489] See *Jamal* v. *Moolla Dawood Sons and Co.* [1916] 1 AC 175, 179.
[490] *Quaere* if they had paid in advance? See the discussion on the date of assessment of damages in the text accompanying nn. 549 ff. below.
[491] N. 485 above.

Saunders.[492] In that case, on a rising market, the buyers refused to accept the seller's offer of mitigation and so were faced with a higher price for crêpe de chine; correlatively, the seller would presumably have disposed of that same quantity of crêpe de chine at an enhanced market price, higher than the figure in the contract and the offer of mitigation. If the buyers and seller did in fact both enter the same market, the one to buy and the other to sell, then there would not have been a loss at all, for the buyers' increased cost would have matched the seller's increased price. The evidence suggested that there was a shortage of crêpe de chine, so it could not be said that the buyers' failure to mitigate robbed the seller of an additional sale of the commodity.[493] A difficulty with the above treatment of mitigation arises where buyer and seller enter the market at different times, or when either or both fail to enter the market at all. This raises another mitigation issue concerning the date of assessment of damages and discussed below. Subject to that, the mitigation rule operates as a condition on the buyer's right to recover expectation losses in full and ought not to be invoked where the buyer alone truly suffers a loss, and justice does not require that the seller be released from liability.

Another point concerning mitigation may be dealt with here. The Sale of Goods Act provisions for assessing damages for non-acceptance by the buyer and non-delivery by the seller lay down, as *prima facie* rules, that the injured party enter the market at the performance date and resell or buy in as the case may be.[494] This is sometimes said to embody a mitigation principle,[495] and indeed there are circumstances where it may do so, as where the injured party has the capacity and the need to act promptly on a continuously adverse market. But this state of affairs is likely to arise more frequently in the case of stable rather than volatile commodities. The value of residential land was perceptibly rising at all material times in *Wroth* v. *Tyler*,[496] but the same could not be said for the value of bulk sugar on the Basrah market in *The Heron II*[497] where, despite some evidence of seasonal decline, the House of Lords held that it was a matter of even probability whether the market in sugar would rise or fall at the material date. That being so, if the injured party is required by law to act promptly if the market is to serve as the measure of his loss, it is difficult to justify this in terms of mitigation. What is important is that a party who delays may equally win or lose by delaying. In reality, he is to be treated as assuming a market risk so that, if he wins, he

---

[492] [1919] 2 KB 581.

[493] The problem of lost volume is discussed in the text accompanying nn. 697 ff. below.

[494] Ss. 50(3) and 51(3).

[495] See, e.g., *Radford* v. *De Froberville* [1977] 1 WLR 1262, 1285; *Asamera Oil Corpn. Ltd* v. *Sea Oil & General Corpn.* [1979] 1 SCR 633, 647 (Can.).

[496] [1974] Ch. 30.		[497] [1969] 1 AC 350.

retains the fruits of his speculation, but if he loses, he may not call in the other party to underwrite that speculation with no hope of reward.[498]

Cost of Mitigation

A corollary of the duty to mitigate is that the plaintiff is entitled to recover as damages the expenses incurred in mitigating, for these are attributable to the defendant's breach of contract.[499] Although a plaintiff placed in a difficult position because of the defendant's breach is not treated too harshly,[500] problems sometimes arise if the plaintiff's peculiarly vulnerable position necessitates heavy expenditures. Plaintiffs in one case were denied recovery for the heavy interest charges they had to bear on securing a bond to release a ship from arrest.[501] These charges, incurred because the plaintiffs ran their own business within unduly tight financial limits, were treated as the subject of a damages claim that failed to comply with the remoteness rule.[502] But in *Bacon* v. *Cooper (Metals) Ltd*,[503] the plaintiff had to purchase a new rotor for his fragmentizer when the wrong sort of steel, supplied in breach of contract by the defendants, was fed into the fragmentizer. A second-hand replacement could not be procured. The plaintiff had no choice but to acquire, on expensive hire purchase terms, a new rotor for the fragmentizer, which was still subject to a hire purchase agreement. The cost of acquiring the replacement rotor was allowed as damages and, moreover, no deduction was made for the 'betterment', or improved position of the plaintiff, supposedly enjoyed from having a new rotor instead of one that had been used for nearly half of its seven year life expectancy. Making such a deduction would have been tantamount to forcing the plaintiff to invest his money in the modernization of his machinery.[504]

---

[498] *Jamal* v. *Moolla Dawood Sons and Co.*, n. 489 above, 179; *Waddell* v. *Blockley* (1880) 4 QBD 478; *British & Commonwealth Holdings Plc* v. *Quadrex Holdings Plc* [1995] CLC 1169; *Campbell Mostyn (Provisions) Ltd* v. *Barnett Trading Co. Ltd* [1954] 1 Lloyd's Rep. 65. This is particularly important where an anticipatory repudiation is accepted: *Kaines (UK) Ltd* v. *Österreichische Warengesellschaft mbH* [1993] 2 Lloyd's Rep. 1; M. G. Bridge [1994] JBL 152.

[499] *Banco de Portugal* v. *Waterlow & Sons Ltd* [1932] AC 452; *Wilson* v. *United Counties Bank* [1920] AC 102; *Erie County Natural Gas and Fuel Co. Ltd* v. *Carroll* [1911] AC 105; *Lloyds and Scottish Finance Ltd* v. *Modern Cars and Caravans (Kingston) Ltd* [1966] 1 QB 764.

[500] *Banco de Portugal*, n. 499 above, 506.

[501] *Cia Financiera Soleada SA* v. *Hamoor Tanker Corpn. Inc. (The Borag)* [1981] 1 WLR 274.

[502] See also *Liesbosch, Dredger* v. *SS Edison* [1933] AC 449; *Radford* v. *De Froberville*, n. 495 above.

[503] [1982] 1 All ER 397.

[504] Citing *Harbutt's 'Plasticine' Ltd* v. *Wayne Tank and Pump Co. Ltd* [1970] 1 QB 447, 472–3 at 401 of *Bacon*, n. 503 above.

Losses Avoided by Mitigation in Fact

Once a plaintiff takes steps to mitigate damages, it follows that he may not recover for losses avoided. Problems sometimes arise where a plaintiff acts after a breach of contract and this action in fact has the effect of diminishing his losses, though the duty to mitigate may not have required such action to be taken and it may be difficult to trace a causal link between this action and the breach of contract. The leading case is *British Westinghouse Electric and Mfg. Co. Ltd* v. *Underground Electric Rys. Co. of London Ltd*,[505] which concerned a contract to sell and erect a number of steam turbines and turbo alternators at various dates between 1904 and 1906. These machines turned out to be non-conforming and defective in design and to consume excessive quantities of coal. Sued for the balance of the price, the buyers abandoned an alternative claim for the actual (to date) plus projected excessive coal consumption by the machines, and claimed instead the cost of excessive coal actually consumed as well as the cost of replacing the seller's machines and substituting them with a much less expensive and efficient new machine made by a competitor. This substitution actually took place in 1908, before the present action was brought. The arbitrator, with some adjustments, found in favour of the buyers, though he also found that it would have been to the buyers' advantage to replace the sellers' machines, as soon as in fact they did, even if the sellers' machines had been in full conformity with the contract. The award, however, was overturned in the House of Lords for reasons appearing in the following passage from Viscount Haldane's speech:

[T]he duty of taking all reasonable steps to mitigate the loss . . . does not impose on the plaintiff an obligation to take any step which a reasonable and prudent man would not ordinarily take in the course of his business. But when in the course of his business he has taken action arising out of the transaction, which action has diminished his loss, the effect in actual diminution of the loss he has suffered may be taken into account even though there was no duty on him to act.[506]

In this passage, Viscount Haldane states that the plaintiff takes action arising out of the 'transaction', whereas in a later passage he states that 'the subsequent transaction, if to be taken into account, must be one arising out of the consequences of the breach'.[507] In *British Westinghouse*, the later substitution could not be said to have arisen from the consequences of the 'breach', since, as the arbitrator found, it would have happened in any event, breach or no breach. But it did arise out of

---

[505] [1912] AC 673.
[506] *Ibid.* 689, citing in support *Staniforth* v. *Lyall* (1830) 7 Bing. 169.
[507] N. 505 above, 690.

the transaction[508] in the sense that the buyers' power requirements were to be satisfied by either the sellers' machines or the competitor's machines but not by both; if the buyers were using the competitor's machines, it would only be because they had no further use for the sellers' machines. Another way of putting it is to say that, apart from the excessive coal consumption up to 1908,[509] the buyers had in fact suffered no loss from the sellers' breach of contract. One can only speculate what the result might have been if the buyers had brought their action before substituting the sellers' machines. The sellers might then have been driven with uncertain prospects of success[510] to argue that the buyers had a duty to mitigate in the way they actually did in this case.

Assuming that the decision taken in 1908 to replace the sellers' machines in *British Westinghouse*, besides turning out to be beneficial, was perceptibly risk-free at that time, a real difficulty emerges in cases where the plaintiff takes a risk that might exacerbate his position. This occurred in a Canadian employment case, *Cockburn* v. *Trusts and Guarantee Co.*,[511] where an employee, dismissed in breach of contract, devoted his time, skill, savings, and credit in purchasing the assets of his former employer, which had gone into liquidation. He then revived the affairs of the company and resold the assets for a figure in excess of the earnings he would have received if his employment contract had not been unlawfully terminated. Because he had made use of his time and skills, which assets would not have been available but for his employer's breach of contract, he was entitled only to nominal damages. It is by no means self-evident that a plaintiff should take a risk the fruits of which, if the risk is beneficial, should first be applied to reducing the defendant's damages. If the plaintiff's enterprise in *Cockburn* had failed, he would never have recovered as damages his lost savings or ruined credit. It is submitted that a plaintiff should not have to surrender to the defendant gains where, if the speculation had been unsuccessful, he would have been unable to charge the defendant with his losses. In *British Westinghouse*, the mitigation principle was repeatedly said by Viscount Haldane to govern only if the later transaction was entered into in the normal course of business.[512] A speculative risk is not something that dismissed salaried employees, or buyers of capital goods, normally undertake.

In the normal run of sale-of-goods contracts, it will be difficult for a defendant seller to show mitigation in fact, taking the form of a substitute

[508] *Ibid.* 691. [509] The buyers were allowed damages for this.
[510] See *Jewelowski* v. *Propp* [1944] KB 510, 511.
[511] (1917) 55 SCR 264. See also *Lavarack* v. *Woods of Colchester Ltd* [1967] 1 QB 278.
[512] N. 505 above, 689–91. See also *Hill & Sons* v. *Edwin Showell & Sons Ltd* (1918) 87 LJ KB 1106, 1115 ('speculative work not in the ordinary course of business').

purchase, that 'aris[es] out of the consequences of the breach'. A buyer's capacity to act is unlikely to be monopolized by a single contract. But the possibility does arise in cases like *British Westinghouse*, where the buyers' needs were confined to one set of machines. In commodities trading, a factual link between a defendant seller's breach and a buyer's subsequent purchase would seem unlikely; merchants conduct their buying and selling activities across a broad front.[513] Nevertheless, in *R. Pagnan & Flli* v. *Corbisa Industrial Agropacuaria Lda*,[514] the buyers lawfully rejected a c.i.f. cargo before purchasing it on a distress basis on shore at the port of discharge. The price was artificially low because the buyers had sequestered the cargo, making it difficult for the sellers to sell to anyone else.[515] Since the later transaction was 'part of a continuous dealing between the same parties in respect of the same goods', and not 'an independent or disconnected transaction',[516] the profit made under it could be offset against the smaller market rise in the goods so that the buyers had suffered no loss in consequence of the sellers' breach.[517] It is unlikely that the same result would have been reached if the buyers had chanced upon another cargo sold by different sellers in distressed circumstances.

Mitigation and Anticipatory Repudiation

A number of problems are presented in cases where the plaintiff has not yet elected to seek relief in damages for the defendant's failure in breach of contract to perform his primary obligations. One such problem arises where the defendant refuses in advance to perform the contract. One somewhat discredited theory, coloured by rescission *ab initio* ideas, is that such an anticipatory repudiation[518] is not a present breach but an offer to rescind on terms.[519] This is consistent with the view that no breach of contract occurs until the repudiation is accepted.[520] There is

---

[513] The difficulties of showing a factual connection between the various purchases and sales is dramatically revealed in a series of soya bean cases arising out of the 1973 US export embargo: see M. G. Bridge, 'The 1973 Mississippi Floods: "Force Majeure" and Prohibition of Export' in E. McKendrick (ed.), *Force Majeure and Frustration of Contract* (2nd edn., 1995).

[514] [1971] 1 All ER 165.

[515] '[T]he sellers were at a disadvantage which the buyers were able to exploit': *Hussey* v. *Eels* [1990] 2 QB 227, 239.

[516] N. 514 above, 169. Cf. *Hussey* v. *Eels*, n. 515 above; *Koch Marine Inc.* v. *D'Amica Societa di Navigazione ARL* [1980] 1 Lloyd's Rep. 75.

[517] The court thereby departed from the normal rule, discussed in the text accompanying nn. 540 ff. below, that damages are assessed by reference to the prevailing market price.

[518] J. M. Nienabr [1962] CLJ 213; F. Dawson [1981] CLJ 83.

[519] *Bradley* v. *H. Newsom, Sons & Co.* [1919] AC 16, 52; *Johnstone* v. *Milling* (1886) 16 QBD 460, 473 (contract ceases to exist except for damages); *Hochster* v. *De la Tour* (1853) 2 E & B 678, 685 (consent to ending of contract). Criticized by Nienabr, n. 518 above, 224.

[520] e.g. *Ripley* v. *M'Lure* (1849) 4 Ex. 345; *Howard* v. *Pickford Tool Co. Ltd* [1951] 1 KB 417, 421 (unaccepted repudiation 'a thing writ in water and of no value to anybody'); *White & Carter (Councils) Ltd* v. *McGregor* [1962] AC 413.

ample support, however, for a different theory, that a refusal to perform in future is a present breach[521] of an implied term to refrain from impeding the other party's contractual expectations or of fidelity to the contract goal. Suppose a seller declares in advance his refusal to deliver goods at a future date as called for by the contract. The innocent party may elect between accepting the repudiation immediately as determining the contract, or awaiting the date fixed for performance. Depending on which of the above theories is accepted, that party is accepting or declining an offer to rescind, or is affirming the contract or terminating it for the breach of the implied term.

No matter which of the above theories is adopted, it is well established that the innocent party is under no compulsion to mitigate damages by electing to terminate the contract. This conclusion is readily supportable if the anticipatory repudiation is not a breach. It is more difficult to justify if a refusal to perform amounts to a present breach, unless the subject of the later damages action is seen as the breach of the primary obligation itself rather than the implied term of fidelity. The inapplicability of mitigation in the face of an anticipatory repudiation is dramatically illustrated by *Tredegar Iron and Coal Co. Ltd* v. *Hawthorn Brothers & Co.*,[522] where an f.o.b. contract called for the supply of coal at a certain price. Unable to nominate an effective ship, the buyers conveyed to the sellers an offer from a third party to buy the same quantity of coal for the domestic market at a price slightly higher than the contract price. The sellers declined to accept this offer and had to sell the coal for less than the contract price shortly after the buyers declined to take delivery at the due date for performance. The sellers were able to recover damages representing the difference between the contract price and the diminished market price. If this result is explicable only according to the technicalities of anticipatory repudiation, it seems extraordinary and argues a case for modifying the substantive law. The result might be less extraordinary, however, if, at the time of the buyers' offer to mitigate, the current market price stands higher than the third party's offer though it later declines, or where the sellers have surplus coal and entertain a legitimate expectation of selling a quantity of coal to that same third party in any event.

Another case where a plaintiff is entitled to ignore a repudiation without feeling the need to mitigate is where he is able to press a claim in

---

[521] e.g. *Frost* v. *Knight* (1872) LR 7 Ex. 11; *Hochster* v. *De la Tour*, n. 519 above; *Maredelanto Cia Naviera SA* v. *Bergbau-Handels GmbH (The Mihalis Angelos)* [1971] 1 QB 164.

[522] (1902) 18 TLR 716. See also *Lusograin Comercio International de Cereas Lda* v. *Bunge AG* [1986] 2 Lloyd's Rep. 654, where the sellers, declining to accept the buyers' repudiation, were allowed to continue earning the carrying charges to which they were entitled during a shipment extension period.

debt. Debt is in principle far from being a discretionary remedy.[523] For example, a plaintiff buyer who has prepaid the price, and who wishes to recover it, as on a failure of consideration, upon terminating the contract, need not mitigate in respect of this money claim,[524] though mitigation may in fact bear upon an ancillary damages claim. This amounts to another way of saying that mitigation does not hamper a plaintiff in exercising termination rights,[525] for the recovery of the pre-paid money is a necessary consequence of termination.

A vivid illustration of the irrelevance of mitigation to debt is afforded by *White & Carter (Councils) Ltd* v. *McGregor*,[526] where the repudiation by a garage of a three-year contract for advertising the garage on municipal waste-paper bins accelerated the garage's payment obligation under the contract. The repudiation occurred before the advertising agents had even prepared the advertising plates, but they went ahead, began displaying them, and sued in debt for the three years' payments. The case shows that mitigation does not destroy the right to sue in debt and, furthermore, it does not prevent the innocent party from proceeding unilaterally with performance so as to qualify under the contract for a debt claim, provided that this can be done in compliance with the letter of the contract. Such compliance will be impossible if the cooperation of the other party is needed to perform conditions precedent to the debt entitlement.[527]

The decision of a bare majority of the House of Lords has been criticized as sanctioning economic waste, but performance in this case was unwanted rather than wasteful; there was nothing to show that the advertising was any the less effective with the general public as a result of the garage's disavowal of it. In the majority, however, Lord Reid qualified his judgment by observing that a plaintiff would need a 'substantial and legitimate interest'[528] if he were unilaterally to qualify for a debt claim in this way: the burden of showing the absence of this would rest upon the defendant. It is nevertheless difficult to see the ground for this qualification, except a vague and innominate principle of equity.[529] The defend-

---

[523] But see Lord Denning in *Attica Sea Carriers Corpn.* v. *Ferrostaal Poseidon Bulk Reederei GmbH (The Puerto Buitrago)* [1976] 1 Lloyd's Rep. 250, 255 (debt claim as specific performance, *sed quaere?*).

[524] What about a plaintiff seeking recovery of the price paid in the form of a damages claim?

[525] *Payzu Ltd* v. *Saunders* [1919] 2 KB 581; *The Solholt* [1983] 1 Lloyd's Rep. 605; *Heaven & Kesterton Ltd* v. *Ets. François Albiac & Cie* [1956] 2 Lloyd's Rep. 316.

[526] [1962] AC 413; cf. *Clark* v. *Marsiglia* (1845) 1 Denio 317 (US).

[527] *White & Carter*, n. 526 above, 429; *Hounslow London BC* v. *Twickenham Garden Developments Ltd* [1971] Ch. 233; *Finelli* v. *Dee* (1968) 67 DLR (2d) 393. *Quaere* where the defendant's breach triggers a clause accelerating the duty to pay to a time before work, needing the defendant's cooperation, falls due?

[528] N. 526 above, 431.

[529] *Ibid.* 430–1: 'some general equitable principle or element of public policy'.

ers in *White & Carter* had failed to lead evidence of the absence of such an interest. One might wonder how such an interest could ever be lacking if it was possessed by the advertising agents in this case, the behaviour of whom is hard to explain, unless they faced difficulty in computing a damages claim.[530] In *Clea Shipping Corp.* v. *Bulk Oil International Ltd (No. 2)*,[531] Lloyd J declined to interfere with an arbitrator's finding that the owner of a ship had no legitimate interest in refusing to accept the time charterer's repudiation by holding the ship at the disposal of the charterer for the remainder of the charter period. The owner should have taken steps to secure an alternative fixture for the ship. The case clearly recognizes that the normally unfettered right to elect in favour of the continuance of a contract where the other party repudiates is qualified in such a case by 'general equitable principles'.[532]

The principle of *White & Carter (Councils) Ltd* v. *McGregor* is of limited significance in sales law. It was seen in an earlier chapter[533] that the co-operation of both parties is needed to pass the property in goods initially unascertained, and that a repudiation by one party is effective in withdrawing his implied assent to the other's unconditional appropriation of the goods to the contract. This combination of assent and unconditional appropriation is required to pass the property in unascertained goods, and the passing of property is the normal case in which a seller is able to sue in debt for the price.[534] Furthermore, as was observed earlier in this Chapter, repudiation is not allowed to negative the requirement that conditions precedent be performed before the right to sue in debt arises.[535]

Mitigation and Specific Performance

Mitigation has emerged in recent times to qualify a plaintiff's entitlement to pursue a claim for the specific performance of the contract. Since specific performance is quite a rare remedy in sales law, this development is therefore of limited interest. The plaintiff house purchaser in *Wroth* v. *Tyler*[536] was able to obtain damages assessed at the judgment date, rather than the breach date, because these were awarded in lieu of

---

[530] For the problem of lost volume (how many litter bins and advertisers could Glasgow absorb?), see discussion in the text accompanying nn. 697 ff. below.

[531] *The Alaskan Trader* [1984] 1 All ER 129.

[532] *Ibid.* 136. And at 137: '*some* fetter, if only in extreme cases' (emphasis in the original). See also *The Puerto Buitrago*, n. 523 above (redelivery of chartered ship and covenant to repair); *Channel Islands Ferries Ltd* v. *Cenargo Navigation Ltd (The Rozel)* [1994] 2 Lloyd's Rep. 161 (damages for breach of repair covenant).

[533] Ch. 3 above.   [534] S. 49(1), above.

[535] *Colley* v. *Overseas Exporters* [1921] 3 KB 302, distinguishing *Mackay* v. *Dick* (1881) 6 App. Cas. 251.

[536] [1974] Ch. 30.

specific performance.[537] That a court might in a proper case require a plaintiff to mitigate, and so award damages assessed at a mitigation date prior to judgment instead of the specific relief it would otherwise be disposed to give, is evident in the Canadian case of *Asamera Oil Corpn. Ltd v. Sea Oil & General Corpn.*[538] In that case, plaintiffs suing in detinue for the return of shares bailed years ago to the defendant company, or for specific performance of this agreement,[539] were not permitted to press their claim for specific relief through years of delay in litigation and in the face of a volatile market in the shares. They were required after a time, admittedly a considerable time, to purchase an equivalent number of shares on the open market. Specific performance is, after all, a discretionary remedy.

Measuring Losses According to the Market

Sections 50 and 51 of the Sale of Goods Act, dealing with the buyer's liability in damages for non-acceptance and the seller's liability in damages for non-delivery, both prescribe in sub-section (3) that the damages due will *prima facie* be the difference between the contract price and the market or current price at the date fixed for acceptance or delivery as the case may be.[540] There has to be an 'available market' for the goods.[541] Sub-section (3) encapsulates two rules: first, the breach date rule, by which the date for calculating damages is the date that the buyer or seller is in breach of his primary obligation of delivery or acceptance of the goods;[542] and secondly, the rule that the contract price is compared with the prevailing market price, rather than with some other standard. Where the contract allows for a flexible quantity of goods, damages will be assessed at the top end of the scale where it is the plaintiff who has the

---

[537] The decision was supported by the wording of the Chancery Amendment Act 1858 (Lord Cairns's Act), 21 & 22 Vict., cap. 27. See however *Johnson* v. *Agnew* [1980] AC 367, where the court preferred a relaxation in the date of assessment of damages at common law to the idea that a difference existed between the equitable and common law approach to damages.

[538] [1979] 1 SCR 633.   [539] The case does not clearly indicate which.

[540] S. 50 (non-acceptance) codifies the decision in *Barrow* v. *Arnaud* (1846) 8 QB 595. If the market price has risen, in the case of a seller's action, or fallen, in the case of a buyer's, the damages will be nominal. See *Erie County Natural Gas and Fuel Co. Ltd* v. *Carroll* [1911] AC 105.

[541] Discussed below.

[542] Where performance takes place over a period, damages will normally be assessed acording to the last date allowed for performance: *Roper* v. *Johnson* (1873) LR 8 CP 167; *Brown* v. *Muller* (1872) LR 7 Ex. 319; *Phoeus D. Kyprianou Co.* v. *Wm. H. Pim Jnr. & Co. Ltd* [1977] 2 Lloyd's Rep. 570; *Bremer Handelsgesellschaft mbH* v. *Vanden Avenne-Izegem PVBA* [1978] 2 Lloyd's Rep. 109 (the next day in the case of default clauses in commodities forms); *Alfred C. Toepfer* v. *Peter Cremer* [1975] 2 Lloyd's Rep. 118; *Tai Hing Cotton Mill* v. *Kamsing Knitting Factory* [1979] AC 91; *Intertradex SA* v. *Lesieur-Tourteaux SARL* [1978] 2 Lloyd's Rep. 509, 518–19.

quantitative option, and at the bottom where the defendant has the option.[543]

Although the two rules in sub-section (3) are contained in a provision stated to be of a *prima facie* nature, they are difficult to displace in practice.[544] They will not be displaced simply because the prospect of a resale or sub-sale satisfies the remoteness of damage test, since the presence of an available market operates as a restraint on recovery.[545] In the absence of an available market, sections 50 to 51[546] apply the standard of remoteness drawn from the first limb of the rule in *Hadley* v. *Baxendale*[547] and permit the assessment of damages by other means. Such assessment, however, must conform to established principles of factual causation, remoteness of damage, and mitigation of damages.[548]

Abstract and Concrete Damages Claims

The breach date rule,[549] as stated earlier in this Chapter, is best explained on the ground that an injured party who chooses not to enter the market is speculating for his own benefit or detriment.[550] The rule does not in fact require the claimant to enter the market and, since in abstract terms it permits the claimant's loss to be crystallized as a market position, without a substitute transaction being made, it is in perfect harmony with the speculation principle. Many of the difficulties that arise in the area of damages stem from uncertainty in characterizing the claimant's loss,

---

[543] *Cockburn* v. *Alexander* (1846) 6 CB 791; *Toprak Mahsullerei Ofisi* v. *Finagrain Cie Commerciale Agricole et Financière SA* [1979] 2 Lloyd's Rep. 98. An option may be subject to an implied limitation as to the quantities of particular types of contract goods: *Paula Lee Ltd* v. *Robert Zehil & [Co.] Ltd* [1983] 2 All ER 390.

[544] S. 50(3) will, however, be displaced in the case of manufactured goods where the seller's claim for damages for non-acceptance is based on the fact that the buyer's default means that the seller has concluded one sale fewer than he would otherwise have done. See *Re Vic Mill Ltd* [1913] 1 Ch. 465 and the lost volume problem, discussed in the text accompanying nn. 697 ff. below.

[545] *Patrick* v. *Russo-British Grain Export Co. Ltd* [1927] 2 KB 535; *Coastal (Bermuda) Petroleum Ltd* v. *VTT Vulcan Petroleum SA (The Marine Star)* [1994] CLC 1019, 1025. But the market is displaced when in fact it is absent, not when it is absent *and* such absence satisfies the remoteness test: *The Marine Star*.

[546] In sub-s. (2).

[547] (1854) 9 Ex. 341. The second limb is to be found in s. 54.

[548] It is common in the absence of a market for sub-sales to be looked at in buyers' actions for non-delivery: *The Arpad* [1934] P 189, 200–2; *Lyon* v. *Fuchs* (1920) 2 Ll. LR 333; *Mott* v. *Muller* (1922) 13 Ll. LR 492; *Patrick* v. *Russo-British Grain Export Co. Ltd*, n. 545 above; *Grébert-Borgnis* v. *J. & W. Nugent* (1885) 15 QBD 85; *Hydraulic Engineering Co. Ltd* v. *McHaffie, Goslett & Co.* (1878) 4 QBD 670; *J. Leavey & Co. Ltd* v. *George H. Hirst & Co. Ltd* [1944] KB 24; *Richmond Western Wineries Ltd* v. *Simpson* [1940] SCR 1 (Can.). But the sub-sale must satisfy the remoteness test: *Kwei Tek Chao* v. *British Traders and Shippers Ltd* [1954] 2 QB 459, 492–9 ; *Coastal International Trading Ltd* v. *Maroil AG* [1988] 1 Lloyd's Rep. 92, 95; *Frank Mott & Co. Ltd* v. *Wm. H. Muller & Co. (London) Ltd* (1922) 13 Ll L R 492.

[549] S. Waddams (1981) 97 *LQR* 445.

[550] See discussion in the text accompanying nn. 494 ff. above.

either as an abstract measure of market disadvantage or as a concrete measure of loss demonstrated by the practical need to enter an adverse market. A claimant in the latter category presses the case for abandoning the philosophy of abstract market disadvantage.

One example of this is the prepaying buyer. In early cases,[551] references were made to the liability of a bailee of shares, unlawfully holding over and sued in detinue by the bailor, where damages were assessed at the date of the subsequent proceedings.[552] These bailment authorities were not followed in sales cases where the buyer had not paid at all[553] and where the buyer had paid in part.[554] But the bailment comparison was followed in another case where the buyer had given acceptances at four months that had been discounted and had fallen due.[555] Further support for departing from the breach date rule in favour of assessment at the date of trial, in the case of prepaying buyers, is afforded in other cases.[556] One of these cases points the way to a rationalization of this departure from the breach date rule, namely, that the rule should not apply where a buyer has been deprived of the financial capacity to enter the market, and this possibility is within the reasonable contemplation of the seller at the contract date as liable to result from his breach.[557] This approach comes close to abandoning the abstract approach of English law to damages assessment in favour of a concrete approach.

A relaxation of the breach date rule to permit damages to be assessed after the breach date is evident in certain sale of land cases,[558] but it will be an exceptional sale of goods case that calls for such treatment. Suppose that the nature of the goods or of the market is such that an instantaneous market transaction cannot occur. An entry into the market may need to be delayed or staggered for reasons concerning shortage, difficulties of communication, or the fear of exciting the market with a large sale or purchase. These difficulties do not detract from the existence of an available market. Nevertheless, the market to be considered remains the one at the breach date and not the later market that the claimant did enter or might have entered.[559] The reason is that the dam-

---

[551] See *Gainsford* v. *Carroll* (1824) 2 B & C 624; *Startup* v. *Cortazzi* (1835) 2 CM & R 164; *Elliot* v. *Hughes* (1863) 3 F & F 387.

[552] See the discussion of these authorities in *Asamera Oil Corpn. Ltd* v. *Sea Oil & General Corpn.* [1979] 1 SCR 633 (Can.).

[553] *Gainsford* v. *Carroll*, n. 551 above.   [554] *Startup* v. *Cortazzi*, n. 551 above.

[555] *Elliot* v. *Hughes*, n. 551 above.

[556] *Aronson* v. *Mologa Holzindustrie A/G Leningrad* (1927) 32 Com. Cas. 276, 290 (Atkin LJ); *Peebles* v. *Pfeifer* [1918] 2 WWR 877; *Asamera Oil Corpn.*, n. 552 above.

[557] *Peebles* v. *Pfeifer*, n. 556 above (purchase of grain seed by a farmer). See also *Asamera Oil Corpn*, n. 552 above, where a buyer who has not paid is said to have his purchasing power released.

[558] *Wroth* v. *Tyler* [1974] Ch. 30; *Johnson* v. *Agnew* [1980] AC 367.

[559] *Garnac Grain Co. Inc.* v. *HMF Faure & Fairclough Ltd* [1968] AC 1130n, 1138

ages assessment under sections 50(3) and 51(3) is based on a 'notional or fictitious sale',[560] which is consistent with English law's preference for an abstract, rather than concrete, approach to these matters. If a pre-paying buyer does have the means to enter the market at the breach date, he can always recover as damages the lost investment value of the prepaid sum from the date of actual mitigation.[561]

Another clear instance of delayed assessment after the performance date is where there has been a waiver or forbearance; there is no need for a binding variation of the contract. The damages will be assessed at the end of the waiver or forbearance when the plaintiff is free to go into the market.[562] Assessment will also be delayed where non-conforming goods have been delivered and subsequently rejected by the buyer, who now seeks damages for non-delivery on a rising market.[563] A buyer unlawfully rejecting goods should be treated as refusing to accept them at that date,[564] which should serve as the reference point for damages.

An interesting case for delaying assessment might also be advanced where the conclusion of the substitute transaction is delayed by currency difficulties. In *Attorney-General of the Republic of Ghana* v. *Texaco Overseas Tankships Ltd*,[565] the plaintiffs sued, under a bill of lading contract,[566] a carrier who had failed to deliver their oil. An alternative cargo would have had to be purchased from the nearest market in US dollars, but the plaintiffs were prevented by internal difficulties from obtaining the requisite foreign currency and effecting the substitute purchase. In the present proceedings, separated from the non-delivery of the plaintiffs' oil by a catastrophic devaluation of the Ghanainan currency, they

(description of trial judge's finding); *Shearson Lehman Hutton Inc.* v. *Maclaine Watson & Co. Ltd (No. 2)* [1990] 3 All ER 723, 731. Cf. *Petrograde Inc.* v. *Stinnes Handels GmbH* [1995] 1 Lloyd's Rep. 142, 152–53 ('weighted average of the prices that would have been obtained during the . . . period').

[560] *Shearson Lehman Hutton*, n. 559 above, 731.

[561] *Startup* v. *Cortazzi*, n. 551 above. Alternatively, the court has a broad discretion, where proceedings have begun, to award simple interest on the pre-paid sum, for part or all of the period, from the time the cause of action arose to the date of payment or of judgment: Supreme Court Act, s. 35A (added by Administration of Justice Act 1982, s. 15 and Sched. 1); County Courts Act 1984, s. 69.

[562] *Ogle* v. *Vane* (1868) LR 3 QB 272; *Hickman* v. *Haynes* (1875) LR 10 CP 598; *Blackburn Bobbin Co. Ltd* v. *T. W. Allen & Sons Ltd* [1918] 1 KB 540; *Toprak Mahsullerei Ofisi* v. *Finagrain Cie Commerciale Agricole et Financière SA* [1979] 2 Lloyd's Rep. 298; *Tyers* v. *Rosedale and Ferryhill Iron Co. Ltd* (1875) LR 10 Ex. 195; *Samuel* v. *Black Lake Asbestos and Chrome Co.* (1921) 62 SCR 472 (Can.); *Petrie* v. *Rae* (1919) 46 OLR 19 (Can.).

[563] *Kwei Tek Chao* v. *British Traders and Shippers Ltd*, n. 548 above, 492–9 (date buyer discovers breach); *Van Den Hurk* v. *Martens & Co. Ltd* [1920] 1 KB 850 (a s. 53 case) (rejection date, despite delay of goods for months on the French railway system, where buyer could not examine goods before use).

[564] S. 50(3).

[565] *The Texaco Melbourne* [1993] 1 Lloyd's Rep. 471 (M. G. Bridge [1994] *JBL* 155), affd. [1994] 1 Lloyd's Rep. 473.

[566] But the case can be treated as a sale of goods for present purposes.

sought to recover the value of the cargo in dollars. This relief was refused because the plaintiffs' loss was suffered in the local Ghanaian currency;[567] they had intended to dispose of the oil in Ghana, where oil transactions were conducted in the local currency. This is in accord with principle.[568] But suppose that the plaintiffs had tried a different approach by claiming as a separate item of damages the added currency cost[569] of the substitute cargo arising out of necessary delays in acquiring it. Although the present plaintiffs would have been in great difficulties explaining the very lengthy delay, it is arguable that a claim of this nature ought to succeed if the claimant does move expeditiously and the loss is not too remote.[570] Delaying the reference to the market in goods and compensating for currency loss amount in a case of this kind to the same thing. Oil and currency are both commodities. On the other hand, allowing a claim of this nature runs counter to the governing principle of abstract damages assessment which eschews concrete transactions of resale and subsale.

Anticipatory Repudiation

The date of assessment of damages has proved particularly troublesome in cases of anticipatory repudiation. Taking first an anticipatory repudiation not accepted by the other party, on one view of the law no breach of contract took place at all until it was accepted by the injured party as terminating the contract.[571] Consequently, there was no need to mitigate damages from the moment of repudiation. Suppose, however, that a repudiation is accepted before the performance date. Is the damages reference to the market in sections 50 to 51 to take place at the due performance date or at the date of the acceptance of the repudiation? And does it make any difference that the plaintiff brings his damages action before the performance date, so that the future market rate cannot be known?

Sections 50 to 51 distinguish between contracts providing for a fixed performance date and those that do not. In the former case, it has been held that damages are to be settled by reference to the market price prevailing at the due date of performance.[572] If an action is brought before

[567] Hence the defendants experienced a very large windfall: their business was conducted in dollars, few of which would now be required to purchase the Ghanaian currency needed to satisfy judgment.

[568] Discussed in the text accompanying nn. 292 ff. above.

[569] *Quaere* could this added cost have been passed on to their purchasers in the local currency so as not to be a loss at all? Or had the steep increase in the price of oil diminished local demand for it?

[570] On the reasonable contemplation of currency movement in modern conditions, see *International Minerals and Chemical Corpn.* v. *Karl O. Helm AG* [1986] 1 Lloyd's Rep. 81, 105.

[571] Discussed in the text accompanying nn. 518–21 above.

[572] *Melachrino* v. *Nickoll and Knight* [1920] 1 KB 693; *Millet* v. *Van Heek & Co.* [1921] 2 KB 369; *Garnac Grain Co. Inc.* v. *HMF Faure & Fairclough Ltd* [1968] AC 1130n, 1140; *Lusograin Comercio International de Cereas Lda* v. *Bunge AG* [1986] 2 Lloyd's Rep. 654.

the due date, a court will make the best surmise that it can of the buyer's loss.[573] As a matter of principle, the same will hold true where the buyer repudiates and the seller brings a damages action for non-acceptance.[574] This approach to damages assessment is quite correct, for the buyer suing for damages for non-delivery may not claim to be put in a better position after the repudiation than if the contract had been performed, and so may not look to the higher market price prevailing at the date of repudiation.[575] Nevertheless, an important reservation must be entered here. In market conditions, a buyer accepting a repudiation before the due performance date is required to mitigate by 'go[ing] into the market and buy[ing] against the defaulting seller if a reasonable opportunity offers',[576] in which event the act of mitigation will provide the standard for quantifying his damages.[577]

Should the buyer fail to mitigate, then the date when he ought to have acted will be taken as the standard for measuring the market.[578] If the buyer buys in before the performance date and the market later falls, it is submitted that the buyer should have his damages assessed according to the repurchase.[579] Alternatively, the difference between the higher mitigation price and the later market price may be treated as the recoverable costs of mitigation.[580] If the market rises, the seller will be spared the added expense of the market rise. This even-handed approach is to be preferred to an assessment of damages based upon the lowest point in the market between the accepted repudiation and the due performance date, which would require the buyer to take risks for the benefit of the seller and is not the law.[581] There is no reason to suppose that the same principles should not apply where it is the buyer who breaches and the seller who mitigates,[582] though from an evidentiary point of view it may be more difficult to establish a causal link between the contract of sale

---

[573] *Melachrino* v. *Nickoll and Knight*, n. 572 above.

[574] *Tai Hing Cotton Mill* v. *Kamsing Knitting Factory* [1979] AC 91, distinguishing, at 103, *Hartley* v. *Hymans* [1920] 3 KB 475 and *Tyers* v. *Rosedale and Ferryhill Iron Co. Ltd*, n. 562 above.

[575] *Tai Hing Cotton Mill*, n. 574 above; *Melachrino*, n. 572 above, 699.

[576] *Melachrino*, n. 572 above.

[577] *Melachrino*, n. 572 above; *Garnac Grain*, n. 572 above; *Kaines (UK) Ltd* v. *Österreichische Warengesellschaft mbH* [1993] 2 Lloyd's Rep. 1.

[578] *Roth and Co.* v. *Tayson, Townsend and Co.* (1895) 73 LT 268; *Kaines (UK) Ltd* v. *Österreichische Warengesellschaft mbH*, n. 577 above.

[579] See *Melachrino*, n. 572 above, 697 (repurchase price sets damages). There is no room for inquiring whether, in market conditions, the buyer's repurchase is reasonable. The market price at any time has factored into it available information about the future and so is *per se* reasonable.

[580] Discussed in the text accompanying nn. 499–504 above.

[581] *Kaines*, n. 577 above.

[582] *Gebrüder Metelmann GmbH* v. *NBR (London) Ltd* [1984] 1 Lloyd's Rep. 614.

and a subsequent contract said to be entered into for the purpose of mitigation.[583]

Where the contract fails to state a clear date for performance, the last two lines of section 50(3) and of section 51(3) provide that the date for assessing damages is the date the buyer refuses to accept and the seller refuses to deliver. If applied literally, this rule would produce a wholly different rule from the one prevailing where a delivery date is fixed, where the market at the due date of performance serves as the basis of a damages award. Although sense might be made of sub-section (3), in the case of an accepted repudiation, as tacitly embodying the mitigation rule, it appears inconsistent with the principle that an innocent party is not required to accept an anticipatory repudiation and terminate the contract in order to mitigate his damages.[584]

In *Tai Hing Cotton Mill Ltd* v. *Kamsing Knitting Factory*,[585] the buyers brought an action for non-delivery of bales of cotton under a contract that required the sellers to deliver within a reasonable time, agreed for present purposes to be one month, of the buyers giving notice of their requirements. The Privy Council concluded that damages should not be assessed at the date of the refusal to deliver.[586] Instead, it applied a rule, drawn from the general remoteness rule in section 51(2), which was consistent with the *prima facie* rule in section 51(3) as it applied to cases of a fixed delivery date, requiring a reference to the market at the due date of delivery.[587] On a rising market, the sellers had repudiated (on 31 July) but the buyers accepted the repudiation only when they issued a writ (on 28 November). In the intervening month of September, the market price of cotton began to fall steadily down to the date of the trial. The buyers sought to argue that they had bought in the cotton against the sellers when the market was high, but this argument could not be maintained, for the transaction in question took place before the sellers repudiated and therefore before the sellers could be said to be in breach at all.[588] In

---

[583] *Gebrüder Metelmann GmbH* v. *NBR (London) Ltd* [1984] 1 Lloyd's Rep. 614. The sellers showed that they had sold on a falling market a quantity of sugar, somewhat larger than the contract quantity, because the buyers' repudiation had left them long. There is no need to appropriate the exact quantity to the repudiated contract.

[584] Discussed in the text accompanying n. 522 above.

[585] N. 574 above.

[586] Various explanations of the closing lines of sub-s. (3) were attempted by the Board, from an empty vessel to a rule of convenience equating the date of refusal with the due date of delivery in uncertain cases: n. 574 above, 104. See also *Millett* v. *Van Heek & Co.*, n. 572 above, 377–8 (Atkin LJ: delivery within a reasonable time is delivery at a fixed date).

[587] Note the way the Board disposed of earlier authority, namely, *Ashmore & Son* v. *C. S. Cox & Co.* [1899] 1 QB 436 and *Kidston and Co.* v. *Monceau Ironworks Ltd* (1902) 18 TLR 320: n. 584 above, 103.

[588] Cf. *Coastal (Bermuda) Petroleum Ltd* v. *VTT Vulcan Petroleum SA (The Marine Star)* [1994] CLC 1019 (no market: substitute cargo already acquired in anticipation of sellers' default).

the opinion of the Board, the damages had to be assessed at one month from the date of acceptance of the repudiation, for the latter date was the last date when the buyers could have called for delivery under the contract; no other date seemed suitable. Although evidence on the point was meagre, the Board was not prepared to accede to the sellers' argument that damages should be nominal since the buyers had failed to prove the state of the market on 28 December. Instead, a market rate was hypothesized for that date, given the evidence of a steady decline of prices to the date of the trial.

Concrete Assessment

Tai Hing demonstrates a measure of judicial flexibility in accepting evidence about the state of the market. It has, however, been questioned whether the market is an altogether appropriate standard for damages assessment, and that a reference to the actual resale price, in a non-acceptance case, or the actual repurchase (or cover) price, in a non-delivery case, might be more appropriate. The obvious advantages of such an approach are that the assessment of damages is simplified and that clear recognition is given to the impracticability of the breach date assessment rule in certain instances, though, as we have seen, shifting the assessment date could meet the latter point.

Article 2 of the Uniform Commercial Code provides that the resale price obtained by the seller in a substitute transaction, provided the resale is conducted in good faith and a commercially reasonable manner, serves as the standard for assessing damages in a non-acceptance case.[589] Where no resale in fact takes place, damages are based on the market price prevailing at the breach date but, if evidence of this market price is not readily available, a reference may be made instead to the market at a reasonable later date.[590] Likewise where the seller fails to deliver, or anticipatorily repudiates his delivery obligation, or the goods are non-conforming and are rightfully rejected by the buyer, damages are assessed according to the reasonable repurchase (or cover) price paid by the buyer.[591] Failing this, the same reference is made to the market as occurs in the case of non-acceptance by the buyer.[592] Resale and cover prices may constitute evidence of the market,[593] but, to the extent

---

[589] UCC, Art. 2–706. The same approach was recommended by the Ontario Law Reform Commission: *Report on Sale of Goods* 1979, ii, 418–23, 521–8.

[590] UCC, Art. 2–708, 723(2).   [591] UCC, Art. 2–712.

[592] UCC, Art. 2–713, 723(2).

[593] *Maclean* v. *Dunn* (1828) 4 Bing. 722; *Ex p. Stapleton* (1879) 10 Ch. D 586; *Whitaker Ltd* v. *Bowater Ltd* (1918) 35 TLR 114; *C. Sharpe & Co.* v. *Nosawa & Co.* [1917] 2 KB 814, 820 (repurchase price will be market price in well-run commodities market); *Esteve Tading Corpn.* v. *Agropec International (The Golden Rio)* [1990] 2 Lloyd's Rep. 273, 279 ('at best, evidence of the market price').

they diverge from the market, English law in fact departs from Article 2 just as does English law in theory.

Available Market

In applying the present market price test, some difficulty has arisen concerning the meaning of 'available market'[594] in sections 50 to 51. The expression was understood in a very tangible way by one of the judges in *Dunkirk Colliery Co.* v. *Lever*, as meaning a particular place in the nature of a corn or cotton exchange where buyers and sellers come together.[595] This dictum proved troublesome in *W. L. Thompson Ltd* v. *Robinson (Gunmakers) Ltd*,[596] which concerned the non-acceptance of a new car, an item not dealt with in such trade circumstances, where the displacement of the *prima facie* market rule was also supported on additional and more justifiable grounds. Upjohn J followed the above approach in *Dunkirk Colliery* with some misgivings and, despite divided judicial opinions in another case dealing with non-delivery,[597] went on to say: 'Had the matter been *res integra* I think I should have found that an "available market" merely means that the situation in the particular trade in the particular area was such that the particular goods could freely be sold.'[598] This statement was later glossed so as to import the additional requirement that the price of goods be settled by the laws of supply and demand.[599] It is submitted that this is a sensible way to read the expression 'available market' in a modern economy and should be followed.

It was noted above that an available market existed even if it took time and planning to organize an entry into it.[600] Provided that a sufficiency of buyers and sellers in touch with each other can be assembled, there is a market.[601] And the market is available if the seller, for example, could find at least one immediate buyer prepared to pay a fair price on the day of entry.[602] Mere volatility of price, and hence market movement if the seller's unwanted goods are made available, does not negative the exist-

---

[594] A matter of 'mixed law and fact': *Shearson Lehman Hutton Inc.* v. *Maclaine Watson & Co. Ltd (No. 2)* [1990] 3 All ER 723, 731. See D. Waters (1958) 36 *Can. Bar Rev.* 360.
[595] (1878) 9 Ch. D 20, 25.   [596] [1955] Ch. 177.
[597] *Marshall & Co.* v. *Nicoll & Son*, 1919 SC 129.   [598] N. 596 above, 187.
[599] *Charter* v. *Sullivan* [1957] 2 QB 117, 128.
[600] *Shearson Lehman Hutton Inc.* v. *Maclaine Watson & Co. Ltd (No. 2)*, n. 594 above.
[601] *ABD (Metals and Waste) Ltd* v. *Anglo Chemical and Ore Co. Ltd* [1955] 2 Lloyd's Rep. 456, 466; *Shearson Lehman Hutton Inc.*, n. 594 above, 728. See also *Borries* v. *Hutchinson* (1865) 18 CB(NS) 445, 460 ('constant demand and supply'); *Heskell* v. *Continental Express Ltd* [1950] 1 All ER 1033, 1056 ('a particular level of trade'); *W. L. Thompson Ltd* v. *Robinson (Gunmakers) Ltd*, n. 596 above, 187 ('a demand sufficient to absorb readily all the goods that were thrust on it').
[602] *Shearson Lehman Hutton Inc.*, n. 594 above, 730.

ence of a market.[603] In determining the existence of a market, the nature of the contract goods is important: they can be specialized to the point of insufficient activity to evidence a market.[604]

In export sales transactions, difficulties can arise out of matters of time and place. For example, because of the seller's default under a forward contract for the supply of goods on c.i.f. terms, the buyer may now be looking for goods of the same description available on spot terms in the country where the unloading port is situated. In *Lesters Leather & Skin Co. Ltd* v. *Home and Overseas Brokers Ltd*,[605] where the buyers rightfully rejected a quantity of non-conforming Indian snake skins sold under a c.i.f. United Kingdom contract, there was no spot market in Indian snake skins so the court had to award damages by reference to the buyers' lost profits, namely the profits they would have made by reselling the individual snake skins or the products thereof.[606] In *Hinde* v. *Liddell*,[607] the buyer of 2,000 pieces of grey shirtings was unable to obtain them on the market when the seller defaulted, since they could be obtained only under a forward manufacturing contract. He obtained the same quantity of other shirtings of a superior quality, for which the price was commensurately higher, and persuaded his sub-buyer to accept these instead of the grey shirtings. The buyer therefore recovered the difference between the contract price for grey shirtings and the price he had to pay for the substitute shirtings, the latter sum representing the value of the contract goods to him.[608] A similar philosophy inspires the view that, in export sales, the market is determined not just by reference to the type of goods but also their delivery terms. Thus, in *The Marine Star*,[609] a c.i.f cargo of Russian fuel oil had to be delivered in the Dutch Antilles in a stated week in August.[610] The sellers' default left the buyers unable to procure

---

[603] *F. C. Bradley & Sons Ltd* v. *Colonial & Continental Trading Ltd* [1964] 2 Lloyd's Rep. 52, 64 (12,000 boxes of Lebanese potatoes).

[604] *Coastal International Trading Ltd* v. *Maroil AG* [1988] 1 Lloyd's Rep. 92 ('July/August Rumanian bunker C 3.5% straight-run atmospheric'); *Harlow & Jones Ltd* v. *Panex (International) Ltd* [1967] 2 Lloyd's Rep. 509 (an f.o.b. cargo of steel blooms in a Soviet Baltic port); *Zepoli Canada Inc.* v. *Zapata Ugland Drilling Ltd* (1985) 53 Nfld. & PEIR 1 (Can.) (huge quantity of anchor chain); *Butler* v. *Countryside Finance Ltd* [1993] 3 NZLR 623 (second-hand goods). But see *Petrograde Inc.* v. *Stinnes Handels GmbH* [1995] 1 Lloyd's Rep. 142 (market in Germany but not other countries for specialized fuel).

[605] [1948] WN 437.

[606] The claim was a speculative one and so was discounted to a degree.

[607] (1875) LR 10 QB 265. See also *Bridge* v. *Wain* (1816) 1 Stark. 504; *Borries* v. *Hutchinson*, n. 601 above; *Elbinger Aktiengesellschaft* v. *Armstrong* (1874) LR 9 QB 473, 476–7; *Blackburn Bobbin Co.* v. *T. W. Allen & Sons Ltd* [1918] 1 KB 540, 554.

[608] *Ibid.* 270.

[609] N. 597 above.

[610] It is common for an arrival range to be specified in oil contracts, though not the case with dry commodities.

another cargo of Russian fuel oil of the same description arriving within the same week. Hence there was no available market.[611]

It may be necessary, in determining market price, for a court to extrapolate from the market price of a similar commodity or the same commodity in a different time and place.[612] The case of *Ströms Bruks Aktiebolag* v. *Hutchison*[613] concerned a carrier's failure to lift a c.i.f. cargo of woodpulp to be shipped from Sweden to Cardiff, but it is analogous to the case of a c.i.f. seller failing to ship or adopt the shipment of a cargo. Damages were calculated according to the cost of acquiring such goods on the spot market in Cardiff, less the value of the goods in Sweden and the freight and insurance charges, these deductions being the equivalent of the price in sale of goods proceedings. This is consistent with the view that the place of destination of goods sets the standard for damages assessment.[614] In *Esteve Trading Corpn.* v. *Agropec International (The Golden Rio)*,[615] a case concerning a bankruptcy clause in a commodities form requiring contracts to be closed out 'at the market price then current for similar goods', the goods (soya beans) had already been shipped from a Brazilian port on f.o.b. Antwerp/Ghent terms when the clause had to be implemented. There was no true market for f.o.b. Antwerp/Ghent soya beans in transit, because, once such goods were shipped, subsequent dealings were conducted on c.i.f. terms. The court's solution was to take the available c.i.f. price and deduct the cost of insurance and freight.

Late Delivery

There is no explicit provision in the Sale of Goods Act dealing with late delivery, and there is little authority. Some support exists for the view that the buyer's damages should be settled according to the difference in the market rates prevailing at the agreed and actual dates of delivery.[616] This could only ever be appropriate, however, if the seller contemplates

---

[611] See also *C. Czarnikow Ltd* v. *Bunge & Co. Ltd* [1987] 1 Lloyd's Rep. 202 ('tenderable goods').

[612] See *British & Commonwealth Holdings Plc* v. *Quadrex Holdings Plc* [1995] CLC 1169, 1227–8 ('if there is *nearly* an available market, that may provide a just method of calculating the damages' (emphasis in the original)).

[613] [1905] AC 515.

[614] *Aryeh* v. *Lawrence Kostoris & Son Ltd* [1967] 1 Lloyd's Rep. 63, 71 (f.o.b. and c.i.f.); *C. Sharpe & Co.* v. *Nosawa & Co.* [1917] 2 KB 814; *Hasell* v. *Bagot, Shakes & Lewis Ltd* (1911) 13 CLR 374 (*ex* ship Adelaide buyer of Japanese phosphates entitled to buy from Australian importer without going to Japan); *Hendrie* v. *Neelon* (1883) 3 OR 603 (Can.); *Amicale Yarns Inc.* v. *Canadian Worsted Manufacturing Inc.* [1968] 2 OR 59; *Graham* v. *Bigelow* (1912) 3 DLR 404.

[615] [1990] 2 Lloyd's Rep. 273.

[616] *The Heron II* [1969] 1 AC 350 (Lord Pearce). This approach was rejected for other reasons in *Wertheim* v. *Chicoutimi Pulp Co.* [1911] AC 301, discussed in the text accompanying nn. 682 ff. below.

that the buyer has bought the goods for resale. Where the goods are bought for consumption, another measure might be more appropriate, such as the loss of profits[617] because of the delay in delivering a profit-earning chattel, or even consequential damages for the buyer having to let machines stand idle or pay employees who have no work to do,[618] or damage to crops incurred while waiting for a promised machine.[619] It may even be appropriate to disregard the market altogether and look to the terms of a sub-sale.[620] Where the buyer is at fault in not taking delivery on time, the likely liability will be for consequential damages arising out of an expense such as the seller's increased storage costs.[621]

Special and Consequential Damages

Liability for special and consequential damages is set out in section 54 of the Sale of Goods Act, a provision common to buyers and sellers alike. It provides that nothing in the Act 'affects the right of the buyer or the seller to recover interest or special damages in a case where by law interest or special damages may be recoverable'. This has been treated as including a statutory reference to the second limb of the rule in *Hadley* v. *Baxendale*[622] and its application to a particular contract of sale is a matter of what can reasonably be imputed, or was disclosed as special knowledge, to the party in breach at the contract date. Section 54, which is merely a saving provision, does not call for any close scrutiny when consequential damages claims are considered; some of these claims could be accommodated under the first limb of the rule. Nothing would be gained by a laborious rehearsal of all the adjudicated cases under the section but a few examples are instructive.

In the nature of things, a buyer's consequential damages are likely to be more varied in their nature than a seller's. Sellers are in appropriate cases entitled to recover the cost of storing or warehousing unwanted goods, and of reselling unwanted goods.[623] Satisfying the remoteness

---

[617] *Cory* v. *Thames Ironworks and Shipbuilding Co. Ltd* (1868) LR 3 QB 181; *Victoria Laundry (Windsor) Ltd* v. *Newman Industries Ltd* [1949] 2 KB 528; *Hydraulic Engineering Co. Ltd* v. *McHaffie, Goslett & Co.* (1878) 4 QBD 670; *Steam Herring Fleet Ltd* v. *S. Richard and Co. Ltd* (1901) 17 TLR 731; *Fletcher* v. *Tayleur* (1855) 17 CB 21.

[618] For the attractions of a liquidated damages clause to avoid problems of proof, see *Clydebank Engineering and Shipbuilding Co. Ltd* v. *Don Jose Ramos Yzquierdo e Castaneda* [1905] AC 6, 11.

[619] *Smeed* v. *Ford* (1859) 1 E & E 602. See also *Watson* v. *Gray* (1900) 16 TLR 308.

[620] *Wertheim* v. *Chicoutimi Pulp Co.*, n. 616 above.

[621] Discussed immediately below.   [622] (1854) 9 Ex. 341.

[623] *Newfoundland Associated Fish Exporters Ltd* v. *Aristomenis Th. Karelas* (1963) 49 MPR 49 (Can.). The buyer's liability for non-acceptance receives particular mention when the time of delivery is at large and the buyer fails to respond to the seller's call for acceptance of delivery: s. 37(1). See *Hal H. Paradise Ltd* v. *Apostolic Trustees of the Friars Minor* (1966) 55 DLR (2d) 671.

rule in such cases will not be unduly difficult; the costs of resale could also be seen as the recoverable costs of mitigation.[624] In one case against a non-accepting buyer, a seller who had concluded a resale on reasonable terms recovered demurrage charges arising out of the delay in delivering the goods.[625]

Indemnity Claims

Buyers may rely upon section 54 in a consequential damages claim where, in breach of the seller's warranty, goods cause them personal injuries[626] or consequential property damage.[627] Where the buyer is claiming in respect of his personal liability to a sub-buyer, the position is more difficult. Consider the case of the first buyer in a distribution chain who wishes to pass on a liability that he has incurred. The liability is imposed under the last contract in the chain and relates to defective goods. By the time the liability snowball reaches the first buyer, it will consist of two principal items, namely, the damages award recovered by the last buyer and the taxed costs of the various successful claimants in the chain below. To this figure, the first buyer will add another item of loss in his claim over against the head seller—his own solicitor and client costs incurred in defending the claim of his sub-buyer.[628] In certain cases, the damages figure will be represented by the amount of a reasonable settlement.[629]

In determining whether a seller's liability may be transmitted back up the chain, a distinction has to be drawn between market loss claims and physical damage claims.[630] For a market loss claim, it seems that the goods must be sold in the various contracts in the chain according to the

---

[624] Discussed in the text accompanying nn. 499–504 above.

[625] *Vitol SA* v. *Phibro Energy AG (The Mathraki)* [1990] 2 Lloyd's Rep. 84.

[626] e.g. *Randall* v. *Newson* (1877) 2 QBD 102; *Wren* v. *Holt* [1903] 1 KB 610; *Preist* v. *Last* [1903] 2 KB 148; *Chaproniere* v. *Mason* (1905) 21 TLR 633; *Grant* v. *Australian Knitting Mills Ltd* [1936] AC 85; *Godley* v. *Perry* [1960] 1 WLR 9; *Vacwell Engineering Co. Ltd* v. *BDH Chemicals Ltd* [1969] 3 All ER 1681.

[627] e.g. *H. Parsons (Livestock) Ltd* v. *Uttley Ingham & Co. Ltd* [1978] QB 791; *Henry Kendall & Sons* v. *William Lillico & Son Ltd* [1969] 2 AC 31; *Ashington Piggeries Ltd* v. *Christopher Hill Ltd* [1972] AC 441.

[628] See *Kasler and Cohen* v. *Slavouski* [1928] 1 KB 78.

[629] *Biggin & Co. Ltd* v. *Permanite Ltd* [1951] 2 KB 314. The onus is on the plaintiff to show the compromise was reasonable: *Seven Seas Properties Ltd* v. *Al-Essa (No. 2)* [1993] 1 WLR 1083, 1089. But not a contractual penalty: *Elbinger Aktiengesellschaft* v. *Armstrong* (1874) LR 9 QB 473. The buyer's defence may serve to extinguish the seller's price claim in full if the goods turn out to be worthless, but in so far as the buyer's claim is for special or consequential damages, it cannot be the subject of a defence but must be pleaded as a counter-claim.

[630] *Biggin & Co. Ltd* v. *Permanite Ltd* [1951] 1 KB 422, 433–4, revd. other grounds at [1951] 2 KB 314.

same warranty and description terms.[631] In the case of physical damage, the question is whether the seller ought to have contemplated the loss at the end of the chain, in accordance with the normal remoteness princi-ples;[632] the length of the chain does not matter, provided that the loss is not too remote.[633] The distinction is defensible, in that relatively minor differences in warranty and description are unlikely to have much of a bearing on physical loss claims. Furthermore, if the seller in the chain has a contractual defence, the indemnification process will be severed at that point on the grounds of familiar privity principles.

The chain of indemnity may be broken, however, in certain circum-stances where an intervening party's negligence severs the causal link between a prior seller's breach of contract and a later buyer's injury.[634] But such a party's failure to notice a defect may not be so causally dis-ruptive as to break the chain.[635] The liability passed back up the chain may be a tort claim or the reasonable cost of defending such a claim.[636] It may also be a criminal penalty,[637] provided that there is no element of fault or negligence on the part of the claimant.[638] Ultimately, the ques-tion is whether the seller ought to have contemplated the various losses being passed back,[639] though the stress sometimes placed on a

[631] Forcefully expressed by Scrutton LJ in *Dexters Ltd* v. *Hill Crest Oil Co. (Bradford) Ltd* [1926] 1 KB 348, 359. The reason given for this is that the effect of a contractual variation on market value is unpredictable: *Biggin & Co.*, n. 629 above. For examples of transmitted liab-ility, see *Hammond & Co.* v. *Bussey* (1887) 20 QBD 79; *Agius* v. *Great Western Colliery Co.* [1899] 1 QB 413. In both cases, the seller was aware of the final use of the goods (bunker coal). See also *Grébert-Borgnis* v. *J. & W. Nugent* (1885) 15 QBD 85; *Frank Mott & Co. Ltd* v. *Wm H. Muller & Co. (London) Ltd* (1922) 13 Ll. LR 492; *Seven Seas Properties Ltd* v. *Al-Essa (No. 2)*, n. 629 above; *Household Machines Ltd* v. *Cosmos Exporters Ltd* [1947] KB 217 (also an indemnity in respect of sub-sale liabilities).

[632] *Biggin & Co.*, n. 629 above. See also *Pinnock Bros.* v. *Lewis & Peat Ltd* [1923] 1 KB 690; *British Oil and Cake Co.* v. *Burstall & Co.* (1923) 39 TLR 406; *G. C. Dobell and Co. Ltd* v. *Barber and Garrett* [1931] 1 KB 219.

[633] *Ibid.* 432; *Kasler and Cohen* v. *Slavouski*, n. 628 above. For a further example of liab-ility being passed back up the chain, see *Sidney Bennett Ltd* v. *Kreeger* (1925) 41 TLR 609. Liability may not be transmitted, however, if the physical loss is due to an unusual use that the seller could not have contemplated: *Bostock & Co. Ltd* v. *Nicholson & Sons Ltd* [1904] 1 KB 725 (with which cf. *Ashington Piggeries Ltd*, n. 627 above).

[634] *Lambert* v. *Lewis* [1982] AC 225, with which contrast *Mowbray* v. *Merryweather* [1895] 2 QB 640. See M. G. Bridge (1982) 6 *Can. Bus. LJ* 184. On contributory negligence and the implied term of fitness, see Ch. 7 above.

[635] *Hammond & Co.* v. *Bussey*, n. 631 above; *British Oil and Cake Co. Ltd* v. *Burstall & Co.* (1923) 39 TLR 406 ('ominous' dark colour of copra cake).

[636] e.g. *Britannia Hygienic Laundry Co. Ltd* v. *John I. Thorneycroft and Co. Ltd* (1925) 41 TLR 667.

[637] *Proops* v. *W. H. Chaplin and Co. Ltd* (1920) 37 TLR 112; *Cointat* v. *Myham & Son* [1913] 2 KB 220.

[638] *Askey* v. *Golden Wine Co. Ltd* [1948] 2 All ER 35 (buyer guilty of gross negligence): any other result would thwart the aims of the criminal law.

[639] See *Hammond & Co.* v. *Bussey*, n. 631 above, 95, for an involved statement of the con-templation chain that the seller hypothetically considers.

claimant's actual conduct in defending an action[640] might suggest that legal costs should be treated as the costs of mitigation.

Other Claims

In principle, sub-sale profits may not be claimed to the extent that they depart from the market standard,[641] but damages for lost profits may usually be recovered if the goods are clearly profit-earning chattels in the hands of the buyer.[642] In certain cases, a lost-profits claim might be allowed, not in respect of the profits directly associated with the contract goods, but because the contract goods so injure the buyer's trade reputation as to blight the possibility of future sales.[643] Unless the seller of machines is alerted to the buyer's exclusive or heavy dependency on his machines, it is unlikely that the buyer will be able to recover for losses incurred because the plant stands idle or workers are paid despite having nothing to do.[644] If the seller's machine breaks down and the buyer has to reinstall his old discarded machine, the cost of reinstallation has been allowed.[645]

Damages have also been given for the accelerated capital expense of installing new equipment because the seller's equipment did not last as long as it should have done.[646] A routine type of buyer's special or consequential loss claim will concern wasted freight charges incurred in connection with rejected goods,[647] or the cost incurred in shipping goods back to the seller,[648] or in repacking and shipping goods already sent on to a third party's premises.[649] In a proper case, a buyer may

[640] e.g. *Agius* v. *Great Western Colliery Co.*, n. 631 above.

[641] See discussion of the market rule in the text accompanying nn. 540 ff. above, and of sub-sales in the text accompanying nn. 658 ff. below.

[642] *Steam Herring Fleet Ltd* v. *S. Richard and Co. Ltd* (1901) 17 TLR 731; *Cullinane* v. *British 'Rema' Manufacturing Co. Ltd* [1954] 1 QB 292; *Sunnyside Greenhouses Ltd* v. *Golden West Seeds Ltd* [1972] 4 WWR 420; *R. G. McLean Ltd* v. *Canadian Vickers Ltd* [1969] 2 OR 249. Cf. *Bunting* v. *Tory* (1948) 64 TLR 353 (seller not informed of buyer's profit-making use). The issue of profit-earning chattels is discussed at length in the text accompanying nn. 750 ff. below.

[643] *GKN Centrax Gears Ltd* v. *Matbro Ltd* [1976] 2 Lloyd's Rep. 555 (defective rear axles and loss of repeat orders from 'dissatisfied and incensed' customers); *Canlin Ltd* v. *Thiokol Fibres Ltd* (1983) 142 DLR (3d) 450 (plaintiff 'deluged with complaints'). For a stricter and probably now superseded view, see *Simon* v. *Pawson and Leafs* (1932) 28 Com. Cas. 151, 157.

[644] *Hydraulic Engineering Co. Ltd* v. *McHaffie, Goslett & Co.* (1878) 4 QBD 670. On appropriate facts, the buyer may recover general damages for disruption, inconvenience and expense: *GKN Centrax Gears Ltd* v. *Matbro Ltd*, n. 643 above.

[645] *British American Paint Co.* v. *Fogh* (1915) 24 DLR 61.

[646] *Sunnyside Greenhouses Ltd* v. *Golden West Seeds Ltd*, n. 642 above.

[647] *D. M. Duncan Machinery Co. Ltd* v. *Canadian National Railways* [1951] OR 578.

[648] *E. Brande (London) Ltd* v. *Porter* [1959] 2 Lloyd's Rep. 161.

[649] *Molling* v. *Dean* (1901) 18 TLR 217.

recover for loss of time and out of pocket expenses.[650] Special damages have also been awarded to cover the additional transaction costs of acquiring substitute goods from multiple sources.[651]

As the embodiment of the second limb of the rule in *Hadley* v. *Baxendale*,[652] section 54 may serve as the justification for compensating a damages claimant who has suffered a currency loss. Notice was taken earlier in the Chapter of the courts' willingness in modern times to formulate debt judgments in a foreign currency.[653] In the case of damages for breach of contract, judgment may also be given in a foreign currency, even if it is not the currency of account in the contract, provided that currency is the one in which the plaintiff's loss is felt and the contract itself does not indicate some other currency.[654] In *The Folias*,[655] the plaintiff charterers were claiming to be indemnified by the shipowner for their liability under a bill of lading contract to cargo receivers whose goods were damaged by the unseaworthiness of the ship. The charterers, whose place of business was in Paris, paid hire under the charterparty in US dollars and had settled with the cargo receivers in Brazilian cruzeiros. But they had purchased those cruzeiros with French francs, and it was within the reasonable contemplation of the shipowner that they should have done so. Consequently, they had suffered their loss in francs and should be indemnified accordingly.

Section 54 may also justify, in exceptional cases, the recovery as damages of the interest that a claimant, for example an unpaid seller, kept out of his money has had to pay a third party in consequence of non-payment.[656] This is distinct from the statutory award of interest that a court may now make, in respect of damages as well as debt claims, where the claimant succeeds for being kept out of his money and not because he has incurred third party obligations.[657]

---

[650] *Lay's Transport Ltd* v. *Meadow Lake Consumers Co-operative Association Ltd* (1982) 20 Sask. R 8 (loss of management time and wasted overhead, and company president's time in meeting lawyer).

[651] *Butler* v. *Countryside Finance Ltd* [1993] 3 NZLR 623.   [652] (1854) 9 Ex. 341.

[653] Discussed in the text accompanying nn. 286–297 above.

[654] *The Folias* [1979] AC 685, 699 ff.; *The Texaco Melbourne* [1993] 1 Lloyd's Rep. 471 (M. G. Bridge [1994] *JBL* 155), affd. [1994] 1 Lloyd's Rep. 473, discussed above.

[655] N. 654 above.

[656] *Wadsworth* v. *Lydall* [1981] 1 WLR 598 (second limb of the rule in *Hadley* v. *Baxendale* (1854) 9 Ex. 341, discussed in the text accompanying nn. 420 ff. above); *President of India* v. *La Pintada Cia Navigacion SA* [1985] AC 104.

[657] Discussed in the text accompanying n. 291 above.

THE SECONDARY OBLIGATION TO PAY DAMAGES: SPECIFIC PROBLEMS

This section of the Chapter will deal with a number of problems that require detailed treatment. For reasons of convenience, because the profit-earning chattel issue will be discussed here, other issues raised by a seller's breach of warranty regarding the quality of the goods will also be considered.

The Sub-sales Problem

It was stated earlier that the market was employed as the standard for measuring the damages in non-acceptance and non-delivery cases. But the Sale of Goods Act states that the market is a standard that expresses in merely presumptive form the remoteness of damage rule. As seen above, there are cases of a breach causing genuine loss where no available market exists. In such cases, courts have been prepared to look even at sub-contracts to gauge the plaintiff's loss. A reading of certain decisions, however, might induce the belief that the law dogmatically refuses ever to look at sub-contracts where a market reference is available. Provided that essential principles of remoteness, causation, and mitigation are kept firmly in view, this pretention should not be accorded unswerving recognition. Some of the following cases demonstrate that an unyielding reference to the market is quite capable of producing under-compensation or over-compensation in a given instance.

Rodoconachi, Sons & Co. v. *Milburn Bros*[658] concerned an action against carriers for non-delivery of cargo when the ship sank because of its master's negligence. The plaintiffs had already sold the cargo on a 'to arrive' basis[659] at a price below the market price prevailing at the anticipated date of discharge. Despite admitting that they could not have been held liable for the extra loss if the plaintiffs had sold above the market price, the carriers argued that their liability should be measured against the lower sub-contract price. Deciding against the carriers, the Court of Appeal made it plain that damages rules should not be tailored to meet the peculiarities of individual cases, but rather should work approximate justice across the broad range of cases. As Lindley LJ put it: '[T]he rules as to damages can in the nature of things only be approximately just, and . . . they have to be worked out, not by mathematicians, but by juries'.[660] The plaintiffs' sale contract was an 'accidental circumstance' and ought to be disregarded, just as the damages of personal injuries litigants were not to

---

[658] (1886) 18 QBD 67.
[659] And thus were not liable to the buyers when the cargo failed to arrive.
[660] N. 658 above, 78.

be reduced when insurance moneys or other collateral benefits were released by the accident.[661] Assuming that the carriers would not have been liable if the sub-contract price had stood higher than the market, the decision in this case has a certain symmetry besides the appeal it presents for ease of administration.

Rodoconachi was not applied in a later case involving a charterparty and a sub-charter of the same ship. In *Andrew Weir & Co.* v. *Dobell & Co.*,[662] the owners of a ship chartered it to the plaintiffs for a particular voyage at a freight rate of 21 shillings per ton. The plaintiffs then entered into a sub-charter with the defendants that was coextensive with the head charter, covering the same ship and the same voyage. But the freight rate in the sub-charter was 28½ shillings. The defendants repudiated the sub-charter by refusing to load and the market rate at the breach date was 17 shillings. Now, the plaintiffs did not have to put the ship on the market at the prevailing rate since they were able to invoke a cancellation right under the head charter. This crystallized their actual loss at 7½ shillings (28½–21 shillings) rather than 11½ shillings (28½–17 shillings) and the former was held to govern the recoverable damages. As Rowlatt J said: 'It all turns, of course, on the circumstance that the plaintiffs' charterparty was coextensive with that of the defendants, otherwise they could not have dealt with the specific interest thrown on their hands, but only with a different and larger interest at 21s.'[663] The key to the result, therefore, was the integrality of the two contracts, which justified the abandonment of any reference to the market at the breach date.

Rodoconachi was extended to the sale of goods in *Williams Bros.* v. *Edward T. Agius Ltd*,[664] which concerned the sellers' failure to ship a cargo of coal from a UK port c.i.f. an Italian port at the price of 16¼ shillings per ton. The contract in question required a shipment every two months in 1911, and the dispute concerned the last such shipment in November. The market price of the coal at the end of November stood at 23½ shillings, but on 28 October the buyers had resold the same quantity of coal on identical c.i.f. terms to sub-buyers at 19 shillings.[665] The question was whether the buyers' damages should be assessed by reference to the sub-contract or to the market. The *Rodoconachi* principle was applied so as to award the higher measure of damages based on the

---

[661] *Bradburn* v. *Great Western Railway Co.* (1874) LR 10 Ex. 1, the case giving birth to the collateral benefits principle in personal injuries litigation.

[662] [1916] 1 KB 722.   [663] *Ibid.* 725.

[664] [1914] AC 510. See also the Canadian cases of *Freedman* v. *French* (1921) 50 OLR 432 and *Merrill* v. *Waddell* (1920) 47 OLR 572, where the seller knew of or contemplated the sub-sales.

[665] The umpire found that the buyers had 'appropriated' their Nov. shipment to the sub-sale contract, but the expression was patently used in a very loose way. The cargo cannot have been appropriated in the c.i.f. sense since no cargo was ever shipped.

market price. Lord Dunedin stressed the merits of a system that ignored the sub-sale price, whether it went up or down:

The buyer never gets [the goods], and he is entitled to be put in the position in which he would have stood had he got them at the due date. That position is the position of a man who has goods at the market price of the day—and barring special circumstances, the defaulting seller is neither mulct in damages for the extra profit which the buyer would have got owing to a forward resale at over the market price . . . nor can he take benefit of the fact that the buyer has made a forward resale at under the market price.[666]

Lord Dunedin went on to observe that there was no merit at all in qualifying liability under the head contract by reference to the sub-contract when the two contracts merely dealt in the same kind of goods.[667] As a matter of causal connection, taking the case of a commodities trader doing business on a wide front, this must be correct, for on what principles could it be asserted that any two contracts, one to buy goods and the other to sell goods, ought to be conjoined? Again, the difficulty of this exercise is emphasized if the contracts concern different quantities or the buyer is disposed to use the goods to fulfil various sub-contracts. The failure of the seller to deliver means that it can never be precisely known what the buyer would have done with the seller's goods.

Lord Dunedin also stated that, even if the head contract and the sub-contract concerned the 'identical article', it would be better to allow the rights and liabilities of buyer and seller under both contracts to be separately adjusted.[668] Where the buyer in the head contract secures special advantages under the terms of the sub-contract, a strong argument may be made that the buyer should not be deprived of such advantages. The market approach would preserve the head buyer's advantage and the sub-sale approach would not.[669] A point that arose in the case was whether the head buyer was to be released from liability under the sub-contract if the head seller failed to deliver. This depended on whether the sub-contract was formed on the basis of the bought-and-sold note, containing an exoneration clause, or of the broker's note, which did not contain such a clause. Ultimately, it was decided that the broker's note governed, but the argument for ignoring the sub-contract would have been even stronger if it had contained such a special clause.

---

[666] *Williams Bros.*, n. 664 above, 522–3. [667] *Ibid.* 523.

[668] *Ibid.* Moreover, the umpire's terms of reference allowed him to look only at the head contract and not to consider the overall effect of the liabilities in the distribution chain. Thus the House of Lords declined to take into account a transaction between the sub-buyer and the head seller, by which either the Nov. shipment was sold back to the latter, or the sub-buyer assigned to the latter the benefit of the sub-sale. This contract was concluded on 28 Nov., at a time, presumably, when the sellers knew they could not make the Nov. shipment.

[669] See in the text accompanying nn. 673 ff. below.

The effect of ignoring the sub-contract and allowing the two sets of litigants—seller and buyer, and buyer and sub-buyer—to settle their differences by reference to the market may be demonstrated by the following hypothetical examples. First of all, suppose the seller agrees to sell to the buyer a quantity of widgets at £10 per ton and the buyer in turn appropriates that same consignment of widgets, so that no other widgets may be supplied, to a sub-contract at the enhanced price of £15 per ton. The date of delivery in both contracts is the same,[670] and the market price at the date of delivery has risen to £20 per ton. If the market price rule is followed in both contracts, the sub-buyer recovers from the buyer £5 per ton (£20–£15) while the buyer recovers from the seller £10 per ton (£20–£10). On balance, the buyer retains £5 per ton (£10–£5). Assume, however, that the sub-sale price is taken as the point of reference in calculating the buyer's damages against the seller. The buyer will still be liable to a market assessment of £5 as regards the sub-buyer, on the assumption that the sub-buyer is not in turn reselling. Under the head contract, the buyer will therefore be limited to recovering £5 per ton, the difference between the two contract prices. But the buyer should also recover, as special or consequential damages,[671] the £5 per ton damages that he has to pay the sub-buyer.[672] On balance, the buyer will be left with a profit of £5 per ton, the same position as that reached under an application of the market rule to the two contracts.

Suppose, however, that the sale price is £10 per ton but that it has risen to £20 per ton under the sub-sale. At the date of performance for both contracts, the market price has fallen back to £15 per ton. The sub-buyer, of course, will not want to sue the buyer and will be relieved to buy in at the lesser price of £15 per ton. If the buyer were allowed to sue the seller on the basis of the sub-sale price, he would recover £10 per ton (£20–£10), but a reference to the market brings in only £5 per ton (£15–£10). In neither case will there be the complicating feature of the buyer's liability to the sub-buyer. On the face of it, the buyer will be under-compensated if the market price is chosen. One response to this is to say that the buyer should be able to go to market and buy in at £15 to fulfil the sub-contract. The profit of £5 made in this way, when added to the £5 per ton damages under the head sale, will give the buyer full compensation. But this cannot be done on the above example, because by appropriating the sale goods to the sub-sale, the buyer has locked himself in and cannot go into

[670] If the buyer staggers the delivery dates, this complicates matters but it should be regarded as his own speculation for reasons given in the text accompanying nn. 494–8 above.

[671] S. 54.

[672] This should not be difficult, given the interdependency of the two contracts and the fact that the seller's whole argument is that the buyer should be indemnified according to how he stands in relation to the sub-buyers.

the market to buy in goods, even if these are in all other respects identical to the sale goods. Once it is established that the market-price rule leaves the buyer under-compensated, the focus is shifted to the remoteness rule and the question is posed whether the seller should reasonably have contemplated that his own non-performance would deny to a sub-selling buyer the opportunity to go into the market. For an enhanced liability, the seller should have to contemplate both the sub-sale and the impossibility of the buyer going to market. Since it goes to the quantum of damages, the seller need not contemplate the subsale price.

A problem of the above sort arose in *Re R. and H. Hall Ltd and W. H. Pim (Jnr.) and Co.'s Arbitration.*[673] The case concerned a string of forward sales of Australian wheat. Acting for an undisclosed principal, Pim agreed on 3 November to sell at 51¾ shillings per quarter to Hall, who on 21 November sold the same quantity and type of wheat to Williams at 56 ¾ shillings. Williams in turn on 25 November agreed to sell the same wheat to Pim again at 59¼ shillings; this time Pim was acting for a different undisclosed principal.[674] All the contracts related to a shipment to be made the following January; it turned out that the market price at the date of delivery[675] had fallen back to 53 ¾ shillings. Wishing to accommodate as far as possible the apparently divergent interests of their two principals, Pim purchased from Rank on 29 January a cargo on board the SS *Indianic* at sixty shillings. They then appropriated this cargo to the contract with Hall and similar notices were passed down the string. Pim, having started the notices of appropriation, immediately resold the same cargo back to Rank at a price securing the latter a modest profit.

The consequence of all this was that, when Pim failed to deliver to Hall, Hall could not buy in to perform the contract with Williams, and Williams could not buy in to fulfil their contract with Pim. Pim's second principal at the end of the string was therefore able to buy in at the market price, which was lower than its contract price, for Pim had correctly anticipated a fall in the market. Pim sought also to protect the interests of their first principal by arguing that Hall's damages should be assessed according to the market rate prevailing at the date of delivery, rather than the higher sub-contract price. But of course Pim had done everything in their power to ensure that Hall could not go to market for the wheat they needed to deliver to Williams. In these circumstances, the House of Lords[676] had little difficulty in ruling that the Hall loss on the Williams contract came within the remoteness rule. The contract between Pim

---

[673] (1928) 33 Com. Cas. 324.
[674] See Lord Blanesburgh for an enlightening explanation of Pim's behaviour.
[675] Presumably, this refers to the latest date the documents could lawfully be tendered.
[676] Including Lords Haldane and Dunedin, who had sat in *Williams Bros.* v. *Edward T. Agius Ltd*, n. 664 above.

and Hall amply recognized the possibility of a sub-sale of the same goods by the notice of appropriation system. Indeed, the entire system of string c.i.f. contracts is based on a principle of linkage so that no commodities dealer in the string is permitted to speculate unfairly in cargoes at the expense of another dealer in the string.

The decision in *Re R. and H. Hall Ltd* was said to have greatly surprised informed commercial and legal opinion.[677] Two members of the Court of Appeal in *James Finlay & Co.* v. *NV Kwik Hoo Tong Handel Maatschappij*[678] seem to have thought it a correct decision and the third,[679] while grudgingly accepting that it might be justified by the application of the remoteness rule to the particular facts, seems to have been more concerned at the failure of the House of Lords in the later case to reconcile its decision with its own earlier statement in *Williams Bros.* v. *Edward T. Agius Ltd*.[680] Any system of law that eschews ironclad rules producing the same result in all cases, regardless of the actual loss suffered by the plaintiff, should find a place for the decision in *Re R. and H. Hall Ltd*, which underlines the role of remoteness and reminds us that the Sale of Goods Act reference to the market remains a *prima facie* rule.[681]

Late Delivery

The Sale of Goods Act contains no damages rules specifically framed to meet the case of late delivery. The problem of market reference presented itself in an acute form in the controversial decision of the Privy Council in *Wertheim* v. *Chicoutimi Pulp Co*.[682] The respondent sellers agreed on 13 March 1900 to sell 3,000 tons of Canadian moist pulpwood to the appellant buyers on f.o.b. Chicoutimi terms. The price was equivalent to twenty-five shillings a ton and the buyer was a German timber merchant; delivery was to take place not later than 1 November 1900. The appellant buyers, meanwhile, had already on 2 March 1900 entered into a contract for the sub-sale of 2,000 tons of pulpwood to a Manchester timber mill, and they had apparently made a number of other sub-sale contracts to account for the whole 3,000 tons due under the head contract. The sub-sale price was sixty-five shillings, and the very large discrepancy between the two prices may be explained only in part by the freight costs of thirteen shillings per ton to transport the timber to the Manchester market. The dearth of evidence in the report concerning

---

[677] '[It] astonished the Temple and surprised St. Mary Axe': *James Finlay & Co.* v. *NV Kwik Hoo Tong Handel Maatschappij* [1929] 1 KB 400, 417.
[678] *Ibid.*, Greer and Sankey LJJ.   [679] Scrutton LJ.   [680] N. 664 above.
[681] General support for *Re R. and H. Hall Ltd* is to be found in *Kwei Tek Chao* v. *British Traders and Shippers Ltd* [1954] 2 QB 459 (late shipment).
[682] [1901] AC 301, sternly criticized by Scrutton LJ in *Slater* v. *Hoyle & Smith* [1920] 2 KB 11, 23–4.

the sub-sale contracts and the circumstances in which they were entered into makes it impossible to explain any further the discrepancy.

The sellers failed to deliver the pulpwood on time in Chicoutimi, with the result that delivery had to be held over until the following season. Delivery actually took place in June 1901, the buyers having affirmed the contract, and the buyers were in turn successful in persuading their sub-buyers to accept late delivery when eventually the pulpwood reached Manchester. The market price at the contractual delivery date was seventy shillings; it had fallen to 42½ shillings per ton by the date the pulpwood was actually delivered. The market price was that prevailing in Manchester, so any calculation of the buyers' damages, if the goods were to be bought in, would have to take account of the buyers' freight costs as well as their purchase costs. By this reckoning, the buyers had paid thirty-eight shillings per ton in order to be in a position to resell and deliver the pulpwood in Manchester.

The buyers contended that their damages should be calculated according to the difference between the market prices at the due and actual dates of delivery. On the other hand, the sellers argued that the buyer had suffered no loss since they had been able to persuade the sub-buyers to accept late the agreed pulpwood; a reference to the market would therefore be irrelevant, and nominal damages would be the appropriate remedy. The court below[683] awarded as damages five shillings per ton (the difference between the market price at the due delivery date and the sub-sale price (70–65 shillings)), a figure both modest and utterly irrelevant in any computation of the buyers' loss. This figure was confirmed by the Privy Council as 'the highest rate at which [the buyers' loss] could properly be fixed',[684] a delphic reference, it seems, to the greater propriety of a nominal damages award. The Privy Council, therefore, rejected the buyers' contention that they ought to receive 27½ shillings as the difference between the two market prices (70 shillings–42½ shillings). It should not be forgotten, however, that, in addition to the five shillings actually awarded, the buyers made twenty-seven shillings profit, as the difference between their purchase and resale prices, making in all a profit on the contract of thirty-two shillings.

An assessment of whether *Wertheim* is correctly decided is in practice impossible, since so little is known of the relationship between the sale contract and the sub-sale contracts. In particular, it cannot be known whether the buyers had actually appropriated the 3,000 tons to the sub-sale contracts, which was unlikely, or whether a shortage of pulpwood on the Manchester market deprived the buyers of a chance to buy in different pulpwood in satisfaction of their sub-sale responsibilities. It is

[683] The Court of King's Bench (Appeal Side) of the Province of Quebec.
[684] N. 682 above, 307.

instructive to consider the hypothetical position if the buyers had been in a position to buy in and had actually done so, and had been able to delay this transaction until the market fell to 42½ shillings.[685] The buyers would presumably then have made a profit on the sub-sales of 22½ shillings (65 shillings–42½ shillings) by buying in. To this figure should be added their recoverable losses on the head contract arrived at with the aid of a market assessment, if they were able to persuade a court that this was the proper measure of damages for late delivery in such a case. This figure would consist of 32 shillings (70 shillings – 38 shillings), less the actual smaller profit of 4½ shillings realized when the buyers sold or should have sold[686] at the reduced market rate (42½ shillings – 38 shillings) making a sum of 27½ shillings. The overall profit of the buyers would thus be fifty shillings per ton (27½ shillings + 22½ shillings).

Wertheim was approved by Lord Dunedin in *Williams Bros.* v. *Edward T. Agius Ltd*[687] on the ground that the outcome of events demonstrated the buyers' actual loss without the need for any judicial speculation. This is certainly correct, it is submitted, if the buyers were locked into the head contract in their dealings with the sub-buyers. It is harder to resolve the case of the buyer whose manifest intentions are plainly at all material times to use the seller's goods in performing the sub-contracts, even though there is no legal compulsion to this end in the sub-contracts. In such a case, though the question is a difficult one, there seems to be no good reason for ignoring the sub-sale when it truly demonstrates the buyer's actual loss. If the buyer is not speculating in commodities, he should not be treated as though he were. Lord Dunedin's statement that there is no need to speculate on the buyer's loss would cover this case too. But harder still is the case of the buyer who, taking advantage of the seller's delay, pointedly buys in to fulfil the sub-sales when otherwise he would not have done.[688] One way of looking at this is to assert that the buyer should not abuse the seller's breach so as to enrich himself. Quite the opposite point of view is that the buyer ought to be able to enter into a particularly beneficial sub-sale, and therefore also to perform a sub-sale in a way particularly beneficial to himself, without being deprived of the benefits of this acumen when he later sues the seller. The call is a close one, but if a buyer actually does buy in and takes a speculative risk in doing so, on familiar principles[689] he should be allowed to take the benefits and burdens associated with this activity.[690]

---

[685] Would the sub-buyers have tolerated this?

[686] Any delay would be a private speculation.   [687] [1914] AC 510.

[688] See the working out of this in the hypothetical example in the previous para.

[689] *Jamal* v. *Moolla Dawood, Sons & Co.* [1916] 1 AC 175, 179.

[690] Suppose in the above example the sellers failed to deliver at all. The liability should be 70–38 shillings. The buyers would also retain the profit on the sub-sales (65–42½

Defective Goods

Rather similar to *Wertheim* is a case involving defective goods, *Slater* v. *Hoyle & Smith*,[691] in that buyers were able to persuade sub-buyers not to exercise their termination rights but to accept non-conforming goods. In the case of breach of warranty, the Sale of Goods Act clearly lays down the presumptive rule that damages are based on the difference between what the goods ought to have been worth if they had answered to the contract and what in fact they were worth at the time of delivery in consequence of the breach.[692] This approach does not as such require a reference to the market:[693] there may not be a market in non-conforming goods of the contract type, or at least in goods failing to conform in the way of those tendered by the seller.[694] More exactly, the relevant provision looks to the question of value at the delivery date. *Slater* concerned a contract entered into by manufacturing sellers to sell 3,000 pieces of unbleached cloth at 129 shillings per piece. The sellers delivered 1,625 pieces before the buyers refused to accept any more because of the inferior quality of the cloth. Now the buyers had entered a contract to sell 2,000 pieces of bleached cloth at a price higher than they had paid the manufacturing sellers for the unbleached cloth. In fulfilment of this sub-sale, the buyers delivered, and were paid in full for, 691 of the 1625 pieces, despite the complaints of the sub-buyer. The market price having fallen, the buyers recovered damages representing the difference between the warranty value and actual value of the goods delivered, even though 691 pieces had been resold in a bleached condition without any actual loss.

The Court of Appeal observed that the buyers were reselling bleached cloth and therefore could not be said to be dealing in the same article, unbleached cloth, as had been sold by the sellers.[695] Furthermore, the buyers were under no obligation to use the sellers' cloth in fulfilling the sub-sales, and the sellers should not be permitted to take advantage of the buyers' good fortune,[696] just as the sellers would not have been responsible for the additional loss if the buyers had to pay the sub-buyers damages greater than the difference in value. The buyers' behaviour in relation to the sub-buyers may be described as an exercise in business judgement. By pocketing the damages due to them from the sellers, the buyers were taking a business risk with regard to the future

---

shillings), making 54½ shillings total profit. The second purchase would clearly be the buyers' private speculation.

[691] N. 682 above.   [692] S. 53(3).

[693] But the language of market is used in *Slater*.

[694] See *Biggin* v. *Permanite Ltd* [1951] 1 KB 422, 438, revd. in part on other grounds [1952] 2 BB 314.

[695] N. 682 above, 15, 17.   [696] *Ibid.* 18, 23.

willingness of the sub-buyers to deal with them after this incident involving sub-standard goods. On balance, for this reason, the actual decision in *Slater* is probably right.

The Lost Volume Problem[697]

This problem concerns a difficulty that sometimes arises when a seller sues a buyer for non-acceptance of the contract goods. Suppose a contract provides for the sale of goods at a certain price and the buyer repudiates his obligations. At all material times, the market is constant and the seller is ultimately able to dispose of the unwanted goods to another buyer at the same price. Taking this resale price as evidence of the market value of the goods at the due date of delivery, the question is whether the seller is entitled only to nominal damages for the buyer's breach, given that there is no difference between the sale and resale prices. An application of section 48(3) of the Sale of Goods Act, the *prima facie* rule that damages are calculated at the difference between the contract and market prices, would produce this result. The same line of reasoning would again produce nominal damages on a rising market and, on a falling market, would produce an award reflecting the market decline since the contract price was negotiated. But the above result ignores the seller's profit margin on his transactions and the concomitant possibility that, in consequence of the buyer's breach, he has made one fewer sale than otherwise he would have done, and thus earned one fewer item of profit.

Supply and Demand

The problem was dealt with at some length in *W. L. Thompson Ltd* v. *Robinson (Gunmakers) Ltd*[698] where the following were the facts agreed by the parties or proved. The buyers agreed to purchase a new Vanguard automobile at the manufacturer's fixed list price; under the distribution scheme, the sellers' profit margin was also fixed at a little over £61. The day after the contract was entered into, the buyers repudiated their obligations. As a result of this, the sellers rescinded the contract of sale that they had with their wholesale suppliers,[699] an associated company. The wholesale suppliers took back the car that they had already delivered

---

[697] C. J. Goetz and R. E. Scott (1979) 31 *Stan. LR* 323; M. Shanker (1973) 24 *Case WRLR* 697 and 712; R. E. Speidel and K. O. Clay (1972) 57 *Corn. LR* 681.

[698] [1955] Ch. 177. For earlier recognition of the problem, see *Re Vic Mill Ltd* [1913] 1 Ch. 465; *Mason & Risch Ltd* v. *Christner* (1920) 48 OLR 8, varying (1920) 47 OLR 52, 54 (Can.); *Cameron* v. *Campbell & Worthington Ltd* [1930] SASR 402.

[699] The report does not say whether this contract was concluded before or after the retail contract, but it should not make a difference.

and did not press a damages claim against the retail sellers.[700] There was no shortage of Vanguard automobiles in the relevant local market and the buyers conceded[701] that the plaintiff sellers had 'lost a sale in the sense that if another purchaser had come into the plaintiff's premises there was available for that other purchaser a 'Vanguard' car for immediate delivery[,] so that . . . the plaintiffs . . . had lost their profit'.[702] The plaintiff sellers claimed as damages their lost profit margin of £61, while the defendant buyers contended that their liability was limited to nominal damages, since the car could have been sold to another customer at the same price or, as actually happened, surrendered to the wholesale suppliers without incurring any damages liability.

Upjohn J concluded that the matter should not be resolved by applying section 48(3), essentially because he understood, in the light of earlier authority, the expression 'available market' in a physical and technical sense as connoting something in the nature of a commodities exchange.[703] Alternatively, if the expression had to be given a broader meaning, it meant a state of supply and demand 'in the particular trade in the particular area . . . such that the particular goods could be freely sold, and that there was a demand sufficient to absorb readily all the goods that were thrust on it'.[704] In the present case, neither of the above statements described the present circumstances, so he felt able to apply a rule reflecting the seller's real loss, which was the loss of a sale and its accompanying profit.

The conditions of supply and demand were quite different in *Charter* v. *Sullivan*[705] where the buyer defaulted on a contract for the sale of a new Hillman automobile. The market price of retail goods was again fixed by the manufacturer and the seller's evidence, that he could sell all of the Hillman automobiles he could obtain, was held to demonstrate that he had suffered no actual loss.[706] The application of the presumptive rule was therefore displaced; there was an additional reason, that systemic price-fixing negatived the very existence of a market based upon supply and demand. Sellers LJ also observed that the seller, subsequently

---

[700] Who therefore did not have a liability to recover from the retail buyer.

[701] The buyer's co-operation is explained by this being a test case with the sellers, win or lose, assuming the costs of the action. Proof is more difficult than principle in this area.

[702] N. 698, above 179.

[703] See discussion in the text accompanying nn. 594 ff. below.

[704] N. 698, above 187.   [705] [1957] 2 QB 117.

[706] But see *Silkstone and Dodsworth Coal and Iron Co.* v. *Joint Stock Coal Co.* (1876) 35 LT 668. The buyer defaulted on a contract to buy coal from a particular mine and the court awarded as damages the whole of the seller's profit margin, even though the coal remained in the mine (whose resources cannot have been infinite) waiting to be brought up for the next buyer. Cf. *Hill & Sons* v. *Edwin Showell & Sons Ltd* (1918) 87 LJ KB 1106 (the buyers defaulting before the sellers manufactures goods, leaving the sellers free to put their limited production facilities to alternative profitable use).

disposing of the unwanted goods to a new buyer, has the burden of proving that he has suffered a real loss;[707] he would thus have to show why the *prima facie* rule in section 48(3) should not apply. This is consistent with the normal forensic principle in damages matters that the plaintiff must prove his loss. The seller, in many cases, will also know more about the state of the market than the buyer.

Profit and Supply Price

Where the supply of goods exceeds demand, in the sense that the seller can readily dispose of all the goods he acquires or makes,[708] so that the buyer's default deprives the seller of a sale and thus of a profit, the efforts the seller makes to resell the unwanted goods in the same market are not to be regarded as acts mitigating the loss of that profit. That does not mean, however, that such efforts are irrelevant from the point of view of mitigation. Suppose that a contract of sale concerns goods priced at £1,500 and that £500 represents the seller's profit margin while £1,000 represents the supply price, that is, the cost of the goods to the seller. This supply price cost may be incurred in the form of the price the seller pays to his supplier. Alternatively, if the seller is himself the manufacturer, it will be the cost of raw materials, as well as the labour and other items of expense, incurred in assembling a product that is fit for sale.

Whichever type of seller is involved, the stock may be handled in more than one way. Goods may be ordered or manufactured by the seller on an 'as required' basis, that is, as soon as a binding contract is concluded with the buyer. Such behaviour is likely where the risks posed by unwanted stock are severe, in the form of physical perishing, heavy capital expenses or technological ephemerality, to name a few examples. Another possibility is that a seller will have on hand a modest stock quota, so that unwanted goods can simply be shunted on the next buyer, and the result of the buyer's default is that the seller retains the last item of this stock in hand longer than would otherwise have been the case. Yet another possibility is the seller who retains on hand a greater supply of goods than can ever be moved in the market. This may reflect poor business judgement on the seller's part, or it may bespeak the economies of sale associated with the purchase or, more likely, the manufacture of goods in bulk. As the unit cost of the goods goes down in such cases in relation to bulk, it cannot be assumed, for example, that a seller who is ultimately able to dispose of forty-nine items out of fifty is left with an item that cost him as much as any one of the earlier forty-nine or the first.[709]

---

[707] N. 705 above, 134.
[708] *W. L. Thompson Ltd* v. *Robinson (Gunmakers) Ltd*, n. 698 above.
[709] *Robophone Facilities Ltd* v. *Blank* [1966] 1 WLR 1428, 1443.

Returning to our example of the goods costing £1,500 to the buyer, a seller stands to lose, not merely the profit margin guaranteed by the contract, but also the supply price if he is left with goods in his hands that decline in value to zero. Such a decline will not happen if his stock figures are modest, either because few items are kept in hand or the goods are ordered or made as required, and they do not perish or deteriorate before the next buyer comes along. Nor, in the case of a manufacturing seller, will it occur if he is able to make adjustments to goods so that they suit the needs of the next buyer. Such action mitigates the seller's damages by averting the loss of the supply price, though it creates a smaller loss in the form of the cost of mitigation incurred when the goods are converted.[710] A further loss will also arise if these same goods are disposed of at a price that secures a smaller profit margin. This will not occur in a market where the price, by one method or another, is fixed,[711] but where it does occur, the seller has suffered an additional recoverable loss.[712]

Suppose, however, that the supply price cannot be recouped in this way and that the seller is left with goods that he cannot sell. The amount of the supply price, relative to the overall price of the goods in the contract of sale, will vary according to whether these goods are single items bought or manufactured, or part of a larger quantity purchased or a lengthy run manufactured. If the seller is unable to mitigate, and assuming the goods decline to a zero value, the seller will recover from the buyer both the supply price and the profit margin, and it will not be necessary to quantify their individual contributions to the overall contract price. Nevertheless, mitigation may require the seller to seek out secondary markets to absorb the goods.[713] The most obvious such market is probably the scrap market, but mitigation may require the seller to do better than this.[714] Taking again the example of the goods costing £1,500, a seller may be able to sell them in a secondary market for £1,100. To the extent that the new buyer was not in the market for goods priced at £1,500,[715] the seller has averted the loss of his supply price but has also

---

[710] These were the facts in *Re Vic Mill Co. Ltd*, n. 698 above, where the sellers recovered as damages the profit margin plus the costs of conversion, since the sellers could instead have manufactured new goods for the next buyer who came along. See also *Sanford* v. *Senger* [1977] 3 WWR 399.

[711] Like the sale of the cars in *W. L. Thompson Ltd*, n. 698 above, and *Charter* v. *Sullivan*, n. 705 above.

[712] This was an additional item allowed in *Re Vic Mill Ltd*, n. 698 above.

[713] In some cases this will not be possible: see *Robophone Facilities*, n. 709 above.

[714] Some goods will have a negligible, even a non-existent, scrap value, like the answering machines in *Robophone Facilities*, n. 709 above, and *Interoffice Telephones Co. Ltd* v. *Robert Freeman Co. Ltd* [1958] 1 QB 190.

[715] Either because he would never have bought at that price, or buys for a particular use that is not worth the price demanded.

recouped £100 of the lost profit margin.[716] Consequently, his damages action against the defaulting buyer is reduced to £400 (£1,500 − £1,100). On given facts, it may be difficult to know whether the second buyer is in a different market. If the seller is able to dispose of his last 1987 model in the 1988 season, in a market where the supply of goods exceeds demand, it may not be possible to ascertain whether the buyer is someone who would have bought a 1988 model if the 1987 model had not been available. The burden is on the seller to prove his loss,[717] but upon the defendant buyer to prove that the seller ought to have mitigated.[718] In effect, this means that the seller carries the burden of showing that a particular course of action taken is not mitigation in fact since it does not abate a loss.

Considerations like those treated in the foregoing paragraphs have emerged in contracts of hire,[719] but hire and sale are alike in the application of principle to this area of law.[720] In particular, it has been convincingly asserted that, in both types of contract, the remoteness of damage rule will support the inference that the defendant buyer, or hirer, ought to have contemplated that the plaintiff might have lost a profit because of the relationship between supply and demand in the market.[721] This is entirely consistent with the way that the remoteness rule is applied. It will be recalled that the defendant need not actually have considered the consequences of any breach on his part and that, if he had considered them, then the plaintiff's loss need not be more probable than not as a consequence of breach, still less a certain loss. Accordingly, the decision of the Court of Appeal in *Lazenby Garages Ltd* v. *Wright*[722] repays close and critical examination.

Second-hand Goods

In that case, a buyer repudiated his contract to purchase a specific used BMW 2002 automobile the day after the contract was concluded. The contract price was £1,670, of which £345 represented the profit margin, but the seller was able to sell the same vehicle two months later for £1,770. The sellers' argument was that they had lost a sale since the second buyer might have bought another of the used BMW 2002s in

---

[716] *Quaere* the seller who has, besides the buyer's unwanted goods, other goods surplus to demand. Why should it be assumed that mitigation in fact concerns the buyer's goods rather than those other goods? The secondary market, however, may be large enough to absorb all unwanted goods.

[717] Which makes it prudent to insert in the contract a liquidated damages clause.

[718] Discussed in the text accompanying n. 467 above.

[719] *Robophone Facilities Ltd* v. *Blank*, n. 709 above; *Interoffice Telephones Co. Ltd* v. *Robert Freeman Co. Ltd*, n. 714 above; *W. & J. Investments Ltd* v. *Bunting* [1984] 1 NSWLR 331.

[720] *Interoffice Telephones*, n. 714 above. [721] *Ibid.* 202.

[722] [1976] 1 WLR 459.

stock at a later date. Seeing this as a matter of even probability, the trial judge did rough justice by awarding the sellers half of their profit margin on the repudiated transaction. Another possibility that does not seem to have been considered is that the sellers, if paid promptly by the defendant buyer, might then have had the liquidity to purchase another used BMW 2002, or even just another used car. This new acquisition might later have been purchased by one of the individuals, not necessarily the eventual buyer, wandering into their showrooms at some future date. In the Court of Appeal, the sellers were denied damages altogether for loss of bargain. Bridge LJ declined to speculate on whether the eventual buyer would have purchased another car if the defendant buyer's BMW 2002 had not been thrown back on the sellers' hands, and so was not convinced that a loss had been shown.[723] Lord Denning went further and denied, contrary to the normal application of the remoteness rule,[724] that the buyer should have contemplated a bargain loss at all.

In *Lazenby Garages Ltd*,[725] nevertheless, there was a very real possibility that the sellers had incurred a loss. It is easy enough to talk of supply exceeding demand, or demand exceeding supply, but difficult indeed to apply it to a sales business consisting of similar goods each of which is unique in its own way. A buyer, not finding the BMW 2002 that he wanted, might purchase instead a Mercedes from another dealer. With the defendant buyer's cash in hand, the seller might have bought a second-hand Mercedes which could later have been resold to a different buyer. If the seller's business is clearly fuelled by his receipts so that turnover is increased with each and every sale, then a buyer's default either costs him an extra sale or the chance of an extra sale. The precise loss should be recoverable if evidence is led by the seller to satisfy the court. As interesting as matters of principle are in damages cases, the issues are often ultimately resolved by the difficulty or impracticability of accumulating the necessary detailed evidence required to bring forth these principles to the point of judicial choice. In cases like *Lazenby Garages Ltd*, the practical answer is that the seller ought to demand a deposit and forfeit it if the buyer defaults. This is greatly superior to a difficult damages inquiry,[726] and superior, too, to a liquidated damages clause.

---

[723] [1976] 1 WLR 463.
[724] Especially as it was applied in *Interoffice Telephones*, n. 714 above.
[725] N. 722 above.
[726] See the radically divergent views in these cases of Denning MR, who fails to see the difference between lost profit and supply price loss, and of Diplock LJ.

Breach of Warranty by the Seller

According to section 53(1) of the Sale of Goods Act, where the seller commits a breach of warranty or of a condition that the buyer is compelled to treat as a breach of warranty,[727] the buyer may 'set up' his warranty entitlement against a seller suing for the price[728] or bring an action for damages against the seller for breach of warranty.[729] A reading of section 53(1) reveals that it is directed towards general damages of the kind that would flow under the first limb of the rule in *Hadley* v. *Baxendale*,[730] namely, a loss of value in the goods, leaving it to section 54 to pick up special or consequential damages flowing through the second limb of the rule in that case. Section 53(1) therefore does not countenance a breach of warranty claim that exceeds in sum the seller's action for the price, which is why the buyer's defence in section 53(1)(a), against a seller's action for the price, is expressed in alternative form to the buyer's warranty action for damages in section 53(1)(b), the latter designed presumably for cases where the price has already been paid. Nevertheless, section 53(4) does go on to recognize the possibility that a buyer who has not yet paid may wish to do more than defend a price action. By stating that the buyer may both defend and sue for damages, it effectively recognizes the separate damages action in section 54.

The rule for asserting the buyer's general damages where goods fail to accord with the contractual warranty standard is found in section 53(3), after section 53(2) restates the first limb of the rule in *Hadley* v. *Baxendale*. According to section 53(3): 'In the case of breach of warranty of quality, such loss is *prima facie* the difference between the value of the goods at the time of delivery to the buyer and the value they would have had if they had answered to the warranty.' The first point to note is that the contract price does not set the ceiling of recovery, in that the buyer is not to be deprived of a later market rise in the value of goods of the kind supplied. If, therefore, the market has so far risen that, even in their defective state, the goods are still worth more than the contract price, damages will nevertheless be awarded according to the difference between their present value and the enhanced value they would have had if they had conformed to the contract.[731] Where the market falls, the buyer's margin of recovery will commensurately diminish and he will

---

[727] Because of his acceptance of the goods.

[728] Sub-s. 1(a). This codifies the decision in *Mondel* v. *Steel* (1841) 8 M & W 858, which overturned the earlier rule that a warranty claim of this kind had to be pleaded separately as a counterclaim: see *Poulton* v. *Lattimore* (1829) 9 B & C 259 and *Bostock & Co. Ltd* v. *Nicholson & Sons Ltd* [1904] 1 KB 725.

[729] Sub-section 1(b).
[730] (1854) 9 Ex. 341.
[731] *Jones* v. *Just* (1868) LR 3 QB 197.

have to take the market loss.[732] So, where the sellers shipped goods beyond the contract period but the buyers later dealt in them so as to lose their right of rejection, it transpired that the only loss actually suffered by the buyers was adverse market movement that would have occurred even if the goods had been shipped in time; the buyers were therefore confined to nominal damages and could not build up a damages claim to recapture a lost opportunity of rejection and termination.[733]

Although section 53(3) does not explicitly mention the market, it appears that in principle value should be determined according to the market.[734] The hypothetical character of the market reference in non-acceptance and non-delivery cases is absent here: the buyer actually does have the contract goods. Evaluating damaged goods is not easy if no market exists in goods of that kind. Experienced trade umpires will often award a price allowance, though the method of calculation is not commonly stated.[735] In the case of second-hand goods, it may be necessary to look at the price of new goods and then subtract for depreciation.[736] For manufactured goods, the absence of price fluctuations would point to the use of the contract price for conforming goods as the appropriate comparator.[737] The absence of a market in damaged or otherwise non-conforming goods[738] will in some cases lead to the cost of repairs being equated with the gap in value between the goods the buyer should have received and those he did receive.[739] When the cost of repairs comes into play, difficulties can be posed by profit-earning chattels. Damages should not be awarded to repair the goods if the expenditure is unreasonable, defined as the incurring of cost that is 'disproportionate to the financial consequences of the deficiency'.[740] In such a case, the buyer may face greater operating costs, which ought to be recoverable in the form of lost profits.[741] For repairs to non-profit-earning chattels, the position would appear to be similar, with the cost of repairs being

---

[732] See the facts of *Cehave NV* v. *Bremer Handelsgesellschaft mbH* [1976] QB 44. Cf. *Naughton* v. *O'Callaghan* [1990] 3 All ER 191, discussed in the text accompanying nn. 747–9 below.

[733] *Taylor & Sons Ltd* v. *Bank of Athens* (1922) 91 LJ KB 776.

[734] See *Sealace Shipping Ltd* v. *Oceanvoice Ltd (The Alecos M)* [1991] 1 Lloyd's Rep. 120 (treated as a case of non-delivery: see in the text accompanying nn. 744–6 below); *Slater* v. *Hoyle and Smith Ltd* [1920] 2 KB 11, 17.

[735] *Cehave NV* v. *Bremer Handelsgesellschaft mbH*, n. 732 above.

[736] *Butler* v. *Countryside Finance Ltd* [1993] 3 NZLR 623.

[737] See *Dingle* v. *Hare* (1859) 29 LJCP 143 for a reference to price; *Naughton* v. *O'Callaghan*, n. 732 above; *White Arrow Express Ltd* v. *Lamey's Distribution Ltd* [1995] CLC 1251 (services), noted by H. Beale (1996) 112 *LQR* 205.

[738] See *Biggin* v. *Permanite Ltd* [1951] 1 KB 422, 438.

[739] *Minster Trust Ltd* v. *Traps Tractors Ltd* [1954] 3 All ER 136; *Channel Island Ferries Ltd* v. *Cenargo Navigation Ltd (The Rozel)* [1994] 2 Lloyd's Rep. 161, 167 (charterparty).

[740] *The Rozel*, n. 739 above, 168.

[741] Discussed in the text accompanying nn. 750 ff. below.

disallowed where the benefits thus yielded would be out of all proportion to the cost.[742]

Where the cost of repair outstrips the benefits that the repairs will bring to the claimant, it is likely that the claimant will keep the money and forgo the repairs, which raises in an acute form the definition of the claimant's contractual expectancy.[743] This same issue arose in *The Alecos M*,[744] where the sellers of a ship failed to supply it with its spare propellor. One issue was whether this was a case of non-delivery or defective delivery. The Court of Appeal concluded that the case was one of non-delivery, which seems not to have affected the result. This is to say the least questionable: the contract was an entire one. Further, to concentrate on the undelivered item courts the risk of taking one's attention away from the defective ship (in the sense of missing its spare propellor) that was delivered. It was common ground that there was no market in which the buyers could have procured a spare propellor. The arbitrator, whose award was restored by the court, was not convinced that the buyers would use a large damages award[745] to purchase a spare when there was only a remote possibility that it would be used, and concluded that the buyers' true loss was the scrap value of the propellor.[746]

Section 53(3) computes damages according to the value of the goods in the buyer's hands at the date of delivery. It was treated as a *prima facie* rule in *Naughton* v. *O'Callaghan*,[747] a case of the sale of a racehorse whose pedigree was misdescribed. The buyer claimed damages for both breach of warranty and for negligent misrepresentation under section 2(1) of the Misrepresentation Act 1967, the court in its judgment blending the two approaches. By the time the buyer discovered the misdescription, he had raced the horse unsuccessfully and it was worth very much less than the sum he paid for it.[748] Impressed by the fact that the buyer, had he known the truth, would never have purchased this horse, so different from its stated pedigree, Waller J took the date of the buyer's discovery as the reference point for comparison with the price paid by

---

[742] See *Ruxley Electronics and Constructions Ltd* v. *Forsyth* [1995] 3 WLR 118. The question of diminution in value *versus* the cost of repair has proved much more troublesome in cases involving works on land, where no statutory text imposes a diminution of value test: see *Tito* v. *Waddell (No. 2)* [1977] Ch. 106; *Radford* v. *De Froberville* [1977] 1 WLR 1262; *Jacob & Youngs* v. *Kent* (1921) 129 NE 889 (US).

[743] See M. G. Bridge, 'Expectation Damages and Uncertain Future Losses' in J. Beatson and D. Friedmann (eds.), *Good Faith and Fault in Contract Law* (1995).

[744] N. 734 above; G. H. Treitel (1991) 107 *LQR* 364.   [745] $150,000.

[746] $1,100. *Quaere* apportionment of the price and recovery on a partial failure of consideration? See *Ebrahim Dawood Ltd* v. *Heath (1927) Ltd* [1961] 1 Lloyd's Rep. 512 and authorities therein considered.

[747] N. 732 above.

[748] The contract price was 26,000 guineas; it would have fetched 23,500 guineas at the sales if its pedigree had been correctly stated; and it was worth only £1,500 (unworthy to be valued in guineas) when the buyer made his discovery.

the buyer. At the time of discovery, the buyer had long since lost the right of rejection for breach of condition and rescission for innocent misrepresentation, so the substantial effect of the judge's generous damages award[749] was to restore to him these lost rights. This meant that the buyer had been racing the horse all along at the seller's risk; had the horse been successful, it is unlikely that the buyer would have turned over the fruits of this success to the seller. The decision, it is submitted, departed from the *prima facie* rule in section 53(3) for no good reason.

   Provided that the buyer's loss falls within the remoteness rule, it will in certain cases be appropriate to displace the *prima facie* value difference rule in section 53(3) and award instead the profits the buyer might reasonably have made, subject to the impact of the mitigation rule. In this case, the buyer's lost profits do not accompany a lost value claim as consequential damages, which was discussed earlier. Rather, they are a substitute for lost value based on the assumption that the price of the contract goods was a cost incurred in earning profits.

   If damages are to be awarded for lost profits, it is vitally important to clarify the working terminology, for a confusion of thought can only lead to under-compensation or, more likely, double recovery.[750] For our present purposes, the expression 'gross profits' may be understood as the sum of all the receipts earned by the buyer in operating the chattel. But it must be recognized that the buyer has to incur certain expenses so as to be able to earn these profits, notably wages and salaries of employees and the overheads (power, lighting etc.) associated with running the buyer's premises. Where the seller delivers a defective chattel, these expenses ought to be ignored,[751]except to the extent that the seller's breach of warranty either abates these costs, for example with the shutting down of the buyer's premises for a period, or increases them, for example by requiring extra labour to operate the chattel. Similarly, the buyer may incur other costs, for example, repairs, not normally associated with operating a chattel that complies with the seller's warranties. One item of expense however, that may never be ignored is the cost of the chattel itself. If the buyer pays £10,000 for a widget-making machine that, but for the seller's breach of contract, would have earned £100,000, the buyer may not recover £110,000, for the £10,000 outlay was a necessary

---

[749] Substantial damages for the upkeep of the horse and its training fees were also awarded to the plaintiff, who must have felt his cup was running over. The plaintiff seems to have sought the recovery of these sums as a surrogate for the unprovable sums that a winning substitute horse would have provided: n. 732 above, 198.

[750] See *Cullinane* v. *British 'Rema' Manufacturing Co. Ltd* [1954] 1 QB 292; *R. G. McLean Ltd* v. *Canadian Vickers Ltd* (1970) 15 DLR (3d) 15 (criticism of trial award); *Sunnyside Greenhouses Ltd* v. *Golden West Seeds Ltd* (1972) 27 DLR (3d) 434.

[751] See *Lay's Transport Ltd* v. *Meadow Lake Consumers' Co-operative Association Ltd* (1982) 20 Sask. R 8 (Can.).

cost incurred by the buyer in putting himself in a position to earn the £100,000.[752] Similarly, if the buyer has not yet paid the price, this liability must be debited against any claim made by the buyer for his gross profits.[753] Again, for present purposes, the expression 'net profits' may be understood as the buyer's gross profits minus the expenses necessarily incurred by the buyer to qualify himself to earn those gross profits.

In so far as the buyer claims gross profits over the warranted period, and the mitigation rule does not enter the picture, a buyer claiming gross profits need not worry about the depreciating value of the chattel in his hands, as its value declines to zero by the end of the warranted period. Depreciation is just an accountancy term useful in producing an annual picture of the buyer's financial position, and is conveniently represented by a straight-line decline in value based upon the historic cost of acquisition of the chattel. It is only when mitigation prevents the buyer from absorbing the total value of the chattel in his product-making activities that depreciation comes into play as a useful device for assessing the capital value of the chattel in his hands. If the buyer has actually resold the chattel, however, then the actual resale price is likely to be a better guide in calculating a benefit in the buyer's hands, cast there by the seller's breach, that has to be offset against the buyer's warranty claim for loss of profits.

Besides the example of price and gross profits stated above, other examples of overlapping claims exist. A buyer, for example, may not recover damages representing both the reduced capital value of a chattel and the loss of production by this chattel, if the reduction in value is but an alternative way of expressing in present terms the loss of future production.[754] Reduced value is realized when the buyer disposes of the chattel and applies his assets to an alternative profit-making venture. Similarly, if the buyer ends up, after receiving an allowance for reduced value, having to pay a lesser sum for the chattel, he may not claim a level of profits associated with a chattel priced at a greater sum.

A useful case study in pointing to the problems of double-counting is the Canadian case of *Sunnyside Greenhouses Ltd* v. *Golden West Seeds Ltd*.[755] It concerned a breach of the sellers' warranty that plastic greenhouse-roof panels would last at least seven years. In fact, half of the panels lasted for only three years (on the south side) while the remaining half lasted for five years (on the north side). The court permitted the buyers to recover four-sevenths of the price paid for the south panels and

[752] *Cullinane*, n. 750 above.

[753] *R. G. McLean Ltd* v. *Canadian Vickers Ltd*, n. 750 above.

[754] *H. Parsons (Livestock) Ltd* v. *Uttley, Ingham & Co. Ltd* [1978] QB 791; *Bunting* v. *Tory* (1948) 64 TLR 353; *Steele* v. *Maurer* (1977) 79 DLR (3d) 764.

[755] N. 750 above.

two-sevenths of the price paid for the north panels. At the same time as it made the award for the south panels, however, it also awarded the buyers damages for the shortfall in gross sales of the buyers' crops in 1969 compared to the crops of other years. Since the buyer was recovering the prorated price of the south panels in that same year, double recovery was clearly taking place; the cost of the panels was the price to be paid for earning gross sales. A further example of double-counting occurred when the court awarded the buyers the whole of their costs in installing the panels, despite the fact that they had a useful life of three years (on the south side) and five years (on the north side). The extent of over-compensation here is revealed in the diametrically opposite view the court took of the cost of removing the panels. Instead of awarding the cost of removal, the court, recognizing that removal would anyway have occurred after seven years, granted damages based on the accelerated expenditure of this sum, namely, interest on the capital sum thus expended for the balance of the seven-year period. This fails to recognize that, over the life of the buyer's business, the seller's breach may have necessitated one extra removal of panels. Whether such a loss has truly occurred is nevertheless a most difficult speculation, and perhaps the addition of the different sums awarded for installation and premature removal works rough justice.

Given the difficulty sometimes presented of proving speculative profit losses, it is understandable that courts permit plaintiffs to claim their wasted capital expenditure in lieu of profits.[756] Nevertheless, this is not permitted where the defendant is able to prove that the plaintiff was engaged upon a losing venture.[757] One issue that has arisen is whether a plaintiff ought to be able to claim both wasted capital expenses and loss of profits, always provided that double-counting is avoided by thus claiming net profits instead of gross profits. The immediate response to this is to assert that this must be acceptable in principle but a pointless thing to do in practice. To revert to the example given earlier of the £10,000 widget-making machine which fails to generate warranted gross profits of £100,000, a buyer wishing to combine capital and profits in one claim is driven to ask for £10,000 plus (£100,000 − £10,000), making £100,000 in all, if he is not to be over-compensated. This calculation is therefore a long-winded way of reproducing a simple £100,000 claim for lost gross profits.

---

[756] *Cullinane*, n. 750 above; *McRae* v. *Commonwealth Disposals Commission* (1950) 84 CLR 377; *CCC Films (London) Ltd* v. *Impact Quadrant Films Ltd* [1985] QB 16; *Anglia Television Ltd* v. *Reed* [1972] 1 QB 60; *Security Stove & Manufacturing Co.* v. *American Railway Express Co.* (1932) 51 SW 2d 572 (US).

[757] *Bowlay Logging Ltd* v. *Domtar Ltd* [1978] 4 WWR 105; *C. & P. Haulage* v. *Middleton* [1983] 3 All ER 94; *CCC Films*, n. 756 above; *Commonwealth of Australia* v. *Amann Aviation Pty. Ltd* (1991) 66 ALJR 123; *Bridge*, n. 743 above.

As simple as the above position ought to be however, it is complicated by the impact of the mitigation rule and by the Court of Appeal decision in *Cullinane* v. *British 'Rema' Manufacturing Co. Ltd*[758] in which the buyers disposed of[759] a clay-pulverising machine sold by the sellers, together with ancillary machinery and buildings, after three years instead of keeping it for the ten years for which it was warranted to produce clay at the profitable rate of six tons per hour. The buyers claimed two major items of loss: first of all, their capital loss, consisting of the purchase price paid for the warranted machine, as well as for the ancillary machinery and buildings, less the residual, break-up capital value of all three items at the end of the three years from the installation of the machine to the trial of the action; and, secondly, their net profits after certain deductions were made, expressed at an annual rate grossed up to the date of statement of claim and stated to be a continuing claim after that date. These deductions included 10 per cent of the purchase price of the three capital items, offset against the annual statement of profits.

The majority of the court[760] understood that the buyers were claiming loss of profits only for a three-year period instead of for the ten-year period warranted by the sellers. This may well not have been the natural way to read the buyer's statement of claim; moreover, it hardly accorded with the assumptions of the official referee, whose calculations of the profits that the machine should have made over that three-year period, if true to its warranty, were clearly based on a slow progression to profitability as initial teething problems were overcome. Accepting that interpretation made by the majority, however, it is plain that the buyers were claiming too much; they were asking for a little over 50 per cent of their capital investment, representing their net capital loss after break-up, and were offsetting only 30 per cent of the capital cost in the form of depreciation at 10 per cent per year against the gross profits figure. In other words, over 20 per cent of their capital cost had not been counted in against the gross profits amount.[761] Despite this, the official referee for unexplained reasons chose to ignore the depreciation factor altogether: he awarded the buyers their net capital loss together with a sum for lost profits that took no account of the capital investment necessarily incurred to earn these profits. The majority of the Court of Appeal,

---

[758] N. 750 above. See *Sunnyside Greenhouses*, n. 750 above; *TC Industrial Plant Pty. Ltd* v. *Robert's Queensland Pty. Ltd* [1964] ALR 1083; H. Street, *Principles of the Law of Damages* (Sweet & Maxwell, London, 1962), 243–5; J. Macleod [1970] JBL 19; M. Baer (1973) 51 *Can. Bar Rev.* 490.

[759] The damages are calculated that they did so in mitigation.

[760] Evershed MR and Jenkins LJ.

[761] This seems to be the point made by the Australian High Court in *TC Industrial Plant*, n. 758 above. See also Jenkins LJ in *Cullinane*, n. 750 above, 309 (capital expenditure wiped out over 10 years at the rate of 10% per year).

seeing an overlapping element in the buyers' claim for net capital loss and lost profits, put the buyers to their election and awarded them only their lost gross profits minus an unpaid portion of the purchase price, as this was a larger figure than their capital loss.

It is submitted that the dissenting member of the court, Morris LJ, was right, assuming that he correctly interpreted the buyers to be claiming lost profits only for three years, without conceding that the machine would have been unprofitable after that time.[762] Morris LJ would have permitted the combination of capital loss and net profits in the form presented by the plaintiff buyers, presumably on the ground that the 20 per cent or so of the capital cost, not offset against the profits claimed over the three years, could be seen as a substitute unclaimed for the profits lost over the remaining seven years of the warranty period. If one accepts that the disagreement in the Court of Appeal centred on the meaning of the buyer's pleadings with regard to the seven-year period, *Cullinane* should not be read as denying the formulation of a capital-loss claim combined with a net-loss-of-profits claim. Indeed, a claim of just this sort is necessitated by the doctrine of mitigation, which requires the buyer to exit from the clay-pulverizing business before the ten-year period has elapsed. Sir Raymond Evershed was quite prepared to countenance a combined claim, if properly made, when he said:

Upon the question whether the plaintiff could have claimed for loss of profits up to the date of the hearing and have claimed an additional sum because he was at that date left with a machine which was less valuable than the machine as warranted I say only that the plaintiff has not so claimed.[763]

On this approach, the plaintiff would be entitled to his gross profits for three years plus the difference between the value of his capital items after three years' wear-and-tear, if the clay-pulverizing machine had answered to the warranty, and their actual value after three years, given the breach of warranty. The capital loss should (presumably) be the depreciated expected value of these capital items, if the warranty had been satisfied, less the price that a purchaser of the business would actually be prepared to pay for them given their sub-warranty performance. If no such purchaser could be found, that second figure would have to be the break-up value of the capital items. In the light of this, the attitude of the majority to the buyer's claim, formulated in difficult circumstances, seems to have been somewhat unaccommodating.

---

[762] See *TC Industrial Plant*, n. 758 above.   [763] *Cullinane*, n. 750 above, 306–7.

Index